Real Essays

Writing Projects for College,
Work, and Everyday Life

Real Essays

Writing Projects for College, Work, and Everyday Life

Susan Anker

BEDFORD/ST. MARTIN'S   *Boston* ◆ *New York*

To Isabel Willey, who gave me the love of language

For Bedford/St. Martin's

Developmental Editors: Michelle M. Clark, Beth Castrodale
Production Editors: Karen Baart, Deborah Baker
Senior Production Supervisor: Dennis Conroy
Marketing Manager: Brian Wheel
Editorial Assistant: Karin Halbert
Copyeditor: Janet Renard
Text Design: Claire Seng-Niemoeller
Cover Design: Billy Boardman
Cover Art: © Photonica, New York, NY.
Composition: Stratford Publishing Services
Printing and Binding: R. R. Donnelley & Sons Company

President: Joan E. Feinberg
Editorial Director: Denise B. Wydra
Editor in Chief: Karen S. Henry
Director of Marketing: Karen Melton
Director of Editing, Design, and Production: Marcia Cohen
Managing Editor: Elizabeth M. Schaaf

Library of Congress Control Number: 2002112252

7   6   5   4   3   2

f   e   d   c   b   a

For information, write: Bedford/St. Martin's, 75 Arlington Street, Boston, MA 02116 (617-399-4000)

ISBN: 0–312–39914–6 (*Real Essays*)
      0–312–39915–4 (*Real Essays with Readings*)
      0–312–39916–2 (*Instructor's Annotated Edition*)

Acknowledgments
Perry W. Buffington. "How to Avoid a Speeding Ticket" and "Get the Raise You Deserve" from *Cheap Psychological Tricks: What to Do When Hard Work, Honesty, and Perseverance Fail* by Perry W. Buffington, Ph.D., illustrated by Mitzi Cartee. Copyright © 1996 by Perry W. Buffington, Ph.D. Published by Peachtree Publishers. Reprinted by permission of Peachtree Publishers, Atlanta, GA.

Acknowledgments and copyrights are continued at the back of the book, which constitutes an extension of the copyright page. It is a violation of the law to reproduce these selections by any means whatsoever without the written permission of the copyright holder.

Preface for Instructors

Too often, students perceive their writing course as a pesky, creaking gate they must pass through in order to move on to "content" courses that, when completed, serve as the way to a good job. The aim of *Real Essays*, as indicated by its subtitle, *Writing Projects for College, Work, and Everyday Life*, is to show students that their writing course is a crucial gateway to success in every arena of their lives. To achieve this aim, *Real Essays* casts writing and editing skills as practical and valuable. Further, it sends the message that strengthening these skills is worth the effort because all the roles students will play in their lives — college student, employee, parent, consumer, community member — require that they write often and well.

Real Essays shares an overarching purpose with its companion, *Real Writing: Paragraphs and Essays for College, Work, and Everyday Life*: to put writing in a real-world context. This two-book series links writing skills to students' own goals in and beyond college. What's more, these books motivate students with photographs, quotes, profiles, and advice from current and former students — people like themselves who have struggled with writing, who have wondered why it was important, and who are learning that good writing is not a mysterious, divinely inspired gift but a skill that can be learned by any person who is willing to pay attention and practice. Together, these books form a foundation for success in the real world based on skills learned in the writing classroom.

Organization

Real Essays is divided into two major sections: writing essays and editing essays. Section I has three parts: "How to Write Essays" (Chapters 1–7); "Writing Different Kinds of Essays" (Chapters 8–16, covering narration, illustration, description, process analysis, classification, definition, comparison and contrast, cause and effect, and argument); and "Writing in College and at Work" (Chapters 17–21). Section II has four parts: "The Four Most Serious Errors" (Chapters 22–26, which includes a basic overview of editing); "Other Grammar Concerns" (Chapters 27–33); "Word

Use" (Chapters 34–36); and "Punctuation and Capitalization" (Chapters 37–41). The longer version of *Real Essays* also includes a final section, "Readings for Writers" (Chapters 42–51), with an introduction to the reading process; twenty high-interest, rhetorically organized readings; and prompts designed to help students comprehend, analyze, and respond to the readings. *Real Essays* ends with three useful appendices that give guidelines for writing email and memos; résumés and letters of application; and for making oral presentations.

These chapters are flexible, allowing you to use them in whatever order suits your course structure and your students' needs.

Features

Real Essays not only presents the information students need but also shows students how and why writing is relevant to them—connecting them to writing, to the content of the book, and to the course. *Real Essays* keeps things practical and lets students in on the fact that not all writing and grammar concepts are of equal importance. The text doesn't mislead students into thinking that writing is a simple process; instead, it presents material in meaningful and manageable chunks.

Motivates Students with a Real-World Emphasis

- **"Profiles of Success."** The writing chapters in Part Two open with photographs of and interviews with former students who have achieved success in the real world. By describing the kinds of work-related writing they do and showing how they actually use the type of writing covered in the chapter, these individuals show students just how valuable writing skills are, both in and beyond college. The "Profiles of Success" also describe how these individuals use technology and teamwork skills in their profession.

- **Real-world models of writing.** Unique to *Real Essays*, all nine writing chapters in Part Two include three essay-length samples—one each from college, work, and everyday life—with guidance and activities for analyzing the structure of the model and opportunities to write similar essays.

- **Problem-solving strategies.** Five real-life scenarios form the core of a unique chapter (Chapter 17) that immerses students in a collaborative problem-solving process—identifying a problem, listing possible solutions, evaluating possible solutions, and choosing and defending a workable solution—and guides them as they write an essay that proposes a solution to one problem. Chapter 17 also provides ample support for working in teams.

- **Assignments that emphasize purpose and audience.** Writing chapters give students opportunities to apply their skills to a document written with a real purpose and targeted to a real audience, putting the writing they do in a real-world context.

Presents Writing in Logical, Manageable Increments

- **A focus on the four basics of each mode promotes successful writing.** Each chapter in Part Two, "Writing Different Kinds of Essays," opens with a list (indicated by this symbol: ▮▮) of four basic features of the type of writing covered. This presentation, which highlights the essential elements needed to understand and use a rhetorical strategy, organizes and simplifies the writing instruction. The writing guide, the questions following the chapter readings, and the chapter-ending Final Check each reinforce the importance of these four basic elements.

- **Step-by-step "Writing Guides" offer real help.** Each chapter in Part Two, the core writing instruction, includes a "Writing Guide" that breaks down the process for a mode into a series of manageable tasks. Each step is accompanied by clear, concise advice for completing the task, and a series of checklist items that guide students as they write the essay and help them keep track of their progress.

- **"Thinking Critically" guides teach college-level thinking skills.** Three-part "Thinking Critically" boxes throughout the text prompt students to *focus* on the basic elements of the task, *ask* themselves some basic questions about it, and then *write* or *edit* after thinking through the questions. These guides help students avoid rushing through a writing, revising, or editing task.

- **Two chapters make the research essay manageable.** Chapter 20 teaches key research skills such as searching databases, taking notes, and avoiding plagiarism. Chapter 21 presents the process for writing a research essay in seven stages. A continuous student example and the student's final MLA-style essay are included.

- **"Use a Computer" sections in Part One ("How to Write Essays") help students use technology to become better writers.** These sections present brief tips and basic strategies for writing with computers. In addition, essay options in Part Two prompt students to investigate specific Web sites or types of sites in preparation for writing an essay. For example, in Chapter 8, "Narration," students are assigned to search a consumer complaint database for samples of written complaints, and write their own essay about a bad experience with a service or product.

Presents Editing in Logical, Manageable Increments

- **The editing section helps students overcome the four most serious errors—and more.** Rather than giving all errors equal weight, *Real Essays* concentrates first, with full coverage and plenty of practice, on the errors identified by teachers across the country as the most serious: fragments, run-ons, subject-verb agreement problems, and verb form problems. These topics, pulled together in Part Four, lead off the editing section of the text. This unique approach teaches students to concentrate on a limited number of major sentence problems as a first step to becoming better editors of their own writing. The remaining chapters include thorough coverage of all standard grammar, usage, punctuation, and mechanics topics—with hundreds of practice items.

- **Reference to Exercise Central provide more opportunities for skill practice.** Marginal references throughout the editing section direct students to Exercise Central for additional exercises. The largest online bank of editing exercises (with more than seven thousand items), Exercise Central offers two levels of skill practice, customized feedback, and instructor monitoring tools.

- **"Quick Review Charts" at the end of each grammar chapter present key information visually.** For students who are visual learners, the editing section presents concepts and strategies in chapter-ending flowcharts for quick comprehension and practical application.

Is Easy to Use

- **"Introduction for Students" offers a quick orientation.** A brief introduction walks students through the text's organization and key features, with sample pages and clear descriptions. It also describes features that students can use while writing and editing their own papers. The introduction ends with an inventory of students' goals and a worksheet that helps students articulate their goals for the writing course.

- **Key chapter elements are clear, accessible, and predictable.** Various elements designed to help students write their papers—step-by-step "Writing Guides," "Critical Thinking" guides, models, practices, checklists, and computer tips—are clearly labeled and easy to use. The chapters follow a consistent three-part organization: *Understand—Read and Analyze—Write* in the writing chapters, and *Understand—Practice—Edit* in the grammar chapters.

- **Marginal references direct students to useful information.** To help students find the assistance they need, *Real Essays* features easy-to-read references in the margins to other material in the text, to the book's companion Web site, and to the "Writing Guide" software.

Ancillaries

Real Essays is complemented by a wide range of useful support materials for both students and instructors. These are all practical tools designed to give real help to busy people.

Print Resources

Instructor's Annotated Edition of Real Essays. Gives practical page-by-page advice on teaching with *Real Essays*, with five types of marginal tips—written by Susan Anker and Susan Naomi Bernstein (University of Houston)—including discussion prompts, strategies for teaching ESL students, and more. Also contains answers to all exercises and suggestions for using the other ancillaries.

Practical Suggestions for Teaching Real Essays by Eddye S. Gallagher, Tarrant County College. Contains information and advice on working with basic writers, bringing the real world into the classroom, building critical-thinking skills, using computers, teaching ESL students and speakers of nonstandard dialects (with a special contribution by James May of Valencia Community College), and assessment (with a special contribution by Karen Eisenhauer of Brevard Community College). Also includes tips for new instructors and ideas for making the most of *Real Essays*.

Additional Resources to Accompany Real Essays by Susan Anker and Eddye S. Gallagher, Tarrant County College. Supplements the instructional materials in the text with a variety of transparency masters and other reproducibles for classroom use.

Teaching Developmental Writing: Background Readings, a Bedford/St. Martin's Professional Resource, by Susan Naomi Bernstein, University of Houston. Offers thirty-five professional essays by Mina Shaughnessy, Mike Rose, Rei Noguchi, and others on topics of interest to basic writing instructors, along with a useful editorial apparatus pointing out practical applications for the classroom.

Real Essays Quick Reference Card. This four-page laminated card, which students can stand up next to their computer monitor, includes editing advice, help with Web searches, and useful word processing tips. (To order this card packaged with your students' copies of *Real Essays with Readings,* use the ISBN 0–312–40751–3. To order the card with the shorter version of *Real Essays,* use the ISBN 0–312–40773–4.)

Media Resources

"Writing Guide" software. Developed specifically to support *Real Essays*, this software leads students step-by-step through the process of writing each of the types of essays covered in the text. Also included are critical reading guides, diagnostic tests, grammar tutorials, and a personalized error log with built-in links to Exercise Central.

Exercise Central <www.bedfordstmartins.com/realessays>. With more than seven thousand items, this is the largest online collection of grammar exercises available. Exercise Central is thorough, easy to use, and convenient for both students and instructors. Multiple exercise sets on every topic, at a variety of levels, ensure that students have as much practice as they need. Customized feedback for all answers assures that skills practice becomes a learning experience, and a reporting feature allows both students and instructors to monitor and assess student progress.

Book companion site <www.bedfordstmartins.com/realessays>. The companion Web site for *Real Essays* provides additional resources for instructors as well as links to Exercise Central and the English Research Room, an online resource for research writers.

Acknowledgments

Real Essays was shaped by cadres of individuals around the country, not by a single voice. A textbook that is workable with diverse populations is, of necessity, the product of vast amounts of input, advice, and hard work on the part of many, and I am grateful to those individuals and groups who participated.

Reviewers

Because we drew upon the philosophy, structure, and content of *Real Writing*, I also want to acknowledge, once again, the many people who helped craft the vision and development of both editions of that book. I first thought to name those friends here, including the individuals who served on the Editorial Advisory Board for each edition, but—given space constraints—I'll just say that you know who you are, and you are as much a part of *Real Essays* as of *Real Writing*. Thank you, thank you.

The following reviewers helped shape *Real Essays* by offering thoughtful comments and specific suggestions for meeting their students' challenges: Leigh Adams, Southwest Missouri State University–West Plains;

Mary Alexander, University of Phoenix; James Allen, College of DuPage; Cathryn Amdahl, Harrisburg Area Community College; Mark Amdahl, Montgomery County Community College; Mary Ann Bernal, San Antonio College; Jan Bone, Roosevelt University; Carol Ann Britt, San Antonio College; Lorraine Page Cadet, Grambling State University; Nandan Choksi, Art Institute of Fort Lauderdale; Sandra Chumchal, Blinn College; Laurie Coleman, San Antonio College; Nancy Davies, Miami-Dade Community College; Rick Dollieslager, Thomas Nelson Community College; Karen Eisenhauer, Brevard Community College; Linda Elaine, College of DuPage; Eileen Eliot, Broward County Community College; Melanie Fahlman-Reid, Capilano College; Katherine Finch, North Shore Community College; Anne Gervasi, DeVry University; Laura Gray-Rosendale, Northern Arizona University; Barbara L. Hamilton, Jones County Junior College; Earl Hawley, College of DuPage; Suzanne R. Hess, Florida Community College at Jacksonville; Lesa Hildebrand, Triton College; Kaaren Holum, University of the District of Columbia; Lennie Irvin, San Antonio College; Florence Johnson, North Dakota State College of Science; Gail Lighthipe, Bloomfield College; Jose Macia, Broward County Community College; Patricia A. Malinowski, Finger Lakes Community College; Gerald McCarthy, San Antonio College; David Merves, Miami-Dade Community College; Terrance Millet, Linn-Benton Community College; Katona Mulholland, Blue River Community College; Kimme Nuckles, Baker College; Amy Penne, Parkland College; Verlene Lee Pierre, Southeastern Louisiana University; Peggy Riley, Las Positas College; P. C. Scheponik, Montgomery County Community College; Tamara Shue, Georgia Perimeter College; Jeff Siddall, College of DuPage; Norman Stephens, Cerro Coso Community College; Denton Tulloch, Miami-Dade Community College; Priscilla Underwood, Quinsigamond Community College; Gail Upchurch, Olive Harvey College; Paul Vantine, Cameron University; Maria C. Villar-Smith, Miami-Dade Community College; Dorothy Voyles, Parkland College; Ted Walkup, Clayton College and State University; Michael Weiser, Thomas Nelson Community College; and Peggy Wogen, Kishwaukee College.

I would also like to thank Jim Rice and Marilyn Martin, both of Quinsigamond Community College, for graciously allowing me to "audit" courses.

Students

Many current and former students have contributed to this book. The nine former students who are "Profiles of Success" and who contributed examples of their real-world writing are Giovanni Bohorquez, Pamela O'Berry Evans, Daigo Fujiwara, Jolanda Jones, Gary Knoblock, Maureen Letendre, Patty Maloney, Salvador Torres, and Wayne Whitaker. I asked for a good deal of these people's time, and I very much appreciate their giving of it willingly and patiently.

Other students and former students contributed model essays to the book: Florence Bagley, Gene Boroski, Emma Brennan, Edna Crespo, Lindsey Ducharme, Roberta Fair, Elena Feltus, Danny Fitzgerald, Jessica Foote, James Freeman, Anna Griffith, George Hanson, Jason Knox, Susan Robinson, Janine Ronzo, and Karron Tempesta.

We asked a number of students to review various parts of the manuscript, and they gave us valuable comments. These students are Michael Joe Blalock, Jean Calixte, Roseann Castillo, Tina Colucci, Mark Coronado, Sandra Curatola, Theresa Dresser, Peggy L. Gamble, Angie Gonzales, Geri Hollinshed, Lizette Iverson, Monet Lasha, Ryan Olson, Michelle Perez, Eric Reese, Yolanda Robinson, Mark E. Skinner, Brenda Sotelo, Travis Tennison, Noel Vargas, and Diana L. Watie.

Contributors

Carolyn Lengel created interesting and grammatically sound exercises—in my mind, the work of a true wizard. Karin Halbert helped greatly with the selection of readings and the author headnotes, and Katie Finch crafted questions and writing prompts to accompany the readings. Marcia Muth edited raw manuscript, line-by-line, smoothing out sharp edges and awkward angles.

Eddye Gallagher (Tarrant County College) wrote the original manuscript for *Practical Suggestions,* a wonderfully savvy and useful guide for instructors, which was updated by Joanne Diaz (Boston University), Karen Eisenhauer (Brevard Community College), and James May (Valencia Community College). Susan Naomi Bernstein (University of Houston) contributed annotations for the *Instructor's Annotated Edition*, bringing to bear her fine sense of classroom practice. She also wrote the popular volume that accompanies the book: *Teaching Developmental Writing: Background Readings.*

Finally, Will Hochman (Southern Connecticut State University) contributed his expert and accessible advice on using computers in the writing process.

Bedford/St. Martin's

With every book I write for Bedford/St. Martin's, I am struck nearly dumb by the unparalleled resources they offer. The people there—to a one—are incredibly intelligent, articulate, and patient. Each also has an active sense of humor. And with the preface of each book, I try to be more succinct in my praise of them. It doesn't always work, but I'm trying.

In her role as editorial assistant, Karin Halbert, mentioned above as a contributor, also ably managed a vast and endless array of projects, including the very extensive review program. She is entirely reliable and competent.

Janet Renard copyedited the manuscript with an enviable ability to see straight to a problem and craft a solution, keeping us consistent throughout many hundreds of pages of manuscript.

The work of the New Media team does not go unnoticed. For their efforts to produce fine electronic resources, I thank Nick Carbone, Harriet Wald, and Coleen O'Hanley.

For the second time, I have been lucky to have Karen Baart to oversee the production process. She is grace under pressure personified and is skillfully devoted to getting things done right, and I appreciate her great worth. Deborah Baker succeeded Karen in this role and ably kept the book on track. I am also thankful to Claire Seng-Niemoeller for designing a student-friendly interior and to Billy Boardman for designing an attractive cover, and for having a kindred sense of humor. Finally, many thanks to Suzi Meyers for photo research and to Sandy Schechter for coordinating permissions.

As always, the talents and input of an array of marketing and sales managers accounted for changes throughout the process. This time, getting a title we could all live with was a Herculean feat. Thanks to Karen Melton, Brian Wheel, Tom Scotty, Bill Soeltz, Steve Patrick, Doug Bolton, John Hunger, Kate Nurre, Guy Geraghty, Rory Baruth, Mike Krotine, and Stacey Luce.

I am forever grateful to and in awe of the talents of Chuck Christensen and Joan Feinberg. During the development of this book, Chuck handed over the reins to Joan, who is now president of Bedford/St. Martin's. Joan brings her own gracious leadership style, and Bedford will forever bear the brand of her and Chuck's joint vision. Karen Henry, editor in chief, ensures that that vision infuses Bedford/St. Martin's publications, including both *Real Writing* and *Real Essays*.

Finally, I thank Michelle Clark, my editor, for her good advice, collaborative spirit, and consistent energy and enthusiasm, which endured through some challenging pressures. She is a terrific help. Beth Castrodale kindly and competently stepped in toward the end of the project and fleetly carried Michelle's baton without missing a beat.

This book would never have been completed without the support of my husband, Jim Anker. Together this year, we have weathered too much sadness. We're both standing, and *Real Essays* is a reality. I couldn't have managed either without him.

Contents

EDITING ESSAYS

*Part Four. The Four Most
Serious Errors*   *343*

22. The Basic Sentence: An Editing Overview   345

23. Fragments: Incomplete Sentences   353

24. Run-Ons: Two Sentences Joined Incorrectly   373

25. Problems with Subject-Verb Agreement: When Subjects and Verbs Don't Match   387

Introduction for Students

Why Should You Read This Introduction First?

These few pages will explain how to use this book. You've just spent a fair amount of money to buy it, so make sure you get your money's worth. This brief introduction will pitch to you the importance of this course and describe *Real Essays: Writing Projects for College, Work, and Everyday Life:* how it is organized, how to find information in it, and how to use certain features that will help you improve your writing. Reading this section will take you no more than twenty minutes — and it'll be worth it.

Why This Course Should Be Important to You

Your life is busy. You attend school, and you may even work full-time while taking classes. Maybe you're also a parent or have other pressing family or community commitments. You have bills to pay and goals to achieve.

And then there's this writing course.

You may be tempted to think of the course as just a nuisance to get through with a passing grade. However, it may be one of your best opportunities to develop the writing skills you need — whatever your current obligations or future plans are.

Here's a true story. When the first book in this series, *Real Writing,* was published, I proudly distributed my author copies to a few friends and relatives. I never thought they'd do much more than look at the pictures and think, "That's my daughter" or "That's my best friend." In fact they did say these things, but soon I started getting emails from people who had seen the book, had actually looked through it, and wanted to know how they could buy a copy. The first request I took as a fluke and wondered why anyone would want to buy this book when they were out of college and already employed in a good position. But the requests kept coming—from people in various occupations, ranging from a police officer to a manager at Verizon to a marketing specialist at IBM to a high-level computer whiz who tests government security programs. Each of them said basically the same thing: "Everyone in this office needs to write, and we're never sure whether what we're writing is right. We're dying for something that will help us, and we like this because it's not just about college writing but about the kinds of writing we really do."

As the title of this book, *Real Essays: Writing Projects for College, Work, and Everyday Life,* indicates, your need to write will not end with this course or with graduation from college. Every one of you will need to write competently for the rest of your life: to continue in college, to get a job and succeed in it, and to get by in your personal life. This course is for you, not for your instructor.

How This Book Is Organized

Real Essays is organized into seven parts:

- Part One (Chapters 1–7) describes the process you use to write any kind of essay for various purposes and audiences.
- Part Two (Chapters 8–16) gives concrete instruction about how to write nine common types of essays—the ones most often assigned in college courses—and guidance about how to apply those same skills to work-related and everyday writing tasks.
- Part Three (Chapters 17–21) presents strategies for completing other kinds of college, workplace, and everyday writing tasks such as taking tests, writing summaries and reports, proposing solutions, and writing from sources.
- Part Four (Chapters 22–26) includes chapters on each of the four most serious grammar errors, the ones that people most often notice: sentence fragments, run-ons, subject-verb agreement problems, and problems with verb forms.
- Part Five (Chapters 27–33) gives you instruction and practice in other areas of grammar, which are important in addition to the four

most serious errors: The book just presents the most important
things first.

- Part Six (Chapters 34–36) includes chapters about words: choosing the right word, not confusing words that sound or look alike, and spelling them correctly.
- Part Seven (Chapters 37–41) covers punctuation—using commas, apostrophes, and quotation marks, for example—and capitalization.

These basic matters are followed by useful appendices with specific advice about and examples of how to write email, memos, résumés, and letters of application, and how to give a good oral presentation.

In addition, your book may have a section called "Readings for Writers," which includes an introduction to critical reading followed by twenty readings on topics such as the use of foul language in our culture and the debate about whether competition is good for children. In addition to giving you practice in reading and—I hope—some enjoyment, these essays and articles will show you how professional writers use the strategies presented in the first two parts of *Real Essays*.

How to Find Information in *Real Essays*

Information is easy to find in *Real Essays*. Knowing where to look is a key first step.

Table of Contents

If you want to find a particular chapter, use the brief table of contents printed on the inside front cover. If you're looking for specific information within a chapter, try the detailed table of contents (pp. xv–xxv), which lists chapter titles and major headings.

Index

If you want to find a particular topic, you can also use the index (p. I-1). Topics are listed alphabetically. To find information on using apostrophes in contractions, look under "apostrophes" and find the subentry "in contractions." The page number will direct you to the right information.

Chart of Correction Symbols

If your instructor uses symbols to indicate grammar, spelling, or punctuation errors in your writing, you can use the chart at the back of the book to get the meaning for each symbol and a chapter reference for more help.

Headings at the Tops of Pages

When you want to know where you are in the book, look at the headings that run along the tops of the pages. The left page gives you the name of the part of the book you're in (for example, Part Seven • Punctuation and Capitalization), and the right page tells you which chapter you're in (for example, Chapter 38 • Apostrophes).

List of Useful Charts and Reference Tools

Turn to the inside back cover for a list of all kinds of review and summary information in the book, with page numbers given so that you can easily access what you need—a checklist, a diagram, a reference chart—without flipping through the whole book or reading the whole table of contents.

References in the Margin

Real Essays includes helpful tips and references printed right in the margin. These direct you to additional information or resources in the book or on the book's companion Web site.

erline the subject of the verb *be, have,* or *do,* and circle
he verb.

(has / have) an important role in many children's

olved in Little League during fifth and sixth grades.

were) happy to cheer at most of the games.

) a Little Leaguer of my own, my daughter Tina.

not a natural athlete.

m / is / are) usually a lot of fun for her.

> For more practice,
> visit Exercise
> Central at <**www**
> **.bedfordstmartins**
> **.com/realessays**>.

How to Use the Features of *Real Essays* to Improve Your Writing

Real Essays is designed to help you to become a better writer. Here are descriptions of charts, checklists, and other helpful features — some with samples from the book.

Thinking Critically Guides

Many chapters include short guides that help you focus on a writing or editing task in order to do it well. These guides make completing the task easier and give you useful practice in thinking about key issues before acting — something you need to do in college but, even more important, in your everyday lives and at work.

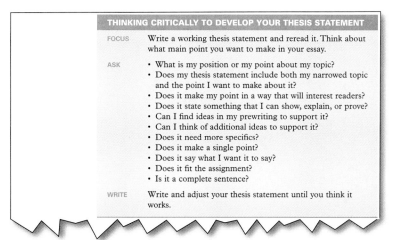

THINKING CRITICALLY TO DEVELOP YOUR THESIS STATEMENT	
FOCUS	Write a working thesis statement and reread it. Think about what main point you want to make in your essay.
ASK	• What is my position or my point about my topic? • Does my thesis statement include both my narrowed topic and the point I want to make about it? • Does it make my point in a way that will interest readers? • Does it state something that I can show, explain, or prove? • Can I find ideas in my prewriting to support it? • Can I think of additional ideas to support it? • Does it need more specifics? • Does it make a single point? • Does it say what I want it to say? • Does it fit the assignment? • Is it a complete sentence?
WRITE	Write and adjust your thesis statement until you think it works.

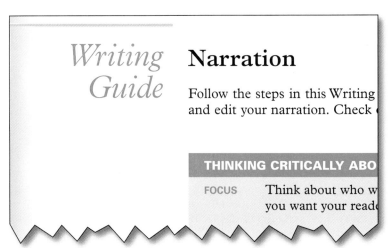

Writing Guides

Writing Guides

Each chapter in Part Two, "Writing Different Kinds of Essays," includes a concrete step-by-step guide that you can follow as you write your essay.

Four Basics of Writing

Each of the chapters in Part Two starts off with a list of the four basic features of the kind of writing covered in the chapter. As you read how a particular kind of writing is developed, keep these four basics in mind. As you do the writing assignments, you can refer to these four basics before, during, and after you write. Focusing on just four key elements for each type of writing will make the assignments easier to manage.

▪▪ Four Basics of Good Argument

1. It takes a strong and definite position on an issue or advises a particular action.
2. It gives good reasons and supporting evidence to defend the position or recommended action.
3. It considers opposing views.
4. It has enthusiasm and energy from start to finish.

The chapter on writing summaries and reports also provides you with the list of basics, as does the appendix on writing emails and memos.

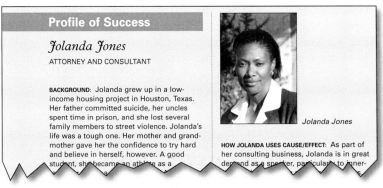

Profile of Success

Jolanda Jones
ATTORNEY AND CONSULTANT

BACKGROUND: Jolanda grew up in a low-income housing project in Houston, Texas. Her father committed suicide, her uncles spent time in prison, and she lost several family members to street violence. Jolanda's life was a tough one. Her mother and grandmother gave her the confidence to try hard and believe in herself, however. A good student, she became an athlete as a

Jolanda Jones

HOW JOLANDA USES CAUSE/EFFECT: As part of her consulting business, Jolanda is in great demand as a speaker, particularly to inner-

Profiles of Success

Each of the chapters in Part Two starts with a brief interview with a former student who struggled with writing. Now successfully employed as nurses, attorneys, small-business owners, and so on, these individuals tell what they write and give an example of the kind of writing they really do — every day. Their stories emphasize the importance of writing skills, computer skills, and the ability to work as part of a team.

Quick Review Charts

The chapters in Parts Four, Five, and Six end with "Quick Review" charts, which enable you, at a glance, to see what to do when you are editing your own writing for a particular type of grammar problem. These are like flowcharts in a how-to manual.

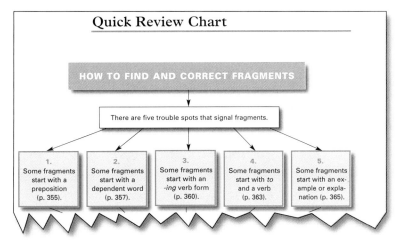

Quick Review Chart

HOW TO FIND AND CORRECT FRAGMENTS

There are five trouble spots that signal fragments.

1.	2.	3.	4.	5.
Some fragments start with a preposition (p. 355).	Some fragments start with a dependent word (p. 357).	Some fragments start with an *-ing* verb form (p. 360).	Some fragments start with *to* and a verb (p. 363).	Some fragments start with an example or explanation (p. 365).

Useful Appendices

At the end of the book are three very practical appendices: How to write email and memos (p. 615); how to write a résumé and a letter of application (p. 622); and how to give a good oral presentation (p. 632). Even if your instructor does not assign the appendices for class, read and save this material. It will come in handy on the job.

Remember the Number Four

Sometimes when you are writing, it may seem as if there is just too much to remember. To make things a little easier on you, remember the number *four;* it's important in this book. Part One covers *four* basic steps in the writing process: prewrite, draft, revise, and edit. Part Two includes a list of *four* key features, called the "Four Basics," for each type of writing. Part Four presents the "*Four* Most Serious Errors" (fragments, run-ons, subject-verb agreement problems, and verb form problems), the most noticeable and potentially damaging errors. *Real Essays*, in an effort to give you practical help, focuses your attention first on the most basic and important issues.

What Do You Want from This Course?

As I said earlier, this course is for you: You need the information and practice it provides if you want to pass the course, succeed in other courses, get a job, or be able to stand up for yourself in your everyday life. As you begin the course, decide what you want to gain from it.

First, what are some of your real-world goals? For example, what kind of job or career do you hope to have? What do you want to do in your everyday life: Find a nice place to live? Buy a car? Travel? Get your money back when you've been overcharged? Make new friends? Do some thinking about your real-life goals and list at least five, the more concrete and specific the better. ("To be happy" may be too general, for example.)

Once you have some real-world goals in mind, particularly the job or career ones, try to link those goals to the writing skills you want to learn or improve in this course. Carefully complete the worksheet that follows.

WRITING QUESTIONNAIRE

NAME _____

COURSE _____ **DATE** _____

Real-World Goals

Use the spaces below to list at least five specific goals you have set for yourself.

_____

_____

_____

_____

_____

Course Goals

Think about your writing and comments you have received about it in the past. What do you think your major problems with writing are? What should you work on improving? List a few answers to these questions in the spaces that follow.

_____

_____

_____

_____

_____

When you have jotted down a few ideas, list three writing skills you want to learn or practice. Be as specific as possible. For example, "Learn to write better" is too general to mean anything much or to help you focus on the areas you want to improve. Based on your answers to the questions above, write three specific skills you want to address and improve during this course.

1. _____

2. _____

3. _____

PART ONE

How to Write Essays

1

The Writing Process

An Overview

Understand Paragraph and Essay Form

DEFINITION: A **paragraph** is a group of sentences that work together to make a point. A good paragraph has three necessary parts—the topic sentence, the body, and the concluding sentence—which serve specific purposes.

PARAGRAPH PART	PURPOSE OF THE PARAGRAPH PART
1. The **topic sentence**	states the **main point**. The topic sentence is often the first sentence of the paragraph.
2. The **body**	supports (shows, explains, or proves) the main point. It usually contains three to six **support sentences**, which present facts and details that develop the main point.

3

3. The **concluding sentence**   reminds readers of the main point and often makes an observation.

Read the paragraph that follows. Standard parts of the paragraph are labeled.

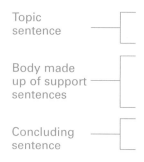

Topic sentence

Body made up of support sentences

Concluding sentence

Asking your boss for a raise doesn't have to be painful if you plan the conversation well. First, think about how you will introduce the subject when you talk with your boss. Then make a list of reasons why you deserve the raise. Be prepared to give specific examples of your achievements. When your plan is ready, make an appointment to meet with your boss. Your plan will allow you to be confident and will increase your chance of success.

DEFINITION: An **essay** is a piece of writing with more than one paragraph. A short essay may be three hundred to six hundred words long with four or five paragraphs. A long essay is six paragraphs or more; the length depends on what the essay needs to accomplish—persuading someone to do something, using research to make a point, or explaining a complex concept.

An essay has three necessary parts: an introduction, a body, and a conclusion.

ESSAY PART	PURPOSE OF THE ESSAY PART
1. The **introduction**	states the **main point** or **thesis**, generally in a single strong statement. The introduction may be a single paragraph or multiple paragraphs.
2. The **body**	supports (shows, explains, or proves) the main point. It generally has at least three **support paragraphs**, each containing facts and details that develop the main point. Each support paragraph begins with a **topic sentence** that supports the thesis statement.
3. The **conclusion**	reminds readers of the main point. It may summarize and reinforce the support in the body paragraphs, or it may make an observation based on that support. Whether it is a single paragraph or more, the conclusion should relate back to the main point of the essay.

The parts of an essay correspond to the parts of a paragraph:

- The **thesis** of an essay is like the **topic sentence** of a paragraph.
- The **support paragraphs** in the body of an essay are like the **support sentences** of a paragraph.
- The **conclusion** of an essay is like the **concluding sentence** of a paragraph.

RELATIONSHIP BETWEEN PARAGRAPHS AND ESSAYS

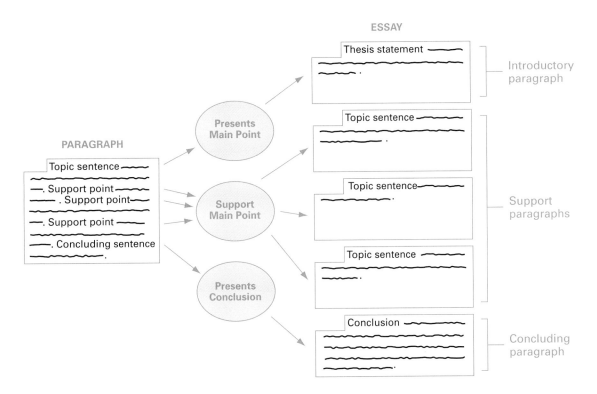

Read the following sample essay, in which the parts are underlined and labeled. It is on the same topic as the paragraph on page 4, but because it is an essay, it goes into greater detail on the topic.

Introductory
paragraph

*Thesis
statement*

At one point or another, you will probably feel that you are entitled to get paid more for your work, but you may not have a clue about how to ask for a raise. Several simple but effective techniques will increase your chances of success.

Topic sentence

Support
paragraph 1

First, you must ask for the raise; don't expect your employer to take the initiative. Before you confront your employer, stand in front of the mirror and rehearse, "I *deserve* a raise." Never say, "May I have a raise?," "Could I have a raise?," or "Is it time for my raise?" Always say, "I *deserve* a raise." You need to believe that before you can convince your employer.

Topic sentence

Support
paragraph 2

Body

Make a list of the reasons why you deserve a raise. Write down exactly what you have done to deserve the raise. Use concrete, observable achievements that cannot be disputed, and be ready with specific examples. If a dollar value in savings to the company has resulted from your work, make sure you have documentation confirming this.

Topic sentence

Support
paragraph 3

You must also consider the amount of the raise you will ask for. Always ask for more than you think you deserve. The key word here is *more*. Rehearse this higher amount while standing in front of a mirror so you won't hesitate or stutter when you ask your boss for the raise. Too many people ask for a modest raise, unaware that this simple request may have negative side effects. When a worker asks for an unusually small raise, the employer has a tendency to devalue the employee, in the same way that people may be skeptical about buying something that is priced too low.

Concluding
paragraph

*Concluding
sentence*

Asking for a reasonably higher raise than you expect may trigger a new thought process in your employer's head. The new thought that you are worth more makes the employer more open to an honest assessment of your value to the company. If you give well-documented reasons why you are valuable to the company, your boss may see you in a new, more positive light. You may not get quite as much as you requested, but your boss is likely to act in some way on the new, positively revised image of you as an employee.

—Adapted from Perry W. Buffington (1996). *Cheap Psychological Tricks: What to Do When Hard Work, Honesty, and Perseverance Fail* (Atlanta, GA: Peachtree Press, 1996), pp. 25–27.

Understand Audience and Purpose

DEFINITION: The **purpose** for a piece of writing is your reason for writing it. In college, your purpose for writing is usually to show something, to explain something, or to create a convincing argument.

DEFINITION: The **audience** for a piece of writing is the person or people who read it, think about it, and respond to it. In college, your audience may be your teacher or your classmates. In order to have an effect on your readers, try to write for real people and address what they need or want to know.

Everything that you write has a **purpose**. Everything you write also has an **audience**. Consider both before you begin to write and at every step along the way.

PRACTICE 1 **UNDERSTANDING AUDIENCE AND PURPOSE**

Read the following description of a writing situation and the notes written in response for two different audiences. Then answer the questions.

SITUATION: Janine Ronzo wakes up and realizes her alarm didn't ring and so she has overslept. She is now going to be late for an interview with Ms. Farina, a supervisor at her company who has a job opening that interests Janine. She leaves a quick note (A) for her roommate, Pat. When she gets to the interview a half hour late, she writes a note (B) for Ms. Farina, who has already left the office to attend a two-day meeting.

A.

AUDIENCE: Janine's roommate, Pat
PURPOSE: To explain

Pat—overslept and am late for work. Cldn't clean up from last nite or feed Sparky. Sorry. J.

B.

AUDIENCE: Ms. Farina
PURPOSE: To explain

Dear Ms. Farina:

I am very sorry that I missed our meeting today. Unfortunately, my usually reliable alarm chose not to go off this morning. When I awoke on my own, I immediately realized that it was later than usual and did everything I could to get here on time. However, I was a half hour late, and I missed our meeting.

    Normally I am very prompt for work, a fact you can verify with my supervisor, Candy Silfer. I hope that we can reschedule our interview as I am very interested in discussing the position with you and I believe I am a strong candidate. I look forward to hearing from you, and I apologize again for inconveniencing you today. I will set a foolproof alarm system before our next meeting.

    Sincerely,

    Janine Ronzo

Answers may vary but should be similar to those supplied.

1. How does the note to Ms. Farina differ from the one to Pat? _____

   _____

2. How do the different audiences affect what the notes say (the content)

   and how they say it (the tone)? _____

   _____

   _____

3. Which note has more detail? _____ Why? _____

   _____

4. What three words in the note to Pat would have been edited had the

   note been to Ms. Farina? _____

THINKING CRITICALLY ABOUT PURPOSE AND AUDIENCE

	PURPOSE	AUDIENCE
FOCUS	Remember that you are writing for a reason.	Remember that someone will read what you write.
ASK	• What is my assignment? • What topic will I be writing about?	• Who will be reading this? • What does my audience already know about the topic?

	PURPOSE	AUDIENCE
ASK	• What point do I want to make about my topic?	• What does my audience want or need to know about my topic?
	• What do I want my audience to think about my topic?	• Does my audience have a particular attitude or opinion about my topic? Do I need to address that specifically?
WRITE	Always write with your purpose and your audience in mind.	

Understand the Writing Process

DEFINITION: The **writing process** consists of a series of steps: exploring ideas, planning, drafting, revising, and editing.

Whenever you are first learning to do something—play a sport, drive a car, ride a bicycle—the steps seem complicated and hard to remember. But after you practice them for a while, they seem to blend together. You no longer have to concentrate to remember the individual steps; you just do them. The same thing will happen as you practice the steps in the writing process.

WRITING ASSIGNMENT

Write an essay on one of the following topics or one of your own choice. Before or as you write, follow a student, Roberta Fair, through the writing process, starting on page 11 and continuing to page 22. Chapters 2 through 7 explain each step of the process in more detail.

A personal goal

How I get through hard times

My biggest responsibility

Something I'm really good at

Everyone in my family _____

I am the only one in my family _____

The Writing Process

1. EXPLORE IDEAS TO MAKE AND SUPPORT A POINT

Ask: What is my purpose in writing? Who will read my essay? What does my audience need to know?

A • Find and explore your topic (Chapter 2).

B • Make your point by stating your thesis (Chapter 3).

C • Support your point with details and topic sentences (Chapter 4).

2 PLAN   Ask: How can I organize my ideas effectively for my reader?

A • Make a plan and arrange your ideas (Chapter 5).

3 DRAFT   Ask: How can I show my reader what I mean?

A • State your main point or thesis (Chapter 3).

B • Write topic sentences for your body paragraphs (Chapter 6).

C • Fill out your draft with details and support (Chapter 6).

D • Add an interesting introduction, a strong conclusion, and a title (Chapter 6).

4 REVISE   Ask: How can I make my draft clearer or more convincing to my reader?

A • Relate ideas or drop ideas that do not fit (Chapter 7).

B • Add more detailed support to make ideas convincing and easy to understand (Chapter 7).

C • Make connections with transitions and key words so that ideas flow smoothly (Chapter 7).

5 EDIT   Ask: What errors could confuse my readers and weaken my point?

A • Find and correct errors in grammar (Chapters 22–33). Focus first on finding sentence fragments (Chapter 23), run-on sentences (Chapter 24), mismatched subjects and verbs (Chapter 25), and problems with verbs (Chapter 26).

B • Look for errors in word use and spelling (Chapters 34–36) and in punctuation and capitalization (Chapters 37–41).

USE THE WRITING PROCESS: A STUDENT WRITER AT WORK

Each step of the writing process is illustrated in this section as student writer Roberta Fair moves from finding an idea to drafting and revising an essay. Chapters 2 through 7 provide more examples and practices for each step as well as additional writing assignments.

Step 1: Narrow and Explore Your Topic

DEFINITION: To **narrow** a topic is to focus on the smaller parts of a general topic until you find a more limited topic or an angle that is interesting, familiar, and specific.

> For more on finding and exploring a topic, see Chapter 2.

DEFINITION: To **explore** a topic is to investigate what you already know about your narrowed topic in order to decide what you want to say. One way to explore a topic is to use a prewriting technique.

DEFINITION: **Prewriting techniques** are strategies you can use to come up with ideas at any point during the writing process: to find a topic, to get ideas for what you want to say about that topic, and to support your ideas.

In the first week of her college writing course, Roberta Fair was given this assignment:

Write an essay about a personal goal.

Her first step was to narrow the general topic, finding a specific idea. She started with the words *personal goals* and made a list of specific personal goals.

NARROWING A TOPIC

Personal Goals

lose some weight

get a better job

get a college degree

get better on the computer

stay patient with my kids

take vitamins

don't argue with my mother

Roberta then read her list and considered each item as a topic for her essay by asking, "Is this narrowed topic important to me?" Roberta decided that her most important personal goal was to get a college degree.

TOPIC	NARROWED TOPIC
a personal goal	*getting a college degree*

Roberta considered using one of five common prewriting techniques to explore her narrowed topic.

For detailed examples of these prewriting techniques, see Chapter 2.

COMMON PREWRITING TECHNIQUES

1. Freewrite
2. List/brainstorm
3. Question
4. Discuss
5. Cluster

Roberta chose to explore her topic by freewriting. For five minutes, she wrote nonstop, writing everything she could think of about her topic without correcting her grammar or crossing anything out.

For a full description of freewriting and another example, see page 28.

ROBERTA'S FREEWRITING

Narrowed Topic: Getting a college degree

I don't know, I don't think about goals more than just handling every day—I don't have time. The kids, my job, laundry, food, school, it's a lot. So I just get by day by day but I know that won't get me or my kids anywhere. I really do wish I could get a better job that was more interesting and I sure wish I could make more money, and get my kids better stuff and live in a better place and not be worried all the time about money and our apartment and all that. I really do need to get that degree cause I know we'd have a better chance then. I know I need to finish college.

 ASSIGNMENT STEP 1   NARROW AND EXPLORE YOUR TOPIC

For more examples showing how to narrow and explore a topic, see Chapter 2.

Narrow one of the general topics in the writing assignment (p. 9) or one of your own choice. Jot down a list of possible topics that are narrower and more specific before choosing one to write about. Then freewrite or use another prewriting technique to explore your narrowed topic.

Step 2: *Make a Point*

DEFINITION: The **main point** of a piece of writing is the message or key idea you want to get across about your topic. Your **thesis** announces your main point or position on your topic to your reader.

> For more on making a point and stating a thesis, see Chapter 3.

Roberta reread her freewriting, trying to figure out what main point she wanted to make. She circled her most important ideas about getting a college degree as she looked for her strongest message.

ROBERTA'S REREADING OF HER FREEWRITING

I don't know, I don't think about goals more than just handling every day — I don't have time. The kids, my job, laundry, food, school, it's a lot. (So I just get by) day by day but I know that (won't get me or my kids anywhere.) I really do (wish I could get a better job) that was (more interesting) and I sure wish I could (make more money,) and (get my kids better stuff) and (live in a better place) and (not be worried all the time about money) and our apartment and all that. I really do need to get that degree cause I know we'd have a better chance then. I know I (need to finish college.)

Roberta's most important ideas made an overall point: Getting a college degree would help her get a good job, which would allow her to improve her life in other ways. Although this specific sentence wasn't in her freewriting, the ideas she circled added up to that point. Roberta stated her point in a working thesis statement, a first-try version of the sentence that would state her main point and let her readers know what she would be writing about.

ROBERTA'S WORKING THESIS

Getting a college degree will help me build a better life for myself and my children.

ASSIGNMENT STEP 2   MAKE A POINT

Reread your freewriting or other prewriting work, and decide what main point you want to make about your narrowed topic. Look for your strongest message, and write a working thesis statement. (Don't worry if it

> For more examples showing how to develop a thesis, see Chapter 3.

doesn't cover every idea you wrote down; you may modify your thesis as you write.)

1 C

Step 3: Support Your Point

For more on sup-
porting a point,
see Chapter 4.

DEFINITION: **Support** is the collection of evidence, examples, or facts that show, explain, or prove your thesis. **Support points** are the major ideas developed in the paragraphs that make up the body of your essay. **Supporting details** are the specifics you provide to explain your major support points to your readers.

Once Roberta had a working thesis for her essay, she began to think about what information would support her point and get it across to her audience. She asked herself a key question: How will getting a college degree help me? She made a list of possible support points; then she reread the list to drop unrelated points or weak ideas.

ROBERTA'S LIST OF IDEAS TO SUPPORT HER THESIS STATEMENT

Thesis: Getting a college degree will help me build a better life for myself and my children.

Key question: How?

make more money

only have one job, won't be so tired

it won't be so boring

more options about jobs

could get that red dress

more respect

move to a better place

feel better about myself

my kids will look up to me, and they're more likely to stay in school

meet guys in class

get kids some clothes they want

might lose weight because I wouldn't have time to eat

When Roberta reviewed her list, she discovered that she could combine her ideas about how a college degree would improve her life into three groups:

Group 1: Getting a better job

Group 2: Providing things for her children

Group 3: Feeling better about herself

She numbered her ideas according to these three groups.

ROBERTA'S GROUPING OF IDEAS

1	make more money	2	move to a better place
1	only have one job, won't be so tired	3	feel better about myself
1	it won't be so boring	3	my kids will look up to me, and they're more likely to stay in school
1	more options about jobs		
3	more respect	2	get kids some clothes they want

Roberta listed her groups as major support points. Then she noted supporting details, more specific information about each support point.

ROBERTA'S MAJOR SUPPORT POINTS	ROBERTA'S SUPPORTING DETAILS
1. Could get a better job	Make more money
	Work one job, not two jobs
	Have more options for jobs
	Get a less boring job
2. Provide for my children	Live in a better place
	Get them some things they want
	Be a good role model for them
3. Feel better about myself	Achieve a goal
	Get respect from others
	Respect myself

As she wrote her essay, Roberta continued to add supporting details to help her readers understand her main point and to bring to life her support points.

ASSIGNMENT STEP 3   SUPPORT YOUR POINT

Using Roberta's steps as a model, find three major support points for your working thesis. Then add three supporting details to each of the major support points.

For more examples showing how to support a point, see Chapter 4.

Step 4: Plan and Make an Outline

For more on planning and outlining, see Chapter 5.

DEFINITION: In writing, **order** means the sequence in which you present your ideas: what comes first, what comes next, and so on. Three common ways of ordering ideas are **chronological order** (by the sequence of time in which events happened), **spatial order** (by the physical arrangement of objects or features), and **order of importance** (by the significance of the ideas or reasons).

There is no one right order for any essay: It depends on your topic and the point you are making about that topic. Ask these two questions as you begin to organize your ideas:

1. Purpose: Why am I writing?
2. Audience: Who will be reading this?

Your answers will help arrange your ideas so that they have the most impact on your readers or so that your readers are most likely to understand your point.

Once Roberta had a body of ideas to work with, she began to plan how to organize them into her essay. Here are her answers to the two questions.

ROBERTA'S RESPONSES TO QUESTIONS ABOUT PURPOSE AND AUDIENCE

1. *Purpose: Why am I writing this?* For an assignment, but also for myself. If I have to spend time writing, I might as well get something out of it. So I'm writing to help me figure out what personal goal is important to me—and why it's important.

2. *Audience: Who will be reading this?* My professor, who doesn't know me at all. She has a college degree, so she probably agrees that getting one is important, but she'll be grading my writing based on the reasons I give and the way I write. I think I should build up to the most important reason for wanting to get a college degree. But what is that?

And also, sometimes professors read essays aloud, so it might be that other students in the class will hear what I've written. I don't want to feel like a fool in front of the class or my professor, so I want to give serious reasons.

Roberta decided to organize her ideas by order of importance, building up to the most important point. Because all of her points were important, she needed to decide which of her reasons for wanting to get a college degree were most important to her. She then put her ideas into outline form so that she had a clear blueprint to use as she wrote her essay.

ROBERTA'S OUTLINE

> *Thesis: Getting a college degree will help me build a better life for myself and my children.*
> 1. Major support, body paragraph #1: *Could get a better job*
>   *Supporting details:*
>   a.   *Get a less boring job*
>   b.   *Have more options for jobs*
>   c.   *Make more money and work one job, not two jobs*
> 2. Major support, body paragraph #2: *Provide for my children*
>   *Supporting details:*
>   a.   *Spend more time with them because I don't have to work two jobs*
>   b.   *Get them some things they want*
>   c.   *Live in a better place*
>   d.   *Be a good role model for them*
> 3. Major support, body paragraph #3: *Feel better about myself*
>   *Supporting details:*
>   a.   *Get respect from others*
>   b.   *Respect myself because I achieved an important goal*
>   c.   *Go on to achieve other goals*
>   Possible Point for Concluding Paragraph: *Won't be easy, but worth the time and effort involved.*

To make her outline, Roberta used the supporting details she had listed earlier. She also added ideas such as 3c (Go on to achieve other goals) and her concluding point (Won't be easy, but worth the time and effort involved).

 ASSIGNMENT STEP 4   MAKE A PLAN

Consider your purpose for writing and the likely audience for your writing as you decide how you want to organize your support. Then make an outline that will serve as a blueprint for your draft.

For more examples showing how to plan and outline, see Chapter 5.

Step 5: Write a Draft

DEFINITION: A **draft** is the first whole version of all your ideas put together in a piece of writing.

Once Roberta had a working outline, she was ready to write a draft of her essay, getting all her ideas on paper in related paragraphs. Roberta used the major support points from her outline to write topic sentences for the paragraphs in the body of her essay.

For more on writing a draft, see Chapter 6.

ROBERTA'S SUPPORT POINTS	ROBERTA'S SUPPORT POINTS AS TOPIC SENTENCES
1. Could get a better job	1. With a college degree, I could get a better job.
2. Provide for my children	2. Having a college degree and a good job would also help me be a better provider for my children.
3. Feel better about myself	3. Having a college degree would make me feel better about myself.

Roberta began writing her draft. Her **introductory paragraph** included her thesis statement and other sentences to interest her readers and give them a preview of what her essay would discuss. Her **concluding paragraph** reminded readers of her main point and made a further observation based on the ideas in the essay. She also wrote a title that fit the topic of her essay.

ROBERTA'S DRAFT ESSAY

A Goal to Live By

Thesis statement

Getting a college degree will help me build a better life for myself and my children. When I think of a personal goal, that is definitely the most important to me. It's not just the degree itself that is important, but also the ways in which it could improve things.

Topic sentence followed by supporting details

With a college degree, I could get a better job. I would have more job options than I do now. That would give me an opportunity to get a job that isn't as boring as the one I have now. It would also mean that I could make more money in one job and wouldn't have to have two.

Topic sentence followed by supporting details

Having a college degree and a good job would also help me be a better provider for my children. I could spend more time with them because I wouldn't have to work two jobs. I could get them some of the things they want so badly. We could move to a better neighborhood that's safer.

Topic sentence followed by supporting deails

Having a college degree would make me feel better about myself. I'd get more respect from others. I'd feel good about myself because I'd achieved an important and hard goal.

> Although it won't be easy, getting my college degree will be worth the time and effort involved. With that degree, I will be able to build a better life and will have the self-esteem that I want for both myself and my children. You have to feel good about yourself.

Concluding sentence

 ASSIGNMENT STEP 5 WRITE A DRAFT

Using your outline from Step 4, write a draft essay.

For more examples showing how to write an introduction, a conclusion, and a full draft, see Chapter 6.

Step 6 *Revise Your Draft*

DEFINITION: **Revising** is changing your ideas to make your writing clearer, stronger, and more convincing. When revising, you might add, cut, re-arrange, or change words and phrases, whole sentences, or paragraphs. It's your chance to move things around and make them work better to get your main point across to your readers.

Roberta put her draft aside for a day or two and then came back to it. She reread it and made some notes about how to improve it. She also visited the writing center at school, where she asked the tutor to read her draft and give her feedback she could use to make her essay more effective. Then she made more notes on her draft, following the tutor's suggestions.

For more on revising — including unity, detail, and coherence — see Chapter 7.

ROBERTA'S NOTES ON HER DRAFT

> Getting a college degree will help me build a better life for myself and my children. When I think of a personal goal, that is definitely the most important to me. It's not just the degree itself that is important, but also the ways in which it could improve things. —————— *What things? Add specific details.*
>
> With a college degree, I could get a better job. I would have more job options than I do now. That would give me an opportunity to get — *Say what I do now.*
> a job that isn't as boring as the one I have now. It would also mean that — *Tell what's boring about my job.*
> I could make more money in one job and wouldn't have to have two.
>
> Having a college degree and a good job would also help me be a better provider for my children. I could spend more time with them — *Say what I mean by "better provider."*

(continued)

Like what? ——————

because I wouldn't have to work two jobs. I could get them some of the things they want so badly. We could move to a better neighborhood that's safer.

Add more detail here; how would I feel, and why would that be new to me?

More; this just seems boring and weak ——————

Having a college degree would make me feel better about myself. I'd get more respect from others. I'd feel good about myself because I'd achieved an important and hard goal.

Although it won't be easy, getting my college degree will be worth the time and effort involved. With that degree, I will be able to build a better life and will have the self-esteem that I want for both myself and my children. You have to feel good about yourself.

Other ideas: doesn't seem to flow very well. It jumps from one paragraph to another. Try making it smoother by adding transitions, both in the paragraph and between paragraphs. Maybe add "most important" to last paragraph?

ROBERTA'S REVISED ESSAY with her changes in bold

A Goal to Live By

Clearer wording ——

Getting a college degree will help me build a better life for myself and my children. **Although I have a number of goals in life,** that is definitely the most important to me. **The degree itself is just a**

Added stronger sentence ——

piece of paper, but it promises concrete, real rewards that I want and am ready to work for.

Added detail in new sentences ——

With a college degree, I could get a better job. I would have more job options than I do now. **I'm a waitress at a restaurant that doesn't even have good tips, and I want to be an assistant manager. The owner said I am a great worker, but an assistant manager has to have a degree. With a degree, I could look for management training programs in many fields.** That would give me an opportunity to get a job that isn't as boring as the one I have

More specific information ——

now, **where I take orders, warm up food in the microwave, and deliver the orders. I actually look forward to folding napkins, just because it's something different!** Being a manager would also mean that I could make more money in one job and wouldn't have to have two. **Right now, in addition to my waitress job, I work at Wal-Mart, but even two minimum-wage jobs don't cover all our expenses. I come up short every month.**

Also, having a college degree and a good job would help me be a better provider for my children. **For example**, I could spend more time with them because I wouldn't have to work two jobs. **I could make sure they do their homework and eat right.** I could get them some of the things they want so badly. **They don't ask for much, but Jilly has wanted a special pair of jeans for months, and Carl's back-pack is about to give out.** We could also move to a better neighbor-hood that's safer. **It worries me that there are gangs, and I want to get Carl, especially, away from them. There's too much easy crime here.**

Most important, having a college degree would make me feel better about myself. I'd get more respect from others, **like the teach-ers and the tutors at Jilly and Carl's school. When I was in for a conference and the teacher found out I was a waitress, she acted as if Carl's low grades were to be expected from the son of an uneducated single parent. I know I'm smart, but people assume I must be dumb, and that wouldn't happen if I had a degree and a better job.** I'd feel good about myself because I'd achieved an important and hard goal. **Sometimes I feel as if I'm just letting life run me, and I want to take more control of it. It's my life, right? I need to respect myself before anyone else will.**

Although it won't be easy, getting my college degree will be well worth the time and effort involved: **It will pay off big-time, both financially and psychologically.** With that degree, I will be able to build a better life and will have the self-esteem that I want for both myself and my children. **Most important of all, I will have choices, and I will be more in charge of my life. As they say, "You only go through once; you should make the most of it." I will.**

For advice on editing a draft, see Chapters 22–41.

Added transition (for example) and more detail

Specific examples

Specific examples

Lots of new information and examples

Even more! I'm on a roll here!

Stronger, more specific opening sentence for conclusion

Much stronger ending!

Roberta completed her essay by working through the following steps of the writing process: exploring ideas, planning, drafting, and revising. Her final step was to edit her paper for correctness in grammar, word use, spelling, punctuation, and mechanics (see Parts 4–7).

▪ **ASSIGNMENT STEP 6** **REVISE YOUR DRAFT**

For more examples showing how to revise a draft, see Chapter 7.

Revise your draft essay, looking for ways to make it stronger, clearer, and more convincing. Think about how you can make your major support points meaningful to your readers. Guide your readers through your ideas so that you accomplish your purpose.

Use a Computer to Write

You may have already used a computer to write. If not, you may be required to do so in this course. With a computer, you will find that a word processing program makes writing much easier than writing everything out by hand. If you are new to computers, ask your teacher or writing center tutor for guidance about how you can quickly learn to use your school's hardware and software. Also, ask other students about how they use computers at school.

In Chapters 2 through 7 you will be practicing the stages of the writing process, and in each chapter you will find tips for practicing that particular stage using word processing software like Microsoft Word or WordPerfect. Here are a few general tips for writing with a computer.

Five Tips for Writing on a Computer

1. *Save your work as you write.* It is very frustrating to lose your work at any stage of the writing process. Saving your work at regular intervals while you are writing—say, every fifteen minutes—is the best way to keep from losing what you have written if there is a power failure or some other interruption on the computer. (In Microsoft Word 2002, you can set Autosave functions by going to the Tools menu, selecting Options, clicking on the Save tab, and checking the boxes to get the functions you want.)

2. *Save your work at the end of every session.* When you are finished using the computer, save your work in two places, if possible:

- Save it on the hard drive of the computer (usually the C: drive if you are on a Windows machine).

- Save it on a disk.

One serves as a backup for the other—computers can crash, and disks can break or malfunction. A plastic carrying case will help you protect and organize your disks. When you are working on a computer in your home, back up your important files once a week. Back it up on the same day each week: That will help you remember to perform this important task.

3. *Name your files so you can find them easily.* Developing an easy-to-remember file naming system will help you make sense of your writing. College students usually use course names or numbers, assignment dates, and key words to help them track the many files and drafts they create. If you are working on a draft of a paper for English 100, naming it "English 100 draft" may help you find it when you return to revise it. What happens when you work on your second assignment, though—your second "English 100 draft"? It's always better to be specific in naming your files by using key words in your file name. Try "Favorite Place first draft 9-28-02" for an essay in which you describe a favorite place, for example. Selecting Save As allows you to create new files—such as "Favorite Place second draft 10-6-02"—from previous drafts so that you won't overwrite anything. Being able to track your drafts will help both you and your instructor see the development of your work.

4. *Label your disks.* If you work regularly on a computer, you may have several different disks that hold your work. On each disk label, write the contents of that disk. If you work on several different computers—at home, at work, and at school, for example—make sure you have disks that are compatible with all of those computers.

5. *Print out your work.* Even though you are saving the electronic version of your writing in two places, also print out your work. Having a paper copy, called a *hard copy*, gives you extra protection against electronic glitches. You may also find it easier to revise and edit on hard copy.

2

Finding and Exploring Your Topic

Choosing Something to Write About

WRITING AS YOU LEARN

Choose one of the following topics and focus on a specific aspect of it with which you are familiar. (For example, focus on one specific pet peeve you have, one specific story about yourself, or one specific event that has affected you personally.)

> Something I find very annoying
>
> A pet peeve
>
> A story about myself
>
> Male/female relationships
>
> An event that affected me personally

With this topic in mind, read this chapter and complete all of the practice activities. When you finish the chapter, you will have found a good topic to write about and explored ideas related to that topic.

GUIDING QUESTIONS

- **PURPOSE:** Why am I writing this essay? What kinds of ideas will help me achieve my purpose?
- **AUDIENCE:** Who are my readers for this essay?

Understand What a Good Topic Is

DEFINITION: A **topic** is who or what you are writing about. A **good topic** is one that interests you, that you know something about, and that you can get involved in.

Any topic that you choose to write about should pass the following test.

FOUR-PART TEST FOR A TOPIC

1. **Does this topic interest me? If so, why do I care about it?**

   It's important that your answer to the first question is yes, because you may have a hard time figuring out what to say about a topic in which you have no interest. If the topic is assigned, you should try to find some interesting element. If you can choose the topic, make sure that it is of interest to you and that you can explain why you care about it.

2. **Do I know something about it? Do I want to know more?**

   Although you can learn about a topic as you write, begin with one that is at least familiar to you and that you want to explore further.

3. **Can I get involved with some part of it?**

   Choose a topic that motivates you to take some kind of action or that is otherwise relevant to your life.

4. **Is it specific enough for a short essay?**

   Look for a topic specific enough that you can make some point about it in a few paragraphs, but not so specific that there is nothing to say about it. If it seems too broad, decide whether you need to break it down into smaller parts; if it seems too narrow, look for a general idea to which it relates.

   PRACTICE 1   FINDING A GOOD TOPIC

Put the writing assignment topic you have chosen to the four-part test. Review your answers and either keep the topic, modify it, or choose another one.

MY TOPIC: _____

Narrow Your Topic

DEFINITION: To **narrow** a topic is to focus on the smaller parts of a general topic until you find a more limited topic or an angle that is interesting, familiar, and specific.

There are several ways to narrow the topic you have chosen.

1. Divide a general category into subcategories.

   GENERAL TOPIC: Cheating

   SUBCATEGORIES: Cheating on a school assignment

   Cheating in a game or sport

   Cheating on a diet

2. Think of specific examples.

   GENERAL TOPIC: Workplace survival skills

   EXAMPLES: Teamwork

   Public speaking

   Communicating by email

3. Focus on events from the last week or day.

   GENERAL TOPIC: Invasions of privacy

   EVENTS: The instructor read aloud parts of our journals that were supposed to be written just for him.

   The person interviewing me asked many very personal questions.

   An email message from a company whose products I'd never bought said that, based on my buying habits, I'd like what it had to offer.

A student, Jason Knox, was given the assignment to write an essay on the general topic of "A memorable accident."

First, he listed some examples of accidents he had experienced:

falling off my bicycle

a car crash on Route 495

dropping a tray of drinks

my first car accident

running a stop sign

falling out of a tree

Then, he asked himself key questions that helped him choose a narrowed topic.

KEY QUESTIONS TO CHOOSE A NARROWED TOPIC

1. Which of the narrowed topics is the most important to me?

2. Is it the right size for a short essay? Is it broad enough that I can make at least several major points about it? Is it narrow enough that I can tell the whole story in detail in a short essay?

Jason chooses "My first car accident" as his narrowed topic.

For an example of another student writer narrowing a topic, see Chapter 1, page 9.

  PRACTICE 2   NARROWING A TOPIC

Use one of the three methods on page 26 to narrow your topic. Then ask yourself the key questions above for choosing a narrowed topic. Write your narrowed topic below.

NARROWED TOPIC: _____

Explore Your Topic

DEFINITION: To **explore** a topic is to investigate what you already know about your narrowed topic in order to decide what you want to say. You can use one of several prewriting techniques to explore a topic, or you can keep a journal.

    DEFINITION: **Prewriting techniques** are strategies you can use to come up with ideas at any point during the writing process: to find a topic, to get ideas for what you want to say about the topic, and to support your ideas.

    Ask yourself: What interests me about this topic? Why do I care about it? What do I know? What do I want to say? Then use prewriting techniques to find the answers.

USE COMMON PREWRITING TECHNIQUES

You can explore your narrowed topic using one or more of five common prewriting techniques. Writers generally don't use all of these at once; instead, they choose the ones that work best for them after considering their assignment, their purpose for writing, and their narrowed topic.

1. Freewrite

2. List/brainstorm

3. Question

4. Discuss

5. Cluster

When using prewriting techniques, don't judge your ideas as you write. Later you can decide whether they're good or not. At this point, your goal is to come up with as many ideas as possible, so don't say "Oh, that's stupid" or "I'm not sure about that." Just get your brain working by writing down all the possibilities.

Student writer Jason Knox uses each of the common prewriting techniques to get ideas about his topic, "My first car accident."

Freewrite

Freewriting is like having a conversation with yourself, on paper. To freewrite, just start writing everything you can think of about your topic. Write nonstop for at least five minutes. Don't go back and cross anything out, and don't worry about using correct grammar or spelling; just write.

FREEWRITING EXAMPLE

So my first accident, what a jerk. I'd just gotten my license that day and was cruising around showing off. I saw my girlfriend, she came over while i was stopped at a red light. The car in back of me honked when the light turned green. My car started rolling back, and instead of hitting the brake I stomped on the gas and ran into the car in front of me. And then I rolled back and hit the car in back. disaster! what an idiot!

List/Brainstorm

List all the ideas about your topic that you can think of. Write as fast as you can for five minutes without stopping.

LISTING/BRAINSTORMING EXAMPLE

Topic: My first car accident

first day with my license

distracted by my girlfriend at a red light

someone behind me honked and startled me

I panicked

car started rolling back

I tried to stomp on the brake, but hit the gas pedal by mistake

plowed into the car in front of me

Ask a Reporter's Questions

Ask yourself questions to start getting ideas. The following questions, which reporters use, give you different angles on a narrowed topic: Who? What? Where? When? Why? How?

QUESTIONING EXAMPLE

Topic: My first car accident

Who? me, age 16

What? a guy with a new license feeling pretty cool gets into a stupid accident

Where? downtown, at the light on the hill

When? 4 years ago, on the same day I got my license

Why? because I was showing off and not paying attention

How? by pounding on the gas pedal instead of the brake and hitting two cars

Discuss

Many people find it helpful to discuss ideas with someone else before they write. As they talk, they get more ideas and they get immediate feedback from the other person.

Team up with another person. If you both have writing assignments, first explore one person's topic, then the other's. The person whose topic is being explored is the interviewee; the other person is the interviewer. The interviewer should ask questions about anything that seems confusing or unclear and should let the interviewee know what sounds interesting. The interviewee should give thoughtful answers and keep an open mind. It is a good idea to take notes when you are the interviewee. If you are writing on a computer, record the notes in your prewriting file.

DISCUSSING EXAMPLE

Jason: I guess I'll write about this car accident.

Tim: What about it?

Jason: Well, it was really stupid.

Tim: Why?

Jason: On the very first day I got my license, I had an accident with two cars. It was my fault, and it wouldn't have happened if I'd been paying attention and not trying to show off.

Tim: What did you do?

Jason: I was stopped at a light on a steep hill and I saw my girlfriend. She came over to the car and I was showing off and stuff because I had a license. The car in back of me honked because the light had turned green, so I took my foot off the brake to go. But then I started rolling back, so I tried to press the brake again really hard to keep from hitting the car in back of me, but I pressed the gas instead. I rammed into the car in front of me and then rolled back and hit the car that had honked. And my girlfriend was standing there the whole time.

Tim: That sounds rough. Sure makes a good story, though.

Jason: Yeah, but too bad I got my license suspended.

Cluster

Clustering, also called mapping, is like listing except that you arrange your ideas in a more visual way. Using a blank sheet of paper, write your narrowed topic in the center and circle it. Then ask yourself some questions, such as *What about this topic is important to me? What do I know about it?* Write your ideas around the narrowed topic, drawing lines from your topic to the ideas and circling them in turn. Add more lines and circles to connect additional ideas, as shown in Jason's example.

CLUSTERING EXAMPLE

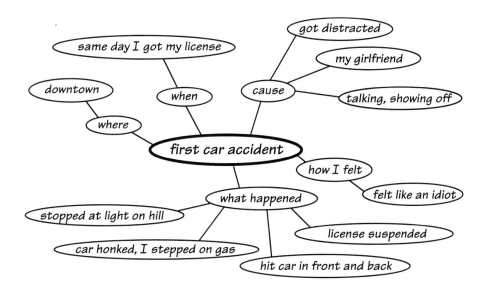

KEEP A JOURNAL

Another good way to explore ideas and topics for writing is to keep a journal. Set aside a few minutes a day or decide on some other regular schedule to write in your journal, which can take the form of a traditional
notebook or a word processing file. Your journal will be a great source of
ideas when you need to find something to write about.

   You can use a journal in many ways:

- To record and explore your personal thoughts and feelings
- To comment on things that happen either to you or in politics, in the
  neighborhood, at work, at your college, and so on
- To list ideas to see what you know and think about them
- To examine situations you don't understand (as you write, you may
  figure them out)

JOURNAL ENTRY EXAMPLE

   *I remember this car accident like it was yesterday. It was one of the
dumbest things I've ever done. I'd just gotten my driver's license and was
cruising around downtown feeling like a real big shot. While I was stopped
at a light on a pretty steep hill, I saw my girlfriend and waved her over.
Instead of paying attention to the light, I was just talking with her. The*

car in back of me honked when the light turned green. I took my foot off the brake to go, but then started rolling back, so I tried to step on the brake but I pressed the gas, hard, instead, and plowed into the car in front of me. Then I rolled back and hit the car in back. And then I lost my license.

PRACTICE 3 PREWRITING

Choose *two* prewriting techniques, and use them to explore your narrowed topic. Keep your readers in mind as you explore your topic; find ideas that will be effective not only for your purpose but also for your readers' understanding.

Use a Computer to Find and Explore Your Topic

Try using a computer as you find and explore your topic. First, open a blank word processor file and write a list of topics that interest you. After testing each one with the Four-Part Test for a Topic on page 25, use your word processing program's drag-and-drop or copy-and-paste feature to bring the most promising topic farther down in your document. Label that topic "General Topic," and then narrow it using the strategies from page 26.

Next, select a specific example, event, or subcategory of your topic, and begin a new section of your document, again using the drag-and-drop or cut-and-paste feature. Choose a prewriting strategy from those listed on page 28, and begin to explore your topic. If you find yourself being concerned with grammar or spelling as you freewrite or brainstorm, for example, darken your monitor or turn it off so that you can't see what you're writing. Save your document so that you can use ideas and information from your prewriting later in your process.

3

Making a Point

Writing Your Thesis Statement

> **You Know This**
> You have lots of experience under-standing and stating main points.
> - You listen to the words of a song and understand the point.
> - You tell a friend about a funny experience. (The point may simply be that it was funny, or it may have a more significant meaning.)
> - You understand the point of a movie.

▪ WRITING AS YOU LEARN

Using your topic and ideas from Chapter 2, develop a strong thesis for your essay.

The explanations, examples, and practices in this chapter will help you write a strong thesis statement. You can either write a thesis now and revise it after working through the chapter, or you can read the chapter and use what you've learned to write a strong thesis.

GUIDING QUESTIONS

- **PURPOSE**: What do I want to show or explain about my topic?

- **AUDIENCE**: What point can I make that would make an impression on my readers?

Understand What a Thesis Is

DEFINITION: The **thesis** of a piece of writing states the main point or idea you want to get across about your topic. It is your position on whatever you are writing about. The basic structure of a thesis is this:

| Narrowed topic | + | Main point/position | = | Thesis |

Eating disorders are caused by both cultural and psychological factors. A strong thesis has four basic features.

FOUR BASICS OF A STRONG THESIS

1. It focuses on a single main point or position about the topic.
2. It is neither too broad nor too narrow.
3. It is specific, not vague, and prepares readers for what is to come.
4. It is a forceful statement written in confident, firm language.

A strong, clearly stated thesis is essential to most good essays. In fact, everything else you write in your essay should be there because it supports the thesis, helping you get your main point across to your readers.

Early in your writing process, you may develop a *working thesis,* a first-try version of the sentence that will state your main point. You can revise the working thesis into a final thesis statement later in the writing process.

Practice Developing a Thesis

The following three-step sequence sets an essay in motion:

1. Narrow the general topic

   GENERAL TOPIC: Public safety

   NARROWED TOPIC: Airport security

2. Determine what point you want to make about the topic. (Use a prewriting technique.)

   For examples of prewriting techniques, see pages 28–31.

   WORKING THESIS: Allowing the federal government to take charge of airport security is a good idea.

3. Rewrite your thesis to make it more specific so that you can explain, show, or prove it with concrete evidence.

   THESIS: Allowing the federal government to take charge of airport security screening is a practical way to make air travel safer.

Once you have chosen your topic and used a prewriting technique to generate some ideas about it, the next step is to determine the point you want to make: You need to develop a thesis. The practices in the next part of this chapter will help you write thesis statements that have the four basics of a strong thesis.

1. WRITE A THESIS THAT STATES A SINGLE MAIN POINT

Your thesis should focus on only one main point. If you try to include more than one main point in a single essay, you will probably not have room to provide adequate support for all of the points. Inadequate support will likely confuse your readers.

THESIS STATEMENT WITH TWO MAIN POINTS

> In the next decade, <u>many schools will have a drastic shortage of teachers,</u> and <u>teachers should have to take competency tests.</u>

The two points are underlined. The writer would need both to explain why there will be a shortage of teachers and to give reasons why teachers should have to take competency tests. These are both meaty points, and any writer would have trouble supporting them equally in a single essay.

THESIS STATEMENT WITH ONE MAIN POINT

> In the next decade, many schools will have a drastic shortage of teachers.

OR

> Teachers should have to take competency tests.

By choosing only one main point, the writer can focus on supporting that point and the essay will be more effective.

PRACTICE 1   IDENTIFY THE MAIN POINT

In each of the following thesis statements, underline the <u>topic</u> and double-underline the <u>main point</u>.

EXAMPLE: The <u>smell of apples</u> always <u>reminds me of fall at home.</u>

1. A visit to New York City will bring many surprises.

2. Many people don't know that this town has lots of free entertainment.

3. Going to the movies is by no means cheap entertainment.

4. Men and women have very different communication styles.

5. People will buy almost anything if it is marked "Clearance."

6. Consignment stores offer an alternative shopping experience.

7. Losing a job can have numerous unexpected results.

8. Executive perks range from the small to the astounding.

9. Being a driver education teacher can make a person crazy.

10. Elder care is the field of the future.

2. WRITE A THESIS THAT IS NEITHER TOO BROAD NOR TOO NARROW

Your thesis should be manageable; that is, it should fit the size of the essay assignment. If it is either too broad or too narrow, it will be hard for you to write an effective essay because you will not be able to show, explain, or prove your thesis with concrete ideas.

A thesis that is too broad is impossible to support fully in a short essay — there is just too much to cover well.

TOO BROAD   Family is an essential part of life.

[Both *family* and *life* are broad concepts, and the thesis would be impossible to explain in a short essay.]

REVISED   Time spent with my children is a welcome balance to time spent at work.

A thesis that is too narrow leaves the writer with little to show, explain, or prove. It can also make the reader think, "So what?"

TOO NARROW   My family members all have the same middle name.

[Once the writer says what the middle name is, there isn't much more to say, *unless* there's an interesting family story explaining why everyone has it.]

REVISED   An interesting event from long ago explains why my family members all have the same middle name.

PRACTICE 2   IDENTIFY THESIS STATEMENTS THAT ARE TOO BROAD OR TOO NARROW

Read the following thesis statements and decide whether they are too broad, too narrow, or the right size for a short essay. For statements that are too broad, write "B" in the space to the left; for statements that are too narrow, write "N"; and for statements that are the right size, write "OK."

EXAMPLE: <u>N</u> My dog will be ten years old next month.

_____ 1. Hinduism is a fascinating religion.

_____ 2. I am a vegetarian.

_____ 3. Being a vegetarian offers a wide range of food choices.

_____ 4. There are many vegetarians in this country.

_____ 5. Another gourmet coffee shop opened last week, the third one on a single block.

3. WRITE A SPECIFIC THESIS STATEMENT THAT PREPARES THE READER FOR WHAT'S TO COME

A strong thesis statement prepares readers by giving them a specific preview of what you will cover in your essay.

GENERAL   I have to write in my job.

[So what? Lots of people do. Why would anyone be interested in that statement?]

SPECIFIC   As a nurse, I take care of people, but my job requires good writing skills.

[Tells the reader that the essay will discuss the amount and probably the type of writing a nurse does.]

MORE SPECIFIC As a nurse, my ability to write clearly is essential in documents such as patient reports, status notes to nurses on other shifts, and emails to other hospital staff.

[Tells the reader what kinds of writing the essay will discuss.]

PRACTICE 3   WRITE SPECIFIC THESIS STATEMENTS

Rewrite each of the following thesis statements by adding at least two specific details.

> **EXAMPLE**: Electronic devices in high schools can be a huge problem. <u>Wireless phones</u> that ring during a high school class <u>disrupt students' concentration and learning.</u>

1. I have a lot of useful skills.

   _____

   _____

2. Tara's new puppy is adorable.

   _____

   _____

3. I have always had trouble writing.

   _____

   _____

4. Children have more allergies now than in the past.

   _____

   _____

5. After I was robbed, I had many feelings.

   _____

   _____

4. WRITE A THESIS STATEMENT THAT IS FORCEFUL

A strong thesis statement should be forceful and definite; a weak one leaves the reader thinking, "So what?" Avoid writing a thesis statement that begins, "In this essay I will show . . ." Don't say you will make a point. Just make it.

WEAK	In this essay, I will prove that high school dropouts have a difficult time in life.
FORCEFUL	High school dropouts can expect to face surprising hardships in life.
WEAK	I think you have to be careful when buying a used car.
FORCEFUL	Before buying a used car, get some basic information so that you don't pay more than you need to.

One way of writing a thesis statement is to announce the number of ideas you will discuss.

THESIS STATEMENT: Before buying a car, get information in three basic areas.

The writer of this thesis statement would go on to identify the three areas and discuss each in a paragraph. The outline of the essay might look like this:

THESIS STATEMENT: Before buying a car, get information in three basic areas.

TOPIC SENTENCE, PARAGRAPH 1: The first area that is important to research is . . .

TOPIC SENTENCE, PARAGRAPH 2: The second area that is important to research is . . .

TOPIC SENTENCE, PARAGRAPH 3: The third area that is important to research is . . .

Note, however, that although this approach ensures that the thesis statement and essay will be organized, it may also make them dull. Before sticking with this kind of thesis statement and topic sentence structure, try to make the thesis more forceful and interesting. For instance, in the thesis statement above, the writer might tell the reader why it is important to get information before buying a car.

PRACTICE 4   WRITE FORCEFUL THESIS STATEMENTS

Rewrite the weak thesis statements that follow to make them more forceful.

EXAMPLE: My dog is great.

My dog, Kayla, understands me better than any human being does.

1. I will explain some examples of history repeating itself.

   _____

   _____

2. This college should provide better parking facilities, I think.

   _____

   _____

3. My new boss is really nice.

   _____

   _____

4. The drug Ecstasy is used by lots of people.

   _____

   _____

5. Working while going to college isn't easy.

   _____

   _____

The four practices you have already completed in this chapter have focused on the four basics of strong thesis statements. The next two practices will help you develop a thesis from prewriting or by narrowing the topic.

PRACTICE 5   DEVELOP A THESIS FROM PREWRITING

Read each example of a narrowed topic with prewriting, and write a possible thesis statement. There is no one right answer.

1. **NARROWED TOPIC**: The popularity of television shows like _Survivor_ and _Temptation Island_

FREEWRITING ON THE TOPIC

   These shows are popular because they're real, not some stupid sitcom. People are really out there, and you feel like they could be you and you know

there's no script, it's really happening and you're watching it. It's like Do
You Want to Be a Millionaire? *Someone just like me could win a lot of
money but sometimes they don't know the easiest answers and then you
feel smarter than they are. But still you're rooting for all the people on
these shows because they are like you.*

THESIS: _____

_____

2. **NARROWED TOPIC:** State proficiency tests required for high school
graduation

BRAINSTORMING ON THE TOPIC

Not fair to kids who don't pass

Very tough tests

Sometimes tests aren't good

Teachers teach only what students need to pass test

I couldn't pass one now

Lots of class time spent on tests

What happens to kids who don't pass?

Can students sue the school if they fail?

THESIS: _____

_____

3. **NARROWED TOPIC:** Lack of privacy on the Internet

CLUSTERING ON THE TOPIC

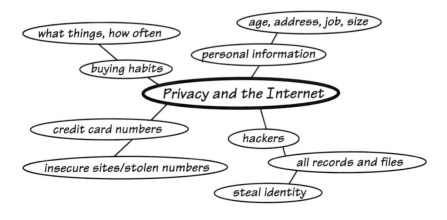

THESIS: _____

_____

▇ PRACTICE 6   DEVELOPING A THESIS BY NARROWING A TOPIC

First, narrow each general topic listed below, and write your answer in the numbered space to its right. Then, in the lettered spaces that follow, write a possible thesis—something you might want to support in an essay—for each narrowed topic.

GENERAL TOPIC	NARROWED TOPIC
Weather	How sun affects people

POSSIBLE THESIS: When the sun is shining, people's moods improve.

GENERAL TOPIC	NARROWED TOPIC
1. Vacations	1. _____
2. Hospitals	2. _____
3. Family problems	3. _____
4. Anger	4. _____
5. Love	5. _____
6. Partnerships	6. _____
7. Cars	7. _____
8. Food	8. _____
9. Parents or parenting	9. _____
10. Holidays	10. _____

POSSIBLE THESIS

a. _____

b. _____

c. _____

d. _____

e. _____

f. _____

g. _____

h. _____

i. _____

j. _____

PRACTICE 7   REVISING A THESIS

Writers almost always need to revise their working thesis statements to make them more specific and more forceful. In the spaces provided below, rewrite each of the possible thesis statements you wrote in Practice 6, making them stronger. Again, think of a statement that you would be interested in writing about. You may want to add more information to your thesis statements to make them more specific and forceful, but short, punchy thesis statements also can be very powerful.

POSSIBLE THESIS: When the sun is shining, people's moods improve.

REVISED THESIS: Bright sunshine dramatically improves people's moods.

1. _____

2. _____

3. _____

4. _____

5. _____

6. _____

7. _____

8. _____

9. _____

10. _____

If you have already written a thesis statement for the writing assignment at the beginning of this chapter, revise it now. If you have waited to write a thesis until you completed the practices, write one now, using the Thinking Critically guide that follows.

THINKING CRITICALLY TO DEVELOP YOUR THESIS STATEMENT

FOCUS   Write a working thesis statement and reread it. Think about what main point you want to make in your essay.

ASK
- What is my position or my point about my topic?
- Does my thesis statement include both my narrowed topic and the point I want to make about it?
- Does it make my point in a way that will interest readers?
- Does it state something that I can show, explain, or prove?
- Can I find ideas in my prewriting to support it?
- Can I think of additional ideas to support it?
- Does it need more specifics?
- Does it make a single point?
- Does it say what I want it to say?
- Does it fit the assignment?
- Is it a complete sentence?

WRITE   Write and adjust your thesis statement until you think it works.

Use a Computer to Write a Thesis Statement

As you review your prewriting, you can practice filtering the ideas you've come up with into possible thesis sentences. You may find it helpful to consider several options before choosing one to build on. To do this, open the document that includes your best prewriting about your topic and narrowed topic, and then save it as a new file with a new name (using Save As in the File menu). This preserves the original file and gives you a new file to use for thesis shaping.

Look through your prewriting in the new file to find several phrases or sentences that come close to stating the main point you want to make. Isolate your best phrases or sentences by putting several spaces between them, and use boldface type to identify any support points. Determine which combinations of words best capture the main point.

Next, use your word processing program's drag-and-drop or copy-and-paste feature to take the best parts of each phrase or sentence to build the thesis statement. When you make your ideas visible on the screen, it will be easier for you to adjust the focus of your working thesis so that your thinking isn't too narrow or too broad. After you draft a thesis statement, read it aloud. Does it sound like a strong, well-thought-out sentence that includes a single main point and is manageable, specific, and forceful?

Supporting Your Point

Finding Details, Examples, and Facts

■ **WRITING AS YOU LEARN**

Develop support for the thesis you wrote in Chapter 3. First, write your thesis here:

THESIS: _____

Then, after working through the chapter, apply what you have learned by writing out three support points and several supporting details for each point.

GUIDING QUESTIONS

- **PURPOSE:** What do I want to accomplish with this essay?

- **AUDIENCE:** In order to accomplish that purpose, what do I need to tell my readers? What do I know about my readers that will help me present support that will be convincing to them? What do they already know or think? What do they need to know in order to grasp my point?

Understand What Support for a Thesis Is

DEFINITION: **Support** is the collection of evidence, examples, or facts that show, explain, or prove your main point. **Support points** are the major ideas developed in the paragraphs that make up the body of your essay. **Supporting details** are the specifics you provide to explain your major support points to your readers.

Without support, you *state* the main point, but you don't *make* the main point. Consider the following statements:

> I didn't break the plates.
>
> I don't deserve an F on this paper.
>
> My telephone bill is wrong.

The statements may be true, but without support they are not convincing. Perhaps you sometimes get papers back with the comment "You need to support (or develop) your ideas"; this chapter will show you how to do so.

Writers sometimes confuse repetition with support. Using the same idea several times in different words is not support: It is just repetition.

> **REPETITION,**
> **NOT SUPPORT**: My telephone bill is wrong. The amount is incorrect. It shouldn't be this much. It is an error.
>
> **SUPPORT**: My telephone bill is wrong. There are four duplicate charges for the same time and the same number. The per minute charge is not the one my plan offers. I did not call Antarctica at all, much less three times.

As you develop support for your thesis, make sure that each point has the following three basic features.

THREE BASICS OF GOOD SUPPORT

1. **It relates to your main point.** The purpose of support is to show, explain, or prove your main point, so the support you use must be directly related to that main point.

2. **It considers your readers.** Aim your support at the people who will read your writing. Supply information that will convince or inform them.

3. **It is detailed and specific.** Give readers enough detail, particularly through examples, so that they can see what you mean.

Practice Supporting a Thesis Statement

A short essay usually has between three and five major points that support the thesis statement. Each major support point becomes the topic sentence in its own paragraph. In turn, each paragraph presents supporting details to back up that major support point.

Follow this sequence to develop support for a thesis:

1. Prewrite to find support.
2. Drop unrelated ideas.
3. Select the best support points.
4. Add supporting details.
5. Write topic sentences for your support points.

For an example of a student writer's use of this sequence, see pages 14–15.

1. PREWRITE TO FIND SUPPORT

To review prewriting techniques, see pages 27–31.

Reread your thesis and imagine your readers asking, "What do you mean?" Use one or two prewriting techniques to come up with as many ideas as you can to answer that question and support your thesis. As you prewrite, just get your ideas down on paper or on screen; don't judge them yet.

 PRACTICE 1   **PREWRITE TO FIND SUPPORT**

Choose one of the following sentences or one of your own, and write for five minutes using one prewriting technique (freewriting, listing/brainstorming, questioning, discussing, clustering). You will need a good supply of ideas from which to choose support points for your thesis. Try to find at least a dozen different ideas.

SUGGESTED THESIS STATEMENTS

1. Valentine's Day gifts can range from the simple and inexpensive to the lavish and costly.
2. Online dating services offer some obvious advantages.
3. Online dating services involve some obvious disadvantages.

4. Discrimination comes in many forms.

5. My parents still don't know about some things I did as a child (teenager).

NOTE: Imagine your reader asking, "What do you mean?"

2. DROP UNRELATED IDEAS

After finishing your prewriting, remind yourself of your main point, as expressed in your thesis statement. Then review your prewriting carefully, and drop any ideas that are not directly related to your main point. (You may want to write the dropped ideas in your journal—in case you want to use them later as writing topics.) Also, cross out any ideas that would confuse your readers or seem meaningless to them. If new ideas occur to you, write them down.

For more on keeping a journal, see pages 31–32.

 PRACTICE 2 **DROP UNRELATED IDEAS**

Each thesis statement below is followed by a list of possible support points. Cross out the unrelated ideas in each list. Be ready to explain your choices.

For an example of a student writer dropping unrelated ideas from prewriting, see page 14.

1. **THESIS STATEMENT**: Written communication must be worded precisely and formatted clearly.

   POSSIBLE SUPPORT POINTS

   use bulleted lists for important short points

   once I wrote a ridiculous memo to my boss but never sent it

   try to keep it to no more than a single page

   write the date

   get it done by the end of the day

   read it over before sending

   hate to put things in writing

   takes too much time

make a copy

getting 40 emails in a day is too many

2. **THESIS STATEMENT**: Just this year, I experienced a day that was perfect in every way.

POSSIBLE SUPPORT POINTS

weather was beautiful

on vacation

we'd had a great meal the night before

slept late

cold but inside fire was burning hot

new snow, all white

the year before we lost electricity

sky cloudless and bright blue

snow shimmering in the sunlight

perfect snow for skiing

no one else on the ski trail, very quiet

next Tuesday the ski resort would close for the season

3. **THESIS STATEMENT**: I know from experience that sometimes the customer is wrong.

POSSIBLE SUPPORT POINTS

work at supermarket

customers often misread sale flyer

they choose something like the item on sale but not it

get mad and sometimes get nasty

why do people bring screaming kids to the supermarket?

they don't have any right to be rude but they are

want to argue but I can't

customers steal food like eating grapes that are sold by the pound

sometimes they eat a whole box of cookies and bring up the empty box

then the kids are always grabbing at the candy and whining, sometimes they just rip the candy open or put it in their mouths

customers misread the signs like ones that say "save $1.50" and think the item is on sale for $1.50

should get a different job

cereal's the worst

3. SELECT THE BEST SUPPORT POINTS

Review your remaining ideas and select the best points to use. Consider which ones will be clearest and most convincing to your readers. As noted earlier, short essays usually have three to five major support points. They will become the topic sentences for your support paragraphs.

PRACTICE 3   **SELECT THE BEST SUPPORT POINTS**

For each item, circle the three points you would use to support the thesis statement. Be ready to explain your answers.

1. **THESIS STATEMENT**: A college degree should not be the only factor in hiring decisions.

   POSSIBLE SUPPORT POINTS

   job experience

   motivation and enthusiasm

   friends who work at the company

   appearance

   age

   reliability and honesty

For an example of a student writer choosing the best support points, see pages 14–15.

good transportation

artistic talents

2. **THESIS STATEMENT**: People have a variety of learning styles.

POSSIBLE SUPPORT POINTS

learn by doing

not interested in learning anything new

learn by seeing

don't bring their books to class

disrupt the class

learn by working with others

get bored

bad learners

gifted students

3. **THESIS STATEMENT**: The beauty and grandeur of the cathedral astonished me.

POSSIBLE SUPPORT POINTS

400 feet high

hundreds of tourists

white, pink, and green marble gleaming in the sun

junky gift shops in the circle around it

interior very plain

beautiful warm day

built hundreds of years ago

intricate carving on all sides

4. ADD SUPPORTING DETAILS

Once you have chosen your major support points, you will need to add details to explain or demonstrate each of those points. These supporting details can be examples, facts, or evidence. As the following example shows, a supporting detail is always more specific than a major support point.

> **THESIS STATEMENT:** I try to eat sensibly, but some foods are just too good to pass up.

> **SUPPORT POINT:** Chocolate in any form is a major temptation for me.
>
> > **SUPPORTING DETAIL:** Peanut M&M's are especially tempting—I could eat a whole pound bag in one sitting.
> >
> > **SUPPORTING DETAIL:** Canned chocolate frosting is great; I can eat it with a spoon right from the can.
> >
> > **SUPPORTING DETAIL:** Big fat truffles with the creamy centers just melt on my tongue.

> **SUPPORT POINT:** Freshly baked bread calls to me from the supermarket shelves.
>
> > **SUPPORTING DETAIL:** I can smell it as soon as I walk in the store.
> >
> > **SUPPORTING DETAIL:** Sometimes it's still warm and soft, with steam on the wrapping.
> >
> > **SUPPORTING DETAIL:** It reminds me of my grandmother making rolls for Thanksgiving dinners at her house in upstate New York.

> **SUPPORT POINT:** I tell myself never to buy boxes of cheese crackers, but sometimes my hand doesn't listen to me.
>
> > **SUPPORTING DETAIL:** Cheddar's my favorite, with lots of salt and shaped in little bite-sized squares.
> >
> > **SUPPORTING DETAIL:** Once I open the box, they'll be gone within a day, maybe even within a couple of hours, especially if I'm working at home.
> >
> > **SUPPORTING DETAIL:** I start by eating one at a time, but I get into handfuls as I go along.

For an example of a student adding supporting details, see pages 20–21.

■ PRACTICE 4   **ADD SUPPORTING DETAILS**

For each major support point, again imagine your readers asking, "What do you mean?" Add specific details to answer that question.

THESIS STATEMENT: I am an excellent baker.

SUPPORT POINT: My chocolate chip cookies are particularly good.

SUPPORTING DETAIL: I bake with the **extra-large double chocolate chips** that are **soft, gooey, and darkly sweet** when they are baked.

In the space indicated, write the points you chose in Practice 3, item 1 (see p. 51), as the best support. Then in the space to the right, add three details that would explain, show, or prove each support point.

THESIS STATEMENT: A college degree should not be the only factor in hiring decisions.

SUPPORT POINT   **SUPPORTING DETAILS**

_____   _____

                                        _____

                                        _____

SUPPORT POINT   **SUPPORTING DETAILS**

_____   _____

                                        _____

                                        _____

SUPPORT POINT   **SUPPORTING DETAILS**

_____   _____

                                        _____

                                        _____

5. WRITE TOPIC SENTENCES FOR YOUR SUPPORT POINTS

For an illustration of the parts of an essay, see pages 4–5.

Your major support points form the topic sentences for the paragraphs that support your thesis statement. Each topic sentence should clearly relate to and support (explain, show, or prove) your thesis by explaining what you mean. In your essay, each topic sentence will begin a new paragraph, and the paragraph will consist of details that explain the topic sentence.

THESIS STATEMENT: Playing a team sport taught me more than how to play the game.

TOPIC SENTENCE (1ST PARAGRAPH): I learned the importance of regular, committed practice.

TOPIC SENTENCE (2ND PARAGRAPH): I also realized that, in order to succeed, I had to work with other people.

TOPIC SENTENCE (3RD PARAGRAPH): Most important of all, I learned the importance of responsibility to others.

A topic sentence should clearly express an idea, one that supports the thesis and can in turn be supported by other details. As you develop major support points for your thesis, it is important to express your ideas in complete, clear topic sentences. Once you have developed your thesis statement and topic sentences, the rest of your essay involves filling in the details to bring your support to life for your readers.

For an example of a student writing topic sentences for her support points, see pages 17–18.

PRACTICE 5   WRITE TOPIC SENTENCES

Using the support points you generated in Practice 4, write topic sentences that support the thesis statement. Then, in the space under each topic sentence, list the details you selected. When you have completed this practice, you will have developed support for an essay.

THESIS STATEMENT: A college degree should not be the only factor in hiring decisions.

TOPIC SENTENCE (SUPPORT POINT 1): _____

_____

   SUPPORTING DETAILS: _____

_____

_____

TOPIC SENTENCE (SUPPORT POINT 2): _____

_____

   SUPPORTING DETAILS: _____

_____

_____

TOPIC SENTENCE (SUPPORT POINT 3): _____

_____

SUPPORTING DETAILS: _____

_____

_____

THINKING CRITICALLY ABOUT SUPPORT FOR YOUR THESIS STATEMENT

FOCUS   Think about the main point you intend to make in your thesis statement.

ASK
- What support can I include that will show, explain, or prove what I mean?
- What do my readers need to know or understand in order to be convinced?
- What examples come to mind?
- What have I experienced myself?
- What major points could I make to convince or inform my readers?
- What details could I use to strengthen the support?
- Do I have enough details to support each major point?
- What could I add?

WRITE   Write for five minutes using a prewriting technique to find as many support points as you can.

For examples of prewriting techniques, see pages 27–31.

Use a Computer to Support Your Point

Open your working thesis statement document and use Save As to create the next document in your writing process—your list of major support points and supporting details. To gather possible support for your thesis thinking, freewrite responses to the questions in the Thinking Critically guide above. Review your freewriting; then use the Comment tool (on the Insert menu in Microsoft Word) to write notes to yourself about which ideas can be used as major support points and which can be supporting details.

In addition to freewriting, try a quick search of World Wide Web resources by going to Google (**<www.google.com>**) and typing your thesis sentence in the Search field. If you find useful details, examples, and facts in any of the links, remember to mention each source by noting its title, author, and Web address—and the date you found the source in your document. Even if you don't find specific details, examples, and facts, the kinds of information your online search produces may help you think more clearly about the support you need for your thesis.

You Know This
You have experience in planning.

- You make a list of things you need to do and put the most important things first.
- You write down what you need at a grocery store according to where the items are in the store.
- You keep track of your appointments or meetings for the day, arranged in sequence from morning to afternoon.

5

Making a Plan

Arranging Your Ideas

▇ WRITING AS YOU LEARN

Write a plan that includes the thesis and support you have developed so far for your essay.

The explanations, examples, and practices in this chapter will help you to write a plan for your essay. Such a plan is also called an outline.

GUIDING QUESTIONS

- **PURPOSE:** Based on what I want to accomplish with this essay, how should I arrange and present the points I plan to make?
- **AUDIENCE:** What sequence of my ideas will work most effectively so that my readers will understand or be convinced of my main point?

Understand Ways of Ordering Ideas

DEFINITION: In writing, **order** means the sequence in which you present your ideas: what comes first, second, third, and so on. Three common ways of ordering your ideas are **chronological order** (by the sequence of time in which events happened), **spatial order** (by the physical arrangement of objects or features), and **order of importance** (by the significance of the ideas or reasons).

After considering the questions about purpose and audience, the next step in planning your essay is to decide how to arrange, or order, your ideas.

CHRONOLOGICAL ORDER

Use **chronological order** (time order) to arrange points according to when they happened. Time order works well when you are telling the story of an event or explaining how an event happened. Usually, you go from what happened first to what happened last; in some cases, though, you can work back from what happened last to what happened first.

EXAMPLE USING CHRONOLOGICAL (TIME) ORDER

The cause of the fire that destroyed the apartment building was human carelessness. The couple in apartment 2F had planned a romantic dinner to celebrate the woman's raise at work. They lit candles all over the apartment and then shared a bottle of wine and ate a delicious meal. After dinner, they decided to go out to a club to continue the celebration. Unfortunately, they forgot to blow out all of the candles, and one of them was too close to a window curtain, which caught fire. First the blaze burned slowly, but because the curtain was not flame retardant, the fire picked up force and spread quickly. It engulfed the apartment and then spread to other floors of the building. By the time another resident smelled smoke, the fire was uncontrollable. Before it was all over, the building was destroyed. Fortunately, rescuers were able to save everyone who was in the building. But all of the tenants lost their homes and most of their possessions. Human carelessness caused much human misery in this situation.

How does the writer use chronological order to arrange information?

SPATIAL ORDER

Use **spatial order** (space order) to arrange ideas so that your readers see your topic as you do. Space order works well when you are writing about a physical object, a place, or a person's appearance. Using the sequence that will give your readers the best picture of what your topic looks like, you can move from top to bottom, bottom to top, near to far, far to near, left to right, right to left, back to front, or front to back.

EXAMPLE USING SPATIAL (SPACE) ORDER

I stood watching in horror while all-powerful flames devoured an entire building, including my apartment and everything I owned. The first few floors looked normal, except that firefighters were racing into the front entry. They wore the long slickers and the helmets that I'd seen on television. They focused only on the building and the fire. A couple of floors up, windows were breaking, and gray, foul-smelling smoke was billowing out, as if to escape the building. I could see shadows of the firefighters moving in and out of the apartments. But my eyes were quickly drawn to the top two floors, where flames of orange and white darted out the windows and flickered in the background. A lone dog with brown and white spots barked furiously from the rooftop. Until you have actually witnessed a severe fire, you can't imagine how engulfing it is and how powerless you feel in its presence.

What type of spatial order does the writer use? _____

ORDER OF IMPORTANCE

Use **order of importance** to arrange points according to their significance, interest, or surprise value. Usually, save the most important point for last. Then you can build up to it as you explain or convince readers to accept your position on a topic.

EXAMPLE USING ORDER OF IMPORTANCE

Fires caused by human carelessness often have disastrous effects on many people's lives. In a recent incident, when an apartment building was completely destroyed by a fire, the owner and tenants had no homes to return to. They also lost all of their possessions: furniture, clothing, and treasured personal items that could never be replaced. Worse than that, however, was that the owner and many of the tenants had no insurance to help them find new housing and replace their possessions. Many had to depend completely on relatives, friends, and a fund that was started for them by neighbors. They would not soon have their own places to live, nor could they buy clothing to replace what they had lost. The most disastrous effect of the fire was that a firefighter lost his life. The thirty-year-old man had a wife and three young children who were robbed of their loved one. Carelessness has no place around fire, as it has the power to destroy.

What is this writer's most important point about the effects of fires?

_____

Practice Ordering Your Ideas

As you arrange your ideas, consider using chronological order, spatial order, or order of importance.

PURPOSE	TYPE OF ORDER
To describe an experience as it happened	Chronological (time)
To help your reader see a person, place, or object as you see it	Spatial (space)
To persuade or convince someone of the significance of your points	Importance

PRACTICE 1   USE CHRONOLOGICAL ORDER TO ARRANGE IDEAS

Arrange the support for each of the thesis statements that follow according to chronological order. Indicate the sequence of ideas by writing a number in the blank at the left. (A number 1 indicates what would happen first, a number 2 indicates what would happen second, and so on.)

1. **THESIS:** Ordering out for pizza is the easiest way to get a good meal, fast.

   _2__ Decide on what kind of toppings you want.

   _3__ Call in the order.

   _1__ Take out the menu for your favorite pizza shop.

   _5__ Pay the delivery person.

   _6__ Eat!

   _4__ Wait for the buzzer and open the door.

2. **THESIS:** Using the following steps will improve your chances of doing well on a test.

   _3__ When you are ready to begin, read the instructions carefully.

   _4__ Answer the easy questions first.

   _6__ Review your answers.

___2___   Before beginning, preview the whole test, noting which parts have the most points.

___1___   Listen to the professor's instructions when you receive the test.

___5___   Allow enough time to answer the hardest, longest items with the most points.

3. **THESIS**: Janeen's experience getting stuck in an elevator was frightening.

___1___   The elevator began to go up but jolted to a stop between floors.

___4___   First the security person told her to press the release button, but nothing happened.

___2___   Janeen waited for a few minutes and then pressed the alarm button.

___7___   Finally, the elevator repair people arrived and got the elevator going again.

___3___   A security person answered through the speaker, and Janeen explained that the elevator had stopped.

___6___   Again, nothing happened.

___5___   Then the security person tried to fix the problem internally.

PRACTICE 2   USE SPATIAL ORDER TO ARRANGE IDEAS

Arrange the support for each of the following thesis statements according to spatial order. Indicate the sequence of ideas by writing a number in the blank to the left. Then indicate the type of spatial arrangement you are using on the line at the end of each item (top to bottom, bottom to top, near to far, far to near, left to right, right to left, back to front, front to back).

1. **THESIS**: Sal wanted to make sure that he looked professional.

___1___   didn't wear one of his baseball caps

___5___   shoes clean and polished

___3___   dress shirt that he had ironed and tucked in carefully

___2___   hair neatly combed and pulled back

___4___   pants belted and not too baggy

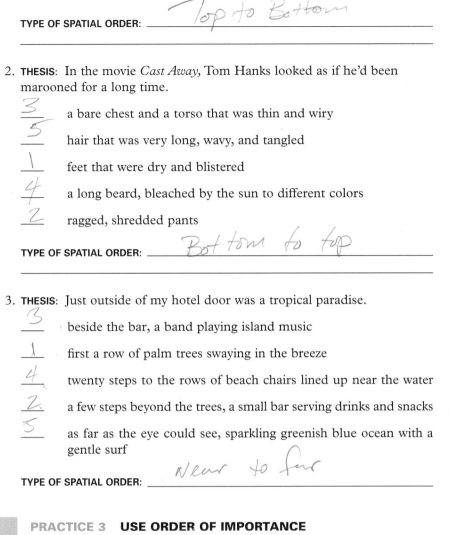

TYPE OF SPATIAL ORDER: _Top to Bottom_

2. **THESIS**: In the movie *Cast Away*, Tom Hanks looked as if he'd been marooned for a long time.

_3_ a bare chest and a torso that was thin and wiry

_5_ hair that was very long, wavy, and tangled

_1_ feet that were dry and blistered

_4_ a long beard, bleached by the sun to different colors

_2_ ragged, shredded pants

TYPE OF SPATIAL ORDER: _Bottom to top_

3. **THESIS**: Just outside of my hotel door was a tropical paradise.

_3_ beside the bar, a band playing island music

_1_ first a row of palm trees swaying in the breeze

_4_ twenty steps to the rows of beach chairs lined up near the water

_2_ a few steps beyond the trees, a small bar serving drinks and snacks

_5_ as far as the eye could see, sparkling greenish blue ocean with a gentle surf

TYPE OF SPATIAL ORDER: _Near to far_

PRACTICE 3 USE ORDER OF IMPORTANCE TO ARRANGE IDEAS

Arrange the support for each of the thesis statements that follow according to order of importance, starting with the *least* important. Indicate the sequence of ideas by writing the number in the blank at the left.

1. **THESIS**: Paying for a class and not getting the most from it is ridiculous.

_3_ You're less likely to try it again.

_1_ You lose the money you paid.

___4___   Worst of all is that you have no one to blame but yourself.

___2___   You don't get the credit or the information from the class.

___3___   You're worse off than before because you've spent money.

2. **THESIS**: People who have a drinking problem should attend Alcoholics Anonymous meetings.

___6___   They're more willing to try to change their behavior.

___4___   They talk with others who haven't had a drink for a while.

___3___   They realize that others have similar problems.

___1___   They may save themselves from great tragedy or death.

___2___   They can take positive steps to change their lives.

___5___   They are assigned a mentor or partner who can help at any time and who understands.

3. **THESIS**: Voting is a right that every U.S. citizen should take advantage of.

___4___   It makes you feel more a part of the community and country.

___5___   It doesn't take very much time.

___2___   It's one of the many rights granted by the Constitution.

___3___   Every vote really does count, as we saw in the 2000 presidential election between Al Gore and George W. Bush.

___1___   Voting gives you a voice in deciding who will shape the government.

Practice Making a Plan

Writing a draft essay is much easier if you work from a written plan than if you just start writing off the top of your head. When you have decided how to order your ideas, make a written plan—an **outline**—starting with your thesis statement. Then state each of your main support points as a topic sentence for one of the body paragraphs of the essay. Add each supporting detail in a sentence that develops or explains the topic sentence for that paragraph. Your plan should also include a possible main point for the concluding paragraph.

Although your outline serves as a good guide or blueprint for you as you draft your essay, don't think of it as inflexible. You can always modify your plan as you draft your essay.

Your outline for your draft essay should look like the one that follows. In this outline, student writer Gene Boroski has written both the support points for the body paragraphs and the supporting details in complete sentences. If you want to use fragments or phrases in your outline and wait to write the complete sentences while you draft, that's fine. Many people, however, find it useful to write complete sentences as they plan so that their outline is a more complete blueprint for the essay.

For a diagram of the relationship between paragraphs and essays, see page 5.

THESIS STATEMENT: As a distance education student, I should not have to pay student activities fees.

1. All of my courses are offered online. — Support point #1

   a. The courses do not exist in real time. — Supporting details

   b. I log on to the course whenever it is convenient for me.

   c. My interaction with the teacher and other students is only through email.

2. Even though I do not go to campus, my tuition is the same as for on-site — Support point #2 students.

   a. This seems reasonable to me because I am getting the same kind of — Supporting details instruction and knowledge.

   b. My tuition helps pay the professors' salaries, which I believe is fair.

   c. Unfortunately, because the courses are online, I am not eligible for academic assistance as on-site students are.

3. I don't use campus facilities, so why should I have to pay for the — Support point #3 services?

   a. I don't use facilities such as the cafeteria. — Supporting details

   b. I also don't need student health services, parking, or campus security.

   c. The computer network is already installed, so there is no extra cost involved for online courses.

POSSIBLE POINT FOR CONCLUDING PARAGRAPH: The college doesn't pay for my online service provider fees or for the electricity I use taking the course online, so why should I pay for services that I don't use?

For an example of a student writer making an outline for her essay, see page 17.

PRACTICE 1   OUTLINING MAJOR SUPPORT POINTS AND SUPPORTING DETAILS

Arrange the major support points and supporting details in the spaces provided, as illustrated in the example below.

THESIS STATEMENT: Being a good customer service representative in a retail store requires several important skills.

ORDER OF IMPORTANCE

PURPOSE AND AUDIENCE: To explain part of the job to someone who is interested in a job as a customer service representative

Filling out paperwork

Looking at person

Listening carefully

Making notes

Asking questions

Being pleasant and polite

Smiling, saying hello

Figuring out how to solve the problem

Calling the right people

Major support points

Supporting details

1. Being pleasant and polite

   a.   Smiling, saying hello

   b.   Looking at person

2. Listening carefully

   a.   Making notes

   b.   Asking questions

3. Figuring out how to solve the problem

   a.   Calling the right people

   b.   Filling out paperwork

1. **THESIS STATEMENT**: I didn't think I was college material.

   ORDER OF IMPORTANCE

   PURPOSE AND AUDIENCE: To explain to a college admissions officer why
   you took time off after high school before applying to college.

   No one in my family had gone to college.

   I'd goofed off in high school.

   I didn't know anyone who could tell me what college was like.

   I've been out of high school for a while.

   My sister said college was a waste of time and money.

   I forgot what school was like.

   I didn't have good high school grades.

   I didn't care about school.

   I'm older than other students.

   1. _I didn't Care_
      a. _I goofed off_
      b. _I didn't have good high School grades._
   2. _I've been out of high school for a while_
      a. _I'm older than other students_
      b. _I forgot what school was like_
   3. _I didn't know anyone who could tell me what College_
      a. _No one in my family had gone to College_
      b. _My Sister said College was a waste_

2. **THESIS STATEMENT**: Be careful of telephone con artists.

   CHRONOLOGICAL ORDER

   PURPOSE AND AUDIENCE: To warn a friend about not getting scammed
   on the phone.

   Ask questions.

   Be realistic.

   What is your address?

Can I call you back?

Personal income is private.

Don't reveal personal information.

Nothing's free.

There's always a catch.

Your social security number can be misused.

1. _____ ASK question _____
   a. _____ Nothing's free _____
   b. _____ There always a catch _____
2. _____ Don't reveal personal info _____
   a. _____ your SSN can be misused _____
   b. _____ personal income is private _____
3. _____ Be realistic _____
   a. _____ Can I call you back _____
   b. _____ what your address _____

PRACTICE 2   OUTLINING AN ESSAY

Outline the essay that follows. Underline the thesis statement, and underline the main point in the concluding paragraph. Double-underline the topic sentences, and put a check mark next to each supporting detail.

We all know people who seem to fall in love, over and over. They love being in love. But others have different patterns. Some people seem to fall in love once and stay there. Others avoid long-term commitment. Until now, we had no way to figure out why some people were steady lovers and others not. Some researchers now believe that the amount and type of certain hormones in a person's brain may determine a person's patterns of love.

Using mice as subjects, the researchers found that when two particular hormones (oxytocin and vasopressin) exist in the pleasure centers of the brain, they produce individuals with a pattern of long-lasting love. Male mice with these hormones in their pleasure centers were faithful to their partners. They stayed with their female mouse partners through pregnancy and the raising of offspring.

In contrast, when those same hormones existed outside of the pleasure center, the male mice sought constant sources of new love. They did not have steady partners and did not stick around when a female mouse became pregnant. The mice with hormones in this location were the ones who ran from commitment.

Unfortunately, the research did not deal with the most common love pattern: individuals involved in relationships that last for some time but not for life. In this pattern, people have a series of serious relationships that are often broken off when one person wants a formal commitment and the other doesn't. Perhaps this research will come next, as it is in these relationships where much of the pain of love exists.

Though these behaviors may be built into the brain, scientists are working on ways to modify the effects. They hope to find a balance so that love patterns can be modified. One humorous researcher suggested that before we select our mates, we should ask them to have a brain scan to determine whether they're likely to stay or go.

THINKING CRITICALLY WHILE MAKING A PLAN

FOCUS   Reread your thesis statement and support points.

ASK
- What would be the best way to organize my support points? (Time? Space? Importance?)
- What point should come first? Next? After that? Last?
- What supporting details will show, explain, or prove each of my main points?
- Does this organization help me get my main point (my position) across? Will it help my readers follow my essay?

WRITE   Write a plan (an outline) that shows how you want to arrange your points.

Use a Computer to Make a Plan

After deciding on an order of organization (chronological, spatial, or importance), you can use your word processing program to help you arrange your ideas. In the View menu, click on Outline View. Notice that a toolbar appears with various arrows (right, left, up, down). Begin your outline with your working thesis statement, and then type in your major support points and supporting details, using the right arrow (→) to indent for details. You can use the left arrow (←) to bring your text back out to the margin.

You'll notice as you type that Outline View formats each level of detail in a different way. In the example shown here, the major support is in large boldface type, supporting details are in italic type, and even finer details are in normal type.

As you create your outline, you'll be able to scan your text for gaps in support. If you decide you want to rearrange the order of your ideas, use the up arrow (↑) and down arrow (↓) to do so.

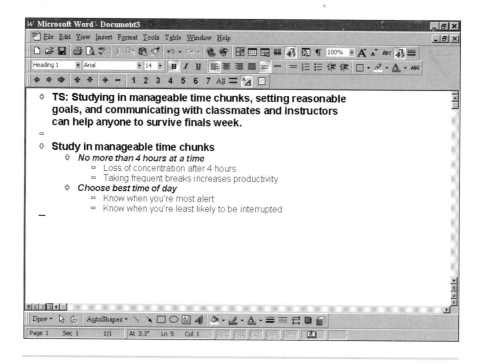

6

Writing a Draft

Putting Your Ideas Together

You Know This
You often rehearse
in advance.
- Your sports team
  plays preseason
  games.
- You practice what
  you're going to
  say to someone.
- You try on
  something you
  might wear to an
  upcoming event.

▓ WRITING AS YOU LEARN

Write a draft of the essay you are working on. Using the outline you created in Chapter 5, concentrate first on drafting the body paragraphs that
support the thesis statement. (You may want to add support or details or
change the order.) Then, write the full introductory paragraph and the
conclusion.

Before writing your draft, read all of this chapter. It explains and illustrates effective introductory and concluding paragraphs. It also provides a
student example, showing how to move from an outline to a draft.

GUIDING QUESTIONS

- **PURPOSE**: What are all my ideas supposed to add up to? What do I want
  to accomplish? Why am I writing this?
- **AUDIENCE**: How can I put myself in my readers' place? Will the facts,
  information, and reasons I've chosen make an impression on them?

Understand What a Draft Is

DEFINITION: A **draft** is the first whole version of all your ideas put together in a piece of writing.

You have been generating and organizing ideas for your draft. Now you need to put them together into essay form. Do the best job you can in drafting, but remember that you will have more chances to make changes. Think of your draft as a dress rehearsal for your final paper.

SIX BASICS OF A GOOD DRAFT

1. It has a thesis statement that presents the main point.
2. Its main support points are stated in topic sentences that develop or explain the thesis statement. (Often, the topic sentences begin each body paragraph.)
3. Its supporting details develop or explain the topic sentence in each body paragraph.
4. Its introduction captures the readers' interest and lets them know what the essay is about.
5. Its conclusion reinforces the main point and makes an observation.
6. It follows standard essay form (introduction, body paragraphs, conclusion) and uses complete sentences.

Practice Writing a Draft

1. WRITE AN INTRODUCTION

The introduction to your essay should capture your readers' interest and present the main point. Think of your introductory paragraph as a marketing challenge. Ask yourself: How can I get my readers to want to continue reading?

THREE BASICS OF A GOOD INTRODUCTION

1. It should catch readers' attention.
2. It should present the essay's thesis statement (narrowed topic + main point).
3. It should give readers a good idea of what the essay will cover.

For more on thesis statements, see Chapter 3.

The thesis statement is often either the first or the last sentence in the introductory paragraph, though you may find essays in which the main point or thesis statement is in the middle of the introductory paragraph.

Here are examples of common kinds of introductions that spark readers' interest.

Start with a Surprising Fact or Idea

Surprises capture people's attention. The more unexpected and surprising something is, the more likely people are to take notice of it and read on.

> Sex sells. This truth is a boon for marketing gurus and the pornography industry but a rather unfortunate situation for women. Every issue of *Playboy*, every lewd poster and even the Victoria's Secret catalog transform real women into ornaments, valued exclusively for their outward appearance. These publications are responsible for defining what is sexy and reinforce the belief that aesthetic appeal is a woman's highest virtue.
> —Amy Beck, "Struggling for Perfection"

Open with a Quotation

A good short quote can definitely get people interested. It must lead naturally into your main point, however, and not just be stuck there. If you start with a quote, make sure that you tell the reader who the speaker or writer is.

> It's "premature to push for federal legislation" to ban cell phone use while driving. That's according to Robert Shelton, executive director of the National Highway Traffic Safety Administration, in congressional testimony this spring. To that, we respond, "Oh, bullfeathers, Robert!"
> —Tom Magliozzi and Ray Magliozzi, "Protecting Its People: Let Our Government Do Its Job"

Give an Example or Tell a Story

People like stories, so opening an essay with a brief story or illustration often draws them in.

> Oh, those oranges arriving in the midst of the North Dakota winters of the forties—the mere color of them, carried through the door in a net bag or a crate from out of the white winter landscape. Their appearance was enough to set my brother and me to thinking that it might be about time to develop an illness, which was the surest way of receiving a steady supply of them. "Mom, we think we're getting a cold."
> —Larry Woiwode, "Ode to an Orange"

Offer a Strong Opinion

The stronger the opinion, the more likely it is that people will pay attention.

> If you're a man, at some point a woman will ask you how she looks. "How do I look?" she'll ask.
>
> You must be careful how you answer this question. The best technique is to form an honest yet sensitive opinion, then collapse on the floor with some kind of fatal seizure. Trust me, this is the easiest way out. You will never come up with the right answer.
>
> —Dave Barry, "The Ugly Truth about Beauty"

Ask a Question

A question needs an answer. If you start your introduction with a question, you engage your readers by inviting them to answer it.

> Is a girl called Gloria apt to be better-looking than one called Bertha? Are criminals more likely to be dark than blond? Can you tell a good deal about someone's personality from hearing his voice briefly over the phone? Can a person's nationality be pretty accurately guessed from his photograph? Does the fact that someone wears glasses imply that he is intelligent?
>
> The answer to all these questions is obviously, "No."
>
> Yet, from all the evidence at hand, most of us believe these things.
>
> —Robert L. Heilbroner, "Don't Let Stereotypes Warp Your Judgments"

PRACTICE 1   **IDENTIFY STRONG INTRODUCTIONS**

In a newspaper, a magazine, a catalog, an advertisement—anything written—find a strong introduction. Explain, in writing, why you think it is a strong introduction.

PRACTICE 2   **MARKET YOUR MAIN POINT**

As you know from watching and reading advertisements, a good writer can make just about anything sound interesting. For each of the following topics, write an introductory statement using the technique indicated. Make that statement punchy and intriguing enough to motivate your readers to stay with you as you explain or defend it. Even if you wouldn't choose to write about the topics given in this practice, try to make fascinating, provocative statements about them.

1. **TOPIC:** Mandatory use of seat belts

   TECHNIQUE: Ask a question.

   Does the mandatory use of seat belts really save lives or is it just another gimmick

2. **TOPIC:** Teenage suicide

   TECHNIQUE: Present a surprising fact or idea (you can make one up for this exercise).

   Teenage suicide has increased due to the lack of a stable family environment.

3. **TOPIC:** Free access to music on the Internet

   TECHNIQUE: Give a strong opinion.

   Free access of Music on the Internet is robbing the artist that produce the music.

4. **TOPIC:** The quality of television shows

   TECHNIQUE: Use a quotation (you can make up a good one for this exercise).
   according to Ted Turner presi the
   of Turner Broadcast → the quality of TV show are becoming worse due to the lack of good writer.

5. **TOPIC:** Blind dates

   TECHNIQUE: Give an example or tell a brief story (you can just sum it up).

   Blind dates should be just that, dates for the blind. If you are ever ask by a friend to go on a blind date, remember to close your eye throughout the date. If you dont, you are subject to see things that you might not like

2. WRITE A CONCLUSION

Your conclusion should build energy and match the force of your thesis statement; it is your last chance to drive your main point home. Fading out with a weak conclusion is like slowing down at the end of a race: You lose ground. In writing, as in sports and other activities, you need to keep up the pace right to the very end. In fact, you should give yourself a last push at the end because people usually remember best what they see, hear, or read last. A good conclusion creates a sense of completion: It not only brings readers back to where they started but also shows them how far they have come.

THREE BASICS OF A GOOD CONCLUSION

1. It should refer to your thesis or main point.

2. It should sum up the support points you have developed in the essay.

3. It should make a further observation or point.

One of the best ways to end an essay is to refer directly to something in the introduction.

- If you asked a question, ask it again and answer it based on what you've said in your essay.

- If you started a story, finish it.

- If you used a quotation, use another one—by the same person or by another person on the same topic.

- If you stated a surprising fact or idea, go back to it and comment on it, using what you have written in the body of the essay.

- Repeat key words that you used in your introduction to remind your reader of your original point.

Look again at two of the introductions you read earlier, each shown here with its conclusion.

Start with an Example or Tell a Story

INTRODUCTION A:

Oh, those oranges arriving in the midst of the North Dakota winters of the forties—the mere color of them, carried through the door in a net bag or a crate from out of the white winter landscape. Their appearance was enough to set my brother and me to thinking that it might be about time to develop an illness, which was the surest way of receiving a steady supply of them. "Mom, we think we're getting a cold."

CONCLUSION A:

"Mom, we think we're getting a cold."

"You mean you want an orange?"

This is difficult to answer or dispute or even to acknowledge, finally with the fullness that the subject deserves, and that each orange bears, within its own makeup, into this hard-edged yet insubstantial, incomplete, cold, wintry world.

—Larry Woiwode, "Ode to an Orange"

Start with a Strong Opinion or Position

INTRODUCTION B:

If you're a man, at some point a woman will ask you how she looks. "How do I look?" she'll ask.

You must be careful how you answer this question. The best technique is to form an honest yet sensitive opinion, then collapse on the floor with some kind of fatal seizure. Trust me, this is the easiest way out. You will never come up with the right answer.

CONCLUSION B:

To go back to my main point: If you're a man, and a woman asks you how she looks, you're in big trouble. Obviously, you can't say she looks bad. But you also can't say that she looks great, because she'll think you're lying, because she has spent countless hours, with the help of the multibillion-dollar beauty industry, obsessing about the differences between herself and Cindy Crawford. Also, she suspects that you're not qualified to judge anybody's appearance. This is because you have shaving cream in your hair.

—Dave Barry, "The Ugly Truth about Beauty"

PRACTICE 3   ANALYZE CONCLUSIONS

After reading the paired introductions and conclusions above, indicate the techniques used in each conclusion to refer back to its introduction.

A. Technique used to link introduction and conclusion: _Mom, we think We're getting a cold_

B. Technique used to link introduction and conclusion: _Repeating the thesis statement_

PRACTICE 4 IDENTIFY GOOD INTRODUCTIONS AND CONCLUSIONS

In a newspaper, magazine, or any other written material, find a piece of writing that has both a strong introduction and a strong conclusion. Answer the following questions about the introduction and conclusion.

1. What method of introduction is used? offer a strong opinion

2. What does the conclusion do? Does it restate the main idea? Sum up the points made in the piece? Make an observation? ____________

3. How are the introduction and the conclusion linked? ____________ It tells a solution

PRACTICE 5 WRITE A CONCLUSION

Read the following introductory paragraphs, and then write a possible conclusion for each one. Your conclusions can be brief, but they should each include the features of a good conclusion and consist of several sentences.

1. **INTRODUCTION:** When it comes to long-term love relationships, I very much believe Anton Chekhov's statement, "Any idiot can face a crisis; it's the day-to-day living that wears you out." When faced with a crisis, couples often pull together. A crisis is a slap in the face that reminds you of who and what is important in your life. It is the routine necessities of living that can erode a relationship as couples argue over who does the laundry, who does the cleaning, or cooking, or bill paying. The constant skirmishes over day-to-day living can do more serious damage over the long term than a crisis.

   CONCLUSION: When it comes to long term relationships, it maybe easier to go out a buy a pet animal and have a good nights sleep that waste the energy,

2. **INTRODUCTION**: Why do so many people feel that they must be available at all times and in all places? Until recently, the only way you could reach someone was by telephone or by mail. Now if you don't have a cell phone, an email account, a beeper, and call waiting, people trying to reach you get annoyed. To me this is just a loss of privacy. I don't want to be available twenty-four hours a day.

CONCLUSION: _being available 24 hours a day will drain the life out of you. It being at someones beckand call is what you like then enjoy, but its not for me._

3. WRITE A DRAFT

Chapter 5 included an outline by student writer Gene Boroski. This outline is reproduced below, followed by the draft Gene wrote from it. Note that while Gene stays close to his outline as he writes his first-try draft, he makes some changes and additions along the way; he isn't just directly copying his outline into essay form.

GENE'S OUTLINE

THESIS STATEMENT: As a distance education student, I should not have to pay student activities fees.

1. All of my courses are offered online. — Support point #1

   a. The courses do not exist in real time.

   b. I log on to the course whenever it is convenient for me. — Supporting details

   c. My interaction with the teacher and other students is only through email.

Support point #2 —— 2. Even though I do not go to campus, my tuition is the same as for on-site students.

Supporting
details
      a. This seems reasonable to me because I am getting the same kind of instruction and knowledge.

      b. My tuition helps pay the professors' salaries, which I believe is fair.

      c. Unfortunately, because the courses are online, I am not eligible for academic assistance as on-site students are.

Support point #3 —— 3. I don't use campus facilities, so why should I have to pay for the services?

Supporting
details
      a. I don't use facilities such as the cafeteria.

      b. I also don't need student health services, parking, or campus security.

      c. The computer network is already installed, so there is no extra cost involved for online courses.

POSSIBLE POINT FOR CONCLUDING PARAGRAPH: The college doesn't pay for my online service provider fees or for the electricity I use taking the course online, so why should I pay for services that I don't use?

GENE'S DRAFT

As a distance education student, I should not have to pay student activities fees. Distance education via computer is relatively new, and I think that college administrators have not adequately thought about what this means for student activities fees, for one thing. In some ways we are like on-site students and should be charged as they are, but I draw the line at student activities fees that benefit only the on-site students.

All of my courses are offered online, so I never come to the campus. The courses don't even exist in real time, so I may log on to the course at 11:00 at night if that's the time that's most convenient for me. I do not interact face-to-face with my professor, but we communicate well, and often, by email. I can also interact with other distance education students that way. It is a very different way of taking classes, but it works well for people like me who can't get to campus during regularly scheduled classes.

Even though I do not go to the campus, my tuition is the same as for on-site students. This seems reasonable to me because I am getting the same kind of instruction and knowledge. My tuition helps pay professors' salaries, which I believe is fair whether I'm taking their classes in the classroom or at a distance. Unfortunately, though, because the courses are online, I am not eligible for academic assistance as on-site students are. There are differences between on-site education and distance education, at least in some people's minds, probably because distance education is so new.

For an example of another student writer's draft, see page 18.

Distance education students do not use campus facilities, so why should we pay for them? For example, I don't use expensive facilities such as the cafeteria, campus health, campus security, or parking. Yes, I use the computer network, but that's already in place; it doesn't cost more to run a course online.

It is time to realize that there are differences in the college "experience" of on-site and distance education students. I don't ask the college to support my online service provider fees or the electricity I use because I am taking the course online, so why should I be asked to pay for services that I don't use?

4. TITLE YOUR ESSAY

Even if your title is the *last* part of the essay you write, it is the *first* thing that readers read. Use your title to get your readers' attention and to tell them what your essay is about. Use concrete, specific words.

THREE BASICS OF A GOOD ESSAY TITLE

1. It makes readers want to read the essay.
2. It does not repeat the same wording in your thesis statement.
3. It may hint at the main point but does not necessarily state it outright.

One way to find a good title is to consider the type of essay you are writing. If you are writing an argument (as you will in Chapter 16), state your position in your title. If you are telling your readers how to do something (as you will in Chapter 11), try using the term *steps* or *how to* in the title. This way, your readers will know immediately both what you are writing about and how you will present it. For example, "Five Steps to Financial Independence" may be a more inviting and more accurate title for a process analysis essay than "Financial Independence."

 PRACTICE 6 **WRITE A TITLE**

Reread the following introductory paragraphs, and write a possible title for the essay each one begins. The first one is done as an example. Be prepared to explain why you worded each title as you did.

EXAMPLE

Sex sells. This truth is a boon for marketing gurus and the pornography industry but a rather unfortunate situation for women. Every issue of *Playboy*, every lewd poster and even the Victoria's Secret catalog transform real women into ornaments, valued exclusively for their outward appearance. These publications are responsible for defining what is sexy and reinforce the belief that aesthetic appeal is a woman's highest virtue.

POSSIBLE TITLE: _Are women becoming ornaments_

1. It's "premature to push for federal legislation" to ban cell phone use while driving. That's according to Robert Shelton, executive director of the National Highway Traffic Safety Administration, in congressional testimony this spring. To that, we respond, "Oh, bullfeathers, Robert!"

POSSIBLE TITLE: _Congressional ban on cell phones this Spring_

2. Oh, those oranges arriving in the midst of the North Dakota winters of the forties—the mere color of them, carried through the door in a net bag or a crate from out of the white winter landscape. Their appearance was enough to set my brother and me to thinking that it might be about time to develop an illness, which was the surest way of receiving a steady supply of them. "Mom, we think we're getting a cold."

POSSIBLE TITLE: _delicious oranges_

3. If you're a man, at some point a woman will ask you how she looks. "How do I look?" she'll ask.

   You must be careful how you answer this question. The best technique is to form an honest yet sensitive opinion, then collapse on the floor with some kind of fatal seizure. Trust me, this is the easiest way out. You will never come up with the right answer.

POSSIBLE TITLE: _When a women ask how do it look dont answer_

4. Is a girl called Gloria apt to be better-looking than one called Bertha? Are criminals more likely to be dark than blond? Can you tell a good deal about someone's personality from hearing his voice briefly over the phone? Can a person's nationality be pretty accurately guessed from his photograph? Does the fact that someone wears glasses imply that he is intelligent?

   The answer to all these questions is obviously, "No."

   Yet, from all the evidence at hand, most of us believe these things.

POSSIBLE TITLE: _You can't tell a book by its cover,_

THINKING CRITICALLY ABOUT WRITING A DRAFT

FOCUS   Reread your outline for the essay.

ASK
- Have I stated my main point or position in a thesis statement?
- Have I written topic sentences for each body paragraph?
- Do I have enough supporting details for each topic sentence?
- Have I arranged my support points as effectively as I can?
- What introductory technique will get my readers' attention and make my point stand out?
- How can I use the conclusion for one last chance to make my point?
- How can I link my conclusion to my introduction? What is the strongest or most interesting part of the introduction that I might refer back to in my conclusion?
- Will my title make readers want to read my essay?

WRITE   Write a draft essay.

Use a Computer to Write Your Draft

You may want to open the file in which you saved your outline and use Save As (in the File menu) to change the file name of your outline and then to begin to draft from it. (This preserves the original outline, and it gives you a new file—the draft file—to work with.) Alternatively, you may want to print your outline and put it next to the computer and begin to write a draft.

You can have multiple documents open in your word processing program—for example, your prewriting, your outline, and your draft—and use the Window menu, checking the appropriate file name, to go back and forth between them. In the example shown on the next page, the writer has a prewriting document open but can easily access an outline or draft by selecting the file name from the drop-down menu.

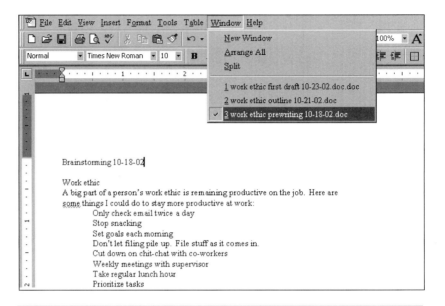

7

Revising Your Draft

Improving Your Essay

You Know This
You already revise in your everyday life.
- You get dressed and then change certain items because they don't look right together.
- You plan what you're going to say to someone, changing your "script" to make it more effective.
- You rework your job application letter and résumé each time you look for a better position.

WRITING AS YOU LEARN

Revise your draft essay. To prepare yourself to revise your essay, read this entire chapter and work through each of the Practices.

GUIDING QUESTIONS

- **PURPOSE**: How can I better accomplish my purpose in this essay — explaining something, showing something, convincing my reader of something, or presenting my position on an issue?

- **AUDIENCE**: How are my readers likely to react to each point I make? What additional support points or supporting details would help them react positively to what I am telling them? What changes can I make so that my main point is stronger, clearer, or more convincing to my readers?

Understand What Revision Is

DEFINITION: **Revising** is focusing on your ideas and looking for ways to make them clearer, stronger, and more convincing. When revising, you might add, cut, move, or change whole sentences or paragraphs.

DEFINITION: **Editing** is finding and correcting problems with grammar, style, usage, and punctuation. While editing, you usually add, cut, or change words and phrases instead of whole sentences or paragraphs (as you might while revising).

Revising and editing are two different ways to improve a paper. Most writers find it difficult to do both at once. It is easier to look first at the ideas in your essay (revising) and then to look at the individual words and sentences (editing). Revising is covered in this chapter, and editing is covered in Chapters 22–41. As you revise, set three goals for yourself.

THREE REVISION GOALS

1. Search for ideas that do not fit (revise for unity, pp. 88–91).
2. Search for ideas that are not as specific or complete as they could be (revise for support and detail, pp. 91–93).
3. Search for ways to connect ideas so that they flow smoothly from one to the next (revise for coherence, pp. 93–101).

Revising—thinking through the ideas in your essay—is a key step in the writing process. It is essential in any kind of writing that you do for college, at work, or in your everyday life. No one gets everything right in one draft, so do not skip the revising stage. Commit yourself to making at least five changes in any draft essay.

FIVE REVISION TIPS

1. Give yourself a break from your draft—set it aside for a few hours or a whole day.
2. Read your draft aloud and listen to what you have written.
3. Imagine yourself as one of your readers.
4. Get feedback from a friend, a classmate, or a colleague (see the following section of this chapter).
5. Get help from a tutor at your college writing center or lab.

To revise your writing, you will need to try to be objective about it. You may need to read what you have written several times before deciding what changes would improve it. Remember to consider your audience (those who will read your essay) and your purpose (your reason for writing it). As you revise, focus on three areas of possible improvement: unity, detail, and coherence.

The following section of this chapter discusses one way for you to gain objectivity—the peer review. The next three sections then give advice on practicing revision.

Understand What Peer Review Is

DEFINITION: **Peer review** is getting feedback on your writing from another person or giving feedback to a fellow student, colleague, or friend.

Other people can look at your work with a fresh perspective and see things that you might not — parts that are good as well as parts that need more explanation or evidence. To say "It's great" without further comment doesn't help you improve your paper. The best reviewers are honest about what could be better, but also sensitive to the writer's feelings.

FOUR BASICS OF USEFUL FEEDBACK

1. It is given in a positive way.
2. It is specific.
3. It offers suggestions.
4. It may be given orally and in writing.

To get useful feedback in your writing class, you can find a partner and exchange papers. Each partner should read the other's paper and jot down a few comments. You may also be able to form a small group, in which you take turns reading the papers aloud while the group members make notes. Then the members of the group should offer comments that will help the writer improve the paper. The first time someone comments on what you

---

Questions for Peer Reviewers

1. What is the main point?
2. After reading the introductory paragraph, do you have an idea of what the essay will cover, and why?
3. How could the introduction be more interesting?
4. Is there enough support for the main point? Where might the writer add support?
5. Are there confusing places where you have to reread something in order to understand it? How might the writer make the points, the organization, or the flow of ideas clearer or smoother?
6. How could the conclusion be more forceful?
7. What do you most like about the essay? Where could it be better? What would you do if it were your essay?
8. What other comments or suggestions do you have?

have written, you may feel a little embarrassed or awkward, but you are likely to feel better about the process once you see how your writing benefits from the comments.

It is useful for peer reviewers to ask or answer a few questions to guide their feedback. Some of these may come from the writer, questions such as "Does my introduction get your attention?" or "What about support for my main point—do I have enough, and is it convincing?" See the box on the previous page for questions peer reviewers might consider as they read through a draft.

Practice Revising for Unity

DEFINITION: **Unity** in writing means that all the points you make are related to your main point; they are *unified* in support of your main point.

As you draft an essay, you might drift away from your main point into something that isn't directly related to it, as the writer of the following paragraph did with the underlined sentences. The diagram after the paragraph shows where readers might get confused.

Just a few years ago online dating services were viewed with great suspicion, but they now have millions of subscribers who say the services offer many advantages over searching for a partner on your own. With an online dating service, people set up their own dates and don't have to cruise the bars. Many people do not like the bar scene, which they describe as a "meat market." Online dating services also give users the opportunity to screen individuals and contact only those who interest them. That screening saves time and also helps people avoid many awkward first dates. Subscribers can exchange email messages to see how they communicate before arranging a meeting. It's almost like the movie *You've Got Mail*. I love Meg Ryan, though she should never have hooked up with that Russell Crowe. With people spending so much time working, it's hard to meet anyone outside of work, so online dating services expand the possibilities greatly. The opportunity to "meet" a wide range of people without leaving your home and to screen out obvious mismatches is, for a growing number of people, the only way to play the dating game.

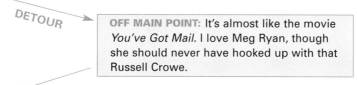

TOPIC SENTENCE: Just a few years ago online dating services were viewed with great suspicion, but they now have millions of subscribers who say the services offer many advantages over searching for a partner on your own.

SUPPORT POINT 1: With an online dating service, people set up their own dates and don't have to cruise the bars.

SUPPORT POINT 2: Online dating services also give users the opportunity to screen individuals and contact only those who interest them.

DETOUR

OFF MAIN POINT: It's almost like the movie *You've Got Mail.* I love Meg Ryan, though she should never have hooked up with that Russell Crowe.

SUPPORT POINT 3: With people spending so much time working, it's hard to meet anyone outside of work, so online dating services expand the possibilities greatly.

CONCLUDING SENTENCE: The opportunity to "meet" a wide range of people without leaving your home and to screen out obvious mismatches is, for a growing number of people, the only way to play the dating game.

Drifting away from your main point shifts your readers' focus and can be confusing. Your essay is much less likely to be effective if the flow of ideas goes off course.

PRACTICE 1   REVISE FOR UNITY

Each of the following essays includes sentences that are off the main point. Underline those sentences. The main point in each of the essays is in bold-face type.

1. Look for four off-the-point sentences.

   Oprah Winfrey is one of the most influential people of our times, but that doesn't mean that life is easy for her. As a child in rural Mississippi, she was dirt-poor and sexually abused. Somehow, she managed to climb out of that existence and become successful. But because she is now a superstar, every aspect of her life is under the media spotlight, and she is frequently criticized for everything from her weight to her attempts to help people spiritually.

Oprah's roller-coaster weight profile is always news. Every supermarket tabloid, every week, seems to have some new information about Oprah and her weight. I can relate to how humiliating that must be. She looked like a balloon in a recent picture I saw, even fatter than my Aunt Greta.

Oprah is also criticized for her wealth, estimated to be at about $800 million. You never hear about the charitable work she does, only about how much money she has. She has a fabulous apartment overlooking Lake Michigan in Chicago. While many businesspeople are as wealthy, few are criticized as often—or as publicly as Oprah.

Even Oprah's book club and magazine, O, bring unwarranted negativity. "Who is she to recommend books?" say some, and "What does she know about publishing?" say others. I especially liked the book *She's Come Undone*. But what could possibly be wrong with recommending books and championing literacy?

Oprah Winfrey, despite her wealth and fame, does not have an easy life. Her critics feel free to cut her down at every turn. Instead, why not celebrate her personal and professional achievements? She deserves respect, not ridicule.

2. Look for three off-the-point sentences.

A recent survey of the places students prefer to study revealed some strange results. We would expect the usual answers, such as the library, a bedroom, a desk, the kitchen, and the survey respondents did in fact name such areas. But apparently some people prefer less traditional places.

One unusual place cited was a church. The respondent said it was a great spot to study when services weren't taking place because it was always quiet and not crowded. Some churches are locked during the day because of vandalism. Other churches have had big problems with theft.

Another unusual study area was the locker room during a football game. Except for half-time, the large area was empty. The person who studies here claims that there's a high energy level in the locker room that, combined with the quiet, helps him concentrate. I wonder what the smell is like, however.

Possibly the most surprising study preference was in the pool area of a gym, sitting up in the bleachers. The light was good, said the student, she loved the smell of chlorine, and the sound of water was soothing.

The results may seem strange — a church, a locker room, and a pool — but they do share some characteristics: quiet, relative solitude, and no interruptions, other than half-time. Perhaps we should all think about new places that might help us study.

Practice Revising for Support and Detail

DEFINITION: **Support** is the collection of evidence, examples, or facts that show, explain, or prove your main point. **Support points** are the major ideas developed in the paragraphs that make up the body of your essay. **Supporting details** are the specifics you provide to explain your major support points to your readers.

For more on support points and supporting details, see Chapter 4.

When you read your draft essay, imagine yourself as the reader and look carefully at the major support points (topic sentences) and the supporting details you have developed. Do you have enough information to understand the main point? Does the writer present enough evidence to convince you of that point? Look for places where you could add more support and detail.

Read the two paragraphs that follow and note the support and details that the writer added to the second one. Notice that she didn't simply add to the paragraph; she also deleted some words and rearranged others to make the story clearer to readers. The additions are underlined; the deletions are crossed out.

This morning I learned that my local police respond quickly and thoroughly to 911 calls. I meant to dial 411 for directory assistance, but by mistake I dialed 911. I hung up after only one ring because I realized what I'd done. A few seconds after I hung up, the phone rang, and it was the police. She said she'd received a 911 call from my number and was checking. I explained what happened and she said she had to send a cruiser over anyway. Within a minute, the cruiser pulled in, and I explained what happened. I apologized and felt very stupid, but I thanked him. I am glad to know that if I ever need to call 911, the police will be there.

REVISED TO ADD SUPPORT AND DETAIL

This morning I tested the 911 emergency system and found that it worked flawlessly. Unfortunately, the test was a mistake. ~~learned that my local police respond quickly and thoroughly to 911 calls.~~ I meant to dial 411 for directory assistance, but without thinking ~~by mistake~~ I dialed 911. I frantically pushed the disconnect button ~~hung up~~ after only one ring because I realized my error. ~~what I'd done.~~ As I reached for the phone to try again for the 411, ~~few seconds after I hung up,~~ it rang like an alarm. ~~the phone rang, and it was the police.~~ The police dispatcher crisply announced ~~She said~~ that she'd received a 911 call from this number. ~~and was checking.~~ I laughed weakly and explained what happened, hoping she would see the humor or at least the innocent human error. Instead, the crispness of her voice became brittle as she said that a cruiser was on its way. I went to meet my fate. Within a minute, the cruiser pulled in, and a police officer swaggered toward me. I explained what had happened, apologized, and thanked him very humbly. I felt guilty of stupidity, at the very least. ~~and felt very stupid, but I thanked him.~~ We learn from our mistakes, and in this case I am glad to know that if I ever need to call 911, the police will be there.

PRACTICE 2 REVISE FOR DETAIL AND SUPPORT

Read the following essay, and write in the space provided at least one additional support point or detail for each body paragraph and for the conclusion. Indicate where the added material should go in the paragraph by writing in a caret (^).

If it's leather, I love it. Anything made of leather makes me want to spend some time admiring it. This appeal is not just limited to coats and jackets but includes furniture, bags, gloves, boots, and any other leather product I find. To me it's an all-around wonderful experience.

The smell of leather is intoxicating. It seems to hang in the air, inviting me to take a big whiff. I smell the leather, especially soft leather, and it is wonderful. I'd like to bury my nose in a soft leather jacket for hours.

Leather also feels wonderful to the touch. It is smooth and silky. It feels soothing against my cheek and hands. When I'm wearing a leather jacket, I have to stop myself from running my hands up and down the sides and sleeves because it just feels so smooth and soft.

Finally, leather is comfortable, whatever form it comes in. A leather coat or jacket doesn't just look good—it's also very warm. Pull on a pair of leather gloves, and your hands won't be cold. And, best of all, sink into a soft, buttery leather easy chair. I guarantee it will relax you.

Just writing this essay about leather makes me want to put on a leather jacket and some soft leather slippers, and find a great leather chair to curl up in. It's my kind of heaven.

Practice Revising for Coherence

DEFINITION: **Coherence** in writing means that all your points and details connect to form a whole. In other words, even when the points and details are assembled in an order that makes sense, they still need "glue" to connect them.

A piece of writing that lacks coherence can sound choppy, like a string of unrelated statements. Revising for coherence improves your essay by helping readers see how one point leads to another. Individual ideas should be so well arranged and connected that they flow easily and leave readers with a clear overall impression. Two major devices can help you increase coherence in your essay.

TWO DEVICES THAT IMPROVE COHERENCE

1. Transitional words, phrases, and sentences that connect one idea to the next

2. Key words that are related to your main point and repeated throughout the essay

1. ADD TRANSITIONS

DEFINITION: **Transitions** are words, phrases, and sentences that connect your ideas so that your writing moves smoothly from one point to another. Transitions can be used to connect sentences and ideas within a paragraph and also to help readers move smoothly from one paragraph to another.

The following paragraphs show how transitional words and phrases are used to join sentences within the same paragraph. The first paragraph includes few transitions. In the second paragraph, added transitions are underlined.

I thought I would never make it to work today. My alarm clock didn't go off. I realized that my only clean shirt was missing two buttons right in front. After finding a sweater that would go over it, I ran for the bus, only to discover that the buses were running late. The one that came was painfully slow and seemed to make stops about every ten feet. The heat was blasting, and I was sweating but couldn't take off my sweater because my shirt was gaping open. I got to work, but the elevator was out of service, so I had to walk. I got to my desk, and I knew that the hardest part of the day was behind me.

TRANSITIONAL WORDS AND PHRASES JOINING IDEAS IN THE SAME PARAGRAPH

I thought I would never make it to work today. <u>First,</u> my alarm clock didn't go off. <u>Then</u> I realized that my only clean shirt was missing two buttons right in front. After finding a sweater that would go over it, I ran for the bus, only to discover that the buses were running late. <u>When one finally came,</u> it was painfully slow and seemed to make stops about every ten feet. <u>To make matters worse,</u> the heat was blasting, and I was sweating but couldn't take off my sweater because my shirt was gaping open. <u>Finally,</u> I got to work, but the elevator was out of service, so I had to walk. <u>By the time</u> I got to my desk, I knew that the hardest part of the day was behind me.

Transitions are also important when you are moving from one paragraph to another. Transitional sentences can connect two paragraphs in an essay. A transitional sentence tells readers, "I'm done with that point, and I'm moving to the next," without saying those words.

Read the following examples to see how transitions are used to move smoothly from one paragraph to the next. The first example includes few transitions. In the second example, added transitions are underlined.

When you are frustrated because you have called the plumber three times and he hasn't come to fix the big leak in your shower, stay calm. Even though you are paying for the service, the leak will not be fixed if you are rude.

Start by saying you know how busy plumbers are and how hard they work. Tell the plumber that you marvel at how he manages to keep track of all his work, and to do it so professionally as well.

Try to find a funny story to tell about the leaky shower and the problems it is causing. Here you might need to stretch the truth a little, but humor helps in most situations.

Say you can be available anytime, at his convenience, to let him in. You just need to know when so you can be there. You are in his hands, at his service. Given that wide window of time, he'd look foolish not booking a time.

Even if you had to work at being nice, you achieved the end result you wanted. If he still doesn't show up, call someone else, and be polite. It works most of the time.

TRANSITIONAL SENTENCES JOINING IDEAS IN DIFFERENT PARAGRAPHS

When you are frustrated because you have called the plumber three times and he hasn't come to fix the big leak in your shower, stay calm. Even though you are paying for the service, the leak will not be fixed if you are rude. <u>Instead, try being polite and friendly.</u>

Start by saying you know how busy plumbers are and how hard they work. Tell the plumber that you marvel at how he manages to keep track of all his work, and to do it so professionally as well. <u>If he is like most people, this opening will soften him up a bit because you are building his ego and being nice.</u>

<u>Now that he feels good,</u> try to find a funny story to tell about the leaky shower and the problems it is causing. Here you might need to stretch the truth a little, but humor helps in most situations. <u>At this point, the plumber is feeling pretty friendly and relaxed—he's in a good mood.</u>

<u>It's time to close the deal.</u> Say you can be available anytime, at his convenience, to let him in. You just need to know when so you can be there. You are in his hands, at his service. Given that wide window of time, he'd look foolish not booking a time.

<u>As a result of your strategy, you are *almost* assured of getting your shower leak fixed.</u> Even if you had to work at being nice, you achieved the end

result you wanted. If he still doesn't show up, call someone else, and be polite. It works most of the time.

In the box on page 97 are some, though not all, of the common transitional words and phrases that often are used to indicate time, space, importance, and other relationships between ideas.

PRACTICE 3   ADD TRANSITIONAL WORDS

Read the following paragraphs. In each blank, add a transition that would smoothly connect the ideas. In each case, there is more than one right answer.

EXAMPLE

Today, many workers are members of labor unions that exist to protect worker rights. _However,_ until the 1930s, unions did not exist. In the 1930s, Congress passed laws that paved the way for unions. _After that,_ workers had the right to organize, bargain, and strike. _Today,_ unions are a powerful force in American politics.

1. The modern-day parking meter is based on an invention by a Greek scientist named Hero, who lived in the first century A.D. The machine that he invented required that the user insert a coin. _____ the coin fell, it hit a lever. _____ out came the desired product: a cup of holy water.

2. Jackie Robinson is considered by many to be the world's greatest baseball player. He got his big start playing for the University of California while he was in college. _____, he was signed by the Brooklyn Dodgers to play second base. _____, in 1995, the Dodgers won the World Series.

3. Robert Goddard is largely responsible for our ability to travel in space. In 1926, Goddard launched the first liquid-fuel rocket in

Auburn, Massachusetts. _____ Goddard's launch, rockets used

solid fuels that required oxygen to burn. _____,

liquid fuel needs no oxygen. _____, it can

operate rockets beyond the Earth's atmosphere, where there is no

oxygen.

Common Transitional Words and Phrases

SPACE

above	below	inside	to the left
across	beside	near	to the right
at the bottom	beyond	next to	to the side
at the top	farther	opposite	under
behind	further	over	where

TIME

after	eventually	meanwhile	soon
as	finally	next	then
at last	first	now	when
before	last	second	while
during	later	since	

IMPORTANCE

above all	in fact	more important	most
best	in particular	most important	worst
especially			

EXAMPLE

for example	for instance	for one thing	one reason

AND

additionally	and	as well as	in addition
also	another	furthermore	moreover

(continued)

BUT			
although	in contrast	nevertheless	still
but	instead	on the other hand	yet
however			
SO			
as a result	finally	so	therefore
because			

■ **PRACTICE 4**   **ADD TRANSITIONAL SENTENCES**

Read the following essay. In the blanks, write a sentence that would provide a smooth transition from the idea in one paragraph to the next. You may add your transitional sentence either at the end of a paragraph or at the beginning of the next. There is no one correct answer.

The tradition of the Snake Dance is one that would rattle many people. It is a practice of the Hopi tribe of Northern California, one of the oldest North American tribes. The Snake Dance, performed in August each year, asked the plumed serpent god to give rain for the crops.

_____

_____

The Snake Dance is an impressive ritual. Participants' faces and bodies are adorned with bright paint in bold designs and images. The prayers are offered as chants, performed in voices and tones that range from hushed and low to echoing and high.

_____

_____

The Snake Dancers hang live rattlesnakes from their mouths as they chant the prayers. These huge poisonous snakes twist and wind themselves around the dancers' painted bodies. The snakes' hisses and writhing coils become a part of the prayer dance.

_____

_____

This ancient tradition is still celebrated each year. August is, in fact, a rainy period in northern California, confirming for the Hopis the success of the ritual prayers. Despite the obvious danger of dancing with a poisonous snake, participants have very rarely been bitten. Nonetheless, the Snake Dance is unlikely to become wildly popular.

2. REPEAT KEY WORDS

DEFINITION: **Key words** are terms that are closely related to your topic and main point.

By repeating key words at various points throughout your essay, you help the reader stay focused on the main point. To add variety, your key words can be different words with the same basic meaning. Be careful, however, not to overuse key words and not to stick them in at random, or your writing may seem repetitious. In the following paragraph, the key words are underlined.

KEY WORDS REPEATED AND UNDERLINED

The SAT, the test many colleges require applicants to take, is at the center of controversy once again—some people claim that the time restrictions are unfair. A group representing the rights of specially challenged test takers claim that the SAT's time limits are unfair to people who, due to physical or mental challenges, cannot complete the test items within the time allotted. For example, someone with multiple sclerosis may simply need more time on the SAT than someone without a physical challenge. Another group disagrees strongly, arguing that the time restrictions are an important part of the test. All students would do better if they had more time. This group maintains that if time limits are eased for anyone, they should be eased for everyone; otherwise the results would be unfair. This new controversy, like past ones, will undoubtedly be settled, and the SAT will remain a key factor in college admissions, fair or unfair.

PRACTICE 5 **IDENTIFY REPEATED KEY WORDS**

Reread the first essay in Practice 1 (p. 89), and circle the key words. Then write those key words in the spaces that follow.

_____

_____

For Gene Boroski's
draft, see pages 80–81.

In his draft essay presented in Chapter 6, student writer Gene Boroski argued that college students who take courses online rather than on-site should not have to pay activities fees. Look back at that draft, and then read the revised version below, which indicates Gene's changes based on the three revision goals (unity, additional support and detail, and coherence).

GENE'S REVISED DRAFT WITH HIS CHANGES IN BOLD

Added to thesis
statement.

Added
explanation.

Added sentence
that emphasizes
thesis.

Added sentence
that emphasizes
thesis.

Added informa-
tion that makes
the sentence
seem smoother.

As a distance education student, I should not have to pay student activities fees **which mainly benefit traditional, on-site students. Distance education is just that: It takes place with a distance between the student and the college classroom.** Distance education via computer is relatively new, and I think that college administrators have not adequately thought about what this means for student activities fees, for one thing. **In some ways we are like on-site students and should be charged as they are, but I draw the line at student activities fees that benefit only the on-site students. I don't mind paying my fair share, but paying for services I will never use is not part of that share.**

Although I am a registered student at Carson, all of my courses are offered online, so I never come to the campus. The courses don't even exist in real time, so I may log on to the course at 11:00 at night if that's the time that's most convenient for me. I do not interact face-to-face with my professor, but we communicate well, and often, by email. I can also interact with other distance education students that way. It is a very different way of taking classes, but it works well for people like me who can't get to campus during regularly scheduled classes.

Even though I do not go to the campus, my tuition is the same as for on-site students. This seems reasonable to me because I am getting the same kind of instruction and knowledge. For example, my tuition helps pay professors' salaries, which I believe is fair whether I'm taking their class in the classroom or at a distance. In that way, on-site and distance education students are equal and should be charged equally. Unfortunately, though, because the courses are online, I am not eligible for academic assistance as on-site students are. **In that way, on-site students have an advantage that I don't have, and no one says that is unfair.**

Added sentence
that makes a
smooth transition
between sup-
porting details.

There are differences between on-site education and distance education, at least in some people's minds, probably because distance education is so new.

One other difference is that distance education students do not use campus facilities, so why should we pay for them? For example, I don't use expensive facilities such as the cafeteria, campus health, campus security, or parking. **I don't benefit from landscaping and building maintenance because I'm never there to see either. I don't use lights or restrooms, and I don't care how prompt snow removal is.** Yes, I use the computer network, but that's already in place; it doesn't cost more to run a course online.

It is time to realize that there are differences in the college experience of on-site and distance education students. I don't ask the college to support my online service provider fees or the electricity I use because I am taking the course online, so why should I be asked to pay for services that I don't use?

Added transition that helps reader follow Gene's essay.

Added detail.

Added detail.

For another example of a student's draft and revision, see pages 18–21.

THINKING CRITICALLY TO REVISE AN ESSAY

FOCUS   After a break, reread your draft with a fresh perspective.

ASK
- What's my point or position? Does my thesis statement clearly state my main point?

- Does my essay have the following?

  —An introductory paragraph

  —Three or more body paragraphs

  —A topic sentence for each paragraph that supports the main point

  —A forceful concluding paragraph that reminds my readers of my main point and makes an observation

- Does my essay have unity?

  —Do all of the major support points relate directly to my main point?

  —Do all the supporting details in each body paragraph relate to the paragraph's topic sentence?

(continued)

—Have I avoided drifting away from my main point?

• Do I have enough support?

—Do the topic sentences together give enough support or evidence for the main point?

—Does each topic sentence have enough support within its paragraph?

—Would more detail strengthen my support?

• Is my essay coherent?

—Have I used transitional words to link ideas?

—Have I used transitional sentences to link paragraphs?

—Have I repeated key words?

—Do both the sentences and the paragraphs flow smoothly?

WRITE   Revise your draft, making any improvements you can.

Use a Computer to Revise Your Draft

Open your draft file and use Save As (in the File menu) to begin a new file for your revision work (these instructions apply to Microsoft Word). Work through the list of questions from the Thinking Critically guide. As you revise your essay, use the highlighting tool to help you concentrate on specific areas, such as your thesis statement, introductory paragraph, and main support points. (To activate highlighting, select [▨] from the formatting toolbar. If this toolbar is not visible, select Customize from the Tools menu, and then select Formatting from the Toolbar options.) Highlighting will help you focus on particular parts of your essay, but remember to deselect highlighting before you begin to make specific changes.

When you have revised as much of your essay as you possibly can, your word processor's Insert and Format menus will help you make certain that your pages are numbered, your margins are correct (usually teachers expect one-inch margins), and that your spacing (usually single or double spacing) is uniform. If your teacher has assigned a certain word length, you can quickly check your essay with Word Count in the Tools menu.

PART TWO

Writing Different Kinds of Essays

8

Narration

Writing That Tells Stories

You Know This
You often use narration.
- You tell a friend about an odd experience you had.
- You tell your boss why you were late.
- You explain what a movie was about.

Understand What Narration Is

DEFINITION: **Narration** is writing that tells a story of an event or experience.

IDEA JOURNAL
Write about the most important thing that happened to you this week.

■■ Four Basics of Good Narration

1. It reveals something of importance to you (your main point).
2. It includes all of the major events of the story.
3. It uses details to bring the story to life for your audience.
4. It presents the events in a clear order, usually according to when they happened.

Sharing stories is one important way in which we communicate with one another. Whether they are serious or humorous, stories provide information and examples that can show, explain, or prove a point. To show that a story is funny, you present events that make this point clear; to explain that you were late for a good reason, you give details; to prove that you have experience, you recall notable moments during that experience.

POINT OF VIEW IN NARRATION

In a narration, the events you include and the way you describe them create a story that is based on your point of view. For example, two people

Profile of Success

Patty Maloney

CLINICAL NURSE SPECIALIST

Patty Maloney

BACKGROUND: Patty says that she was "always a terrible student who was very shy and lacking in confidence." She hated to read, hated to write, and hated school. After graduating from high school, she took one course at a community college, but she quit because she didn't think she could do it.

She worked as a typist for an insurance company but soon realized she wanted to work with young children. She got a job as a nursing assistant at Shriner's Burn Center in Boston, working with children in the intensive care unit. She loved the children and was impressed by how much the nurses helped them.

Patty completed a one-year program and became a licensed practical nurse (LPN). She continued to work at Shriner's as an LPN for another six years, but she wanted to go beyond this level of nursing. While continuing to work, she became certified as a registered nurse (RN) and got a job in the newborn intensive care unit at Children's Hospital in Boston. As she worked, she took more courses and earned bachelor's and master's degrees in nursing.

In the various nursing degree programs she completed, Patty had to do lots of writing: long papers, summaries of articles, analyses of diseases and of case studies. Because she still felt that she was not a strong writer (particularly when it came to grammar), she always had a couple of other people read her papers before she turned them in.

EMPLOYER: Children's Hospital, Boston

COLLEGE(S)/DEGREES: Massachusetts Bay Community College, Labouré Junior College, Massachusetts College of Pharmacy (B.S.N.), Northeastern University (M.S.N.)

TYPES OF WRITING ON THE JOB: Observations of patients, notes about patients, memos to colleagues, instructions for junior staff, lots of email

HOW PATTY USES NARRATION: Notes on patients are usually narratives. They need to be concise, precise, and clear, as both Patty and others will need to refer to them for patients' treatment. For an example of how Patty uses narration, see Narration in the Workplace, page 112.

COMPUTER SKILLS: Word processing and spreadsheet programs

TEAMWORK ON THE JOB: Most of the nursing work at Children's Hospital is teamwork, with primary teams of four nurses assigned to children. Team members have regular conferences, write weekly summaries of patient care and patients' conditions, and write reports that they share with each other. They must work together well and communicate well, both in speech and in writing; children's lives depend on their effective cooperation.

FUTURE GOAL: Patty has held her current position only for a short time, and her goal is to be successful in her many new roles: consultant, direct patient care provider, researcher, and new staff educator.

who witness or participate in the same series of events may give very different accounts because they focus on different aspects of the events or perceive the whole series differently. The stories that Gloria and Mason tell in the following two paragraphs reflect their different points of view regarding the same experience.

GLORIA'S STORY

This morning Mason and I set out for a day at the beach. It was supposed to be great, but Mason's stubborn behavior ruined everything. First, he took the longest route, so we hit traffic that we would have avoided by going the short route. Then we got lost. I suggested that we stop and ask directions, but Mason said he could get us there. After another hour of driving, we passed an intersection that we'd crossed earlier. I again suggested that we stop and ask directions, but Mason wasn't buying it. So we drove some more. Finally, we were about to run out of gas, so we pulled into a gas station. While Mason was filling the tank, I asked the attendant for directions. I swear if we hadn't needed gas, we'd still be driving around looking for that beach!

MASON'S STORY

This morning Gloria and I set out for a day at the beach. It would have been a great day if Gloria hadn't wanted to pick a fight. First she insisted I was going the wrong way, it was going to take us longer, and we'd hit more traffic. Then she decided we were lost. I knew about where we were going and knew I could figure it out. Gloria kept on nagging me to stop and ask directions. When we were almost there, I decided to get gas, and she had to ask the attendant for directions. I don't know what was going on with her, but she was really on my case.

As you can see, the events are the same, but the stories aren't; they are told from two very different points of view. When you write a narration, be careful to describe events in a way that will tell the story you want to tell.

MAJOR EVENTS AND DETAILS IN NARRATION

The support for the main point of your narration is the presentation and explanation of the major events in the story. These major events are your support points and will become the topic sentences for the body paragraphs in your essay. Ask yourself what the major events are and what was so important about them.

For more on supporting a point, see Chapter 4.

If you give only the major events, your readers will not be able to experience those events as you did. You must also supply **supporting details** that bring the experience to life for the readers.

For example, one student stated the main point of an event in the following thesis: *Skydiving is the most thrilling experience I have ever had.* Then that student presented major events and supporting details about those events.

MAJOR EVENTS	SUPPORTING DETAILS
opening door	rush of cold air
	flapping of suit
jumping	lump in throat
	goosebumps
parachute	drifting to ground

CHRONOLOGICAL (TIME) ORDER IN NARRATION

Because narration tells a story, it uses chronological (time) order. Start at the beginning of the story, and describe the events in the sequence in which they occurred.

Introduction (including thesis)

First major event

    Details about the first event

Second major event

    Details about the second event

Third major event

    Details about the third event

Conclusion

For more on chronological order, see page 59.

Time transitions (see p. 109) are important in narration because they make the order of events clear to readers. Writers of narration use these common transitions not only within a paragraph to move from one detail about the event to the next but also between paragraphs to move from one major event to the next.

When you are writing narration, particularly for college or work, make sure that your essay has a main point that readers can recognize. Your readers should not come to the end of your narration and think, "So what?" Here are some ways you might use narration:

COLLEGE

- In a marketing course, you recount the history of Coca-Cola's advertising strategies.

Common Time Transitions

after	eventually	meanwhile	soon
as	finally	next	then
at last	first	now	when
before	last	second	while
during	later	since	

WORK

For more on transitions, see pages 94–99.

• You write up what took place in a staff meeting.

EVERYDAY LIFE

• You write an accident report for your insurance company.

Read and Analyze Narration

Read the following examples of narration — one each from college, the workplace, and everyday life — and answer the questions that accompany each. Reading and analyzing the examples will help you understand how to write a good narration essay.

1. NARRATION IN COLLEGE

The following essay was part of Giovanni Bohorquez's application to business schools. (Bohorquez is featured in the Profile of Success in Chapter 12.) Read the essay and complete the questions that follow it.

From the time I was very young, I saw challenge in difficult situations and always tried my best to meet that challenge. If lemonade stands made millions, I would be rich. I have made lemonade out of the many lemons that life has tossed me, and that experience has served me well.

My teenage parents divorced after a year of marriage, and virtually all of my relatives took their turns raising me. At the age of eleven, I left Colombia to come to the United States. I arrived in the poor town of Elizabeth, New Jersey, to find that my dad was not excited to have me living with him. Those days opened my eyes to poverty. I didn't know it at the time, but hardship was just what I needed. I became a hard worker and helped my family greatly by becoming monetarily self-sufficient at age twelve.

I learned the value of work, knowledge, time, and money. With my work money, I managed to send my mother school money and to get cool clothes, two cars, three guitars, and lots of records. I became responsible, but I was just making the best out of a bad situation.

At fourteen, I got a job in a bicycle shop and came up with the idea of forming a cycling team sponsored by the shop. It was a great success, and the shop owner loved having us advertise to the local aficionados. We never won awards, but we had great fun and got in great shape during the two years I was there. I understood then that I could help other people like me who were trying to find a positive escape from their problems.

When I was fifteen, I came to California and started a guitar club in my high school. I got support from music companies and the school, and in just a month we had a budget, facilities, and twenty members. To culminate the year, we had two concerts. We had a sound engineer, lighting, the school theater, photographers, and videographers—and we even appeared in the local newspaper.

When I got to junior college, I was working sixty hours a week. I managed to become a Business Senator, though, and the vice president of a chapter of the Society of Hispanic Professional Engineers (SHPE). In student government we decided how to use the student funds and helped a lot of school initiatives get started. At SHPE I headed events to help at-risk high school students and organized trips to events at universities. These were some of my hardest times in terms of work and school, but the school activities kept me going. Out of my groups, a good 80 percent of us went to top universities.

When I transferred to UCLA, I wanted to take the hardest, most marketable classes. So I minored in computer programming, specialized in econometrics (data analysis), and even took half a year of Mandarin Chinese. It all paid off. A year before finishing school I already had an offer from the consulting group at Ernst & Young. In order to help other students, I started the UCLA Student Consulting Society. We guided students into the world of consulting through workshops and a course roadmap. A good ten members (50 percent of the group) went into Big Five accounting firms and *Fortune* 100 companies.

I am still the same person today. I still like to help my community and the programs that got me where I am. At Ernst & Young, I got the company to participate in SHPE's national yearly event in which more than seven thousand young professionals from all over the world meet top firms. I led EY's participation at the Stanford Career Day for two years. I often participate in Habitat for Humanity events, and I have been an active mentor for the Puente Program (an outreach program for college students at risk of dropping out) for many years. Through programs such as UCLA's Riordan Fellows, I have helped put together community events for needy children and the homeless. I get great joy out of contributing and helping out. I hope to contribute to my business school the same things I have contributed to other programs. I have a great deal of positive experience in the challenge of excelling in difficult situations and have learned to welcome these challenges.

1. Who is Giovanni's **audience** for this essay? _____

_____

For more on audience and purpose, see pages 7–9.

2. What is Giovanni's **purpose** in telling this story? _____

_____

_____

3. Fill in the blanks with the topic and the main point of Giovanni's essay

   TOPIC: _____

   MAIN POINT: _____

4. Double-underline the **thesis statement**.

5. Put a check mark (✓) at the beginning of each **topic sentence**.

6. Underline the **supporting details** that Giovanni uses, and indicate which you think are the most effective by starring them. Be prepared to discuss your choices.

7. Circle the (transitions) that Giovanni used in his essay.

For a list of the four basics of good narration, see page 105.

8. Does Giovanni's essay have the **four basics of good narration**?

Why or why not? _____

2. NARRATION IN THE WORKPLACE

As a neonatal clinical nurse specialist, Patty Maloney cares for at-risk infants. The following is a narrative that describes her experience with a patient, the patient's parents, and her staff. Nurses need to write accounts of their patients regularly, and those accounts must be clear, descriptive, and accurate. The narration that follows was part of a seminar for nurses interested in becoming managers.

In the neonatal intensive care unit, we work with high-risk infants. Because we are health care professionals, we must maintain objectivity and clinical distance, a tall order when patients are tiny humans just beginning life. As a clinical nurse specialist who manages other staff, I am responsible for helping others see the complete picture when they may be too involved with a patient to do so. Late one recent Christmas Eve, my management skills were put to a painful test.

The patient was a premature infant who weighed only 700 grams and who had been in critical condition since birth. On Christmas Eve, the patient went into shock and experienced respiratory failure. Because of the holiday, the complete medical team wasn't on-site, but the physician and nurse who were caring for this child were unsure about how much longer the child would live. They were faced with a difficult question: Will maximum invasive medical therapy help this child?

The attending physician and nurse concluded that they had exhausted all treatment options. They then decided to call the family in to spend time with the infant and to discuss redirection of support (which means, in essence, acknowledging that most avenues have been exhausted). Redirection of support would avoid any treatment that would be both radical and unlikely to save the patient.

Before contacting the parents, however, the nurse sought my advice. She asked me if I felt there was anything more that she and the doctor could offer the infant. Based on the information I had received, I believed that further treatment was unlikely to change the child's condition. I offered that opinion.

The situation was particularly painful for the team: They did not want to unnecessarily prolong the inevitable death of the infant, so they were inclined to call the parents right away to discuss redirection of support. At this point, I realized that the caregivers' discomfort was preventing them from considering all aspects of the situation. It was my responsibility to fill in the whole picture.

I wanted to ease the pain of my colleagues, which I well understood, but I did not believe that calling the family on Christmas Eve was the best course of action. I explained that I fully appreciated why the team wanted to act quickly, but I also called upon my experience in working with bereaved families, which taught me that the most intense bereavement comes when a loved one dies on a holiday. In this particular case, I reasoned, the child was not going to die in the next few days, so the only reason to call the parents was to ease the medical team's pain. Then I suggested that we wait until after Christmas to meet with the parents, which would also mean that the rest of the medical team could be present and involved in the decision-making process. My colleagues agreed, and they planned a care conference for the day after Christmas.

Personally, I wanted to ease my colleagues' discomfort. Professionally, I couldn't do that, I had to give advice based on a range of circumstances that included my responsibilities to the patient, the patient's family, and my staff. Certainly I won't forget that Christmas Eve, but I know we made the right decisions.

1. What is Patty's **purpose** for writing? _____

   _____

For more on purpose, see pages 7–9.

2. Double-underline the **thesis statement**.

3. Put a check mark (✓) at the beginning of each **topic sentence**.

4. Underline the **supporting details** that Patty uses, and place a star by those you think are the most effective. Be prepared to discuss your choices.

5. Circle the (time transitions) that Patty uses.

6. What key words does she repeat? _____

_____

7. Underline the sentence in the concluding paragraph that relates back to the introduction.

3. NARRATION IN EVERYDAY LIFE

The following is a report to an insurance company following a car accident.

The details of my accident involving a truck on the afternoon of June 1, 2002, will indicate that the truck driver was at fault. I hope this account will help clarify the matter for insurance purposes. I do not want to have my rates raised when another person was at fault.

I was driving north on Route 16 and was following a large truck with the license plate 3819KG. I had followed the truck for about one mile when its left turn indicator started blinking. The truck slowed, and I slowed behind it.

Then the truck pulled into the left lane. I thought the driver was getting ready to make the left turn that he had indicated by turning on his left blinker. The truck then stopped.

Because the truck was mostly in the left lane, I had plenty of room in my lane to continue on, which I did at a very slow pace. All of a sudden the truck turned right and slammed into my car. Fortunately, the truck was going very slowly, but my small Ford Escort was left with significant damage on the left side.

The driver and I then exchanged licenses. He claimed that, during this whole time, it was his intention to turn right and that he had moved left in order to allow clearance for his truck. When I said that he had signaled a left turn, he denied it and refused further discussion.

I would not have pulled to the side of a huge truck just as it was turning in my direction. But all indications were that the driver was making a left turn, not a right one. As I explained to the police officer who came to the accident scene, the truck driver's actions clearly caused this accident. Please consider my letter carefully because I do not want to be charged higher insurance rates for an accident that I did not cause. Thank you for your consideration.

1. What is the writer's **purpose** in preparing this report?

   _____

   _____

   For more on purpose and audience, see pages 7–9.

2. Who is the **audience**? _____

3. Double-underline the **thesis statement**.

4. Identify each of the **major events** with a check mark.

5. Underline the **supporting details**.

6. Circle the **transitions**, including transitional sentences.

7. Underline the sentence in the concluding paragraph that relates back to the introduction.

Write a Narration Essay

In this section, you will write your own narration essay. To do so, follow this sequence:

REVIEW the four basics of good narration (p. 105).

CHOOSE your writing assignment (p. 116).

WRITE your narration using the step-by-step Writing Guide (p. 118).

CHECK your final essay (p. 122).

WRITING ASSIGNMENT 1 **COLLEGE, WORK, EVERYDAY LIFE**

Write a narration essay on *one* of the following topics, or on a topic of your own choice.

COLLEGE

- Tell a story about one of your professors that shows something significant about this person.
- Explain the most important or interesting event that has happened to you in college.
- Recount the events of one historic day.

WORK

- Tell the story of something positive you did at work (some achievement).
- Explain what you learned from getting or doing your first job.
- Describe an incident that shows your boss as _____ (supportive, fair, unfair, clueless, sharp, unrealistic, honest, dishonest).

EVERYDAY LIFE

- Tell the story of your first love (or your most recent one), showing how it changed or influenced you.
- Write about an event when you were proud of someone in your family.
- Write about an event when you were proud or ashamed of your behavior.

 WRITING ASSIGNMENT 2 **USE THE INTERNET**

For advice about how to cite a source, see Chapter 20.

WRITE A COMPLAINT: The Web site Complaints.com (**<www.complaints. com>**) contains complaints about all kinds of products and services. Select either "Read Complaints by Date Posted" or "List of Most Recent Complaints," and read some examples of complaints. As you read, think of similar complaints that you have had, and then write an essay that traces your experience with a particular product or service.

WRITING ASSIGNMENT 3 **YOUR JOB INTERVIEW**

Read the situation that follows, and then choose *one* of the assignment options (3A or 3B) that appear after it.

> **SITUATION:** You have an interview at a company where you really want to work. You are determined to get this job, so you search the library and the Web for information on interviewing, and you find a source that includes sample preparation questions. You can easily answer the first few sample questions (about job history, for example), but then you come to some questions that require you to talk about yourself. You realize that you are less prepared for these, and you decide to write out some answers to help you prepare for your interview.

ASSIGNMENT OPTION 3A: RESPONSE TO THE SITUATION

Write a narration essay in response to the following interview question: What is your greatest personal or professional strength? Your essay should include a chain of specific events that shows this strength in action. Remember that you want to present yourself as a strong candidate for the job. To do so, you must not only present your strengths as an employee but also support your claims with concrete details and examples.

ASSIGNMENT OPTION 3B: ANOTHER PERSPECTIVE

Addressing a possible future employer, write a letter that traces a chain of specific events that demonstrate one of your personal or professional strengths. Begin your letter with this opening sentence:

I believe that I am ideally suited for the position at _____

(fill in the name of the company or organization) and look forward to

meeting the challenges of the _____ job (include

position for which you would like to interview).

Writing Guide

Narration

Follow the steps in this Writing Guide to help you prewrite, draft, revise, and edit your narration. Check off each step as you complete it.

THINKING CRITICALLY ABOUT NARRATION	
FOCUS	Think about who will read your narration and what point you want your readers to understand from your story.
ASK	• What experience or series of events do I want to write about? • What is important about the story from my point of view? • What main point do I want to make with this story? • To make that point, what major events do I need to include? • What details, examples, and facts will bring these events to life and show my readers what the point is and why it is important? • Should I include conversation (something that was said)?

PREWRITE TO EXPLORE YOUR TOPIC

Prewriting for narration involves considering several possible experiences or stories to retell and deciding on the one that you can bring to life for your readers. Your topic should also reveal something important.

For more on purpose and audience, see pages 7–9.

_____ Determine your purpose for writing.

_____ Identify the audience for your essay.

_____ Decide what story you want to tell.

_____ Use a prewriting technique (freewriting, listing/brainstorming, questioning, discussing, clustering) to explore your impressions and thoughts about what happened; how it affected you or others; and what the story shows, explains, or proves.

WRITE A THESIS STATEMENT

The thesis statement in narration includes the topic and the main point you want to make about it.

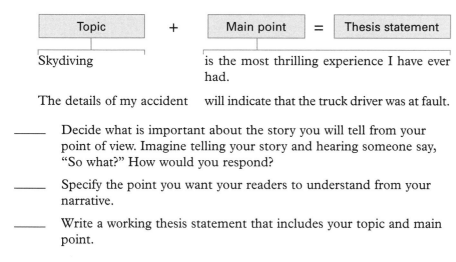

| Topic | + | Main point | = | Thesis statement |

Skydiving   is the most thrilling experience I have ever had.

The details of my accident   will indicate that the truck driver was at fault.

_____ Decide what is important about the story you will tell from your point of view. Imagine telling your story and hearing someone say, "So what?" How would you respond?

_____ Specify the point you want your readers to understand from your narrative.

_____ Write a working thesis statement that includes your topic and main point.

SUPPORT YOUR POINT

Your support in narration includes the major events in your story and the supporting details that explain the events for readers.

_____ List all of the major events in the story.

_____ Review your working thesis statement, and drop any events that do not help you explain, show, or prove your main point. Make your thesis more specific.

_____ Choose at least three major events that will help your readers understand your main point.

_____ Add supporting details about each event that will help your reader experience it as you did. It might help to think about how familiar your readers are with your topic and what details would bring your major events to life for them.

MAKE A PLAN

Making a written plan—an outline—helps you decide how to order your narration. Narration usually tells a story in chronological (time) order, presenting events in the order in which they happened.

_____ Arrange your major events according to when they occurred (in chronological order, first to last).

_____ Write a plan or an outline for your narration that includes your main support points (the major events) and supporting details for each event.

DRAFT

Drafting a narration means writing in complete sentences and including the following:

- An introduction
- A thesis statement that communicates your topic and main point
- The major events in the story, supported by concrete, specific details
- A conclusion that reminds your readers of the main point and makes an observation about the importance of the story

_____ Think about how you can show your readers what's important about the story you are telling.

_____ Write an introduction that hooks your readers' interest and presents your thesis statement.

_____ Using your plan or outline, write a topic sentence for each of the main events. Be sure that each topic sentence is directly related to your thesis statement.

_____ Write body paragraphs that include concrete, specific details that further explain your support points and bring the major events of your story to life. Your readers should be able to experience the events of the story as you did through the supporting details.

_____ Write a concluding paragraph that reminds your readers of your main point and makes a final observation about the importance of the story.

_____ Title your essay.

REVISE

Revising means changing whole sentences or paragraphs to make your writing clearer or stronger. To revise a narration, imagine that you do not know the events in the story or their importance. Read your draft, looking for the following:

- Places where the ideas are off the main point (revising for unity)
- Gaps in information or detail (revising for support and detail)
- Areas in need of "glue" to move readers smoothly from one point to the next (revising for coherence)

_____ Ask another person to read your draft and give you feedback.

_____ Begin revising by considering how you can make the main point of the story clearer or more convincing to your readers.

For more on peer review, see pages 87–88.

_____ Reread your thesis statement. Revise to make it clearer, more concrete, and more forceful.

_____ Reread the body of your narration to see if the events and details support your thesis. If you have left out key events that would show, explain, or prove your thesis, add them now. Add any additional supporting details that would help your readers experience the events as you did or as you want them to.

_____ Reread your introduction. Make changes if the opening is dull or lacks force.

_____ Reread your conclusion to make sure that it is energetic and convincing, reminds readers of your main point, and makes an observation on the importance of the story you have told. Your purpose in telling the story should be clear to your readers.

_____ Add transition words and sentences to connect your ideas smoothly.

_____ Make at least five changes to your draft to improve the unity, support, or coherence of your narration or to make the introduction, thesis statement, or conclusion stronger or more convincing.

EDIT

Some grammar, spelling, word use, or punctuation errors may confuse your readers and make it difficult for them to understand a point you are trying to make. Even if they do not confuse your readers, errors detract from the effectiveness and overall quality of your writing. Edit your narration carefully, correcting any errors you find.

_____ Ask a classmate or a friend to read your narration and highlight any errors.

_____ Use the spell checker or grammar checker on your computer, but do not rely on those programs to catch all errors.

_____ Read your narration carefully, looking for errors in grammar, spelling, word use, or punctuation. Focus first on sentence fragments, run-on sentences, problems with subject–verb agreement, problems with verbs, and other areas where you know you often make errors.

_____ Print a clean, final copy.

_____ Ask yourself: Is this the best I can do?

A FINAL CHECK BEFORE HANDING IN YOUR NARRATION ESSAY

If you've followed the Writing Guide for narration, your essay will already include the four basics of good narration. Use this list to double-check each basic.

_____ My thesis statement reveals what is important about the story.

_____ Each of my paragraphs has a topic sentence that presents a major event in the story.

_____ Each paragraph in the body of my essay has supporting details to show or explain the major event. (I have found at least three supporting details.)

_____ My narration presents the major events in chronological order and uses transitions to connect ideas. (I have found at least three transitions.)

9
Illustration

Writing That Shows Examples

You Know This
Anytime you give examples to explain what you mean, you are using illustration.
- You tell a friend why you like or dislike your job.
- You answer the question "Like what?"
- You select incidents from your experience to show that you are qualified for a different job or new responsibilities.

Understand What Illustration Is

DEFINITION: **Illustration** is writing that uses examples to show, explain, or prove a point. Giving examples is the basis of all good writing and speaking. You make a statement, and then you give an example that shows what you mean.

IDEA JOURNAL
Write about the things that keep your life busy.

▪▪ Four Basics of Good Illustration

1. It makes a point.
2. It gives specific and detailed examples to show, explain, or prove the point.
3. It uses examples that the readers will understand.
4. It uses enough examples to get the writer's point across.

   Illustrations make explanations clear and general statements powerful. They draw readers into essays by providing specifics that make the point.

EXAMPLES FOR ILLUSTRATION

For effective illustration, focus on finding examples that show, explain, or prove your thesis. Listing/brainstorming and clustering are particularly useful prewriting techniques for exploring an illustration topic.

For more on prewriting techniques, see pages 27–31.

123

Pamela O'Berry Evans

DEPUTY COMMONWEALTH ATTORNEY

Pamela O'Berry Evans

BACKGROUND: Pam grew up in a low-income housing project in Philadelphia, one of five children raised by a working mother. Early in school, she was a gifted student but was ridiculed by her friends for doing well and for speaking standard English. In high school, she wanted to be popular, so she turned away from academics and took business prep classes. She had fun, but three months before graduating Pam realized that she wanted to go to college. She had not taken the SAT and did not have good grades. Fortunately, her high school counselor pointed her in the direction of the ACT 101 program. She entered Shippensburg University through this special program and had to work hard on her study skills in order to pass courses.

EMPLOYER: Virginia Commonwealth Attorney's Office

COLLEGE(S)/DEGREES: Shippensburg University (B.A.), American University (J.D.L.)

TYPES OF WRITING ON THE JOB: Letters to crime victims, letters and email among many state and city agencies, legal briefs, correspondence with judges, indictments (summary of the crime), reports tracking crimes and court dates

HOW PAM USES ILLUSTRATION: Legal briefs must include examples of behaviors, actions to be taken, or restrictions. For an example of how Pam uses illustration, see Illustration in the Workplace, page 128.

COMPUTER SKILLS: Word processing, Excel, PowerPoint

TEAMWORK ON THE JOB: Pam leads several teams of attorneys who share information and experience with each other while building prosecution cases against defendants.

FUTURE GOAL: Pam says her goal is to always keep learning. She is also planning to move from the public sector into a private firm that handles civil, rather than criminal, cases.

For example, the writer of the thesis *Homeschooling is beneficial to both the child and the parent* would focus her prewriting on finding examples of benefits of homeschooling. Here are some examples from her brainstorming:

individualized to child	*parent and child have control*
parent and child together	*more flexibility*
at child's own pace	*considers child's learning style*
one-on-one	*education as part of regular life*

SUPPORT FOR ILLUSTRATION

For more on support, see Chapter 4.

An illustration essay may use several examples as support points. The writer of the prewriting on the previous page selected "individualized to child" as one support point and asked herself, "What do I mean? How? In what ways?" to find supporting details.

She also chose "parent and child have control" as another major example that would support the thesis. She then asked herself, "How do they have more control?" and listed potential supporting details:

control over materials used (what books, what computer programs,

what approach)

control over time of instruction (what hours of the day, based on

child's natural rhythms, vacations—not tied to a school's calendar)

ORDER OF IMPORTANCE FOR ILLUSTRATION

For more on order of importance, see page 60.

An illustration often uses order of importance to organize several examples, saving the most vivid, convincing one for last. Keep your readers in mind as you arrange your examples. A typical plan for an illustration essay might look like this:

Introduction (including thesis)

First example

    Supporting details that explain the first example

Second example

    Supporting details that explain the second example

Third (and most important) example

    Supporting details that explain the third example

Conclusion (refers back to your main point and makes an observation)

Illustrations often use transitions such as the following to lead from one major example to the next or from one supporting detail to the next.

For more on transitions, see pages 94–97.

Common Illustration Transitions

also	finally	for instance	in addition
another	for example	for one thing	one example

Whenever we explain something, we use examples to show what we mean. Here are some ways that you might use illustration:

COLLEGE

- In a criminal justice course, you are asked to discuss and give examples of the most common criminal violations.

WORK

- Your written self-evaluation includes specific and measurable examples of how well (or poorly) you performed your job and achieved your goals.

EVERYDAY LIFE

- You take your car to a mechanic, and you give the mechanic examples that show how the car is not running properly.

Read and Analyze Illustration

Read the following examples of illustration—one each from college, the workplace, and everyday life—and answer the questions that accompany each. Reading and analyzing the examples will help you understand how to write good illustration.

1. ILLUSTRATION IN COLLEGE

Read the essay by Lindsey Ducharme, a student in a first-year writing course, and answer the questions that follow it.

Italy: My Dream Destination

Lindsey Ducharme

Where would you go if you had the opportunity to travel anywhere in the world? If I could visit any location, I would go somewhere filled with fascinating sights. I would visit a place I have seen often in movies and magazines. I would visit Italy, an enchanting country of diverse landscapes, historic landmarks, and inspiring art masterpieces.

Italy's first allure is its diverse landscapes, with cosmopolitan cities, small villages, and silent countrysides all within its boundaries. One day I could be exploring an ancient, walled hill town, and the next day I could be purchasing jewelry from a vendor on a crowded street in front of a small restaurant in Florence. Later in my visit, I could be having lunch on the rocky cliff of a very quiet and peaceful fishing village that overlooks the Mediterranean Sea.

In addition to its many diverse cities and villages, Italy is filled with historic landmarks. In Rome alone, there are many places I would visit, such as the remnants of the ancient Roman Forum. There I would observe the meeting place where noblemen gathered in the times of Julius Caesar and Cleopatra. Across from the ruins of the Forum is the great Colosseum, a stadium where gladiators fought to the death to entertain the upper class. The living quarters of former Italian leader Benito Mussolini would be a quick stop on my way to the home of the Catholic Church's living authority: the Vatican. While visiting places important in Italy's history would be a large part of my agenda, I would also like to view some of the world's greatest works of art.

Not only is Italy a land of assorted landscapes and historical sites, it is also an art connoisseur's dream. Italy is home to Michelangelo's extraordinary sculpture of David, which resides in the Academy, an art museum in Florence. Another famous work of Michelangelo's that I would love to see, the *Pietà*, is in St. Peter's Church in Rome. It is a moving and incredibly lifelike sculpture of Christ dying. My last stop would be the Sistine Chapel, which houses hundreds of great works of art that depict biblical stories.

Where would I go if I could travel anywhere? I would set out for Italy, land of diverse scenery, historical landmarks, and majestic artwork. It is filled with places to go and sights to see, all of which are different from what I have known. But Italy would just be my first choice: I hope to travel widely to experience the world's rich wonders and diverse cultures.

1. Who is Lindsey's **audience** for this essay? _*anyone who loves to travel*_

2. What is Lindsey's **purpose** for writing? _*to explain why traveling is so wonderful*_

For more on audience and purpose, see pages 7–9.

3. Fill in the blanks with the **topic** and **main point** of Lindsey's essay.

   TOPIC: _Where would I go_

   MAIN POINT: _go somewhere with fascinating sights_

4. Double-underline the **thesis statement**.

5. Put a check mark (✓) next to the **topic sentences** that present the major examples supporting Lindsey's thesis.

6. Underline the **supporting details** that Lindsey uses to describe her examples.

7. What **introductory technique** does Lindsey use?

   where would I go

8. Circle the (transitions) and (transitional sentences) in Lindsey's essay.

9. How does Lindsey relate the **conclusion** back to the introduction?

   where would I go

For a list of the four basics of good illustration, see page 123.

10. Does Lindsey's essay have the **four basics of good illustration**?

    Why or why not? _____

2. ILLUSTRATION IN THE WORKPLACE

The following is an example of a legal brief of the type that attorney Pamela O'Berry Evans writes nearly every day. (The names have been changed.) Although this document is not written in essay form, it is an example of illustration in the workplace. Read the brief, and answer the questions that follow it.

<table>
<tr><td>1</td><td></td></tr>
<tr><td>2</td><td></td></tr>
</table>

1 | **VIRGINIA:**
IN THE CIRCUIT COURT FOR
2 | **THE CITY OF RICHMOND**

3 | **JANE PARSONS, Petitioner,**
versus
4 | **HECTOR RAZO, Respondent.**

5 | **Preliminary Protective Order**
     This day pursuant to Virginia Code sections 19.2-
6 | 152.9-10, Petitioner's affidavit, and good cause having
     been shown, it is ordered that a preliminary protective
7 | order be issued against the Respondent, Hector Razo,
     commanding that any acts of stalking cease immediately.

8 |
     a. That the Respondent (Razo) shall have no
9 | contact whatsoever with the Petitioner (Parsons). This
     includes, but is not limited to contact by letter,
10 | telephone, in person or through agents or confederates
     of the Respondent.

11 |
     b. That the Respondent (Razo) shall not follow,
12 | contact, telephone, or harass family, friends or co-
     workers of the Petitioner (Parsons) for the purpose of
13 | discussing or making contact, with the Petitioner.

14 |
     c. That the Respondent (Razo) shall not come
     within 100 feet of the Petitioner (Parsons).
15 |
     It is further ordered that a full hearing on the
16 | protective order shall be held within fifteen (15) days of
     the issuance of this order on _____.
17 |

18 | _____   _____
     Date   Judge
19 |

1. Who is the **audience** for this document? __Hector Raza__

For more on audience and purpose, see pages 7–9.

2. What is the **purpose** of this document? ___to inform___

3. How do Pamela O'Berry Evans's audience and purpose make the tone of this document different from the tone used by student writer Lindsey Ducharme in her illustration essay? (See p. 126.)

more formal

4. What is the **main point** of the document? *to inform*

5. The document gives **examples** of *a, b, c*

6. Underline each **specific example**.

7. Which example gives the most **details**? *A*

8. If you were to add one more detail to an example of "contact," what would you add?

3. ILLUSTRATION IN EVERYDAY LIFE

The following is an example of a letter written by a town resident and father of a high school student to the editor of the local newspaper. It shows how you might use illustration in your everyday life to explain your point of view. Read it, and answer the questions that follow.

TO THE EDITOR:

Last week this paper reported in great detail the episode of drug dealing at the high school. An entire page was devoted to a description of what happened, interviews with the principal and the arresting police officer, and a disturbing picture of two handcuffed students being led out of school. While I know that this is news, I wonder why this paper doesn't give equal coverage to some of the many positive activities at the high school.

Earlier this year, a group of high school students organized a fundraiser to help families who were left homeless after a fire. They worked nights and weekends planning the event, a flea market. They solicited donations from residents and local businesses, and they baked items to sell. They placed notices in the paper, the school newsletter, and buildings around town. They worked the night before setting up, all the next day, and the next night cleaning up. The paper reported the event in a single paragraph on page 10.

Another example of positive behavior is the students' ongoing relationship with the senior center. Several times this year, students have organized events to entertain the seniors, including a performance by the jazz band, a humor night, and three dinners. In addition, the students organized a book drive for the senior center's library and collected hundreds of books and videos. Also, a group of students regularly visits the senior center to read to its residents. These activities weren't covered at all by this newspaper.

One last example of positive behavior is the tribute to a young teacher who suddenly passed away this year. The students put together a memorial for Ms. Sessions, with written stories and testimonials. For this event, they organized a class donation to a memorial scholarship fund and student speeches. They invited the teacher's family to the memorial, and the family was very moved.

Yes, we have problem students and, yes, they make sensational news. I don't suggest that this paper ignore the problems or gloss them over, but in the interest of balanced reporting, I ask that you give the good news equal time.

1. Who is the **audience** for this essay? _____ the Editor _____

2. What is the writer's **purpose** for writing? _____ to inform _____

For more on audience and purpose, see pages 7–9.

_____

3. Double-underline the **thesis statement**.

4. Put a check mark (✓) next to each of the major **examples**.

5. Underline the **details** that support the examples.

6. Circle the (**transitions**.)

Write an Illustration Essay

In this section, you will write your own illustration. To do so, follow this sequence:

REVIEW the four basics of good illustration (p. 123).

CHOOSE your writing assignment (below).

WRITE your illustration using the step-by-step Writing Guide (p. 134).

CHECK your final essay (p. 138).

WRITING ASSIGNMENT 1   COLLEGE, WORK, EVERYDAY LIFE

Write an illustration essay on *one* of the following topics or on a topic of your own choice.

COLLEGE

- Make a point about your college to a prospective student and back it up with examples.

- Assess the value of a course you have taken, giving specific examples.

- Explain how _____ (someone you learned about in a college course) made a meaningful contribution to society.

WORK

- Tell a job applicant what the typical responsibilities might be in your job.

- Explain to your supervisor your claim that there is too much work to be done in the time allotted.

- Demonstrate the following statement: "I am a very _____ person." Your audience is a potential employer.

EVERYDAY LIFE

- Write a letter to your landlord about how your apartment needs more regular maintenance.

- Write a letter to a friend in which you explain that your _____ _____ (mother, father, sibling, sweetheart) is the most _____ (selfish, generous, irresponsible, capable) person you know.

- Write a report explaining your living costs and expenses in order to show how well (or how poorly) you are managing your money.

WRITING ASSIGNMENT 2   **USE THE INTERNET**

Write an illustration essay in which you complete the following sentence and use it as your thesis statement:

For advice about how to cite a source, see Chapter 20.

If you are interested in finding information about _____,

the Internet _____.

Use examples to show a reader why you hold the view expressed in this thesis.

WRITING ASSIGNMENT 3   **HARASSMENT ON THE JOB**

Read the problem and the situation that follow, and then choose *one* of the assignment options (3A or 3B) that appear after it.

PROBLEM: Although most companies have written policies designed to prevent sexual harassment, problems still occur frequently in the workplace. Sexual harassment situations are always uncomfortable, and often the person being harassed doesn't know what to do. Victims want to stop the unwanted advances, but they may fear that making a formal complaint will hurt their chances for success at work—or worse, will lead to their getting fired.

SITUATION: Kim Alleya, a young woman with whom you work, asks for your advice one day during lunch. She is an administrative assistant, and she started with the company just two months ago. She tells you the following:

> Jerry Churney is bothering me. He asked me out a month or so ago, and I said no. I think he was mad, and since then he's been harassing me. Recently he's been coming up to me and saying or doing stuff that makes me uncomfortable; I dread coming to work.
>
> You know, he's good friends with my boss, and I'm afraid if I say anything that I'll get in trouble. I'm still technically in the probation period, and I really need this job. What would you do if you were me?

You advise Kim to write a report for your company's human resources department that illustrates (gives detailed examples of) the harassing behavior, and you offer to help her write it. This is a very sensitive subject, but the writing should be professional and objective in tone. The conclusion should emphasize both the victim's concern about the inappropriate behavior and her willingness to work cooperatively to solve the problem.

ASSIGNMENT OPTION 3A: DOCUMENTING A COMPLAINT

Using what you know about illustration, assume you are Kim and write a report for the human resources department.

ASSIGNMENT OPTION 3B: ANOTHER PERSPECTIVE

Write an illustration essay from the perspective of Jerry Churney, who has been informed of Kim's complaint of harassment. Again, the audience is the human resources department.

Illustration

Follow the steps in this Writing Guide to help you prewrite, draft, revise, and edit your illustration. Check off each step as you complete it.

THINKING CRITICALLY ABOUT ILLUSTRATION

FOCUS	Think about what you want to explain and who will read your illustration essay.
ASK	• What main point am I trying to illustrate (explain with examples)? • Which examples will most clearly and vividly explain my point? • What examples will my readers most easily understand? • How can I make the examples specific and detailed? • How should I order my examples so that they will be the most effective?

PREWRITE TO EXPLORE YOUR TOPIC

Prewriting for illustration involves considering what aspect of a topic you know well enough to illustrate. Then you need to select good examples and make sure that they demonstrate your main point.

_____ Decide on your purpose for writing.

_____ Identify the audience for your essay.

_____ After you select a writing assignment, use a prewriting technique (freewriting, listing/brainstorming, questioning, discussing, clustering) to get some ideas about the topic.

_____ Narrow your ideas to a topic you can write about in a short essay, and then generate examples that would demonstrate your point about the topic.

For more on purpose and audience, see pages 7–9.

WRITE A THESIS STATEMENT

The thesis statement in illustration usually includes the topic and the main point you want to make about it.

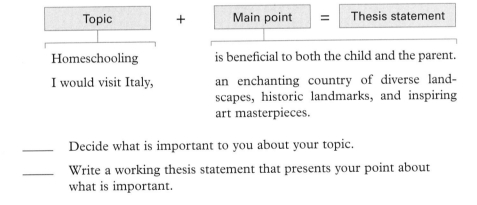

| Topic | + | Main point | = | Thesis statement |

Homeschooling   is beneficial to both the child and the parent.

I would visit Italy,   an enchanting country of diverse land-scapes, historic landmarks, and inspiring art masterpieces.

_____ Decide what is important to you about your topic.

_____ Write a working thesis statement that presents your point about what is important.

SUPPORT YOUR POINT

The major support points in illustration are the examples you give to demonstrate or prove your thesis. These examples will become the topic sentences for the body paragraphs. To come up with examples, assume someone has read your thesis and asked, "What do you mean?" or "Like what?"

_____ Use a prewriting technique to help you get ideas for examples.

_____ Choose at least three examples that will show your readers what you mean.

_____ Reread your prewriting to find supporting details that you may have already generated.

_____ Find additional supporting details by asking yourself more questions: What do I mean? How? In what ways?

_____ For each of your examples, add supporting details that will help your readers understand how the example demonstrates your main point. Give your readers specific and detailed information about each major example.

MAKE A PLAN

Making a written plan—an outline—helps you decide how to order your illustration. An illustration essay with several examples is often organized by order of importance, building up to the most significant or persuasive example.

_____ Arrange your major support examples in order of importance, leading up to the one that you think will have most impact on your readers.

_____ Make a plan or outline for your illustration essay that includes your main support points (your examples) and supporting details for each example.

DRAFT

Drafting in illustration means writing in complete sentences and including the following:

• An introduction with a thesis statement that communicates your topic and your main point about that topic
• The examples that demonstrate or prove your main point
• Supporting details that explain the examples for your reader

_____ Reread your thesis so that it is fresh in your mind.

_____ Write an introductory paragraph that includes your thesis statement and hooks your readers' interest.

_____ Using your plan or outline, write a topic sentence for each of your major examples.

_____ Fill in the supporting details that explain your major support points, your examples. Add any details that occur to you as you write and think about your thesis. Ask yourself what other specific, concrete details would help your readers understand each example as you would like them to.

_____ Write a strong conclusion that refers back to your main point and makes a final observation or recommendation.

_____ Title your essay.

REVISE

Revising means changing whole sentences or paragraphs to make your writing clearer or stronger. To revise an illustration, imagine that you are a reader with no idea how your topic is what your thesis claims it is. Read your draft, looking for the following:

- Examples and details that don't really demonstrate your thesis (revise for unity)
- Places where you would stop and think, "I don't get it," because there isn't enough concrete information (revise for support and detail).
- Places where the examples need transitions to connect ideas and move a reader smoothly from one idea to the next (revise for coherence).

_____ Get feedback from others through peer review.

For more on peer review, see pages 87–88.

_____ Begin by asking, "If a reader didn't know much about this topic, would my examples give that reader enough information to understand my main point?"

_____ Reread your thesis statement. Revise it so that your point is clearer, more concrete, and more forceful.

_____ Reread the body paragraphs of your illustration essay to see if the examples and supporting details demonstrate your thesis to your readers. Suppose that, after reading your thesis, a reader asked, "How? Give me some examples." Would your body paragraphs supply the answer?

_____ Reread your introduction and make changes if it is dull or weak.

_____ Reread your conclusion to make sure it is energetic and drives home your thesis.

_____ Add transitions, words and sentences that connect your examples and details.

_____ Make at least five changes to your draft, to improve its unity, support, or coherence or to make the introduction, thesis statement, or conclusion stronger or more convincing.

EDIT

Some grammar, spelling, word use, or punctuation errors may confuse your readers and make it difficult for them to understand a point you are trying to make. Even if they do not confuse your readers, errors detract from the effectiveness and overall quality of your writing. Edit your illustration carefully, and correct any errors you find.

_____ Ask a classmate or friend to read your illustration and highlight errors.

_____ Use the spell checker or grammar checker on your computer, but do not rely on them to catch all errors.

_____ Read your illustration carefully, looking for errors in grammar, spelling, word use, or punctuation. Focus first on sentence fragments, run-on sentences, problems with subject–verb agreement, problems with verbs, and other areas where you know you often make errors.

_____ Print a clean, final copy.

_____ Ask yourself: Is this the best I can do?

A FINAL CHECK BEFORE HANDING IN YOUR ILLUSTRATION ESSAY

If you've followed the Writing Guide for illustration, your essay will already include the four basics of good illustration. Use this list to double-check each basic feature.

____ My thesis statement reveals the point of my illustration essay.

____ Each of the paragraphs in the body of my essay presents a detailed example that supports and explains my main point.

____ My examples are clear, detailed, and specific so that my readers can understand them.

____ My illustration essay includes enough examples to get my point across.

10

Description

Writing That Creates Pictures in Words

You Know This
You use description every day.
- You describe what someone looks like.
- You describe an item you have lost.
- You describe a place you have visited.

Understand What Description Is

IDEA JOURNAL
Write about the most beautiful, the most interesting, or the ugliest chair, car, T-shirt, or other object you've ever seen.

DEFINITION: Description is writing that creates a clear and vivid impression of the topic. Description translates your experience of a person, place, or thing into words, often by appealing to the senses: sight, hearing, smell, taste, and touch.

▐▐ Four Basics of Good Description

1. It creates a main impression—an overall effect, feeling, or image— about the topic.
2. It uses specific sensory images to support the main impression.
3. It uses concrete details that appeal to the senses: sight, hearing, smell, taste, and touch.
4. It brings a person, place, or physical object to life for the reader.

In a description, you create an impression for your audience through the sensory images and details you present. These details help your audience share your experience and understand your impression of the topic.

Daigo Fujiwara

ASSISTANT ART DIRECTOR

Daigo Fujiwara

BACKGROUND: Daigo came to the United States from Japan as an exchange student when he was a senior in high school. After graduation he remained—against the wishes of his parents—to continue his education. Although he wanted to go to college, his English-language test scores were low, so he took writing courses in English as a second language (ESL) at Becker Junior College and then enrolled there. Although he could speak English fairly well, his writing skills were still poor. Through continuing on with ESL writing courses, Daigo improved his skills and graduated first from Becker and then from Northeastern University. In addition to his job as an assistant art director, Daigo is a photographer and plays bass in a band.

EMPLOYER: *Inc.* magazine

COLLEGE(S)/DEGREES: Becker Junior College (A.A.), Northeastern University (B.A.)

TYPES OF WRITING ON THE JOB: Summaries of articles for illustrators, memos to illustrators, follow-up letters to illustrators, notes about layout, directions for interns, forms describing necessary changes in artwork

HOW DAIGO USES DESCRIPTION: Daigo has to write detailed descriptions of what he needs for the magazine's art program. These descriptions, called specifications, are written for freelance artists. For an example of Daigo's use of description, see page 145.

COMPUTER SKILLS: Word processing, photo imaging software (Photoshop), illustration software, Internet

TEAMWORK ON THE JOB: Daigo works with *Inc.*'s art director and editor to develop a concept, to decide whether to use photographs or illustrations for each article, and to make individual selections.

FUTURE GOAL: Daigo hopes, first, to remain interested in whatever he's doing by learning new skills and, second, to continue his bass playing.

For more on prewriting techniques, see pages 27–31.

SPECIFIC DETAILS FOR DESCRIPTION

Good description uses specific, concrete details to present the sights, sounds, smells, tastes, and touches that contribute to vivid sensory images and a clear overall impression. You can use prewriting techniques to generate or recall effective details that will help readers to understand your experience.

SIGHT	SOUND	SMELL
Colors	Loud/soft	Sweet/sour
Shapes	Piercing/soothing	Sharp/mild
Sizes	Continuous/off-and-on	Good (like what?)

SIGHT	SOUND	SMELL
Patterns	Pleasant/unpleasant (how?)	Bad (rotten?)
Brightness	Does it sound like anything else?	New (like what?)
Does it look like anything else?		Does it smell like anything else?

TASTE	TOUCH
Good (What does good taste like?)	Hard/soft
Bad (What does bad taste like?)	Liquid/solid
Bitter/sugary	Rough/smooth
Metallic	Dry/oily
Burning/spicy	Textures
Does it taste like anything else?	Does it feel like anything else?

SUPPORT POINTS FOR DESCRIPTION

As you think about the main impression you want to convey, ask yourself what major sensory images your details might bring to life. Look for clusters or groups of details that describe the major sensory images as you recall them. Add other details to convey each sensory image more accurately or vividly.

For example, one student wrote this thesis statement, *When I take her coat from the closet, it's as if my grandmother is standing beside me.* To support this main impression, the writer might describe sensory images such as the smell of the coat, the feel of the fabric, or the candy left in the pocket. She might give details about the smell of the coat (*sweet like Grandma's perfume, with a faint odor of mothballs and home-baked bread*); the feel of the fabric (*nubby and rough, with some smooth spots where the fabric has worn thin*); and the candy in the pocket (*single pieces of butterscotch that rustle in their wrappings, and a round cylinder that is a roll of wintergreen Life Savers*).

ORDER OF IDEAS FOR DESCRIPTION

Description may use any of the orders of organization: time, space, or importance, depending on the purpose of the description. If you are describing what someone or something looks like, you might use spatial order. If you are describing a main impression that is more than visual, you might use order of importance.

For more on ordering ideas, see pages 58–64.

For example, the student who is writing about her grandmother's coat might use order of importance, saving for last the sensory image and the details that most vividly bring her grandmother to life. Her plan for her description might be as follows:

Introduction (including thesis)

First sensory image (candy in the pocket)

>   details

Second sensory image (feel of fabric)

>   details

Most important sensory image (smell of coat)

>   details

>   why most important

Conclusion

>   Remind reader of the main impression (coat reminds me of grandmother)

>   Make an observation (to others just an old coat, but the feel and smell of it belong to my grandmother)

Add transitions to be certain that your reader can move smoothly from sensory image to sensory image and detail to detail.

For more on transitions, see pages 94–99.

Common Transitions in Description

TRANSITIONS TO SHOW ORDER OF IMPORTANCE	TRANSITIONS TO SHOW SPACE ORDER
the most	to the left/right
more	in front of/behind
even more	beyond
the strongest	above/underneath
the most intense	

Being able to describe something or someone accurately and in detail is important not only in school but also in other settings. Describing something well involves using specific, concrete details. Here are some ways that you might use description:

COLLEGE

- For a science lab report, you have to describe the physical and chemical properties of an element.

WORK

- You write a letter to your office cleaning contractor describing the unacceptable conditions of the office.

EVERYDAY LIFE

- You describe a jacket that you want a friend to buy for a birthday gift for you.

Read and Analyze Description

Read the following examples of description—one each from college, work, and everyday life—and answer the questions that accompany each. Reading and analyzing the examples will help you understand how to write a good description.

1. DESCRIPTION IN COLLEGE

Read the following description essay, written by a student for a course assignment, and complete the questions following it.

Photograph of My Father

Florence Bagley

This old black-and-white photograph of my father fills me with conflicting emotions. He died very young, and this photo is one of the few that my family has of him. The picture seems to show a strong, happy man, young and smiling, but to me it also reveals his weakness.

Looking at this picture of my father, I feel how much I have lost. In it, my father is sitting upright in a worn plaid easy chair. It was "his" chair, and when he was at work I'd curl up in it and smell his aftershave lotion and cigarette smoke. His pitch-black hair is so dark that it blends into the background of the photo. His eyes, though indistinct in this photo, were a deep, dark brown. Although the photo is faded around my father's face, I still can make out his strong jaw and the cleft in his chin. In the photo my father is wearing a clean white T-shirt that reveals his thick, muscular arms. Resting in the crook of his left arm is my younger brother, who was about one year old at the time. Both of them are smiling.

However, when I study the photo, my eyes are drawn to the can of beer that sits on the table next to him. Against my will, I begin to feel resentful. I have so many wonderful memories of my father. Whether he was carrying me on his shoulders, picking me up from school, or teaching me to draw, he always made time for me. All of these memories fade when I see that beer. From what I remember, he always made time for that beer as well. The smell of beer was always on him, the cool, sweating can always within reach.

In this photo, my father appears to be a strong man; however, looks are deceiving. My father died at the age of thirty-seven because he was an alcoholic. I was eleven when he died, and I really did not understand that his drinking was the reason for his death. I just knew that he left me without a father and the possibility of more memories. He should have been strong enough to stop drinking.

In spite of the resentment I may feel about his leaving me, this photo holds many loving memories as well. It is of my father—the strong, wonderful man and the alcoholic—and it is the most precious thing I own. Although I would much rather have him here, I stay connected to him when I look at it.

For more on purpose and audience, see pages 7–9.

1. What is Florence's **purpose** for writing this essay?

    _____

2. Who is Florence's **audience** for this essay? _____

3. Fill in the blanks with the **topic** and the **main impression** from Florence's essay.

    TOPIC: _____

    MAIN IMPRESSION: _____

    _____

4. Double-underline the **thesis statement**.

5. Each major support point should be a topic sentence for a paragraph in the body of the essay. Put a check mark (✓) next to each **topic sentence** in this essay.

6. Underline some of the **details** that create a picture of Florence's father.

7. What, to you, is the strongest image in the essay? Why?

   _____

8. What type of **organization** does the writer use? _____

9. Does Florence's essay have the **four basics of good description**? Why or why not? _____

For a list of the four basics of good description, see page 139.

2. DESCRIPTION IN THE WORKPLACE

The following is an example of the kind of description that Daigo Fujiwara writes in his job as graphic artist and assistant art director. Although the memo to the photo researcher is not in standard essay form, it is a clear example of description in the workplace.

> May 8, 2002
>
> TO: Jonathan Kuvicek, Photo Researcher
>
> FR: Daigo Fujiwara, Assistant Art Director
>
> RE: Photographs to accompany article
>
> As we discussed earlier today, we need four photographs to accompany the article on innovative work spaces. Overall, the photos should be colorful, upbeat, and somewhat playful, demonstrating the positive attributes of the spaces.
>
> The photographs should include people working in them. We would like to have a representative group of people: a variety of racial and ethnic groups balanced by gender. Probably most of the people will be younger, in that the companies piloting these innovative spaces tend to attract younger employees. As we discussed, the opening photo might contrast a traditional cubicle arrangement with the newer arrangements.

All photographs should be in full color. The opening photograph will be sized at 3" × 6"; the other three will be 5" × 4". When you submit photos for our consideration, please indicate any cropping suggestions.

As we agreed, you will submit a group of photographs for our consideration by May 20.

For more on audience and purpose, see pages 7–9.

1. Who is Daigo's **audience** for this memo? _____

2. What is his **purpose** for writing? _____

   _____

3. Like Florence's essay, Daigo's memo is an example of descriptive writing. How does his purpose for writing make his memo different from Florence's essay? _____

   _____

4. Double-underline the **thesis statement**.

5. Circle at least three **specific details**.

For a list of the four basics of good description, see page 139.

6. Does this memo have the **four basics of good description**? Why or why not? _____

3. DESCRIPTION IN EVERYDAY LIFE

The following essay is a description of water damage to the writer's apartment and possessions. The writer took pictures of the damage but wanted to have a written backup for the photos.

On Wednesday, February 10, I returned to my apartment (275 Marlboro Avenue, #3D) to find significant water damage in my bedroom. I was not completely surprised because the leaky shower in the apartment above me has been a problem for over six months. This time, however, it wasn't a matter of a few spots on the ceiling. Part of the ceiling had caved in, leaving my room and my possessions a soggy mess.

The floor was covered with chunks of plaster. Larger pieces of the falling plaster had scratched and chipped my dresser and night table. Plaster dust mixed with water formed a gluey substance that was caked on my floor, the television, the CD player, and my computer. Not only did this make a disgusting mess, but it also gummed up my computer and keyboard, which now are nonfunctional.

In addition to the plaster, rancid, rusty brown water filled with who knows what had come through the hole in the ceiling and through the light fixture. It permanently soaked some texts and notebooks lying on the bed, as well as the blankets and sheets—it even soaked through and stained the mattress. Replacing these items will mean significant cost.

The worst, though, is that my guitar was also ruined, with nicks and scratches from the falling plaster and warped, stained wood and strings. That rusty stinking water ruined my most valuable possession. The worst part of the soggy mess is not the cost or the time involved in replacing damaged items. It is the permanent loss of that guitar. When I saw my guitar that night, I stood there aching.

1. What is the writer's **purpose** in this essay? _____

_____

For more on purpose and audience, see pages 7–9.

2. Who is the writer's **audience** for this essay? _____

_____

3. What is your strongest reaction to the essay? Why? _____

4. What is the **main impression** that the thesis statement creates?

_____

5. Double-underline the **thesis statement**.

6. Put a check mark (✓) next to each **topic sentence** that supports the thesis statement.

7. Underline at least four **supporting details**.

8. Circle the (transitional words).

9. How does the concluding paragraph relate back to the main point?

Write a Description Essay

In this section, you will write your own description essay. To do so, follow this sequence:

REVIEW the basics of good description (p. 139).

CHOOSE your writing assignment (below).

WRITE your description using the step-by-step Writing Guide (p. 150).

CHECK your final essay (p. 154).

WRITING ASSIGNMENT 1   COLLEGE, WORK, EVERYDAY LIFE

Write a description essay on *one* of the following topics or on a topic of your own choice.

COLLEGE

- Describe the setting of your college to someone who has never seen it but is interested in attending.
- Describe your favorite place on campus so that a reader understands why you like to be there.
- Describe an average student at your college in order to create an impression of your school.

WORK

- Describe an area of your workplace that is not worker-friendly.
- Describe a product or service that your company produces.
- Describe your boss or another person with whom you work.

EVERYDAY LIFE

- Describe a favorite place.
- Describe someone in your family.
- Describe a favorite photograph.

WRITING ASSIGNMENT 2   **USE THE INTERNET**

Write a description essay about a place you would like to visit—a geographic area, a resort, a museum, a theme park. To get information about the location, visit its Web site. (For instance, visiting **<www.grandcanyon. com>** will lead you to information about one of America's most traveled sites.) You will need to cite, or acknowledge, any source information that you include in your essay.

For advice about how to cite a source, see Chapter 20.

 WRITING ASSIGNMENT 3   **WRITE A REPORT**

Read the problem and the situation that follow, and then choose *one* of the assignment options (3A or 3B) that appear after it.

> PROBLEM: Increasingly, companies are being urged to provide more attractive workplaces for their employees. This initiative grows out of recent research that indicates that employees' productivity increases and the amount of sick time taken by employees decreases when a workplace is attractive and comfortable.

> SITUATION: Your boss has asked you to be part of a task force that will recommend how a specific area of the workplace could be made more attractive and comfortable for employees.

ASSIGNMENT OPTION 3A: RESPONSE TO THE SITUATION

Choose a specific area of your workplace (or your college, if you are not working). Using what you know about description, recommend some ways in which this area could be made more worker-friendly (or student-friendly). Your recommendations should be detailed enough that your boss (or a college official) could visualize what you have in mind.

ASSIGNMENT OPTION 3B: ANOTHER PERSPECTIVE

Read assignment option 3A. Instead of writing from your own perspective, write a description essay from the perspective of the other gender. For example, if you are a man, make recommendations from the perspective of a woman; if you are a woman, make them from a man's perspective. Talk to a member of the opposite sex to understand how he or she may see things differently. Would you focus on the same area? What kinds of changes would make the area more appealing to the other person?

Writing Guide

Description

Follow the steps in this Writing Guide to help you prewrite, draft, revise, and edit your description. Check off each step as you complete it.

THINKING CRITICALLY ABOUT DESCRIPTION	
FOCUS	Think about what you want to describe and the overall impression you want to give your readers.
ASK	• What person, place, or thing do I want to write about? Why? What main impression about it do I want to convey? • Who will be reading this essay, and what do they know or need to know about my topic? • What thesis statement would introduce my topic and state my main impression? • To convey my main impression, what aspects of my topic do I need to describe? • What sensory images will my readers need in order to understand my topic? What details might create those sensory images?

PREWRITE TO EXPLORE YOUR TOPIC

Prewriting for description involves selecting a topic about which you have strong impressions and then getting ideas about those impressions. Description creates strong sensory images in words, allowing your reader to see, feel, or experience your topic as intensely as you have.

For more on purpose and audience, see pages 7–9.

_____   Decide on your purpose for writing.

_____   Identify the audience for your essay.

_____   Jot down some ideas about what you see when you visualize your topic.

_____   Think about what main impression you want to convey to your readers.

_____   Use a prewriting technique (freewriting, listing/brainstorming, questioning, discussing, clustering) to explore your impressions and visual or other sensory images.

WRITE A THESIS STATEMENT

The thesis statement in description includes the topic and the main impression about it that you want to convey to your reader.

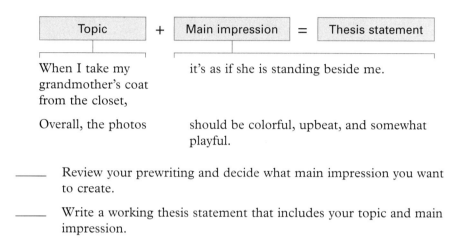

| Topic | + | Main impression | = | Thesis statement |

When I take my grandmother's coat from the closet,   it's as if she is standing beside me.

Overall, the photos   should be colorful, upbeat, and somewhat playful.

_____ Review your prewriting and decide what main impression you want to create.

_____ Write a working thesis statement that includes your topic and main impression.

SUPPORT YOUR POINT

The major support points in description are the sensory images that, together, create the main impression. The sensory images will become the topic sentences for the body paragraphs.

The sensory images are supported by concrete details that allow readers to see, hear, or feel the topic as you do.

_____ Review your thesis statement and prewriting, and make other notes. Try to find strong sensory images that will support your main impression and make the topic come alive for your readers.

_____ Choose at least three sensory images that will help to convey your main impression.

_____ Add specific, concrete details that vividly describe each sensory image. Try to appeal to the senses: sight, sound, smell, touch, taste.

MAKE A PLAN

Making a written plan—an outline—helps you decide how to order your description. A description may use time order, space order, or order of importance, depending on the purpose.

For more on ordering ideas in description, see page 141.

_____ Arrange your support points—your sensory images—in a logical order.

_____ Identify vivid details that will describe each sensory image for your readers.

_____ Make a plan or outline for your description essay.

DRAFT

Drafting a description means writing in complete sentences and including the following:

- An introduction with a thesis that states your topic and main impression
- Body paragraphs with topic sentences that identify the major sensory images
- Supporting details that show readers each sensory image
- A conclusion that refers back to the main impression and makes a further observation

_____ Close your eyes and try to experience the topic and main impression you are writing about.

_____ Write an introduction that draws your readers in and makes them want to know about your topic.

_____ Write a topic sentence for each of the major sensory images.

_____ Add specific details in each paragraph to bring the sensory images and main impression to life.

_____ Write a conclusion that reminds your readers of your main impression of your topic and makes an observation based on the sensory images you have presented.

_____ Title your essay.

REVISE

Revising means changing whole sentences or paragraphs to make your writing clearer or stronger. To revise a description, imagine that you are a reader who has never seen or experienced the topic. Read your draft, looking for the following:

- Places where the ideas are off the main point (revise for unity)
- Gaps in information or detail (revise for support and detail)

- Areas in need of transitions to connect ideas and move your readers smoothly from one point to the next (revise for coherence)

_____ Get feedback from others through peer review.

For more on peer review, see pages 87–88.

_____ Begin revising by considering how you can make your description more lively or vivid for your readers.

_____ Reread your thesis statement. Revise to convey your main impression more concretely and forcefully.

_____ Reread the body of your essay to see whether the sensory images and details support your thesis. Replace or cut any sensory images that do not support your main impression. Add any supporting details that would help readers understand your main impression of the topic.

_____ Reread your introduction. Make changes if the opening is dull or vague.

_____ Reread your conclusion to make sure that it is energetic and vivid, reminds readers of your main impression, and makes an observation on the topic you have described. Your purpose in describing the topic should be clear to your readers.

_____ Add transition words and sentences to connect your details and lead readers smoothly from one sensory image to another.

_____ Make at least five changes to your draft to improve the unity, support, or coherence of your description or to make the introduction, thesis statement, or conclusion stronger or more interesting.

EDIT

Some grammar, spelling, word use, or punctuation errors may confuse your readers and make it difficult for them to understand a point you are trying to make. Even if they do not confuse your readers, errors detract from the effectiveness and overall quality of your writing. Edit your description carefully, and correct any errors you find.

_____ Ask a classmate or friend to read your description and highlight any errors.

_____ Use the spell checker or grammar checker on your computer, but do not rely on those programs to catch all errors. Check spelling and grammar yourself as well.

_____ Reread your essay, looking for errors in grammar, spelling, word use, or punctuation. Concentrate especially on finding fragments, run-on sentences, problems with subject–verb agreement, and problems with verb tense.

_____ Print a clean final copy.

_____ Ask yourself: Is this the best I can do?

A FINAL CHECK BEFORE HANDING IN YOUR DESCRIPTION ESSAY

If you've followed the Writing Guide for description, your essay will already include the four basics of good description. Use this list to double-check each basic feature.

_____ My essay creates a clear main impression about my topic.

_____ Each paragraph in the body of my essay presents a strong sensory image that supports the main impression.

_____ The details in my essay create strong sensory images by appealing to several senses—sight, hearing, smell, taste, and touch.

_____ My description brings my topic to life.

11

Process Analysis

Writing That Explains How Things Happen

You Know This
You already use process analysis.
- You learn or teach someone how to do something (drive, operate a DVD player, or assemble a bookcase).
- You give directions to your home.
- You explain a process to a child, like leaves turning color.

Understand What Process Analysis Is

DEFINITION: **Process analysis** either explains how to do something (so your readers can do it) or explains how something works (so your readers can understand it). Both types of process analysis present the steps involved in the process.

IDEA JOURNAL
Write about a goal you have for yourself and what you will do to accomplish it.

■■ Four Basics of Good Process Analysis

1. It helps readers either perform the steps themselves or understand how something works.
2. It presents the essential steps in the process.
3. It explains the steps in detail.
4. It arranges the steps in a logical order (usually in chronological order).

Process analysis is an important way to help readers either follow or understand a series of steps. It helps empower others, and it gets things done.

Maureen Letendre

DIRECTOR OF HUMAN RESOURCES

Maureen Letendre

BACKGROUND: After graduating from a commercial studies program in high school, Maureen spent several years at a small, family-owned business before taking a clerical position for the court system and putting herself through college. She then got a job at Digital Equipment Corporation in the clerical placement group. She stayed at Digital for more than twenty years, moving into increasingly higher-level positions. In each of those positions, she looked for someone to learn from, and that person became her informal mentor. She took a lot of initiative and found that Digital consistently rewarded her hard work and commitment.

When Digital was bought out by Compaq, Maureen moved to Inforonics, a rapidly growing and fast-paced e-commerce consulting firm, where she is now the director of human resources.

EMPLOYER: Inforonics, Inc.

COLLEGE(S)/DEGREES: Framingham State College

TYPES OF WRITING ON THE JOB: Maureen writes many personnel-related reports and statements about the company for job fairs; explanations to managers of how to implement new plans; letters to prospective employees and outside sources; and, as she says, "tons of email." She is particularly careful in writing her email messages because, although they seem informal and casual, the emails often become part of a permanent record. According to Maureen, something as small as a misplaced comma has actually slowed down projects and caused misunderstandings.

HOW MAUREEN USES PROCESS ANALYSIS: Maureen uses process analysis often in her position when she writes to managers and employees, explaining how to implement a new program or policy or how a new plan (such as a pension or profit-sharing plan) works. For an example of how Maureen uses process analysis, see Process Analysis in the Workplace, page 161.

COMPUTER SKILLS: Word processing, Excel and other spreadsheets, Microsoft Office, and human resource–specific applications

TEAMWORK ON THE JOB: Inforonics uses teams at all levels: It is an essential part of the company's operational philosophy. The company believes that involving people at all levels in decision making makes implementation of any new policy, plan, or procedure much more effective than it would be otherwise.

FUTURE GOAL: Inforonics, like most companies, has very specific performance goals, and Maureen is committed to exceeding them each year. One of her personal goals is to make more time for analyzing a situation before responding or reacting. She wants always to be evaluating what's working and what's not, in every area of her life, rather than coasting along without seeking growth.

COMPLETE STEPS FOR PROCESS ANALYSIS

A clear process analysis presents all the essential steps in the process. Each step is explained by supporting details. For example, the writer of the thesis *Learning how to use the advanced functions on my computer is frustrating*, might identify several essential steps and the details to explain each step.

WHAT ARE THE ESSENTIAL STEPS OF THE PROCESS?

- Using the Help feature or a tutorial
- Consulting a reference book such as *Word 98 for Dummies*
- Trying to undo automatic functions

For more on supporting your thesis, see Chapter 4.

WHAT IS INVOLVED IN EACH OF THOSE STEPS?

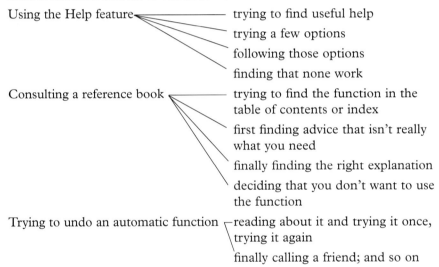

Using the Help feature — trying to find useful help
trying a few options
following those options
finding that none work

Consulting a reference book — trying to find the function in the table of contents or index
first finding advice that isn't really what you need
finally finding the right explanation
deciding that you don't want to use the function

Trying to undo an automatic function — reading about it and trying it once, trying it again
finally calling a friend; and so on

Sometimes you will need to write about a process that you are very familiar with, but your readers are not. Make sure you include all of the essential steps in the process, particularly if you want your readers to be able to do something based on your instructions. Read the following process analysis example. What essential step is missing?

You shouldn't have any trouble doing a load of laundry before I get home. The clothes are in the baskets next to the machine. One of the baskets has all dark clothes. Put these in the washing machine, with the heaviest, biggest items on the bottom. You can fill the machine to the top, but don't mash the clothes down. If you put in too many clothes, the machine will stall out. As you load the machine, check to make sure that there aren't any white things mixed in by mistake. After all of the clothes are in, set the level on Extra High. Then turn the knob on the left to Warm Wash, Cool Rinse. Press the Start button. After about half an hour the laundry should be done, and you can transfer it to the dryer.

Although these directions cover loading the machine and operating it, they leave out adding the soap.

CHRONOLOGICAL ORDER FOR PROCESS ANALYSIS

For more on chronological order, see page 59.

Because process analysis explains how to do something or how something works, it usually uses chronological order. Start with the first step, and then explain each step in order as it should occur. The plan for a process analysis often looks like this:

> Introduction (including thesis)
> First step
>> details about the first step
> Second step
>> details about the second step
> Third step
>> details about the third step
> Conclusion

Add transitional words to your essay to help your readers follow your process analysis as you move from step to step.

For more on transitions, see pages 94–99.

Common Transitions in Process Analysis

after	eventually	meanwhile	soon
as	finally	next	then
at last	first	now	when
before	last	second	while
during	later	since	

Whenever you give someone directions about how to do something or explain how something works, you are using process analysis. Here are some ways you might use process analysis:

- In an information management course, you must write an essay explaining the process for implementing a new data management system.

- The office has a new security system, and you are asked to write a memo explaining to employees how to access their work areas during and after normal business hours.

- You write directions telling your child how to operate the microwave oven.

Read and Analyze Process Analysis

Before writing your own process analysis essay, read the following examples—one each from college, the workplace, and everyday life—and answer the questions that accompany each. Reading the examples and answering the questions will help you understand how to write a good process analysis.

1. PROCESS ANALYSIS IN COLLEGE

The following is an essay that student Jessica Foote wrote for her first-year composition class.

How to Fall Out of Love

Jessica Foote

Falling in love is easy; people do it every day. Most "love" doesn't last though, and after the initial period of passion, many romances fall apart. Unfortunately, in most cases one person falls out of love before the other, and that can result in a very painful breakup. If you learn how to fall out of love, you will minimize the pain of a breakup.

First of all, don't blame yourself. You will probably ask yourself what you did or what you said or what's wrong with you to cause the breakup. Analyzing the situation isn't bad, but assuming that it's your fault is. Don't assume you are to blame: It happens all the time. So don't beat yourself up, because that won't change a thing. Take some time for yourself to do things that will help you heal. Go out for a walk, write down your feelings, watch a movie, eat a pint of rocky road ice cream. Whatever you do, just remember that the hurt will lessen with time. Give yourself that time to put things in perspective.

Next, accept what happened. It's not the end of the world, even though at first it may seem that way. To love and lose is part of the relationship cycle. We learn from each experience. Remember the old saying "It is better to have loved and lost than never to have loved at all." You will be wiser because of your experience, and you are better prepared to face life's future challenges.

Finally, see friends and have fun; don't isolate yourself and sulk. Have people over to watch a movie; or go to a movie, a restaurant, a party; or go on a blind date. Give yourself the opportunity to meet new people.

Falling out of love is much harder than falling in love. But there are ways to help yourself heal. Many people believe that there is someone out there for everybody; perhaps now you are closer to finding that person.

For more on audience and purpose, see pages 7–9.

1. Who is Jessica's **audience** for this essay? _____

2. What is her **purpose** for writing? _____

_____

3. Fill in the blanks with the **process** and the **main point** of Jessica's essay.

   PROCESS: _____

   MAIN POINT: _____

4. Double-underline the **thesis statement**.

5. Put a check mark (✓) next to each **topic sentence**.

6. Underline the **details** that Jessica gives to help the reader understand each step of the process.

7. Circle the (**transitions**) (words, phrases, and sentences) that Jessica uses to guide readers from one step to the next.

8. What **key words** does Jessica repeat? _____

9. Describe how Jessica links the concluding paragraph to the introductory

   paragraph. _____

10. Does Jessica's essay have the **four basics of good process analysis**?

    Why or why not? _____

For a list of the four basics of good process analysis, see page 155.

2. PROCESS ANALYSIS IN THE WORKPLACE

Maureen Letendre, a human resources director at a high-tech company, often has to write directions for how to implement a new policy or procedure. While this piece of writing is not in essay form, it is a good example of process analysis.

PURPOSE

The Performance Review Program is designed to be a dynamic, ongoing process of open and constructive communication between managers and employees focusing on discussion and documentation of each employee's goals, progress, and performance. Both managers and employees are responsible for the success of this program. Please read, understand, and follow the steps of the Performance Review Program as outlined below.

PROCESS

1. Goal Setting, February

As a first step, the employee and manager use the Goals Worksheet to establish and agree upon expectations for the coming year. When a new employee starts, the manager needs to initiate the goal-setting process.

The employee and manager each keep a copy of the completed worksheet and use it in their goal review meetings.

Employee Feedback

Employees may use the recommended Employee Feedback Form to track their progress. This form then can be used as a basis for discussion during quarterly manager/employee meetings.

2. Goals Review, March–September

The next step is to hold goal review meetings, where the manager and employee meet to discuss progress and accomplishments. The results of these discussions are documented on the Goals Worksheet. This is an opportunity to recognize good performance as well as to address performance problems. It is also an opportunity to adjust goals when necessary.

3. Annual Review, December

Next, the manager requests completed **recommended** Employee Feedback Forms and any supporting documentation from the employee. Using this information in addition to the Goals Worksheets, the manager evaluates the employee's performance and completes the Employee Annual Performance Review Form.

Following the annual review, the manager and employee meet to discuss the manager's final review and rating. The Annual Performance Review is signed by both employee and manager and forwarded to Human Resources. At this same meeting, the manager and employee discuss and agree upon expectations for the coming year and document their agreements on the Goals Worksheet.

Escalation Process

When the employee and manager cannot agree on the final evaluation, the employee may request a review by his or her manager's manager.

When the employee, manager, and manager's manager cannot agree on the final evaluation, the employee may request an objective review of the process and evaluation by contacting HR.

This revised Performance Review Program is the product of your input, and we believe the review process will be fair, satisfying, and productive. As we go through the first year of this new program, we welcome continued input on the various stages of the process.

1. What is the **purpose** of Maureen's memo? _____
   _____

   For more on purpose and audience, see pages 7–9.

2. Who is Maureen's **audience**? _____

3. Double-underline the **thesis statement**.

4. Put a check mark (✓) next to each **major step** in the process.

5. What order of organization does Maureen use? _____

6. Circle the (transitions) that Maureen uses.

7. Describe how the concluding paragraph relates back to the thesis.

3. PROCESS ANALYSIS IN EVERYDAY LIFE

The following essay is an example of a process analysis that provides practical advice on how to do something—in this case, how to avoid a speeding ticket.

How to Avoid a Speeding Ticket

Perry Buffington

The best and safest advice about how to get out of a speeding ticket is simply DON'T SPEED. If, however, you are stopped for speeding and you'd like to avoid the punishment, or you feel the ticket is genuinely unfair, there are several psychological tricks or steps you can use to your advantage.

The best thing you can do is try to reduce the officer's anxiety. *You* are feeling anxiety because you've been caught, and another person now has control of you. The patrol officer is experiencing anxiety because he or she knows nothing about you. The officer may even fear that your behavior is unpredictable. His or her life may be in jeopardy, and in these violent times, that is a very understandable apprehension. As you ease the police officer's anxiety, you will reduce the probability that you will be given a ticket. There are several steps you can follow.

First, stop immediately after seeing the blue lights. Then show both hands as quickly as possible. Put both hands on the steering wheel or even wave out the window. It is not necessary to hold your hands above your head; that makes you look like a criminal. Greet the officer and call him or her by name if identification is visible. This turns the officer into a fellow human being instead of an authority figure.

Don't try to immediately talk your way out of it. Patrol officers are taught to keep conversation to a minimum. For legal reasons, this makes sense (the case may go to court, and the less said now, the better). Officers also are trained to keep their objectivity; if they talk to you they are more likely to identify with you. In other words, trying to talk your way out of a ticket is probably not going to work. Crying can actually *increase* your chances of receiving a ticket; the officer is forced into an uncomfortable and anxious position and may want to remove him- or herself from the scene as soon as possible. It is also easier for officers to view you as a subordinate when you are bathed in tears.

Next, if it looks as if you are going to get a ticket, ask the officer for a warning, and state your reasons for leniency. *Make sure the reasons are plausible.* If you believe you were stopped unfairly, tell the officer courteously, but only after you've reduced his or her anxiety. Never argue: If you do, you immediately start a power struggle, and you will lose.

Finally, turn the officer into a helper. If the officer gives you a warning instead of a ticket, immediately ask for directions—even if you know where you are. Most patrol officers would prefer to be helpers rather than enforcers. Providing you with directions helps him or her deal with "caving in" to your wish for a warning.

It's best not to speed, but if you are stopped for speeding, think before acting. Try to get the officer to see you as a person rather than a speed demon and scofflaw. Put yourself in his or her shoes, and try a little psychology.

> —Perry W. Buffington, *Cheap Psychological Tricks*
> (Atlanta, GA: Peachtree, 1996).

1. What **audience** is Perry Buffington writing for? _____

For more on audience and purpose, see pages 7–9.

2. What is his **purpose**? _____

3. Double-underline the **thesis statement**.

4. Which does the essay tell the reader: how to do something or how something works? _____

5. Put a check mark (✓) next to the **topic sentence** in each paragraph.

6. Circle the **transitions**.

7. What **key words** are repeated? _____

_____

8. How does the author's **concluding paragraph** relate back to his main point or thesis statement? _____

_____

Write a Process Analysis Essay

In this section, you will write your own process analysis essay. To do so, follow this sequence:

REVIEW the four basics of good process analysis (p. 155).

CHOOSE your writing assignment (below).

WRITE your process analysis using the step-by-step Writing Guide (p. 168).

CHECK your final essay (p. 172).

WRITING ASSIGNMENT 1   COLLEGE, WORK, EVERYDAY LIFE

Write a process analysis essay on *one* of the following topics or on a topic of your own choice.

COLLEGE

- How to use the computers in the computer lab
- How to get an A in a course
- How _____ (a process in your major field of study) works

WORK

- How to do one of your major tasks at work
- How a benefit plan works (a 401k, another retirement plan, a medical plan)
- How the human resources department can help with a problem

EVERYDAY LIFE

- How to calm down or get to sleep
- How to buy or sell a car (or some other item)
- How a checking account works

WRITING ASSIGNMENT 2   USE THE INTERNET

Search the Internet for information on one of the following topics. Then write a process analysis essay on how to find information about the topic.

- Your family tree (Try the National Genealogical Society's Web site at <**www.ngsgenealogy.org**>.)
- Getting a job (Try Career Builder's site at <**www.careerbuilder.com**>.)
- Getting medical information online (Try the U.S. National Library of Medicine's MEDLINEplus site at <**www.nlm.nih.gov/medlineplus**>.)

For advice about how to cite a source, see Chapter 20.

▮ WRITING ASSIGNMENT 3   HOW TO KEEP A JOB

Read the problem and situation that follow, and then choose *one* of the assignment options (3A or 3B) that appear after it.

PROBLEM: Many people, even those who have worked for some time, do not understand either the basic rules for keeping a job (things you do in order not to get fired immediately) or the behaviors that employers value. As a result, they get passed over for promotions or salary increases, or they get fired.

SITUATION: Your company has agreed to work with a social services agency in town and to hire former welfare recipients in a welfare-to-work program. Your boss has found that although the individuals have gone through a brief training program, they often jeopardize their continued employment because they don't understand what being a responsible employee means.

Your boss asks you to write a report that helps these new employees understand what is expected of them.

ASSIGNMENT OPTION 3A: RESPONSE TO THE SITUATION

Using what you know about process analysis, write an essay that explains the basics of holding a job. First make a list of basic expectations of any employee. Within the essay, suggest steps an employee can take that go beyond the minimum of keeping a job to becoming a valuable employee.

ASSIGNMENT OPTION 3B: ANOTHER PERSPECTIVE

Assume you are a manager, and write an essay that gives advice about how to get a promotion. If you have never been a manager, this assignment will get you to think about what makes an employee a valuable, promotable asset to a manager. If you can't come up with ideas yourself, do a little

For advice about doing research, see Chapter 20.

research. You can find articles on this subject online, or you could go to a company or store and ask to interview a manager.

Writing Guide

Process Analysis

Follow the steps in this Writing Guide to help you prewrite, draft, revise, and edit your process analysis. Check off each step as you complete it.

THINKING CRITICALLY ABOUT PROCESS ANALYSIS

FOCUS   Think about the process you want to explain to your readers, the steps involved in the process, and the main point you want to make.

ASK
- What process do I know well?
- Who will be reading this, and how much are they likely to know about the process?
- What do I want my readers to be able to do? Should they be able to perform the process themselves? Or should they understand how the process happens?
- Can I write a thesis statement that identifies the process and the main point I want to write about it?
- What steps in the process do my readers need to know about? What details, facts, and examples will help them understand each step?
- How should I arrange the steps?

PREWRITE TO EXPLORE YOUR TOPIC

Prewriting in process analysis involves considering all of the steps involved in doing something or in explaining how something works.

For more on purpose and audience, see pages 7–9.

_____ Decide on your purpose for writing.

_____ Identify the audience for your essay. Consider whether your readers will need to follow the steps necessary for the process or want only to understand the process.

_____ Choose a process you understand well. You will need to know all the steps and write about the essential ones in your essay.

_____ Once you know what process you want to explain, use a prewriting technique (freewriting, listing/brainstorming, questioning, discussing, clustering) to jot down some ideas about how to explain that process to a reader who isn't familiar with it.

WRITE A THESIS STATEMENT

The thesis statement in a process analysis usually identifies the process and the main point you want to make about that process.

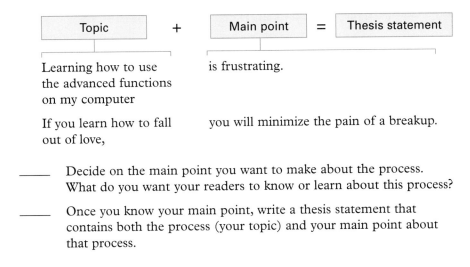

| Topic | + | Main point | = | Thesis statement |

Learning how to use the advanced functions on my computer   is frustrating.

If you learn how to fall out of love,   you will minimize the pain of a breakup.

_____ Decide on the main point you want to make about the process. What do you want your readers to know or learn about this process?

_____ Once you know your main point, write a thesis statement that contains both the process (your topic) and your main point about that process.

SUPPORT YOUR POINT

The major support points in a process analysis are the essential steps involved in explaining how to do the process or how the process works. These steps should demonstrate the main point about the process that you have stated in your thesis. The supporting details in process analysis explain each of the essential steps to your readers.

_____ List all the essential steps in the process.

_____ Review your thesis statement, and drop any steps that are not essential.

_____ Choose the steps that are necessary for readers to perform this activity or to understand how it works.

_____ Add details that describe the steps and would help your readers do this activity correctly. Imagine that you are not already familiar with the process, and ask yourself whether you could do it or understand how it works after reading the essay.

MAKE A PLAN

Making a written plan—an outline—helps you decide how to order your process analysis. A process analysis generally uses chronological (time) order, presenting each step from first to last as it would take place.

_____   Arrange the steps in the process in chronological order.

_____   Make a plan or an outline for your process analysis essay.

DRAFT

Drafting in process analysis means writing in complete sentences and including the following:

- An introduction with a thesis statement that identifies the process and the point you want to make about the process
- The essential steps in the process, supported by explanations of those steps
- A conclusion that reminds your readers of your main point and makes another observation about the process

_____   Think about how you can show your readers your main point about the process.

_____   Write an introductory paragraph that includes your thesis statement and hooks your readers' interest.

_____   Write a topic sentence for each of the steps.

_____   Write body paragraphs that explain each step in detail to your readers.

_____   Write a concluding paragraph that has energy, refers back to your point about the process, and makes a final observation or recommendation.

_____   Title your essay.

REVISE

Revising means changing whole sentences or paragraphs to make your writing clearer or stronger. To revise a process analysis, imagine that you have no idea how to perform the process or how the process works. Read your draft, looking for the following:

- Places where the essay strays from the essential steps and details about those steps (revise for unity)
- Places where readers might not understand the steps (revise for support and detail)
- Places where transitions are needed to help readers move smoothly from one step to the next (revise for coherence)

_____ Get feedback from others through peer review.

For more on peer review, see pages 87–88.

_____ Begin revising by asking yourself how you could make the steps of the process clearer for your readers.

_____ Reread your thesis statement to see whether it clearly identifies the process and your main point about it.

_____ Reread the body of your essay to make sure you haven't left out any essential steps. Add any details that would make the steps clearer.

_____ Reread your introduction, and make changes if it is dull.

_____ Reread your conclusion to be certain that it is energetic and reinforces your opening and your thesis.

_____ Add your transition words and sentences to connect your steps and lead readers smoothly from one to another.

_____ Make at least five changes to your draft to improve the unity, support, or coherence of your process analysis or to make the introduction, thesis statement, or conclusion stronger or more convincing.

EDIT

Some grammar, spelling, word use, or punctuation errors may confuse your readers and make it difficult for them to understand a point you are trying to make. Even if they do not confuse your readers, errors detract from the effectiveness and overall quality of your writing. Edit your process analysis carefully, and correct any errors you find.

_____ Ask a classmate or friend to read your process analysis and highlight any errors.

_____ Use the spell checker or grammar checker on your computer.

_____ Look yourself for additional errors in grammar, spelling, word use, or punctuation. Focus first on sentence fragments, run-on sentences, problems with subject–verb agreement, problems with verbs, and other areas where you know you often make errors.

_____ Print a clean, final copy.

_____ Ask yourself: Is this the best I can do?

For more on editing, see Chapters 22–41.

A FINAL CHECK BEFORE HANDING IN YOUR PROCESS ANALYSIS ESSAY

If you've followed the Writing Guide for process analysis, your essay will already include the four basics of good process analysis. Use this list to double-check each basic feature.

_____ My process analysis helps readers follow the steps in the process themselves or understand how the process works.

_____ The paragraphs in the body of my essay present the essential steps in the process.

_____ Each paragraph that presents a step also includes a detailed explanation of how that step works.

_____ The steps are arranged in chronological order, as they occur, or in some other logical order.

12

Classification

Writing That Puts Things into Groups

You Know This
You already use classification.
- You walk into a video store where movies are classified in categories such as comedy, drama, and horror.
- You use the college bookstore, where books are classified by discipline (English, biology, economics) and by course number.
- You shop at the drugstore where products are classified by use, such as hair, skin, or dental care.

Understand What Classification Is

DEFINITION: **Classification** is writing that organizes, or sorts, people or items into categories.

DEFINITION: The **organizing principle** for a classification is *how* you sort the group of people or items, not the categories themselves. For example, you might sort clean laundry using one of the following organizing principles: by ownership (yours, your roommate's, and so on); by where it goes (the bedroom, the bathroom).

IDEA JOURNAL
Write about the different kinds of friends you have.

▪▪ Four Basics of Good Classification

1. It makes sense of a group of people or items by organizing them into categories.
2. It has useful categories.
3. It uses a single organizing principle.
4. It gives examples of the people or items that fit into each category.

173

Giovanni Bohorquez

TECHNICAL CONSULTANT

Giovanni Bohorquez

BACKGROUND: At the age of eleven, Giovanni left Colombia, where he was born and lived with his mother, and came to the United States to live with his father in New Jersey. His father was poor and wasn't particularly happy to have responsibility for taking care of anyone else, so Giovanni worked several jobs and was earning significant wages by the age of twelve.

After high school, Giovanni went to a community college and then transferred to the University of California–Los Angeles (UCLA), where he finished his bachelor's degree. He then went to work for Ernst & Young, a financial consulting company, and is now pursuing a master's degree in business administration (M.B.A.) at UCLA's Anderson School while continuing to work.

EMPLOYER: Hewlett-Packard Consulting

COLLEGE(S)/DEGREES: El Camino College (A.A.), UCLA (B.S.)

TYPES OF WRITING ON THE JOB: Proposals, project plan reports, contracts, sales letters, documentation of business processes, change order reports, email

HOW GIOVANNI USES CLASSIFICATION: As a consultant, Giovanni must perform a good deal of analysis for clients. For example, he recently completed a detailed analysis of the types of emerging technologies. For an example of how Giovanni uses classification, see Classification in the Workplace, page 179.

COMPUTER SKILLS: Word processing, UNIX, BroadVision, Advanced PL/SQL, Java, HTML, statistical analysis software

TEAMWORK ON THE JOB: Giovanni's analytical work often involves both Ernst & Young employees and employees from the client's company. Teamwork is essential in compiling all of the technical information necessary to generate a thorough analysis. As the team leader, Giovanni is responsible for pulling together varied bits of data gathered from across the office and across the country.

FUTURE GOAL: Giovanni hopes to complete his M.B.A. program and to successfully manage a high-tech product.

ORGANIZING PRINCIPLE FOR CLASSIFICATION

A classification applies an organizing principle—a method of sorting—to a group. Imagine the following situation, in which the classification system does not arrange things in useful categories following a single organizing principle.

You go into your local video store to find that it has been rearranged. The signs indicating the location of different types of videos—comedy, horror, drama—are gone. You take a look around, but you can't figure out how the videos are now classified, so you don't know where to look for what you want.

When you ask the clerk at the desk how to find a video, she says, "The videos over on this side are arranged by length of the film, starting with the shortest. The videos on the other side are arranged alphabetically by the leading actor's last name."

This new arrangement is confusing for two reasons:

- It doesn't have useful categories. (Who's likely to select a video based on its exact length?)
- It doesn't have a single organizing principle. (Even if you know the length of the video and the actor's last name, you still don't know on which side of the store to start looking.)

The following diagram shows how videos at most stores are classified, following a single organizing principle.

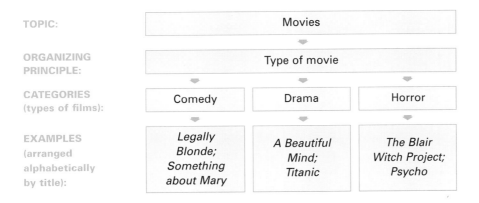

TOPIC:	Movies		
ORGANIZING PRINCIPLE:	Type of movie		
CATEGORIES (types of films):	Comedy	Drama	Horror
EXAMPLES (arranged alphabetically by title):	Legally Blonde; Something about Mary	A Beautiful Mind; Titanic	The Blair Witch Project; Psycho

SUPPORT POINTS FOR CLASSIFICATION

Once you decide on a group to classify and select an organizing principle, your categories provide support points for your essay. Examples of the things or people in each category provide the supporting details that help explain your categories to readers. The following plan is often used to organize a classification essay. Arrange your categories and examples logically, according to your purpose and your readers' expectations.

Topic
Organizing principle
Category
    examples
Category
    examples
Category
    examples

As you write your essay, the following transitions may be helpful in leading from one category to the next or from one example to another.

For more on transitions, see pages 94–99.

Common Transitions in Classification

another	first, second, third, and so on
another kind	for example
for instance	

Whenever you organize or sort things to make sense of them, you are classifying them. Here are some ways you might use classification:

COLLEGE

- In a nursing course, you are asked to discuss three types of antibiotics used to treat infections.

WORK

- For an inventory report, you have to list the types of software the store carries and report how many of each type you have in stock.

EVERYDAY LIFE

- You look at the types of payment plans that are available with your car loan.

Read and Analyze Classification

Before writing your own classification essay, read the following examples—one each from college, the workplace, and everyday life—and answer the questions that accompany each. Reading the examples and answering the questions will help you understand how to write a good classification.

1. CLASSIFICATION IN COLLEGE

The following is an essay that a student, Danny Fitzgerald, wrote for his English composition class.

Blood Type and Personality

Danny Fitzgerald

In Japan, the question "What's your blood type?" is as common as "What's your sign?" in the United States. Some Japanese researchers claim that people's personalities can be classified by their blood types. You may be skeptical about this method of classification, but don't judge its validity before you read the descriptions the researchers have put together. Do you see yourself?

If you have blood type O, you are a leader. When you see something you want, you strive to achieve your goal. You are passionate, loyal, and self-confident, and you are often a trendsetter. Your enthusiasm for projects and goals spreads to others who happily follow your lead. When you want something, you may be ruthless about getting it or blind to how your actions affect others.

Another blood type, A, is a social, people person. You like people and work well with them. You are sensitive, patient, compassionate, and affectionate. You are a good peacekeeper because you want everyone to be happy. In a team situation, you resolve conflicts and keep things on a smooth course. Sometimes type A's are stubborn and find it difficult to relax. They may find it uncomfortable to do things alone.

People with type B blood are usually individualists who like to do things on their own. You may be creative and adaptable, and you usually say exactly what you mean. Although you can adapt to situations, you may choose not to do so because of your strong independent streak. You may prefer working on your own to being part of a team.

The final blood type is AB. If you have AB blood, you are a natural entertainer. You draw people to you because of your charm and easygoing nature. ABs are usually calm and controlled, tactful and fair. On the downside, though, they may take too long to make decisions. And they may procrastinate, putting off tasks until the last minute.

Classifying people's personalities by blood type seems very unusual until you examine what researchers have found. Most people find the descriptions fairly accurate. When you think about it, classification by blood type isn't any more far-fetched than classification by horoscope sign. What will they think of next? Classification by hair color?

For more on audience and purpose, see pages 7–9.

1. What type of **audience** is Danny writing for? _____

2. What is the **purpose** of his classification of blood types? _____

   _____

3. Fill in the blanks with the **topic** and the **method of classifying** (the organizing principle) for Danny's essay.

   TOPIC: _____

   HOW CLASSIFIED: _____

4. Double-underline the **thesis statement**.

5. What **introduction techniques** does Danny use to get the reader's

   attention? _____

6. What **categories** does Danny present? _____

7. Put a check mark next to each **topic sentence** identifying a category.

8. Underline the **examples** of each category that Danny gives.

9. What **key words** are repeated? _____

   _____

10. Does Danny's essay have the **four basics of good classification**? Why | For a list of the four basics, see page 173.

or why not? _____

2. CLASSIFICATION IN THE WORKPLACE

The following essay was part of Giovanni Bohorquez's application for the Anderson School, the graduate business school at UCLA. Notice how Giovanni presents the types of key skills he has learned.

One day I would like to manage a high-tech product, so over the last ten years I have learned the types of skills that product managers must have: production management, system design, and entrepreneurism.

I learned the first type of skill—production management—when I worked as a plant controller for three years with control over production of modem components and responsibility for more than one hundred employees. As a plant controller, I managed the raw materials, created production schedules, and oversaw inventory.

I learned the second type of skill—system design—by designing and implementing Enterprise Resource Planning (ERP) systems, which are integrated information-sharing software programs that serve the needs of all departments within a single company. Companies such as ConAgra, SUN, Genentech, and Hewlett-Packard are currently benefiting from systems that I have designed.

The third type of skill—entrepreneurism—I learned by consulting with start-up and middle-market projects. Though entrepreneurial environments need to cultivate creativity and vision, they also need to recognize and meet the realities of a business environment. Many good entrepreneurial ventures fail because, though they have a wealth of good ideas, they do not understand accounting, production, and the need for good systems. As a consultant, I have been able to help entrepreneurs recognize business necessities.

With these types of key skills, I am closer to being able to attain my goal of managing a product. I have worked steadily and purposefully to acquire these types of skills, and now I am ready to learn the other skills that will allow me to successfully manage a product. It is for this reason that I am applying to the Anderson School, where I believe I can develop the expertise I need to become a well-rounded, responsible member of the business community.

For more on purpose and audience, see pages 7–9.

1. What is Giovanni's **purpose** for writing? _____

   _____

2. Who is Giovanni's **audience**? _____

3. Double-underline the **thesis statement**.

4. Put a check mark (✓) next to the topic sentences that present the **categories** in Giovanni's essay.

5. Underline the **supporting details** that give examples of items in each category.

6. What observation does the concluding paragraph make? _____

   _____

   _____

3. CLASSIFICATION IN EVERYDAY LIFE

The following essay was written by a student who considers herself an expert in yard sale bargain hunting.

Yard Sale Treasures

Susan Robinson

When I started attending yard sales several years ago, I bought a lot of items that were inexpensive but turned out to be low-quality junk. Now I search only for the treasures that I know are real deals. As part of my education as a bargain hunter, I have learned to look for three kinds of items.

The first kind of yard sale treasure is kid stuff. You can find lots of nearly new equipment, furniture, toys, and clothing at yard sales. Often there's nothing wrong with the merchandise; owners just want to sell items that take up room in the house or the basement once their children have outgrown them. Last year one of my friends found a nearly new name-brand baby stroller at a yard sale and paid $15 for it. Others have found good cribs, swings, and baby clothing that has never been worn— all at bargain prices.

Another treasure I've come to respect is costume jewelry. People tend to collect tons of inexpensive jewelry over the years, and jewelry doesn't wear out. In the $1 box at a recent yard sale, I bought a "pearl" necklace and matching earrings for $2. They weren't real pearls, but they looked so real that no one but an expert would know the difference. In the same box, my friend found a "ruby" ring that looked authentic, with a small, well-shaped stone and an antique-like setting.

A third kind of treasure is kitchen stuff, especially sets of plates, sets of glasses, serving pieces, and vases. When you are setting up an apartment, there is no better place than a yard sale to find dishes and glasses. Maybe a set of dishes that originally had twelve pieces is down to ten, but who really needs twelve of the same dish?

When people have yard sales, they put out all kinds of things, and shoppers should beware of junk. Instead, look for the things that you know are good values, and avoid the odd knickknacks or old Christmas decorations or worn-down shoes. You can get great bargains at yard sales if you choose carefully. A word of caution to the buyer of junk: You will soon have to have your own yard sale.

1. What type of **audience** is Susan writing for? _____

For more on audience and purpose, see pages 7–9.

2. What is Susan's **purpose** for writing? _____

_____

3. Fill in the diagram using the elements of Susan's essay.

TOPIC: _____

ORGANIZING PRINCIPLE: sorted by _____

CATEGORIES: _____   _____   _____

EXAMPLES: _____ _____ _____

_____ _____ _____

_____ _____

_____

_____

4. Double-underline the **thesis statement**.

5. Circle the **transitions** in the essay.

6. Put a check mark (✓) next to the **topic sentences** that present the categories.

Write a Classification Essay

In this section, you will write your own classification essay. To do so, follow this sequence:

REVIEW the four basics of good classification (p. 173).

CHOOSE your writing assignment (below).

WRITE your classification using the step-by-step Writing Guide (p. 184).

CHECK your final essay (p. 188).

WRITING ASSIGNMENT 1   COLLEGE, WORK, EVERYDAY LIFE

Write a classification essay on *one* of the following topics or on a topic of your own choice.

COLLEGE

Types of
- Degree programs
- Student services
- Choose a classifiable subject from another course

WORK

Types of
- Work spaces
- Customers or clients
- Skills needed for a particular job

EVERYDAY LIFE

Types of
- Drivers
- Restaurants in your town
- Wireless phone calling plans

 WRITING ASSIGNMENT 2   **USE THE INTERNET**

Visit Amazon.com (**<www.amazon.com>**), or the Web site of another major retailer, and write a classification essay in which you explain how the site is organized.

For advice about how to cite a source, see Chapter 20.

 WRITING ASSIGNMENT 3   **MAKE A BUDGET**

Read the problem and situation that follow, and then choose *one* of the assignment options (3A or 3B) that appear after it.

PROBLEM: Many people, even those with a good salary, have trouble managing their money. Because they have no idea how to organize their expenses, at the end of the week or month they wonder where their money has gone. They know only that they seem to be spending lots of money, have trouble making ends meet, and can't ever seem to save.

SITUATION: You finally decide that you need to create a budget for yourself. The first thing you need to do is to figure out how you spend your money.

ASSIGNMENT OPTION 3A: RESPONSE TO THE SITUATION

Using what you know about classification, write an essay that sorts your monthly expenses. (Hint: You might begin by making a list of all the monthly expenses you have. The idea is to account for as much of what you spend in a month as possible and then to give examples of or details about those expenses.)

ASSIGNMENT OPTION 3B: ANOTHER PERSPECTIVE

Using what you know about classification, discuss the kinds of expenses that are associated with going to college.

Writing Guide

Classification

Follow the steps in this Writing Guide to help you prewrite, draft, revise, and edit your classification essay. Check off each step as you complete it.

THINKING CRITICALLY ABOUT CLASSIFICATION	
FOCUS	Think about what you want to classify (sort) for your readers and the main point you want to make about that topic.
ASK	• Who will be reading this piece of writing, and what do they know or need to know about my topic? • What is my purpose—my reason for sorting or classifying? What is my main point about the topic? • To accomplish my purpose, how should I sort things? What should my organizing principle be? • What categories will help my readers make sense of my topic? • What people or items fit into each category? What examples, facts, and details will my readers need to understand how I have classified things?

PREWRITE TO EXPLORE YOUR TOPIC

Prewriting in classification involves considering how to sort your topic into useful categories and thinking about how to give good examples of or details about those categories.

For more on purpose and audience, see pages 7–9.

_____ Decide on your purpose for writing.

_____ Identify the audience for your essay.

_____ Select the topic or group that you want to classify.

_____ Once you have decided on a narrowed topic, use a prewriting technique (freewriting, listing/brainstorming, questioning, discussing, clustering) to generate useful categories for sorting your topic. In classification, a variation on the technique of clustering is often useful: filling in a diagram like the one shown at the top of the next page.

WRITE A THESIS STATEMENT

The thesis statement in a classification essay can take one of several forms:

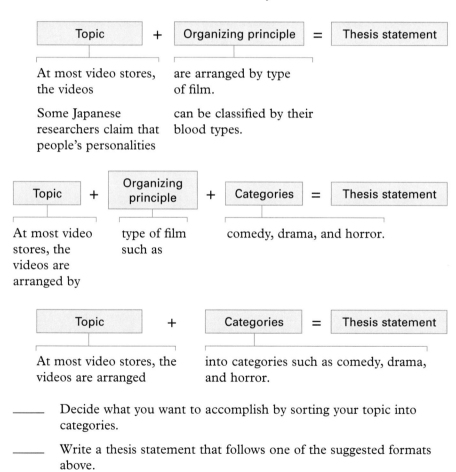

_____ Decide what you want to accomplish by sorting your topic into categories.

_____ Write a thesis statement that follows one of the suggested formats above.

SUPPORT YOUR POINT

The support points in classification are the categories into which you choose to sort your topic. These will become the topic sentences for the body paragraphs in your essay. The supporting details will be specific examples of people or items that fit into the categories. Fill in below categories you want to use and examples of each category.

Topic _____

Organizing principle _____

Category _____

    examples _____

Category _____

    examples _____

Category _____

    examples _____

_____ Choose at least three useful categories into which you can sort your topic.

_____ Add facts and details for each example you want to use under the categories.

MAKE A PLAN

Making a written plan—an outline—helps you decide how to order your classification. If you filled in the list above, you already have a written plan. Now you need to decide on a logical sequence of categories that accomplishes your purpose and will make sense to your readers. (Writers of classification essays may or may not use standard organizational patterns such as chronological order, spatial order, and order of importance.)

_____ Arrange the categories in a logical order.

_____ Make a new outline that shows the order you have chosen.

DRAFT

In classification, drafting involves writing in complete sentences and including the following:

- An introduction with your thesis statement
- The categories you have chosen with examples and details of items that fit into those categories

- A conclusion that reminds your readers of your main point and makes an observation about your classification

_____ Write an introductory paragraph that includes your thesis statement and hooks your readers' interest.

_____ Write a topic sentence for each of the categories.

_____ Write body paragraphs that include the topic sentence and the specific examples and details.

_____ Write a concluding paragraph that reminds your readers of the purpose of classifying your topic into these categories and makes a further observation.

_____ Title your essay.

REVISE

Revising means changing whole sentences or paragraphs to make your writing clearer or stronger. To revise a classification essay, imagine that you have no idea how or why one might sort your topic. Read your draft, looking for the following:

- Places where the ideas are off the main point (revising for unity)
- Gaps in information or detail (revising for support)
- Areas in need of transitions that will help readers move smoothly from one point to the next (revising for coherence)

_____ Get feedback from others through peer review.

For more on peer review, see pages 87–88.

_____ Begin revising by considering how to make your classification clearer or more interesting for your readers.

_____ Reread your thesis statement. See whether it is clear about what the single organizing principle is, the categories into which you will sort your topic, or both.

_____ Reread the body paragraphs of your classification essay. Replace or cut any categories that do not follow your organizing principle.

_____ Look at the examples you have used in each category. Add details or replace examples to make sure that they will help your readers understand the kinds of things that fit into the category.

_____ Reread your introduction, and make changes if it is dull. Even when you're just introducing categories, be enthusiastic about what you're classifying.

_____   Reread your conclusion with the same goal: to make it energetic and memorable to your readers. Make your final observation a personal comment about the classification system.

_____   Add transitions and transitional sentences to help your readers move smoothly from one category to another.

_____   Make at least five changes to your draft, to improve the unity, support, and coherence of your classification or to strengthen your introduction, thesis statement, or conclusion.

EDIT

Some grammar, spelling, word use, or punctuation errors may confuse your readers and make it difficult for them to understand a point you are trying to make. Even if they do not confuse your readers, errors detract from the effectiveness and overall quality of your writing. Edit your classification carefully, and correct any errors you find.

For more on editing, see Chapters 22–41.

_____   Ask a classmate or friend to read your classification and highlight any errors.

_____   Use the spell checker and grammar checker on your computer, but do not rely on those programs to catch all the errors.

_____   Look yourself for errors that the spell checker or grammar checker didn't catch. Focus first on sentence fragments, run-on sentences, problems with subject–verb agreement, problems with verbs, and other areas where you know you often make errors.

_____   Print a clean final copy.

_____   Ask yourself: Is this the best I can do?

A FINAL CHECK BEFORE HANDING IN YOUR CLASSIFICATION ESSAY

If you've followed the Writing Guide for classification, your essay will already include the four basics of classification. Use this list to double-check each basic feature.

_____   My thesis statement explains how I organize a group into categories.

_____   My categories are useful and make sense.

_____   My categories follow only one organizing principle.

_____   The body of my essay gives examples, members of the group that fit into each category.

13

Definition

Writing That Tells What Something Means

You Know This

You already use definition.
- You tell a friend, "That new movie is disgusting," and she asks, "What do you mean by disgusting?" You then define the word.
- Your child hears the word *tornado* and asks what it means. You define the word.
- You train someone new at work and define the company's names for the procedures everyone follows.

Understand What Definition Is

DEFINITION: Definition is writing that explains what a term means. Having a clear understanding of what a term means can help you avoid confusion and mistakes.

IDEA JOURNAL
Write about what success means.

▉ Four Basics of Good Definition

1. It tells readers what term is being defined.
2. It presents a clear and precise basic definition.
3. It includes examples to show what the writer means.
4. It uses words and examples that readers will understand.

Definition helps you convey what you mean so that you are understood. It also helps you understand what other people mean. Before you define a term for a reader, you need to understand the meaning yourself. Start by reading the dictionary definition; then try to explain the meaning in your own words. Your definition essay needs to include a good basic definition of the term as you are using it for your reader.

Profile of Success

Gary Knoblock

BUSINESS OWNER

BACKGROUND: Gary grew up in New Orleans, and while neither of his parents had much formal education themselves, they valued education. After high school, Gary tried college for a year but was told by a professor that he wasn't college material and should try manual labor. Gary left college and moved to Fort Worth, Texas, where he took law enforcement exams. He passed the exams and joined the Fort Worth Police Department. During his ten years with the force, he attended a junior college at night, earning an associate's degree. He also had numerous promotions at work and became a member of the force's SWAT team.

"Believe it or not," said Gary, "police work can be boring [because] you're not always involved in a case." In 1999, Gary decided to start his own business. He moved to Mississippi, where his parents now live, and started a sign company, Lightning Quick (LQ) Signs. Since then the company has grown steadily into a successful business.

EMPLOYER: Self

COLLEGE(S)/DEGREES: Tarrant County Junior College (A.A.)

TYPES OF WRITING ON THE JOB: Proposals to get jobs, advertising copy, follow-up reports and letters, loan applications, correspondence with clients and prospective clients, precise and descriptive specifications for government jobs

Gary Knoblock

HOW GARY USES DEFINITION: Gary often needs to define terms for clients. In addition, his letter about the company that he uses in sales situations defines how LQ Signs is "customer-oriented." For an example of Gary's use of definition, see Definition in the Workplace, page 194.

COMPUTER SKILLS: WordPerfect, Quicken, and Adobe Photoshop and Illustrator, two types of design software

TEAMWORK ON THE JOB: Teamwork saved Gary's life a number of times when he was a police officer and SWAT team member. He brings the value of teamwork to his own small business. He and his employees work as a team to prioritize and schedule activities, assign responsibilities, prepare job sites, secure any necessary permits, and plan graphics. Even as company president, Gary feels his role is to be part of the team.

FUTURE GOAL: Gary says, "Never to feel *too* comfortable, because that can lead to stagnation and boredom. I am constantly reevaluating things, because I never want to coast or get stale."

POINT OF VIEW IN DEFINITION

You can depend on a dictionary to discover the definitions of words like *desk, chair,* and *paper*—which have definite, concrete meanings. The meanings of other words—like *love, success,* or *freedom*—depend on a person's point of view. These words need to be carefully explained, or they could be misunderstood.

For example, if a friend says, "Summer in New York City is awful," you don't know what she means by *awful*. Is it the weather? The people? The transportation? Until you ask, you won't know whether you would think New York City in the summer is awful or not.

SUPPORT IN DEFINITION

When you write a definition essay, your thesis statement may present your basic definition. It may also tell what larger class or category the word belongs to and what details distinguish it from other words in that class. Just as a terrier is one member of the class of dogs, so Jo-Jo, your dog, is one member of the class of terriers.

Your major support points in a definition are your examples. You develop your examples by adding details and explanations that will show your readers what you mean by a term. The examples in a definition are often organized by importance, or the impact you think the examples will have on your readers. Save the most important example for last.

For more on order of importance, see page 60.

The plan for a definition essay might look like this:

Introduction (including thesis)

First Example of Your Meaning

> specific details that show how that example demonstrates your definition

Second Example of Your Meaning

> specific details that show how that example demonstrates your definition

Third Example of Your Meaning

> specific details that show how that example demonstrates your definition

As you write, add transitions to connect one example to the next.

For more on transitions, see pages 94–99.

Common Transitions for Definition

another	for example
another kind	for instance
first, second, third, and so on	

Many situations—in college, at work, or in everyday life—require you to explain the meaning of a term, particularly how you are using it. Here are some ways you might use definition.

COLLEGE

• On a U.S. history exam you are asked to define the term *carpetbagger*.

WORK

• In a conversation with a benefits customer, you have to define *reasonable and customary charges*.

EVERYDAY LIFE

• You explain the term *fair* to your child in the context of games or sports.

Read and Analyze Definition

Before writing your own definition essay, read the following examples—one each from college, the workplace, and everyday life—and answer the questions that accompany each. Reading the examples and answering the questions will help you understand how to write a good definition essay.

1. DEFINITION IN COLLEGE

The following is an essay that a student wrote in an introductory psychology course. This was the assignment:

> Define a term from Part One of the textbook, and give examples of that term in a well-organized essay that demonstrates your understanding of the term.

Two Intelligences

Emma Brennan

Until this semester, I thought that intelligence was just being smart academically. Over the course of the semester, I learned that while intelligence means "acquired or applied knowledge," there are different types of intelligence, two of which I will discuss here.

The first type, crystallized intelligence, is the knowledge an individual has built up and stored in memory. This intelligence includes information, skills, and experiences that a person can draw on to operate in this world. The basic math skills that we learn and use in a variety of ways—to add a tip to a restaurant bill, to add the prices of items we want to purchase, to calculate whether we have enough gas to get home—are examples of crystallized intelligence. Another is the ability to read. Once we know how to read, we don't have to relearn that skill every time we need to do it. We also store information such as what dates are holidays or important events in history, what substances are poisonous, what our social security number is. We have learned how to handle situations such as being hurt (emotionally or physically), being in danger, and being hungry. We walk around with a whole universe of facts, information, skills, and strategies that we can call up at any time. These things are just with us, part of our past experiences.

Fluid intelligence, on the other hand, is the ability to deal with new problems and situations. Although fluid intelligence may draw upon information and experience that is actually crystallized intelligence, it is an individual's ability to meet completely new challenges and contexts and learn how to work within them. For example, if at work you have a problem that you've never experienced before, the amount of fluid intelligence you have will determine whether you try to solve the problem or just give up. If you have a new computer program and something goes wrong, for example, fluid intelligence would prompt you to try to figure out a solution and move forward. If your fluid intelligence is not highly developed, you will likely either call the help line or sit there frustrated.

Both types of intelligence are important as one, crystallized intelligence allows us to incorporate the sum of what we have learned into our supply of skills and behaviors while the other, fluid intelligence, allows us to continue to learn and rise to new challenges. Though an individual may have natural abilities (and natural weaknesses) in a variety of areas, it is the preservation and balance of these two basic types of intelligence that allow him or her to be successful in the world.

For more on audience and purpose, see pages 7–9.

1. Who is Emma's likely **audience**? _____

2. What is Emma's **purpose** in this essay? _____

_____

3. Double-underline the **thesis statement**.

4. Put a check mark (✓) next to each **topic sentence** in the body paragraphs.

5. Underline the **examples** that Emma provides.

6. Circle any (**transitions**) that Emma has used.

7. What **key words** are repeated? _____

_____

For a list of the four basics of good definition, see page 189.

8. Does Emma's essay have the **four basics of good definition**? Why or

   why not? _____

2. DEFINITION IN THE WORKPLACE

The following is a piece of writing that Gary Knoblock has incorporated into a variety of situations: when trying to get a contract for his sign company, as part of advertising copy, and as part of his company's mission statement.

The fundamental principle of Lightning Quick (LQ) Signs is customer orientation. While most companies claim that they are customer-oriented, most have no idea what that really means. I tell my employees that I would like to have a customer giggle at the completion of the job, delighting in the product and service we have delivered, his every expectation met and exceeded. For all of us at LQ Signs, *customer-oriented* means that from start to finish to follow-up, the customer comes first.

Our customer orientation begins before the job begins. Before doing anything, we interview the customer to learn what his or her needs are and to determine the most cost-effective route to meet those needs. No job for us is "standard." Each is unique.

Our customer orientation means that we produce high-quality products quickly. We keep signs simple, because our customers want their prospective customers to be able to read the sign in a glance. We use the most current digital printing processes to produce sharp, readable signs quickly. Because we have previously determined, with the customer, the most cost-effective method of producing the signs, the high quality and rapid return do not come at extra cost.

Our customer orientation means that our products are thoroughly checked for flaws and installed at the customer's convenience. Our signs leave our workshop in perfect condition, as the customer has ordered. Our well-trained team of installers works with the customer to determine the installation schedule.

Finally, our customer orientation means that the job is not complete when the sign is in place. We follow up every sale to make sure that the product is in top shape and that the customer is pleased.

LQ Signs is truly customer-oriented, from start to finish to follow-up. Our customers are our partners.

1. Who is the **audience** for this piece of writing? _____

2. What is Gary's **purpose**? _____

   _____

For more on audience and purpose, see pages 7–9.

3. Double-underline the **thesis statement**.

4. Put a check mark (✓) next to each **topic sentence** that supports Gary's thesis statement.

5. Were you familiar with the term that Gary defined? Restate the meaning of *customer-oriented* in your own words.

   _____

3. DEFINITION IN EVERYDAY LIFE

With the rapid growth of residential development, some new homes are poorly built, even those situated in very affluent communities. The following example is a letter written by a woman who had recently moved into a new home. She sent this letter both to her lawyer and to the local newspaper.

To Whom It May Concern:

I am writing to protest the careless workmanship that has resulted in my new home being substandard. According to the *American Heritage Dictionary, substandard* means failing to meet a standard or falling below standard, and my home meets that definition in many areas. I write not only in hopes of some correction of the problems, but also to warn potential buyers of things to watch for.

The siding on my home is substandard. I was told that the siding would be actual stucco, but in reality the siding is an artificial stucco that falls off and allows water damage. After six months, the siding on my house hangs off in some places, and the structure underneath is severely water damaged. This is substandard, to be sure.

In addition to the exterior siding, the roof is also substandard. The tiles, of the lowest quality, were not affixed properly, and, like the siding, are falling off and allowing water to damage the structure. Not only do I have a leaky roof, but a roofing specialist whom I consulted says the entire roof must be replaced immediately. This roof is substandard.

Finally, the landscaping is not only substandard, it's just plain missing. The contract promises a seeded, thriving lawn. Instead, I have lived with churned up dirt and mud. Not only is there no seeding or evidence of grass, but the entire area is littered with nails and razor blades left on the site by the builders. I discovered the razor blades after my five-year-old daughter was injured by one of them. As I investigated the yard, I found these were all around. Surely, this meets the definition of substandard.

These are just three examples of the many substandard areas in my new home, which was to be the fulfillment of my American dream. As a single parent, I have put my entire savings into this house that I wanted for my family. My dream, like those of others in this development, has become a nightmare, and an extremely expensive one. The builders are wholly unresponsive. Their work defines the word *substandard*. I write in hopes that they will live up to basic standards and remedy their substandard practices.

Sincerely,

Elena Fetzer

1. What is Elena's **purpose** for writing this letter? _____

_____

_____

For more on purpose and audience, see pages 7–9.

2. Who is Elena's **audience**? _____

_____

3. Double-underline the **thesis statement**.

4. Put a check mark (✓) next to the **topic sentences** for the support paragraphs.

5. From Elena's description, can you visualize the areas she cites as substandard? Using what you know about description, add another detail to each body paragraph to make the image stronger.

6. Circle the transitions in the letter.

7. What **key word** does Elena repeat? _____

8. Reread the **concluding paragraph**. Imagine this has happened to you: that you spent everything you had on something that turns out to be junk. Rewrite the conclusion, making it stronger.

Write a Definition Essay

In this section, you will write your own definition essay. To do so, follow this sequence:

REVIEW the four basics of good definition (p. 189).

CHOOSE your writing assignment (p. 198).

WRITE your definition using the step-by-step Writing Guide (p. 199).

CHECK your final essay (p. 204).

WRITING ASSIGNMENT 1   **COLLEGE, WORK, EVERYDAY LIFE**

Write a definition essay on *one* of the following topics or on a topic of your own choice.

COLLEGE

Define

- A term or concept from another course you have taken
- A good teacher
- Cheating

WORK

Define

- Any term you use at work
- Probationary period
- A model employee

EVERYDAY LIFE

Define

- An attitude or behavior (such as assertiveness, generosity, negativity, optimism, and so on)
- Scam
- Road rage

WRITING ASSIGNMENT 2   **USE THE INTERNET**

For advice about how to cite a source, see Chapter 20.

Basic computer skills are necessary for most jobs today. Many job descriptions, whether in the newspaper or on the Web, list *computer literacy* among the requirements for a position. Go to the Web to find out more about computer literacy, and then write a definition of the term in your own words. You might start by entering the key words "information literacy" or "computer literacy" into search engines such as Google (**<www.google.com>**) or AltaVista (**<www.altavista.com>**). In your essay, define and give examples of the term. Assume your audience is someone who is seeking a job in your company.

WRITING ASSIGNMENT 3   **WRITE A SECTION IN A MANUAL**

Read the problem and situation that follow, and then choose *one* of the assignment options (3A or 3B) that appear after it.

PROBLEM: Most people are aware that communication skills are ranked among the top skill sets that employers seek and value. But what exactly are communication skills? While most people have a good general idea of what the term *communication skills* means, they don't have a clear idea of what those skills are, specifically, and how they should be applied.

SITUATION: Your company is putting together a new employee handbook. To make the handbook both realistic and relevant, the company has decided that the contents will come directly from the employees. Your department has been assigned the section on communication.

ASSIGNMENT OPTION 3A: RESPONSE TO THE SITUATION

Using what you know about definition, write an essay that defines *communication skills* and gives specific examples of how you apply those skills in your job. Of course, you'll also want your essay to demonstrate the use of good communication skills. Think of the various people with whom you need to communicate at work and what defines good communication with those people.

First look up the meaning of *communication* in a dictionary. Then list the various types of communication skills. (Remember, communication is not just the ability to speak well.) Next, make a list of communication skills you need in your job. Give specific examples from your workplace of how a communication skill is used or needed.

ASSIGNMENT OPTION 3B: ANOTHER PERSPECTIVE

Instead of writing about your own communication skills on the job, write an essay about what skills a new employee will need. Use the same process that is outlined in assignment option 3A.

Definition

Follow the steps in this Writing Guide to help you prewrite, draft, revise, and edit your definition. Check off each step as you complete it.

Writing Guide

For more on purpose
and audience, see
pages 7–9.

THINKING CRITICALLY ABOUT DEFINITION

FOCUS   Think about what the term you are defining means to you
and what it is likely to mean to your readers.

ASK   • Who am I writing this for, and how familiar are my
readers likely to be with the term I'm defining?
• What is my purpose in defining this term? Do I want to
give a formal definition, or do I want to explain what I
mean when I use the word?
• What basic definition should I use?
• What examples or other information about the term will
make the meaning clear to my readers?

PREWRITE TO EXPLORE YOUR TOPIC

Prewriting for definition involves coming up with various meanings of the
term or concept you are going to define. Most words have more than one
meaning, and you want to decide how you want to present your topic.

_____   Decide on your purpose for writing.

_____   Identify the audience for your essay.

_____   Look up the dictionary meaning of the word you might define.

_____   Use a prewriting technique (freewriting, listing/brainstorming,
questioning, discussing, clustering) to come up with the different uses
of the word. Decide on the meaning you will develop in your essay.

WRITE A THESIS STATEMENT

The thesis statement in a definition essay often follows one of three basic
patterns. You do not have to follow these patterns exactly, but they provide
a simple guide to what a thesis statement in a definition essay might include.

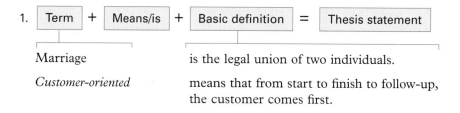

1.   Term + Means/is + Basic definition = Thesis statement

Marriage   is the legal union of two individuals.

Customer-oriented   means that from start to finish to follow-up,
the customer comes first.

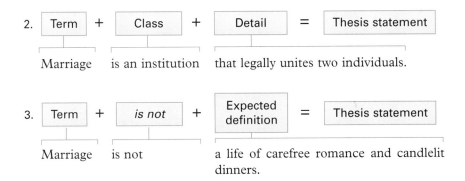

2. Term + Class + Detail = Thesis statement

Marriage   is an institution   that legally unites two individuals.

3. Term + *is not* + Expected definition = Thesis statement

Marriage   is not   a life of carefree romance and candlelit dinners.

This last pattern is a little tricky, but if used correctly, it can grab your readers' attention.

_____ Review your ideas about the term, and decide what basic definition you will give or whether you want to give several different meanings.

_____ Do not just copy the dictionary definition. Write the definition in your own words, and think about what wording will make sense to your readers.

_____ Write a thesis statement that includes both the term and your basic definition.

SUPPORT YOUR POINT

The major support points in definition are the examples that show what you mean by your use of the term or concept you are defining. The supporting details are the explanations and specific details that you give about each of your examples. These examples and explanations show your readers what you mean by the term. Think about what kinds of examples will make sense to them.

_____ Use a prewriting technique to find examples and details that explain what you mean by the term.

_____ Choose at least three good examples that demonstrate your use of the term being defined.

_____ Explain each example with details that clearly show how the example demonstrates your definition.

MAKE A PLAN

Making a written plan—an outline—helps you decide how to order your definition. A definition generally uses order of importance, arranging the examples to build up to the one with the most impact on readers.

_____ Arrange your examples (your support points) according to which you think best demonstrates the meaning of your term.

_____ Make a plan or outline for your definition essay.

DRAFT

Drafting a definition means writing in complete sentences and including the following:

- An introduction with a thesis statement
- Examples of the term with specific details that demonstrate your definition of the term
- A conclusion that reminds your readers about your definition

_____ Write an introductory paragraph that includes your thesis statement and gets your readers' interest.

_____ Write a topic sentence for each of the examples.

_____ Write body paragraphs with topic sentences and specific, concrete details about each example.

_____ Write a concluding paragraph that reminds your readers of the term and its meaning and that makes a final observation.

_____ Title your essay.

REVISE

Revising means changing whole sentences or paragraphs to make your writing clearer or stronger. To revise a definition essay, remember that most words can mean different things, depending on how they are being used. Remind yourself of other possible meanings so that you can make sure that your examples clearly explain your particular definition. Read your draft, looking for the following:

- Places where the ideas are off the main point (revising for unity)
- Gaps in information or detail (revising for support and detail)

- Areas in need of transitions to help readers move smoothly from one point to the next (revising for coherence)

_____ Get feedback from others through peer review.

For more on peer review, see pages 87–88.

_____ Begin revising by considering how you can make your definition clearer and more precise for your readers.

_____ Reread your thesis statement. Revise it so that both the term and your definition are clear.

_____ Reread the body of your essay to make sure the examples support your definition and the details about the examples demonstrate what you mean. Add other examples and details that would help explain what you mean by the term.

_____ Reread your introduction to make sure that it has energy and uses concrete words to define your topic.

_____ Reread your conclusion, again judging its energy and interest level. Make a further comment or observation about the topic or definition.

_____ Add transitions and transitional sentences to connect your examples.

_____ Make at least five changes to your draft to improve the unity, support, or coherence of your definition, or to make the introduction, thesis statement, or conclusion clearer or more interesting.

EDIT

Some grammar, spelling, word use, or punctuation errors may confuse your readers and make it difficult for them to understand a point you are trying to make. Even if they do not confuse your readers, errors detract from the effectiveness and overall quality of your writing. Edit your definition carefully, and correct any errors you find.

_____ Ask a classmate or friend to read your definition essay and highlight any errors.

_____ Use the spell checker and grammar checker on your computer.

_____ Look yourself for errors that the spell checker or grammar checker didn't catch. Focus first on sentence fragments, run-on sentences, problems with subject–verb agreement, problems with verbs, and other areas where you know you often make errors.

_____ Print a clean final copy.

_____ Ask yourself: Is this the best I can do?

A FINAL CHECK BEFORE HANDING IN YOUR DEFINITION ESSAY

If you've followed the Writing Guide for definition, your essay will already include the four basics of good definition. Use this list to double-check each basic feature.

____ My definition essay tells readers what term I am defining.

____ My thesis statement presents a clear, precise definition.

____ Each paragraph in the body of my essay presents an example with supporting details to help show what the term means.

____ My definition uses examples and words that my readers can easily understand.

14

Comparison and Contrast

Writing That Shows Similarities and
Differences

You Know This
You already use comparison and contrast to help make decisions.
• You compare and contrast features of several DVD players.
• You compare and contrast two job offers.
• You compare and contrast two courses you might want to take.

Understand What Comparison and Contrast Are

DEFINITION: **Comparison** is writing that shows the similarities among subjects — people, ideas, situation, or items; **contrast** shows the differences. In conversation, we often use the word *compare* to mean either compare or contrast, but as you work through this chapter, the terms will be separated.

IDEA JOURNAL
Write about some differences you see between men and women when it comes to movies they like.

∷ Four Basics of Good Comparison and Contrast

1. It uses subjects that have enough in common to be usefully compared and contrasted.

2. It serves a purpose — either to help readers make a decision or understand the subjects.

3. It presents several important, parallel points of comparison and contrast.

4. It arranges points in a logical organization.

205

Salvador Torres

FINANCIAL CONSULTANT

BACKGROUND: Salvador is the son of farm-workers who moved to California from rural Mexico. He spoke only Spanish at home and did not learn English until he was in the fourth grade. He worked with his parents at times, which taught him that the life of a manual laborer is extremely difficult. His parents always insisted he should try to do better for himself. A high school teacher and counselor encouraged Salvador academically and introduced him to several people who, like Salvador, had started with poor grades and English skills but had attended community college and were successful working professionals. Salvador was part of and later worked with the Puenté Project, a program for Hispanic students who are at risk of not completing college. He is now a mentor who helps others like him to stay—and succeed—in college.

EMPLOYER: Public Financial Management, Inc.

COLLEGE(S)/DEGREES: Gavilan College (A.A.), Stanford University (B.A.), Princeton University (M.P.A.)

TYPES OF WRITING ON THE JOB: Memos to clients on a variety of financial topics, financial reports and analyses, email

HOW SALVADOR USES COMPARISON/CONTRAST: Because Salvador is a financial consultant, he has to compare and contrast investment

Salvador Torres

options for clients. For an example of the type of comparison/contrast writing Salvador does on the job, see page 212.

COMPUTER SKILLS: Microsoft Office (Word, Excel, PowerPoint, Front Page, Outlook, Access); DBC Finance, Groupwise; Lexis-Nexis; STATA statistical software; Visual Basic programming

TEAMWORK ON THE JOB: Being able to work in a team is vital to success as a financial consultant because on any given project, a consultant works with various other advisers—experts in investment banking, law, insurance, and credit. All of these individuals must pool their knowledge to advise a client who has hired Public Financial Management, Inc.

FUTURE GOAL: Salvador says, "[My goal is] to reach my full personal potential and to help other Chicanos and Latinos meet theirs. I also want to help preserve existing institutions and create new institutions that will aid in the success of members of our community."

A comparison/contrast essay shows how things are alike or different, helping readers understand or choose between alternatives. For example, you might want to compare and contrast two restaurants so that readers can choose between them. Or you might want to compare and contrast two friends or two of your children; your purpose then is not to help your readers choose between them but to give them an understanding of both people.

POINTS FOR COMPARISON AND CONTRAST

You may have heard people say, "That's comparing apples and oranges," meaning that two things aren't alike enough to result in any meaningful comparison. For example, comparing a DVD player and a toaster would not help explain either. Although they are both electronic appliances, they are so different that showing similarities or differences makes no sense. When you write comparison/contrast, choose subjects that are similar enough to be compared or contrasted.

Once you have selected comparable subjects, you need to find **points of comparison**—parallel or matched points that will show how the subjects are similar or different. Supporting details then explain these support points for each subject. For example, the student who wrote the thesis *The ages of twenty and forty are both enjoyable, but they represent very different stages in life*, might go on to list several points of contrast between twenty and forty:

For more on supporting your thesis, see Chapter 4.

>   appearance
>
>   place in life
>
>   perspective

For each point of comparison, the writer would then come up with details to explain the differences:

AGE TWENTY	AGE FORTY
appearance	
smooth skin	some wrinkles
trendy haircut	classic hairstyle
rounded features	well-defined features
place in life	
just starting out	established
single, no children	married with children
living at home	own home
perspective	
self-centered	more thoughtful
choices to make	many choices made
uncertainty	wisdom

ORGANIZATION IN COMPARISON AND CONTRAST

DEFINITIONS: A **point-by-point organization** first presents one point of comparison or contrast between the two subjects with examples of each and then moves to the next point of comparison or contrast. A **whole-to-whole organization** first presents all the points of comparison or contrast for one subject and then all the points for the second subject.

After you have developed points of comparison and supporting details, you need to decide how to present them in your essay. There are two ways to organize a comparison/contrast essay: point-by-point or whole-to-whole. You have to decide which of the two organizations will best serve your purpose. Choose one and stick with it throughout the essay; otherwise you will confuse your readers.

The two organizations look like this:

POINT-BY-POINT	WHOLE-TO-WHOLE
Thesis statement	Thesis statement
Topic sentence, point 1	Topic sentence, subject 1
subject 1	point 1
subject 2	point 2
Topic sentence, point 2	point 3
subject 1	Topic sentence, subject 2
subject 2	point 1
Topic sentence, point 3	point 2
subject 1	point 3
subject 2	Concluding statement
Concluding statement	

Although the whole-to-whole organization looks as if it might be shorter, the organization has little effect on the length. Select the organization that will be clearest and easiest for readers to follow. Arrange the points and details in a sequence that suits what you have to say — chronological order, space order, order of importance, or any logical order.

As you write your essay, add transitions to lead from point to point and subject to subject.

For more on transitions, see pages 94–99.

> ### *Common Transitions in Comparison/Contrast*
>
> | COMMON COMPARISON TRANSITIONS | COMMON CONTRAST TRANSITIONS |
> | --- | --- |
> | one similarity | one difference |
> | another similarity | another difference |
> | similarly | in contrast |
> | like | now/then |
> | both | unlike |
> | | while |

Many situations require you to understand similarities and differences. Here are some examples of how you might use comparison and contrast.

COLLEGE

- In a business course, you compare and contrast practices in e-commerce and traditional commerce.

WORK

- You compare and contrast two health insurance options offered by your company in order to select the one that is best for you.

EVERYDAY LIFE

- Before choosing an Internet service provider, you compare and contrast the fees, services, and options each offers.

Read and Analyze Comparison/Contrast

Before writing your own comparison/contrast essay, read the following examples — one each from college, the workplace, and everyday life — and answer the questions that accompany each. Reading the examples and answering the questions will help you understand how to write a good comparison/contrast essay.

1. COMPARISON AND CONTRAST IN COLLEGE

The following essay was written for this assignment in a sociology class:

> Compare some aspect of two different cultures, using your own experience, the video that was shown in class, or the material from Chapter 4 of your textbook.

My Observations on Mexican and American Children

Anna Griffith

In the past few years I have been privileged to go on several mission trips to the Yucatan Peninsula. There our group worked with some Mexican children who live in poverty in the city of Merida. In observing and getting to know the children, I was struck by several diferences in the situations, behaviors, and attitudes of the Mexican children compared to children I know here in Hattiesburg, Mississippi.

The most obvious difference was in the living situations. The children here in Hattiesburg live in sturdy houses or apartments. The houses are of different sizes, and not all are in great shape, but they have multiple rooms, and they are made of wood, brick, or stucco. None of the children I know here share a bedroom with their parents. In contrast, as I arrived with my group to organize a basketball camp and Bible school in one of the neighborhoods of Merida, I was shocked by the homes I saw. Children of all ages peeped out from the doors of their homes: small tin shacks that were roughly the size of my bedroom at home. Many people lived together in these wobbly structures, where one room served for eating, sleeping, bathing, and anything else that takes place inside.

Another difference is in the amount of parental supervision the Meridan children get versus the children in Hattiesburg. Like the children I know here in the States, at our first event the Mexican children were shy, reserved, and a little cautious with us because we were strangers. But that didn't last more than a few minutes, after which they were eager to find out everything about us. Most parents here in the States would accompany their small children to an event such as ours, but these children were rarely seen with adults. Every night I watched a little girl of about five walk down the road holding her little sister's hand. It was common to see several battered strollers with babies around the open-air basketball courts we set up. We realized soon that no one had been at home when the children left, and they were given no time to return—they were on their own. This lack of supervision simply doesn't happen at home, where parents want to keep a close eye on their children's whereabouts. Interestingly, the

Mexican children knew very early that it was their responsibility to take care of their younger siblings, and they did so willingly and with a sense of duty. In contrast, this seems to be a behavior that children here have lost.

The difference that had the most impact on me, though, was the appreciation the Mexican children had for very simple things. They do not have the elaborate, high-tech toys that American children take for granted. Items that are ordinary to American children, such as flashlights, disposable cameras, and marker pens, fascinated Mexican children. One little boy picked up one of our flashlights and ran around clicking it on and off. He had never seen anything like it. When we said he could have it, he stared at us open-mouthed, amazed at his luck. He was giddy with delight and appreciation. Cameras with flashes produced similar responses. But we were most surprised at the children's reactions to Crayola marker pens. One night after a child had been fascinated with a marker, we gave it to her. After thanking us, she ran into the night to show off her new treasure. Within moments, we were surrounded by a crowd of eager faces and reaching hands. Like children anywhere, they were impatient and greedy to have what another child has, but this was just a marker, something American children would not get excited about or appreciate. The Mexican children were grateful for and appreciated simple things.

Through my experiences with children here in America and in Mexico, I have come to realize how much different economic situations affect the children. Although the most obvious difference between American children I know and Mexican children was in their poorer living conditions, the thing that most affected me was how much more thankful and appreciative the Mexican children were. There is much to be said in favor of simplicity, something most American children do not experience.

1. What is Anna's **purpose** for writing? _____

2. Who is Anna's **audience**? _____

For more on purpose and audience, see pages 7–9.

3. Fill in the blanks with the **subjects** and the **main point** of Anna's essay.

SUBJECT 1: _____

SUBJECT 2: _____

MAIN POINT: _____

4. Double-underline the **thesis statement**.

5. Does Anna use **point-to-point** or **whole-to-whole** organization?

   _____

6. What **order** (time, space, or importance) does Anna use to arrange her

   points? _____

7. Put a check mark (✓) next to each **topic sentence** Anna uses to introduce a similarity or a difference.

8. Underline the **details** that Anna gives to help the reader understand each difference.

9. Circle the (**transitions**) (words, phrases, and sentences) that Anna uses.

10. What **key words** does Anna repeat? _____

    _____

11. Double-underline the **sentence in the concluding paragraph** that ties the concluding paragraph to the introductory paragraph.

For a list of the four basics of good comparison and contrast, see page 205.

12. Does Anna's essay have the **four basics of good comparison and contrast**? Why or why not? _____

2. COMPARISON AND CONTRAST IN THE WORKPLACE

The following memo is similar to those that Salvador Torres, a financial consultant at Public Financial Management, Inc., prepares for clients. Although it is not in essay form, it is an example of how comparison/contrast is used in the workplace.

TO: Investment Client

Based on our discussion of your investment needs, I would recommend that you invest in Stock Mutual Funds rather than Bond Mutual Funds. Your three expressed preferences were 1) to hold on to the stock for more than ten years, 2) that the funds you invest in be professionally managed, and 3) that you wanted a high potential for gain and were not overly concerned with risk and the daily fluctuations of funds. You have no need for present annual income from your investments. We determined, after reviewing numerous options, that either Bond Mutual Funds or Stock Mutual Funds would meet your criteria.

There are several similarities between Bond Mutual Funds and Stock Mutual Funds. One is that they both offer investment horizons greater than ten years. Another is that both are professionally managed. A third is that either fund may pay annual income. Based on these factors, either fund fulfills your investment needs.

However, there are differences worth noting. One is that Stock Mutual Funds have higher potential gains over a ten-year period, though they have more risk and fluctuation in the shorter term. Additionally, though both funds may pay annual income, the Bond Mutual Fund is more likely to do so, at the expense of greater long-term appreciation.

Both funds meet some of your criteria, but the Stock Mutual Funds are more tailored to your expressed preferences than the Bond Mutual Funds. The Stock Mutual Funds are likely to have a greater return on investment over a ten-year period. Since this is a high priority for you, I suggest that you invest in Stock Mutual Funds. I can monitor this investment and inform you of its status at any time.

If you have questions or need further clarification, please do not hesitate to ask. I will look forward to meeting with you again to determine the precise funds in which to invest. Thank you.

1. Who is the **audience** for this memo? _____

2. What is the **purpose** of the memo? _____

_____

For more on audience and purpose, see pages 7–9.

3. Double-underline the **thesis statement**.

4. Does the writer use **point-by-point** or **whole-to-whole** organization?

_____

5. Put a check mark next to the **topic sentences**.

3. COMPARISON AND CONTRAST IN EVERYDAY LIFE

The following comparison and contrast was done by Karron Tempesta to help her decide which of two job offers to accept. When comparing things in order to make a decision, it is often helpful to list the points of comparison next to each other so that the differences are easy to see. First look at Karron's list (which is like prewriting), and then read the essay she wrote, which is more casual than a formal essay.

COMPANY A	COMPANY B
• higher salary	• lower salary, but a good bonus plan
• big company	• small company
• farther away but on bus line	• near home
• more jobs at the company because it's big	• fewer jobs because it's small, but maybe more chance to do more and be rewarded
• nice people	• nice people
• entry-level job	• more responsibilities and challenge
• good benefit plan	• okay benefit plan

The job offers I received from Company A and Company B are both good, but they differ on a number of points. I'm writing this because sometimes I think better when I can see things in print, and this is an important decision that I want to think about seriously.

   The first difference is the location of the companies. Company A is way across town. It's on a bus line, and that's good, but it would still take me anywhere from thirty to forty-five minutes to get there. It makes for a longer day. Company B, on the other hand, is very close by. I could ride my bicycle and be there in ten minutes. I'd also save the bus fare. But what about when it's raining or really hot?

Another difference is in the salaries. The actual salary at Company A is higher than that at Company B. However, Company B is experiencing rapid growth, and it has a good bonus plan. Although I can't count on it, I have the opportunity with Company B to actually make more than at Company A. But then again, maybe I wouldn't get a good bonus.

Probably the most important difference is really the size of the two companies: Company A is a big company, and Company B is small. Size is probably the reason that Company A has a better benefit plan—there are more people to enroll, so it gets a good rate. In contrast, Company B has fewer people and probably pays a higher rate because there are fewer people.

Size also affects the type of job and where it will lead. At Company A, the job is an entry-level position with clearly defined responsibilities that aren't that interesting. But the company has lots of jobs, so I'd have more opportunities once I was there. At Company B, the job has more responsibility, and I'd learn more and be more interested. Because it's small, people are more likely to let me try new things—and to notice when I've done well. So there are good opportunities there, too.

So there are the differences. Which of those differences are most important to me, and where will I be the happiest? The location isn't really very important. I need money, so a higher salary is attractive, but I like the idea of being rewarded with a bonus if I do well. I might make more at Company B that way, and it's good motivation. Also, I like smaller companies better; I just felt better there, and I like that I get to do more on the job and be noticed. The benefit difference isn't good for Company B, but I think, overall, Company B is best. I'll go with it.

1. What is Karron's **purpose** for this comparison? _____

   _____

   For more on purpose and audience, see pages 7–9.

2. Who is Karron's **audience**? _____

3. Double-underline the **thesis statement**.

4. Does Karron use **point-by-point** or **whole-to-whole** organization?

   _____

5. What order of **organization** (chronological, spatial, or importance) does Karron use? _____

6. Put a check mark (✓) next to each **topic sentence**.

7. Circle the (**transitions**) that Karron uses.

8. What **key words** does she repeat? _____

_____

Write a Comparison/Contrast Essay

In this section, you will write your own comparison/contrast essay. To do so, follow this sequence:

REVIEW the basics of good comparison/contrast writing (p. 205).

CHOOSE your writing assignment (below).

WRITE your comparison/contrast essay using the step-by-step Writing Guide (p. 219).

CHECK your final essay (p. 223).

WRITING ASSIGNMENT 1   COLLEGE, WORK, EVERYDAY LIFE

Write a comparison/contrast essay on *one* of the following topics or on a topic of your own choice.

COLLEGE

• Being a working student/Being a nonworking student

• Two topics from another course

• Being an older, returning student/Coming right from high school

WORK

• Two jobs you have had

• Two companies you have worked for

• A job and a career

EVERYDAY LIFE

- Two different kinds of families

- Good customer service and bad customer service

- Your feeling about commitment in a relationship now versus ten years ago

WRITING ASSIGNMENT 2 **USE THE INTERNET**

Choose two Internet search engines from the following list of popular search engines or your list of personal favorites. Write an essay in which you compare and contrast the two.

For advice about how to cite a source, see Chapter 20.

AltaVista: **<www.altavista.com>**   Google: **<www.google.com>**

Excite: **<www.excite.com>**   Lycos: **<www.lycos.com>**

Fast Search: **<www.alltheweb.com>**   Yahoo: **<www.yahoo.com>**

Compare or contrast them on these three points: (1) ease of use, (2) types of search help offered, and (3) quality of results.

WRITING ASSIGNMENT 3 **COMPARING OFFERS**

Read the problem and situation that follow, and then choose *one* of the assignment options (3A or 3B) that appear after it.

PROBLEM: These days there are many laptop computers available. But there are significant differences among them that you should consider before buying. What facts and features should you compare?

SITUATION: You decide that you need a laptop computer that you can bring to class and use at home. You check a recent issue of *Consumer Reports* that rates laptops and you find the chart on page 218.

Overall Ratings

Within types, in performance order

Rating key: ● Excellent ◕ Very good ○ Good ◐ Fair ● Poor

KEY NO.	BRAND & MODEL	PRICE	OVERALL SCORE (0 P F G VG E 100)	APPLICATION SPEED	DISPLAY QUALITY	MULTIMEDIA	FEATURES AND USABILITY	EXPANSION AND UPGRADES	BATTERY LIFE (HR.)	POWER CONSERVATION	MANUALS	WARRANTY AND SUPPORT
WINDOWS LAPTOPS												
1	**Compaq** Presidio 1800T	$2,300	▬▬▬	●	●	◕	◕	◕	4	●	●	○
2	**Toshiba** Satellite 2805-S401	2,200	▬▬▬	●	●	◕	◕	◕	3	◕	●	○
3	**HP** Pavilion n5270	2,000	▬▬▬	●	◕	◕	●	◕	2 3/4	◕	◕	○
4	**Sony** Vaio PCG-FX170	3,000	▬▬▬	●	●	◕	●	◕	3	○	◕	○
5	**Dell** Inspiron 8000	2,460	▬▬▬	◕	●	◕	◕	●	2 3/4	○	○	◐
6	**Sony** Vaio PCG-Z505LS	2,550	▬▬▬	●	●	◕	◕	◕	2 1/4	○	●	◐
7	**Dell** Inspiron 4000	1,725	▬▬▬	◕	◕	◕	◕	◕	3 1/2	○	○	◐
8	**Gateway** Solo 5300	2,230	▬▬▬	◕	◕	◕	○	◕	3 1/4	◕	●	◐
9	**IBM** ThinkPad i1200	1,850	▬▬▬	◕	◕	○	○	○	4 1/4	●	●	◐
10	**Toshiba** Satellite 1735	1,200	▬▬▬	◕	○	○	◕	○	2 1/2	○	●	◐
11	**Compaq** Presario 1200 12XL400	1,400	▬▬▬	◕	○	◕	◕	○	2	○	◕	◐
12	**Toshiba** Portegé 3480CT	2,000	▬▬▬	◕	◕	○	○	◕	2 1/4	○	●	○
MACINTOSH LAPTOPS												
13	**Apple** PowerBook G4 Titanium	3,200	▬▬▬	●	◕	●	○	○	3	●	◕	○
14	**Apple** iBook 466 Special Edition	1,950	▬▬▬	◕	●	◕	○	◐	3 1/4	◕	◕	○

ASSIGNMENT OPTION 3A: RESPOND TO THE SITUATION

Read the rating chart about laptop computers, and contrast two of the models. Identify three important points of difference, and look at what the chart says about each model for each point. Explain why these points are important to you. After analyzing the points, choose the laptop you would buy. In the concluding paragraph, review what you have learned about the two models of laptop, state which you would select, and tell why.

ASSIGNMENT OPTION 3B: ANOTHER PERSPECTIVE

Read the rating chart about laptop computers. Instead of comparing models for yourself, imagine that you are recommending a model that would be good for your company. Consider what functions you would need most for work, and then choose points to contrast. Explain why each point is important, and in the last paragraph make a recommendation to your boss about what model to purchase and why.

Comparison and Contrast

Writing Guide

Follow the steps in this Writing Guide to help you prewrite, draft, revise, and edit your comparison and contrast. Check off each step as you complete it.

THINKING CRITICALLY ABOUT COMPARISON AND CONTRAST	
FOCUS	Think about what you want to compare or contrast and the main point you want to make about your subjects.
ASK	• What are my readers likely to know about these subjects? • What do I want my readers to be able to do: make a decision or understand my subjects? • What are some parallel points of comparison or contrast between my two subjects? Which points will best help me to achieve my purpose? • Which of the two organizations would best help me get my point across: point-by-point or whole-to-whole?

PREWRITE TO EXPLORE YOUR SUBJECTS

Prewriting for comparison and contrast involves considering what subjects to compare or contrast and then coming up with some points of comparison or contrast for them.

_____ Decide on your purpose for writing.

_____ Identify the audience for your essay.

_____ Select two subjects with similarities and differences you want to explore.

_____ Decide whether you want readers to choose between or to understand your two subjects.

_____ Consider whether the subjects have enough in common to allow a valid comparison or contrast between them.

_____ Once you decide what subjects to compare or contrast, use a prewriting technique (freewriting, listing/brainstorming, questioning, discussing, clustering) to explore in what ways the subjects are alike or different.

For more on purpose and audience, see pages 7–9.

WRITE A THESIS STATEMENT

The thesis statement in a comparison/contrast essay includes the two subjects you are comparing or contrasting and the main point you want to make about them.

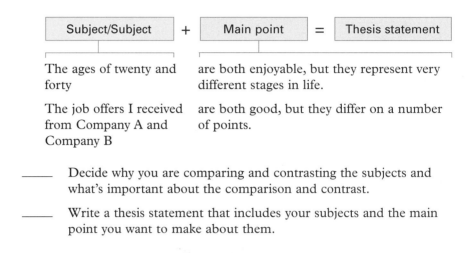

| Subject/Subject | + | Main point | = | Thesis statement |

The ages of twenty and forty — are both enjoyable, but they represent very different stages in life.

The job offers I received from Company A and Company B — are both good, but they differ on a number of points.

_____   Decide why you are comparing and contrasting the subjects and what's important about the comparison and contrast.

_____   Write a thesis statement that includes your subjects and the main point you want to make about them.

SUPPORT YOUR POINT

The major support points in comparison and contrast are the points of comparison that you use. The supporting details are the specific details and explanations you give about the points of comparison or contrast.

_____   Review your ideas about the subjects.

_____   List some differences or similarities, depending on whether you are comparing, contrasting, or doing both.

_____   Select from your list the points of comparison that you will use in the essay, choosing points that your readers will understand and that serve your purpose. These points of comparison are the major support points for your thesis statement.

_____   Add supporting details and examples to explain the points of comparison.

MAKE A PLAN

Making a written plan—an outline—helps you decide how to order your comparison and contrast. A plan for a comparison/contrast essay must use either point-by-point organization or whole-to-whole organization. Your plan should follow one of the structures shown here:

POINT-BY-POINT	WHOLE-TO-WHOLE
Thesis statement	Thesis statement
Topic sentence, point 1	Topic sentence, subject 1
subject 1	point 1
subject 2	point 2
Topic sentence, point 2	point 3
subject 1	Topic sentence, subject 2
subject 2	point 1
Topic sentence, point 3	point 2
subject 1	point 3
subject 2	Concluding statement
Concluding statement	

_____ Decide whether you will use a point-by-point or whole-to-whole organization.

_____ Make a plan or outline that follows the point-by-point or whole-to-whole structure as shown here.

DRAFT

Drafting a comparison/contrast essay means writing in complete sentences and including the following:

- An introductory paragraph that includes your thesis statement about your two subjects
- Body paragraphs that explain your points of comparison
- A concluding paragraph that reinforces your thesis

_____ Think about what is interesting about the comparison you are about to make.

_____ Write an introductory paragraph that introduces your two subjects and the main point you will make about them. Try to spark your readers' attention.

_____ Write a topic sentence for each of the points of comparison or contrast.

_____ Write body paragraphs that provide specific details about the points of comparison so that your readers can understand the similarities or differences between your two subjects.

_____ Write a concluding paragraph that refers back to your main point and makes a further comment or observation based on your points of comparison or contrast.

_____ Title your essay.

REVISE

Revising means changing whole sentences or paragraphs to make your writing clearer or stronger. To revise your comparison/contrast essay, imagine that you know little about the subjects. Read your draft from that perspective, looking for ways to make the similarities or differences clearer. Read your draft, looking for the following:

- Places where the ideas are off the main point (revising for unity)
- Gaps in information or detail (revising for support and detail)
- Areas in need of transitions to help readers move smoothly from one point to the next (revising for coherence)

For more on peer review, see pages 87–88.

_____ Get feedback from others through peer review.

_____ Reread your thesis. Make sure it presents the two subjects forcefully and clearly, and states the point you want to make in your essay.

_____ Reread the body paragraphs. Add other points of comparison and contrast or details that would clearly demonstrate your main point. Add details that would show the similarities or differences between the subjects.

_____ Make sure that you have followed either point-by-point or whole-to-whole organization all the way through your essay.

_____ Reread your introduction. If it lacks energy or clarity, rewrite it to give it some life.

_____ Reread your conclusion to make sure that it sounds energetic, confirms your main point about the two subjects, and makes a further observation.

_____ Add transitions that move your readers from one point of comparison to another, and decide whether you want to repeat key words.

_____ Make at least five changes to your draft to improve the unity, support, or coherence of your comparison and contrast or to make the introduction, thesis statement, or conclusion stronger or more convincing.

EDIT

Some grammar, spelling, word use, or punctuation errors may confuse your readers and make it difficult for them to understand a point you are trying to make. Even if they do not confuse your readers, errors detract from the effectiveness and overall quality of your writing. Edit your comparison and contrast carefully, and correct any errors you find.

_____ Ask a classmate or friend to read your essay and highlight any errors.

_____ Use the spell checker and grammar checker on your computer.

_____ Look yourself for errors that the spell checker or grammar checker didn't catch. Focus first on sentence fragments, run-on sentences, problems with subject–verb agreement, problems with verbs, and other areas where you know you often make errors.

_____ Print a clean final copy.

_____ Ask yourself: Is this the best I can do?

**A FINAL CHECK BEFORE HANDING IN YOUR COMPARISON/
CONTRAST ESSAY**

If you've followed the Writing Guide for comparison and contrast, your essay will already include the four basics of good comparison and contrast. Use this list to double-check each basic feature.

_____ My thesis statement identifies two subjects that can be usefully compared and contrasted.

_____ The purpose of my essay is to help readers make a decision or understand the subjects.

_____ The body of my essay presents several major points of comparison, supported by details about both subjects.

_____ My essay arranges the points of comparison in a logical order.

You Know This
You already use cause and effect to understand things.
- You try to figure out what caused your partner to get angry.
- You explain to a child why she shouldn't eat too fast.
- You think about what will happen if you change jobs.

15

Cause and Effect

Writing That Explains Reasons or Results

Understand What Cause and Effect Are

DEFINITION: A **cause** is what makes an event happen. An **effect** is what happens as a result of an event.

■■ Four Basics of Good Cause and Effect

1. It clearly distinguishes between a cause and an effect.
2. It discusses real causes, not just something that happened before another event.
3. It discusses real effects, not just something that happened after another event.
4. It gives clear and detailed examples of causes, effects, or both.

Analyzing causes and effects goes beyond asking "What happened?" to also ask "Why?" and "How?"

SITUATION: On a hot summer day, you leave a video you need to return on the front seat of your car while you are at work. When you come out of work, you find the video has melted.

Jolanda Jones

ATTORNEY AND CONSULTANT

Jolanda Jones

BACKGROUND: Jolanda grew up in a low-income housing project in Houston, Texas. Her father committed suicide, her uncles spent time in prison, and she lost several family members to street violence. Jolanda's life was a tough one. Her mother and grandmother gave her the confidence to try hard and believe in herself, however. A good student, she became an athlete as a teenager and is a three-time NCAA heptathalon champion, two-time Academic All-American, and a 1989 U.S. heptathalon champion. She participated in the 1996 U.S. Olympic Team Trials and won the high jump, beating Jackie Joyner-Kersee, an elite track and field athlete and gold medalist.

Jolanda went to college and to law school, and then went on to practice law. In 2000, she received the NAACP's Award for Legal Excellence for dedication to community service. She still practices law, and recently she has started her own consulting business.

EMPLOYER: Self

COLLEGE(S)/DEGREES: University of Houston, Central Campus (B.A.), University of Houston—Bates School of Law (J.D.L.)

TYPES OF WRITING ON THE JOB: Legal briefs, proposals, letters, evaluations, emails, Web site content, speeches

HOW JOLANDA USES CAUSE/EFFECT: As part of her consulting business, Jolanda is in great demand as a speaker, particularly to inner-city youth. When she addresses students, she emphasizes the importance of understanding that for every action they take there is a consequence that they should consider. For an example of how Jolanda uses cause and effect, see Cause and Effect in the Workplace, on pages 230–32.

COMPUTER SKILLS: WordPerfect, Microsoft Word, Excel, Internet

TEAMWORK ON THE JOB: Jolanda says, "In my legal practice, my clients and I must work together as a team to be the most effective. I also consult with schools and school districts, where it is important for administrators, teachers, parents, and students to work together to achieve common goals."

FUTURE GOAL: Jolanda hopes to set up a nonprofit organization to teach young people how to empower themselves to accomplish all their goals and to be the best and most positive people they can be.

CAUSE: The **cause** of the video melting was **leaving it all day in a hot car**.

EFFECT: The **effect** of leaving the video in a hot car all day was that **it melted**.

Jim Rice of Quinsigamond Community College helps his students visualize the cause/effect relationship by suggesting that they think of three linked rings:

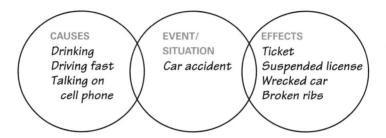

CLEAR CAUSES AND EFFECTS

When you are writing about causes, be careful that you don't say something caused an event or situation just because it happened beforehand. For example, one summer night when I was a child, my family went out for ice cream, and I got a chocolate cone. Later that night I was sick to my stomach. It turned out that I had the flu, but it was many years before I would again eat chocolate ice cream, despite my mother's assurance that the cone I'd eaten did not cause my sickness. I had confused something that happened before a situation with its cause. In fact, one thing just happened before another. I would have been sick from the flu whether I had eaten chocolate ice cream or not.

When you are writing about effects, do not confuse something that happens after something else with the effect. Just as the chocolate ice cream did not cause me to get the flu, getting the flu was not the effect of eating the ice cream.

SUPPORT FOR CAUSE AND EFFECT

In a cause/effect essay, the causes and effects that you explain are the support points. They demonstrate the main point stated in your thesis. For example, the student who wrote the thesis *Irresponsible behavior caused my car accident* goes on to write about the following causes and explanations:

CAUSE: Driving too fast	**CAUSE**: Talking on my cell phone
It was rainy and slippery	Not paying close attention
Going too fast to control car	Hit a curve while laughing
Couldn't stop	Didn't react fast enough

CAUSE: Drinking

Not focused

Slowed reaction time

Each cause (or effect) is developed by supporting details that explain exactly how the situation happened.

ORDER OF IDEAS FOR CAUSE AND EFFECT

Cause/effect essays are often organized by **order of importance**, saving the most important or intense cause or effect for last in order to create a strong impression on the readers. The plan for a cause/effect essay generally looks like this:

For more on order of importance, see page 60.

Introduction (including thesis)

First cause or effect

explanation of cause or effect

Second cause or effect

explanation of cause or effect

Most important cause or effect

explanation of cause or effect

Conclusion

As you write your essay, add transitions to show how each cause or effect relates to your main point. Here are some common transitions that are used in cause/effect writing.

For more on transitions, see pages 94–96.

Common Transitions for Cause and Effect

one cause, reason, effect, result	first, second, third, and so on
also	as a result
another	because

Many situations require you to determine causes or effects. Here are some examples showing how you might find yourself considering causes and effects:

COLLEGE

- In an information technology course, you must discuss the effects of a virus on a local-area computer network.

WORK

- You analyze the likely effects of laying off 15 percent of your department's employees.

EVERYDAY LIFE

- You try to figure out what is causing your computer to freeze.

Read and Analyze Cause/Effect

Before writing your own cause/effect essay, read the following examples—one each from college, the workplace, and everyday life—and answer the questions that accompany each. Reading the examples and answering the questions will help you understand how to write a good cause/effect essay.

1. CAUSE AND EFFECT IN COLLEGE

A student wrote the following cause/effect essay for a political science course. The assignment, given in January 2002, asked students to write about the effects of the September 11, 2001, terrorist attacks on the World Trade Center in New York City and the Pentagon in Washington, D.C.

Life after the World Trade Center and Pentagon Attacks

James Freeman

As Americans watched the attacks on the World Trade Center and the Pentagon, many were heard to say, "The world as we know it will never be the same." Several months later, that statement is perhaps a little strong, but the terrorist attacks have produced significant changes in Americans' attitudes and behaviors.

One immediate effect of the attacks was felt by the airlines, as people shied away from flying. Airports were like ghost towns, even over the Thanksgiving holiday, which is traditionally the busiest air travel weekend of the year. Instead of flying, people drove to their destinations, took buses or trains, or simply stayed home. The bottom line for many commercial airlines, already in financial distress, plummeted even further. Some airlines consolidated, some went bankrupt, but all were significantly affected by the events of September 11.

The attacks also resulted in a recession much worse than what was already on the horizon. People stayed at home rather than going out for entertainment or to make unnecessary purchases. As people became more conservative and cautious, less money was flowing into an already unstable economy. Businesses closed up, and many people lost their jobs through the fall and into the winter. As a result, people's fiscal conservatism increased even more. More businesses have gone bankrupt in the new year, and we seem to be caught in a vicious cycle of decline as one bankruptcy stems from another.

The most significant, and perhaps the longest-lasting effect of September 11, however, is the loss of the naively secure attitude that most Americans—especially younger Americans—felt when they believed, "Nothing like that can happen here." It has happened, and it has forever changed the way we perceive our personal safety and security. As a student, I am now uncertain about what my major will be and what the future will, should, or could bring. For the first time, I feel that terrorist acts could occur at any time and to anyone. I'm more cautious, as if I'm always looking over my shoulder. I don't feel as certain about the future—even if there will be one. I go about my life, but I will never feel the same level of personal safety that I did before September 11, and that influences everything I do.

The world that most Americans knew never will be the same. Some of the effects of September 11, particularly on the economy or the airlines or the postal service, will lessen as time passes. But the belief that we are living at risk because we are within the reach of terrorism is here to stay. My world is still a very good one, but make no mistake, it is forever changed.

1. What is James's **purpose** for writing? _____

_____

For more on purpose and audience, see pages 7–9.

2. Who is James's **audience**? _____

3. Fill in the blanks with the **topic** and the **main point** of James's essay.

   TOPIC: _____

   MAIN POINT: _____

4. Double-underline the **thesis statement**.

5. Put a check mark (✓) next to each **topic sentence**. The topic sentences should be the causes or effects that the writer presents.

6. Underline the **details** that James gives to help the reader understand each effect.

7. What kind of **organization** (chronological, spatial, or importance) does

   James use? _____

8. Circle the (**transitions**) (words, phrases, and sentences) that James uses.

9. What **key words** does James repeat? _____

10. Double-underline the **sentence in the concluding paragraph** that ties the concluding paragraph to the introductory paragraph.

For a list of the four basics of good cause and effect, see page 224.

11. Does James's essay have the **four basics of good cause and effect**? Why or why not?

   _____

   _____

2. CAUSE AND EFFECT IN THE WORKPLACE

The following piece of writing is representative of the kinds of inspirational presentations that Jolanda Jones makes to students. She wants students to learn to think through their decisions and choices, so she talks about the causes and effects of certain actions, giving examples from her own experience. The piece is a speech—meant to be spoken and heard.

Some of the worst life situations I've seen were caused simply by people failing to consider the effects of their actions. Each of you in this room must learn for yourselves that every single decision you make has

consequences, whether you think much about it or not. It is super important that you think about the decisions you make **before** you make them
because if you don't, then you will end up somewhere you didn't plan for.
Take charge of your life by making informed and well-thought-out
decisions.

For me it seems like my best decisions are the ones I make when I
think my grandmother might find out about them. If I would be proud for
her to know the decision I've made, then it's probably a good decision. If
I have to sneak or would be ashamed for her to know my decision, then it
is probably a bad decision. In any case, here are some examples of the
thought process in good decision making. They show what happens when
you don't consider consequences.

Some of you girls might be getting pressured by your boyfriends to
have sex. What should you think about? Well, you're probably wondering
what he'll say if you don't sleep with him. Will he break up with you or
call you "Prude"? Well, don't let him define you. What if you get pregnant?
What if you get a sexually transmitted disease? What if you get AIDS?
What if you break up after you have sex with him? Will he tell everyone
how good you were in bed? Will everyone know your business?

Single parenthood is hard. I know from personal experience. I had
graduated from college, was working as a minority recruiter and admissions counselor and was training for the Olympics. I also planned to go to
law school at Stanford. Then I got pregnant without planning for it. All of
a sudden I was expecting a child with a man who was both abusive and
unsupportive. I was not married. I was disappointed in myself. I was
ashamed of the shame I brought on my grandmother. I was a coward. I
fled the United States and hid my pregnancy in Spain. I absolutely love
my son, but I gave up my Olympic aspirations and Stanford Law School.

Some of you might be thinking about using drugs. Think long and
hard. I have crackheads in my family whose lives have been destroyed.
Some are homeless. Some are dying of AIDS. My aunt was murdered
in a drug house. My brother was murdered buying marijuana. I have an
alcoholic cousin who does not take care of her children, and she is on
welfare. People who do drugs come to love drugs more than they love

anyone or anything else. Then the drugs control you. You lose control of your life.

What about crime, just little stuff, like shoplifting that little pair of earrings at the neighborhood Target. When I was sixteen, I'd worked to earn money to buy stuff I wanted. I wanted a pair of jeans. Instead my mother took my check for herself. I still thought I was entitled to the jeans, so I went to Target and took a pair. I got caught. I was arrested, handcuffed, put in the back of a patrol car and detained. I ducked my head down in the back of the patrol car. I just knew the whole world was looking at me. I was humiliated. I should have thought about the consequences. It wasn't right to steal from Target even if my mother took my check. You best believe I've thought about that ever since that date because I've never shoplifted again. I even told my son about it. I don't want him to make the same mistake that I did.

You have choices in life, and it's up to you to make the decisions that will most positively benefit your life. We are all capable of thinking through stuff and making the right decision. The question is: Are you gonna do it or are you gonna just take the easy road through life? My grandmother said, "If you make a bad decision, learn from it and move on, that way it's not your fault. If, however, you make the same mistake twice, you're stupid and it is your fault." I don't know about you, but I'm not stupid.

I've made good and bad decisions in my life. Thankfully, I've made more good ones than bad. I hope to continue to make good decisions by considering consequence and learning from my mistakes. I hope that's your philosophy too.

For more on audience and purpose, see pages 7–9.

1. Who is Jolanda's **audience**? _____

2. What is Jolanda's **purpose**? _____

_____

3. Double-underline the **thesis statement**.

4. Put a check mark (✓) next to each **topic sentence** for the body paragraphs of the essay.

5. Use the ring diagrams to show one of the situations Jolanda presents, along with the causes or effects.

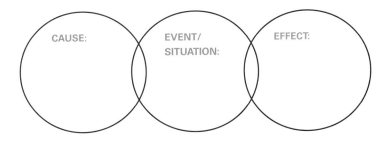

3. CAUSE AND EFFECT IN EVERYDAY LIFE

The following is an example of cause/effect writing in everyday life. In this case, a man has consulted his physician about several health problems that he believes might be caused by the new carpeting and cubicles at his workplace. The doctor writes a letter to the man's employer.

July 2, 2002

To Whom It May Concern:

The health of one of my patients, George Hanson, is being seriously affected by conditions in the offices of Kirkland Brothers. I am recommending that Mr. Hanson apply immediately for short-term disability to separate himself from the unhealthful environment that allegedly includes harmful chemicals and poor ventilation. Over the course of the next few weeks, I will closely monitor his symptoms, all of which have appeared since Mr. Hanson began work at Kirkland Brothers.

One of the symptoms is a dull but constant headache that Mr. Hanson develops each day within an hour of arriving at work. The pain is centered in the sinus passages above the eyes and is a growing annoyance, making it difficult for Mr. Hanson to concentrate on his work.

A more severe symptom is a chronic watering and stinging of Mr. Hanson's eyes. This condition is not merely unpleasant; it has advanced to a burning sensation and has affected Mr. Hanson's eyesight. The condition disappears a few hours after his shift ends every night.

The most serious medical effect is the impact on Mr. Hanson's lungs. His breathing is labored, and he has become asthmatic, although he has no previous history of lung or breathing problems. Unlike his sight, Mr. Hanson's asthma is progressively worsening, and he now depends on the frequent use of inhalers.

Given the range and intensity of Mr. Hanson's symptoms and the appearance that they are connected to the interior of Kirkland Brothers, I recommend that he remain away from the building until further medical testing can be completed. If you have further questions, please do not hesitate to contact me.

Sincerely,

Althea Sedoris, M.D.

For more on purpose and audience, see pages 7–9.

1. What is the **purpose** of the doctor's letter? _____

_____

2. Who is the **audience**? _____

3. Which does the doctor discuss: causes or effects? _____

4. Put a check mark (✓) next to the **topic sentences** that are the major causes or effects.

5. Underline the **details** that support the causes or effects.

6. Circle the (**transitions**).

7. What **key words** are repeated? _____

Write a Cause/Effect Essay

In this section, you will write your own cause/effect essay. To do so, follow this sequence:

REVIEW the four basics of good cause/effect writing (p. 224).

CHOOSE your writing assignment (p. 235).

WRITE your cause/effect essay using the step-by-step Writing Guide (p. 237).

CHECK your final essay (p. 241).

WRITING ASSIGNMENT 1   **COLLEGE, WORK, EVERYDAY LIFE**

Write a cause/effect essay on *one* of the following topics or on a topic of your own choice.

COLLEGE

- Immediate effects of being in college, or the desired long-term effects of going to college
- Causes of a legitimate absence that resulted in your missing a test (directed to your professor)
- Probable causes of a poor grade or a good grade

WORK

- Causes of low employee morale
- Causes, effects, or both of a situation at work
- Causes and effects of stress at work

EVERYDAY LIFE

- Causes of an argument with a friend or a member of your family
- Effects of a bad decision you or someone you know made (refer to the idea journal assignment at the start of this chapter)
- Effects of a particular drug

 WRITING ASSIGNMENT 2   **USE THE INTERNET**

Choose an illness or disorder that has affected you or someone you know. Use the Internet to find out about why it occurs and what happens because of it. Then, in your own words, write an essay in which you discuss the causes, effects, or both of the illness or disorder you have chosen to investigate.

As you search, be as specific as possible about the topic. For example, if you want to find out what causes abuse in families, try entering a term such as *spouse abuse, domestic abuse,* or *child abuse* in the search field of a search engine such as Google or Lycos. Keep narrowing your search until you find information that you want, and bookmark useful sites you may want to return to later.

For advice about how to cite a source, see Chapter 20.

WRITING ASSIGNMENT 3   AN ACTION PLAN

Read the problem and situation that follow, and then choose *one* of the assignment options (3A or 3B) that appear after it.

> PROBLEM: Some of us are so busy just trying to cope with our present lives that we don't have time to think about or plan for the future. As a result, we don't always act in ways that will get us where we want to be.

> SITUATION: You have finally decided to make planning your future a priority. You know you need to think carefully about where you want to be or what you want to do and how you might get there. Start by identifying a particular goal you have for yourself. Consider the actions or behaviors that will result in (cause) that goal to happen or the benefits that will come from (be effects of) achieving that goal. Use a ring diagram like the one on page 226 to help you do this.

ASSIGNMENT OPTION 3A: RESPOND TO THE SITUATION

First think hard about something concrete that you would like to achieve, something that will be a challenge but that you believe will be worth the time and effort it takes. Choosing a topic may be the most difficult part of the assignment because it involves thinking about a future goal instead of living only in the present. The goal should be something that really matters to you. It doesn't have to be unique or earth shattering: Maybe you want to lose weight, stop smoking, get some regular exercise, or spend more time with your family. Maybe you want to make more money, spend less on useless things, or get a new car or new job. Spend some time thinking about a goal that is important to you.

    Then write an essay that identifies and gives details about what actions you could take to make this goal happen.

ASSIGNMENT OPTION 3B: ANOTHER PERSPECTIVE

Rather than making an action plan for yourself, consider instead another person whom you care about (pick a real friend or family member with a real problem). One way in which friends can help each other is to suggest alternatives to destructive behaviors. In this essay, identify a problem that a friend or family member has, and then suggest positive effects of addressing the problem or changing the behavior.

Cause and Effect

Writing Guide

Follow the steps in this Writing Guide to help you prewrite, draft, revise, and edit your cause and effect essay. Check off each step as you complete it.

THINKING CRITICALLY ABOUT CAUSE AND EFFECT

FOCUS   Think about a topic that matters to you and whether you want to describe its causes, its effects, or both.

ASK   • Who are my readers? Who are the people I am writing for?
   • Are my causes *real* causes, not just events that happened before? Are my effects *real* effects, not just events that follow?
   • What examples and details do I need to give in order to make the causes and effects stand out?
   • How should I organize the essay? Should I arrange the causes and effects by order of importance, chronologically, or in some other way?

PREWRITE TO EXPLORE YOUR TOPIC

Prewriting for cause and effect involves thinking about the actual causes of an event or the actual results of it, as opposed to an event that came before another event but didn't really cause it or came after it but was not an effect of it.

_____ Decide on your purpose for writing.

_____ Identify the audience for your essay.

_____ Jot down some ideas about a situation that affects you. Using the ring diagram as a prewriting technique works well for cause and effect.

_____ Consider how the situation occurred and what will happen because of it.

For more on purpose and audience, see pages 7–9.

WRITE A THESIS STATEMENT

The thesis statement in a cause/effect essay usually includes the topic and your main point about it. To state your main point clearly in a cause/effect essay, you might use a word such as *because, cause, reason, result,* or *effect* in your thesis statement.

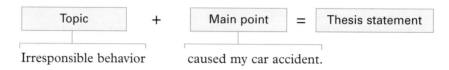

| Topic | + | Main point | = | Thesis statement |

Irresponsible behavior   caused my car accident.

Note that the above writer groups the items in the "causes" ring in the ring diagram (see page 226) for this topic into the more general term *irresponsible behavior.*

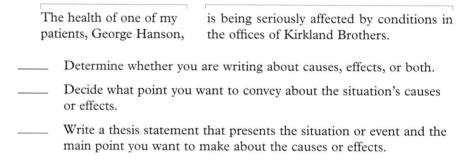

The health of one of my patients, George Hanson,   is being seriously affected by conditions in the offices of Kirkland Brothers.

_____ Determine whether you are writing about causes, effects, or both.

_____ Decide what point you want to convey about the situation's causes or effects.

_____ Write a thesis statement that presents the situation or event and the main point you want to make about the causes or effects.

SUPPORT YOUR POINT

The major support points in a cause/effect essay are the causes, effects, or both that you present to demonstrate your main point.

The supporting details explain how the cause or effect you have identified directly caused the situation or resulted from it. The explanations are important because they tell your readers *how* the causes or effects relate to the situation.

_____ List the most important causes or effects of a situation.

_____ For each cause or effect, give an example and details about how it caused or resulted from the event or situation. Think about what information and explanation your reader needs to know.

MAKE A PLAN

Making a written plan—an outline—helps you decide how to order your cause and effect. A cause/effect essay often uses order of importance to arrange causes or effects. By building up to the most important point, the essay creates a strong final impression on readers.

_____ Make a plan or outline for your essay that arranges the causes and effects in order of importance, from least to most significant, or in some other logical order.

_____ Include explanations of each cause and effect in your plan.

DRAFT

Drafting a cause/effect essay means writing in complete sentences and including the following:

- An introduction with a thesis statement that communicates your topic and main point about it
- The causes, effects, or both for the situation, with detailed explanations
- A conclusion

_____ Think about how you can present the causes or effects so that your readers clearly understand your main point.

_____ Write an introductory paragraph that includes your thesis statement and interests your readers in finding out more about the causes or effects of a particular situation or event.

_____ Write a topic sentence for each of the causes or effects.

_____ Write body paragraphs that present and carefully explain each cause or effect.

_____ Write a strong conclusion that refers back to your main point and makes a final observation.

_____ Title your essay.

REVISE

Revising means changing whole sentences or paragraphs to make your writing clearer or stronger. To revise a cause and effect essay, imagine that you have no idea what caused or resulted from the situation. Read your draft, looking for the following:

- Places where the ideas are off the main point (revising for unity)
- Gaps in information or detail (revising for support and detail)

• Areas in need of transitions to move readers smoothly from one point to the next (revising for coherence)

For more on peer review, see pages 87–88.

_____ Get feedback from others through peer review.

_____ Begin revising by asking yourself how you could make your causes and effects clearer for your readers.

_____ Reread your thesis statement, and make changes so that it has more impact on your readers.

_____ Reread the body of your cause and effect essay to see whether the causes or effects are directly related to the situation or event. Be sure that each is clearly explained, based on what you know about your readers. Add other details that would help explain the causes or effects.

_____ Reread your introduction to make sure that it is as effective as possible.

_____ Reread your conclusion to make sure that it is energetic and convincing, that it reminds your readers of your main point, and makes a final observation.

_____ Add transition words and sentences to connect your ideas and lead readers smoothly from one to another.

_____ Decide whether repeating key words would increase your emphasis.

_____ Make at least five changes to your draft to improve the unity, support, or coherence or to make the introduction, thesis statement, or conclusion stronger or more convincing.

EDIT

Some grammar, spelling, word use, or punctuation errors may confuse your readers and make it difficult for them to understand a point you are trying to make. Even if they do not confuse your readers, errors detract from the effectiveness and overall quality of your writing. Edit your cause/effect essay carefully, and correct any errors you find.

_____ Ask a classmate or friend to read your cause/effect essay and highlight any errors.

_____ Use the spell checker and grammar checker on your computer.

_____ Look yourself for errors that the spell checker or grammar checker didn't catch. Focus first on sentence fragments, run-on sentences, problems with subject–verb agreement, problems with verbs, and other areas where you know you often make errors.

_____ Print a clean, final copy.

_____ Ask yourself: Is this the best I can do?

A FINAL CHECK BEFORE HANDING IN YOUR CAUSE/EFFECT ESSAY

If you've followed the Writing Guide for cause and effect, your essay will already include the four basics of good cause and effect. Use this list to double-check each basic feature.

_____ My thesis clearly distinguishes causes and effects.

_____ The causes in my essay are real causes, not just events that happened before another event.

_____ The effects in my essay are real effects, not just events that happened after another event.

_____ The body of my essay includes clear and detailed examples of the causes, effects, or both that I have considered.

16

Argument

Writing That Persuades

Understand What Argument Is

DEFINITION: **Argument** is writing that takes a position on an issue and offers reasons and supporting evidence to persuade someone else to accept, or at least consider, the position. Argument is also used to convince someone to take an action (or not to take an action).

■■ Four Basics of Good Argument

1. It takes a strong and definite position on an issue or advises a particular action.
2. It gives good reasons and supporting evidence to defend the position or recommended action.
3. It considers opposing views.
4. It has enthusiasm and energy from start to finish.

Knowing how to argue is critical. We use argument every day as a way to persuade someone to lend us something or to do something for us. We present an argument to persuade someone to give us a job, or not to give us a parking ticket, to buy something we're selling, or to give us more time. And we argue when something important is at stake, like keeping a job or

Profile of Success

Wayne Whitaker

ASSISTANT DIRECTOR OF ADMISSIONS

Wayne Whitaker

BACKGROUND: Wayne grew up in New York City's South Bronx and Brooklyn. School was difficult for him, and most of his classes were in the vocational/technical program. At the end of his senior year, Wayne told his guidance counselor that he wanted to go to college. Although his grades weren't good, he was admitted to Bloomsburg University through a special admissions program, ACT 101. Wayne, now a recruiter for the school he attended, helps others also gain admission to Bloomsburg University.

EMPLOYER: Bloomsburg University

COLLEGE(S)/DEGREES: Bloomsburg University (B.A. and M.S.)

TYPES OF WRITING ON THE JOB: Letters to students telling them about Bloomsburg and encouraging them to apply; federal and state grant proposals for recruitment programs; reports to administration and granting agencies; frequent emails; presentations to prospective students

HOW WAYNE USES ARGUMENT: It is part of Wayne's job to convince students to apply to and attend Bloomsburg. He does this through persuasive letters, presentations, and personal conversations. For an example of how Wayne uses argument, see Argument in the Workplace, on page 254.

COMPUTER SKILLS: Word processing, PowerPoint, Web design

TEAMWORK ON THE JOB: Wayne says, "Recruitment can't be done by a single person: It requires a unified team effort." As a recruiter, he works with high school guidance counselors, colleagues, the athletic department, and other offices. To ensure successful campus visits, he works with everyone from maintenance and cafeteria staff to faculty and administration.

FUTURE GOAL: Wayne says, "[My goal is] to be director of admissions and then to broaden my role and become a dean of student life."

protecting our rights. To argue effectively, we need to do more than just say what we want or believe; we need to give solid reasons and evidence.

Argument is the method you use to persuade people to see things your way, or at least to understand your position. Argument helps you to take action in problem situations, rather than standing by, silent and frustrated. Although knowing how to argue won't eliminate all such situations, it will help you to defend your position.

ENERGY AND ENTHUSIASM FOR A STRONG POSITION

The topic of an argument is the issue you are writing about. In order for something to be an issue, it has to be something that people have different opinions about. A good argument starts with a strong and definite position on an issue. As a writer, you need to be very clear about what your position is so that you can take a stand and defend that position with energy.

When you are free to choose an issue to write about, choose something you care about or are interested in. But even when you are assigned an issue, you still need to defend it powerfully by finding some aspect of it that you care about.

Take a few minutes to either think about the issue, talk it over with a partner, or jot down ideas related to it. Here are some tips to get you started.

Tips for Building Energy and Enthusiasm

- Imagine yourself arguing your position with someone who holds the opposite position.
- Imagine that your whole grade rests on persuading your teacher of your position.
- Imagine how this issue could affect you or your family personally.
- Imagine that you are representing a large group of people who very much care about the issue and whose lives will be forever changed by it. It's up to you to win their case.

A THESIS STATEMENT OF YOUR POSITION

Your thesis statement in an argument presents your position on the issue. It should include the topic (the issue you are writing about) and your position.

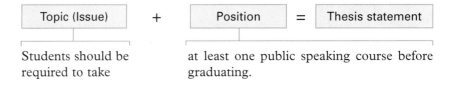

| Topic (Issue) | + | Position | = | Thesis statement |

Students should be required to take   at least one public speaking course before graduating.

Many thesis statements for arguments use words such as the following because they clearly express a position:

could (not)	ought (not)
must (not)	requires
must have	should (not)
needs	would

For more on writing a thesis statement, see Chapter 3.

PRACTICE 1   WRITING A STATEMENT OF YOUR POSITION

Write your position on the following issues.

Lowering the drinking age to eighteen _____

_____

Mandatory drug testing as a requirement for employment _____

_____

Bilingual education at every grade level _____

_____

_____

Now take one of the position statements that you just wrote and put more

energy into it. _____

_____

When you start to write your argument, you need to be clear about your position—and make your readers clear about it too.

SUPPORT FOR YOUR POSITION

DEFINITION: **Reasons** are the points that support your position, points that must be backed up with evidence.

　DEFINITION: **Evidence** consists of the **facts and statistics, examples,** and **expert opinions** that support your reasons.

　The strength of your argument depends on the quality of the reasons and evidence that you present to support your position.

For more on supporting a thesis, see Chapter 4.

Facts: Accurate information that can be verified. Statistics—numerical facts based on research—can be persuasive evidence to back up your position.

> POSITION: It pays to stay in college.
>
> REASON: College graduates earn more than high school graduates.
>
> > EVIDENCE/FACT: College graduates earn 58 percent more than high school graduates and 320 percent more than high school dropouts.

Examples: Stories and experiences that directly support your position.

> POSITION: It pays to stay in college.
>
> REASON: Students learn up-to-date skills that they will need to find a job.
>
> > EVIDENCE/EXAMPLE: Understanding how to use technology in your field may make the difference between getting a job and coming in second.

Expert Opinion: The testimony of someone who is considered knowledgeable in the field. The person must be known for his or her expertise in the area you are writing about. For example, a doctor's opinion on the effects of a certain drug is more convincing support than a movie star's. *Note:* Just because a person's opinion appears on a Web site does not mean that he or she has any expertise. Find out about the person's credentials before using his or her words as expert opinion.

> POSITION: It pays to stay in college.
>
> REASON: An increasing number of jobs require college degrees.
>
> > EVIDENCE/EXPERT OPINION: John Sterling, president of one of the largest recruiting agencies, said recently, "Ten years ago, a college degree was perceived as an advantage. Today, the college degree is the basic ticket of entry for the majority of jobs." *Note:* When you use expert opinion, you need to identify the source of the quote.

For more on using quotations and citing sources, see Chapters 20 and 21.

For more on finding sources, see Chapter 20.

As you choose reasons and evidence to support your position, consider what your audience is likely to think about your stand on the issue. Are they likely to agree with you, to be uncommitted, or to be hostile? Think about what kinds of reasons and evidence would be most convincing to a typical member of your audience.

OPPOSING POSITIONS

When you write your thesis, you state your position on the issue. The rest of your essay should be devoted to supporting that position. Part of supporting your own position, however, is acknowledging the opposing position and presenting some evidence against it.

If, for example, you are arguing in favor of lowering the drinking age in your state to eighteen, you should not ignore the position that it should be kept at age twenty-one. If you don't say anything about the other position, you are leaving your argument unprotected. To defend your own position, you need to acknowledge the opposing view and address it by showing some weakness in it or another way of looking at it.

POSITION:	The drinking age should be lowered to eighteen.
OPPOSING POSITION:	The drinking age should not be lowered because people begin drinking before the legal age. If the age were lowered to eighteen, more sixteen-year-olds would drink.

RESPONSE TO THE OPPOSING POSITION: Laws should not be based on the extent to which they are abused or broken. Enforcement (or lack of enforcement) should not influence the law itself.

STATEMENTS THAT ACKNOWLEDGE AND ADDRESS OPPOSING POSITION:

Some people feel strongly that the drinking age should not be lowered because, if drinking is legal at eighteen, teenagers will start drinking at sixteen. While many teenagers do in fact drink before it is legal to do so, there is no evidence to show that the higher legal age has anything to do with the age at which teenagers start to drink. Other factors involved, such as peer pressure and the availability of fake ID's, have more impact on whether teenagers drink. Laws should not be based on ease of enforcement. Otherwise, our legal system would be a joke.

Acknowledge opposing position

Address the opposing position

While some people believe that lowering the legal drinking age will lower the age that teenagers start drinking, there is no evidence to show that the legal age is a major influence on teenaged drinking. (Writer then gives other evidence such as in the above paragraph.)

PRACTICE 2   ACKNOWLEDGING AND ADDRESSING THE OPPOSING VIEW

For each of the following positions, in the spaces indicated, state the opposing position and at least one point someone holding the opposing view might make against your position.

ISSUE:	The "Three Strikes and You're Out" rule in some high schools that says students are expelled after three serious offenses
POSITION:	Against it

OPPOSING POSITION: _____

POINT THAT SOMEONE HOLDING THE OPPOSING POSITION WOULD MAKE: _____

_____

ISSUE: Mandatory retirement at age sixty-five
POSITION: In favor of it

OPPOSING POSITION: _____

POINT THAT SOMEONE HOLDING THE OPPOSING POSITION WOULD MAKE: _____

_____

ISSUE: Stricter gun control laws
POSITION: Against it

OPPOSING POSITION: _____

POINT THAT SOMEONE HOLDING THE OPPOSING POSITION WOULD MAKE: _____

_____

Writing a good argument is like arguing a case in court. A lawyer representing one side not only builds his or her own case but also tries to anticipate what the opposing lawyer will say and how to weaken the opposing lawyer's case. In a short essay, you may not be able to address all the points of the opposing view, but you should know what they are and address at least the most important point.

As you gather support for your position, keep the opposing position in mind and follow the tips given in the box.

Tips for Supporting Your Position by Addressing the Opposing Position

•   Visualize someone who holds the opposing position and what that person would say to defend it.

•   In part of the body of your essay, acknowledge the opposing position. Do so politely; if you try to ridicule the opposing view, you will alienate people and immediately weaken your argument.

•   Poke some holes in the opposing position by addressing it head-on and showing what's wrong, or misguided, about the position. Again, do this politely; don't make your opposition look foolish.

•   Return to the reasons and the evidence that support your position.

ORDER OF IDEAS FOR ARGUMENT

Argument most often uses order of importance to organize reasons for the writer's position on the issue. Consider what you think your readers will find your most convincing reason. Think about how you can arrange the reasons and evidence so that they build the strongest case for your position. Save the most convincing reason for last.

For more on order of importance, see page 60.

Do not forget to acknowledge and address the opposing position. Where you do that within the body of your essay depends on where it will have the most impact on your readers. Some writers acknowledge and address the opposing position for each reason they give; others may choose to do so in a separate paragraph. You have to be the judge of where and how, but you must acknowledge and address the opposing position or your argument is not adequately supported.

The plan for an argument often looks like this:

Introduction (including thesis)

First reason

    evidence and information to back up reason

Second reason

    evidence and information to back up reason

Most important reason

    evidence and information to back up reason

Conclusion

    reminds readers of your position on the issue and makes a final pitch for that position

    may also make a further recommendation or issue a warning about what will happen if your position is ignored or defeated

As you write your argument, use transitions to connect your reasons to your thesis and your evidence to your reasons.

For more on transitions, see pages 94–97.

Here are some transitions often used for argument.

Common Transitions in Argument

TRANSITIONS FROM ONE POINT TO ANOTHER	TRANSITIONS TO ADD EMPHASIS
also	above all
another fact to consider	best of all
another reason	especially

(continued)

Common Transitions in Argument

TRANSITIONS FROM ONE POINT TO ANOTHER	TRANSITIONS TO ADD EMPHASIS
another thing	in fact
consider that	in particular
for example	more important
in addition	most important
in the first place	remember
	the last point to consider
	worst of all

Putting together a good argument is one of the most useful skills you can learn. Knowing how to argue well will equip you to defend effectively what you believe and to convince others to support your opinion. Many situations require good argument skills:

COLLEGE

- An essay exam question in a human services course asks you to agree or disagree, using information from the course, with the following statement: "Government agencies should not have the authority to separate families."
- You present reasons why you should be able to make up a test that you missed.
- An exit essay from a writing course contains the following instruction: "Develop a well-balanced argument on the subject of free speech on the Internet."

WORK

- You present reasons why you should get a raise.
- You negotiate a better benefits package than the one that was offered.
- You give a customer or client reasons why he or she should invest in your company's product or services.

EVERYDAY LIFE

- You convince a large company that it has made a mistake on your bill.
- You persuade a child to share a favorite toy with a friend.
- You take a stand on a local issue or policy that you believe is unfair.

Read and Analyze Argument

Before writing your own argument essay, read the following examples—one each from college, the workplace, and everyday life—and answer the questions that accompany each. Reading the examples and answering the questions will help you understand how to write a good argument essay.

1. ARGUMENT IN COLLEGE

The following is an essay written by a student for her English composition course. Since the writer, Edna Crespo, consulted several sources as she wrote, her essay includes a list of works cited.

For more on writing from sources, see Chapter 21.

How Violence on TV Affects Children and Adolescents

Edna Crespo

"Children who watch the violent shows, even 'just funny cartoons,' are more likely to hit out at their playmates, argue, disobey class rules, leave tasks unfinished, and be less willing to wait for things than those who watch nonviolent programs," says Aletha Huston, Ph.D., now at the University of Kansas. Nearly five violent scenes are displayed during one hour of prime time shows. There is violence even in many cartoons. Several studies in North America of children who watch violent television programs consistently reveal that they are directly affected by televised violence. Violent programming negatively affects youth, changing children's interests, making them less sensitive to the pain of others, and teaching them to be aggressive toward others.

The impact of aggressive television programs upon children may be so strong that it can cause them to lose interest in many other activities. The passive activity of watching violence on television often becomes more attractive to children than socializing or participating in outdoor activities. Specifically, community programs, such as various sports or outdoor excursions, appear less interesting to them. They also spend less time playing with friends, reading, and doing homework. Because of their lack of activity, they have the tendency to become idle and overweight. Furthermore, "many adolescents admit that they just find it very difficult to turn off the TV. . . . They recognize the seductive power of the medium" (Ledingham).

In addition, several studies have shown that most children who are exposed to violent scenes become less sensitive to the suffering of people and more tolerant of aggressiveness. For example, studies of some children who watched heavy violence on television found them "slower to intervene or to call for help when they saw younger children fighting or playing destructively" (Huston). They seem not to be bothered by violent acts. Actually, they tolerate aggressive behavior as if it were common and acceptable.

Worst of all is that too much exposure to television violence induces aggressiveness in children. By watching violent television shows, children's aggressiveness is increased, sometimes to dangerous levels. It seems that they think this is the normal pattern of behavior in everyday life, and they copy this hostile conduct at home with family members and friends. There are cases in which children have harmed classmates in an attempt to mimic a fight or a particular maneuver shown on a television program. For example, Aaron Auffhammer, an eight-year-old boy, was victimized by his own classmates when they tried to imitate some violent actions they had seen in a television show. Aaron's mother, Mykie Auffhammer, explained, "After being tripped by a kid, Aaron was trying to get up when a third kid picked up his legs so that he was upside down, and then slammed his head on the ground" (Brossett). Aaron was harmed and could have been seriously injured by children of his own age who were simply trying out something they had seen.

While some people argue that any monitoring of violent behavior in television goes against the principle of free speech, I wonder what those people say about the impact on children. Is free speech more important than helping children to become good, responsible, healthy adults? Is the violent content of so many television programs necessary to ensure free expression?

For eighteen years, I have worked in the marketing and advertising business, and I know how powerful television can be in influencing and teaching values and shaping behaviors in children and adolescents. The television broadcasts in the intimacy of our homes can help to establish close relationships between parents and children. Unfortunately, this power is not frequently used to build positive qualities and feelings.

Instead, violent scenes predominate in a culture where billions of dollars are made by this industry. What is violent television doing to us? It is making lots of money while destructively shaping the values of children.

Works Cited

Brossett, Tonja. "Does Violence on Television Affect Our Kids?" 23 Apr. 2001 <www.parenthoodweb.com>.

Huston, Aletha, Ph.D. "Violence on Television." 23 Apr. 2001 <www.apa.org/pubinfo/violence.html>.

Ledingham, Jane, Dr. "The Effect of Media Violence on Children." The National Clearinghouse on Family Violence. 23 Apr. 2001 <www.media.awareness.ca/eng/med>.

1. What is Edna's **purpose**? _____

_____

For more on purpose and audience, see pages 7–9.

2. Who is Edna's **audience**? _____

3. Fill in the blanks with the **issue** and Edna's **position** on the issue.

   ISSUE: _____

   POSITION: _____

4. Double-underline the **thesis statement**.

5. What kind of **introductory technique** does Edna use to get the

   reader's attention? _____

6. Put a check mark (✓) next to each **topic sentence**.

7. What kinds of **support** (facts, examples, expert opinion) does Edna use

   to demonstrate her thesis statement? _____

   _____

8. In what paragraph does Edna acknowledge the **opposing position**?

   _____

9. What **order of organization** does Edna use? _____

10. Circle the (transitions) in the essay.

For a list of the four basics of good argument, see page 242.

11. Edna does not have a sentence in her concluding paragraph that relates back to her introduction. Write one that would do so, and indicate where you would place it in the concluding paragraph.

_____

_____

_____

12. Does Edna's essay have the **four basics of good argument**? Why or why not?

_____

_____

2. ARGUMENT IN THE WORKPLACE

Some of the argument writing you do in college will involve issues that you are passionate about and that directly affect you. In the workplace, you may be less passionate about the topic, but you still use the principles of good argument regularly, perhaps even more than you do in college. When you work with others and your success depends on what they do, hardly a day will go by when you don't use argument strategies to persuade someone of something.

The following letter to a student is similar to ones that Wayne Whitaker writes when he is trying to convince a student to apply to Bloomsburg University. One measure of Wayne's success at his job is how many students enroll for each new class, so it is important that he convince people to apply. Note how Wayne uses what he knows about his audience, the student Ms. Petrona, to present reasons that will be important to her.

Dear Ms. Petrona:

I'm glad that we had an opportunity to talk during your recent visit to Bloomsburg University. Based on our conversation, I am convinced that Bloomsburg is the ideal college for you. I hope to convince you of that, too.

Bloomsburg University will offer you unparalleled support that will help you adjust to and succeed in college. We discussed the fact that you feel a little intimidated by the whole idea of college. Well, Ms. Petrona, you certainly aren't alone in that feeling, and I can assure you that we have the resources you need to set you on the strong course. Our ACT 101 summer program will ensure that you have the basic skills you need for your first-year courses. Your ACT 101 counselor will be your mentor and adviser throughout college, a wise and savvy guide who is there to help you with any issue. As one of our ACT 101 graduates, Roberta Connoni, said, "I wouldn't have made it in college without ACT 101. The people there gave me the information and confidence I needed to believe I could get a college degree."

Bloomsburg University also has a very strong business program that should be attractive to you since you are interested in majoring in business. Our courses are small, so you receive individual attention. Many of our faculty members are also working professionals who have real-life experience to bring to the classroom. And the university has strong relationships with local and state businesses. Last year, 85 percent of our business majors had received job offers prior to graduation.

Bloomsburg University is a community, not just an institution. Our rural location helps us focus on our shared purpose: to learn and develop as citizens. We are a community of learners rather than some buildings set among other city buildings. This setting reinforces our mission and joins us all in the mission of learning.

Ms. Petrona, you will thrive here. Based on your background and the needs you cited, Bloomsburg is a perfect match. We are eager to welcome you to our community and will look forward to helping you achieve your best.

1. What is Wayne's **purpose**? _____

_____

For more on purpose and audience, see pages 7–9.

2. What do you learn about Wayne's **audience** from his letter? _____

_____

3. What issue is Wayne writing about? What is his position on that issue?

_____

_____

4. Double-underline his **thesis statement**.

5. Put a check mark (✓) next to his **topic sentences.**

6. Underline the **evidence** that supports his reasons.

7. Is there any obvious organization to the argument? _____

_____

3. ARGUMENT IN EVERYDAY LIFE

The following is the body of a letter that one Philadelphia-area resident wrote to the chair of the school committee in her town.

I am painfully aware that violence in schools is a clear and present danger, in our town as everywhere. I realize that schools must take precautions to ensure the safety of their students. However, recent events in our schools make me wonder whether we have overreacted to the threat of violence and have lost our common sense. With the enactment of new rules, we must make sure that common sense still prevails as the judge of what is punishable behavior.

Common sense dictates that there are legitimate exceptions to every rule. Many items are banned from school for good reason: guns, knives, and so on. The penalty for having any contraband item is immediate suspension. These rules make sense. But what of the young woman, a diabetic, at the high school who was suspended for having a needle? It was part of her medical kit—she gives herself daily injections of insulin. Does it make sense to suspend her without consideration of the circumstances?

Common sense also dictates that a student should not be punished for fulfilling an assignment. What about the student whose teacher made an assignment to write an imaginative short story, a horror story, with details that made it lifelike and truly scary. When the student wrote a powerful short story about a student who stalks and then murders an English teacher, the student was suspended because of the threat to the teacher. Maybe the student didn't use the best judgment, but was there a punishable act?

In both of the above cases, the students were eventually reinstated, but not without a good deal of trauma and embarrassment for everyone involved. What message does that send to our students? I believe that common sense is a key element to good judgment, something I want my children to learn. What are they learning when common sense goes out the window? As adults, we need to apply common sense, particularly in the schools, our institutions of learning.

1. What is the writer's **purpose** in this letter? _____

_____

For more on purpose and audience, see pages 7–9.

2. What does the letter suggest about the writer's **audience**? _____

_____

3. What is the issue that the writer discusses? _____

_____

4. What is the writer's position on the issue? _____

_____

5. Double-underline the **thesis statement**.

6. Put a check mark (✓) next to each **topic sentence**.

7. Does the writer offer convincing evidence? Why or why not? _____

_____

Write an Argument Essay

In this section you will write your own argument essay. To do so, follow this sequence:

REVIEW the basics of good argument (p. 242).

CHOOSE your writing assignment (below).

WRITE your argument using the step-by-step Writing Guide (p. 261).

CHECK your final essay (p. 265).

WRITING ASSIGNMENT 1   COLLEGE, WORK, EVERYDAY LIFE

Write an argument essay on *one* of the following topics or on a topic of your own choice. Select an issue that you care about so that you can argue powerfully.

COLLEGE

- Persuade the college president to make a change that would help students.
- Persuade one of your teachers to raise the grade on your last assignment (in a course you are currently taking).
- Defend the following statement: "A college degree means something."

WORK

- Argue against a company policy that you believe is unfair.
- Laws in many states prohibit an employer from sharing information with another employer about a former employee—even if the individual was dangerous. Agree or disagree with that policy.
- Argue that you should get a promotion.

EVERYDAY LIFE

- Argue for or against a 7:00 A.M. starting time at the local high school.
- Argue against a rent increase.
- Argue for or against tobacco companies being sued by cancer patients.

WRITING ASSIGNMENT 2 USE THE INTERNET

For advice about how to cite a source, see Chapter 20.

Visit a Web site devoted to taking action on some controversial issue. Spend time reading through the site's home page, mission statement, action plan, and headlines. Then write an essay in which you take a position on the issue. You can agree or disagree with the sponsors of the site you have investigated. Here is a brief list of Web sites that tackle controversial issues:

People for the Ethical Treatment of Animals **<www.peta.org>** (Click on "Action alerts" or "Campaigns" from the home page.)

The American Civil Liberties Union's Freedom Network page on racial profiling **<www.aclu.org/profiling>**

Freedom From Religion Foundation page on school prayer **<www.ffrf.org/issues>**

Physicians for Compassionate Care, an organization of health professionals against assisted suicide **<www.pccef.org>**

WRITING ASSIGNMENT 3   **ARGUMENT WRITING TESTS**

Many states and colleges require students to take a timed writing test. Often the test calls for an argument essay on an assigned topic, and students must argue pro (for) or con (against), as directed. Many people believe that a good writer should be able to argue either side of an issue regardless of his or her personal feelings. Choose one of the following questions, come up with evidence to support both sides of the issue, and write an essay defending one side or another. *Note:* Part of the requirement of the essay is to be able to support each side, so you will need to turn in the support you develop for each side of the position.

- Should students be penalized for poor attendance?
- Should the government make it more difficult for couples to divorce?
- Should personal email messages written on a company's computer be company property or personal property?

 WRITING ASSIGNMENT 4   **THE COLLEGE COUNCIL**

Read the problem and situation that follow, as well as "David's Problem," and "The President's Instructions." Then choose *one* of the assignment options to write about.

PROBLEM: At some point, we all find ourselves in ethical dilemmas, where we are presented with a situation that pulls us in different directions, but about which we need to make a decision one way or the other. Understanding argument helps us make thoughtful choices as we weigh evidence to reach a conclusion. Although in difficult situations we may not feel completely easy with our decision, we know that that decision is based on careful consideration of everything involved and that we've done our best.

SITUATION: You are a student representative to the College Council, which reviews requests and issues that affect the college as a whole. The college president opens today's session by saying, "We have before us a difficult question to consider that affects not only the student involved but others as well." The president then describes the situation.

Professor McNamara teaches English 100A, the basic writing course in the English department. All students must pass the course before they can be accepted into a degree program. A student in Professor McNamara's course, David K., has made a request that the professor does not feel she can grant without advisement by the College Council.

DAVID'S PROBLEM: David is a mechanic at a large automotive repair center. He has a wife and four children, one of whom has a chronic illness that requires expensive medical treatments. In order to pay for the treatments, David must either make more money or sign up for welfare assistance. David recently applied for a supervisor position at the center where he works. The position includes a substantial pay raise, but the company requires its management to have a degree in automotive engineering. Because David is a good worker, the boss will make an exception to the rule *if* David enrolls in a degree program.

David is failing English 100A, a prerequisite for enrolling in the automotive engineering degree program. He attends every class, does all the homework, and completes all the writing assignments, but his writing is so poor that he receives F's. He has finally approached Professor McNamara, hoping that she will give him a passing grade if she knows how important it is. Professor McNamara is caught between the very real needs of this student and her responsibility both to the college and to other students.

THE PRESIDENT'S INSTRUCTIONS: "I would like your recommendation about what should be done. But first, here are some of the angles of the situation that I would like you to consider. I'm sure there are others; please raise them in your written opinion."

- The college recognizes that the student's reasons for wanting to enter the program are very serious.
- If the student fails English 100A, he will not get a much-needed promotion.
- Other students in the basic writing course also have good reasons for needing a passing grade.
- The college made a passing grade in English 100A necessary for good reasons. For the college degree to mean anything, certain basic skills must be guaranteed.
- As a supervisor at the automotive center, David has to write weekly production reports.

ASSIGNMENT OPTION 4A: RESPONSE TO THE SITUATION

Consider the facts of the case, and then write an argument essay either in favor or against giving David a passing grade.

ASSIGNMENT OPTION 4B: ANOTHER PERSPECTIVE

Imagine that you are a local businessperson who sits on the College Council. From this perspective, write an argument essay either in favor or against giving David a passing grade.

Argument

Follow the steps in this Writing Guide to help you prewrite, draft, revise, and edit your argument. Check off each step as you complete it.

THINKING CRITICALLY ABOUT ARGUMENT	
FOCUS	Before and as you write, think about your position on the issue and how you can persuade your readers.
ASK	• Who will be reading this essay, and what are they likely to know about the issue? • Why is this issue important to me? What do I have at stake? • What is my position on the issue? • What are my reasons for taking this position? • What are some reasons for the opposing position? • What is my readers' position? • How can I build and maintain enthusiasm for my position? • What facts, statistics, examples, and expert opinions can I include to convince readers of my position?

PREWRITE TO EXPLORE YOUR ISSUE

Prewriting for argument involves exploring an issue you care about and deciding what your position on that issue is. As you prewrite, also think about the reasons you hold a particular view.

_____ Decide on your purpose for writing.

_____ Identify the audience for your argument.

_____ Jot down some ideas about an issue that is important to you, focusing on what your position is and why. Various prewriting techniques work well for argument, so you should choose the one that you are most comfortable with. Freewriting, listing/brainstorming, and clustering work well for many writers.

_____ Take a few minutes to build some energy about the issue. How does

For more on purpose and audience, see pages 7–9.

this issue affect you personally? Why does it matter to you?

WRITE A THESIS STATEMENT

The thesis statement of an argument essay usually includes the issue and the writer's position on that issue. Writers may also use a thesis statement to preview the reasons they will offer to support their position.

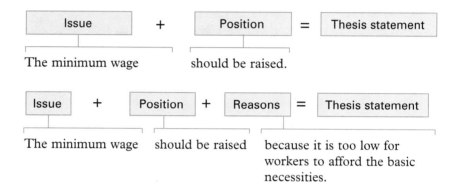

| Issue | + | Position | = | Thesis statement |

The minimum wage   should be raised.

| Issue | + | Position | + | Reasons | = | Thesis statement |

The minimum wage   should be raised   because it is too low for workers to afford the basic necessities.

As you develop and revise your argument, you will also need to revise your thesis statement, right up to the very end, making it clearer and more forceful each time.

SUPPORT YOUR POINT

The major support points in an argument are the reasons you give for your position on the issue. These reasons will become the topic sentences for the body paragraphs of your essay. The supporting details in argument are the evidence and information you provide for each of your reasons. To come up with convincing support, keep a specific audience in mind, particularly readers who may not care about the issue or (if they do care) may not share your position on the issue.

_____ Use a prewriting technique to come up with support (convincing reasons and evidence) for your position. Look for persuasive facts, statistics, examples, and expert opinions to support your position.

_____ Clearly state each reason and give specific evidence and details to back it up.

_____ Acknowledge the opposing position and show weaknesses in it by addressing points an opponent might raise.

_____   Consider whether you will need to use outside sources.

_____   Test your reasons and evidence.

_____   Reread your reasons and evidence from your opponent's point of view, looking for their weaknesses. Anticipate your opponent's objections, and include evidence to answer those objections.

_____   Consider every important angle of the issue.

_____   Make sure that your reasons support your position and that your evidence supports your reasons.

MAKE A PLAN

Making a written plan—or outline—helps you decide how to order your argument. An argument generally uses order of importance to arrange the reasons it discusses. As you organize, think about what your audience will find most convincing. Be sure to acknowledge and address opposing positions, too.

_____   Arrange your reasons according to their importance to your position. End with the most important reason.

_____   Make a plan or outline with your reasons and evidence in order.

DRAFT

Drafting an argument essay means writing in complete sentences and including the following:

- An introduction, including a thesis statement that presents your position on an issue
- Major reasons for your position
- Evidence and information that support your reasons
- An acknowledgment of the opposing view with responses to it
- A conclusion

_____   Think about how your readers might react to each point you make.

_____   Write an introductory paragraph that includes your thesis statement and interests your readers in the issue.

_____   Using your outline or plan, write a topic sentence for each of the reasons that will support your position on the issue.

——— Write body paragraphs that give facts, examples, and expert opinion that support your reasons.

——— End on a strong note. Before writing your conclusion, build up your energy and enthusiasm again (see p. 244). Save your best reason for last, and write a conclusion that refers back to your issue and position, reviews the support you give, and makes a final strong statement urging your readers to see it your way and act accordingly.

——— Title your essay.

REVISE

Revising means changing whole sentences or paragraphs to make your writing clearer or stronger. To revise an argument, assume that you are someone who holds the opposing view but is willing to listen to the other side. Think about how to make your reasons and evidence more convincing to that kind of a reader. Read your draft, looking for the following:

- Places where the ideas are off the main point (revise for unity)
- Gaps in information or detail (revise for support and detail)
- Areas in need of transitions to help the reader move smoothly from one reason to the next (revise for coherence)

For more on peer review, see pages 87–88.

——— Get feedback from others through peer review. Ask one or more readers to listen carefully to your reasons and to challenge any that they find weak or don't understand. Find new reasons and evidence if needed.

——— Begin revising by asking yourself how you could make your argument clearer and more persuasive for your readers.

——— Reread your thesis to make sure that you clearly state your position on the issue.

——— Reread your topic sentences to make sure that they clearly support your position and are written in strong, concrete language. Focus on whether you could provide additional reasons that would convincingly support your position.

——— Reread each body paragraph to see if the evidence you give clearly explains and backs up your reasons. Add other evidence and information that might further persuade your reader that your reasons are valid.

——— Reread your introduction to make sure that it states a definite opinion, with confidence, and hooks your readers' interest.

_____ Reread your conclusion to make sure that it sounds energetic and convincing, reminds your readers of your position, and makes a final attempt to persuade your readers.

_____ Add transitions to help your readers move smoothly from one reason to the next and to connect the backup evidence you provide.

_____ Decide whether repeating key words would increase your emphasis.

_____ Make at least five changes to your draft to improve the unity, support, or coherence of your argument or to make the introduction, thesis statement, or conclusion stronger or more convincing.

EDIT

Some grammar, spelling, word use, or punctuation errors may confuse your readers and make it difficult for them to understand a point you are trying to make. Even if they do not confuse your readers, errors detract from the effectiveness and overall quality of your writing. Edit your argument carefully, and correct any errors you find.

_____ Ask a classmate or friend to read your argument and highlight any errors.

_____ Use the spell checker and grammar checker on your computer.

_____ Look yourself for errors that the spell checker or grammar checker didn't catch. Focus first on sentence fragments, run-on sentences, problems with subject–verb agreement, problems with verbs, and other areas where you know you often make errors.

_____ Print a clean final copy.

_____ Ask yourself: Is this the best I can do?

A FINAL CHECK BEFORE HANDING IN YOUR ARGUMENT ESSAY

If you've followed the Writing Guide for argument, your essay will already include the four basics of good argument. Use this list to double-check each basic feature.

____ My argument has a thesis statement that takes a definite position or advises a particular action on a clear issue.

____ The body paragraphs in my argument present good reasons and evidence to support my position.

____ My essay acknowledges and addresses opposing views.

____ My argument is enthusiastic and energetic.

PART THREE

Writing in College and at Work

17

Solving Problems

Case Studies for Writing and Teamwork

You Know This
You've probably solved all kinds of problems.
- There's a traffic jam on your way to work, and you determine what alternative route to use.
- You figure out how to pay your bills when you're a little short on cash.
- You work with a friend to get a big job done on a tight schedule.
- You and a brother or sister decide how to get your parents to agree to something.

Understand What Problem Solving Is

IDEA JOURNAL
Write about a problem that you have encountered at work or in your everyday life.

DEFINITION: **Problem solving** is the process of identifying the problem and figuring out a good solution.

Think of the situations in your life that you might classify as problems. Perhaps you're falling behind in one of your courses. Or maybe you are managing a sales staff that hasn't met its quota for the third straight month. It could be that your child's day care center is having trouble retaining quality staff. While they often disrupt our lives, problems give us opportunities to tackle difficult situations with confidence. Being able to find reasonable solutions to problems is critical to success in every arena of life.

Sometimes you may be paralyzed by a problem. You may freeze because you don't have strategies for attacking it. Backing away from a problem is rarely a good solution; you simply become a victim, often feeling helpless and angry. When you know how to approach a challenging situation, you are better able to take charge of your life. Problem-solving skills are life skills that you'll use in college, at work, and in everyday life. Here are some ways in which you might use problem solving:

COLLEGE

- You have been working on a major assignment, and your computer breaks down the night before it is due.
- You lose your notebook near the end of the semester.
- Your college is eliminating its career services center when you need its services most.

WORK

- Your work schedule changes three weeks before the end of the semester and conflicts with class time.
- When several coworkers are laid off, you are assigned more work than you can handle.
- You have to work on a project with a colleague whom you don't like.

EVERYDAY LIFE

- You know you need major dental work, but you don't have insurance.
- Your child is afraid to go to school because two other children are making fun of him and taking his things during recess.
- You rely on public transportation, and you've just discovered that bus service in your town is being suspended indefinitely.

Problem solving, the process of identifying a problem and figuring out a reasonable solution to it, includes several basic steps.

THE PROBLEM-SOLVING PROCESS

1. Identify the problem. You should be able to describe it, orally or in writing, in a few sentences.

2. List people, information, and other resources that can help you solve the problem.

3. Identify possible solutions.

4. Evaluate each possible solution.
   - Identify the steps the solution would require.
   - List possible obstacles to the solution (e.g., money or time constraints).
   - List the advantages and disadvantages of the solution.

5. Choose the most reasonable solution, one that seems realistic and sensible. Keep in mind that problems seldom have right and wrong

solutions—just better and worse ones. Be able to explain and support your choice.

The problem-solving process can be used effectively by either an individual or a group. Increasingly in college, and particularly in the workplace, the task of solving a problem is assigned to a team, so it's important that you learn how to work with others toward a common goal of solving a problem.

Understand What Teamwork Is

DEFINITION: **Teamwork** is the combined effort of two or more individuals to solve a problem and achieve a common goal.

Working with others has many benefits: more ideas and perspectives, more possible solutions, more people to share the work. But being part of an effective team requires more than simply meeting with people: You need to understand how a team functions well. In order to achieve a common goal, members of a team need to work *as* a team rather than trying to showcase their individual efforts and talents.

Sports teams don't win just because the individual players are talented; they win because the players pool their talents into a coordinated whole. Each player on the team works hard and supports the other players.

The same is true of teamwork in other arenas as well: To benefit from teamwork in college, work, and everyday life, individuals must not only understand and perform their own responsibilities well but also mesh those responsibilities with the work of the team. Take a moment to look back at a few of the Profiles of Success in Chapters 8–16. Notice that each of the people in the profiles emphasizes the importance of teamwork and gives examples of how he or she uses team skills on the job.

FIVE BASICS OF EFFECTIVE TEAMWORK

1. The team establishes ground rules to ensure that each person on the team can contribute.

2. Members listen to each other and respect different points of view.

3. Although one person may function as team leader, all individuals participate and are equally appreciated.

4. Members recognize that they must depend on one another.

5. All members contribute and feel responsible for their own work as it affects the outcomes of the team's effort.

You will work in a team to complete the problem-solving assignments in this chapter. After your instructor forms the teams, you and your teammates should work together to decide who will play which team roles. If the members of your group do not know each other, your instructor may plan some activities to help you get acquainted before the team determines roles. Each team member will play an active role as a **contributor**, but teams should also select people to fulfill the following additional roles:

Team leader: The leader keeps the group focused on the task. He or she leads the team as a facilitator, or one who helps move the process along, not as a bully. For example, the leader might help the group stay focused on listing possible solutions to a problem, like this:

> Rob and Shawna think we should write a letter to the college president, and Paolo says we should collect students' signatures on a petition instead. What other ideas can we come up with?

not like this:

> I think we need to have a fund-raiser. Does anyone have a problem with that?

The team leader's opinions carry no more weight than those of other team members, and it's the team leader's responsibility to make sure that every team member has an opportunity to participate.

Recorder: The recorder takes notes on the group's work, keeping track of the agreed-on outcomes of each step. He or she does not write down everything that is said—just the ideas that the group agrees are the best and most helpful. If each group member is required to write an essay or report, the recorder's notes can be photocopied or typed and printed so that everyone has a copy to use.

Timekeeper: Sometimes teams find that they are spending more time on a task than they had planned. When this happens, it is the timekeeper's responsibility to interrupt the group and report the time spent and the time remaining in the meeting. The team can then decide, collectively, to either continue the task or move on to the next step.

If your assignment stretches over a number of days or weeks, your team may need to meet several times. If this is the case, try rotating roles.

Solve Problems from Real-World Case Studies

Using the problem-solving process and working as part of a team, you will suggest a reasonable solution to a real-life problem presented in one of the following case studies. Once you have chosen or been assigned a case, read the case carefully. Then the team can meet to start working through the process of problem solving.

CASE STUDIES

1. Network Administrator

You are a network administrator for a large corporation and have the ability, though not the authority, to read all messages sent to and from employees using company email. Your company has a strict policy that safeguards the privacy of personal email, and the last network administrator was fired for reading other employees' mail. During one of your routine monitoring sessions, you notice an unusually large number of messages being sent from one internal email address to another. Out of curiosity, you open and read some of these email messages. The messages are from the boss's son to his girlfriend (both of whom are employees of the company), but they are not love letters. In his email, the young man talks about hurting his girlfriend, and each message is more threatening than the one before it. What do you do?

2. College Ice Hockey Coach

It is two nights before the conference game that will decide whether or not your ice hockey team advances to the championship playoffs. You learn that four key players have violated their curfew. Curfews are an important part of the discipline program created by the coaching staff. Both the rules of the curfew and the school's zero-tolerance policy for rule breaking are clearly established during preseason training. The punishment for breaking curfew is a one-game suspension. The group of players facing punishment includes the team's leading scorers. The team, which includes fourteen other players, has worked hard all season to achieve the school's best record in more than two decades. What do you do?

3. High School Principal

You are the principal of a high school. One of your best English teachers comes to you, very upset, and tells you that she fears for her safety. Around Halloween, she had assigned students in her creative writing class to write a story that was truly frightening and descriptive. One of her students had turned in a story that was indeed bloodcurdling—a detailed, graphic, gory account of a student who had executed his English teacher. The teacher has taken this story as a real threat and demands that the student be reported to the authorities and expelled. You read the story and agree that it is threatening. However, the student who wrote it has good grades, positive relationships with teachers and other students, and no history of violence. The school has a written policy that informs students that any threats to the school community will result in suspension, expulsion, or possible legal action. What do you do?

4. Warehouse Floor Supervisor

You are the floor supervisor at a warehouse. One day a coworker you supervise tells you that he has tested HIV-positive. The man, John, tells you that he has already informed the Human Resources Department of his diagnosis, and its administrators are following the company's policy of nondiscrimination and privacy that requires the diagnosis to be kept confidential. You confirm this fact with the Human Resources Department and assure the employee that you will maintain his privacy.

A few months later, there is an accident in the warehouse. A person on one of the high ladders is loading heavy boxes onto a vehicle when two boxes drop from a height of 25 feet. One lands on John. He collapses onto the concrete floor, unconscious and bleeding. While one worker goes to call for help, several others rush to help John, wiping the blood from his cuts with their hands or shirttails. You know John is HIV-positive; you are also bound to confidentiality. What do you do?

 WRITING ASSIGNMENT   SOLVE A PROBLEM

Using the problem-solving process (p. 270) and the basics of good teamwork (p. 271), propose a reasonable solution to the case study you have chosen or been assigned. As your team works through the problem-solving process, make sure that you keep good records of the ideas you agree on during every step. Though each team member will write his or her own essay, each essay should present what the team agrees is the most reasonable solution. Each essay should also explain the reasons for your team's choice of that solution. Before turning in your essays, you may want to read one another's drafts to suggest revisions and point out errors.

THINKING CRITICALLY ABOUT SOLVING A PROBLEM	
FOCUS	Read the case study carefully. Make a genuine effort to take on the team role you have chosen or been assigned.
ASK	• What is the core of the problem? • What factors make the situation a problem? • What people or information might help the team identify a solution to the problem?

- What are all the possible solutions?
- What are the advantages and disadvantages of each possible solution?
- What does the team see as the most reasonable and realistic solution? Why?
- What is the best way to explain the solution so that readers will understand what the problem is, what the proposed solution is, and why it is a reasonable solution?

WRITE   Write an essay that summarizes the problem, explains the possible solution, and supports your choice of this solution.

Tips for the Assignment

1. Try to be as specific as possible in identifying the problem.

2. When listing possible solutions, avoid censoring yourself. Be bold, daring, and imaginative. List as many possible solutions as your team can think of before you begin to discuss the advantages and disadvantages of any single possibility.

3. Once you've identified the most promising solution, work together to come up with the strongest reasons why the chosen solution is the best one. You might take turns defending that solution from readers who might say, "Your solution isn't fair," or "That would just cause more problems," or even "It's a good idea, but it's not practical." As a team, you should generate at least three strong reasons to support your choice.

4. Your introductory paragraph should state the problem and your proposed solution. It should also state why the situation is a problem.

5. The body paragraphs should serve two basic purposes: explain your proposed solution and give reasons that support your choice of this solution. Your instructor may specify which method of development to use in writing your proposal essay. If not, you may find it helpful to review the following chapters: Chapter 9, Illustration; Chapter 11, Process Analysis; Chapter 15, Cause and Effect; and Chapter 16, Argument.

6. Your conclusion should restate your solution and confirm that it is the most reasonable course of action.

18

Writing under Pressure

Tests, Essay Exams, and Timed Writing

Studying for Tests

Everyone, no matter how well prepared, gets nervous about taking tests. The trick is to turn that nervousness into positive energy by learning test-taking strategies. This chapter will give you tips on studying for different kinds of tests as well as specific advice about essay exams and other timed writing assignments.

Here are five reliable tips to help you study for any exam:

FIVE TIPS FOR STUDYING

1. Ask about the test.
2. Study with a partner or group.
3. Predict what will be on the exam.
4. Use study aids.
5. Review actively.

1. ASK ABOUT THE TEST

When you know you are having a test, ask your instructor about it. Just make sure you ask reasonable questions.

ASK	**NOT**
• What part of the course or text will it cover?	• What's on the test?
• Will the format be multiple choice, short answer, or essay?	• You're not going to give us an essay question, are you?
• Will we be allowed to use notes or books?	• We can just look up the answers, right?
• What percentage of my course grade will this count for?	• Is this test important?
• Can you recommend what to review?	• Do I need to read the book? Is the stuff you said in class important?
• Will we have the whole period to complete the test?	• How long is it?
• I know I have to miss class that day (give your reason). Can I arrange to take the test at another time?	• Is there a makeup test?

Write down your instructor's answers to your questions. Don't rely on your memory; you will be busy enough remembering the material for the exam without having to remember what your instructor said.

2. STUDY WITH A PARTNER OR GROUP

Although everyone is busy, forming a study group is well worth the time and effort it takes. Setting a time to study with others guarantees that you'll study, and pooling ideas improves everyone's ability to predict what will be on the test. List the names of three people in the class you might like to study with. Contact them by phone, by email, or in person to ask if they would be interested in joining a study group.

Do some preparation before group meetings so that you make the most of the study time. The following are some tips on how study group members can prepare for a meeting:

For more on teamwork, see Chapter 17.

- Each person could take responsibility for a particular section of the material, preparing a list of five to ten questions that might be on the test. Questions and possible responses could then be discussed in the group.
- Each person could copy his or her notes on a particular chapter, section, or topic and distribute them to the members of the group.
- Each person could come up with a list of "the five most important things we learned during the course."
- Each person could come up with a list of "things I don't understand."

3. PREDICT WHAT WILL BE ON THE EXAM

Whether you are studying with other people or by yourself, it's a good idea to make a list of what you think will be covered on the exam. Look over your notes, assignments, and any previous tests or quizzes. What has your instructor stressed? Try writing questions for that material, and then try answering your own questions.

If you are confused about any material, ask about it either in class, after class, or during your instructor's office hours. Your instructor will probably welcome questions by email as well. Do not go into an exam knowing that you don't understand a major concept.

PRACTICE 1   PREDICTING THE CONTENT OF A TEST

Imagine that you are having a quiz in this class next week. With a partner or in a small group, identify three topics that might be on that quiz, and write one question for each.

TOPIC: Process for solving a problem

QUESTION: List the steps involved in the problem-solving process.

TOPIC: _____

QUESTION: _____

TOPIC: _____

QUESTION: _____

TOPIC: _____

QUESTION: _____

4. USE STUDY AIDS

Use one or more of the following study aids — or any other that is available to you — to ensure your success:

- Reread your notes, looking especially for anything you've underlined or marked in some other way.
- If you are being tested on material from your textbook, reread any chapter reviews, summaries, or boxes containing key concepts.
- Review any handouts from your instructor.
- Consider other available ways to review material — audiotapes, videos, computer exercises, study guides, the course or textbook Web site, and so on.

5. REVIEW ACTIVELY

The following are some suggestions for reviewing material actively:

- If you're reviewing material from a book, take notes. Improve your memory by putting information in your own words, writing it down, and seeing it on the page of your notebook, on the screen of your computer, or in the margin of a book.
- If you're reviewing handouts, use a colored pen or highlighter to mark the most important ideas, most useful facts, or any other key information.
- Say important material aloud. Many people learn well by hearing something in addition to seeing it.
- If you are studying from notes, rewrite your notes. For example, if you've written an outline, transform it into a concept map.

What I will do to study more actively: _____

_____

Doubling Your Chances of Passing Exams

Some students fail exams or get low grades because they don't understand the material. Others know the material but still score low because they don't have any useful strategies for taking exams.

FIVE STRATEGIES FOR TAKING EXAMS

1. Be prepared.
2. Manage your nerves.
3. Understand the directions.
4. Survey the whole exam before starting.
5. Develop a plan.

1. BE PREPARED

If you have found out all the particulars about the exam and have studied for it using the five tips listed on page 276, you've already done the most important preparation. But don't arrive at the exam and discover that you've left something essential at home. Take some time the night before to think about what you need. Make a list of what to bring (pen? books? calculator? notebook? textbook? computer disk? watch?), and assemble everything so that it's ready to go.

2. MANAGE YOUR NERVES

Get as much rest as possible the night before the exam, and allow extra time to get to class. Arrive early enough to settle in. Sit up straight, take a deep breath, and remind yourself that you know the material. You're prepared; you're ready; you will pass. When your instructor starts to talk, look up and listen.

3. UNDERSTAND THE DIRECTIONS

First, listen to the spoken directions your instructor gives. It's tempting to start flipping through the exam as soon as you get it rather than listening to what your instructor is saying. Resist the temptation. Your instructor may be giving you key advice or information that's not written elsewhere, and you may miss it if you're not paying attention.

Second, when you begin the test, carefully read the written directions for each part. Sometimes students answer all of the questions in a section only to find out afterward that the directions said to answer only one or two. If you don't understand any part of the directions, be sure to ask your instructor for clarification.

4. SURVEY THE WHOLE EXAM BEFORE STARTING

To survey means to examine something as a whole before approaching any single part. Surveying an exam before starting to answer questions is a crucial step that will help you budget your time. Often the toughest questions (and the ones worth the most points) are at the end. You don't want to answer all the two-point questions and leave the thirty-point ones unanswered. Ask yourself the following questions:

- *How many parts does the test have?* Be sure to look on both sides of all exam pages.
- *How many points is each part worth?* This information will help you decide how much time to spend on each part.
- *What questions can I answer quickly and easily?* Start with these. Answering them will assure you of some good points and build your confidence and momentum.

5. DEVELOP A PLAN

First, **budget your time**. After surveying the whole test, write down how much time you will allow for each part. You might even find it helpful to calculate what time you want to start each section: Part 1 at 9:40, Part 2 at 9:55, and so on. Make sure you leave enough time for the parts with the highest point values. Also leave enough time to answer essay questions: They can take longer than you think they will. As you plan your time, keep in mind how much time you *really* have for the exam: A "two-hour" exam may be only one hour and fifty minutes once your instructor finishes giving directions and so on. Remember also to leave a few minutes to check your work.

Second, **decide on an order**: where you should start, what you should do second, third, and so on. Start with the questions you can answer quickly and easily.

Finally, **monitor your time** during the exam. If you find you're really stuck on a question and you're going way over your time budget, move on. If you have time at the end of the exam period, you can always go back to it.

Answering an Essay Question or a Timed Writing Assignment

DEFINITION: An **essay question** is an examination item that asks you to write one or several paragraphs explaining and illustrating your answer.

DEFINITION: A **timed writing** is an assignment that requires writing one or several paragraphs in response to a question or prompt within a set amount of time.

Essay questions on an exam are usually worth more points than short-answer or multiple-choice questions, so they deserve special strategies. The following strategies apply also to timed writing.

FIVE STRATEGIES FOR ANSWERING AN ESSAY QUESTION OR TIMED WRITING ASSIGNMENT

1. Read the question carefully.
2. Write a thesis statement.
3. Make an outline.
4. Write your answer.
5. Reread and revise your answer.

1. READ THE QUESTION CAREFULLY

Be sure to read an essay question carefully so that you know exactly what to write. Look for three kinds of key words in an essay question:

- Words that tell you *what subject* to write on.
- Words that tell you *how to write about it*.
- Words that tell you *how many parts* your answer should have.

Discuss two major causes of personal bankruptcy in this country.

Tells how to write the response   Tells how many parts the answer should have   Tells what subject to write about

Define and give examples of the phenomenon of global warming.

Tells how to write the response   Tells what subject to write about

Once you understand the type of answer expected, you can both follow the directions and draw on your experience writing similar essays.

Common Key Words in Essay Exam Questions

KEY WORD	WHAT IT MEANS
Analyze	Break into parts (classify) and discuss
Define	State the meaning and give examples
Describe the **stages** of	List and explain steps in a process
Discuss the **causes** of	List and explain the causes
Discuss the **concept** of	Define and give examples
Discuss the **differences between**	Contrast and give examples
Discuss the **effects/results** of	List and explain the effects
Discuss the **meaning** of	Define and give examples
Discuss the **similarities between**	Compare and give examples
Discuss the **stages/steps** of	Explain a process
Explain the **term**	Define and give examples
Follow/Trace the **development** of	Give the history; narrate the story
Follow/Trace the **process** of	Explain the sequence of steps or stages in the process
Identify	Define and give examples
Should	Argue for or against
Summarize	Give a brief overview of narrative

 PRACTICE 2   IDENTIFYING KEY WORDS

Read the following samples from essay tests. Circle the key words that tell what subject to write about, how to write about it, and how many parts to write. In the space below each item, explain what the question asks a writer to do. Example:

(Define) and (illustrate) (dependency.)

Give the meaning of the term dependency and give examples of it.

1. Identify three causes of the Persian Gulf War.

   _____

2. Trace the stages of grieving.

   _____

3. Discuss the problem of the current energy crisis.

   _____

4. Should drivers be banned from using handheld cell phones while driving? Why or why not?

   _____

2. WRITE A THESIS STATEMENT

A thesis statement lets the reader know what your topic is and what your position or main point about that topic is. Your response should include a thesis statement that is simple and clear. You may want to preview what you plan to cover in your answer, as in some exams you may get partial credit for information contained in the thesis statement even if you run out of time to explain fully.

For more on writing a thesis statement, see Chapter 3.   The best way to stay on track in an essay exam is to write a thesis statement that contains the key words in the essay question and restates its main idea. It also helps to reread your thesis statement several times as you write your exam response.

PRACTICE 3   WRITING THESIS STATEMENTS

Write possible thesis statements in response to the following sample essay exam questions. Even if you do not know the answer to the question, write a thesis statement that responds to the question and lets the reader know what you will cover.

ESSAY EXAM QUESTION: Discuss the concept of First Amendment (free speech) protection related to pornography on the Internet.

POSSIBLE THESIS STATEMENT: The protection of First Amendment rights is often cited as a reason not to ban pornography on the Internet.

1. Discuss the causes of the decline of the traditional "nuclear family" (two married parents and their children living under the same roof, without others).

   _____

2. Explain the effects of binge drinking.

   _____

3. Trace the development of the Industrial Revolution in Lowell, Massachusetts.

   _____

4. Describe the atmospheric conditions that precede a thunderstorm.

   _____

5. Discuss three advantages and/or disadvantages of reliance on email.

   _____

3. MAKE AN OUTLINE

Before you answer an essay question, jot down some notes on how you will answer it. Write down any important names, dates, or facts that occur to you. Make a short informal outline that you can use as a basic map for laying out the parts of your answer. These notes will help you stick to your main points and remember essential details as you write.

For more on outlining, see Chapter 5.

4. WRITE YOUR ANSWER

Your answer to an essay question should always be in essay form, with an introductory paragraph, several support points, and a concluding paragraph.

Here is an essay written by Brenda White of Quinsigamond Community College, in response to the essay prompt "Discuss your role model."

For more on the parts of an essay, see page 4 and Chapters 5 and 6.

My role model is my best friend, Tanya, a single mother. Although young unmarried parents are often looked down upon in our society, Tanya has overcome many obstacles and is doing an excellent job raising her son. I admire her patience, independence, and willingness to work hard. With these qualities, she defies the stereotype of the teen parent.

Introduction states thesis and previews support points

Support point 1

Support point 2

Support point 3

Conclusion sums up and strengthens response to essay prompt

Tanya could have made the choice to terminate her pregnancy, but she decided not to because she knew that she had the patience to raise a child, even under difficult circumstances. She has incredible patience with her son, Quentin. For example, when he's crying—even for a long time—she'll just rock him until he sleeps. Tanya also has patience with her friends. She understands that they have other things to do and can't always be counted on to watch Quentin. Tanya never gets mad if we can't help her out. She is also patient with her mother, who is very critical. Tanya's steady patience has gotten her through many difficult situations.

Independence is another trait that makes Tanya a good role model. She is raising her son without the help of her parents and mostly without Quentin's father. Tanya does not rely on others to care for her son or make decisions about his care; she does what needs to be done. She is also financially independent. She spends the money she earns wisely, only on things that are necessary. She pays her own tuition, rent, and, of course, the expenses of bringing up Quentin. Tanya has earned her independence and is wise about the actions she takes.

Tanya is a very hard worker, pushing herself to the maximum. She works two jobs so she can provide for her growing son. Tanya also maintains an A average in her college courses. She has always gone beyond the normal, everyday achievements. For example, she graduated from high school on the honor roll while living on her own and supporting her son. She works hard and sticks to her belief that education is valuable. Tanya has gone beyond the traditional definition of hardworking.

In some people's eyes, Tanya is just a single, teenage mother, a burden on society. But to me, Tanya is a wonderful role model. She has accomplished a lot in her young life. She has also gained control of her life and her surroundings by being patient, independent, and hardworking. Tanya is a single, teenage parent, but she is also a worthy role model.

5. READ AND REVISE YOUR ANSWER

After you have finished writing your answer to an essay question, reread it carefully. Make corrections or changes so that your response is clearer, more precise, and more detailed.

Teachers sometimes use a *scoring rubric*, which consists of the criteria—or standards—they use to judge the quality of an essay. Although scoring rubrics vary from one teacher to the next, most rubrics used to evaluate writing include some basic elements:

- Adherence to the assignment. (Has the writer followed the assignment and answered the question? Does the essay stay focused on the topic?)

- Thesis statement. (Does the essay clearly state the topic and the writer's main point about it?)
- Accuracy. (Does the essay include correct answers or reliable information?)
- Development. (Are explanations clear and supported with examples?)
- Language and expression. (Is the essay free of major errors in grammar, mechanics, and usage?)

Scoring rubrics often have points or percentages attached to each element. A typical scoring rubric might look like this:

ELEMENT	TOTAL POINTS POSSIBLE	STUDENT SCORE
Adherence to assignment	20	18
Thesis statement	15	15
Accuracy	30	25
Development	25	20
Language and expression	10	10
TOTAL POSSIBLE POINTS	**100**	**88**

If your teacher provides you with a rubric, use it to set priorities as you review and revise your essay. Otherwise, consider the elements in the sample rubric above as you revise your essay exam.

If on a test you are writing by hand (rather than using a computer), you can revise your essay by neatly crossing out mistakes and adding extra words or sentences between the lines or in the margin, like this:

Groups of people living together have expectations about how the

group should function and how to keep order within the group.

~~Societies need to have rules and laws.~~ This semester, we learned about

social deviance, which is any behavior that does not conform to

expectations of the group and which violates the group's sense of order. For
                     , those who break society's rules,
example, criminals are social deviants. Rather than thinking that we can

or should eliminate deviant behavior altogether, I agree with sociologist
                          a necessary element of any healthy social group.
Emile Durkheim that deviance is ~~necessary.~~

WRITING ASSIGNMENTS

Choose one of the following topics and write an essay on it, using the five strategies for answering an essay question or timed writing assignment introduced on page 282. To practice with timed writing, give yourself a one-hour time limit.

1. Write an essay agreeing or disagreeing with one of the following statements:

   Schoolchildren have too many vacations.

   Most students cheat.

   People should be required to retire at age sixty-five.

   People should live together before they get married.

   There are no valuable lessons to be learned from studying history.

2. Define *responsibility*.

3. Propose a solution to a major problem in your town or city.

4. Discuss a person who has had great influence on you.

5. Discuss an event that changed your life.

19

Writing Summaries and Reports

Important College Writing Tasks

Writing a Summary

DEFINITION: A **summary** is a condensed version of a piece of writing, a conversation, or an event. A summary presents main ideas and key support points, stripping down the information to its essential elements. A summary is stated in your own words, generally without opinion or judgment.

To summarize something—an event, an article, a chapter in a book, a movie plot, or a conversation—you have to understand it thoroughly so that you can explain its important parts in your own words. Think of a summary as making a long story short, as when you tell a friend about the plot of a television program or a movie, or about something that happened to you. There are many uses for summarizing.

COLLEGE

- You answer exam questions that ask you to summarize information.

- You may summarize recent findings on a topic for a research project.

- You summarize readings in your notes and written assignments.

WORK

- You summarize events or situations for a manager who needs to know what's going on but doesn't have the time to hear every small detail.
- You write a memo that summarizes the issues discussed and decisions made at a meeting.
- You prepare monthly or quarterly reports that summarize achievements, trends, and goals.

EVERYDAY LIFE

- You summarize for a partner your conversation with a plumber who was at your home to fix a pipe.
- You write a résumé and a job application letter summarizing your work experience and educational accomplishments.
- You summarize a novel that you recommend to your book group.

FIVE BASICS OF A GOOD SUMMARY

1. It includes a thesis statement that identifies what is being summarized and the main idea of the original piece of writing, event, or conversation.
2. It concisely identifies the key support points presented in the original.
3. It includes any final observations or recommendations made in the original.
4. It is objective in tone, presenting information without opinions.
5. It is written (or stated) in your own words.

READ AND ANALYZE A SUMMARY

A typical assignment in college is to summarize something you have read. Here is a summary of the student essay in Chapter 16 (p. 251). Reread the original essay ("How Violence on TV Affects Children and Adolescents"), read the summary here, and answer the questions that follow the summary.

In her essay, "How Violence on TV Affects Children and Adolescents," Edna Crespo argues that violence has definite negative effects on children and adolescents. She identifies three significant effects and presents evidence of them.

Crespo reports that frequent viewing of violent television causes children to become passive and to lose interest in more healthy activities such as playing with friends, getting physical exercise, and enjoying outdoor activities. She bases her statement on evidence from a physician who says that children themselves admit they are addicted to television. Crespo also discusses how TV leads children to become insensitive to violence and more tolerant of aggressiveness. She cites a study showing that students who watched a lot of violent television were less likely to help other students who were the victims of aggressive behavior. The worst effect of television violence, according to Crespo, is that children themselves become more aggressive. She points out that children often try out behaviors they have seen on television, without seeming to realize they might hurt other children.

The author concludes by drawing upon her eighteen years of work experience in the marketing and advertising industry, where, she says, she has learned exactly how powerful—and destructive—television can be. She makes the powerful statement that we are spending millions of dollars to destroy our children's values.

1. Double-underline the **thesis statement**.

2. Underline the **key points** of the summary. Do they match the key points in Crespo's essay? _____ Does the summary leave out any of the essay's key points? _____

3. Do you think that this summary gives you a good understanding of the original piece? Why or why not? _____

_____

4. Is the summary written in the writer's words or in Crespo's? _____

_____

5. Does this piece have the five basics of a good summary? _____

_____

Writing a summary is not a mysterious process: It just requires that you understand the key points of a piece of writing, a conversation, or an event and communicate them simply and accurately. Follow the five steps here to write a good summary.

FIVE STEPS FOR WRITING A GOOD SUMMARY

1. Preview the original piece of writing, looking for visual clues to what is important, such as the title, headings, words in bold or italics, quotations, or boxed information.
2. Read the entire original piece carefully, first for overall meaning. Then reread to note key points. If you are summarizing an event or conversation, recall and review the entire happening.
3. Make an outline of the writer's or speaker's key points.
4. Write your summary.
5. Revise your summary.

PRACTICE 1   WRITE A SUMMARY

Apply the five steps for writing a good summary as you read the following article and respond to the questions about it.

1. Preview the Writing

Before reading, skim over the article, looking for visual clues to what is important (title, headings, words in bold or italics, quotations, and so forth). What visual clues in the article below suggest items of importance?

_____

2. Read and Reread the Article

First read the article to understand its overall meaning. As you read, you might want to make check marks next to points you think might be important. But your purpose in reading right now is to understand the overall content, not to figure out the specific points.

Survey Finds Many Firms Monitor Staff

Your employer could be watching you. Such are the findings of a new study released last week by the American Management Association (AMA) in New York. The survey of 1,626 large and midsize companies found that nearly 80 percent of major US firms routinely check their employees' email, Internet, or telephone connections, and some regularly videotape them at work.

"It's not just a matter of corporate curiosity," said Eric R. Greenberg, director of management studies at the American Management Association. "Personal email can clog a company's telecommunications system, and sexually explicit or other inappropriate material downloaded from the Internet can lead to claims of a hostile work environment."

Researchers have found that companies are more likely to conduct random checks versus 24-hour surveillance of messages, phone conversations, or Internet usage. Even so, the AMA advises that employees use discretion at work.

According to the survey, 63 percent of US companies check employees' Internet connections, up 54 percent since last year. Forty-seven percent read workers' email, up from 38 percent in the year 2000. Forty percent have installed firewalls to prevent employees from using the Internet inappropriately, up from 29 percent last year.

When asked whether they had fired workers because of inappropriate use of electronic equipment, 27 percent of the employers said they had dismissed staff for misuse of office email or Internet connections. Sixty-five percent of the companies had disciplined offenders.

Ellen Bayer, the AMA's practice leader on human rights issues, said the findings indicate that privacy in the modern-day workplace is "largely illusory."

"In this era of open space cubicles, shared desk space, networked computers, and teleworkers, it is hard to realistically hold onto the belief in private space," said Bayer. She added that some employees do not understand that their employers have a legal right to monitor equipment that workers use on the job.

Employers also reported other forms of surveillance, such as monitoring telephone numbers called (43 percent), logged computer time (19 percent), and video surveillance for security purposes (38 percent).

> This article uses direct quotations from personal interviews conducted by the writer.

> "In this era of open space cubicles, shared desk space, networked computers, and teleworkers, it is hard to realistically hold onto the belief in private space," said Bayer.

"In previous years, the growth in monitoring went hand in hand with increases in the share of employees gaining access to email and the Internet," added AMA's Greenberg. "This year, the average share of employees with office connections barely grew at all, while monitoring of those activities rose by nearly 10 percent. It is important to note, however, that 90 percent of the companies engaging in any of these practices inform their employees that they are doing so."

But companies don't have to inform employees of any monitoring practice. In fact, most US courts have ruled in favor of employers who routinely monitor telephones, computers, or other electronic equipment used on the job. It is best not to misuse company media: Your employer may be watching you.

> — Staff reporter, "Survey Finds Many Firms Monitor Staff,"
> *Boston Sunday Globe,* April 29, 2001.

What is the subject of the article? _____

_____

What is the main point of the article? _____

_____

Reread the Article.   Now go back and reread the article, placing a check mark by each major point that your summary should include and making notes to yourself about how to present the information.

3. Make an Outline of Key Points

Now review your notes, and make an outline for the summary you will write. Note both the writer's key points and any examples that you might include.

Key points/examples: _____

_____

_____

_____

_____

Final observation or recommendation that article makes: _____

_____

4. Write Your Summary

Using your outline as a guide, write a summary of the article in your own words. This is a draft, so just try to capture the key points of the article. Reread parts of the original article as necessary.

5. *Revise Your Summary*

Read over your summary carefully to see if it has the five basics of a good summary (p. 290). If not, add necessary information or modify what you have written so that your summary accurately and clearly represents the original. Because a summary is a shortened version of a longer piece, using transitions (such as "first," "second," "next," and "finally") to help your reader move smoothly from one key point to another is especially important.

While your summary should focus on the main points, make sure you provide enough detail (examples) so that your reader, who has not read the piece, will understand each point.

Finally, read your answer to make sure that it is free of errors in grammar, spelling, and punctuation.

WRITING ASSIGNMENTS

1. Summarize the cover story of a recent issue of a magazine (print or online).
2. Summarize the plot of a movie you have seen recently.
3. Summarize an article from today's newspaper.
4. Summarize an essay or article, either from this book (if you are using the version with readings; see pp. 615–717) or from another book you use in a course.
5. Summarize Giovanni Bohorquez's narration essay from Chapter 12 (p. 174).

Writing a Report

DEFINITION: A **report** usually begins with a summary that condenses a piece of writing, a conversation, or an event and then goes on to give some type of analysis. Recall that a summary is objective: You present a brief version without stating your opinions. In contrast, a report summarizes key points and also includes reactions to, opinions about, or recommendations based on the piece, conversation, or event. A **review** is a type of report in which the writer evaluates a film, performance, product, or piece of writing.

COLLEGE

• Your theater class reviews a play opening on campus.
• An instructor in a business class assigns you to write a report based on a campus event, such as a presentation on marketing trends by a local professional.
• You review a film for the student paper.

WORK

- Your manager asks you to review software from different suppliers who want your company's business. Your review must recommend which supplier to use.

- Your committee reviews last year's employee awards program and recommends changes.

- You write a report on your company's insurance options, reviewing each plan.

EVERYDAY LIFE

- You informally review a new restaurant for your friends.
- You report on a nonfiction book for your book club.
- You review a performance for your local newspaper.

In order to write a good report, you must thoroughly understand the original event, conversation, or piece of writing. Because you will also include your opinions, think carefully about what your reactions were and why you had those particular reactions.

FOUR BASICS OF A GOOD REPORT

1. It includes a thesis statement that identifies the subject and the main idea of the original piece of writing, event, or conversation.

2. It includes the key support points.

3. It includes your opinion of or recommendations concerning the piece of writing, event, or conversation, along with your specific support for that opinion. Reviews of books or films often include specific passages or quotations in supporting statements.

4. It is written or stated primarily in your own words. Specific quotations may be used to support your opinions.

For example, in an English class, you may be asked to write a book report or a film review. You would need to summarize the work, but your instructor would also expect you to include your opinions about the piece and provide reasons or examples for those opinions.

Read the following example of a film review.

Delay Gives "Damage" a Fighting Chance

Wesley Morris

What a difference six months makes. Nixed from the fall 2001 schedule in the haze of Sept. 11, *Collateral Damage* reemerges—jaw clenched—ready to take terrorism down. And who but Arnold Schwarzenegger is a more apt action figure for the "new patriotism" conducted on a global scale?

Playing a Los Angeles firefighter who treks to the Colombian jungles to punish the terrorist who killed his wife and child in a bombing, Schwarzenegger bounds out of obsolescence like a figure from the cover of a Marvel comic book. Accordingly, *Collateral Damage* is an SUV of a movie driven by a one-man National Guard.

The film is directed by Andrew Davis ("The Fugitive"), a man who never met a bus under siege, a death-defying leap down a waterfall, or a quest for a spouse's murderer that didn't turn him on. The story itself is recyclable, right down to Elias Koteas—Tommy Lee Jones to Schwarzenegger's Harrison Ford—playing a seemingly crooked CIA operative trying to catch Schwarzenegger before he nabs his prey.

Despite its action-in-a-can mentality, the movie's generic roots gain a new post-terror specificity that lends it an almost bombastic level of relevance it was never meant to have. Initially, Warner Bros.'s postponement had a glum take-one-for-the-team dimension: It was the right thing to do when the wrong thing happens. It was a gesture that seemed designed to save the movie from terrible timing by releasing it later the following year, and there may have been something to it.

Six months ago, *Collateral Damage* was another dated attempt to relaunch Schwarzenegger out of the moribund-action-star silo as another heat-seeking missile. Now the movie, incidentally but not insignificantly, taps into its audience's own revenge fantasies—not unlike the domestic drama *In the Bedroom*—only with a cartoonish blur around its moral edges.

Sensing the necessity to represent the alternative side to Schwarzenegger's unrelenting need for personal justice, the movie deigns to give a human face to its terrorist, an embittered guerrilla bomb-maker who calls himself El Lobo. The face belongs to Cliff Curtis, the alluring New Zealand changeling whose American career has oscillated between troubled ethnicities (Saudi, Iraqi, Nicaraguan) in such movies as *Three Kings* and *Blow*.

Here, he's playing not a monster so much as a revolutionary with money to burn and a political ax to grind against America. But you can tell El Lobo is a gentleman caught in the gears of a formula flick when he barely bats an eyelash at his wife's bond with the man trying to kill him.

Curtis lets the mask slip on his villain long enough for it to be jarring when El Lobo reverts to his bomb-planting self and heads back to America for more mayhem — in time, of course, for our hero to try to stop him.

This brings us back to Schwarzenegger, finally making good on his decade-old "I'll be back" promise. There had been some concern that we'd lost him. After an on-set accident and heart problems, Arnold had recently taken a back seat to the subject of his mortality. His plunge into millennial outlandishness, once battling not simply the Bad Guy but Satan himself in "End of Days," was as desperate as Michael Jackson naming his first new album in five years "Invincible."

In *Collateral Damage,* the metaphysical lunacy is gone, and so are the shades, leather tunics, and heavy artillery. In fact, Schwarzenegger at 55 — in a shirt and khakis, and serving homemade knuckle-sandwiches — is decidedly dress-casual for the proceedings. Vengeance, the movie seems to say, is the new normal.

His physique, still mighty, but only discreetly alluded to, is secondary to his extended emotional capacity. He's still a rock, but it seems you can squeeze blood and tears from this stone. If this film is a hit — and judging from the fact that it strikes all the right populist notes, even the sour ones, it will be — that will be because Schwarzenegger's mortality for the first time suits him.

Not only does he feel your pain, he's living through it — the erstwhile last action hero, born again.

To write a report on a piece of writing, an event, or a conversation, you need to understand its key points and to communicate them simply and accurately. You also need to include your own opinions or recommendations based on the original work or happening and to provide support for those opinions or recommendations. Use the seven steps here to write a report.

SEVEN STEPS FOR WRITING A REPORT

1. Preview the original, looking for visual clues to what is important, such as headings, words in bold or italics, boxed quotations, or other elements.

2. Read the original piece carefully, making note of key points as you read. If you are reporting on an event, conversation, performance, or something that isn't a written work, recall and review the entire happening.

3. Make an outline of the writer's or speaker's key points.

4. Make notes on your outline about your reactions to the work. Note your opinions about both the main idea and the key points. Include the main point you want to make about it and examples that support your point.

5. Write a thesis statement that includes the title of the work, its purpose, and the main point you want to make about the piece.

6. Write your report.

7. Revise your report.

WRITING ASSIGNMENTS

1. Write a review of a book that you have read for either this class or another one.

2. Write a review of a movie or live performance that you either very much liked or very much disliked.

3. Write a report that includes a summary of and reaction to a recent or proposed change in your town or on your campus.

4. Write a report of a class that you have taken recently.

5. Attend a public event and report on it.

20

Finding, Evaluating, and Documenting Sources

Key Research Skills

DEFINITION: Conducting **research** means finding information that will help you or others understand a subject. Knowing how to find information that you need is an important skill, not just for college but for all areas of your life. Here are a few examples of the kinds of research you might need to do.

COLLEGE

- For your history class, you need to investigate different accounts of an event.
- In your psychology course, you are required to write a paper using outside sources, such as books, periodicals, or the Internet.
- For a business course, you need to interview an entrepreneur and learn about his or her product or industry.

WORK

- You need to plan a customer survey, asking people for their opinions of a new product.
- You have been asked to research the sales history of a competitor's product.
- You need to gather demographic data to support your company's plans to expand into a new region.

EVERYDAY LIFE

- You want to trace your family history and start a family tree.
- A doctor diagnoses a family member's illness and recommends a certain method of treatment. You want to find out more about both the illness and the possible treatments.
- You need to buy a new television and want to find a reliable but inexpensive model.

As you find information, you'll need to take two additional steps. First, you must evaluate your sources to determine if the information within them is reliable. Second, to avoid plagiarism, you must give credit to your sources by documenting them.

Find Sources

Finding reliable information about your research topic may seem like an overwhelming job, but keeping in mind a process for conducting research can help guide your work. As you start your search, try the strategies described in the following sections.

For more on finding and narrowing a topic for a research essay, see page 325.

CONSULT A REFERENCE LIBRARIAN

Although much information is available on the Internet, you will still need to use the library for books and some other materials. If you are not familiar with finding materials in the library, you will save yourself time and possible frustration by talking with the reference librarian. If your library allows, schedule an appointment with the librarian. Before your appointment, jot down some questions you want to ask, such as those listed below. Begin your conversation by telling the librarian your research topic.

QUESTIONS FOR THE LIBRARIAN

- How do I use an online catalog or a card catalog? What information will the library's catalog give me?
- What other reference tools would you recommend as a good starting place for research on my topic?
- Once I identify a source that might be useful, how do I find it?
- Can I get onto the Internet from a library computer? If so, how?
- Can you recommend an Internet search engine that will help me find information on my topic? Can you also recommend some useful key words?

- I've already found some articles related to my topic. Can you suggest some other places to look for sources?

USE THE ONLINE CATALOG OR CARD CATALOG

Most libraries now list their holdings on a computer rather than in a card catalog, but both systems give the same information: titles, authors, subjects, publication data, and call numbers. If you are working with a librarian, he or she may offer step-by-step instructions for using the online catalog. If you are working on your own, the online catalog help is usually easy to find (generally on the screen or in a Help menu) and easy to follow. Catalogs allow you to search by author, title, subject, or key word. If you are just beginning your research, you will probably use the subject heading or a key word because you may not know specific authors or titles.

For more on conducting key word searches, see page 305.

Florence Bagley, a student whose research process and completed essay appear in Chapter 21, searched her library's online catalog using the name *Aretha Franklin* as a key word. Here is one source she found.

```
Record 6 of 11


Author:          Sheafer, Silvia A.

Title:           Aretha Franklin: Motown superstar / Silvia
                    A. Sheafer.

Publisher:       Detroit : Enslow, 1996.

Subject:         Franklin, Aretha.

                 Motown music.

                 Rhythm and blues -- Soul music -- United
                    States -- 20th century.

                 Women singers.

                 Women musicians -- United States -- 20th
                    century.

Location:        Worcester Greendale

Call Number:     899.304b

Status:          Available
```

A call number is a book's identification number. Knowing the call number will help you to locate a source in the library. Once you do locate the source, browse the nearby shelves. Since a library's holdings are organized by subject, you may find other sources related to your topic.

USE OTHER REFERENCE MATERIALS

The reference section of the library has many resources that will help you find information on your topic. Here is a sampling of common databases and other reference sources. Most are available online or on CD-ROM.

Periodical Indexes

Periodical indexes help you locate information published in magazines, journals, and newspapers. If your topic is a current one, periodicals may be more useful than books. The following are some of the most popular periodical indexes:

- *InfoTrac*
- *LexisNexis*
- *NewsBank*
- *New York Times Index*
- *Readers' Guide to Periodical Literature*

General Encyclopedias

Encyclopedias can offer information when you are seeking an overview of a subject. Some encyclopedias, like the *Encyclopædia Britannica,* are available in print, online, and on CD-ROM. An encyclopedia entry is generally followed by a bibliography of other useful sources. In addition to general encyclopedias, your library may have specialized encyclopedias that give more detailed information on your topic. An example would be the *Encyclopedia of Psychology* for a research paper in a social sciences course.

Specialized Indexes

Specialized indexes—either in book form, online, or on CD-ROM—direct you to resources in various broad subject areas. A few of the many indexes are the following:

- *America: History and Life*
- *Biological Abstracts*
- *Educational Resources Information Center (ERIC)*
- *MLA International Bibliography of Books and Articles on the Modern Languages and Literatures*
- *PsycLIT*

Visit <**www.census .gov**>, the official Web site of the U.S. Census Bureau, for current state and national statistical data related to population, economics, and geography.

Statistical Sources

Some research essays use statistical data, or facts and figures, as excellent support. As one example, the *Statistical Abstract of the United States* (published annually by the U.S. Census Bureau) can help you locate useful statistics related to social issues, population, economics, and other topics.

USE THE INTERNET

The Internet, a vast global computer network, now provides access to all kinds of information. The biggest part of the Internet is called the World Wide Web, which allows users to jump from site to site using links. If you are new to using the Internet and the World Wide Web to search for sources, this section will offer some basics. You may also want to work with a librarian, a writing-center tutor, or a knowledgeable friend as you continue to search.

Uniform Resource Locator (URL)

When you discover a Web site that you might want to return to, bookmark it or add it to your list of favorites. Doing so ensures that you don't have to remember the URL each time you want to go to the site. Different browsers have different ways of bookmarking; choose "Bookmarks" in Netscape or "Favorites" in Microsoft Internet Explorer.

Every site on the World Wide Web has an address, called a uniform resource locator (URL). You may already be familiar with some frequently advertised URLs, such as <**www.amazon.com**> (the Internet address for bookseller Amazon.com) or the URL for your college's Web site. If you know the URL of a Web site that you think would be helpful for your research, enter it into the Address field of your Web browser. (Web browsers, like Microsoft Internet Explorer and Netscape Navigator, are software programs that allow a computer to read Web pages.) If you do not know the URL of a particular site you want to visit, you will need to use a search engine.

Search Engines

Search engines function very much like the electronic catalogs and databases in your college or local library. You can conduct searches for information by subject, title, or author, or by key words. It's important to know that all search engines have a Help feature that offers guidance in using the engine, selecting key words, and refining your search.

POPULAR SEARCH ENGINES AND THEIR URLS

- AltaVista <**www.altavista.com**>
- Ask Jeeves <**www.askjeeves.com**>
- Excite <**www.excite.com**>
- Google <**www.google.com**>
- HotBot <**www.hotbot.com**>
- Lycos <**www.lycos.com**>
- Yahoo! <**www.yahoo.com**>

Searching with Key Words

One drawback of typing key words into a search engine is having to sift through the number of matches, or "hits," that often result from a search. For example, when student writer Florence Bagley used *Aretha Franklin* as a key word on Yahoo, her search returned 54,728 hits. As she scrolled through those hits, she quickly realized that many were not related to her topic—the role that music has played in Aretha's life. For example, her results included sites that auctioned celebrity items, a site for the church where her father was the minister, and a site for the history of rhythm and blues.

Although she would certainly have found some useful sites, Florence didn't want to scroll through 54,728 possibilities. Instead, she made her keyword search more specific: *Aretha Franklin's life*. This search produced 1,070 hits, which was still more than enough. However, Florence found some promising sources: the Aretha Franklin home page, fan-club sites, and a link to Amazon.com's list of books on Aretha Franklin's life.

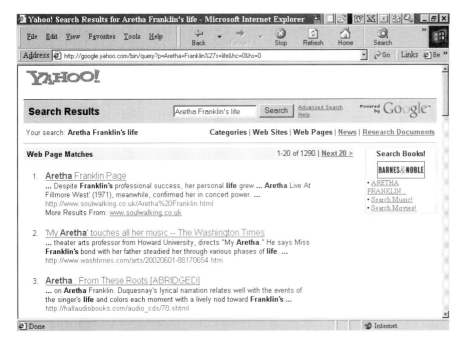

RESULTS FROM A KEYWORD SEARCH ON YAHOO USING *ARETHA FRANKLIN'S LIFE* IN THE SEARCH BOX

If you find too much information or, worse, too little, try making your key words more specific or using different combinations of key words. Consult the search engine's built-in Help feature for tips on conducting successful searches.

Use a Computer to Build Research Skills

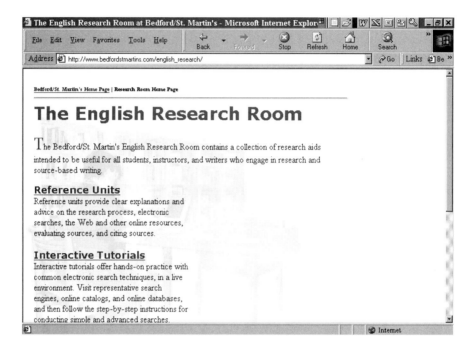

For help with research, visit the *English Research Room* at **<www.bedford stmartins.com/english_research>**. The site is organized into three main areas designed to help you to develop stronger research writing skills. The "reference units" offer concise information to help you understand your research process and conduct research online. The "interactive tutorials" guide you through the most important parts of online research as if you had a librarian and teacher sitting next to you. The "research links" connect you to many of the basic tools research writers are likely to use, such as online writing labs and popular search engines. Use Bookmarks in Netscape or Favorites in Internet Explorer to keep this important Web site handy.

INTERVIEW PEOPLE

Personal interviews can be excellent sources of information. Before interviewing anyone, however, plan carefully. First consider what kind of person to interview. Do you want information from an expert on the subject or from a person directly affected by the issue? How would the experience or comments of each person help support your points? The person should be knowledgeable about the subject and have firsthand experience. When you have decided whom to interview, schedule an appointment.

Next, to get ready for the interview, prepare a list of five to ten questions. Ask more open-ended questions (What is your position on regulating cell-phone use by drivers?) than closed ones that require only a simple "yes" or "no" response (Do you favor regulating cell-phone use by drivers?). Leave space for notes about the person's responses and for additional questions that may occur to you during the interview. Include the person's full name and qualifications and the date of the interview in your research notes.

As you conduct the interview, listen carefully and write down any important ideas. If you plan to use any of the interviewee's exact words (i.e., direct quotations), make sure to put them in quotation marks in your notes. Doing so will help you figure out if your notes are the exact words of the person you interviewed, your own interpretation of something he or she said, or a thought you had during the interview.

> For more on using quotation marks correctly, see Chapter 39.

NOTE: Recording what a person says without notifying him or her first is unethical and, in some states, is against the law. If you plan to record an interview on videotape or audiotape, get your subject's permission first.

Evaluate Sources

Evaluating sources means judging them to determine how reliable they are—a critical skill in college, on the job, and in everyday life. Reliable sources are those that present accurate, up-to-date information written by authors with appropriate credentials for the subject matter. Reliable sources support claims with evidence and use objective, reasonable language. Research materials found in a college library (books, journals, and newspapers, for example), are generally considered reliable sources.

When you are using the Internet, don't assume that a source is reliable just because it exists there. Just about anyone can create a Web site and put whatever he or she wants on it. If you are searching the Web for information about the psychological benefits of weight loss, for example, you may find a range of sources—reliable ones such as an article published by the *Journal of the American Medical Association* or a report by faculty at Johns Hopkins University and questionable ones such as an individual's personal weight-loss story or an advertisement for a product that claims to "eliminate pounds while you sleep." Whether you are doing research for a college course, a work assignment, or personal use, you need to make sure that the source is reliable and legitimate for your purpose. Otherwise, you may receive a failing grade on a paper, make a big mistake at work, or foul up something in your personal life.

When you're viewing a Web site, try to determine its purpose. A Web site set up solely to provide information may be more reliable than an online product advertisement. A keyword search for attention-deficit/ hyperactivity disorder (ADHD), for example, would point a researcher to thousands of sites; the two shown here are just samples. Which do you think contains more reliable information?

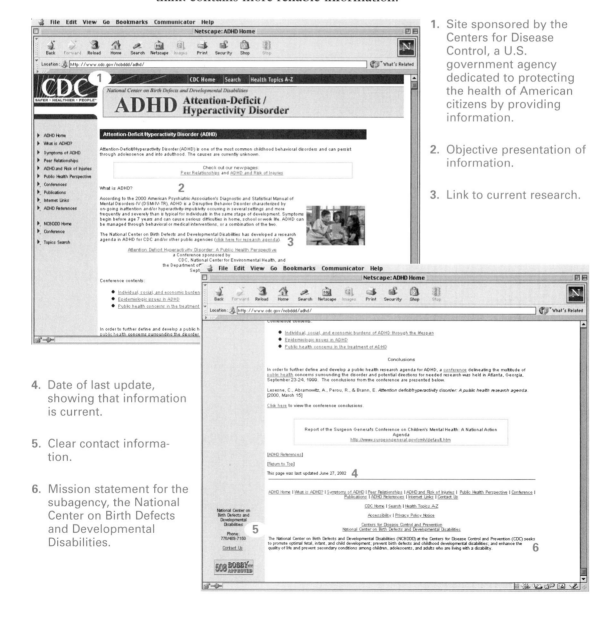

1. Site sponsored by the Centers for Disease Control, a U.S. government agency dedicated to protecting the health of American citizens by providing information.

2. Objective presentation of information.

3. Link to current research.

4. Date of last update, showing that information is current.

5. Clear contact information.

6. Mission statement for the subagency, the National Center on Birth Defects and Developmental Disabilities.

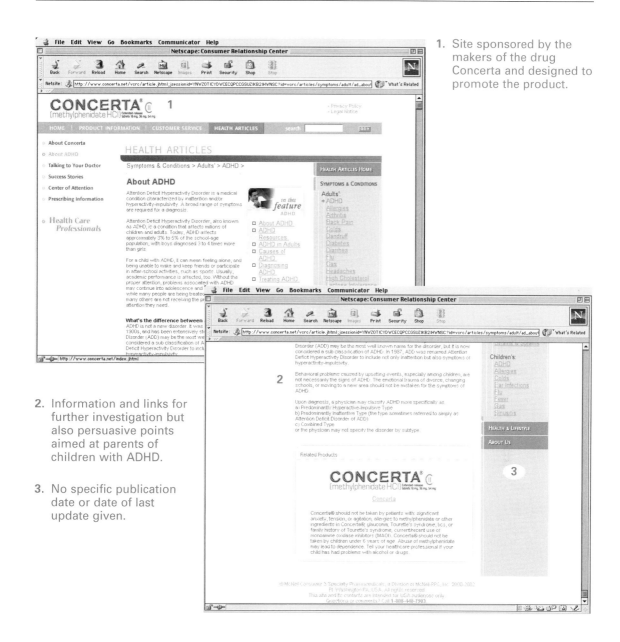

1. Site sponsored by the makers of the drug Concerta and designed to promote the product.

2. Information and links for further investigation but also persuasive points aimed at parents of children with ADHD.

3. No specific publication date or date of last update given.

Here are some questions you can ask to evaluate a source. If you answer "no" to any of these questions, think twice about using the source.

TEN QUESTIONS FOR EVALUATING A PRINT OR ELECTRONIC SOURCE

1. Is the source up-to-date?

2. Is the source one that you know is reliable (such as a well-known magazine or a reputable Web site)?

3. Has the author published other material on this subject?

4. Does the author offer other sources to support his or her ideas?

5. Does the author present only information that will support his or her point, ignoring other perspectives? (If the author presents all sides of the topic but lets the reader know his or her own views, the source may still provide good information.)

6. Does the author have a balanced, objective tone? (An objective author does not make other points of view seem wrong or dangerous.)

7. Does the author provide adequate support for his or her thesis?

8. If the source is a Web site, is the site's sponsoring organization well known and generally well respected?

9. Will using this source actually strengthen the point you want to make?

10. Can the information in the source be verified by checking other sources?

One way to evaluate a source is to consider the URL extension, the part of the URL that follows the "dot."

Guide to URL Extensions

EXTENSION	TYPE OF SITE	HOW RELIABLE?
.com	A commercial, or business, organization	Varies. Consider whether you have heard of the organization, and be sure to read its home page carefully.
.edu	An educational institution	Reliable, but may include many varied course materials.
.gov	A government agency	Reliable.
.net	A commercial, or business organization, or a personal site	Varies. This extension indicates just the provider, not anything about the source. Go to the source's home page to find out what you can about the author or the sponsor.

EXTENSION	TYPE OF SITE	HOW RELIABLE?
.org	A nonprofit organization	Generally reliable, although each volunteer or professional group promotes its own view or interests.

PRACTICE 1   **EVALUATING WEB SITES**

To practice analyzing two sites that address the same subject, visit <**www.whitehouse.gov/nsc**> and <**www.edreport.com**>. Which site is more likely to offer valid information about the National Security Council? How can you tell which site is legitimate and which one is phony?

_____

_____

_____

Avoid Plagiarism

DEFINITION: **Plagiarism** means passing off ideas and information you gather from another source as your own. Writers who plagiarize, either deliberately or by accident, risk failing a course, being expelled from school, losing their jobs, or damaging their reputations. You must be careful to avoid plagiarism when you are writing a research essay.

DELIBERATE PLAGIARISM

When you copy someone's work with no intention of crediting your source, you make a deliberate choice to plagiarize. Here are several examples of deliberate plagiarism:

1. A friend has a paper that fits your assignment, and you turn it in as your own work.
2. You find a paper on the Internet that fits your assignment, and you print it out and turn it in as your own work.

3. You see a great article in a newspaper or magazine, and you copy it word for word and turn it in as your own work.

As described, these three cases are plagiarism, plain and simple—you have intentionally put your name to someone else's work. Even crediting the source would not solve the problem: Your instructor would not want you to use someone else's paper. Plagiarism can be avoided, however, by quoting parts of the sources in your own essay and crediting them properly.

ACCIDENTAL PLAGIARISM

Too often, plagiarism results from taking sloppy notes, as illustrated in the following scenarios:

1. When it is time to write your paper, you find that you have forgotten to note the exact source of a useful fact or detail.
2. You can't remember whether a statement in your notes is a direct quotation or a paraphrase (a statement putting another person's ideas into your own words).
3. You can't remember whether an idea is yours or another person's, and you can't tell from your notes.

Accidental plagiarism that results from a poor note-taking process is still considered unethical or, in some cases, illegal. It often takes several weeks to write a research paper, and during this time many other events are going on in your life. Don't rely on your memory; use a trustworthy system for taking notes. Some such systems are described in the following section.

USE A SYSTEM FOR TAKING NOTES

Some writers take notes by hand on notecards (or index cards). These writers may enjoy the ease with which they can shuffle their notes as they organize and draft their essay. Others prefer to take notes in a word processing program. Doing so enables writers to cut and paste directly from notes to a draft. Use whatever method you find most comfortable, but be systematic about it. In other words, use a consistent format for all of your notes. Doing so will ensure that you have the information you need to avoid plagiarism.

Florence Bagley, a student writer, took notes on index cards. On one side of the card she noted the author and title of the source, the page numbers on which she found key information, and the parts of the source she wanted to use in her essay. She also clearly indicated what each note contained: a summary, a paraphrase, or a direct quotation. (She recorded full details about each source in her running bibliography, illustrated on p. 314.)

SAMPLE NOTE CARD—FRONT SIDE

Page number

Name of source

Type of information

> *Sheafer, Aretha Franklin: Motown Superstar*   *pp. 95–110*
>
> *Summary*
>
> *Aretha's career flourished, but her personal life was a mess.*
>
> *Marriage to Ted White (controlling and abusive).*
>
> *Divorce, 1969, shortly after birth of 3rd child.*
>
> *1969 — father arrested and charged with drug possession.*
>
> *Meanwhile, she won Grammy awards 1969–1975.*
>
> *Had 4th child (not married).*
>
> *Father died (from gunshot wound he'd gotten earlier).*

Florence used the back side of each note card to record her own comment about the source or a plan for using the information in her paper.

SAMPLE NOTE CARD—BACK SIDE

> *— What songs came out during those years?*
>
> *— How did her father get shot?*
>
> *— What happened to these kids?*

KEEP A RUNNING BIBLIOGRAPHY

If you are using a computer, you can alphabetize sources as you list them or use the Sort option in the Table menu in Microsoft Word. If you are not using a computer, add each source to your list as you use it, and don't worry about alphabetizing until you have finished.

DEFINITION: A **bibliography** is a complete list, alphabetized by author, of the sources you consulted as you investigated your topic. A **list of works cited** is a complete list, alphabetized by author, of the sources that you actually mention within your essay. Most instructors require a list of works cited at the end of a research essay. Some may require a bibliography as well.

To help you manage your sources, keep a running bibliography and add to it as you examine each source. Make sure that you include all of the information you will need to correctly identify the source in your bibliography or list of works cited.

BOOKS	ARTICLES	WEB SITES
Author name(s)	Author name(s)	Author name(s)
Title and subtitle	Title and page numbers	Title of page or site
Year of publication	Title of magazine, journal, or newspaper	Date of publication or latest update
Publisher and location of publisher	Year, month, day of publication (1999, December 9)	Name of sponsoring organization
		Date on which you accessed the source
		The URL (online address) in angle brackets (</>)

Here is a sample entry from Florence Bagley's running bibliography:

        Sheafer, Silvia A. Aretha Franklin: Motown Superstar. Detroit:
            Enslow, 1996.

Using a Computer to Avoid Plagiarism

Avoiding plagiarism is necessary in college, work, and everyday writing tasks. In the age of computers and the Internet, it is easy to cut and paste chunks of writing from sources. This mechanical ease of moving text may seem to make it easier for students to plagiarize, but computer resources also make it easier than ever before for teachers to detect plagiarism. Many teachers discover that a student has copied material from a Web source simply by using a search engine like Google and typing in a sentence or two from the student's paper. Search engines are now so powerful that they often find the source of a sentence in a fraction of a second.

In some cases though, teachers may suspect plagiarism when all that really happened was revision. In addition to learning to be careful about noting your sources, you should also be careful about saving each draft of your research essay and maintaining control of your research notes. By doing so, you can prove to your teacher that you aren't plagiarizing by showing how your writing has improved draft by draft.

CITE SOURCES AS YOU TAKE NOTES

Your running bibliography will help you keep track of the sources of all the facts, details, and examples you may want to use in your essay. If you are writing a paper in Modern Language Association (MLA) style (the style most commonly used in English courses), you will use parentheses to identify the author (or title) and page number for each source within your paper — immediately following the fact, detail, or example you borrow. At the end of your paper, you will list full information about each source.

EXCERPT FROM A RESEARCH ESSAY

Many American college students today go to a computer rather than to campus for a lecture, exam, or class discussion. A recent survey revealed that "more than half of the nation's colleges and universities deliver some courses over the Internet" (Press and Washburn 34).

ENTRY IN THE LIST OF WORKS CITED

Press, Eyal, and Jennifer Washburn. "Digital Diplomas." Mother Jones Jan.-Feb. 2001: 34+.

Besides identifying sources accurately, think about how each source can best help you explain or prove your thesis. Would using exact words from a source lend strength to your argument? Perhaps your essay needs technical evidence written in everyday language. Or maybe a source contains key information that you would be better off condensing. For each source you read, take notes in the form you think will be most useful in your research essay — direct quotation, paraphrase, or summary.

For an example of notes with proper source publication information, see page 332.

Direct Quotation

DEFINITION: When you use a person's exact words, you are using a **direct quotation**. Use these guidelines when you write direct quotations:

- Record the exact words of the source.
- Record the name of the writer or speaker so that you can use it later to introduce the quotation in your paper. If there is more than one author or speaker, record all names.
- Enclose the writer or speaker's words in quotation marks.
- For written sources, include the page number on which the quote appeared in the original source in parentheses after the end quotation mark but before the period. If the person quoted is not the author of the book or the article (that is, if you're quoting a quotation), give the author's name in parentheses along with the page number.

Identifying phrase   Quotation marks

DIRECT QUOTATION: According to Dr. Min Xiao, "The psychological benefits of a well-lit workspace are significant" (28).

Parenthetical citation

Paraphrase

DEFINITION: **Paraphrasing** is putting someone else's idea into your own words and restating it. Be careful if you choose to paraphrase. It is easy to think you are using your own words while you are actually using only some of your own and some of the author's or speaker's. When you paraphrase, follow these guidelines:

- Don't look at the source while you are writing the paraphrase.
- Check your paraphrase against the original source to make sure you have not used the author's words or copied the author's sentence structure.
- Cite your source in parentheses after your paraphrase.

Read the examples that follow to see acceptable and unacceptable paraphrases.

ORIGINAL SOURCE

Not unlike drugs or alcohol, the television experience allows the participant to blot out the real world and enter into a pleasurable and passive mental state. To be sure, other experiences, notably reading, also provide a temporary respite from reality. But it's much easier to stop reading and return to reality than to stop watching television. The entry into another world offered by reading includes an easily accessible return ticket. The entry via television does not. In this way television viewing, for those vulnerable to addiction, is more like drinking or taking drugs—once you start it's hard to stop.

—Marie Winn, "Cookies or Heroin?"

UNACCEPTABLE PARAPHRASE, TOO CLOSE TO ORIGINAL

Marie Winn says that like drugs or alcohol, television allows people to blot out reality and escape into the passive world of television. Reading also provides a break from the real world, but it's easier to put down a book than to turn off the television. Therefore, in people susceptible to addiction, television viewing is more like drinking or taking drugs than reading: It's much harder to stop once you've started.

This paraphrase is unacceptable for several reasons:

- The first sentence uses the same structure and some of the same words as the first sentence of the original.
- The paraphrase too closely follows the sentences and ideas of the original source.
- The writer hasn't cited the source.

The writer has obviously written the paraphrase while looking at the original source rather than expressing the ideas in his or her own words.

ACCEPTABLE PARAPHRASE

Marie Winn says that although television and reading both offer a break from reality, television watching is harder to stop and can therefore be considered "addictive," in a way that reading cannot (32).

The acceptable paraphrase presents Winn's basic ideas, but in the writer's own words and structures. It also includes a parenthetical citation. The writer carefully read Winn's paragraph but then wrote the paraphrase without looking at the original. Then the writer checked the original again to make sure she hadn't missed any ideas or repeated words or sentence structures.

Summary

DEFINITION: A **summary** presents only the main points of a source in your own words.

Let's say you read a three-page article on rhythm and blues singers. Although it supports your thesis and contains useful background information, the article doesn't contain any one person's words or ideas you want to include in your paper. Overall, though, the article does offer support because it appears in a reputable source and is current. If you decide to summarize and cite the source, you will need to do the following:

- State the source's main points briefly, in your own words.
- Note author's name so that you can use it in your paper to introduce your summary.
- Include in parentheses the page numbers of the entire section you have summarized.

For more on writing summaries, see Chapter 19.

SUMMARY OF AN ARTICLE: As reported in a recent issue of *Psychology Today*, people often listen to music when they are feeling depressed or are trying to work out a problem or move on from a difficult situation (Rayne 16–18).

Document Sources

DEFINITION: Responsible researchers **document**, or give credit to, their sources. Each source cited or mentioned in a research essay should also be fully credited in a list of works cited, bibliography, or reference list at the end of the paper. When you write research papers in college courses, you will be required to document your sources using a particular documentation style. Ask your instructor which one to use for your assignment. Most English instructors prefer the MLA (Modern Language Association) system. The last few pages of this chapter present the MLA system of documenting twenty common types of sources.

The model entries in this section are presented in four groups: books, periodicals, electronic sources, and other nonprint sources. If you cannot find a model for a type of source you are using in your essay, consult the *MLA Handbook for Writers of Research Papers*, fifth edition, or Research and Documentation online at <**www .bedfordstmartins .com/hacker/resdoc**>.

Use the following section as you add sources to your running bibliography. Look for the type of source (book, journal, Web site, and so on), and then format your source as shown, paying attention to the information required, the order of information, and the punctuation. Few people can remember the specifics of how to document sources; the key is to refer to this section as you gather your running bibliography and prepare your list of works cited.

BOOKS

1. **BOOK WITH ONE AUTHOR**   Author   Title

Anker, Susan. Real Essays: Writing Projects for College, Work, and Everyday Life. Boston: Bedford/St. Martin's, 2003.

Publisher   Publication date

2.   BOOK WITH TWO OR THREE AUTHORS

Piccioto, Richard, and Daniel Paisner. Last Man Down: A New York
     City Fire Chief and the Collapse of the World Trade Center.
     New York: Berkley, 2002.

Quigley, Sharon, Gloria Florez, and Thomas McCann. You Can Clean
     Almost Anything. New York: Sutton, 1999.

3.   BOOK WITH FOUR OR MORE AUTHORS

(Note: *et al.* means "and others.")

Roark, James L., et al. The American Promise: A History of the
     United States. Boston: Bedford/St. Martin's, 1998.

4.   BOOK WITH AN EDITOR

Tate, Parson, ed. Most Romantic Vacation Spots. Cheyenne:
     Chandler, 2000.

5.   WORK IN AN ANTHOLOGY

Cisneros, Sandra. "Barbie Q." Literature. Ed. Robert DiYanni.
     5th ed. New York: McGraw Hill, 2002. 235-36.

6.   ENCYCLOPEDIA ARTICLE

"Kosovo." Encyclopædia Britannica. 16th ed. 1999.

PERIODICALS

7.   MAGAZINE ARTICLE   Author   Title of article   Name of periodical

Kluger, Jeffrey. "Hunting Made Easy." Time 11 Mar. 2002: 62-63.

                                            Date   Inclusive pages

8.   NEWSPAPER ARTICLE

Fox, Maggie. "Scientists Report Experiment Creating Immune
     Cells." Boston Globe 1 May 2002: A20.

9.   SIGNED EDITORIAL IN A MAGAZINE OR NEWSPAPER

Udall, Don. "When Someone Is Alive but Not Living." Editorial.
     Newsweek 14 June 1999: 12.

10. **UNSIGNED EDITORIAL IN A MAGAZINE OR NEWSPAPER**

> "The Fall of a Telecom Gunslinger." Editorial. New York Times
>   1 May 2002: A22.

ELECTRONIC SOURCES

Electronic sources include Web sites; reference databases (online or on CD-ROM); works from subscription services such as LexisNexis, Electric Library, or PsycLIT; and electronic communications such as email. Because many electronic sources change often, always note the date you accessed or read the source as well as the date on which the source was posted or updated online. To make sure your records are accurate, you may want to bookmark, download, or print out hard copies of the pages you have used.

11. **AN ENTIRE WEB SITE**   Author   Title of Web site or description, such as home page

> Keely, Meg. The Basics of Effective Learning. 1 Mar. 1999. Bucks
>   County Community College. 1 May 2002 <http://www.bucks.edu/
>   ~specpop/time-manage.htm>.

Sponsor of the site, if listed   Date of access   URL   Date of most recent update

12. **A PART OF A LARGER WEB SITE**   Title of specific document within larger Web site

> Keely, Meg. "Managing Your Time and Study Environment."
>   The Basics of Effective Learning. 1 Mar. 1999. Bucks County
>   Community College. 1 May 2002
>   <http://www.bucks.edu/~specpop/time-manage.htm>.

13. **ARTICLE IN AN ONLINE PERIODICAL**   Author   Title of source   Name of online periodical

> Weine, Stevan M. "Survivor Families and Their Strengths:
>   Learning from Bosnians after Genocide." Other Voices: The
>   (e)Journal of Cultural Criticism. 2.1 (2000). 1 May 2002
>   <http://www.othervoices.org/2.1/weine/bosnia.html>.

Volume number and publication date   Date of access   URL

14. **WORK FROM A SUBSCRIPTION SERVICE**   Author   Title of source   Title of periodical

> Rex, Lesley A. "The Remaking of a High School Reader." Reading
>   Research Quarterly 36.3 (2001): 288-314. Expanded Academic
>   ASAP. InfoTrac. Clement C. Maxwell Lib., Bridgewater State
>   College, Bridgewater, MA. 23 Mar. 2002.

Publication information   Date of access   Name of library holding the subscription   Name of database and service

15. ELECTRONIC MAIL (EMAIL) OR ONLINE POSTING

Eisenhauer, Karen. "Learning Styles." Email to Susan Anker. 24
     Apr. 2002.

Collins, Terence. "Effective Grammar Activities." Online posting.
     14 Dec. 2001. CBW Listserv. 3 May 2002 <cbw-l@tc.umn.edu>.

OTHER SOURCES

16. PERSONAL INTERVIEW

Okayo, Margaret. Personal interview. 16 Apr. 2002.

17. SPEECH

Glenn, Cheryl. "Toward an Understanding of Silence and
     Silencing." Conf. on Coll. Composition and Communication
     Convention. Minneapolis Convention Center, Minneapolis.
     13 Apr. 2000.

18. FILM OR VIDEO

To the Limit. Dir. Nandana Krishna. Perf. Kristin Peri, Sarah
     Saltrick, and Jason Willey. Universal, 2000.

19. TELEVISION OR RADIO PROGRAM

"Playing Cards." Ally McBeal. Fox. KTTV, Rancho Cucamonga. 30
     Nov. 2001.

20. RECORDING

Keys, Alicia. "A Woman's Worth." Songs in A Minor. J-Records,
     2001.

You Will Know This

Okay, so maybe you've never written a research essay. But you've already done research on your own before to find out information you need (see p. 301), so you have a start. This chapter will show you how to do the rest.

21

Writing the Research Essay

Working with Sources

This chapter will guide you through the process of writing a research essay. Many stages are demonstrated by the work of student writer Florence Bagley, who wrote her essay, "The Queen of Soul," on the influence of music in Aretha Franklin's life.

THE RESEARCH WRITING PROCESS

1. Get organized.

For Florence Bagley's completed essay, "The Queen of Soul," see pages 338–42.

2. Find and narrow your topic.

3. Explore your topic, and write a thesis statement.

4. Take careful notes to build support.

5. Organize your notes, and plan your draft.

6. Draft and revise your essay.

7. Edit your essay.

Get Organized

Writing a good research essay requires organization from the very beginning. Two ways to get—and stay—organized are (*a*) to make a schedule and (*b*) to keep all of your research material in one place.

MAKE A SCHEDULE

After you receive your assignment, create a schedule that divides your research assignment into small, manageable tasks. Keep the schedule handy; you will need to refer to it often.

You can use the following schedule as a model for making your own:

SAMPLE RESEARCH ESSAY SCHEDULE

Assignment: _____

_____
(Write out what your instructor has assigned.)

Length: _____

Draft due date: _____

Final due date: _____

My general topic: _____

My narrowed topic: _____

TASK	DO BY
Review some of the information available about my general topic.	_____
Narrow my general topic, and write a research question.	_____
Find sources.	_____
Evaluate my sources; decide which ones to use.	_____
Take notes, and record publication information for each source.	_____
Review all notes; choose the best support for my working thesis.	_____

(continued)

For an electronic version of this schedule, visit the *Real Essays* Web site at <**www .bedfordstmartins .com/realessays**>.

Organize notes; make an outline.   _____

Write a draft.   _____

Review the draft; get feedback; add more support if needed.   _____

Revise the draft.   _____

Prepare a list of works cited using correct documentation form.   _____

Edit the revised draft.   _____

Print out and submit the final copy.   _____

KEEP ALL OF YOUR RESEARCH MATERIAL IN ONE PLACE

As you do your research, you will accumulate numerous items: a schedule, print material, electronic material, index cards or notes, an outline, and so on. Keeping everything together will help you manage your project successfully.

Managing Print Material

Some research writers prefer to keep hard copies, or paper copies, of sources, notes, schedules, and other project materials. If this system appeals to you, keep everything together in a file folder or large envelope. Label it "Research" or, more specifically, label it with your topic—such as "The Effects of Workspace on Workplace Productivity." Within the folder or envelope, use binder clips to hold together groups of materials.

Managing Electronic Material

Some research writers prefer to save sources, notes, schedules, and other project materials to a disk, a hard drive, or a list of bookmarks on their computer. If this system appeals to you, be sure to name your files as descriptively as possible (for example, "Notes on Turner article Feb-03" is better than "res. notes"). Then organize individual files within folders in your word processor. The following example shows a well-organized system for managing research materials:

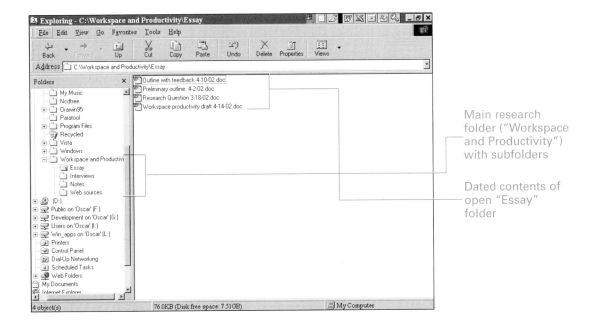

Main research folder ("Workspace and Productivity") with subfolders

Dated contents of open "Essay" folder

Find and Narrow Your Topic

In college, your instructor may want you to think of your own topic for a research paper assignment. If you are free to choose your topic, find a subject that you are personally interested in or curious about. If your instructor assigns a topic, you can skip ahead to the next main section, "Explore Your Topic, and Write a Thesis Statement," on page 330.

FIND YOUR TOPIC

If your instructor has not assigned a general topic but has said something like "Write about something that interests or affects you," consider it an opportunity. The best research essays often start with a personal connection. Ask and answer questions like the following to find a topic connected to your life:

1. What is going on in my own life that I want to know more about?
2. What have I heard about lately that I'd like to know more about?
3. What possible careers am I interested in?
4. What famous person—living or deceased—most interests me?

5. What do I daydream about? What frightens me? What do I see as a threat to me or my family? What inspires or encourages me?

6. Is there something I do in my spare time (sports, music, computer games) that I'd like to know more about?

Also look back at the writing you have done so far in this class. Are you personally interested in any of the topics you have already written about? What topics could you explore further by using research sources? Try rereading the paper you most liked to see if it includes a topic you can research.

For more on prewriting techniques, see page 27.

If you can't think of anything right away, take a little break and flip through a magazine or newspaper, watch the news, think about things that have mattered to you and made you react. Try a prewriting technique such as freewriting or brainstorming to find a general topic.

See the box below for some current topics and issues that you might want to explore.

Possible Topics for a Research Essay

A contemporary or historical figure	Free speech and the Internet
ADHD	Gang membership
Advertising	Gay marriage
An illness	Homeschooling
Assisted suicide	Mandatory drug testing
Cell phones	Road rage
Competitive sports in schools	Sexual harassment
Dating services	Standardized testing/placement testing
Dieting/eating disorders	Uniforms in school
Discrimination	Violence in the media
The draft for military service	Women in military combat
Executive salaries	Working parents
The family in America	

Write before You Research

When you have a general topic, write answers to these questions:

1. Why is this topic important to me or of interest to me? How does it affect me? What do I hope to gain by exploring it?
2. What do I know about the topic? What do I want to find out?

Florence Bagley, a second-year college student, was assigned a research paper on the general topic "A contemporary figure who has influenced your life." As she listened to CDs late one night, she thought about how much she loved Aretha Franklin's music and always had. She didn't know much about the singer and wondered if writing about her life would be a good topic for a research essay. She knew it couldn't just be a biography, like an encyclopedia entry, but thought she might be able to think of some part of Aretha's life she could write about.

After writing some notes to herself about Aretha's songs and how they really meant something to her, she then answered the two sets of questions listed above, applying them to her general topic.

1. Why is this topic important to me or of interest to me? How does it affect me? What do I hope to gain by exploring it?

FLORENCE'S RESPONSE (FREEWRITING)

> Ever since I can remember, I loved Aretha Franklin's music. It's more than just the music, though. It's the words and the way Aretha puts her heart into her music. It's like she knows about how life can be tough, and she's able to get that across in her music. A bunch of times when I'm going through something bad, I just put on her music and listen, and it really helps me. I feel like I know her, but I don't. I just know I love her music.

2. What do I know about the topic? What do I want to find out?

FLORENCE'S RESPONSE (FREEWRITING)

> I really don't know anything about her which is funny because we usually know a lot about most famous people. I know she started singing in a church, but that's all I know. Since her songs have been so important to me, I'd like to know a bit more about her.

■   **PRACTICE 1   FINDING YOUR TOPIC**

Write your general topic here: _____

With your general topic in mind, write your answers to these two questions about your general topic.

1. Why is this topic important to me or of interest to me? How does it affect me? What do I hope to gain by exploring it?

_____

_____

_____

2. What do I know about this topic? What do I want to find out?

_____

_____

_____

NARROW YOUR TOPIC

For more narrowing and exploring a topic, see Chapter 2.

The general topic you choose is likely to be too big to cover in a short research paper. It would be impossible, for example, to write a good five-page essay on the general topic "Crime." A more specific topic — something like "Neighborhood watch programs as crime deterrents" — is more manageable. To narrow your general topic to one that is more specific, you need to get an overview of the topic and find out what kinds of sources are available.

Ask and Answer Questions

You probably know more than you think you do about your general topic. One way to narrow your topic is to determine what you already know. Ask and answer the following questions to narrow your general topic.

1. What do I know or what have I heard about this topic?
2. What can I write about in a short research essay?

Now read Florence's answers to the questions about her general topic, "A contemporary figure who has influenced your life."

1. What do I know or what have I heard about this topic?

FLORENCE'S RESPONSE

> *I only know that Aretha Franklin started singing in church. I don't know anything else about her life. I'd like to find out more about it because her singing has been so important to me. I wonder how she put so much into her music and whether what she sang about was related to her life. Maybe she had a whole other life apart from her music, but I bet music was a key part of her life. Otherwise, I don't know how it could be so powerful.*

2. What can I write about in a short research essay?

FLORENCE'S RESPONSE

> *I can write about the basic facts of her life and music's role in it, maybe what it meant to her.*

PRACTICE 2   NARROWING YOUR TOPIC

Write your answers to these two questions to narrow your topic:

1. What do I know or what have I heard about this topic?

_____

2. What can I write about in a short research essay?

_____

Review Possible Sources

As you narrow your topic, spend a little time in the library, on the Internet, or with someone who is an authority on the subject to find out what information is available. With some help from a reference librarian, Florence found several articles and a book about Aretha Franklin, as well as a few promising Web sites. She discovered a good deal of information on Franklin's life and her music. After skimming and thinking about the information, Florence was able to narrow her topic.

FLORENCE'S NARROWED TOPIC: How music helped Aretha Franklin throughout her life, including some bad times.

THINKING CRITICALLY TO NARROW YOUR TOPIC

FOCUS   Think about the general topic you have chosen; then use the following questions to narrow your general topic.

ASK   • What part of my topic do I find interesting? What was I really thinking about when I chose it?
• On what aspects (or parts) of the topic could I find sources?
• Which of these aspects am I most interested in?

WRITE   Write your narrowed topic.

Explore Your Topic, and Write a Thesis Statement

Once you have a narrowed topic, you need to write a working thesis statement—a sentence that identifies your narrowed topic and the main point you want to make in your essay. If you have trouble deciding on your main point, try exploring your narrowed topic by asking a guiding research question.

ASK A GUIDING RESEARCH QUESTION

When you ask a guiding research question, your goal is to arrive at a single question about your narrowed topic that you will address in your paper. Write as many possible questions as you can think of before you decide on one.

FLORENCE'S NARROWED TOPIC: How singing helped Aretha Franklin throughout her life, including some bad times

POSSIBLE GUIDING RESEARCH QUESTIONS

How did Aretha's singing affect her life?

Was singing always a part of her life?

How important a part was it?

What role did singing play in Aretha's life?

How did Aretha become famous?

What was Aretha's childhood like?

What is Aretha's place in musical history?

FLORENCE'S GUIDING RESEARCH QUESTION: What role has singing played in Aretha Franklin's life?

PRACTICE 3   WRITING A RESEARCH QUESTION

Write at least three possible guiding research questions for your narrowed topic, and choose the most promising one.

WRITE A THESIS STATEMENT

Although your thesis statement may change as you find out more about your topic, it is important to start with a good working thesis statement. Before writing your thesis, remind yourself of what your purpose (or reason) for writing is and who your readers are. Your thesis statement should contain your narrowed topic and your main point. To find a good working thesis statement, try answering your guiding research question.

For more on writing a thesis statement, see Chapter 3.

FLORENCE'S THESIS STATEMENT: Aretha Franklin's life wasn't easy, but music helped her at every stage.

PRACTICE 4   WRITING A THESIS STATEMENT

Think about your narrowed topic and research question, and come up with a good working thesis statement.

1. What is the single main point about my narrowed topic that I want to show, explain, or prove?

   _____

2. Write a working thesis statement.

   _____

Take Careful Notes to Build Support

As in any other kind of writing, the quality of your research essay depends on the support you present to explain or prove your thesis. As you read possible sources, take notes that might help you answer your guiding research question. If you find later that you don't want to use some of the information, you can discard it. But start with a good supply of potential support.

For more on supporting your thesis, see Chapter 4.

As Florence read her sources, she noted examples and details that she could use to support her thesis. The following notecard includes a paraphrase of source information that Florence used to support her point that music helped Aretha Franklin through difficult periods in her life.

Author and title of source

Date of access and URL

Type of note

Source information in the student's own words

Layne, "Aretha Franklin Biography."	March 16, 2001
<www.rollingstone.com/artists/bio.asp?oid=457&cf=457>	
Paraphrase	
Aretha Franklin recorded "Bridge over Troubled Water" during some of her most difficult times. Her father was arrested on drug charges, and Franklin herself was abusing alcohol.	

For more on paraphrasing, summarizing, and using direct quotations, see pages 316–18.

As you work with sources, think about how source information can help you explain or prove your thesis. Writers generally support their points by using exact words, or direct quotations, from a source or by paraphrasing or summarizing source material.

Organize Your Notes, and Plan Your Draft

For more on making a plan, see Chapter 5.

When you think you have enough support for the thesis of your research essay, you need to make a plan, just as you would for any other essay. First, review your notes to decide what your major support points will be. Then make an outline that includes your thesis statement and the major support points.

Once you've completed this much of your outline, group your research notes under the major support points. Then review the notes for each major support point and arrange them in the most logical order (chronological, spatial, or importance). If you have taken notes using a word processor, cut and paste to place your notes within each section. If you are using index cards, arrange them in sequence and then number them according to the order in which you will use them in each paragraph. You may find that it helps to indicate source information within your outline. Student writer Florence Bagley carried her citations over from her notes to her outline (see below).

After you have arranged your notes, fill in the rest of the outline. If you haven't already done so, write a topic sentence for each of the major support points. During this step, you may notice gaps in your support. If you find that you need more information or support, return to your sources or seek out additional sources.

FLORENCE'S OUTLINE

I.   Introduction

Song lyric sung to Aretha by her father (quoted in Sheafer 9)

Thesis: Aretha Franklin's life hasn't been easy, but music has helped her at every stage.

II. How song and soul music became important: the early years

    A. Music at New Bethel Baptist Church

        1. Father was a Baptist minister whose sermons drew people from all around, very soulful

        2. Famous gospel singers came to the church (Bego 14)

        3. Singing at church

    B. Music at home

        1. Famous musicians would visit and play

        2. Mother's desertion; music was solace (Bego 12)

    C. Singing at church revivals

        1. Traveled around the country

        2. Met founders of Motown Music and recorded for them (Bego 30)

III. How music helped Aretha Franklin through hard times

    A. Pregnant at 15

        1. Dropped out of school

        2. Music career on hold

        3. At 17, single mother of two children

      B. Her grandmother encouraged her singing

         1. Got her to make tapes

         2. Scraped together money for Aretha to go to NYC

         3. Met Jerry Wexler, rhythm and blues (Franklin and Ritz 90)

      C. Problems with her father (Sheafer 85–110)

         1. Arrested for possession of marijuana

         2. Died from a gunshot wound

  IV. How she became known as the "Queen of Soul"

      A. Fame

         1. Wexler, "mysterious lady of sorrow" (Bego 8)

         2. First woman inducted into Rock and Roll Hall of Fame

         3. Cover of *Time*

         4. Lifetime achievement award

      B. "Respect," her most famous song

         1. Women and African Americans

         2. Two Grammy awards

      C. "A Bridge over Troubled Water"

         1. Drinking heavily

         2. Quote from *Rolling Stone* (Layne)

  V. Conclusion

      A. Relate back to introduction, maybe the opening song lyric

      B. Her special ability to reach us and help all of us

Draft and Revise Your Essay

For more on writing a draft, see Chapter 6.

Use your outline to help you draft your research essay from your notes, writing in complete sentences and paragraphs. As you draft your essay, you will need to work the source material into your writing smoothly. If you just drop a quotation, paraphrase, or summary into a paragraph with no explanation or context, you risk confusing your readers. Instead, you should add an identifying phrase at either the beginning or the end of the source material to distinguish your ideas from those of your source.

SAMPLE IDENTIFYING PHRASES

Sheafer reports . . .

As Sheafer writes . . .

According to a recent article in *Psychology Today,*

A recent survey in *Psychology Today* shows that...

"She was the mysterious lady of sorrow," said...

You may be able to work a fact or detail into your paragraph without an identifying phrase. In either case, though, you need to cite the source immediately afterward by giving the last name of the author and the page number in parentheses. (If a source does not have an author, use a short title instead.)

Tips for Writing an Essay Based on One Source

You may have been assigned to write an essay on a single source, such as one of the selections in "Readings for Writers" at the end of this book. If so, keep these guidelines handy.

- Read the source carefully. Identify the main idea and supporting ideas presented in the source.

- Take careful notes.

  - Record your own ideas about the topic. Note the ideas with which you agree and those with which you disagree.

  - Identify direct quotations that may help you to show or prove your own point. Place quotation marks around the passage in your notes, and write down the page number.

  - Write paraphrase notes or summary notes when you need to borrow ideas but not exact language from the source. Note the page number on which you find the material.

- Write a thesis statement that includes your narrowed topic and the point you want to make about it.

- As you draft, be certain that you are using the ideas in the source to support your own idea. Unless you have been asked simply to summarize a source (see Chapter 19), avoid stringing together ideas from the source without any indication of the point you are making.

- As you draft, use identifying phrases to distinguish your ideas from those of your source.

- Unless required by your instructor, do not include a list of works cited in a paper that uses only one source. Instead, cite the title of the source and the author's name early in your essay, and then use exact page numbers in parentheses for quotations, paraphrases, and summaries.

For more on revising a draft, see Chapter 7.

As you revise your research essay, ask yourself many of the same questions you ask when revising other types of essays.

THINKING CRITICALLY TO REVISE A RESEARCH ESSAY

FOCUS   After a break, reread your draft with a fresh perspective.

ASK   What's my point or position? Does my thesis statement clearly state my main point?

Does my essay have the necessary parts?
- Do I have an introductory paragraph that presents my research topic and states my main point about it?
- Do I have three or more body paragraphs, each with a topic sentence that supports the main point?
- Do I have a forceful concluding paragraph that reminds my readers of my main point and makes an observation?
- Do I use information and ideas from reliable sources?

Does my essay have unity?
- Do all of the major support points in my essay relate directly to the main point in my thesis?
- Do all the supporting details in each body paragraph relate to the paragraph's topic sentence?
- Have I avoided drifting away from my main point?

Do I have enough support?
- Do the quotations, summaries, and paraphrases drawn from source material provide ample support for my thesis?
- Does each paragraph have enough support for its topic sentence?
- Would more information or information from different types of sources strengthen my support?

Is my essay coherent?
- Have I used appropriate identifying phrases to integrate quotations, paraphrases, and summaries into my text?
- Have I used transitional words to link ideas within paragraphs and transitional sentences to link paragraphs?
- Do both the sentences and the paragraphs flow smoothly?

WRITE   Revise your draft, making any improvements you can.

Edit Your Essay

After you have carefully revised your research essay, take the time to edit and proofread it thoroughly. After all of your hard work, you don't want to be marked down for errors in grammar, spelling, punctuation, word use, or documentation format. Keep in mind that errors are unacceptable in research writing at work as well.

For more on editing, see Chapters 22–41.

Be sure to follow the documentation system required by your instructor. In your English classes, you will probably use the Modern Language Association (MLA) format for documentation. As you edit, be sure that you have correctly identified in parentheses the source for every quotation, paraphrase, summary, or other detail from a source. At the end of your research essay, also be sure that you have included a page headed "Works Cited," listing all the sources you have used in your essay.

For more on MLA style, see pages 318–21.

Sample Student Research Essay

Here is Florence Bagley's final research essay, "The Queen of Soul: The Influence of Music in Aretha Franklin's Life." You may notice that she has added some sections that did not appear in her outline. Before getting to this stage — the final paper — Florence wrote two drafts. She carefully reread each draft and got feedback before revising the essay thoroughly.

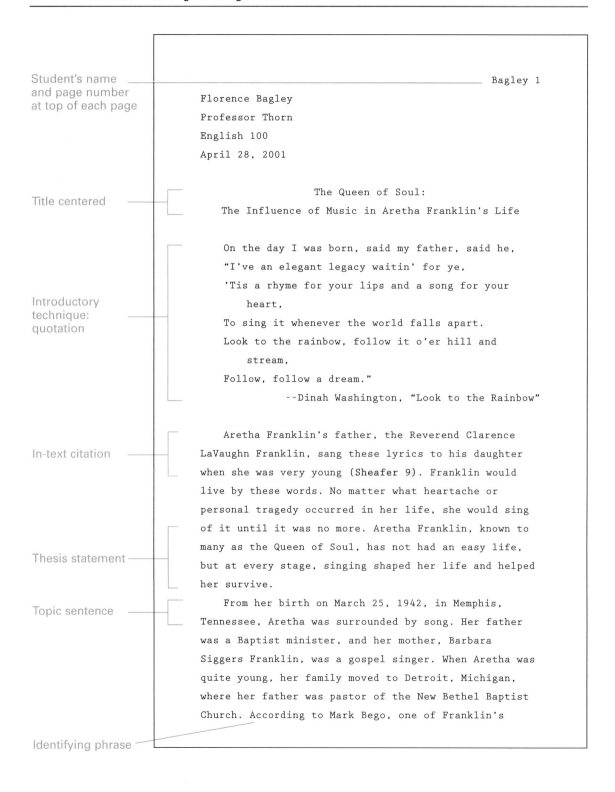

Student's name and page number at top of each page

Bagley 1

Florence Bagley

Professor Thorn

English 100

April 28, 2001

Title centered

The Queen of Soul:

The Influence of Music in Aretha Franklin's Life

Introductory technique: quotation

On the day I was born, said my father, said he,

"I've an elegant legacy waitin' for ye,

'Tis a rhyme for your lips and a song for your
    heart,

To sing it whenever the world falls apart.

Look to the rainbow, follow it o'er hill and
    stream,

Follow, follow a dream."

--Dinah Washington, "Look to the Rainbow"

In-text citation

Aretha Franklin's father, the Reverend Clarence LaVaughn Franklin, sang these lyrics to his daughter when she was very young (Sheafer 9). Franklin would live by these words. No matter what heartache or personal tragedy occurred in her life, she would sing of it until it was no more. Aretha Franklin, known to many as the Queen of Soul, has not had an easy life, but at every stage, singing shaped her life and helped her survive.

Thesis statement

Topic sentence

From her birth on March 25, 1942, in Memphis, Tennessee, Aretha was surrounded by song. Her father was a Baptist minister, and her mother, Barbara Siggers Franklin, was a gospel singer. When Aretha was quite young, her family moved to Detroit, Michigan, where her father was pastor of the New Bethel Baptist Church. According to Mark Bego, one of Franklin's

Identifying phrase

Bagley 2

biographers, this is where her lifelong passion for
singing began. People from all over came to this
church to hear the Reverend Franklin's sermons and to
sing in the choir (Bego 14). Famous gospel singers,
such as Mahalia Jackson and Clara Ward, sang in the
church and were among Aretha's early inspirations. The
Franklins' home, too, was full of music. Song artists
Sam Cooke, Dinah Washington, and Lionel Hampton were
among the many who came to the Franklin home to eat,
play the piano, and sing. Into this life of song came
Aretha's first heartache: her mother left her family
when Aretha was six (Bego 18). Song carried her through
the pain of an early disappointment.

> Paraphrase of source information

    Singing became Aretha's passion. Standing on a
chair, she would belt out gospel songs and, at the age
of twelve, she sang her first solo. People would flock
around her father, praising his daughter's talent. She
expanded her world to church revivals, traveling around
the country to sing. All the while, she remained
friends with Sam Cooke, who introduced her to Berry
Gordy and Billy Davis, the founders of Motown Music. On
hearing Aretha sing, the two men invited her to record
with them, though she was only fifteen. This she did,
over the objections of her father, who protested that
she was too young (Bego 20-30).

> Topic sentence

> Summary of source information

    Singing would see Aretha through the toughest times
of her life. At fifteen, she became pregnant and
dropped out of school. By the age of seventeen, Aretha
was a single parent of two children. Although she had
to put her musical career on hold, she continued to
sing for her life. With the encouragement of her
grandmother, Aretha went to New York to jump-start her
career while her children stayed in her grandmother's

> Topic sentence

Bagley 3

care. In 1960, she began recording tapes that brought her many contract offers; she signed a contract withColumbia Records as a pop singer. Still, however, pop was not the music that she sang from her soul. In 1966, Aretha met Jerry Wexler, a famous record producer, who repackaged her as a rhythm and blues singer. From then on, there was no turning back. Over the next three years, she would sell millions of albums (Franklin and Ritz 90).

While Aretha's career flourished, her personal life was once again in turmoil, as another biographer, Silvia Sheafer, tells us. Her brief marriage to Ted White, a controlling and abusive man, ended in 1969, shortly after the birth of her third child. In that same year, her father was arrested and charged with drug possession. Aretha's album sales soared, her songs became deeper and more powerful, and she won Grammy awards for six successive years, 1969 to 1975. In the meantime, however, she had a fourth child out of wedlock, and her father died from an earlier gunshot wound (Sheafer 95-110).

It seems that Aretha's many personal tragedies fueled the passion of her singing and were key to her success. Her producer, Jerry Wexler, would refer to her as "the mysterious lady of sorrow" (Bego 8), singing through the most dire personal traumas, as if compelled to do so. Her accomplishments are unmatched: She was the first woman inducted into the Rock and Roll Hall of Fame, the first African American woman to appear on the cover of *Time* magazine, and the recipient in 1996 of the Lifetime Achievement Award (Fanclub.com 1-3). Her greatest success sprang from her hardship.

Topic sentence

Identifying phrase

Identifying phrase

Direct quotation

Bagley 4

Aretha's songs and powerful lyrics help us deal
with serious issues in our lives and culture. One of
her greatest, "Respect," is a song of equality for
African Americans and women. It earned Aretha two of
her fifteen Grammy awards. She recorded "Bridge over
Troubled Water" during some of her most difficult
times, when she was rumored to have been drinking
heavily. Of the words "Like a bridge over troubled
water, I will lay me down," Aretha says, "What it says
to me is even though you may want to give up, just be
strong and things will get better. The storm will pass"
(qtd. in Layne).

    The way each of us interprets music and song lyrics
is very similar to how we interpret other language: It
may mean different things to different people. What I
hear in a song may not be what you hear. Whatever our
individual interpretations, however, the vibrating soul
in Aretha's voice has touched many lives. Her natural
ability to reach into our hearts and minds to create a
feeling of wellness and hope is a special gift. Her
deep expression of language and feeling through her
soul music is, for many of us, the most expressive
language of our time.

    Aretha Franklin has followed her father's message,
singing "whenever the world falls apart," following it
as a dream. Song has made her a strong person who will
be remembered long after her time. The Queen of Soul's
music not only helped her through but has also touched
many of our lives. Her ability to reach into our hearts
and minds to create a feeling of well-being and
connectedness is a special gift. Her soul reaches into
ours and brings us together in times of joy and sorrow.
She is truly the Queen of Soul.

Annotations:
- Topic sentence
- Franklin's words quoted in another source—in this case, a Web source
- Topic sentence
- Refers back to introduction
- Refers to introduction and makes an observation
- Another observation
- Reference to title, also tying conclusion back to introduction

Bagley 5

Works Cited

<u>Aretha Franklin: The Life Story</u>. 2001. VH1. 16 Mar.

2001 <http://www.vh1.com/fanclubs/

bio.jhtml?id=7622>.

Bego, Mark. <u>Aretha Franklin: The Queen of Soul</u>. New

York: St. Martin's, 1989.

Franklin, Aretha, and David Ritz. <u>From These Roots</u>.

New York: Crown, 1989.

Layne, Anni. <u>Aretha Franklin: Biography</u>. 2000.

Rollingstone.com. 16 Mar. 2001. <http://www

.rollingstone.com/artists/bio.asp?oid=457&cf=457>.

Sheafer, Silvia Anne. <u>Aretha Franklin: Motown Super-

star</u>. Detroit: Enslow, 1996.

Web site with
unknown author

For all entries,
indent after first
line

Book by two
authors

Titles of books are
either underlined
or italicized

PART FOUR

The Four Most Serious Errors

22

The Basic Sentence

An Editing Overview

The Four Most Serious Errors

This book puts special emphasis on the four grammar errors that people most often notice. These four errors may make your meaning harder to understand, but even if they don't, they give a bad impression of you.

THE FOUR MOST SERIOUS ERRORS

1. Fragments (see Chapter 23).
2. Run-ons (see Chapter 24).
3. Problems with subject–verb agreement (see Chapter 25).
4. Problems with verb form and tense (see Chapter 26).

If you can edit your writing to correct the four most serious errors, your sentences will be clearer and your grades will improve. Learning how to correct these errors will make a big difference in your writing.

This chapter will review the basic element of the sentence; the next four chapters cover the four most serious errors.

Understand What a Sentence Is

DEFINITION: A **sentence** is the basic unit of written communication. A complete sentence written in standard English must have three elements:

1. It must have a **subject**.
2. It must have a **verb**.
3. It must express a **complete thought**.

To edit your writing, you need a clear understanding of what *is* a sentence and what *is not* a sentence. You can find out if a group of words is a complete sentence by checking to see if it has a subject, if it has a verb, and if it expresses a complete thought.

SUBJECTS

For a list of pronoun types, see page 440.

DEFINITION: The **subject** of a sentence is the person, place, or thing that the sentence is about. The subject of the sentence can be a noun (a word that names the person, place, or thing) or a pronoun (a word that replaces the noun, such as *I, you, she,* or *they*).

To find the subject, ask yourself, *Who or what is the sentence about?*

In this section on subjects, only the subject is underlined.

PERSON AS SUBJECT   <u>Vivian</u> works for the police department.

[*Who* is the sentence about? *Vivian*]

THING AS SUBJECT   The <u>tickets</u> cost $65 apiece.

[*What* is the sentence about? The *tickets*]

A compound subject consists of two (or more) subjects joined by *and, or,* or *nor.*

TWO SUBJECTS   <u>Marty</u> and <u>Kim</u> have a new baby girl.

SEVERAL SUBJECTS   The <u>jacket</u>, <u>pants</u>, and <u>sweater</u> match perfectly.

For a list of common prepositions, see page 347.

DEFINITIONS: A **prepositional phrase** is a word group that begins with a preposition and ends with a noun or pronoun. A **preposition** is a word that connects a noun, pronoun, or verb with some other information about it.

The subject of a sentence is *never* in a prepositional phrase.

preposition

The <u>check</u> is in the mail,

prepositional phrase

The subject of the sentence is *check.* The subject can't be the word *mail,* which is in the prepositional phrase *in the mail.*

Common Prepositions

about	beneath	like	to
above	beside	near	toward
across	between	next to	under
after	by	of	until
against	down	off	up
along	during	on	upon
among	except	out	with
around	for	outside	within
at	from	over	without
before	in	past	
behind	inside	since	
below	into	through	

preposition

One of my best friends is a circus clown.

prepositional phrase

Although the word *friends* may seem to be the subject of the sentence, it isn't. *One* is the subject. The word *friends* can't be the subject because it is in the prepositional phrase *of my best friends.*

When you are looking for the subject of a sentence in your writing, it may help you to cross out any prepositional phrases, as in the following sentences.

The rules ~~about smoking~~ are posted everywhere.

The sound ~~of lightning striking a tree~~ is like gunfire.

Many ~~of the students~~ work part-time.

PRACTICE 1   IDENTIFYING SUBJECTS AND PREPOSITIONAL PHRASES

In each of the following sentences, cross out any prepositional phrases and underline the subject of the sentence.

For more practice, visit Exercise Central at <www.bedfordstmartins.com/realessays>.

EXAMPLE: For many, a first <u>apartment</u> is a welcome taste of independence.

1. Every year, thousands of young people from all over the country move to New York City.

2. Each of them hopes to become successful in the big city.

3. These young artists with big talent and very little money soon discover the difficulty of finding an apartment in New York.

4. Every apartment listing in the newspaper will be seen by hundreds of other apartment-seekers.

5. The advice of a real estate broker can be helpful.

6. Naturally, the apartment of a young person's dreams is likely to be out of his or her price range.

7. Unfortunately, even a tiny apartment with no closets and no view can be unaffordable on the island of Manhattan.

8. The salary for an entry-level position is unlikely to be enough to rent even a small, shabby apartment.

9. Many young people without money share their apartments with roommates.

10. Sadly, living among total strangers is usually more fun in movies and on television than in real life.

VERBS

DEFINITION: Every sentence has a **main verb,** the word or words that tell what the subject does or that link the subject to another word that describes it. Verbs do not always immediately follow the subject: Other words may come between the subject and the verb.

There are three kinds of verbs: action verbs, linking verbs, and helping verbs.

In the examples throughout this chapter, the subject is underlined once, and the <u>verb</u> is underlined twice.

Action Verbs

DEFINITION: An **action verb** tells what action the subject performs.

To find the main action verb in a sentence, ask yourself, *What action does the subject perform?*

ACTION VERBS   The <u>puppy</u> <u><u>cried</u></u> all night.

The <u>building</u> <u><u>collapsed</u></u> around midnight.

After work, <u>we</u> often <u><u>go</u></u> to Tallie's.

My <u>aunt and uncle</u> <u><u>train</u></u> service dogs.

Linking Verbs

DEFINITION: A **linking verb** connects (links) the subject to a word or group of words that describe the subject. Linking verbs show no action. The most common linking verb is *be,* along with all its forms (*am, is, are,* and so on). Other linking verbs such as *seem* and *become* can usually be replaced by the corresponding form of *be,* and the sentence will still make sense.

LINKING VERBS   The <u>dinner</u> <u><u>is</u></u> delicious.

<u>I</u> <u><u>felt</u></u> great this morning.

This <u>lasagna</u> <u><u>tastes</u></u> just like my mother's.

The <u>doctor</u> <u><u>looks</u></u> extremely tired.

Some words can be either action verbs or linking verbs, depending on how they are used in a particular sentence.

ACTION VERB   The <u>dog</u> <u><u>smelled</u></u> Jake's shoes.

LINKING VERB   The <u>dog</u> <u><u>smelled</u></u> terrible.

Common Linking Verbs

FORMS OF *BE*	FORMS OF *BECOME* AND *SEEM*	FORMS OF SENSE VERBS
am	become, becomes	appear, appears
are	became	appeared
is	seem, seems	feel, feels, felt
was	seemed	look, looks
were		looked
		smell, smells
		smelled
		taste, tastes, tasted

Helping Verbs

DEFINITION: A **helping verb** joins with the main verb in the sentence to form the **complete verb**. The helping verb is often a form of the verb *be, have,* or *do.* A sentence may have more than one helping verb along with the main verb.

Sunil <u><u>was talking</u></u> on his cell phone.

[The helping verb is *was;* the complete verb is *was talking.*]

Charisse <u><u>is taking</u></u> three courses this semester.

Tomas <u><u>has missed</u></u> the last four meetings.

My brother <u><u>might have passed</u></u> the test.

Common Helping Verbs

FORMS OF *BE*	FORMS OF *HAVE*	FORMS OF *DO*	OTHER
am	have	do	can
are	has	does	could
been	had	did	may
being			might
is			must
was			should
were			will
			would

PRACTICE 2   **IDENTIFYING THE VERB (ACTION, LINKING, OR HELPING + MAIN)**

In the following sentences, underline each subject and double-underline each verb. Then identify each verb as an action verb, a linking verb, or a helping verb + a main verb.

EXAMPLE: At first, <u>Miguel</u> <u>did</u> not <u>want</u> to attend his high school reunion. *helping verb + main verb*

1. Miguel's family moved to Ohio from Guatemala ten years ago.

2. He was the new kid at his high school that fall.

3. Miguel was learning English at that time.

4. The football players teased small, quiet boys like him.

5. After graduation, he was delighted to leave that part of his life behind.

6. Recently, the planning committee sent Miguel an invitation to his high school reunion.

7. His original plan had been to throw the invitation in the trash.

8. Instead, he is going to the party to satisfy his curiosity.

9. His family is proud of Miguel's college degree and his new career as a graphic artist.

10. Perhaps some of the other students at the reunion will finally get to know the real Miguel.

COMPLETE THOUGHTS

DEFINITION: A **complete thought** is an idea, expressed in a sentence, that makes sense by itself without other sentences. An incomplete thought leaves readers wondering what's going on.

INCOMPLETE THOUGHT	as I was leaving [*What's going on?*]
COMPLETE THOUGHT	The <u>phone</u> <u>rang</u> as I was leaving.
INCOMPLETE THOUGHT	the people selling the car [*What's going on?*]
COMPLETE THOUGHT	The <u>people</u> selling the car <u>placed</u> the ad.

To identify a complete thought, ask yourself: *Do I know what's going on, or do I have to ask a question to understand?*

INCOMPLETE THOUGHT   in the apartment next door

[Do I know what's going on, or do I have to ask a question to understand? *You would have to ask a question, so this is not a complete thought.*]

COMPLETE THOUGHT   Carlos lives in the apartment next door.

PRACTICE 3   IDENTIFYING COMPLETE THOUGHTS

Some of the following items contain complete thoughts, and others do not. In the space to the left of each item, write either "C" for complete thought or "I" for incomplete thought. If you write "I," add words to make a sentence.

I cleaned the bathroom

EXAMPLE: __I__ Because my mother asked me to do it.

_____ 1. Smiling broadly as the cameras flashed all around him.

_____ 2. Nobody spoke.

_____ 3. The man who lives in the big brick house on Valley Street.

_____ 4. Her shoes were tight.

_____ 5. It's raining.

_____ 6. After the last customer had gone home.

_____ 7. Which explains why she missed class last week.

_____ 8. Although you could have gotten away with cheating.

_____ 9. Leave them alone.

_____ 10. On the five o'clock train.

23

Fragments

Incomplete Sentences

Understand What Sentence Fragments Are

DEFINITIONS: A **sentence** is a group of words that has a subject and a verb and expresses a complete thought, independent of other sentences. A **sentence fragment** is a group of words that is missing a subject or a verb or that does not express a complete thought.

SENTENCE	I'm going to a concert on Friday at Memorial Arena.
FRAGMENT	I'm going to a concert on Friday. *At Memorial Arena.*
	[*At Memorial Arena* does not have a subject or a verb.]

IN THE REAL WORLD, WHY IS IT IMPORTANT TO CORRECT FRAGMENTS?

A sentence fragment is one of the grammatical errors that most people notice. When people outside of the English classroom notice errors such as fragments, they don't assign you a course grade, but they do judge you by your communication skills. Prospective employers sometimes rule out candidates who make certain kinds of errors. For this reason, make sure you know how to edit your writing for fragments and how to correct them before you turn in any piece of writing, either in college or in the work-place.

SITUATION: James is responding to an ad he has seen for a job at a consulting firm. He sends the following cover letter, along with his résumé.

Dear Ms. Letendre:
   I am interested in the computer technician position I saw. In the *Lowell Sun*. I have held two similar positions that I have described. In my attached résumé. I believe I have the skills you are looking for. I would like an opportunity to meet with you. To discuss possible employment opportunities.
   Thank you for your consideration.
   Sincerely,
   James Cosentini

RESPONSE: Maureen Letendre, the human resource director who is profiled in Chapter 11, had the following response to James's letter.

This letter and résumé go right into the "reject" pile.

Find and Correct Fragments

To find fragments in your own writing, look for the five fragment trouble spots listed below. If you find a potential trouble spot, read the sentence carefully to make sure it has a subject, has a verb, and expresses a complete thought.

FIVE FRAGMENT TROUBLE SPOTS

1. A word group that **starts with a preposition**, such as *in, at, with* (for a list, see p. 355).
2. A word group that **starts with a dependent word** such as *although, because, who, that.*
3. A word group that **starts with an -*ing* verb form**.
4. A word group that **starts with *to* and a verb**.
5. A word group that **starts with an example or explanation**.

When you are editing your own writing and find a fragment, you can usually correct it in one of two ways.

TWO WAYS TO CORRECT FRAGMENTS

1. Add what is missing (a subject, a verb, or both).
2. Attach the fragment to the sentence before or after it.

1. FRAGMENTS THAT START WITH A PREPOSITION

Finding Fragments

Whenever a preposition starts what you think is a sentence, check for a subject, a verb, and a complete thought. If any one of those is missing, you have a fragment.

Remember, the subject of a sentence is *never* in a prepositional phrase (see p. 346).

FRAGMENT   The plane crashed into the house. *With a deafening roar.*

[*With a deafening roar* is a prepositional phrase starting with the preposition *with* and ending with the noun *roar*. The phrase has neither a subject nor a verb. It is a fragment.]

FRAGMENT   Take the second left and head west. *Toward the highway.*

[*Toward the highway* is a prepositional phrase starting with the preposition *toward* and ending with the noun *highway*. The phrase has neither a subject nor a verb. It is a fragment.]

Common Prepositions

about	beneath	like	to
above	beside	near	toward
across	between	next to	under
after	by	of	until
against	down	off	up
along	during	on	upon
among	except	out	with
around	for	outside	within
at	from	over	without
before	in	past	
behind	inside	since	
below	into	through	

Correcting Fragments

Correct a fragment that starts with a preposition by connecting it to the sentence either before or after it. If you connect a fragment to the sentence after it, put a comma after the fragment to join it to the sentence.

FRAGMENT	The plane crashed into the house. *From a height of eight hundred feet.*
CORRECTED	The plane crashed into the house. /From a height of eight hundred feet.
CORRECTED	From a height of eight hundred feet, the plane crashed into the house.

PRACTICE 1   CORRECTING FRAGMENTS THAT START WITH PREPOSITIONS

In the following items, circle any preposition that appears at the beginning of a word group. Then correct any fragment by connecting it to the previous or the next sentence.

EXAMPLE: (Since) the discovery of fingerprint ~~evidence. Police~~ depart-
evidence, police
ments all over the world have used it to convict wrongdoers.

For more practice, visit Exercise Central at <www.bedfordstmartins.com/realessays>.

1. Fingerprinting must have seemed like magic. To the public a hundred years ago.

2. On most surfaces, such as the handle of a weapon. Fingerprints are nearly invisible.

3. With the development of techniques for finding and preserving fingerprints. Detectives gained an advantage over criminals who did not wear gloves.

4. For most juries. Fingerprint evidence was absolute proof.

5. Until recently. Few people realized that identifying fingerprints was not an exact science.

6. Fingerprint experts can sometimes disagree. On whether two prints match.

7. When two prints were very similar, there have even been a few cases. Of mistaken fingerprint identification.

8. To most investigators. Fingerprint evidence is no longer the most reliable tool for identifying criminals.

9. DNA evidence has become the new industry standard. In the past decade.

10. DNA identification is much more exact than fingerprinting, and it is very difficult. For a criminal to avoid leaving his or her DNA at a crime scene.

2. FRAGMENTS THAT START WITH A DEPENDENT WORD

DEFINITIONS: A **dependent word** is the first word in a dependent clause. A **dependent clause** has a subject and a verb but does not express a complete thought.

DEPENDENT CLAUSE	because the apartment was already rented

[*because* is the dependent word that begins the clause]

FRAGMENT THAT STARTS WITH A DEPENDENT WORD	I didn't fill out an application. *Because the apartment was already rented.*
DEPENDENT CLAUSE IN A SENTENCE	I didn't fill out an application *because the apartment was already rented.*
DEPENDENT CLAUSE	who came into the restaurant last week

[*who* is the dependent word that begins the clause]

FRAGMENT THAT STARTS WITH A DEPENDENT WORD	The server remembered the two sets of twins. *Who came into the restaurant last week.*

DEPENDENT CLAUSE IN A SENTENCE	The server remembered the two sets of twins *who came into the restaurant last week.*

Finding Fragments

A word group that starts with a dependent word (see list below) is a dependent clause, not a complete sentence. Although a dependent clause has a subject and a verb, it does not express a complete thought. It is a fragment unless it is connected to a complete sentence.

FRAGMENT   Last night we went to a movie. *After we had dinner at Luigi's.*

[Does the word group have a subject? Yes, *we.* A verb? Yes, *had.* Then why isn't it a sentence? Because it isn't a complete thought: After we had dinner at Luigi's, what happened?]

FRAGMENT   I'll go pick up the pizza and soda. *While you put the baby to bed.*

[Does the word group have a subject? Yes, *you.* A verb? Yes, *put.* Then why isn't it a sentence? Because it isn't a complete thought: While you put the baby to bed, what will happen?]

Common Dependent Words

after	if	what(ever)
although	since	when(ever)
as	so that	where
because	that	whether
before	though	which(ever)
even though	unless	while
how	until	who/whose

Correcting Fragments

Correct a fragment that starts with a dependent word by connecting it to the sentence before or after it. If the dependent clause is connected to the sentence before it, you usually do not need to put a comma in front of it. If the dependent clause is joined to the sentence after it, put a comma after the dependent clause.

FRAGMENT   Chris looked for a job for a whole year. *Before he found the right one.*

CORRECTED   Chris looked for a job for a whole year. *b* Before he found the right one.

CORRECTED   Before he found the right ~~job.~~ *one,* Chris looked for a whole year. *a job for*

FRAGMENT   My boss docked my pay for the half hour I was late. *Even though I worked through my lunch hour.*

CORRECTED   My boss docked my pay for the half hour I was late. *e* Even though I worked through my lunch hour.

PRACTICE 2   FINDING AND CORRECTING FRAGMENTS THAT START WITH A DEPENDENT WORD

In the following items, circle any dependent word that appears at the beginning of a word group. Then correct any fragment by connecting it to the previous or the next sentence.

EXAMPLE: (Since) many jobs involve working on a computer all ~~day. Some~~ *day, some* employees can work wherever a computer is available.

1. If a company mainly sells information. Its workers are more likely than employees of other businesses to be allowed to do their jobs at home.

2. Before a worker begins telecommuting. He or she must often convince the company that there is a good reason for the change.

3. Some companies are reluctant to approve telecommuting. Unless their workers already have the necessary computer equipment at home.

4. Telecommuting sounds like a wonderful idea to many employees. Who do not look forward to getting dressed for work and commuting to the office.

5. While going to work in a bathrobe may be appealing. Telecommuters sometimes discover that working at home also has drawbacks.

6. Some telecommuters discover that they are not as productive at home. As they are at the office.

7. A telecommuter needs motivation and discipline. So that he or she can concentrate on the job while surrounded by all the distractions of home.

8. Telecommuters sometimes feel isolated. When they are not in daily contact with other employees.

9. Finally, telecommuters may find the pace of their work slowed down by their home Internet connection. Which may not be as fast as an office's high-speed line.

10. Even though telecommuting is not for everyone. A growing percentage of workers are on the job at home one or two days a week.

3. FRAGMENTS THAT START WITH *-ING* VERB FORMS

DEFINITION: An ***-ing* verb form** is the form of a verb that ends in *-ing: walking, writing, swimming.* When this verb form is part of a complete verb, it must be used with a helping verb (*am, is, was*—for a complete list see p. 350). By itself, it can act as a subject but not as a verb. An *-ing* verb form acting as a subject or other noun is also known as a *gerund.*

-ING FORM USED WITH A HELPING VERB AS A VERB

I am swimming every day this summer.

[In this sentence, *am* is the helping verb; *am swimming* is the complete verb.]

Tom *was running* when he saw the accident.

[In this sentence, *was* is the helping verb; *was running* is the complete verb.]

-ING FORM USED ALONE AS A SUBJECT

Swimming is a wonderful form of exercise.

[In this sentence, *swimming* is the subject, not the verb; *is* is the verb.]

Running strains the knees.

[In this sentence, *running* is the subject, not the verb; *strains* is the verb.]

Finding Fragments

Whenever a word group begins with a word in *-ing* form, look carefully to see if the word group contains a subject and a verb and if it expresses a complete thought.

FRAGMENT   Snoring so loud I couldn't sleep.

[If *snoring* is the main verb, what is the subject? There isn't one. Is there a helping verb used with *snoring*? No. It is a fragment.]

FRAGMENT   *Hoping to make up for lost time.* I took a back road to school.

[If *hoping* is the main verb, what is the subject? There isn't one. Is there a helping verb used with *hoping*? No. It is a fragment.]

Correcting Fragments

Correct a fragment that starts with an *-ing* verb form either by adding whatever sentence elements are missing (usually a subject and a helping verb) or by connecting the fragment to the sentence before or after it. Usually, you will need to put a comma before or after the fragment to join it to the complete sentence.

-ING FRAGMENT   The audience applauded for ten minutes. *Whistling and cheering wildly.*

CORRECTED   The audience applauded for ten minutes, *Whistling and cheering wildly.*

CORRECTED   The audience applauded for ten minutes. *They were whistling and* ~~Whistling and~~ cheering wildly.

-ING FRAGMENT   *Working two jobs and going to school.* I am tired all the time.

CORRECTED   Working two jobs and going to school, I am tired all the time.

CORRECTED

I am working

~~Working~~ two jobs and going to school. I am tired all the
time.

PRACTICE 3   CORRECTING FRAGMENTS THAT START WITH A DEPENDENT WORD

In the following items, circle any *-ing* verb that appears at the beginning of a word group. Then correct any fragment either by adding the
missing sentence elements or by connecting it to the sentence before or
after it.

EXAMPLE: (Quilting) with a group of other ~~women. My~~ *women, my* grandmother

found a social life and a creative outlet.

1. My grandmother spent her entire life. Living on a farm in eastern
   Wyoming.

2. Growing up during World War II.   She learned from her mother
   how to sew her own clothes.

3. She was a natural seamstress. Creating shirts and dresses more beautiful
   than anything available in a store.

4. Joining a quilting circle at the age of twenty.   My grandmother learned
   how to make quilts.

5. The quilting circle made quilts for special occasions. Using scraps of
   cloth left over from other sewing projects.

6. Laying the scraps out in an interesting pattern. The women then chose
   a traditional design for the stitching that joined the top and bottom
   parts of the quilt.

7. Celebrating the birth of her first child, my father. The quilting circle
   gave my grandmother a baby quilt that is now a treasured heirloom.

8. She told me that the quilt was made of memories. Incorporating fabric from her wedding dress, her maternity outfits, and all of the baby clothes she had stitched.

9. Looking at each bit of cloth in that quilt. My grandmother could still describe, years later, the garment she had made it from.

10. Trying to ensure that those memories would survive. I asked her to write down everything she recalled about my father's baby quilt.

4. FRAGMENTS THAT START WITH *TO* AND A VERB

DEFINITION: An **infinitive** is the word *to* plus a verb: *to hire, to eat, to study.* If a word group begins with *to* and a verb, it must have another verb or it is not a complete sentence.

FRAGMENT   I will go to the store later. *To buy a card.*

[The first word group is a sentence, with *I* as the subject and *will go* as the verb. There is no subject or verb in the word group *to buy a card.*]

FRAGMENT   I ate nothing but popcorn for a week. *To lose ten pounds, my goal.*

[The word group that begins with *to lose* has no subject and no verb.]

Finding Fragments

When you have written what you think is a sentence, and it begins with the word *to* and a verb, check to see if there is another verb. If there is not another verb in the word group, it is a fragment.

FRAGMENT   Last week a couple in New York fulfilled their wedding fantasy. *To get married on the top of the Empire State Building.*

[Is there another verb in addition to *to get married* in the word group that starts with *to* and a verb? No; the word group is a fragment.]

FRAGMENT   David brought a magazine to the post office. *To read in the long line of customers.*

[Is there another verb in addition to *to read* in the word group that starts with *to* and a verb? No; the word group is a fragment.]

Correcting Fragments

To correct a fragment that starts with *to* and a verb, connect it to the sentence before or after it, or add the missing sentence elements (a subject and a verb.)

FRAGMENT	Geri climbed up on the roof. *To watch the fireworks.*
CORRECTED	Geri climbed up on the roof., *t* To watch the fireworks.
CORRECTED	*She wanted to* Geri climbed up on the roof. To watch the fireworks.
FRAGMENT	*To save on her monthly gas bills.* Tammy sold her SUV and got a Honda Civic.
CORRECTED	To save on her monthly gas bills., Tammy sold her SUV and got a Honda Civic.
CORRECTED	*Tammy wanted to* *She* To save on her monthly gas bills. Tammy sold her SUV and got a Honda Civic.

▪ **PRACTICE 4   FINDING AND CORRECTING FRAGMENTS THAT START WITH *TO* AND A VERB**

In the following items, circle any examples of *to* and a verb that begin a word group. Then correct each fragment either by adding the missing sentence elements or by connecting it to the previous or the next sentence.

> **EXAMPLE:** Convincing Americans to use less energy is one way, *t* To ensure that there is enough for everyone.

1. In 1976, several oil-producing countries in the Middle East made an agreement. To refuse to sell oil to the United States.

2. During the energy crisis that followed, drivers could not always buy enough gasoline. To fill the tanks of their cars.

3. American automakers increased the fuel efficiency of their cars. To meet consumers' demands for vehicles with better gas mileage.

4. To use less fuel. Homeowners in the mid-1970s kept their homes cooler in the winter and warmer in the summer.

5. Oil and gasoline soon became widely available again, so many Americans made a decision. To stop worrying about conserving energy.

6. To drive a giant sport utility vehicle. This was a goal of large numbers of middle-class Americans at the end of the twentieth century.

7. To deal with energy shortages in California and rising gas prices across the country in 2001. Some people suggested that Americans needed to consume less energy.

8. Others argued that the United States needed to invest in new technology. To develop renewable sources of energy, such as wind and solar power.

9. Perhaps the booming economy of the 1990s convinced too many Americans that there would never be a need for them. To consider a less wasteful lifestyle.

10. To combat rising energy prices in the winter of 2001–2002. American politicians wanted to tap into the country's emergency fuel reserves, not to urge citizens to use less.

5. FRAGMENTS THAT START WITH EXAMPLES OR EXPLANATIONS

As you edit your writing, pay special attention in each sentence to groups of words that are examples or explanations of information you have given in the previous sentences. These word groups may be fragments.

FRAGMENT   Shoppers find many ways to save money on food bills. *For example, using double coupons.*

[The second word group has no subject and no verb. The word *using* is an -*ing* verb form that needs either to be the subject of a sentence or to have a helping verb with it.]

FRAGMENT   Parking on this campus is a real nightmare. *Especially between 8:00 and 8:30 A.M.*

[The second word group has no subject and no verb.]

Finding Fragments

Finding fragments that start with examples or explanations can be difficult because there is no single kind of word to look for. The following are a few starting words that may signal an example or explanation, but fragments that are examples or explanations do not always start with these words:

especially   for example   like   such as

When a group of words that you think is a sentence gives an example of information in the previous sentence, stop to see if it has a subject and a verb and if it expresses a complete thought. If it is missing any of these elements, it is a fragment.

FRAGMENT   The Web has many job search sites. *Such as Monster.com.*

[Does the second word group have a subject? No. A verb? No. It is a fragment.]

FRAGMENT   I wish I had something to eat from Chipotle's right now. *A giant burrito, for example.*

[Does the second word group have a subject? Yes, *burrito.* A verb? No. It is a fragment.]

FRAGMENT   I had to push seven different voice-mail buttons before I spoke to a real person. *Not a helpful one, though.*

[Does the second word group have a subject? Yes, *one.* A verb? No. It is a fragment.]

Correcting Fragments

To correct a fragment that starts with an example or an explanation, connect it either to the previous or to the next one. Sometimes you can add the missing sentence elements (a subject, a verb, or both) instead. When you connect the fragment to a sentence, you may need to reword or to change some punctuation. Many fragments that are examples are set off by commas.

FRAGMENT   The Web has many job search sites. *Such as Monster.com.*

CORRECTED   The Web has many job search sites, such as Monster.com.

FRAGMENT   I had to push seven different voice-mail buttons before I
                    spoke to a real person. *Not a helpful one, though.*

CORRECTED   I had to push seven different voice-mail buttons before I
                    He was not
                    spoke to a real person. ~~Not a~~ helpful ~~one~~, though.
                                            ^

PRACTICE 5   CORRECTING FRAGMENTS THAT ARE EXAMPLES OR EXPLANATIONS

In the following items, circle any word groups that are examples or explanations. Correct each fragment either by connecting it to the previous sentence or by adding the missing sentence elements.

EXAMPLE: Some studies estimate that the number of teenage girls

suffering dating abuse is very high. (Perhaps as many as one)
experiences some type of abuse from her boyfriend.
(out of three girls.)
                  ^

1. Many parents believe that they would know if their daughters were
   being abused. Either physically or emotionally.

2. Most parents would certainly be concerned to see signs of violence on
   their children. Such as bruises or scratches.

3. A young man can be abusive without laying a finger on his girlfriend.
   A guy who monitors her actions and keeps her from spending time
   with other friends.

4. Abusive boyfriends often want to control their partners. Make sure that
   their girlfriends dress conservatively for example.

5. Around her parents, a teenager's boyfriend may act like a perfect
   gentleman. Polite, attentive, and kind to the young woman.

6. When the couple is alone, however, he may be subjecting her to verbal
   abuse. Like telling her that she is fat, stupid, and ugly.

7. A young woman with an abusive boyfriend may develop psychological problems that will be difficult to treat. Such as low self-esteem.

8. Parents should look for signs that their daughter needs help. Slipping grades, loss of interest in her friends, and unwillingness to confide in parents.

9. Friends who think that a young woman is involved in an abusive relationship should try to be supportive of her. Not turn away even if she will not leave her boyfriend.

10. Young women need to know that help is available. From parents, guidance counselors, women's support services, and even the police, if necessary.

Edit Paragraphs and Your Own Writing

As you complete the practices and edit your own writing, use the Thinking Critically guide that follows. You may also want to refer to the Quick Review Chart on page 372.

THINKING CRITICALLY TO EDIT FRAGMENTS	
FOCUS	Whenever you see one of the five trouble spots in your writing, stop to check for a possible fragment.
ASK	• Does it have a subject? • Does it have a verb? • Does it express a complete thought?
EDIT	If your answer to any of these questions is "no," you have a fragment that you must correct.

PRACTICE 6   **EDITING PARAGRAPHS FOR FRAGMENTS**

Find and correct any fragments in the following paragraphs.

1. (1) Genetically modified foods are being marketed. (2) As the foods of the future. (3) For the past decade, gene technology has been advancing dramatically. (4) Inserting a gene from one species into the DNA of another species is easily possible. (5) A gene from a fish may be found. (6) To make tomatoes more resistant to disease. (7) Of course, this genetic modification may have unintended effects. (8) As in the case of genetically modified corn. (9) Which may harm monarch butterfly caterpillars. (10) Arguing that the long-term effects of genetic modification may not be known for years to come. (11) Some scientists urge caution before marketing genetically modified foods.

2. (1) The year 2001 brought more bad news. (2) For beef eaters and for British cattle farmers struggling to overcome the bad publicity brought on by mad cow disease. (3) Cattle in England and Scotland suffered an epidemic of an extremely contagious illness. (4) Hoof-and-mouth disease. (5) Many people were frightened of eating British beef even though the disease does not harm humans. (6) To contain the outbreak. (7) Hiking trails were closed. (8) Because the disease could travel on the shoes or clothing of people walking from one region to another. (9) Before the epidemic was contained, thousands of infected cattle were slaughtered. (10) In the end, many farmers wondered how they would be able to survive. (11) After losing so many of their livestock.

3. (1) The term *organic* means different things. (2) To different people. (3) Organic foods are supposed to be grown without pesticides. (4) A

method that reduces a farm's impact on the environment. (5) But is organic food a healthier choice for the person eating it? (6) Most people who buy organic food think so. (7) They pay premium prices for organic products because they think the food is good for their own well-being. (8) Not just that of the environment. (9) Surprisingly, however, some foods labeled *organic* today are highly processed. (10) The label merely means that the ingredients meet a certain government standard. (11) While guaranteeing nothing about the nutritional content or health benefits of the food.

4.   (1) For several years. (2) The U.S. Department of Agriculture has permitted the irradiation of certain foods sold in American supermarkets. (3) Irradiating produce kills bacteria on the food. (4) Increasing its shelf life. (5) Without irradiation, a strawberry may last only a day or two after being purchased. (6) An irradiated strawberry, on the other hand, can last a week or more. (7) Because the bacteria that would cause it to spoil are killed by radiation. (8) While some consumers worry about buying irradiated food. (9) Others dismiss these concerns as the effect of too many science-fiction movies. (10) In stores where irradiated fruits and vegetables are sold under banners announcing the radiation treatment. (11) The owners report a booming market.

5.   (1) Bacteria that resist antibiotics could be a real health threat in the next century. (2) Doctors have begun to explain to their patients. (3) That antibiotics are useful only for certain kinds of infections and that patients must finish every course of antibiotics they start. (4) Antibiotic use in agriculture, however, has continued. (5) To increase. (6) The government does not even keep records. (7) Of antibiotic use in farm animals. (8) Many

cattle, pigs, and chickens get antibiotics for economic reasons. (9) Such as to keep them healthy and to make them grow faster. (10) Many scientists fear that antibiotic residue in the meat Americans eat may contribute to antibiotic resistance. (11) If so, agricultural antibiotics could eventually endanger human health.

PRACTICE 7   EDITING YOUR OWN WRITING FOR FRAGMENTS

As a final practice, carefully read a piece of your own writing—a paper you are working on for this class, a paper you've already finished, a paper for another course, or a recent piece of writing from your work or everyday life. Use the Thinking Critically guide on page 368 and the Quick Review Chart that follows as you edit for fragments.

Quick Review Chart

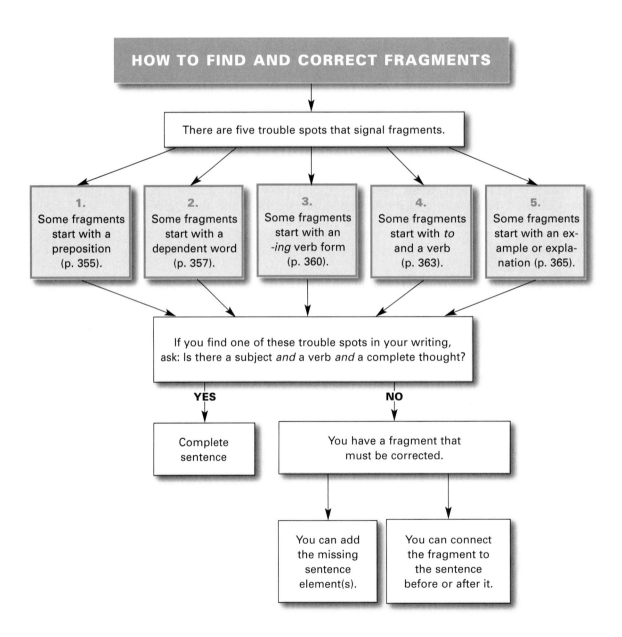

HOW TO FIND AND CORRECT FRAGMENTS

There are five trouble spots that signal fragments.

1.
Some fragments start with a preposition (p. 355).

2.
Some fragments start with a dependent word (p. 357).

3.
Some fragments start with an -*ing* verb form (p. 360).

4.
Some fragments start with *to* and a verb (p. 363).

5.
Some fragments start with an example or explanation (p. 365).

If you find one of these trouble spots in your writing, ask: Is there a subject *and* a verb *and* a complete thought?

YES

NO

Complete sentence

You have a fragment that must be corrected.

You can add the missing sentence element(s).

You can connect the fragment to the sentence before or after it.

24

Run-Ons

Two Sentences Joined Incorrectly

Understand What Run-Ons Are

DEFINITION: A sentence is also called an **independent clause**, a group of words with a subject and a verb that expresses a complete thought. Sometimes two independent clauses can be joined in one sentence.

SENTENCE WITH TWO INDEPENDENT CLAUSES

independent clause　　　independent clause

The <u>fog</u> <u><u>was</u></u> very thick, so the <u>airport</u> <u><u>closed</u></u>.

DEFINITIONS: A **run-on** is two sentences (each containing a subject and a verb and expressing a complete thought) that are joined incorrectly and written as one sentence. There are two kinds of run-ons: **fused sentences** and **comma splices**.

A **fused sentence** is two complete sentences joined without any punctuation.

In the examples throughout this chapter, the <u>subject</u> is underlined once and the <u><u>verb</u></u> is underlined twice.

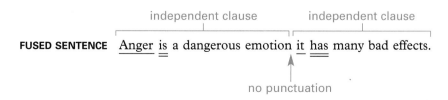

FUSED SENTENCE <u>Anger</u> <u><u>is</u></u> a dangerous emotion <u>it</u> <u><u>has</u></u> many bad effects.

no punctuation

A **comma splice** is two complete sentences joined by only a comma instead of a comma and one of the following words: *and, but, for, nor, or, so, yet*.

COMMA SPLICE   <u>Anger</u> <u>is</u> a dangerous emotion, <u>it</u> <u>has</u> many bad effects.

comma

IN THE REAL WORLD, WHY IS IT IMPORTANT TO CORRECT RUN-ONS?

Run-ons, like fragments, are errors that people notice. Their presence in your writing can result in a bad grade on a paper or, worse, a rejection from a potential employer. Because a run-on is one of the four most serious errors you can make, an important editing task is to find and correct both fused sentences and comma splices.

SITUATION: Marion is new to her position as a licensed practical nurse at a large hospital. Each day she updates patients' records and writes brief summaries of their progress for other nurses. The following is a report that Marion wrote in her first week on the job.

Trudari Kami is a premature infant she was born with a birth weight of 1.7 pounds her lungs were not fully developed and she was not able to breathe on her own. As of 2:15 A.M. on Thurday, April 6, she remains in stable condition her condition is still critical though she is being carefully monitored.

RESPONSE: Patty Maloney, the clinical nurse specialist profiled in Chapter 8, had the following response to Marion's report.

I had to meet with Marion, who is obviously not sure how to communicate clearly in medical documents. I explained to her that what she had written was very difficult to understand, and I worked with her on revising the report so that the next person would understand what Marion was trying to say. I had to do this because the reports must be clear; otherwise, the next person might not be sure how to treat the baby.

Find and Correct Run-Ons

FINDING RUN-ONS

There is only one good way to find run-ons in your writing: Read each sentence carefully, checking specifically to make sure that you have not fused two sentences or created a comma splice. As you get used to correcting run-ons in your writing, you won't have to spend as much time looking for them because you will write fewer of them with each new assignment or project.

Read the following paragraph. Does it include any run-ons? _Yes_

If so, how many? ___5___

> The concert to benefit AIDS research included fabulous musicians and songs. One of the guitarists had six different guitars they were all acoustic. One had a shiny, engraved silver shield on it, it flashed in the lights. The riffs the group played were fantastic. All of the songs were original, and many had to do with the loss of loved ones. At the end of some songs the audience was hushed, too moved with emotion to begin the applause right away. When the concert was over the listeners, many of them in tears, gave the performers a standing ovation.

CORRECTING RUN-ONS

When you are editing your writing and find a run-on, you can correct it in one of four ways.

FOUR WAYS TO CORRECT A RUN-ON

1. Add a period.
2. Add a semicolon.
3. Add a comma and a coordinating conjunction.
4. Add a dependent word.

1. Add a Period

You can correct a run-on by adding a period to make two separate sentences.

FUSED SENTENCE	I tried to call about my bill I got four useless recorded messages.	
COMMA SPLICE	I finally hung up, my question remained unanswered.	

2. Add a Semicolon

You can correct a run-on by adding a semicolon (;) to join the two independent clauses into one sentence. Use a semicolon only when the two independent clauses express closely related ideas that make sense in a single combined sentence.

FUSED SENTENCE	My father had a heart attack he is in the hospital.
COMMA SPLICE	My mother called 911 the ambulance was there in four minutes.

A semicolon is sometimes used before a transition from one independent clause to another, and the transition word is followed by a comma.

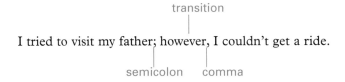

I tried to visit my father; however, I couldn't get a ride.

■ **PRACTICE 1**   **CORRECTING A RUN-ON BY ADDING A PERIOD OR A SEMICOLON**

For more practice, visit Exercise Central at <www .bedfordstmartins .com/realessays>.

For each of the following run-ons, indicate in the space to the left whether it is a fused sentence (FS) or a comma splice (CS). Then correct the run-on by adding a period or a semicolon.

EXAMPLE: _CS_   A cellular phone in the car can be a lifesaver in an

emergency; a cell phone may also contribute to

an accident.

_FS_   1. The invention of cell phones made telephoning from a car

possible, people could telephone for help if they were stranded on

the highway.

_FS_   2. Almost as soon as cell phones became common, people began to

use them in traffic, some drivers were undoubtedly distracted by

their telephones, creating a danger.

_CS_   3. Some communities in the United States have banned drivers from

talking on handheld cell phones, a driver must stop the car to

place a call legally in those areas.

_CS_   4. Cell-phone makers have come up with hands-free phones even in

places with cell-phone restrictions, these phones can be used by

the driver of a moving car.

_FS_   5. No one debates that drivers can be distracted by cell phones.

some people wonder, however, whether the problem is really the

fact that a driver is holding the phone.

_FS_   6. If lawmakers simply want to make sure that drivers have their

hands free, they should ban eating while driving as well, they

could also stop people from shaving or putting on makeup behind

the wheel.

_FS_   7. Some people worry that drivers are distracted not by holding the

telephone, but by having a conversation, a tense discussion with the boss or good news from a relative can take the driver's attention from traffic.

FS

_____ 8. Cell-phone supporters argue that the same kinds of distractions can come from elsewhere in the car, music and talk radio, for example, can suddenly make a driver lose concentration.

CS

_____ 9. There are differences, however, between talking on a cell phone and listening to music in the car, the telephone requires interaction from the driver, but the radio calls for passive listening.

FS

_____ 10. Drivers who love making calls on the road will resist cell-phone restrictions, many other people will feel safer in communities that do not allow driving while telephoning.

3. Add a Comma and a Coordinating Conjunction

DEFINITION: Coordinating conjunctions are the words used to combine two independent clauses of equal importance into one sentence. There are only seven coordinating conjunctions: *and, but, for, nor, or, so, yet.*

To correct a comma splice, keep the comma but add a coordinating conjunction. If the run-on is a fused sentence, add both a comma and a coordinating conjunction. Before adding just any coordinating conjunction, read the independent clauses to see which of the seven makes the most sense.

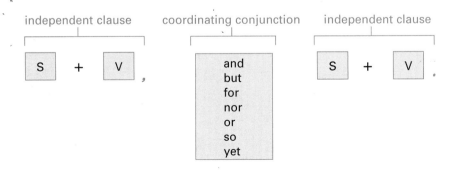

, but

FUSED SENTENCE   We warned Tim to wear a seat belt ‸ he never did.

and

COMMA SPLICE   He got into an accident, ‸ he went through the windshield.

PRACTICE 2   CORRECTING A RUN-ON BY ADDING A COMMA AND A COORDINATING CONJUNCTION

Correct each of the following run-ons. First underline the subjects and double-underline the verbs to find the separate sentences. Then add a comma (unless the run-on already includes one) and a coordinating conjunction.

EXAMPLE: Tasmania, an island off the coast of Australia, is the home

but

of many unusual kinds of wildlife, ‸ it also has been the site

of several oil spills.

and

1. Fairy penguins, a small breed of penguin, live in Tasmania these birds have often been the victims of oil spills.

and

2. The birds clean their feathers with their beaks they swallow the oil on their feathers.

for

3. Unfortunately, the penguins' attempts to clean off their feathers can be fatal, crude oil is poisonous to penguins.

4. Wildlife conservationists in Tasmania expected future spills, they created a plan to save the penguins.

5. One of the conservationists created a pattern for a sweater for the penguins, volunteers from around the world knitted these unusual sweaters.

6. The sweaters cover everything but the penguins' heads and feet, they can't lick the oil-poisoned feathers.

7. Most of the sweaters were made by elderly nursing-home residents in Tasmania, some were sent from as far away as Japan.

8. After future spills, a fairy penguin may wear a sweater it also might wear a tiny football jersey.

9. Some creative knitters made tuxedo-patterned sweaters a few of these penguin suits even have bow ties.

10. The penguins have a variety of protective outfits they don't like any of the garments.

4. Add a Dependent Word

The fourth way to correct a run-on is to make one of the independent clauses a dependent clause.

Common dependent words are listed below.

DEFINITION: A **dependent clause** is a group of words with a subject and a verb. However, it is not a complete sentence because it begins with a dependent word and does not express a complete thought. It is dependent on a sentence or independent clause to do that.

dependent clause

The ice cream melted fast because it was really hot out.

dependent word

Common Dependent Words

after	if	what(ever)
although	since	when(ever)
as	so that	where
because	that	whether
before	though	which(ever)
even though	unless	while
how	until	who/whose

When you add a dependent clause to an independent clause, place the addition where it makes more sense. If the dependent clause starts off the sentence, you need to add a comma after it. If the dependent clause is added to the second part of the sentence, you don't need a comma. Always begin a dependent clause with a dependent word.

until
COMMA SPLICE   I took deep breaths, I was calmer.

In this case, the sentence would not make much sense if the word *until* was added to the first independent clause: Until I took deep breaths, I was calmer.

In other cases, though, the dependent word can be added to either independent clause. The writer can choose where to place the word according to what part of the sentence he or she wants to emphasize.

Although   ,
FUSED SENTENCE   I ordered a salad I wanted the fried clam plate with fries.

In this example, the dependent word *although* would also make sense before the second independent clause:

I ordered a salad although I wanted the fried clam plate with fries.

PRACTICE 3   CORRECTING A RUN-ON BY MAKING A DEPENDENT CLAUSE

Correct each of the following run-ons. First underline the subjects and double-underline the verbs to find the separate sentences. Then make one of the clauses a dependent clause by adding a dependent word. Add a comma after the dependent clause if it comes first in the sentence.

before
EXAMPLE: Mr. Johnson was a sheet-metal worker, he retired.

1. My neighbor, Mr. Johnson, began his hobby his children were worried about his ability to keep busy after retirement.

2. In his basement, he built small replicas of local buildings, the buildings were familiar to him and his family.

3. He made the models out of sheet metal, he was used to working with that material.

4. He made a copy of his own house, he used wire mesh for the porch railing.

5. He finished the metal work Mr. Johnson painted the house white with a green roof, just like the original.

6. Mr. Johnson drove by our town's century-old sandstone courthouse he had planned to make just one model house.

7. He was working on the model courthouse, he found photographs of his childhood home.

8. He found enough photographs, he had a view of every part of the old farmhouse.

9. He finished his model of the old house his family began to show the models to other people.

10. Mr. Johnson's retirement suddenly became busier than his working life, everyone in town seemed to want a model house.

5. *A Word That Can Cause Run-Ons:* Then

Many run-ons are caused by the word *then.* You can use *then* to join two sentences, but if you add it without the correct punctuation, your sentence will be a run-on. Often writers mistakenly use just a comma before *then,* but that makes a comma splice.

To correct a run-on caused by the word *then,* you can use any of the four methods presented in this chapter.

COMMA SPLICE   I grabbed the remote, then I ate my pizza.

CORRECTED   I grabbed the remote, then I ate my pizza.   [added period]

CORRECTED   I grabbed the remote, then I ate my pizza.   [semicolon added]

and

CORRECTED   I grabbed the remote, then I ate my pizza.   [coordinating conjunction *and* added]

before

CORRECTED   I grabbed the remote, then I ate my pizza.   [dependent word *before* added to make a dependent clause]

Edit Paragraphs and Your Own Writing

As you complete the practices and edit your own writing, use the Thinking Critically guide that follows. You may also want to refer to the Quick Review Chart on page 386.

THINKING CRITICALLY TO EDIT RUN-ONS

FOCUS	Read each sentence aloud, and listen carefully as you read.
ASK	• Am I pausing in the middle of the sentence? • If so, are there two subjects and two verbs? • If so, are there two complete sentences in this sentence? • If there are two sentences (independent clauses), are they separated by punctuation? If the answer is "no," the sentence is a **fused sentence**. • If there is punctuation between the two independent clauses, is it a comma only, with no coordinating conjunction? If the answer is "yes," the sentence is a **comma splice**.
EDIT	If the sentence is a run-on, correct it using one of the four methods for editing run-ons.

██   **PRACTICE 4   EDITING PARAGRAPHS FOR RUN-ONS**

Find and correct any run-ons in the following paragraphs. Make the corrections using whichever of the four methods seems best to you. You may want to refer to the preceding Thinking Critically guide or the Quick Review Chart on page 386.

1.   (1) Your memory can play tricks on you. (2) It's often easy to forget things you want desperately to remember them. (3) You have probably had the experience of forgetting an acquaintance's name the name comes to your mind only when it's too late. (4) You have also probably been unable to find your keys once in a while, you put them down somewhere without thinking. (5) At other times, however, you may find it difficult to forget some things, you wish you could never think of them again. (6) If you have an annoying song in your mind, you may spend hours wishing desperately to forget it. (7) Sometimes you may find yourself forced to relive your most embarrassing moment over and over again in your mind your memory won't let you leave that part of your past behind. (8) Some scholars believe that these annoying habits of memory evolved for a reason, it's hard to imagine, though, any good reason for developing the ability to forget where you left your keys.

2.   (1) Most scientists now agree that human beings are changing the climate industrial activities release gases into the air that trap heat in the earth's atmosphere. (2) The number one problem gas is carbon dioxide, factories and gasoline engines release tons of it into the air. (3) In international discussions of global warming, industrial countries like the United States have argued that planting forests might reduce the amount of carbon dioxide in the air. (4) Trees absorb carbon dioxide, then they release oxygen. (5) A recent study tested trees in North Carolina it exposed them to high levels of carbon dioxide. (6) At first, the trees grew rapidly, after a while, their growth returned to normal. (7) Dead trees did not release their accumulated carbon into the soil instead, the carbon went back into the air as carbon dioxide. (8) The study will continue for

years, this is not the last word on the subject. (9) However, perhaps reducing carbon dioxide in the atmosphere will be difficult the United States may yet have to come up with a way to reduce the amount of the gas getting into the air in the first place.

PRACTICE 5   EDITING YOUR OWN WRITING FOR RUN-ONS

As a final practice, carefully read a piece of your own writing—a paper you are working on for this class, a paper you've already finished, a paper for another course, or a recent piece of writing from your work or everyday life. For extra help in editing for run-ons, use the Thinking Critically guide on page 383 and the Quick Review Chart that follows.

Quick Review Chart

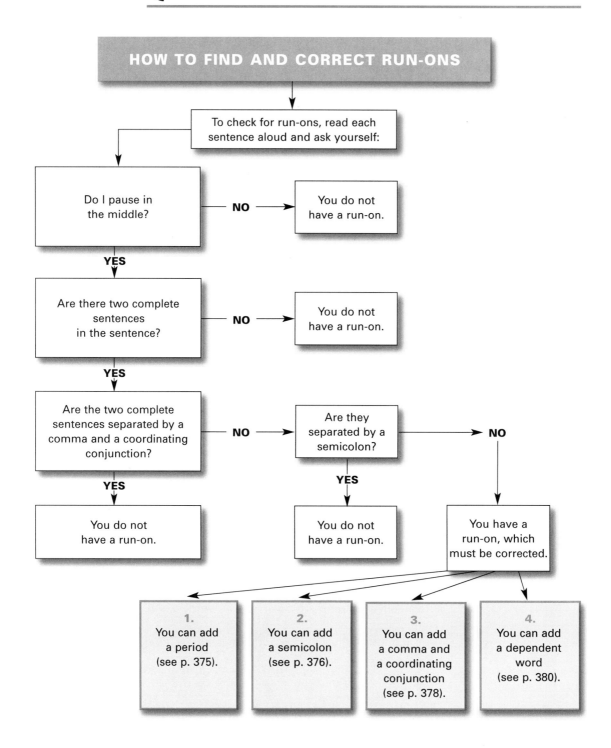

HOW TO FIND AND CORRECT RUN-ONS

To check for run-ons, read each sentence aloud and ask yourself:

Do I pause in the middle?

NO → You do not have a run-on.

YES

Are there two complete sentences in the sentence?

NO → You do not have a run-on.

YES

Are the two complete sentences separated by a comma and a coordinating conjunction?

NO → Are they separated by a semicolon?

NO

YES (first branch)

You do not have a run-on.

YES (second branch)

You do not have a run-on.

You have a run-on, which must be corrected.

1.
You can add a period (see p. 375).

2.
You can add a semicolon (see p. 376).

3.
You can add a comma and a coordinating conjunction (see p. 378).

4.
You can add a dependent word (see p. 380).

25

Problems with Subject-Verb Agreement

When Subjects and Verbs Don't Match

Understand What Subject-Verb Agreement Is

DEFINITION: In any sentence, the subject and the verb must agree or match in number. If the subject is singular (one person, place, or thing), then the verb must also be singular in form. If the subject is plural (more than one), the verb must also be plural in form.

> **SINGULAR**   The phone rings constantly at work.
>
> [The subject, *phone,* is singular—just one phone—so the verb must take the singular form: *rings.*]
>
> **PLURAL**   The phones ring constantly at work.
>
> [The subject, *phones,* is plural—more than one phone—so the verb must take the plural form: *ring.*]

DEFINITION: **Regular verbs** are verbs with forms that follow standard English patterns. They have two forms in the present tense: one that does not add an ending and one that ends in -*s*.

In the examples throughout this chapter, the subject is underlined once and the verb is underlined twice.

387

Regular Verbs, Present Tense

	SINGULAR FORM	PLURAL FORM
First person	I walk.	We walk.
Second person	You walk.	You walk.
Third person	He/she/it walks.	They walk.
	Percy walks.	Percy and Don walk.
	The dog walks.	The dogs walk.

First-person (*I, we*) subjects, second-person (*you*) subjects, and plural (more than one person, place, or thing) subjects have verbs with no *-s* ending. Third person singular subjects (*he, she, it,* and singular nouns) always have a verb that ends in *-s*.

IN THE REAL WORLD, WHY IS IT IMPORTANT TO CORRECT SUBJECT-VERB AGREEMENT PROBLEMS?

Like fragments and run-ons, errors in subject-verb agreement are widely considered to be one of the four most serious grammar errors. When people notice them, they form a negative impression of your writing ability. It is important that you learn to edit your writing for problems with subject-verb agreement.

SITUATION: Daigo Fujiwara, the assistant art director profiled in Chapter 10, communicates frequently with freelance artists and designers. The following email message from one designer caught his attention.

Today we talk about specs for the photographs. I has several possibilities that I be sending you by the end of the week.

RESPONSE: I had to reread this message a few times to make sure I understood. These kinds of mistakes make me stop, so it takes longer for me to process the message. On the one hand, I sympathize with the person because I also had to learn to write correct English. On the other hand, when my writing was really bad, I reread anything I wrote very carefully to make sure that it was right, and I think this person should have taken the time to do that.

Find and Correct Errors in Subject-Verb Agreement

To find problems with subject-verb agreement in your own writing, learn to look for five trouble spots that often signal errors in subject-verb agreement. The best way to find these errors is to read your writing carefully, looking specifically for these trouble spots.

TROUBLE SPOTS IN SUBJECT-VERB AGREEMENT

1. The verb is a form of *be*, *have*, or *do*.
2. Words or phrases come between the subject and the verb.
3. The sentence has a compound subject.
4. The subject is an indefinite pronoun.
5. The verb comes before the subject.

1. THE VERB IS A FORM OF *BE, HAVE,* OR *DO*

The verbs *be*, *have*, and *do* do not follow the regular patterns for forming singular and plural forms; they are **irregular verbs** (irregular because they do not conform to the regular patterns).

Forms of the Verb Be

PRESENT TENSE	SINGULAR	PLURAL
First person	I am	we are
Second person	you are	you are
Third person	she/he/it is	they are
	the student/Joe is	the students are
PAST TENSE		
First person	I was	we were
Second person	you were	you were
Third person	she/he/it was	they were
	the student/Joe was	the students were

Forms of the Verb Have, *Present Tense*

	SINGULAR	PLURAL
First person	I have	we have
Second person	you have	you have
Third person	she/he/it has	they have
	the student/Joe has	the students have

Forms of the Verb Do, *Present Tense*

	SINGULAR	PLURAL
First person	I do	we do
Second person	you do	you do
Third person	she/he/it does	they do
	the student/Joe does	the students do

These verbs are difficult for many writers because in casual conversation people sometimes use the same form of the verb, no matter what *person* the subject is in and no matter whether the subject is singular or plural. For example, in conversation, one friend might say to another:

He be the craziest person I've ever known.

Johnson have the best car in the lot.

Valery do the bill paying on the first of every month.

In college or professional situations, you need to use the correct form of the verbs *be, have,* and *do.* The verb must agree with the subject.

_is_
He be the craziest person I've ever known.

has
Johnson have the best car in the lot.

does
Valery do the bill paying on the first of every month.

PRACTICE 1   **CHOOSING THE CORRECT FORM OF *BE, HAVE, OR DO***

In each sentence, underline the subject of the verb *be, have,* or *do,* and circle the correct form of the verb.

> **EXAMPLE:** A <u>sport</u> (has / have) an important role in many children's lives.

1. I (was / were) involved in Little League during fifth and sixth grades.

2. My parents (was / were) happy to cheer at most of the games.

3. Now I (has / have) a Little Leaguer of my own, my daughter Tina.

4. She (am / is / are) not a natural athlete.

5. Still, the games (am / is / are) usually a lot of fun for her.

6. She (does / do) not see too many parents who can't control their tempers.

7. Once in a while, incidents (does / do) happen because of angry parents.

8. The local Little League organization (has / have) very strict rules about parents' interference.

9. Children (does / do) not need to see parents cursing at the opposing team or threatening the coaches.

10. Sports teams (am / is / are) supposed to be a way to learn about good sportsmanship, not an opportunity for parents to be terrible role models.

For more practice, visit Exercise Central at <www .bedfordstmartins .com/realessays>.

PRACTICE 2   **USING THE CORRECT FORM OF *BE, HAVE, OR DO***

In each sentence, underline the subject and fill in the correct form of the verb (*be, have,* or *do*) indicated in parentheses.

> **EXAMPLE:** Our <u>professor</u> *has* (*have*) forty papers to grade this weekend.

1. Most students _are_ (be) used to the idea that computers sometimes grade tests.

2. You _have_ (have) probably taken standardized tests and filled in small ovals with a pencil.

3. A computer _does_ (do) not have to be sophisticated to read the results of a test like the SAT or ACT.

4. Surprisingly, a new software program _is_ (be) designed to grade student essays.

5. The program _has_ (have) the ability to sort words in an essay and compare the essay to others in its database.

6. The software _does_ (do) not check grammar or spelling.

7. Teachers _are_ (be) still needed to supplement the computer grade, according to the software manufacturer.

8. If a computer grades your essay, you _are_ (have) to write about one of five hundred specified topics.

9. How _does_ (do) a computer check the organization, clarity, and style of your writing?

10. Some teachers _are_ (be) excited about their new computerized assistant, but I _do_ (do) not like the idea of a computer grading my essays.

2. WORDS COME BETWEEN THE SUBJECT AND THE VERB

When the subject and the verb aren't right next to each other, it can be difficult to make sure that they agree. Most often, what comes between the subject and the verb is either a prepositional phrase or a dependent clause.

Prepositional Phrase between the Subject and Verb

DEFINITION: A **prepositional phrase** starts with a preposition and ends with a noun or pronoun: The line *for the movie* went *around the corner.*

For a list of common prepositions, see page 347.

Remember, the subject of a sentence is never in a prepositional phrase. When you are looking for the subject of a sentence, you can cross out any prepositional phrases. This strategy should help you find the real subject and decide whether it agrees with the verb.

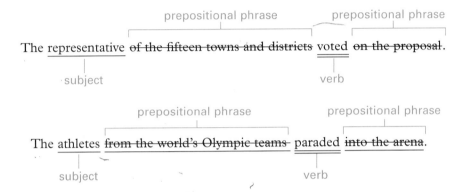

PRACTICE 3   MAKING SUBJECTS AND VERBS AGREE WHEN THEY ARE SEPARATED BY A PREPOSITIONAL PHRASE

In each of the following sentences, first cross out the prepositional phrase between the subject and the verb, and then circle the correct form of the verb. Remember, the subject of a sentence is never in a prepositional phrase.

EXAMPLE: Twenty-eight million people ~~in the United States~~ (am / is / are) deaf or hard of hearing.

1. Ninety percent of parents ~~with hearing loss~~ (has / have) children who can hear.

2. Many of these children (learns / learn) sign language ~~as a first~~ language.

3. Communication ~~with words~~ (comes / come) later.

4. Few people ~~in the hearing world~~ (understands / understand) the lives of deaf people completely.

5. Many deaf people ~~in this country~~ (feels / (feel)) closer to deaf people from other parts of the world than to hearing Americans.

6. The hearing children ~~of deaf parents~~ (comes / (come)) closer to understanding deaf culture than most hearing people.

7. A hearing child ~~in a deaf household~~ ((resembles) / resemble) a child of immigrant parents in many ways.

8. Adapting to two different cultures ((makes) / make) fitting in difficult for some young people.

9. Sometimes ties to the ~~hearing world~~ and the ~~deaf world~~ ((pulls) / pull) in opposite directions.

10. Bridges ~~between cultures~~ (am / is / (are)) more easily built by people who understand both sides.

Dependent Clause between the Subject and the Verb

DEFINITION: A **dependent clause** has a subject and a verb, but it does not express a complete thought. When a dependent clause comes between the subject and the verb, it usually starts with the word *who, whose, whom, that,* or *which.*

The subject of a sentence is never in the dependent clause. When you are looking for the subject of a sentence, you can cross out any dependent clauses.

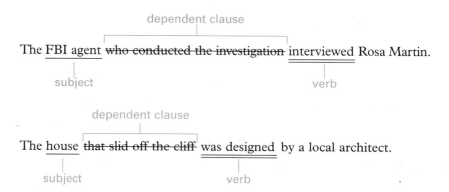

■   **PRACTICE 4   MAKING SUBJECTS AND VERBS AGREE WHEN
THEY ARE SEPARATED BY A DEPENDENT CLAUSE**

In each of the following sentences, cross out any dependent clauses. Then correct any problems with subject-verb agreement. If a sentence has no problem, write "OK" next to it.

is

EXAMPLE: A person ~~who lies in job applications~~ are likely to get caught.

1. A résumé, ~~which is a job applicant's first contact with many~~ prospective employers, contains details about past work experience and education.

2. Many people ~~who write résumés~~ are tempted to exaggerate.

3. Perhaps an applicant ~~who held a previous job for two months~~ claim to have spent a year there.

4. A job title ~~that sounds impressive~~ looks good on a résumé, whether or not it is accurate.

5. Often, a person ~~who never completed a college degree~~ wants to add it to a résumé anyway.

6. A person ~~who is considering untrue résumé additions~~ needs to think twice.

7. Employers ~~who like a résumé~~ checks the information provided by the applicant.

8. A résumé ~~that contains false information~~ goes in the reject pile.

9. In addition, many people ~~who invent material on a résumé~~ forgets the inventions when they face a prospective employer in an interview.

10. Even a company ~~that does not check all of the information on résumés~~ will pays attention when interviewees seem to forget some of their qualifications.

3. THE SENTENCE HAS A COMPOUND SUBJECT

DEFINITION: A **compound subject** consists of two (or more) subjects joined by *and, or,* or *nor.*

If two subjects are joined by *and,* they combine to become a plural subject, and the verb must take a plural form as well.

subject *and* · subject plural form of verb

The <u>director</u> and the <u>producer</u> <u>decide</u> how the film will be made.

If two subjects are separated by the word *or* or *nor,* they are not combined, and the verb should agree with whatever subject is closer to it.

subject *or* singular subject singular form of verb

The <u>director</u> or the <u>producer</u> <u>decides</u> how the film will be made.

subject *or* plural subject plural form of verb

The <u>director</u> or his <u>assistants</u> <u>decide</u> how the film will be made.

PRACTICE 5 CHOOSING THE CORRECT VERB IN A SENTENCE WITH A COMPOUND SUBJECT

In each of the following sentences, underline the word (*and, or,* or *nor*) that joins the parts of the compound subject. Then circle the correct form of the verb.

EXAMPLE: A child <u>and</u> an adult (has / (have)) different nutritional needs.

1. Fruits <u>and</u> vegetables (does / (do)) not make up enough of most Americans' diets.

2. The U.S. Food <u>and</u> Drug Administration and other government organizations (recommends / <u>recommend</u>) that people eat at least five servings of fruits and vegetables a day.

3. Whole-grain cereal <u>or</u> bread ((is) / are) another important part of a healthy diet.

4. Neither vitamins nor fiber (is / are) found in many popular snack foods.

5. Potato chips and candy (contains / contain) few useful nutrients.

6. Neither fat nor sugar (helps / help) build a healthy body.

7. However, in small amounts, fat and sugar (contributes / contribute) beneficially by making food taste good.

8. Only motivated dieters and certain health fanatics (eats / eat) nutritious food that tastes terrible.

9. Neither dieters nor health fanatics (is / are) likely to keep eating the unappetizing food for a lifetime.

10. Choosing nutritious food and preparing it well (allows / allow) a person to feel healthy and satisfied.

4. THE SUBJECT IS AN INDEFINITE PRONOUN

DEFINITION: An **indefinite pronoun** does not replace the name of a specific person, place, or thing. It is a general word. Most indefinite pronouns are either always singular or always plural.

Indefinite Pronouns

ALWAYS SINGULAR			ALWAYS PLURAL
another	everyone	nothing	both
anybody	everything	one (of)	few
anything	much	somebody	many
each (of)*	neither (of)*	someone	several
either (of)*	nobody	something	
everybody	no one		

*When one of these words is the subject, mentally replace it with the word *one*. *One* is singular and must have the singular form of the verb to agree with it.

SINGULAR	Everyone loves vacations.
PLURAL	Many prefer beach vacations.
SINGULAR	Either of the vacation locations is fine with me.

Often an indefinite pronoun is followed by a prepositional phrase or a dependent clause; remember that the subject of a sentence is never found in either of these. To choose the correct verb, you can cross out the prepositional phrase or dependent clause to focus on the indefinite pronoun.

Much ~~of a mechanic's work~~ requires precision.

Few ~~of the people in the building~~ favor the rent increase.

Several ~~who are longtime~~ residents recommend a rent strike.

PRACTICE 6   CHOOSING THE CORRECT VERB WHEN THE SUBJECT IS AN INDEFINITE PRONOUN

In each of the following sentences, cross out any prepositional phrases or dependent clauses that come between the subject and the verb. Then underline the subject, and circle the correct verb.

> **EXAMPLE:** One ~~of the best things about the Internet~~ (is / are) the way people can use it to get information from around the world.

1. Anyone ~~who wants to take college courses~~ (needs / need) access to a college campus.

2. Today, nobody ~~with a computer and Internet access~~ (lives / live) too far from a college to get a degree.

3. Several ~~of the hundreds of accredited colleges in the United States~~ (offers / offer) online degree programs.

4. Everything ~~that students need to pass the course~~ (is / are) available online.

5. Everyone who takes online courses (has / have) to participate in email discussions and write papers.

6. No one in an online class (gets / get) to sit silently in the back of the room.

7. Someone who learns best by listening (is / are) probably not a good candidate for an online college course.

8. Some students learn well by reading or by working independently; either of these types (has / have) a good chance to pass an online course.

9. Anybody who is considering an online class (needs / need) to work well without supervision.

10. Some of the people in online college classes (expects / expect) to earn a degree without ever visiting the campus.

5. THE VERB COMES BEFORE THE SUBJECT

In most sentences, the subject comes before the verb. Two kinds of sentences reverse that order: questions, and sentences that begin with *here* or *there*. In these two types of sentences, you need to check carefully for errors in subject-verb agreement.

Questions

In questions, the verb or part of the verb comes before the subject. To find the subject and verb, you can turn the question around as if you were going to answer it.

Where is the nearest gas station? The nearest gas station is . . .

Are the keys in the car? The keys are in the car.

Sentences That Begin with Here or There

When a sentence begins with *here* or *there*, the subject always follows the verb. Turn the sentence around to find the subject and verb.

Here are the hot dog rolls. The hot dog rolls are here.

There is a fly in my soup. The fly is in my soup.

PRACTICE 7   CORRECTING A SENTENCE WHEN THE VERB COMES BEFORE THE SUBJECT

Correct any problems with subject-verb agreement in the following sentences. If a sentence is already correct, write "OK" next to it.

EXAMPLE: There ~~is~~ *are* several openings for bilingual applicants.

1. Where ~~is~~ *are* the corporation's main offices located?

2. There ~~is~~ *are* branch offices in Paris, Singapore, and Tokyo.

3. How well ~~do~~ *does* the average employee abroad speak English?

4. What ~~do~~ *does* the company manufacture?

5. How many languages ~~are~~ *is* the manual written in?

6. Does the company employ college graduates as translators? *OK*

7. There ~~is~~ *are* some machines that can do translation.

8. Does learning a second language give an applicant a special advantage? *OK*

9. There is never a disadvantage in knowing another language. *OK*

10. Here ~~is~~ *are* the names of several qualified people.

Edit Paragraphs and Your Own Writing

As you edit paragraphs and your own writing, use the Thinking Critically guide that follows. You may also want to refer to the Quick Review Chart on page 404.

THINKING CRITICALLY TO EDIT FOR SUBJECT-VERB AGREEMENT

FOCUS   Whenever you see one of the five trouble spots in your writing, stop to check that the subject and the verb agree.

ASK   • Where is the subject in this sentence? Where is the verb?
         • Do the subject and verb agree in number? (Are they both singular or both plural?)

EDIT   If you answer "no" to the agreement question, you need to correct the sentence.

PRACTICE 8   **EDITING PARAGRAPHS FOR SUBJECT-VERB AGREEMENT**

Find and correct any problems with subject-verb agreement in the following paragraphs. You may want to refer to the preceding Thinking Critically Guide or the Quick Review Chart on page 404.

1. (1) School systems around the country ~~is~~ *are* embracing educational standards. (2) The idea of standards sound reasonable. (3) Does anyone want to argue that students should not have to meet certain requirements to graduate? (4) A national standard for all American students ~~have~~ *has* many supporters, too. (5) If the requirements for graduation in Oregon and Tennessee ~~is~~ *are* the same, everyone with a high school diploma ~~gets~~ *will* a similar education. (6) There is a catch, of course. (7) Not everyone with a professional or personal interest in school quality is able to agree on these requirements. (8) Mathematics and writing ~~is~~ *are* important, but so is music and physical education. (9) How ~~is~~ *are* parents, teachers, and administrators ever going to find standards that everyone accepts?

2. (1) Agreeing on school standards are only part of the battle over education. (2) How ~~is~~ *are* students going to prove that they have met the

standards before graduation? (3) The answer, in many cases, are testing. (4) School tests that are required by state law is becoming more and more common. (5) These tests are standardized, so all of the students taking an eighth-grade test in a particular state is given the same test. (6) Both the individual student and his or her school district is evaluated by the scores. (7) The parents of a student learns not only what their child's score is but also how the school compares to others around the state. (8) Then children who need extra help is supposed to receive it, and schools with very low scores year after year becomes eligible for additional resources.

3.   (1) In reality, standardized tests for schools have many problems. (2) Most school districts that have a testing program uses tests that can be scored by a computer. (3) Computers cannot read, so the tests that they grade usually offers multiple-choice questions. (4) A multiple-choice test in science or mathematics do not allow students to demonstrate critical thinking. (5) How does students show their writing ability on such a test? (6) There is tricks to answering multiple-choice questions that many students learn. (7) Frequently, a high score on such a test says more about the student's test-taking ability than about his or her knowledge of a subject. (8) Nevertheless, the quick results and low cost of a multiple-choice computer-graded test means that this imperfect testing system is used in many school systems.

4.   (1) Another problem with standardized tests are that test material can begin to change the curriculum. (2) Everyone who teaches wants his or her students to get high scores on the tests. (3) For one thing, a teacher of underperforming students are likely to be criticized for not preparing them better. (4) One result of teachers' fears are that they spend most of

the class time preparing students for the test. (5) In some cases, the phenomenon of "teaching to the test" become school policy. (6) A creative teacher or one who ~~has~~ *have* been teaching for years are no longer trusted to engage students with a subject. (7) School officials, who also want high scores for their districts, encourage teachers to focus on material that the test will cover. (8) Other material, which may be fascinating to students, are ignored because the test does not require it.

5.   (1) Many parents who send their children to public school fears that the schools are not teaching the students adequately. (2) As these fears increase, the number of states that require tests rise as well. (3) But there ~~has~~ *have* been some teachers and parents willing to resist standardized testing. (4) A few parents ~~has~~ *have* kept their children home on test days. (5) In rare cases, teachers who oppose testing ~~has~~ *have* refused to administer standardized tests to their students. (6) In the places that require students to pass tests in order to graduate, rebellion against tests have serious consequences for the student. (7) Elsewhere, however, a parent or student has the option to refuse. (8) People who believe that standardized testing is not the answer is still trying to change this growing national trend.

PRACTICE 9   EDITING YOUR OWN WRITING FOR SUBJECT-VERB AGREEMENT

As a final practice, carefully read a piece of your own writing—a paper you are working on for this class, a paper you've already finished, a paper for another course, or a recent piece of writing from your work or everyday life. For extra help in making your subjects and verbs agree, use the Thinking Critically guide on page 401 and the Quick Review Chart that follows.

Quick Review Chart

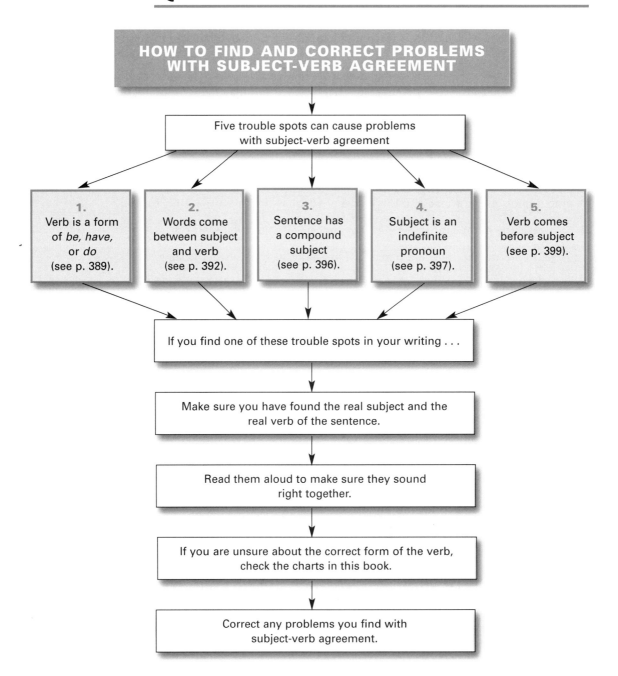

**HOW TO FIND AND CORRECT PROBLEMS
WITH SUBJECT-VERB AGREEMENT**

Five trouble spots can cause problems
with subject-verb agreement

1.
Verb is a form
of *be, have,*
or *do*
(see p. 389).

2.
Words come
between subject
and verb
(see p. 392).

3.
Sentence has
a compound
subject
(see p. 396).

4.
Subject is an
indefinite
pronoun
(see p. 397).

5.
Verb comes
before subject
(see p. 399).

If you find one of these trouble spots in your writing . . .

Make sure you have found the real subject and the
real verb of the sentence.

Read them aloud to make sure they sound
right together.

If you are unsure about the correct form of the verb,
check the charts in this book.

Correct any problems you find with
subject-verb agreement.

26

Verb Problems

Mistakes in Verb Form and Verb Tense

Understand What Verb Form and Verb Tense Are

DEFINITION: **Verb forms** are the different ways a verb can be spelled and pronounced. For example, here are three different forms of the same verb:

talk   talks   talked

DEFINITION: **Verb tense** indicates *when* the action of a sentence occurred: in the present, in the past, or in the future. Verbs change their form and use helping verbs to indicate different tenses.

PRESENT TENSE   I worry about my mother's health.

PAST TENSE   She worried about me when I was a child.

FUTURE TENSE   We will worry about each other forever, I guess.

To choose the correct form when you are writing, you need to use the singular or plural form of the verb that agrees with the subject of the sentence. You also need to select the form that shows the time of the action — past, present, and so on.

I talk to my mother every day.

She talks about the past a lot.

I talked to her this morning and will talk to her tomorrow.

For more on subject-verb agreement, see Chapter 25.

In the examples throughout this chapter, the subject is underlined and the verb is underlined twice.

405

IN THE REAL WORLD, WHY IS IT IMPORTANT TO USE CORRECT VERBS?

Using the wrong form of the verb is a mistake that people notice and tend to take seriously. Using incorrect forms may create a negative impression of you as a student or prospective employee. Learning to find and correct errors with verb forms or, better, learning to avoid them in your own writing is worth the effort.

SITUATION: A college student submits an essay to a contest hoping the piece will be published in the school's literary magazine and that she will win the $100 prize. Here is the beginning of the student's essay:

> I had just beginned to work when I heared a loud explosion that came from inside the building. That was the start of a night that I will not forgot.

RESPONSE: One of the judges, a professional journalist, said this to his fellow judges: "I read exactly two lines, not even enough to really get an idea of what the essay was about. Clearly, the person is a poor writer, and I just couldn't bear the idea of having to read the whole piece: It isn't worth my time."

Find and Correct Verb Problems

English verbs can be complicated. You can learn some general rules about them, but some verb forms must simply be practiced until they are memorized and you don't even have to think about them. The best way to learn the correct forms is to read, write, and speak them as often as possible.

1. REGULAR VERBS

DEFINITION: Most verbs in English are **regular verbs**—they follow a few basic, standard patterns.

Two Present-Tense Forms for Regular Verbs: -s Ending and No Added Ending

DEFINITION: The **present tense** is used for actions that are ongoing or that are happening at the same time that you are writing about them.

There are two forms for the present tense of regular verbs: -*s* ending or no added ending. Use the -*s* ending when the subject is *he, she,* or *it,* or the name of one person or thing. Do not add any ending for other subjects.

In the chart on page 407, note that only *she, he, it,* and *baby* (the name of one person or thing) have verbs with an -*s* ending. All the rest (*I, we, you, they,* and *babies*) have verbs with no added ending.

Regular Verb Forms in the Present Tense

	SINGULAR	PLURAL
First person	I laugh.	We laugh.
Second person	You laugh.	You laugh.
Third person	She/he/it laugh**s**.	They laugh.
	The baby laugh**s**.	The babies laugh.

PRACTICE 1   **USING THE CORRECT FORM FOR REGULAR VERBS IN THE PRESENT TENSE**

In each of the following sentences, first underline the subject, and then circle the correct verb form.

EXAMPLE: My son (attends / attend) day care while I am at work.

1. I (enjoys / enjoy) both working and spending time with my four-year-old.

2. My mother (watches / watch) my little boy when I go to school at night.

3. During the day, I (works / work) in the billing department of our local hospital.

4. My son (passes / pass) the time at the hospital's day-care center.

5. He (loves / love) the activities and the other children there.

6. The children (plays / play) games every morning.

7. They (uses / use) crayons, chalk, and paint during their art period.

8. I (misses / miss) him when I'm working.

9. However, the hospital (allows / allow) me to eat lunch in the day-care center with him.

10. The arrangement (enables / enable) my son and me to enjoy some family time during the day.

For more practice, visit Exercise Central at <www .bedfordstmartins .com/realessays>.

One Past-Tense Form for Regular Verbs: -ed Ending

DEFINITION: The **past tense** is used for actions that have already happened. An *-ed* ending is needed for all regular verbs in the past tense.

	PRESENT TENSE	**PAST TENSE**
First person	I rush to work.	I rush**ed** to work.
Second person	You lock the door.	You lock**ed** the door.
Third person	Rufus seems strange.	Rufus seem**ed** strange.

√ **PRACTICE 2   USING THE CORRECT FORM FOR REGULAR VERBS IN THE PAST TENSE**

In each of the following sentences, fill in the correct past-tense form of the verb in parentheses.

EXAMPLE: Between 1830 and 1860, about fifty thousand people ___escaped___ (*escape*) from slavery in the United States.

(1) Before the Civil War, many African Americans __faced__ (*face*) lives as unwilling, unpaid slaves on American farms and plantations. (2) When northern states __abolished__ (*abolish*) slavery, many southern slaves __tried__ (*try*) to escape to freedom in the North. (3) The journey __covered__ (*cover*) hundreds of miles, and anyone who __wanted__ (*want*) to make the trip __realized__ (*realize*) that it __involved__ (*involve*) terrible danger. (4) Both enslaved and free Americans __worked__ (*work*) to find safe hiding places for escaping slaves along a path leading to the free states of the North. (5) The people aware of this path __called__ (*call*) it the Underground Railroad.

(6) Many slaves in the South __helped__ (*help*) others to escape; they __provided__ (*provide*) fugitive slaves with shelter, food, and clothing whenever they could. (7) Escaping slaves also __needed__ (*need*) information about the route and guides to lead the way. (8) One fugitive, Harriet Tubman, repeatedly __returned__ (*return*) to the South to lead more than three hundred slaves to freedom. (9) Slaveholders __offered__ (*offer*) a

reward of $40,000 for her capture, but they _____ *failed* (*fail*) to find her.

(10) In addition to Tubman and other African Americans, some white Americans, especially Quakers, who _____ *believed* (*believe*) that slavery was evil, _____ *assisted* (*assist*) the fugitives. (11) Before the Civil War finally _____ *freed* (*free*) the slaves, the Underground Railroad _____ *carried* (*carry*) thousands of them north to freedom.

One Regular Past Participle: -ed Ending

DEFINITION: The **past participle** is a verb form that can be used with helping verbs, such as *have*. For all regular verbs, the past-participle form is the same as the past-tense form: It needs an *-ed* ending.

PAST-TENSE FORM	PAST-PARTICIPLE FORM
My brother and I argu**ed**.	We have argu**ed** before.
Karen help**ed** me.	She has help**ed** often.

PRACTICE 3   USING THE CORRECT FORM FOR THE PAST PARTICIPLES OF REGULAR VERBS

In each of the following sentences, underline the helping verb (a form of *have*), and fill in the correct form of the verb in parentheses.

   EXAMPLE: My father has _*served*_ (*serve*) in the army for twenty years.

1. My father's military career has _____ *forced* (*force*) our family to move many times.

2. We have _____ *lived* (*live*) in seven towns that I remember.

3. I had _____ *attended* (*attend*) three different high schools before I turned seventeen.

4. None of the towns have ever really _____ *seemed* (*seem*) like home.

5. I have never _____ *objected* (*object*) to my family's traveling life.

6. None of us has ever _____ *expected* (*expect*) to stay in one place for long.

7. My closest friends have all _*travel*_ (*travel*) a lot, too.

8. One of them has _*visited*_ (*visit*) Egypt, Australia, Turkey, Pakistan,

and seventeen other countries.

9. She had once _*hoped*_ (*hope*) for a career as a travel agent.

10. Now, however, she has _*decided*_(*decide*) to accept a position with a

large international corporation that will allow her to travel.

2. IRREGULAR VERBS

DEFINITION: **Irregular verbs** do not follow the regular patterns for verb endings (the ones that you have just practiced in this chapter). Instead, they may change spelling as the chart on pages 410–12 shows.

Irregular Verb Forms

PRESENT-TENSE FORM	PAST-TENSE FORM	PAST PARTICIPLE
am/are/is	was/were	been
become	became	become
begin	began	begun
bite	bit	bitten
blow	blew	blown
break	broke	broken
bring	brought	brought
build	built	built
buy	bought	bought
catch	caught	caught
choose	chose	chosen
come	came	come
cost	cost	cost
do	did	done
draw	drew	drawn
drink	drank	drunk
drive	drove	driven

PRESENT-TENSE FORM	PAST-TENSE FORM	PAST PARTICIPLE
eat	ate	eaten
fall	fell	fallen
feed	fed	fed
feel	felt	felt
fight	fought	fought
find	found	found
forget	forgot	forgotten
get	got	gotten
give	gave	given
go	went	gone
grow	grew	grown
have/has	had	had
hide	hid	hidden
hit	hit	hit
hold	held	held
hurt	hurt	hurt
keep	kept	kept
know	knew	known
lay	laid	laid
leave	left	left
let	let	let
lie	lay	lain
light	lit	lit
lose	lost	lost
make	made	made
mean	meant	meant
meet	met	met
pay	paid	paid
put	put	put
quit	quit	quit
read	read	read
ride	rode	ridden

(continued)

Irregular Verb Forms (continued)

PRESENT-TENSE FORM	PAST-TENSE FORM	PAST PARTICIPLE
run	ran	run
say	said	said
see	saw	seen
sell	sold	sold
send	sent	sent
show	showed	shown
shut	shut	shut
sing	sang	sung
sink	sank	sunk
sit	sat	sat
sleep	slept	slept
speak	spoke	spoken
spend	spent	spent
stand	stood	stood
steal	stole	stolen
stick	stuck	stuck
sting	stung	stung
swim	swam	swum
take	took	taken
teach	taught	taught
tear	tore	torn
tell	told	told
think	thought	thought
throw	threw	thrown
understand	understood	understood
wake	woke	woken
wear	wore	worn
win	won	won
write	wrote	written

Irregular Present-Tense Forms

Only a few verbs are irregular in the present tense. The ones most commonly used are the verbs *be* and *have*.

Present-Tense Forms for Two Irregular Verbs

	BE		**HAVE**	
First person	I am	we are	I have	we have
Second person	you are	you are	you have	you have
Third person	he/she/it is	they are	he/she/ it has	they have
	the dog is	the dogs are	the dog has	the dogs have
	Chris is	Chris and Dan are	Chris has	Chris and Dan have

PRACTICE 4 **USING THE CORRECT FORMS FOR *BE* AND *HAVE* IN THE PRESENT TENSE**

In each of the following sentences, fill in the correct form of the verb indicated in parentheses.

EXAMPLE: Disc golf _is_ (*be*) a game played with Frisbees.

1. I ___am___ (*be*) a fanatical disc golfer.

2. The game ___has___ (*have*) eighteen holes, like regular golf, but uses a Frisbee instead of a ball.

3. A disc golf course ___has___ (*have*) fairways and holes.

4. A tee ___is___ (*be*) at the beginning of each fairway.

5. Players ___are___ (*be*) eager to get the Frisbee from the tee into a metal basket in the fewest possible throws.

6. Some disc golfers ___have___ (*have*) special Frisbees for teeing off and putting.

7. My brother, who also plays disc golf, ___has___ (*have*) thirty different Frisbees for the game.

8. His wife ___*is*___ (*be*) surprisingly patient with his enthusiasm for the sport.

9. "You ___*are*___ (*be*) in the middle of a second adolescence," she tells him.

10. However, she, too, ___*has*___ (*have*) formidable Frisbee technique.

Irregular Past-Tense Forms

Irregular verbs do not use the *-ed* ending for the past tense.

PRESENT-TENSE FORM	PAST-TENSE FORM
Tony makes hats.	Tony made hats.
You write well.	You wrote well.
I ride a bike.	I rode a bike.

The verb *be* is tricky because it has two different forms for the past tense: *was* and *were*.

There is no simple rule for forming irregular verbs in the past tense. Until you know them well, you will need to consult the chart on pages 410–12.

The Verb Be, *Past Tense*

	SINGULAR	PLURAL
First person	I was	we were
Second person	you were	you were
Third person	she/he/it was	they were
	the car was	the cars were
	Jolanda was	Jolanda and Ti were

PRACTICE 5   **USING THE CORRECT PAST-TENSE FORM OF THE VERB *BE***

In the paragraph that follows, fill in each blank with the correct past-tense form of the verb *be*.

EXAMPLE: Your father and I __were__ struggling to make ends meet.

\

(1) Before you __were__ born, your father and I __were__ very wor-

ried. (2) He _____ still in school at the time. (3) I _____ a part-

time waitress, so we _____ not exactly rich in those days. (4) Having

a baby _____ a big step for us. (5) My mother _____ thrilled

that she would be a grandmother, but she _____ not even in the

same state. (6) Your other grandparents _____ no longer living. (7) I

_____ terrified that we would not be able to take good care of you.

(8) But when you _____ born, your father's friends and my cowork-

ers _____ an amazing support system. (9) They _____ all as

much in love with you as we _____ . (10) You _____ the most

beautiful thing that any of us had ever seen.

PRACTICE 6   USING THE CORRECT FORM FOR IRREGULAR VERBS IN THE PAST TENSE

In each of the following sentences, fill in the correct past-tense form of the irregular verb in parentheses. If you do not know the answer, find the word in the chart of irregular verb forms on pages 410–12.

EXAMPLE: The *Titanic* __set__ (*set*) out from England in 1912.

1. The White Star Line _____ (*build*) the *Titanic,* which was the

   biggest moving object in the world at that time.

2. The huge ship _____ (*hold*) over 2,200 passengers on its maiden

   voyage.

3. Twenty lifeboats, which could hold 1,178 people altogether, _____

   (*hang*) from the upper deck of the *Titanic.*

4. The shipbuilders _____ (*feel*) that the giant liner was the safest

   ship in the world and that more lifeboats were simply unnecessary.

5. On April 14, 1912, during its first trip across the Atlantic, the *Titanic*

_____ (*strike*) an iceberg.

6. The sharp ice _____ (*tear*) a gaping hole in the bottom of the ship.

7. Icy ocean water _____ (*begin*) to pour into the hold, dragging the

Titanic down in the water.

8. Few passengers _____ (*understand*) the danger at first.

9. Half-empty lifeboats _____ (*leave*) the sinking ship while other

passengers _____ (*stand*) on deck, refusing to depart.

10. Hundreds of people _____ (*freeze*) to death in the ocean before the

nearest ship _____ (*come*) to rescue the *Titanic*'s 705 survivors.

PRACTICE 7   USING THE CORRECT FORM FOR PAST-TENSE IRREGULAR VERBS

In the following paragraph, replace any incorrect present-tense verb forms with the correct past-tense form of the verb. If you do not know the answer, look up the verbs in the chart of irregular verb forms on pages 410–12.

> **EXAMPLE:** Dewayne faced a judge and jury of his fellow high school
>   *hit*
> students after he ~~hits~~ a boy in the classroom.
>   ^

(1) Two years ago, my high school sets up a student court to give students a voice in disciplining rule breakers. (2) Before the court opened its doors, adults teach students about decision making and about courtroom procedures. (3) Some of us served as members of juries, and others become advocates or even judges. (4) I sit on a jury twice when I was a junior. (5) Then, last spring, my friend Dewayne appeared before the student court after he loses his temper and strikes a fellow student. (6) I agreed to

be his advocate because I think he truly regretted his behavior. (7) I

tell the jury that he knew his violent reaction was a mistake. (8) The jury

sends Dewayne for counseling to learn to manage his anger and made him

write an apology to the other student. (9) After hearing the verdict,

Dewayne shakes hands with all the jurors and thanked them for their fair-

ness. (10) The experience makes me eager to learn more about America's

system of justice.

Irregular Past Participles

DEFINITION: For regular verbs, the **past-participle form** (used with helping verbs such as *have*) is the same as the past-tense form; they both use
the -*ed* ending. For irregular verbs, the past-participle form may be different from the past-tense form.

	PAST-TENSE FORM	PAST-PARTICIPLE FORM
REGULAR VERB	Danielle smiled.	Danielle has smiled.
IRREGULAR VERB	Lara drove fast.	Lara has driven fast.

Until you know the right form for a verb, check the chart of irregular
verb forms on pages 410–12.

**PRACTICE 8   USING CORRECT PAST-PARTICIPLE FORMS FOR
IRREGULAR VERBS**

In each of the following sentences, underline the helping verb (a form of
have) and fill in the correct past-participle form of the verb in parentheses. If you do not know the correct form, find the word in the chart on
pages 410–12.

 EXAMPLE: Hector has ___*found*___ (*find*) that a dot-com career has ups
and downs.

1. By the time Hector graduated from college in 1998, he had _____

   (*take*) dozens of hours of computer courses.

2. He had _____ (*choose*) a career in programming.

3. Before getting his diploma, Hector had _____ (*begin*) to work for an Internet service provider.

4. By the end of the summer, a rival online service had _____ (*steal*) Hector away from his employer.

5. His new bosses had _____ (*be*) in business for only a few months.

6. After a year, the company still had never _____ (*make*) a profit.

7. However, hundreds of investors had _____ (*buy*) shares of the company's stock.

8. By early 2000, the stock's prices had _____ (*grow*) to more than fifty times their original worth.

9. Hector often wishes that he had _____ (*sell*) his shares then and retired a rich man.

10. Instead, the company went bankrupt, and Hector has _____ (*go*) to work for an old-fashioned but secure banking firm.

3. USING PAST PARTICIPLES

A **past participle**, by itself, cannot be the main verb of a sentence. But when it is combined with another verb, called a **helping verb**, it can be used to make the **present perfect tense**, the **past perfect tense**, and the **passive voice**.

Have/Has + *Past Participle* = *Present Perfect Tense*

DEFINITION: The **present perfect tense** of a verb is used for an action begun in the past that is ongoing into the present or that was completed at some unspecified time in the past.

PAST TENSE   My <u>car</u> <u>stalled</u>.

[The car stalled at some point in the past but does not stall now, in the present.]

helping verb   past participle

PRESENT PERFECT TENSE   My car has stalled often.

[The car began to stall in the past but may continue to do so into the present.]

✓   PRACTICE 9   **USING THE PRESENT PERFECT TENSE**

In each of the following sentences, circle the correct verb form.

> **EXAMPLE:** Dishonest people (found / have found) new ways to cheat since the Internet became widely available.

1. As long as there have been grades, some students (were / have been) willing to cheat.

2. For the past ten years, the Internet (made / has made) all kinds of resources available to students.

3. By now, many students (found / have found) that term papers are available online.

4. Some of the sites that help students cheat (operated / have operated) for years.

5. Cheating is so easy now that teachers are at a disadvantage, but some (began / have begun) to fight back.

6. Two years ago, a professor at the University of Virginia (created / has created) a program to check student papers for plagiarism.

7. In the spring of 2001, he (discovered / has discovered) dozens of plagiarized papers.

8. Since it was founded in the eighteenth century, the University of Virginia (made / has made) students agree to obey a strict honor code.

9. For more than two hundred years, University of Virginia students caught cheating (faced / have faced) expulsion; in the case of graduates, diplomas (were / have been) revoked.

10. Cheating (got / has gotten) easier with Internet availability, but students who believe that cheating is risk-free are fooling themselves.

Had + *Past Participle* = *Past Perfect Tense*

DEFINITION: The **past perfect tense** is used for an action that was begun in the past but completed before some other past action took place. Use *had* (the past-tense form of *have*) plus the past participle to make the past perfect tense.

past tense of helping verb   past participle

PAST PERFECT TENSE   My head had ached for a week before I called a doctor.

[Both of the actions (head ached and I called) happened in the past, but the ache happened before the calling.]

Neither the past tense nor the present perfect tense uses *had*.

PAST TENSE   My head ached.

PRESENT PERFECT TENSE   My head has ached often.

PRACTICE 10   USING THE PAST PERFECT TENSE

In each of the following sentences, circle the correct verb form.

EXAMPLE: By the time I reached home, rolling blackouts (darkened / had darkened) the city.

1. The temperature was unseasonably hot when I (got / had gotten) out of bed that morning.

2. By noon, the air conditioners at the office (were running / had been running) at high power for three hours.

3. My boss told me that she (heard / had heard) that energy use that day was skyrocketing.

4. I (asked / had asked) how we could conserve energy.

5. I mentioned that I (just learned / had just learned) that some household and office machines use power even when they are turned off.

6. My boss (read / had read) the same information, so we unplugged computers in the office that were not in use.

7. We also (raised / had raised) the office temperature from sixty-eight degrees to seventy-two, and then we turned off some of the lights.

8. We (did / had done) everything we could think of to save energy, but it was not enough.

9. We knew that the city (warned / had warned) residents that rolling blackouts were possible.

10. However, when the office (suddenly darkened / had suddenly darkened), everyone was stunned.

Be + *Past Participle* = *Passive Voice*

DEFINITION: A sentence that is written in the **passive voice** has a subject that performs no action. Instead, the subject is acted upon. To create the passive voice, combine a form of the verb *be* with a past participle.

helping verb   past participle

PASSIVE   The memo was written by an employee.

[The subject, *memo,* did not write itself. An employee wrote the memo, but the subject in the sentence, *memo,* performs no action.]

DEFINITION: In sentences that use the **active voice**, the subject performs the action.

ACTIVE   An employee wrote the memo.

Use the passive voice when no one person performed the action, when you don't know who performed the action, or when you want to emphasize the receiver of the action. Use active voice whenever possible, and use passive voice sparingly.

PASSIVE   The dog was hit by a passing car.

[If the writer wants to focus on the dog as the receiver of the action, the passive voice is acceptable.]

ACTIVE   A passing car hit the dog.

▓   **PRACTICE 11   CHANGING FROM PASSIVE VOICE TO ACTIVE VOICE**

Rewrite the following sentences in the active voice.

　　　　　　Someone stole my
EXAMPLE: My umbrella˙ was stolen.

1. Robert Bork's nomination to the Supreme Court was denied by the Senate.

2. Annoyingly loud music was being played in the apartment downstairs.

3. Eighty employees are being laid off by Genzyme, Inc.

4. My feelings were hurt by your joke.

5. The check was mailed by me last Tuesday.

4. CONSISTENCY OF VERB TENSE

DEFINITION: Consistency of tense means that all the verbs in your sentence that are happening (or happened) at the same time are in the same tense. If all of the actions happen in the present, use the present tense for all verbs in the sentence. If all of the actions happened in the past, use the past tense for all verbs in the sentence.

	past tense　　present tense
INCONSISTENT TENSE	The bell chimed just as I am running up the stairs.
CONSISTENT PRESENT TENSE	The bell chimes just as I am running up the stairs.
CONSISTENT PAST TENSE	The bell chimed just as I was running up the stairs.

PRACTICE 12   USING CONSISTENT TENSE

In each of the following items, double-underline the verbs in the sentence, and correct any unnecessary shift in verb tense. Write the correct form of any incorrect verb in the blank space provided.

EXAMPLE: ___*become*___ As suburban sprawl increases, downtown areas and urban centers became emptier.

1. _____ Americans love their cars because they wanted independence and convenience.

2. _____ As people bought more and more cars, the traffic in cities and downtown areas seems to get worse every day.

3. _____ A strip mall on the edge of town is rarely beautiful, but convenience counted for a lot.

4. _____ Big stores with big parking lots usually offered low prices, and they also allow customers to do most of their shopping in one place.

5. _____ These discount stores appear everywhere; most communities had one close by.

6. _____ Some Americans worried that these chain stores are changing the country's landscape for the worse.

7. _____ Once, small towns had unique stores owned by local people, and the residents go downtown to shop.

8. _____ A small local business in those days probably provided only a limited selection of products at standard prices, but the customers get personalized service for their money.

9. _____ Today, discount superstores had the ability to sell products for a lower price than their small local competitors can offer.

10. _____ Convenience and low prices win customers, but the atmosphere in American towns and cities would never be the same.

Edit Paragraphs and Your Own Writing

As you edit paragraphs and your own writing, use the following Thinking Critically guide and the Quick Review Chart on page 427.

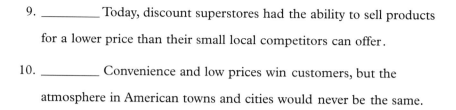

THINKING CRITICALLY TO EDIT FOR VERB PROBLEMS	
FOCUS	Read all of your sentences carefully, looking for verb problems.
ASK	• Is my sentence about the present? About the past? About something that happened before something else? • Is each verb a regular verb or an irregular verb? • Have I used the tense that tells the reader when the action happened? • Have I used the correct form of the verb? • If the verbs in the sentence are not all in the same tense, is it because the actions actually happened at different times?
EDIT	Edit to correct any problems with verb form or verb tense.

▣ PRACTICE 13   EDITING PARAGRAPHS FOR CORRECT VERB USE

Find and correct any problems with verb form or tense in the following paragraphs.

1. (1) Since 1835, trapeze artists consider the triple somersault the most dangerous maneuver. (2) That year, a performer tried to do a triple somersault on a trapeze for the first time and dies in the attempt.

(3) Only one person has managed to do the trick successfully for the next sixty-three years. (4) That man, a trapeze artist named Armor, did a triple somersault in 1860 and is afraid to try it again. (5) According to circus legend, the second person to survive the triple, Ernie Clarke, once done a quadruple somersault in private. (6) Ernie Lane, the third person to complete a triple somersault, was later killed by the maneuver when his catcher missed. (7) Circus historians now believed that Alfredo Codona, a performer in the 1920s and 1930s, was the greatest master of the triple somersault. (8) He has went down in history as the King of Trapeze.

2.   (1) Many people go through life without even knowing that there is a record for peeling an apple or hopping on a pogo stick. (2) However, some people are very aware of such records, and ordinary folks around the world have did some peculiar things to qualify for the *Guinness Book of World Records*. (3) For example, a New Jersey disc jockey, Glen Jones, recently setted a new record for the longest continuous radio broadcast. (4) In the spring of 2001, he has stayed on the air for one hundred hours with only a few fifteen-minute breaks. (5) Another world record, for hopping up steps on a bicycle, is hold by Javier Zapata of Colombia. (6) He climbed 943 steps without letting his feet touch the ground, breaking a record that he has previously set. (7) Ashrita Furman of New York also be a record breaker. (8) She balanced a milk bottle on her head and then walks almost eighty-one miles around a track. (9) These strange endurance contests may not make Jones, Zapata, and Furman famous, but their names had entered the record book.

3.   (1) The Olympic Games first let women compete in swimming events in 1912, and with that, the swimsuit revolution begun. (2) In 1913, the

first mass-produced women's swimsuit hit the market. (3) Before that year, women have only been able to wade at the beach in bathing costumes with long, baggy legs. (4) The 1913 suits, designed by Carl Jantzen, was ribbed one-piece outfits that allowed actual swimming. (5) An engineer, Louis Réard, comed up with the next major development in swimwear in 1946 while working in the lingerie business. (6) He has called it the "bikini," after a Pacific island used for testing the atomic bomb. (7) In the 1950s, few Americans had dared to wear bikinis, which was considered scandalous. (8) Two-piece swimsuits catch on in the 1960s and 1970s. (9) The bikini losted some popularity in the last decades of the twentieth century, but it has made a triumphant return in the new millennium.

PRACTICE 14   EDIT YOUR OWN WRITING FOR CORRECT VERB TENSE AND FORM

Use a piece of your own writing—a paper you are working on for this class or another class, a paper you've already finished, or a recent piece of writing from work or everyday life. For extra help, use the Thinking Critically guide on page 424 and the following Quick Review Chart.

Quick Review Chart

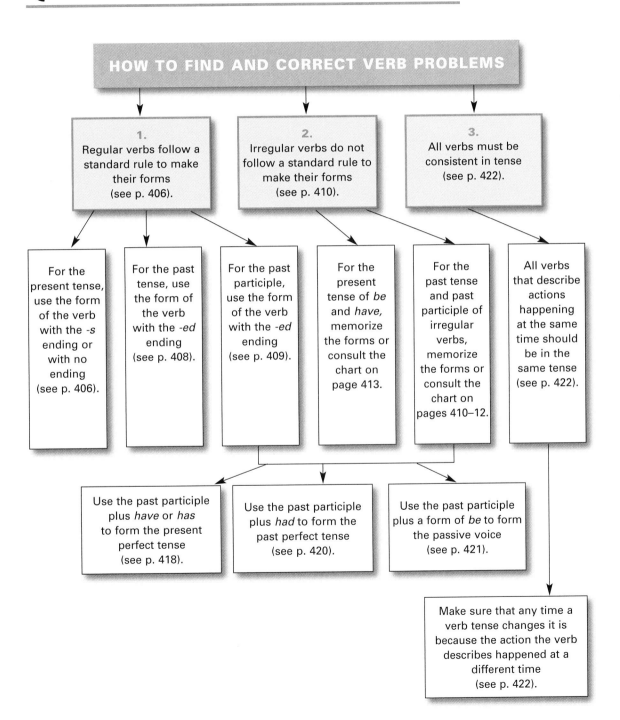

HOW TO FIND AND CORRECT VERB PROBLEMS

1.
Regular verbs follow a standard rule to make their forms
(see p. 406).

2.
Irregular verbs do not follow a standard rule to make their forms
(see p. 410).

3.
All verbs must be consistent in tense
(see p. 422).

For the present tense, use the form of the verb with the *-s* ending or with no ending
(see p. 406).

For the past tense, use the form of the verb with the *-ed* ending
(see p. 408).

For the past participle, use the form of the verb with the *-ed* ending
(see p. 409).

For the present tense of *be* and *have,* memorize the forms or consult the chart on page 413.

For the past tense and past participle of irregular verbs, memorize the forms or consult the chart on pages 410–12.

All verbs that describe actions happening at the same time should be in the same tense
(see p. 422).

Use the past participle plus *have* or *has* to form the present perfect tense
(see p. 418).

Use the past participle plus *had* to form the past perfect tense
(see p. 420).

Use the past participle plus a form of *be* to form the passive voice
(see p. 421).

Make sure that any time a verb tense changes it is because the action the verb describes happened at a different time
(see p. 422).

PART FIVE

Other Grammar Concerns

27

Pronouns

Using Substitutes for Nouns

Understand What Pronouns Are

DEFINITION: Nouns are words that name people, places, or things. **Pronouns** replace nouns or other pronouns in a sentence so that you do not have to repeat them.

> Tessa let me borrow ~~Tessa's~~ *her* jacket.

> You have met Carl. ~~Carl~~ *He* is my cousin.

DEFINITION: The noun or pronoun that a pronoun replaces is called the **antecedent**, which means "something that comes before." In most cases, a pronoun refers to a specific antecedent nearby.

> I filled out the health form. It was complicated.

antecedent   pronoun replacing antecedent

PRACTICE 1   IDENTIFYING PRONOUNS

In each of the following sentences, circle the pronoun, underline the antecedent (the noun to which the pronoun refers), and draw an arrow from the pronoun to the antecedent.

431

EXAMPLE: My uncle is a hard-working entrepreneur who knew he could succeed with a business loan.

1. Many poor people don't feel as if they can depend on big banks.

2. A bank in an underdeveloped area, however, needs to find customers wherever it can.

3. Microlending has become a popular banking trend. It has helped people in impoverished neighborhoods all over the world.

4. Microlending has succeeded because it involves lending very small amounts of money.

5. For many poor owners of a small business, microlending helps them to get a jump start.

6. For example, street vendors sell small quantities and earn small profits, so they may never save up enough to expand.

7. Yet a woman selling tacos from a cart may have enough experience to manage her own business successfully.

8. If the taco vendor gets a microloan, she may be able to open a storefront restaurant and earn larger profits.

LEARNING JOURNAL
Use your learning journal as a place to record sentences with pronoun problems that you find in your writing. Also write down edited versions of the sentences, with the problems corrected.

9. After receiving a small loan, a young entrepreneur can make his or her business more successful.

10. According to my uncle, getting a microloan allowed him to pursue a childhood dream.

Practice Using Pronouns Correctly

CHECK FOR PRONOUN AGREEMENT

DEFINITION: A pronoun must agree with (match) the noun or pronoun it refers to in number. **Number** tells how many of something, either one (singular) or more than one (plural).

If a pronoun is singular, it must also match its noun or pronoun in gender (*he, she,* or *it*).

>   **CONSISTENT**   Sherry talked to *her* aunt.
>
>   [*Her* agrees with *Sherry* because both are singular and feminine.]
>
>   **CONSISTENT**   The Romanos sold *their* restaurant.
>
>   [*Their* agrees with the *Romanos* because both are plural.]

Watch out for singular nouns that are not specific. If a noun is singular, the pronoun must be as well.

>   **INCONSISTENT**   Any cook has had *their* disasters.
>
>   [*Cook* is singular, but the pronoun *their* is plural.]
>
>   **CONSISTENT**   Any cook has had *his* or *her* disasters.
>
>   [*Cook* is singular, and so are the pronouns *his* and *her.*]

As an alternative to using the phrase *his or her,* make the subject plural if you can. (For more on this, see the note on p. 434.)

>   **CONSISTENT**   All cooks have had *their* disasters.

Two types of words often cause errors in pronoun agreement: indefinite pronouns and collective nouns.

Indefinite Pronouns

DEFINITION: An **indefinite pronoun** does not refer to a specific person, place, or thing; it is general. Most indefinite pronouns are either always singular or always plural. Whenever a pronoun refers to an indefinite person, place, or thing, check for agreement.

>   *his*
>   Someone forgot ~~their~~ coat.
>
>   *his or her*
>   Everybody practiced ~~their~~ lines.

Indefinite Pronouns

ALWAYS SINGULAR			ALWAYS PLURAL
anybody	everyone	nothing	both
anyone	everything	one (of)	few
anything	much	somebody	many
each (of)	neither (of)	someone	several
either (of)	nobody	something	
everybody	no one		

NOTE: Although still grammatically correct, using a masculine pronoun (*he, his,* or *him*) alone to refer to a singular indefinite pronoun such as *everyone* is now considered sexist. Here are two ways to avoid this problem:

1. Use *his or her.*

   Someone forgot his or her coat.

2. Change the sentence so that the pronoun refers to a plural noun or pronoun.

   The children forgot their coats.

PRACTICE 2   USING INDEFINITE PRONOUNS

Circle the correct pronoun or group of words in parentheses.

(1) Everyone who has battled an addiction to alcohol has (his or her / their) own views of the best ways to stop drinking. (2) Millions of former problem drinkers have quit, and many have made (his or her / their) way through recovery programs. (3) Few begin the road to recovery without attending (his or her / their) first Alcoholics Anonymous (AA) meeting. (4) With its famous twelve-step program, AA has helped countless alcoholics, but someone who is not religious may have (his or her / their) difficulties with one of the twelve steps. (5) No one can complete the whole

AA recovery program without turning (himself or herself / themselves) over to a "higher power." (6) In addition, everybody who joins AA is asked to admit that (he or she is / they are) powerless over alcohol. (7) Many object that (he or she needs / they need) to feel empowered rather than powerless in order to recover. (8) Anyone who does not feel that (he or she / they) can believe in a higher power might participate instead in a group like Secular Organizations for Sobriety. (9) Some can take responsibility for (his or her / their) drinking and stop more easily with groups such as Smart Recovery. (10) Different approaches work for different people, but former problem drinkers offer this sober advice to others with alcohol problems: Anyone can quit drinking if (he or she wants / they want) to stop badly enough.

Collective Nouns

DEFINITION: A **collective noun** names a group that acts as a single unit.

Common Collective Nouns

audience	company	group
class	crowd	jury
college	family	society
committee	government	team

Collective nouns are usually singular, so when you use a pronoun to refer to a collective noun, it too must usually be singular.

its
The class had their final exam at 8:00 A.M.

its
The group turned in their report.

If the people in a group are acting as individuals, however, the noun is plural and should be used with a plural pronoun.

The audience took *their* seats.

PRACTICE 3   USING COLLECTIVE NOUNS AND PRONOUNS

Fill in the correct pronoun (*their* or *its*) in each of the following sentences.

> EXAMPLE: The basketball team was playing all of _____*its*_____ games in a damp, dark gymnasium.

1. The downtown branch of the university needed to overhaul several buildings on _____*its*_____ campus.

2. The theater department wanted to enlarge the auditorium used for _____*its*_____ productions.

3. In the present theater, the audience had to wait in _____*its*_____ seats until the performance was over and then exit through the stage door.

4. A sorority also needed more space to house _____*its*_____ members.

5. In addition, the football team could not go to any out-of-town games because _____*its*_____ bus had broken down.

6. The science teachers had to hold _____*their*_____ office hours in the student cafeteria.

7. The university president appointed a commission to study renovations and agreed to abide by _____*its*_____ findings.

8. The graduating class agreed to ask _____*its*_____ parents to make contributions.

9. One wealthy family donated _____*its*_____ slightly used luxury car to a fund-raising auction.

10. A record homecoming crowd shouted _____*their*_____ approval as the

renovation plans were announced.

MAKE PRONOUN REFERENCE CLEAR

If the reader isn't sure what a pronoun refers to, the meaning of a sentence may be confusing. You should edit any sentence that has an ambiguous, vague, or repetitious pronoun reference.

Avoid Ambiguous or Vague Pronoun References

DEFINITION: An **ambiguous pronoun reference** is one in which the pronoun could refer to more than one noun.

AMBIGUOUS   Michelle told Carla that she should get a better hourly wage.

[Did Michelle tell Carla that Michelle herself should get a better hourly wage? Or did Michelle tell Carla that Carla should get a better hourly wage?]

EDITED   Michelle told Carla that she wanted to get a better hourly wage.

AMBIGUOUS   I threw my bag on the table and it broke.

[Was it the bag or the table that broke?]

EDITED   My bag broke when I threw it on the table.

DEFINITION: A **vague pronoun reference** is one in which the pronoun does not refer clearly to any particular person or thing. (To correct a vague pronoun reference, substitute a noun for the pronoun.)

VAGUE   After an accident at the intersection, they installed a traffic light.

[Who installed the traffic light?]

EDITED   After an accident at the intersection, the highway department installed a traffic light.

VAGUE   When I heard it, I laughed.

[Heard what?]

EDITED   When I heard the message, I laughed.

PRACTICE 4   AVOIDING AMBIGUOUS OR VAGUE PRONOUN REFERENCES

Edit each of the following sentences to eliminate any ambiguous or vague pronoun references. Some sentences may be revised correctly in more than one way.

EXAMPLE: In a recent study, ~~they~~ *scientists* found that people do not always see objects that are in unexpected places.

1. In a psychology study, volunteers watched a video of two basketball teams, and they had to count the number of passes.

2. As the volunteers focused on the players, some of them did not notice a person in a gorilla suit walking onto the basketball court.

3. Later, when the volunteers met with the researchers, many of them asked, "What gorilla?"

4. At the end of the study, the researchers had learned that if it was unexpected, many people simply could not see it.

5. The way the human brain processes visual information may keep people from using it wisely.

6. For example, if a car crosses into the lane facing oncoming traffic, it may not register in the mind of a driver who expects a routine trip.

7. A stop sign appearing at an intersection cannot prevent an accident if drivers do not see it.

8. Before the psychology study, they thought that drivers who missed signs of danger were simply not paying attention.

9. However, the study indicates that drivers make mistakes because they may not see them ahead.

10. Traffic safety regulations cannot make people's brains and eyes work differently, but they can make them wear seat belts.

Avoid Repetitious Pronoun References

DEFINITION: In a **repetitious pronoun reference**, the pronoun repeats a reference to a noun rather than replacing the noun. Such pronouns should be removed.

The police officer ~~he~~ told me I had not stopped at the sign.

The sign, ~~it~~ was hidden by a tree.

PRACTICE 5   AVOIDING REPETITIOUS PRONOUN REFERENCES

Correct any repetitious pronoun references in the following sentences.

EXAMPLE: The science of robotics ~~it~~ already has practical applications.

1. Robots ~~they~~ have been part of many science-fiction classics, from *The Jetsons* to *Star Wars.*

2. Is there any child who ~~he~~ hasn't wished for a robot friend, a robot tutor, or a robot maid?

3. In some industries, robots ~~they~~ are already part of the workforce.

4. Robots ~~they~~ make sushi for some Japanese fast-food restaurant chains.

5. A factory might use robots to handle substances that ~~they~~ are dangerous for humans to touch.

6. But business ~~it~~ is not the only area in which the robot population is increasing.

7. Some children who ~~they~~ wanted a robot friend have already gotten their wish.

8. Toy manufacturers have created a robot dog that ~~it~~ can respond to human commands.

9. The robot dog ~~it~~ was first on many holiday and birthday gift lists for children in the past few years.

10. The day it may still arrive when people can have friendly robot

assistants around the house.

USE THE RIGHT TYPE OF PRONOUN

There are three types of pronouns: subject pronouns, object pronouns, and possessive pronouns. These different types show the way pronouns can be used in a sentence. Note that the pronouns in the following sentence are all different types.

her (possessive)
When Mariah sang at the Super Bowl, Mariah's voice sounded beautiful,

her (object)   *she (subject)*
the crowd loved Mariah, and Mariah looked thrilled.

Pronoun Types

	SUBJECT	OBJECT	POSSESSIVE
First person	I/we	me/us	my, mine/ our, ours
Second person	you/you	you/you	your, yours/ your, yours
Third person singular	he, she, it	him, her, it	his, her, hers, its
Third person plural	they	them	their, theirs
	who/who	whom/whom	its, whose

Subject Pronouns

DEFINITION: A **subject pronoun** refers to the person, place, or thing that is the subject of a verb.

She took my parking space.

I honked my horn.

Object Pronouns

If a pronoun in a sentence is not a subject pronoun or a possessive pronoun, it is probably an object pronoun.

DEFINITION: **Object pronouns** either receive the action of a verb (the object of the verb) or are part of a prepositional phrase (the object of the preposition).

OBJECT OF THE VERB	Carolyn asked *me* to drive.
	Carolyn gave *me* the keys.
OBJECT OF THE PREPOSITION	Carolyn gave the keys to *me*.

Possessive Pronouns

DEFINITION: **Possessive pronouns** show ownership.

> Giselle is *my* best friend.

> Don't forget to bring *your* book.

Three trouble spots make it difficult to know what type of pronoun to use.

Never put an apostrophe in a possessive pronoun.

THREE PRONOUN TROUBLE SPOTS

1. Compound subjects and objects.
2. Comparisons.
3. Sentences that need *who* or *whom*.

Pronouns Used with Compound Subjects and Objects

DEFINITION: A **compound subject** has more than one subject joined by a conjunction such as *and* or *or*.
   DEFINITION: A **compound object** has more than one object joined by a conjunction.

In grammar, the word *compound* means containing two or more equal elements.

| COMPOUND SUBJECT | Tim and *I* work together. |
| COMPOUND OBJECT | Joan baked the cookies for Jim and *me*. |

To decide what type of pronoun to use in a compound construction, try leaving out the other part of the compound and the conjunction. Then say the sentence aloud to yourself.

When you are writing about yourself and someone else, always put yourself after everyone else. *My friends and I went to a club,* not *I and my friends went to a club.*

> ~~Jerome and~~ (me/I) like chili dogs.   [Think: *I* like chili dogs.]

> The package was for ~~Karen and~~ (she/her).   [Think: The package was for *her*.]

If a pronoun is part of a compound object in a prepositional phrase, use an object pronoun.

> I will keep that information just between you and (I/me).

> [*Between you and me* is a prepositional phrase, so an object pronoun, *me*, is required.]

Many people make the mistake of using *I* in the phrase *between you and (me/I)*. The correct pronoun with *between* is the object *me*. If *between me* sounds odd to you, try thinking *with me*.

■ PRACTICE 6   EDITING PRONOUNS IN COMPOUND CONSTRUCTIONS

Edit each sentence using the proper type of pronoun. If a sentence is already correct, write "C" next to it.

EXAMPLE: Getting an MBA was one choice ~~him~~ *he* and ~~me~~ *I* had.

1. I met Jun when we were students in an engineering program, and ~~him~~ *we* and ~~me~~ *I* both decided that we were interested in business careers.

2. It seemed to Jun and ~~I~~ *me* that we should finish our engineering degrees first.

3. The day they handed diplomas to Jun and me, we started looking into corporate consulting.

4. Some people told Jun and ~~I~~ *me* that we needed master's degrees in business administration.

5. ~~Him~~ *He* and I were convinced that smart people with degrees in engineering would be useful in the business world, with or without an MBA.

6. In just a few weeks, Jun and ~~me~~ *I* were accepted as management consultant trainees.

7. He and I were not the only trainees who did not have MBA degrees.

8. Nancy had a degree in philosophy, and Andrew was a lawyer; both ~~him~~ *he* and ~~her~~ *she* had decided to look for jobs in business.

9. Nancy said that ~~her~~ *she* and Andrew had learned that people without MBAs perform just as well in corporate America as people who have business degrees.

10. Our new employer told her and him that intelligence was a better predictor of success in business than an MBA was.

Pronouns Used in Comparisons

Using the right type of pronoun in comparisons is particularly important because using the wrong type can change the meaning of the sentence. Editing comparisons can be tricky because they often imply words that aren't actually included in the sentence.

> To find comparisons, look for the words *than* or *as*.

> Bill likes Chinese food more than *I*.

[This sentence means Bill likes Chinese food more than I like it. The implied words after *I* are *like Chinese food.*]

> Bill likes Chinese food more than *me*.

[This sentence means Bill likes Chinese food more than he likes me. The implied words after *than* are *he likes.*]

To decide whether to use a subject or object pronoun in a comparison, try adding the implied words and saying the sentence aloud.

> Add the implied words to the comparison when you speak and write. Then your meaning will be clear.

> The professor knows more than (us/we).

[Think: The professor knows more than *we know.*]

> Jen likes other professors more than (he/him).

[Think: Jen likes other professors more than *she likes him.*]

PRACTICE 7 EDITING PRONOUNS IN COMPARISONS

Edit each sentence using the correct pronoun type. If a sentence is correct, put a "C" next to it.

EXAMPLE: Gardening was a competitive sport for my mother, and I
                                           she
take it almost as seriously as ~~her~~.

1. My mother and father had a garden in their backyard, but she spent
                                      he
   much more time there than ~~him~~.

2. My father always said that my mother had a greener thumb than he.

3. The garden was filled with tomatoes because my mother loved no other
                                  them
   vegetable as much as ~~they.~~

4. No one I have ever known has had as many tomato recipes as ~~her~~. *she*

5. She won many blue ribbons at the county fair with her garden produce, and nothing in our house was displayed more proudly than they.

6. My brother, who is two years older than ~~me~~ *I*, began helping her when he was a little boy.

7. He made sure that the leaf of each plant was free of slugs, for few other garden pests are as destructive as ~~them~~ *they*.

8. To this day, he is a better gardener than ~~me~~ *I*.

9. I spend just as much time as ~~him~~ *he* working in the garden, however.

10. Every summer, we compare notes to see if I have grown as many tomatoes as ~~him~~ *he*.

Choosing between Who *and* Whom

Who is always a subject; use this form if the pronoun performs an action. *Whom* is always an object; use this form if the pronoun does not perform an action.

> **WHO = SUBJECT**   I don't know *who* rang the alarm.

> **WHOM = OBJECT**   Billy is the person to *whom* I report.

Whoever is a subject pronoun; *whomever* is an object pronoun.

In sentences other than questions, when the pronoun (*who* or *whom*) is followed by a verb, use *who*. When the pronoun (*who* or *whom*) is followed by a noun or pronoun, use *whom*.

> The person (**who**/whom) spoke was boring.
> [The pronoun is followed by the verb *spoke*. Use *who*.]
> The person (who/**whom**) I met was boring.
> [The pronoun is followed by another pronoun: *I*. Use *whom*.]

▨ PRACTICE 8   **CHOOSING BETWEEN *WHO* AND *WHOM***

In each sentence, circle the correct word, *who* or *whom*. Remember, if the pronoun is followed by a verb, use *who*. If it is followed by a noun or pronoun, use *whom*.

EXAMPLE: Chester Himes was the writer (who / whom) created the characters Coffin Ed Johnson and Grave Digger Jones.

1. Chester Himes, (who / whom) readers know best as a detective novelist, wrote several novels in the 1940s and 1950s analyzing race relations in the United States.

2. Himes, (who / whom) was the youngest son of a middle-class family, spent many years living in Los Angeles.

3. Like many African American writers (who / whom) he knew, Himes moved to Paris in the 1950s.

4. One of his novels about two African American detectives (who / whom) work in Harlem, *Cotton Comes to Harlem,* was made into a successful movie.

5. Himes, (who / whom) died in Spain in 1984, actually knew other parts of the United States and of Europe much better than he knew Harlem.

MAKE PRONOUNS CONSISTENT IN PERSON

DEFINITION: **Person** is the point of view a writer uses—the perspective from which he or she writes. Pronouns may be in first person *(I, we)*; second person *(you)*; or third person *(he, she, it, or they)*. (See the chart on p. 440.)

> **INCONSISTENT PERSON**   *I* wanted to use the copy machine, but the attendant said *you* had to have an access code.

[The sentence starts in the first person *(I)* but shifts to the second person *(you)*.]

> **CONSISTENT PERSON**   *I* wanted to use the copy machine, but the attendant said *I* had to have an access code.

[The sentence stays with the first person, *I*.]

> **INCONSISTENT PERSON**   After *a caller* presses 1, *you* get a recording.

[The sentence starts with the third person *(a caller)* but shifts to the second person *(you)*.]

CONSISTENT PERSON	After *a caller* presses 1, *he* or *she* gets a recording.
CONSISTENT PERSON, PLURAL	After *callers* press 1, *they* get a recording.

PRACTICE 9   MAKING PRONOUNS CONSISTENT IN PERSON

In the following items, correct the shifts in person. There may be more than one way to correct some sentences.

> **EXAMPLE:** I have a younger brother with an allergy to peanuts, and
> *I*
> ~~you~~ have to be very careful with his food.

1. Experts agree that the percentage of people with allergies to foods is rising, but we don't know why.

2. Someone who has a mild allergic reaction the first time you eat a food may develop more severe allergies from future contacts with the food.

3. If a person has a severe allergy to a food and unknowingly eats even a small amount of that food, you could die.

4. However, if people with allergies are protected from any contact with the food for several years, his or her allergies may disappear or become milder.

5. When a young child has severe allergies, their parents can be extremely cautious.

6. My little brother is severely allergic to peanuts, so you are not allowed to eat anything containing peanuts while he is nearby.

7. He carries an adrenaline pen that can save your life if you go into shock from a food allergy.

8. I love peanut butter, but you can't eat a peanut butter sandwich in my house.

9. My mother will not take my brother to any public place where you can even smell peanuts.

10. Some people think that her precautions are extreme, but she knows that you can't be too careful when your child's life is at stake.

Edit Paragraphs and Your Own Writing

PRACTICE 10 EDITING PARAGRAPHS FOR PRONOUN USE

Find and correct any problems with pronoun use in the following paragraphs. You may want to use the Quick Review chart on page 450.

1. (1) The picture phone never caught on with consumers, but videoconferencing it uses the same idea. (2) Anyone whom has a video camera hooked up to a home computer can connect to someone else with a similar setup. (3) A person simply sits in front of the camera and talks; a person or group of people on the other end is able to see and hear them. (4) It has been wonderful for both businesses and families.

(5) In the new global economy, a company often has their offices all over the world. (6) Once, a businessperson might have had to travel a great deal to keep in touch with their clients, suppliers, and fellow employees around the globe. (7) Today, much of it can be done with videoconferencing. (8) Anyone can attend a meeting and see their clients face to face while remaining on a different continent. (9) The technology has improved so that you can transmit high-quality images and sound, and the cost of videoconferencing continues to drop. (10) And of course, a videoconferencing businessperson with competitors who travel the world will save much more money than them on airfare and accommodations.

(11) Businesses are not the only ones to benefit from videoconferencing technology. (12) A family today may find that it often must spend time apart. (13) A parent traveling for business may not see their spouse or children for days at a time. (14) People move across the country from where you grew up, leaving parents and siblings behind. (15) Parents they sometimes divorce, and sometimes one starts a new job far away from the children. (16) Today, however, someone who cannot be present to kiss their children goodnight or wish their sister a happy birthday can see family members across the miles through videoconferencing. (17) Divorced parents who judges have allowed to move to another state have actually been required by law to buy videoconferencing technology to keep in touch with their children.

(18) Most people do not feel that videoconferencing can replace being physically present with family members and clients, but it costs less than regular visits while offering more intimacy than a telephone call. (19) They say that the eyes are the windows of the soul, and videoconferencing helps people look into those windows and stay connected.

2.   (1) Some people travel the world without ever leaving his or her house by reading books about exotic locations. (2) A person who is afraid to fly can nevertheless immerse themselves in a far-off place. (3) Someone whom does not speak a word of any foreign language can pretend to fit in like a native while reading travel literature. (4) At the end of a good travel book, you can feel as if you know a place you've never visited—even if you never want to go there. (5) Armchair travel is, in fact, less dangerous and more comfortable than much actual tourism. (6) Unfamiliar customs and food that might make a traveler feel out of place often seem very

amusing when it is described in a good book. (7) And many people who read avidly about a traveler getting food poisoning in a strange place or sitting on a plane that nearly crashes say to themselves, "I am glad that happened to him rather than I!" (8) Armchair travel books are one genre that it often turns up on best-seller lists. (9) A growing audience will continue to demand such books from its local bookstores and libraries.

PRACTICE 11   EDITING YOUR OWN WRITING FOR PRONOUN USE

As a final practice, edit a piece of your own writing for pronoun use. It can be a paper you are working on for this course, a paper you've already finished, a paper for another course, or a recent piece of writing from your work or everyday life. Record in your learning journal any problem sentences you find, along with their corrections. You may want to use the following Quick Review Chart.

LEARNING JOURNAL
Do you understand the terms *pronoun agreement* and *pronoun reference?* How would you explain them to someone else?

Quick Review Chart

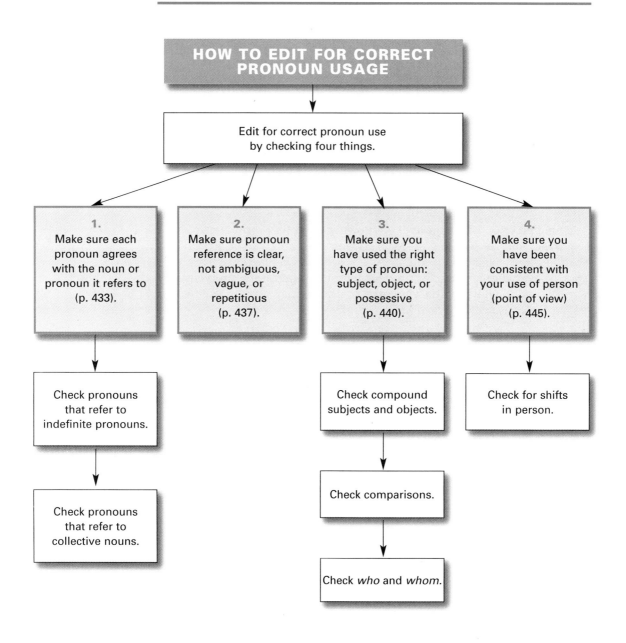

HOW TO EDIT FOR CORRECT PRONOUN USAGE

Edit for correct pronoun use by checking four things.

1.
Make sure each pronoun agrees with the noun or pronoun it refers to (p. 433).

2.
Make sure pronoun reference is clear, not ambiguous, vague, or repetitious (p. 437).

3.
Make sure you have used the right type of pronoun: subject, object, or possessive (p. 440).

4.
Make sure you have been consistent with your use of person (point of view) (p. 445).

Check pronouns that refer to indefinite pronouns.

Check compound subjects and objects.

Check for shifts in person.

Check pronouns that refer to collective nouns.

Check comparisons.

Check *who* and *whom*.

28

Adjectives and Adverbs

Describing *Which One?* or *How?*

Understand What Adjectives and Adverbs Are

DEFINITION: **Adjectives** describe or modify nouns (words that name people, places, or things) and pronouns (words that replace nouns). They add information about what kind, which one, or how many.

City traffic was *terrible* last night.

The highway was *congested* for *three* miles.

Two huge old tractor trailers had collided.

DEFINITION: **Adverbs** describe or modify verbs (words that tell what happens in a sentence), adjectives, or other adverbs. They add information about how, how much, when, where, why, or to what extent. Adverbs often end with *-ly*.

MODIFYING VERB	Dave drives *aggressively*.
MODIFYING ADJECTIVE	The *extremely* old woman swims every day.
MODIFYING ANOTHER ADVERB	Dave drives *very* aggressively.

LEARNING JOURNAL
Use your learning journal to record sentences with adjective and adverb problems that you find in your writing. Also write down edited versions of the sentences, with the problems corrected.

Note that both adjectives and adverbs can come before or after the words they modify, and that you can use more than one adjective or adverb to modify a word.

Practice Using Adjectives and Adverbs Correctly

CHOOSING BETWEEN ADJECTIVE AND ADVERB FORMS

Many adverbs are formed by adding -*ly* to the end of an adjective.

ADJECTIVE	ADVERB
The *new* student introduced himself.	The couple is *newly* married.
That is an *honest* answer.	Please answer *honestly*.

It can be difficult to decide whether to use the adjective form or the adverb form of a word. To decide which form to use, find the word you want to describe or modify. If that word is a noun or pronoun, use the adjective form. If it is a verb, adjective, or another adverb, use the adverb form.

PRACTICE 1 CHOOSING BETWEEN ADJECTIVE AND ADVERB FORMS

In each sentence, underline the word in the sentence that is being described or modified, and then circle the correct word in parentheses.

> **EXAMPLE:** Teenagers who want a summer job (usual / (usually)) can find work.

1. Even in a slowing economy, many summer jobs for unskilled workers are (easy / easily) to find.

2. Of course, teenaged workers without much experience should not have (extreme / extremely) rigid requirements for a summer job.

3. Fast-food restaurants are a (frequent / frequently) employer of teenagers.

4. The wages at a fast-food restaurant will not be (high / highly) for a starting position, however.

5. In addition, the work may not be very (interesting / interestingly).

6. However, teenagers can learn (valuable / valuably) lessons from going to almost any job.

7. Arriving on time and behaving (responsible / responsibly) will impress any supervisor.

8. Working (close / closely) with other employees also may teach a teenage worker to get along with people who are not friends or family.

9. Earning money can make a high school student feel more (financial / financially) independent.

10. Saving for college tuition is one way in which a teenager can use money from a summer job (wise / wisely).

USING COMPARATIVE AND SUPERLATIVE FORMS

DEFINITION: To compare two persons, places, or things, use the **comparative** form of adjectives or adverbs.

Sheehan drives *faster* than I do.

Francis is *more gullible* than Tara is.

DEFINITION: To compare three or more persons, places, or things, use the **superlative** form of adjectives or adverbs.

Sheehan drives the *fastest* of all our friends.

Francis is the *most gullible* of the children.

Comparatives and superlatives can be formed either by adding an ending to an adjective or adverb or by adding a word. If an adjective or adverb is short (one syllable), add *-er* to form the comparative and *-est* to form the superlative. Also use this pattern for adjectives that end in *-y* (but change the *-y* to *-i* before adding *-er* or *-est*). If an adjective or adverb is longer than one syllable, add the word *more* to make the comparative and the word *most* to make the superlative.

Comparative and Superlative Forms

ADJECTIVE OR ADVERB	COMPARATIVE	SUPERLATIVE
ADVERBS AND ADJECTIVES OF ONE SYLLABLE		
tall	taller	tallest
fast	faster	fastest
ADJECTIVES ENDING IN *-Y*		
happy	happier	happiest
silly	sillier	silliest
ADVERBS AND ADJECTIVES OF MORE THAN ONE SYLLABLE		
graceful	more graceful	most graceful
gracefully	more gracefully	most gracefully
intelligent	more intelligent	most intelligent
intelligently	more intelligently	most intelligently

For more on changing a final *-y* to *-i* when adding endings, and on other spelling changes involving endings, see Chapter 36.

Use either an ending (*-er* or *-est*) or an extra word (*more* or *most*) to form a comparative or superlative—not both at once.

One of the ~~most~~ easiest ways to beat stress is to exercise regularly.

◼ PRACTICE 2   USING COMPARATIVES AND SUPERLATIVES

In the space provided in each sentence, write the correct form of the adjective or adverb in parentheses. You may need to add *more* or *most* to some adjectives and adverbs.

> **EXAMPLE:** One of the _most beautiful_ *(beautiful)* sights in the West is a herd of wild horses.

1. Mustangs live in several western states, but Nevada is the place where

    they are _____ *(commonly)* found.

2. Thousands of wild horses live on public lands in the West, but cattle are

   seen _____ *(frequently)* than horses are.

3. Horses have lived in the Nevada mountains for a _____ *(long)* time

   than cattle have; some may be descendants of Spanish conquistadors'

   horses.

4. Soon, the Bureau of Land Management expects to conduct one of the

   _____ *(big)* roundups of wild mustangs in recent decades.

5. Government officials believe that the land should have a _____

   (small) population of horses than it now supports.

6. Many people find a mustang roundup, which often involves helicopters

   and horseback riders, one of the _____ *(exciting)* events

   they have ever witnessed.

7. After government roundups, mustangs are sold at auction to the

   _____ *(high)* bidder.

8. Experienced horse trainers find that they can get horses _____

   _____*(cheaply)* at government auctions than at many other sales.

9. Wild mustangs may be _____ *(difficult)* to train than

   domestic horses, but some mustangs have gone on to become champions.

10. Horse lovers may view the mustangs _____ *(romanti-*

    cally) than cattle ranchers do; cattle ranchers see the horses as

    competition for scarce food.

GOOD, WELL, BAD, AND BADLY

Irregular means not
following a standard
rule.

Four common adjectives and adverbs have irregular forms: *good, well, bad,*
and *badly.*

Forms of Good, Well, Bad, *and* Badly

	COMPARATIVE	SUPERLATIVE
ADJECTIVE		
good	better	best
bad	worse	worst
ADVERB		
well	better	best
badly	worse	worst

People often get confused about whether to use *good* or *well*. *Good* is an adjective, so use it to describe a noun or pronoun. *Well* is an adverb, so use it to describe a verb or an adjective.

ADJECTIVE   She is a *good* friend.

ADVERB   He works *well* with his colleagues.

Well can also be an adjective to describe someone's health:

I am not *well* today.

PRACTICE 3   USING *GOOD* AND *WELL*

Complete each sentence by circling the correct word in parentheses. Underline the word that *good* or *well* modifies.

EXAMPLE: A (good / well) storyteller can hold an audience's attention.

1. Mark Twain's ability to tell an amusing story is (good / well) known.

2. Twain's famous story "The Notorious Jumping Frog of Calaveras County" is a (good / well) example of traditional American tale-telling.

3. The story is narrated by an Easterner whose proper speech contrasts (good / well) with the country dialect of Simon Wheeler, a storyteller he meets.

4. Wheeler may not be (good / well) <u>educated</u>, but he is a master of the tall tale.

5. The narrator claims that Wheeler has told him a "monotonous" story, but the <u>tale</u> is apparently (good / well) enough for the narrator to repeat.

6. The frog in the story is famous for being a (good / well) <u>jumper</u>.

7. Wheeler explains that the frog's owner <u>lives</u> (good / well) by gambling on the frog's jumping ability.

8. The frog's owner, Jim Smiley, makes the mistake of leaving the frog with a man whom Smiley does not <u>know</u> (good / well).

9. The stranger makes the frog swallow heavy shot so that he can no longer jump (good / well).

10. In Twain's story, Simon Wheeler has such a (good / well) <u>time telling</u> stories that the narrator has to escape from him at the end.

PRACTICE 4   USING COMPARATIVE AND SUPERLATIVE FORMS OF *GOOD* AND *BAD*

Complete each sentence by circling the correct comparative or superlative form of *good* or *bad* in parentheses.

EXAMPLE: The (better / best) way my family found to learn about another culture was to allow an exchange student to live in our home.

1. Simone, a French high school student, spent last summer getting to know the United States (better / best) by living with my family.

2. She had studied English since the age of five, and her understanding of grammar was (better / best) than mine.

3. She told me that she had the (worse / worst) accent of any student in her English classes, but I liked the way she spoke.

4. Her accent was certainly no (worse / worst) than mine would be if I tried to speak French.

5. My (worse / worst) fear was that she would find our lives boring.

6. However, the exchange program's administrator explained that the (better / best) way for Simone to learn about our country was for us to do ordinary things.

7. For me, the (better / best) part of Simone's visit was the chance to see my world through fresh eyes.

8. I felt (better / best) about my summer job, trips to the supermarket, and afternoon swims at the pool because Simone found all of these things exotic and fascinating.

9. Simone even liked summer reruns on television; she claimed that French television was much (worse / worst).

10. The (worse / worst) part of the visit was having to say goodbye to Simone at the end of the summer.

Edit Paragraphs and Your Own Writing

PRACTICE 5   EDITING PARAGRAPHS FOR CORRECT ADJECTIVES AND ADVERBS

Find and correct any problems with adjectives and adverbs in the following paragraphs. You may want to use the Quick Review Chart on page 461.

1.   (1) For an average European in the Middle Ages, wearing stripes was not simple a fashion mistake. (2) According to Michel Pastoureau, a scholar of the medieval period, wearing stripes was one of the worse

things a European Christian could do in the thirteenth and fourteenth centuries. (3) Stripes might be taken as a sign that the wearer was ~~more~~ sillier than other people; jesters, for example, often wore them. (4) Prostitutes also wore striped clothes, so stripes might be seen as an indication that the person was ~~sinfuller~~ *more sinful* than others. (5) Wearing stripes was ~~dangerousest~~ *most dangerous* for clergymen. (6) At least one clergyman in fourteenth-century France was executed because he had been foolishly enough to wear striped clothes. (7) Carmelite monks who wore striped cloaks were frequent attacked, and several popes insisted that the monks change to a more simple costume. (8) People in medieval Europe certainly took their clothing serious. (9) The only reason some people don't wear stripes today is that they are afraid of looking fat.

2. (1) Many people no longer find it embarrassingly to admit that they have seen a psychotherapist. (2) Some patients argue that it is gooder to seek mental help than to suffer silently. (3) Others seem to feel that needing a therapist is a sign that their lives are interestinger than other people's. (4) At any rate, the stigma that some people once attached to psychotherapy is disappearing quick. (5) Therapists have lately become visibler in popular culture, and this visibility may result in even wider acceptance of psychotherapy. (6) For example, when a mobster on the cable television show *The Sopranos* asks a therapist to treat his panic attacks, viewers see that the most tough of men is still able to discuss his relationships and feelings with a mental health specialist. (7) If Tony Soprano can do it, what ordinary person is going to feel badly about seeking help for ordinary problems?

(8) However, people considering seeing a therapist are not the only ones who love to watch Tony Soprano trying to work through his problems. (9) Indeed, *The Sopranos,* which is one of the bigger hits ever on cable television, includes many psychologists in its audience. (10) One online magazine regular publishes a therapist's analysis of each episode. (11) Other therapists chat online about whether or not the psychologist on the television show is practicing psychology. (12) The audiences of psychological professionals seem to agree that therapy is portrayed accurrer on the show than in many popular films. (13) As they point out, at least the therapist is not in love with her patient, unlike several psychiatrists in recently movies. (14) Although Mr. Soprano, like many actual therapy patients, does things that are not good for his mental health, his therapist thinks that he is functioning best now than before. (15) Perhaps someday he will honest discuss his criminal day job with her—and if he does, even the therapists tuning in might have trouble figuring out the bestest possible response.

■ PRACTICE 6   EDITING YOUR OWN WRITING FOR CORRECT ADJECTIVES AND ADVERBS

LEARNING JOURNAL
What kind of mistake in using adjectives or adverbs do you make most often in your writing? What are some ways to avoid or correct this mistake?

As a final practice, edit a piece of your own writing for correct use of adjectives and adverbs. It can be a paper you are working on for this course, a paper you've already finished, a paper for another course, or a recent piece of writing from your work or everyday life. Record in your learning journal any problem sentences you find, along with their corrections. You may want to use the following Quick Review Chart.

Quick Review Chart

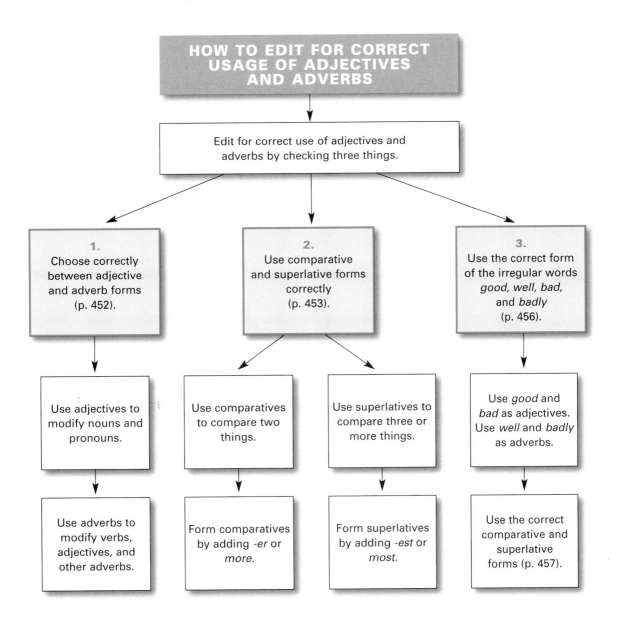

HOW TO EDIT FOR CORRECT USAGE OF ADJECTIVES AND ADVERBS

Edit for correct use of adjectives and adverbs by checking three things.

1. Choose correctly between adjective and adverb forms (p. 452).

2. Use comparative and superlative forms correctly (p. 453).

3. Use the correct form of the irregular words *good, well, bad,* and *badly* (p. 456).

Use adjectives to modify nouns and pronouns.

Use comparatives to compare two things.

Use superlatives to compare three or more things.

Use *good* and *bad* as adjectives. Use *well* and *badly* as adverbs.

Use adverbs to modify verbs, adjectives, and other adverbs.

Form comparatives by adding *-er* or *more.*

Form superlatives by adding *-est* or *most.*

Use the correct comparative and superlative forms (p. 457).

29

Misplaced and Dangling Modifiers

Avoiding Confusing Descriptions

Understand What Misplaced and Dangling Modifiers Are

LEARNING JOURNAL
Use your learning journal to record sentences you find in your writing that have misplaced or dangling modifiers. Also write down edited versions of the sentences, with the problems corrected.

DEFINITION: **Modifiers** are words or word groups that describe or give more information about other words in a sentence. So that this information is clear, the modifier must be near the words it modifies and must modify only one sentence element. In most cases, the modifier should be right before or right after that sentence element.

DEFINITION: A **misplaced modifier** ends up describing the wrong sentence element because it is incorrectly placed within the sentence.

MISPLACED   Lorene saw my dog *driving her car on the highway.*

[Was my dog driving her car?]

CLEAR   *Driving her car on the highway,* Lorene saw my dog.

DEFINITION: A **dangling modifier** is said to "dangle" because it has nothing to attach itself to; the sentence element it is supposed to modify may be implied, but it is not actually stated in the sentence. A dangling

462

modifier usually appears at the beginning of a sentence and seems to modify the noun or pronoun that immediately follows it.

DANGLING   *Talking on my cell phone,* my car drove into a ditch.

[Was the car talking on the cell phone?]

CLEAR   *Talking on my cell phone,* I drove my car into a ditch.

Even if readers can guess what you are trying to say, misplaced and dangling modifiers are awkward. Be sure to look for and correct misplaced and dangling modifiers in your writing.

Practice Correcting Misplaced and Dangling Modifiers

MISPLACED MODIFIERS

To correct a misplaced modifier, move the modifier as close as possible to the sentence element it modifies. The safest choice is often to put the modifier directly before the sentence element it modifies.

Using her computer, Suzy illustrated the story.
Suzy illustrated the story using her computer.

Three constructions in particular often lead to misplaced modifiers. Be sure to check your writing for these three trouble spots.

Trouble Spots: Misplaced Modifiers

1. Limiting modifiers such as *only, almost, hardly, nearly,* and *just.* These words need to be right before—not just close to—the words or phrases they modify.

ordered only
I only ordered half a pound.

collected nearly
Griffin nearly collected 100 cans.

2. Phrases

PREPOSITIONAL PHRASES

to the house for his sister.

Jim was carrying the bags ~~for his sister to the house.~~

for ice cream in her glove compartment.

Julie found money ~~in her glove compartment for ice cream.~~

PHRASES BEGINNING WITH *-ING* VERB FORMS

Using cash,

Timothy bought the car ~~using cash.~~

Wearing an oven mitt,

Elena took out the hot pizza ~~wearing an oven mitt.~~

3. Clauses beginning with *who, whose, that,* or *which*

that was missing

I finally found the sock stuck to a T-shirt ~~that was missing.~~

PRACTICE 1   CORRECTING MISPLACED MODIFIERS

Find and correct any misplaced modifiers in the following sentences. If a sentence is correct, write a "C" next to it.

who work in U.S. hospitals

EXAMPLE: Many nurses are being trained to perform therapeutic touch ~~who work in U.S. hospitals.~~

1. Are there energy fields that can be touched by trained professionals in a human body?

2. People claim to be able to feel and move invisible energy fields who practice therapeutic touch.

subject

3. According to believers in therapeutic touch, an energy field can cause pain and illness that is out of alignment.

4. A practitioner treating a patient does not touch the sick person.

5. After a session of therapeutic touch, many patients just report that they felt better without knowing why.

   report just

6. Emily Rosa, the twelve-year-old daughter of a nurse, made news when her experiment appeared in an important medical journal to test practitioners of therapeutic touch.

7. In her experiment, practitioners were supposed to use the invisible energy field to determine when her hands were near theirs who could not see Emily.

8. Even though guessing should have allowed a 50 percent accuracy rating, the practitioners Emily tested were correct only 44 percent of the time.

9. Anyone who can demonstrate the ability to detect a human energy field can claim a million-dollar prize in a similar experiment.

10. The prize has not been awarded yet, which is offered by a foundation that investigates supernatural claims.

DANGLING MODIFIERS

DEFINITION: When an opening modifier does not modify any word in the sentence, it is a **dangling modifier**. Writers often fail to include the word being modified because they think the meaning is clear. To be certain that your sentence says what you intend it to say, be sure to include the word being modified.

I was
While watching the movie, my purse was stolen.

There are two basic ways to correct dangling modifiers. Use the one that makes the most sense.

1. You can add the word being modified right after the opening modifier so that the connection between the two is clear.

I twisted

Running to catch up, my ankle ~~twisted.~~

2. You can add the word being modified in the opening modifier itself.

As I was running

~~Running~~ to catch up, my ankle twisted.

 PRACTICE 2   CORRECTING DANGLING MODIFIERS

Find and correct any dangling modifiers in the following sentences. If a sentence is correct, write "C" next to it. It may be necessary to add new words or ideas to some sentences.

the owner will get a better price for

EXAMPLE: Selling a used car, a resale ~~will bring a better price~~ than a

trade-in.   *Dealer*

1. Trading in a used car, a buyer will offer a better price if the car is clean.   *on a used*

2. Hiring a professional detailer, a used car can still impress potential buyers.

3. Looking like new, the owner can get the best price for a trade-in or a resale.   *if the car*

4. With essential repairs completed, a used car should be in good working order to be sold.

5. Approved as safe and drivable by a reputable mechanic, minor mechanical problems may not have to be fixed.

6. Winning points for honesty, prospective buyers should know about a used car's minor problems.

7. Deducted from the asking price, the owner can be fair with a buyer.

8. No matter how expensive, decorative lighting and other details usually do not add to the value of a car.

9. With higher than usual mileage, the owner may have to reduce the asking price.

10. Advertising in a local newspaper, a used car is likely to reach its target market.

Edit Paragraphs and Your Own Writing

PRACTICE 3   EDITING PARAGRAPHS FOR MISPLACED AND DANGLING MODIFIERS

Find and correct any misplaced or dangling modifiers in the following paragraphs. You may want to refer to the Quick Review Chart on page 470.

1.   (1) When ordering items online, shipping and handling costs can make or break a business. (2) By charging too much, customers may abandon their order. (3) A customer may never return to the site who feels that shipping and handling charges are too high. (4) Most people have shipped packages, so they know how much shipping costs at least occasionally. (5) Going too far in the other direction, some online customers get free shipping and handling. (6) The sites lose money that offer free shipping, and may have to either close down for good or start charging shipping fees. (7) Most shipping companies charge by weight. (8) Buying from the sites that use these shippers, the online sites must either charge a flat fee, which may be too much or too little, or make the customer wait until the order is complete to find out the shipping fee. (9) Neither option is per-

fect, so a business must choose the least unattractive solution that wants to keep expanding its customer base online.

2.   MEMO

To: All staff

From: Sara Hollister

Re: Dress code

(1) After encouraging employees to wear casual clothing on Fridays, the casual dress code was soon in force all week long. (2) With some uncertainty about what was appropriate casual wear, a memo was circulated last year with guidelines for dress. (3) Wearing khakis and polo shirts, suits and ties became very rare in the halls of Wilson and Hollister. (4) Some younger staff members almost never wore anything but jeans. (5) Arriving in the office in a Hawaiian shirt, some employees hardly recognized Mr. Wilson without his trademark pinstriped suit. (6) Believing that informality improved productivity and morale, the casual dress code was well liked.

(7) Recommending changes in the dress policy now, for several reasons. (8) The human resources department feels that the relaxed attitude toward dress may have contributed to the recent increases in absenteeism and lateness at Wilson and Hollister. (9) Other problems have also surfaced. (10) Clients have sometimes expressed surprise who have dropped in unexpectedly. (11) Hoping to keep their respect and their business, the clients appear to feel more comfortable with employees in suits. (12) Finally, fearing an increase in sexual harassment, sleeveless shirts, shorts, miniskirts, and halter tops will no longer be permitted. (13) Human resources almost

recommends a complete change in the casual-dress policy. (14) While continuing to wear casual clothing on Friday, business attire on Monday through Thursday, effective immediately. (15) As an employee who prefers casual clothing, this news is rather sad, but the decision is for the best. (16) Certain that you will understand the necessity for these changes, necessity for these changes, I appreciate your cooperation.

■ PRACTICE 4   **EDITING YOUR OWN WRITING FOR MISPLACED AND DANGLING MODIFIERS**

As a final practice, edit a piece of your own writing for misplaced and dangling modifiers. It can be a paper you are working on for this course, a paper you've already finished, a paper for another course, or a recent piece of writing from your work or everyday life. Record in your learning journal any problem sentences you find, along with their corrections. You may want to use the following Quick Review Chart.

LEARNING JOURNAL
Which is more difficult for you, finding misplaced and dangling modifiers or correcting them? What can you do to help yourself find or correct them more easily?

Quick Review Chart

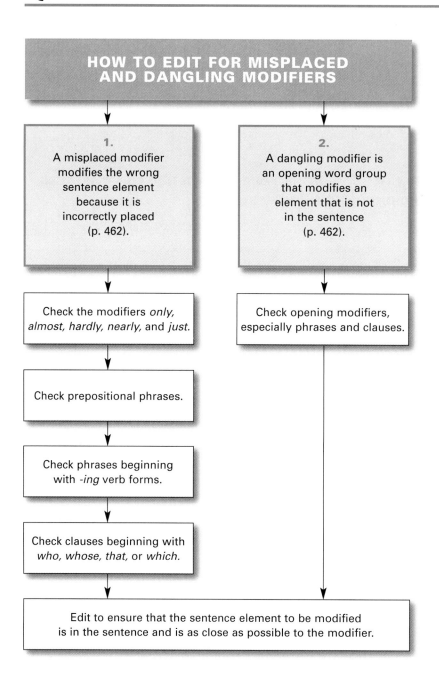

HOW TO EDIT FOR MISPLACED AND DANGLING MODIFIERS

1.
A misplaced modifier modifies the wrong sentence element because it is incorrectly placed (p. 462).

2.
A dangling modifier is an opening word group that modifies an element that is not in the sentence (p. 462).

Check the modifiers *only, almost, hardly, nearly,* and *just.*

Check opening modifiers, especially phrases and clauses.

Check prepositional phrases.

Check phrases beginning with *-ing* verb forms.

Check clauses beginning with *who, whose, that,* or *which.*

Edit to ensure that the sentence element to be modified is in the sentence and is as close as possible to the modifier.

30

Coordination and Subordination

Joining Ideas

Understand Coordination and Subordination

DEFINITION: Coordination can be used to join two sentences when the ideas in them are equally important.

TWO SENTENCES	The internship at the magazine is very prestigious. Many interns have gone on to get good jobs.
JOINED THROUGH COORDINATION	The internship at the magazine is very prestigious, *and* many interns have gone on to get good jobs.

DEFINITION: Subordination can be used to join two sentences when one idea is less important than the other. Adding a dependent word (such as *although, because, if,* or *that*) to one sentence shows that it is subordinate to, or less important than, the other.

TWO SENTENCES	The internship was advertised last week. The magazine received many calls about it.

The word *subordinate* means "lower in rank" or "secondary." In the workplace, for example, you are subordinate to your boss. In the army, a private is subordinate to an officer.

LEARNING JOURNAL
Use your learning
journal as a place to
record short, choppy
sentences that could
be joined by coordi-
nation or subordina-
tion. Also, once you
have connected them,
write down the edited
versions of the sen-
tences.

**JOINED THROUGH
SUBORDINATION**

When the internship was advertised last week, the magazine received many calls about it.

[The word *when* makes the first sentence dependent, or subordinate, and puts more emphasis on the second part, the idea that the magazine received many calls.]

If all of your sentences are short, they will seem choppy and hard to read. To vary the rhythm and flow of your writing and to clarify the relationship between ideas, use coordination or subordination to join sentences with related ideas.

Practice Using Coordination and Subordination

COORDINATION USING COORDINATING CONJUNCTIONS

DEFINITIONS: A **conjunction** is a word that joins words, phrases, or clauses. **Coordinating conjunctions** are the words *and, but, for, nor, or, so,* and *yet.* (You can remember them by thinking of FANBOYS—*for, and, nor, but, or, yet, so.*) They join ideas of equal importance. To join two sentences with ideas that are equally important, put a comma and one of these conjunctions between the sentences.

Choose the conjunction that makes the most sense for the meaning of the two sentences.

Equal idea	, and , but , for , nor , or , so , yet	Equal idea

My friend is coming to town   , and   I'm excited to see her.

[*And* simply joins two ideas.]

We used to be best friends   , but   I haven't seen her for years.

[*But* indicates a contrast.]

I'm a little nervous	, for	we may not have anything in common anymore.

[*For* indicates a reason or cause.]

We haven't talked much	, nor	have we written.

[*Nor* indicates a negative.]

Maybe we will pick up our friendship	, or	we may be like strangers.

[*Or* indicates alternatives.]

We are having dinner tonight	, so	we will know soon.

[*So* indicates a result.]

It's hard to keep old friends	, yet	they are very important.

[*Yet* indicates a reason.]

PRACTICE 1   JOINING IDEAS WITH COORDINATING CONJUNCTIONS

In each of the following sentences, fill in the blank with an appropriate coordinating conjunction. There may be more than one correct answer for some sentences.

> **EXAMPLE:** Some students may not be ready for promotion at the end of the school year, *but* teachers, principals, and parents are often reluctant to keep them back.

1. Is social promotion in American schools a problem, _OR_ is it better for students to remain with classmates their own age than for them to repeat a grade?

2. In almost every school, some children will not be able to keep up with the required work, _NOR_ will they have the skills to move on to the next grade when the school year ends.

3. Many schools promote such children to the next grade anyway, _and_ they continue to advance with the rest of their classmates.

4. Social promotion may be harmful, _for_ the student may never learn the material without repeating a grade.

5. Socially promoted students may graduate from high school without basic skills, _And_ they may never be able to function well in society.

6. Other students earn the right to graduate, _but_ their diplomas may even be less valuable because unprepared students have the same certificates.

7. On the other hand, holding students back can cause terrible harm, _for_ the students lose friends and respect when their classmates go on without them.

8. People need self-respect to accomplish their goals, _So_ students who are left back may feel worthless or stupid.

9. Students who are left back are likely to be bigger and stronger than their younger classmates, _and_ some people have suggested that holding students back can endanger younger children.

10. Perhaps summer school can help some underprepared students catch up with classmates, _Or_ perhaps schools should provide students with additional help throughout the school year.

PRACTICE 2   COMBINING SENTENCES WITH COORDINATING CONJUNCTIONS

Combine each pair of sentences into a single sentence by using a comma and a coordinating conjunction. As you choose a coordinating conjunction, consider how the ideas in the two sentences are related to each other. In some cases, there may be more than one correct answer.

EXAMPLE: Americans have recently experienced unpleasant shocks at
                                , but people
           the gas station./People in the United States still pay lower

           gas prices than much of the world.

1. Gasoline prices are lower in the United States than in many other industrialized countries, Most Americans do not find this news comforting.

2. People in the United States are used to low gas prices, Many drivers feel cheated when prices increase.

3. In 2000, Hong Kong drivers paid over three times as much as Americans paid for gasoline, Italians and Japanese were buying gas at more than four dollars a gallon.

4. Canadians also pay higher gas prices than Americans pay, The taxes on gasoline are higher in Canada than they are in this country.

5. Few people would argue that gasoline prices in the United States are too low, The reason for these relatively cheap prices is that gasoline is not heavily taxed.

6. In many countries, taxes on gasoline support social services, The money may also pay for research on reducing air pollution.

7. Gasoline taxes can help to pay for roads, They can raise money for research into fuel efficiency.

8. However, taxes on gasoline are very unpopular with most drivers, Politicians are not eager to vote for gasoline taxes.

9. Many Americans do not want to pay gas taxes of even two or three cents per gallon, Most also do not want to spend tax money on mass transit systems.

10. Gasoline prices will probably never be as high in the United States as they are in Asia, A few Americans are not sure that this is a good thing.

COORDINATION USING SEMICOLONS

DEFINITION: A **semicolon** is a punctuation mark that can join two sentences through coordination. When you use a semicolon, make sure that the ideas in the two sentences are not only of equal importance but also very closely related.

EQUAL IDEA	;	EQUAL IDEA
My computer crashed	;	I lost all of my files.
I had just finished my research paper	;	I will have to redo the whole thing.

DEFINITION: A semicolon alone does not tell readers much about the relationship between the two ideas. To give more information about the relationship, use a semicolon followed by a word that indicates the relationship; such words are known as **conjunctive adverbs**. They must be followed by a comma.

Here are some of the most common conjunctive adverbs, along with some examples of how they are used.

Equal idea	; afterward, ; also, ; as a result, ; besides, ; consequently, ; frequently, ; however, ; in addition, ; in fact, ; instead, ; still, ; then, ; therefore,	Equal idea

My computer crashed	; as a result,	I lost all my files.
I should have made backup files	; however,	I did not.
The information is lost	; therefore,	I will have to try to rebuild the files.

■ **PRACTICE 3** **JOINING IDEAS WITH SEMICOLONS**

Join each pair of sentences by using a semicolon alone.

                                                         ; a

EXAMPLE: Different countries have different laws/A law school usually

            teaches students about the laws of a particular country.

1. Legal differences can cause problems in the global marketplace. Businesses from two different countries working together will probably not use the laws of either country when they draw up a contract.

2. Businesspeople need to decide which laws to follow in creating international contracts and deals. U.S. law is often the one they choose.

3. The American legal system is set up to deal with corporations and business interests. It is not surprising that many international businesses choose to follow U.S. laws.

4. Lawyers with experience in the U.S. system are now in demand. Bright people from all over the world are applying to law schools in the United States.

5. International students can often find good jobs after finishing law school. They usually know more than one language and understand more than one culture.

■ **PRACTICE 4** **COMBINING SENTENCES WITH SEMICOLONS AND CONNECTING WORDS (CONJUNCTIVE ADVERBS)**

Combine each pair of sentences by using a semicolon and a connecting word. Choose a conjunctive adverb that makes sense for the relationship between the two ideas. In some cases, there may be more than one correct answer.

           EXAMPLE: High school graduation is the unofficial end of adoles-

                  ; afterward, graduates

           cence/ Graduates choose different paths.

1. Some high school graduates want to grow up as quickly as possible. Others want to enjoy a period with limited responsibilities.

2. Many high school students intend to go directly to college. They must spend their junior and senior years reading brochures, filling out applications, and taking standardized tests.

3. Some students are not ready to think about college yet. They should choose another option.

4. Working attracts many high school graduates. A job can help a young person to feel independent and adult.

5. Many high school graduates have minimal living expenses. They can experiment with careers and find out what they enjoy doing.

6. Young graduates may not be committed yet to a family or a particular place. They can travel and seek interesting opportunities.

7. Volunteer work allows many high school graduates to help causes they believe in. They may get to visit other parts of the world.

8. Many young Americans choose to serve their country by joining the military. Such service can teach them skills and help them earn money.

9. Some high school graduates work, volunteer, or join the military as an intermediate step. They may plan to go to college after spending some time away from school.

10. Some young graduates want more education from an academic institution. Others prefer to learn from life's experiences.

SUBORDINATION USING SUBORDINATING CONJUNCTIONS

DEFINITIONS: A **conjunction** is a word that joins words, phrases, or clauses. **Subordinating conjunctions** are dependent words that can join two sentences when one is more important than the other. The sentence with the subordinating conjunction in front of it becomes a subordinate or dependent clause; because of the subordinating conjunction, it no longer expresses a complete thought and cannot stand by itself as a sentence.

Choose the conjunction that makes the most sense with the two sentences. Here are some of the most common subordinating conjunctions.

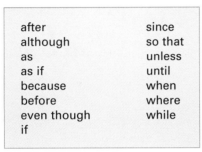

Main idea	after	since	Subordinate idea
	although	so that	
	as	unless	
	as if	until	
	because	when	
	before	where	
	even though	while	
	if		

| I decided to go to work | although | I had a terrible cold. |
| I hate to miss a day | unless | I absolutely can't get there. |

When a subordinate idea ends a sentence, it usually does not need to be preceded by a comma unless it is showing a contrast. When a subordinate idea begins a new sentence, use a comma to separate it from the rest of the sentence.

Subordinating conjunction	Subordinate idea	,	Main idea
Although	I had a terrible cold	,	I decided to go to work.
Unless	I absolutely can't get there	,	I hate to miss a day.

▨ PRACTICE 5   JOINING IDEAS THROUGH SUBORDINATION

In the following sentences, fill in the blank with an appropriate subordinating conjunction. In some cases, there may be more than one correct answer.

EXAMPLE: Smokey Bear spent most of his life in the National Zoo in Washington, D.C., _where_ he received so much mail that he had his own zip code.

1. Smokey Bear began reminding people that "Only you can prevent forest fires" in 1944 _____ government officials during World War II were concerned about preserving valuable resources like trees.

2. However, Smokey Bear existed only as a cartoon _____ a tragedy occurred six years later.

3. _____ a fire destroyed part of Lincoln National Forest near Capitan, New Mexico, in 1950, forest rangers found a badly burned bear cub clinging to a tree.

4. The "real" Smokey Bear became a celebrity _____ the public heard his story.

5. After his death, Smokey Bear's body was returned to New Mexico _____ he could be buried near his former home.

6. The character of Smokey Bear has been used continuously in U.S. and Canadian fire safety campaigns _____ it first appeared more than fifty years ago.

7. Smokey has also appeared in public service announcements in Mexico, _____ he is known as Simon.

8. Recently, Smokey's famous line was changed to "Only you can prevent wildfires" _____ research indicated that most adults did not believe they could cause a wildfire.

9. However, humans can easily set fires _____ they discard cigarettes carelessly, burn trash on windy days, or even park a car with a catalytic converter in a dry field.

10. _____ the Smokey Bear campaign heads for its sixtieth anniversary,

Smokey is as recognizable to most Americans as Mickey Mouse and

Santa Claus.

PRACTICE 6   COMBINING SENTENCES THROUGH SUBORDINATION

Combine each pair of sentences into a single sentence by using an appropriate subordinating conjunction either at the beginning or between the two sentences. Use a conjunction that makes sense with the two sentences.

EXAMPLE: Children like to assert themselves. ~~They~~ *when they* are between one

Although and four years old.

1. Toddlers do not get to make many decisions. They want to have some

    power over their own lives.

2. Young children often become frustrated. *when* Parents do not let them have

    their own way.

IF 3. Parents want to avoid power struggles with their toddlers. The parents

    should learn to pick their battles.

4. Experts recommend letting even young children make some choices. *so that* The

    children will feel that they have some control.

5. Parents should not let a child do anything dangerous. *Even though* The child may

    want to.

Even though 6. Toddlers can be difficult to handle. Most parents worry more about

    power struggles with their teenagers.

7. Adolescents need to establish their independence from their parents. They

    also want their parents to set some limits.

Since 8. Teenagers can be skilled at arguments. Parents should learn not to

    argue about or renegotiate rules that the household has established.

9. Food, sleep, clothes, and grooming are often battlefields for children and parents. Parents remember their own rebellious phases and try to understand what their children are feeling.

10. Parents and children can work through power struggles. They have respect for each other.

Edit Paragraphs and Your Own Writing

PRACTICE 7   EDITING PARAGRAPHS FOR COORDINATION AND SUBORDINATION

In the following paragraphs, join the underlined sentences by using either coordination or subordination. Be sure to punctuate correctly. You may want to use the Quick Review Chart on page 484 to help you.

1.   (1) Lyme disease is carried by deer ticks. (2) The disease appears most frequently in the northeastern United States. (3) Hikers, gardeners, and other lovers of the outdoors in that area often become victims of the illness. (4) People venture into tall grass or brush against other foliage. (5)   They should inspect any exposed skin carefully for the minuscule ticks. (6) Researchers now know that the disease is more widespread than was once thought. (7) Limiting exposed skin by wearing socks, long pants, and long sleeves gives ticks fewer chances to attach themselves. (8) So does washing exposed skin within about ninety minutes of being outdoors. (9) These simple precautions can prevent most cases of potentially dangerous Lyme disease.

2.   (1) Al-Qurain is a community in the small Middle Eastern country of Kuwait. (2) Thirty years ago, Kuwait City officials began to use an abandoned quarry in al-Qurain as a garbage dump. (3) None of them thought the

area would ever be populated. (4) Fifteen years ago, the government began to build subsidized housing in al-Qurain. (5) The dump was supposed to be closed. (6) Kuwaitis continued to use the al-Qurain landfill. (7) People soon lived all around the foul-smelling garbage pit. (8) Residents of the area were teased and insulted for living in the neighborhood. (9) Al-Qurain now houses sixty thousand people.

(10) For years, the dump sickened people around it. (11) Sometimes the garbage caught fire and sent fumes into the homes nearby. (12) Finally, the Kuwaiti Environmental Protection Agency decided to try to help. (13) The agency gets little government funding. (14) It needed to rely on donations for the cleanup effort.

(15) Soon, a mountain of garbage had been removed. (16) The leveled site was covered with pebbles from the desert. (17) Engineers found a way to siphon methane gas from the seventy-five-foot-deep garbage pit. (18) Kuwait is famous for oil production. (19) A methane-powered generator may soon provide electricity for al-Qurain residents. (20) The air in the neighborhood now ranks among the country's cleanest. (21) For many environmentalists and residents of this neighborhood, the cleanup of al-Qurain is almost a miracle.

PRACTICE 8   EDITING YOUR OWN WRITING FOR COORDINATION AND SUBORDINATION

As a final practice, edit a piece of your own writing for coordination and subordination. It can be a paper you are working on for this course, a paper you've already finished, a paper for another course, or a recent piece of writing from your work or everyday life. Record in your learning journal any choppy problem sentences you find, along with the edited versions. You may want to use the following Quick Review Chart.

LEARNING JOURNAL
How would you explain coordination and subordination to someone who had never heard of them?

Quick Review Chart

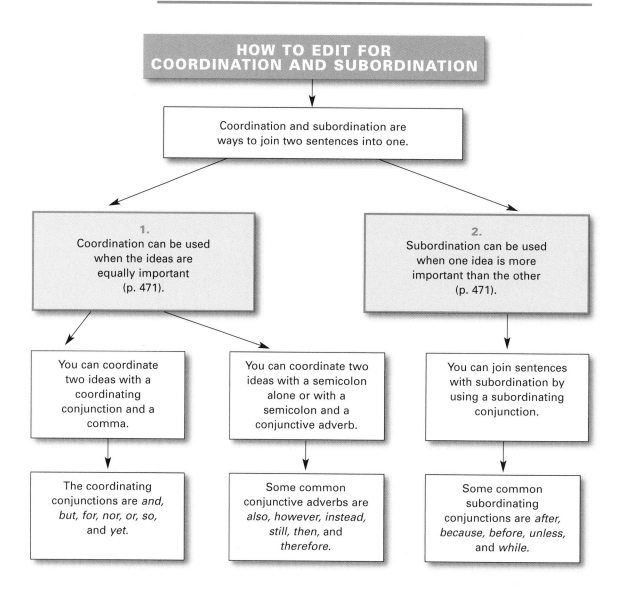

HOW TO EDIT FOR COORDINATION AND SUBORDINATION

Coordination and subordination are ways to join two sentences into one.

1.
Coordination can be used when the ideas are equally important (p. 471).

2.
Subordination can be used when one idea is more important than the other (p. 471).

You can coordinate two ideas with a coordinating conjunction and a comma.

You can coordinate two ideas with a semicolon alone or with a semicolon and a conjunctive adverb.

You can join sentences with subordination by using a subordinating conjunction.

The coordinating conjunctions are *and, but, for, nor, or, so,* and *yet.*

Some common conjunctive adverbs are *also, however, instead, still, then,* and *therefore.*

Some common subordinating conjunctions are *after, because, before, unless,* and *while.*

31

Parallelism

Balancing Ideas

Understand What Parallelism Is

DEFINITION: **Parallel** means having evenly matched parts. If you have ever watched a gymnastics meet, you might have seen parallel bars. The bars match in height, and the gymnasts' performances depend on the bars being correctly lined up and evenly balanced.

DEFINITION: **Parallelism** in writing means that similar parts in a sentence have the same structure: Their parts are comparable and balanced. Parallelism makes your writing flow smoothly and helps your readers understand your meaning. To create parallelism, use similar structures to express similar ideas. Put nouns with nouns, verbs with verbs, and phrases with phrases.

NOT PARALLEL   I like math more than studying English.

[*Math* is a noun, but *studying English* is a phrase.]

PARALLEL   I like math more than English.

NOT PARALLEL   On vacation, we swam, snorkled, and were eating at great restaurants.

[Verbs must be in the same tense to be parallel.]

PARALLEL   On vacation, we swam, snorkled, and ate at great restaurants.

LEARNING JOURNAL
Use your learning journal as a place to record sentences with problems in parallelism that you find in your writing. Also record edited versions of these sentences, with the problems corrected.

485

NOT PARALLEL   Last night we went <u>to a movie</u> and <u>dancing at a club</u> after.

[*To a movie* and *dancing at a club* are both phrases, but they have different forms. *To a movie* should be paired with another prepositional phrase: *to a dance club*.]

PARALLEL   Last night we went <u>to a movie</u> and <u>to a dance club</u>.

Practice Writing Parallel Sentences

PARALLELISM IN PAIRS AND LISTS

When you present two or more items in a series joined by the word *and* or *or*, use a similar form for each item.

NOT PARALLEL   The fund-raiser included <u>a bake sale</u> and <u>also holding an auction</u>.

PARALLEL   The fund-raiser included <u>a bake sale</u> and <u>an auction</u>.

NOT PARALLEL   Students got items for the auction <u>from local businesses</u>, <u>from their own families</u>, and <u>ran an advertisement in the newspaper</u>.

PARALLEL   Students got items for the auction <u>from local businesses</u>, <u>from their own families</u>, and <u>from their advertisement in the newspaper</u>.

> **PRACTICE 1**   **USING PARALLELISM IN PAIRS AND LISTS**

In each sentence, underline the parts of the sentence that should be parallel. Then edit the sentence to make it parallel.

EXAMPLE: Sometimes even a well-maintained car can <u>break down</u> or *run out of gas.*
~~you might forget to fill up the gas tank.~~

1. When your car breaks down on the road, you should follow simple rules to <u>remain safe</u> and <u>so that assistance will come quickly.</u>

2. When contacting a garage for help, you should give your location accurately by identifying <u>the street or highway</u>, <u>the nearest cross street or exit</u>, and <u>which landmarks or stores are nearby.</u>

3. All of the cars in a parking lot look similar, so a mechanic may have trouble finding your car unless you open the hood, put on emergency flashers, or ~~you could~~ tie a handkerchief to the antenna.

4. If you decide to read a book or ~~a nap sounds good~~ *take a* while you wait for the mechanic, *OR* you may not see the tow truck.

5. A mechanic who sees no obviously broken-down car and ~~he or she has~~ *has other* other calls to deal with may simply go on to the next customer.

6. You should leave a cell-phone number ~~or~~ a nearby business *Number* with the garage so the mechanic can call you back.

7. Most pay phones nowadays do not receive incoming calls, so the garage may not be able to call you back on a pay phone to let you know about problems or ~~if there are~~ delays.

8. The garage will not be able to reach you on your cell phone if you make a lot of calls or ~~it is time for a~~ *have* long talk with your best friend.

9. Sitting ~~in a car~~ or ~~if you~~ stand behind ~~it~~ *ing your car* can be very dangerous when a breakdown occurs on the side of the highway.

10. Relying on common sense, patience, and ~~remembering~~ basic safety guidelines will help you get through your car's breakdown.

PARALLELISM IN COMPARISONS

In comparisons, the items being compared should have parallel structures. Comparisons often use the word *than* or *as*. When you edit for parallelism, check to make sure that the items on either side of the comparison word are parallel.

NOT PARALLEL	Driving downtown is as fast as the bus.
PARALLEL	Driving downtown is as fast as taking the bus.
NOT PARALLEL	Reasonable dieting is better than fasts.

PARALLEL	Reasonable <u>dieting</u> is better than <u>fasting</u>.
OR	A reasonable <u>diet</u> is better than a <u>fast</u>.

In order to make the parts of a sentence parallel, you may need to add or drop a word or two.

NOT PARALLEL	<u>A multiple-choice test</u> is easier than <u>answering an essay question</u>.
PARALLEL, WORD ADDED	*Taking* a multiple-choice test is easier than <u>answering an essay question</u>.
NOT PARALLEL	<u>The cost</u> of a train ticket is less than <u>to pay the cost</u> of a plane ticket.
PARALLEL, WORDS DROPPED	<u>The cost</u> of a train ticket is less than <u>the cost</u> of a plane ticket.

PRACTICE 2 USING PARALLELISM IN COMPARISONS

In each sentence, underline the parts of the sentence that should be parallel. Then edit the sentence to make it parallel.

EXAMPLE: New <u>appliances</u> are usually much more energy-efficient than <u>~~running~~ old ones</u>.

1. For many people, <u>getting the household electric bill</u> is more worrisome
   than <u>~~to~~ pay the rent each month</u>.

2. <u>The amount of the rent bill</u> usually changes much less from month to
   month than <u>what an energy company charges</u>.

3. <u>Saving money</u> appeals to many consumers more than <u>to use less electricity</u>.

4. Compact fluorescent light bulbs use less energy than <u>continuing to use</u>
   regular incandescent bulbs.

5. In most households, <u>~~running~~ the refrigerator</u> uses more energy than
   <u>the use of all other appliances</u>.

6. Many people worry that buying a new refrigerator is more expensive

   than ~~if they simply~~ keep the old one.

7. However, ~~an~~ energy-efficient new refrigerator uses much less electricity

   than running an inefficient older model.

8. Some new refrigerators use only as much energy as ~~keeping~~ a 75-watt

   light bulb burning.

9. Householders might spend less money to buy an efficient new refrigerator

   than it would take to run the old one for another five years.

10. Researching information about energy efficiency can save consumers as

    much money as ~~when they~~ remember to turn off lights and air conditioners.

PARALLELISM WITH CERTAIN PAIRED WORDS

DEFINITION: When a sentence uses certain paired words, called **correlative conjunctions**, the items joined by them must be parallel. These words link two equal elements and show the relationship between them. Here are the paired words:

both . . . and	neither . . . nor	rather . . . than
either . . . or	not only . . . but also	

NOT PARALLEL	Brianna dislikes *both* fruit *and* eating vegetables.
PARALLEL	Brianna dislikes *both* fruit *and* vegetables.
NOT PARALLEL	She would *rather* eat popcorn every night *than* to cook.
PARALLEL	She would *rather* eat popcorn every night *than* cook.

PRACTICE 3   USING PARALLELISM WITH CERTAIN PAIRED WORDS

In each sentence, circle the paired words and underline the parts of the sentence that should be parallel. Then edit the sentence to make it parallel. You may need to change the second part of the correlative conjunction.

EXAMPLE: A recent survey of young women reported that a majority of them would rather lose twenty pounds permanently than to live to be ninety.

1. People in the United States are both pressed for time and have gotten used to convenient but fattening foods.

2. Many Americans are neither willing to exercise regularly nor do they have to do anything physical during a normal day.

3. Being overweight can be unhealthy, but many Americans would rather look thinner than to stay the same size and get in better shape.

4. In fact, some Americans are not only out of shape but are dangerously obsessed with being thin.

5. The idea that thinner is better affects both overweight people and it even influences people of normal weight.

6. In their quest to lose weight, many Americans have tried either fad diets or have taken prescription drugs.

7. Dozens of healthy, average-sized Americans in the past ten years have died from either surgical procedures to remove fat or they have died from dangerous diet drugs.

8. A thin person is neither guaranteed to be attractive nor is he or she necessarily healthy.

9. Some people who are larger than average are not only in good health but also can be physically fit.

10. Americans who would rather pay for risky drugs and surgery and prefer not to eat moderately and exercise may have hazardous priorities.

■ PRACTICE 4   **COMPLETING SENTENCES WITH PAIRED WORDS**

The following practice items contain only the first part of a correlative conjunction. Complete the correlative conjunction and add more information to form a whole sentence. Make sure that the structures on both sides of the correlative conjunction are parallel.

> **EXAMPLE:** I am both enthusiastic about your company *and eager to* *work for you* .

1. I could bring to this job not only youthful enthusiasm _____

   _____

2. I am willing to work either in your Chicago office _____

   _____

3. My current job neither encourages creativity _____

4. I would rather work in a difficult job _____

5. In college I learned a lot both from my classes _____

Edit Paragraphs and Your Own Writing

■ PRACTICE 5   **EDITING PARAGRAPHS FOR PARALLELISM**

Find and correct any problems with parallelism in the following paragraphs. You may want to refer to the Quick Review Chart on page 494.

1.   (1) Some employees who want to advance their careers would rather transfer within their company than looking for a new job elsewhere. (2) In-house job changes are possible, but employees should be sure that they both meet the criteria of the job and to avoid making their present boss angry. (3) Because businesses invest money in each person they hire,

many companies would rather hire from within and not bring an outsider into a position. (4) By hiring an employee from another department, a company neither needs to make an investment in a new employee but may also prevent the current employee from leaving. (5) Transfers usually go more smoothly now than in the past; however, an in-house job move can still require diplomacy and being honest. (6) Experts caution employees who are considering an in-house transfer to tell their current manager the truth and that they should discuss their wish to transfer with the potential new manager. (7) Employees should neither threaten to quit if they do not get the new job nor is it a good idea to spread the word around the department that they are anxious to leave their present job. (8) Employees' goals for in-house transfers should be career advancement and making sure that they create no bad feelings with the move.

2.   (1) Black motorists frequently arouse police suspicion either when driving in neighborhoods that are mainly white or when they are driving an expensive car. (2) A higher percentage of African Americans than among people who are white are pulled over by the police. (3) Many African Americans feel insulted, endangered, and react with anger when they are accused of "driving while black." (4) African Americans are liable to be singled out by police who suspect they are criminals not only while in a car but African Americans also report being wrongly stopped on foot. (5) Racial profiling is illegal yet a fairly common phenomenon. (6) According to a 2001 poll, among black women the figure is 25 percent, and 52 percent of black men have been singled out by police. (7) Victims of racial profiling have done nothing wrong, yet they are made to feel that others are either afraid or do not trust them. (8) Law-abiding African Americans should neither expect such treatment nor should they

put up with it from public officials who are supposed to protect citizens.
(9) Police departments around the country must make their employees
aware that automatically stopping, asking them questions, and searching
African Americans will not be tolerated. (10) Treating all citizens fairly is
a more important American value than that there is a high arrest rate for
the police.

PRACTICE 6   EDITING YOUR OWN WRITING FOR PARALLELISM

As a final practice, edit a piece of your own writing for parallelism. It can
be a paper you are working on for this course, a paper you've already finished, a paper for another course, or a recent piece of writing from your
work or everyday life. Record in your learning journal any problem sentences you find, along with their corrections. You may want to use the following Quick Review Chart.

LEARNING JOURNAL
How would you
explain parallelism to
someone who had
never heard of it? How
would you explain how
to edit for it?

Quick Review Chart

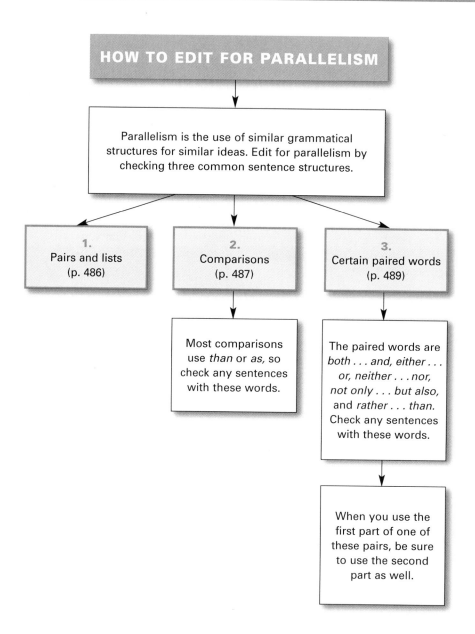

HOW TO EDIT FOR PARALLELISM

Parallelism is the use of similar grammatical structures for similar ideas. Edit for parallelism by checking three common sentence structures.

1.
Pairs and lists
(p. 486)

2.
Comparisons
(p. 487)

3.
Certain paired words
(p. 489)

Most comparisons use *than* or *as,* so check any sentences with these words.

The paired words are *both . . . and, either . . . or, neither . . . nor, not only . . . but also,* and *rather . . . than.* Check any sentences with these words.

When you use the first part of one of these pairs, be sure to use the second part as well.

32

Sentence Variety

Putting Rhythm in Your Writing

Understand What Sentence Variety Is

DEFINITION: Having **sentence variety** in your writing means using assorted sentence patterns, lengths, and rhythms. Most of us like variety: We don't want to eat the same dinner every night, own ten shirts of the same style and color, or listen to the same song ten times in a row.

If your sentences all have the same pattern and are the same length, your readers will quickly tire of them and may not keep reading long enough to understand your point. Many writers use too many short, simple sentences, mistakenly thinking that short is always easier to understand than long. In fact, that is not true, as the following examples show.

LEARNING JOURNAL
Use your learning journal as a place to record an example of a brief passage with short, similar-sounding sentences. Also record an edited version after you have introduced sentence variety.

WITH SHORT, SIMPLE SENTENCES

Age discrimination can exist even in unpaid jobs. The newspaper today reported that a magazine has been accused of age discrimination. The magazine is *The Atlantic Monthly*. A woman was told she was too old to be an unpaid intern. The woman was forty-one. The position was for a senior in college. The woman was a senior. She had raised three children before going to college. She is suing the magazine. The next day another woman, age fifty-one, reported that the same thing had happened to her a year earlier. She had filed a discrimination suit. The suit was brought to court by the Council on Age Discrimination. The magazine never showed up. The court never took any follow-up action against the magazine. Apparently the matter was not of great importance to either the magazine or the justice system.

WITH SENTENCE VARIETY

Age discrimination can exist even in unpaid jobs. The newspaper today reported that a magazine, *The Atlantic Monthly,* has been accused of age discrimination by a forty-one-year-old woman. This woman, who raised three children before going to college and is now in her senior year, was told she was too old to be an unpaid intern, even though the position was for a college senior. She is suing the magazine. The next day another woman, age fifty-one, reported that the same thing had happened to her a year earlier and she, too, had filed an age discrimination suit. The suit was brought to court by the Council on Age Discrimination, but the magazine didn't appear for the court date, and the court never took any follow-up action. Apparently the matter was not of great importance to either the magazine or the justice system.

Good writing results when you mix long and short sentences and use a variety of sentence patterns. Sentence variety is what gives your writing good rhythm and flow.

Practice Creating Sentence Variety

For two additional techniques used to achieve sentence variety—coordination and subordination—see Chapter 30.

To create sentence variety, you need to edit your writing so that it has sentences of different types and lengths. Because many writers tend to write short sentences that start with the subject, this chapter will focus on techniques for starting with something other than the subject and for writing a variety of longer sentences.

Remember that the goal is to use variety to achieve a good rhythm. Do not simply change all your sentences from one pattern to another, or you still won't have variety: You'll have just another set of similar-sounding sentences. When you are changing the patterns of your sentences, make sure that your revised sentences are correct.

START SOME SENTENCES WITH ADVERBS

DEFINITION: **Adverbs** are words that modify or describe verbs, adjectives, or other adverbs; they often end with *-ly.* As long as the meaning is clear, an adverb can be placed at the beginning of a sentence instead of in the middle. An adverb at the beginning is usually followed by a comma. If an adverb indicates time, such as *often* or *always*, a comma may not be needed. How-ever, always use a comma if the reader should pause slightly after reading the adverb.

For more about ad-verbs, see Chapter 28.

ADVERB IN MIDDLE	Stories about haunted houses *frequently* surface at Halloween.
STARTS WITH ADVERB	*Frequently,* stories about haunted houses surface at Halloween.
ADVERB IN MIDDLE	These tales *often* reveal the life stories of former inhabitants.
STARTS WITH ADVERB	*Often* these tales reveal the life stories of former inhabitants.

■ **PRACTICE 1** **STARTING SENTENCES WITH AN ADVERB**

Edit each sentence so that it begins with an adverb.

EXAMPLE: *Frequently, hurricanes*
Hurricanes ~~frequently~~ strike barrier islands.

1. Harsh weather takes a toll annually on sandy beaches.

2. That island house once stood on solid ground.

3. The ocean eventually washed the ground out from under it.

4. The house was finally condemned as unsafe.

5. It is now going to be demolished.

■ **PRACTICE 2** **STARTING SENTENCES WITH AN ADVERB**

In each sentence, fill in the blank with an adverb that makes sense. Add a comma when necessary. There may be several good choices for each item. In the example sentence, *luckily, thankfully,* or any of several other adverbs also would have been a good choice.

EXAMPLE: _*Fortunately,*_ no one was living in the house at the time.

1. _____ a row of houses stood on the east side of the channel.

2. _____ a hurricane washed away most of the land nearby.

3. _____ most of the houses vanished.

4. _____ the house stood alone on a sandy peninsula.

5 _____ maps of the island were redrawn.

■ **PRACTICE 3**   **WRITING SENTENCES THAT START WITH AN ADVERB**

Write three more sentences that start with an adverb. Use commas as necessary. Choose from the following adverbs: *often, sadly, amazingly, luckily, lovingly, gently, frequently, stupidly, quietly.*

EXAMPLE: *Luckily, I remembered to save my file on a disk.*

1. _____

2. _____

3. _____

JOIN IDEAS USING AN *-ING* VERB FORM

One way to combine sentences is to turn one of them into a phrase using an *-ing* **verb form** (such as *walking* or *racing*). The *-ing* verb form indicates that the two parts of the sentence are happening at the same time. The more important idea (the one you want to emphasize) should be in the main clause, not in the phrase you make by adding the *-ing* verb form.

TWO SENTENCES   Jonah did well in the high jump. He came in second.

JOINED WITH *-ING*   Jonah did well in the high jump, *coming* in second.
VERB FORM

To combine sentences this way, add *-ing* to the verb in one of the sentences and delete the subject. You now have a modifier phrase that can be added to the beginning or the end of the other sentence, depending on what makes sense.

                                        , breaking
He also won the long jump./ ~~He broke~~ the record.

If you add the phrase to the end of a sentence, you will usually need to put a comma before it, as in the preceding example, unless the phrase is essential to the meaning of the sentence. If you add a phrase starting with an *-ing* verb form to the beginning of a sentence, put a comma after it. Be sure that the word being modified follows immediately after the phrase. Otherwise, you will create a dangling modifier.

> For more on finding and correcting dangling modifiers, see Chapter 29.

TWO SENTENCES	I dropped my bag. My groceries spilled.
DANGLING MODIFIER	Dropping my bag, my groceries spilled.
EDITED	Dropping my bag, I spilled my groceries.

PRACTICE 4   JOINING IDEAS USING AN *-ING* VERB FORM

Combine each pair of sentences into a single sentence by using an *-ing* verb form. Add or delete words if necessary.

Wanting the guests at his fourth birthday party to stay away from his toys, he

EXAMPLE: He hit the other children. ~~He wanted the guests at his fourth~~
                    ^

~~birthday party to stay away from his toys.~~

1. Children pay attention to role models. Some children learn aggression from people at home, at school, or on television.

2. I react to some frustrating situations with fury. I forget that my son Sean watches and learns from me.

3. His favorite television characters do not model good behavior, either. They act violently under stress.

4. I wanted expert advice on anger management. I feared that Sean would not learn to control his temper.

5. I punished my son for his angry outbursts. I used to take away his toys and privileges.

6. An expert told me that angry children need positive lessons in how to cope. She said that punishing Sean for losing his temper was ineffective.

7. I taught my son concrete ways to react to his anger. I gave him something to focus on before lashing out.

8. I did not try to reason with my son when he was furious. I saved the lessons for his calm moods.

9. Sean counts to ten when he gets angry. He now gives himself time to cool off.

10. Preschoolers can learn ways to handle their anger. They can modify their reactions before they understand why they should.

PRACTICE 5   JOINING IDEAS USING AN *-ING* VERB FORM

Fill in the blank in each sentence with an appropriate *-ing* verb form. There are many possible ways to complete each sentence.

EXAMPLE: ____*Lounging*____ in his cubicle, Franklin tossed pencils aimlessly at the ceiling.

1. _____ at the computer screen, Franklin tried to concentrate.

2. In the next cubicle sat Martina, _____ Franklin with a loud telephone conversation.

3. _____ on the wall between them, he tried to get her attention.

4. A stapler flew over the wall into Franklin's cubicle, _____ on his head.

5. _____ the stapler, Franklin thanked Martina for waking him up.

PRACTICE 6   JOINING IDEAS USING AN *-ING* VERB FORM

Write two sets of sentences, and join each set using an *-ing* verb form.

EXAMPLE: a. *Teresa signed onto eBay.com.* _____

b. *She used her password.* _____

COMBINED: *Using her password, Teresa signed onto eBay.com.*

Teresa signed onto eBay.com using her password.

1. a. _____

    b. _____

    COMBINED: _____

    _____

2. a. _____

    b. _____

    COMBINED: _____

    _____

JOIN IDEAS USING AN *-ED* VERB FORM

For more on helping verbs, see Chapters 25 and 26.

DEFINITION: Another way to combine sentences is to turn one of them into a phrase using an **-ed verb form** (such as *waited* or *walked*). You can join sentences this way if one of them has a form of *be* as a helping verb along with the *-ed* verb form.

TWO SENTENCES   Leonardo da Vinci was a man of many talents. He was noted most often for his painting.

JOINED WITH *-ED* VERB FORM   Noted most often for his painting, Leonardo da Vinci was a man of many talents.

To combine sentences this way, drop the subject and the helping verb from a sentence that has an *-ed* verb form. You now have a modifier phrase that can be added to the beginning or the end of the other sentence, depending on what makes the most sense.

Interested   *, Leonardo*
~~Leonardo was interested~~ in many areas./ He investigated problems of geology, botany, mechanics, and hydraulics.

If you add a phrase that begins with an *-ed* verb form to the beginning of a sentence, put a comma after it. Be sure the word that the phrase

For more on finding and correcting dangling modifiers, see Chapter 29.

modifies follows immediately. Otherwise, you will create a dangling modifier. Sometimes, as in the preceding example, you will need to change the word that the phrase modifies from a pronoun to a noun. If you add the phrase to the end of the sentence, you will need to put a comma before it unless the meaning of the sentence would change without the phrase.

PRACTICE 7   JOINING IDEAS USING AN *-ED* VERB FORM

Combine each pair of sentences into a single sentence by using an *-ed* verb form.

EXAMPLE: ~~Alligators are~~ *Hatched* ~~hatched~~ from eggs when they are only a few

inches long. ~~Alligators~~ *, alligators* can reach a length of ten feet or

more as adults.

1. An alligator was spotted in a pond in Central Park in New York in June of 2001. Many New Yorkers refused to believe in the existence of the alligator.

2. Alligators were released by their owners for growing too large to be pets. These alligators were sometimes said to be living in New York City sewers.

3. Rumors were believed by some gullible people. The rumors about giant sewer alligators were untrue.

4. The story of the alligator in Central Park was denied by city officials. The story sounded like another wild rumor.

5. Central Park alligator sightings were reported by several New Yorkers. The sightings were confirmed when a television news crew filmed a reptile in the pond.

6. A professional alligator wrestler was hired to catch the reptile. He came to New York from Florida.

7. The pond in Central Park was surrounded by news cameras and curious onlookers. It was brightly lit just before 11:00 P.M. on June 22.

8. The creature was captured in just a few minutes by the alligator wrestler's wife. The so-called alligator turned out to be a spectacled caiman, a species native to Central and South America.

9. Some New Yorkers were surprised to find that the caiman was only two feet long. They may have felt a bit foolish for expecting to see a giant alligator in the park.

10. The caiman was removed from Central Park. It soon found a home in a warmer climate.

PRACTICE 8   JOINING IDEAS USING AN *-ED* VERB FORM

Fill in the blank in each sentence with an appropriate *-ed* verb form. There are several possible ways to complete each sentence.

     EXAMPLE: ___*Decorated*___ in unusual colors and textures, fingernails are sometimes as stylish as clothing.

1. _____ to perform manicures, nail stylists are setting up shop all over the United States.

2. Style-conscious women today are seldom satisfied with old-fashioned fingernails _____ with a simple solid color.

3. _____ as an art form, manicures have become a new fashion trend.

4. Some expensive manicures turn fingernails into exotic little sculptures _____ to last only a few days.

5. _____ to create fingernail designs to match the latest fashions,

a manicurist with an artistic touch can make a good living today.

■ **PRACTICE 9   JOINING IDEAS USING AN *-ED* VERB FORM**

Write two sets of sentences and join them using an *-ed* verb form.

EXAMPLE: a. *Lee is training for the Boston Marathon.*_____

b. *It is believed to have the most difficult hill to run.*_____

COMBINED: *Lee is training for the Boston Marathon, believed to have the most*

*difficult hill to run.*_____

1. a. _____

b. _____

COMBINED: _____

_____

2. a. _____

b. _____

COMBINED: _____

_____

JOIN IDEAS USING AN APPOSITIVE

DEFINITION: An **appositive** is a phrase that renames a noun. Appositives can be used to combine two sentences into one.

TWO SENTENCES   Elvis Presley continues to be popular many years after his death. He is "the King."

JOINED WITH AN APPOSITIVE   Elvis Presley, "the King," continues to be popular many years after his death.

[The phrase *"the King"* renames the noun *Elvis Presley.*]

To combine two sentences this way, turn the sentence that renames the noun into a phrase by dropping its subject and verb. The appositive phrase can appear anywhere in the sentence, but it should be placed before or after the noun it renames. Use a comma or commas to set off the appositive.

Elvis's home is visited by millions of people each year. ~~It is~~

, Graceland,

~~called Graceland.~~

![PRACTICE 10] **PRACTICE 10   JOINING IDEAS USING AN APPOSITIVE**

Combine each pair of sentences into a single sentence by using an appositive. Be sure to use a comma or commas to set off the appositive.

EXAMPLE: A decade ago, a majority of college students wanted one

thing from their ~~education. They wanted~~ a high-paying job.

education,

1. In the late 1980s, political activists were a rare breed. They were almost unknown on many college campuses.

2. Political demonstrations had once been a common sight. They seemed as outdated as the hippie lifestyle by 1990.

3. Protests made the news again in 1999. That was the year activists targeted the Seattle meeting of the World Trade Organization.

4. The destruction of property did not win many supporters to the Seattle protesters' cause. It was an unpopular tactic.

5. But the Seattle protests publicized the idea of social activism. It was a concept that was out of fashion at the time.

6. Young Americans today are not united by a single political cause. They are a diverse group with diverse interests.

7. Most social activists share a common goal. That goal is to have a positive effect on others' lives.

8. Many young people interested in making a difference nationally or globally turn to their college campuses. These are the traditional training grounds for social activism.

9. College courses can provide young activists with a knowledge of history. This is an essential subject for anyone who hopes to improve society.

10. Some college students are motivated and idealistic. They dream of a fairer and more tolerant world.

PRACTICE 11   JOINING IDEAS USING AN APPOSITIVE

Fill in the blank in each sentence with an appropriate appositive. There are many possible ways to complete each sentence.

> **EXAMPLE**: My sister Clara, _____*a busy mother of three*_____, loves to watch soap operas.

1. Clara's favorite show, _____, comes on at three o'clock in the afternoon.

2. Clara, _____, rarely has the time to sit down in front of the television for the broadcast.

3. Instead, she programs her VCR, _____, and tapes the show for later.

4. Clara's husband, _____, used to tease her for watching the soaps.

5. But while he was recovering from the flu recently, he found her stack of tapes, _____, and Clara insists that he watched every show of the previous season.

Use *who* to refer to a person, *which* to refer to places or things (but not to people), and *that* for people, places, or things. When referring to a person, *who* is preferable to *that*.

JOIN IDEAS USING AN ADJECTIVE CLAUSE

DEFINITION: An **adjective clause** is a group of words with a subject and a verb that modifies or describes a noun. Adjective clauses often begin with the word *who*, *which*, or *that* and can be used to combine two sentences into one.

TWO SENTENCES   Lorene owns an art and framing store. She is a good friend of mine.

JOINED WITH AN   Lorene, who is a good friend, owns an art and framing
ADJECTIVE CLAUSE   store.

> An adjective clause is sometimes called a relative clause. The word it begins with is called a relative adjective because it *relates* the word group to a specific word in the sentence.

To join sentences this way, use *who, which,* or *that* to replace the subject of a sentence that describes a noun in another sentence. Once you have made this change, you have an adjective clause that you can move so that it follows the noun it describes. The sentence with the more important idea (the one you want to emphasize) should become the main clause. The less important idea should be in the adjective clause.

TWO SENTENCES   Rosalind is director of human services for the town of Marlborough. Marlborough is her hometown.

[The more important idea here is that Rosalind is director of human services. The less important idea is that the town is her hometown.]

JOINED WITH AN   Rosalind is director of human services for the town of
ADJECTIVE CLAUSE   Marlborough, her hometown.

NOTE: Punctuating adjective clauses can be tricky. If an adjective clause can be taken out of a sentence without completely changing the meaning of the sentence, put commas around the clause.

Lorene, who is a good friend, owns an art and framing store.

[The phrase *who is a good friend* adds information about Lorene, but it is not essential; the sentence *Lorene owns an art and framing store* means almost the same thing as the sentence in the example.]

If an adjective clause is an essential part of the meaning of a sentence, do not put commas around it.

Lorene is a good friend who saved my life.

[*Who saved my life* is an essential part of this sentence. The sentence *Lorene is a good friend* is very different in meaning from the whole sentence in the example.]

PRACTICE 12   **JOINING IDEAS USING AN ADJECTIVE CLAUSE**

Combine each pair of sentences into a single sentence by using an adjective clause beginning with *who, which,* or *that.*

Allergies that

EXAMPLE: ~~Some allergies~~ ⌃cause sneezing, itching, and watery eyes. ~~They~~
can make people very uncomfortable.

1. Cats produce a protein. It keeps their skin soft.

2. This protein makes some people itch and sneeze. The protein is the
   reason for most allergic reactions to cats.

3. Some cat lovers are allergic to cats. They can control their allergies with
   medication.

4. Allergic cat lovers may get another option from a new company. The company
   wants to create a genetically engineered cat.

5. Scientists have successfully cloned mice. Some mice have been
   genetically engineered for scientific study.

6. Researchers may soon have the technology to clone cats. Cats could be
   genetically engineered to remove the allergen.

7. Many people have allergic reactions to cats. According to cat experts,
   more than 10 percent of those people are allergic to something other
   than the skin-softening protein.

8. A single gene produces a cat's skin-softening protein. Scientists are not
   sure whether the gene is necessary for the cat's good health.

9. However, owning a genetically engineered cat would allow an allergic
   person to avoid taking allergy medications. The medications can
   sometimes cause dangerous side effects.

10. Cloning and genetic engineering raise ethical questions. These are
    difficult to answer.

PRACTICE 13   JOINING IDEAS USING AN ADJECTIVE CLAUSE

Fill in the blank in each of the following sentences with an appropriate adjective clause. Add commas, if necessary. There are many possible ways to complete each sentence.

EXAMPLE: Interactive television _____, *which may soon be available to* _____ *consumers,* _____ is a potential threat to viewers' privacy.

1. Many Web sites _____

   try to make a profit by selling information about visitors to the site.

2. Consumers _____ must provide information to

   retail Web sites before being allowed to complete a purchase.

3. Consumer privacy _____ may suffer

   further when interactive television stations begin to operate.

4. A viewer _____ may

   not realize that the television station is collecting information about him

   or her.

5. The sale of personal information _____

   _____ can bring huge profits.

Edit Paragraphs and Your Own Writing

 PRACTICE 14   EDITING PARAGRAPHS FOR SENTENCE VARIETY

Create sentence variety in the following paragraphs. Join at least two sentences in each of the paragraphs. Try to use several of the techniques discussed in this chapter. There are many possible ways to edit each paragraph. You may want to refer to the Quick Review Chart on page 512.

(1) Lotteries were illegal until recently in most U.S. states. (2) They have now been legalized in most parts of this country. (3) The lotteries are run by state governments in many places. (4) Lotteries allow the

governments to raise money without raising taxes. (5) The money can help fund education and other projects. (6) These projects are necessary and expensive. (7) Many citizens consider lotteries an ideal way to raise funds. (8) These people reason that no one is forced to buy a lottery ticket. (9) However, lotteries have a dark side that should be discussed more often.

(10) Many experts on gambling worry about the increasing numbers of state lotteries. (11) Lotteries are difficult for many people to resist. (12) The games offer prizes of millions of dollars. (13) They make people fantasize about easy wealth. (14) Lottery tickets cost very little. (15) They are sold in grocery stores and shops in every neighborhood. (16) Unfortunately, the people least able to afford lottery tickets spend the most money on them. (17) They are convinced that they will strike it rich someday. (18) In many impoverished areas, large numbers of people regularly buy several lottery tickets each week. (19) They hope to escape boring, low-paying jobs.

(20) Nor are the poor the only victims of lottery fever. (21) Many people are addicted to gambling. (22) They do not consider the nearly impossible odds of winning a lottery jackpot. (23) They are hooked by occasional small payoffs of two or three dollars. (24) Addicted gamblers will keep buying tickets until they have no money left.

(25) Lotteries promise a big payoff for a little investment. (26) They bring vast amounts of money into state treasuries. (27) Many people believe that lotteries save everyone money. (28) But lottery supporters seldom think about the victims of lotteries. (29) When taxes fund state programs, wealthier people must contribute more than poorer people. (30) But

gambling addicts and people desperate to escape poverty pay more heavily than anyone else into state lottery funds. (31) Governments should not rely on the poor and addicted to come up with money to run essential state programs.

![] PRACTICE 15   **EDITING YOUR OWN WRITING FOR SENTENCE VARIETY**

As a final practice, edit a piece of your own writing for sentence variety. It can be a paper you are working on for this course, a paper you've already finished, a paper for another course, or a recent piece of writing from your work or everyday life. Record in your learning journal any examples of short, choppy sentences you find, along with the edited versions. You may want to use the following Quick Review Chart.

LEARNING JOURNAL
Do you tend to write short, similar-sounding sentences? Which sentence patterns covered in this chapter do you think you will use most often when you are editing for sentence variety?

Quick Review Chart

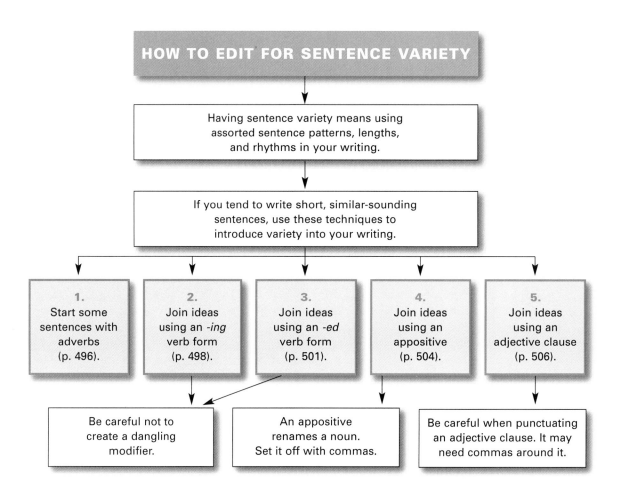

HOW TO EDIT FOR SENTENCE VARIETY

Having sentence variety means using assorted sentence patterns, lengths, and rhythms in your writing.

If you tend to write short, similar-sounding sentences, use these techniques to introduce variety into your writing.

1. Start some sentences with adverbs (p. 496).

2. Join ideas using an *-ing* verb form (p. 498).

3. Join ideas using an *-ed* verb form (p. 501).

4. Join ideas using an appositive (p. 504).

5. Join ideas using an adjective clause (p. 506).

Be careful not to create a dangling modifier.

An appositive renames a noun. Set it off with commas.

Be careful when punctuating an adjective clause. It may need commas around it.

33

ESL Concerns

Areas of Special Interest
to Nonnative Speakers and
Speakers of Nonstandard English

If English is not your first language or if you grew up speaking a different version of English than what is expected in college papers, you may need some help with certain aspects of English that may be very different from your own first or your current spoken language. This chapter will focus on those areas.

Nouns and Articles

SUBJECTS

DEFINITION: The **subject** of a sentence is the person, place, or thing the sentence is about. It is either a noun, a pronoun (a word that substitutes for a noun), or a word or phrase that functions like a noun. Be sure to include a subject in every sentence and every dependent clause.

> *It is*
> I̶s̶ hot outside.

> *she does*
> My teacher makes us write a lot, although not grade us.

This chapter focuses on problems that many nonnative speakers of English have when they write papers for college, but native speakers may find it useful as well.

513

COUNT AND NONCOUNT NOUNS

DEFINITION: A **noun** is a word that names a person, place, or thing. English nouns fall into two categories: those naming things that can be counted, and those naming things that cannot be counted.

Singular means one; plural means more than one.

COUNT NOUN	I sold ten of my old *CD*s at the yard sale.
NONCOUNT NOUN	I sold lots of *music* at the yard sale.

DEFINITION: A **count noun** names a distinct individual item that can be counted. The noun *CD* is a count noun.

DEFINITION: A **noncount noun** names a general category or group that cannot be divided easily into distinct, countable items. The noun *music* is a noncount noun. In English, it would not make sense to say *I bought ten new musics.* Here are some more examples.

LEARNING JOURNAL
Use your learning journal as a place to record sentences with the types of problems covered in this chapter or other problems that you think may be related to the fact that you speak English as a second language or that your spoken English differs from the English expected in college writing. Also record edited versions of these sentences, with the problems corrected.

COUNT	NONCOUNT
apple/apples	fruit
tree/trees	grass
dollar/dollars	money
beach/beaches	sand
fact/facts	information

Count nouns can be made plural. Noncount nouns usually cannot be plural; they are usually singular.

COUNT/SINGLE	I got a *ticket* for the concert.
COUNT/PLURAL	I got two *tickets* for the concert.
NONCOUNT	The Internet has all kinds of *information.*

NOTE: Some noncount nouns, such as *fruit, money,* and *sand,* are occasionally treated as count nouns *(the sands of time)*.

ARTICLES

DEFINITION: The words *a, an,* and *the* are called **articles**; they are used with nouns. You can choose *a, an, the,* or no article at all. Use *a* before words that start with a consonant sound; use *an* before words that start with a vowel sound: *a* dog, *an* elevator. The box that follows shows how to use articles and when to use no article at all.

Never use *a* or *an* with noncount nouns.

Articles with Count and Noncount Nouns

COUNT NOUNS	ARTICLE
SINGULAR	
Identity known	*the*
	I want to read *the book* on taxes that you recommended.
	[The sentence refers to one particular book: the one that was recommended.]
	I can't stay in *the sun* very long.
	[There is only one sun.]
Identity not known	*a* or *an*
	I want to read *a book* on taxes.
	[It could be any book on taxes.]
PLURAL	
Identity known	*the*
	I enjoyed *the books* we read.
	[The sentence refers to a particular group of books: the ones we read.]
Identity not known or a general category	**(no article at all or another kind of word such as *this, these, that, some*)**
	I usually enjoy *books*.
	[The sentence refers to books in general.]
	She found *some books*.
	[I don't know which books she found.]

NONCOUNT NOUNS	ARTICLE
SINGULAR	
Identity known	*the*
	I put away *the food* we bought.
	[The sentence refers to particular food: the food we bought.]
Identity not known or a general category	**(no article at all or another kind of word such as *this, these, that, some*)**
	There is *food* all over the kitchen.
	[The reader doesn't know what food the sentence refers to.]
	Give *some food* to the neighbors.
	[The sentence refers to food in general.]

PRACTICE 1   EDITING NOUNS AND ARTICLES

Edit the following paragraph, adding and changing articles and nouns as necessary. Also, add a subject to any sentence that is missing one.

EXAMPLE: Restaurant work is not an easy way to earn ~~the~~ money.

(1) I am waitress at the restaurant four days a week. (2) My shift is at lunchtimes, and is usually very busy then. (3) Is an university close by, so the many college students eat at my restaurant because it serves cheap foods. (4) I am college student too; however, some of my student customers do not treat me as a equal. (5) They seem to think that is okay to be rude to person serving them. (6) Many of them do not tip me well even though I am very good waitress and take good cares of my customers. (7) I do not make high salaries, so I need the tips from my customers to make good living. (8) I understand that college students are often pinching penny. (9) However, I think that peoples who cannot afford to leave tip should not eat in a restaurant.

Verbs

DEFINITION: **Verbs** tell what action the subject in a sentence performs or link the subject to a word that describes it.

USING THE *-ING* FORM OR THE *TO* FORM AFTER CERTAIN VERBS

To improve your ability to write and speak standard English, read magazines and your local newspaper, and listen to television and radio news programs. Also read magazines and newspaper articles aloud; it will help your pronunciation.

DEFINITIONS: A **gerund** (or *-ing* form of the verb) is a verb form that ends in *-ing* and acts as a noun. An **infinitive** is a verb form that is preceded by the word *to* but has no ending added. These verb forms (gerunds and infinitives) cannot be the main verbs in sentences; each sentence must have another word that is the main verb.

In the sentences that follow, the gerund and the infinitive are objects—they receive the action of the verbs.

GERUND   I enjoy *skating*.

INFINITIVE   I like *to skate*.

How do you decide whether to use a gerund or an infinitive as the object of a verb? The decision often depends on the main verb in a sentence. Some verbs can be followed by either a gerund or an infinitive, some can be followed only by a gerund, and some can be followed only by an infinitive. Knowing which to use can be tricky because the correct form is based on common practice, not logic. Practice using the correct structures for the verbs you use most often.

For advice on verbs with prepositions, see page 520. For more on the position of verbs in questions, see page 523. For other problems with verbs, see Chapter 26.

In the examples in this section, the <u>verbs</u> in the sentences are double-underlined.

Verbs That Are Followed by Either an Infinitive or a Gerund

begin	hate	remember	try
continue	like	start	
forget	love	stop	

These verbs can be followed by either an infinitive or a gerund. Sometimes the meaning is about the same.

He loves to drive. = He loves driving.

Sometimes the meaning changes depending on whether you use an infinitive or a gerund.

Mario stopped to smoke.

[This sentence means that Mario stopped what he was doing and smoked a cigarette.]

Mario stopped smoking.

[This sentence means that Mario no longer smokes cigarettes.]

Verbs That Are Followed by an Infinitive

agree	decide	need	refuse
ask	expect	offer	want
beg	fail	plan	
choose	hope	pretend	
claim	manage	promise	

Aunt Sally <u>wants</u> to help.

Cal <u>hopes</u> to become a millionaire.

Verbs That Are Followed by a Gerund

admit	discuss	keep	risk
avoid	enjoy	miss	suggest
consider	finish	practice	
deny	imagine	quit	

The representative <u>risks</u> losing the election.

Sophia <u>considered</u> quitting her job.

PROGRESSIVE TENSE

DEFINITION: The **progressive tense** consists of a form of the verb *be* plus the *-ing* form of a verb. It is used to indicate a continuing activity. Use the present progressive tense to indicate that an action is in progress now.

Lottie <u>is learning</u> to paint.

Our instructor <u>is posting</u> grades today.

Not all verbs can form the progressive tense. Certain verbs that indicate sensing or a state of being are not generally used this way.

Verbs That Cannot Form the Progressive Tense

appear	have	mean	taste
believe	hear	need	understand
belong	know	see	want
cost	like	seem	weigh

appears
The dog is ~~appearing~~ angry.

costs
That bag is ~~costing~~ too much.

PRACTICE 2   EDITING VERBS

Edit the following paragraph to make sure that the verbs are used correctly.

(1) Marlene and Agnetha wanted seeing a certain movie after they saw the advertisement for it in the newspaper. (2) David Manning, the reviewer who was quoted in the ad, was liking the film a lot. (3) The two women did not want to miss to see the film at their neighborhood theater, so they arranged their schedules carefully. (4) They managed attending the first show on Saturday afternoon. (5) After they were seeing the movie, they were very angry that they had wasted their time and money. (6) They were not understanding how the reviewer could have enjoyed to watch such a stupid film. (7) Then Marlene read in a different newspaper that the movie studio had admitted to invent David Manning. (8) Every well-known film critic was hating the movie. (9) Therefore, the studio executives had decided publishing advertisements that contained a made-up quotation saying that the film was wonderful. (10) Marlene and Agnetha were so disgusted by this deception that they planned to write to the head of the movie studio and ask getting their money back.

Prepositions

For more on prepositions, see Chapter 22. For a list of prepositions, see page 347.

DEFINITION: A **preposition** is a word (such as *of, above, between, about*) that connects a noun, pronoun, or verb with some other information about it. Knowing which preposition to use can be difficult because the correct preposition is often determined by idiom or common practice rather than by its actual meaning.

DEFINITION: An **idiom** is any combination of words that is always used the same way, even though there is no logical or grammatical explanation for it. The best way to learn English idioms is to listen and read as much as possible and then to practice writing and speaking the correct forms.

PREPOSITIONS WITH ADJECTIVES

Adjectives are often followed by prepositions. Here are some common examples.

afraid of	full of	scared of
ashamed of	happy about	sorry for
aware of	interested in	tired of
confused by	proud of	
excited about	responsible for	

Tanya is excited *about* ~~of~~ going to Mexico.

However, she is afraid *of* ~~by~~ taking time off.

PREPOSITIONS WITH VERBS

Many verbs consist of a verb plus a preposition (or adverb). The meaning of these verbs usually has nothing to do with the literal meanings of the verb and the preposition. Taken together, however, the verb and the preposition have a particular meaning in English. Often, the meaning of the verb changes completely depending on which preposition is used with it.

You must *take out* the trash. [*take out* = bring to a different location]

You must *take in* the exciting sights of New York City. [*take in* = observe]

Here are a few common examples.

call off (cancel)	They *called off* the pool party.
call on (choose)	The teacher always *calls on* me.
drop in (visit)	*Drop in* when you are in the area.

fill in (refill)	Please *fill in* the holes in the ground.
fill out (complete)	Please *fill out* this application form.
fill up (make something full)	Don't *fill up* with junk food.
go over (review)	He wants to *go over* our speeches.
grow up (age)	All children *grow up*.
hand in (submit)	You may *hand in* your homework now.
look up (check)	I *looked up* the word in the dictionary.
pick out (choose)	Sandy *picked out* a puppy.
pick up (take or collect)	When do you *pick up* the keys?
put off (postpone)	I often *put off* doing dishes.

PRACTICE 3   EDITING PREPOSITIONS

Edit the following sentences to make sure that the correct prepositions are used.

> **EXAMPLE:** Several U.S. presidents have said that they were sorry of the mistreatment of Japanese Americans during World War II. *(for)*

1. During World War II, more than 120,000 Japanese Americans were shut down in internment camps.

2. Many young Japanese Americans still chose to sign away for the U.S. military.

3. These soldiers often had to fight for prejudice as well as the enemy.

4. About eight hundred Japanese American soldiers gave in their lives during the fighting.

5. After the war, many Japanese Americans who had been interned were ashamed for their experience.

6. More than fifty years after the war, some Americans of Japanese descent became interested on creating a memorial to the Japanese Americans of the war years.

7. They wanted to make other Americans aware on the sacrifices of Japanese Americans during World War II.

8. A city full with memorials to the country's past, Washington, D.C., was chosen to be the site of the National Japanese American Memorial.

9. For the center of the memorial park, the designers picked on a sculpture by a Japanese American artist, Nina Akamu, featuring two cranes tangled in barbed wire.

10. Visitors to the park will be reminded on Japanese Americans' struggle for acceptance in the United States.

PRACTICE 4 EDITING PREPOSITIONS

Edit the following paragraph to make sure that the correct prepositions are used.

(1) Students who are anxious on mathematics take fewer math classes and perform worse in them than students who do not have math anxiety. (2) Scientists used to believe that students were afraid about math because they were not good at it, but that belief was incorrect. (3) It turns up that worry prevents students from understanding mathematics as well as they could. (4) Fear interferes in the working memory that is necessary for math, making students less able to think about math problems. (5) Starting on about the age of twelve, students with math anxiety become less able to compensate for the loss of working memory. (6) The good news is that effective treatment is available for math anxiety. (7) Students who once thought they would never be able to understand math may someday find up that they can conquer their anxiety and cope with numbers.

Negatives and Questions

NEGATIVES

To form a negative statement, you can usually use one of these words:

never	nobody	no one	nowhere
no	none	not	

DEFINITION: The word *not* is often combined with a verb in a shortened form called a **contraction**. Contractions are common in spoken English and in informal written English, but they may not be appropriate in all papers.

They aren't finished. = They are not finished.

In standard English, there can be only one negative word in each clause.

Johnetta will ~~not~~ call no one.

anyone
Johnetta will not call ~~no one~~.

> A clause is a group of words with a subject and a verb. It may or may not be able to stand on its own as a sentence. For more on clauses, see Chapter 22.

When you write a negative statement using the word *not*, the *not* must come after the first helping verb in the sentence. If there is no helping verb, you must add a form of *do* as well as *not* to make a negative statement.

Common Helping Verbs

FORMS OF *BE*	FORMS OF *HAVE*	FORMS OF *DO*	OTHER VERBS
am	have	do	can
are	has	does	could
been	had	did	may
being			might
is			must
was			should
were			will

POSITIVE	Candace *will go* with us.
NEGATIVE	Candace *will not go* with us.
POSITIVE	I *enjoyed* the party.
NEGATIVE	I *did not enjoy* the party.

[Notice that the verb *enjoyed* changed to *enjoy* once the verb *did* was added.]

QUESTIONS

To turn a statement into a question, move the helping verb in the statement so that it comes before the subject. If the only verb is a form of *be*, it should also be moved before the subject. If there is no helping verb or form of *be* in the statement, you must add a form of *do* and put it before the subject. Be sure to end the question with a question mark.

STATEMENT	Tory *can work* late.
QUESTION	*Can* Tory *work* late?
STATEMENT	Cia *is* smart.
QUESTION	*Is* Cia smart?
STATEMENT	You *helped* my sister.
QUESTION	*Did* you *help* my sister?

[Notice that the verb *helped* changed to *help* once the verb *did* was added.]

PRACTICE 5   WRITING NEGATIVE STATEMENTS AND QUESTIONS

For each positive statement, write one negative statement and one question.

EXAMPLE:

Positive statement: *The weather forecast calls for rain tomorrow.*

Negative statement: *The weather forecast does not call for rain tomorrow.*

Question: *Does the weather forecast call for rain tomorrow?*

1. **Positive statement:** We will have to cancel the picnic.

Negative statement: _____

Question: _____

2. **Positive statement:** The forecast on television could be wrong.

   Negative statement: _____

   Question: _____

3. **Positive statement:** The garden needs water this year.

   Negative statement: _____

   Question: _____

4. **Positive statement:** The children liked playing in the rain.

   Negative statement: _____

   Question: _____

5. **Positive statement:** Carrying an umbrella was a good idea.

   Negative statement: _____

   Question: _____

Adjectives

DEFINITION: **Adjectives** modify or describe nouns and pronouns. Many sentences have several adjectives that modify the same word.

> For more on adjectives, see Chapter 28.

The happy old brown dog slept on the sidewalk.

ORDER OF ADJECTIVES

When you use more than one adjective to modify the same word, you should use the conventional order for adjectives in standard English. The list that follows indicates this order.

1. Judgment or overall opinion: *awful, friendly, intelligent, strange, terrible.*
2. Size: *big, huge, tiny, small, large, short, tall.*
3. Shape: *round, square, fat, thin, circular.*
4. Age: *old, young, new, youthful.*

5. Color: *blue, green, yellow, red.*

6. Nationality or location: *Greek, Italian, California, southern.*

7. Material: *paper, glass, plastic, wooden.*

EXAMPLE, ORDER OF ADJECTIVES

The (1) friendly (4) old (5) black terrier was chasing the squirrel.

I lost a (2) small (3) round (6) Italian (7) leather purse on the subway.

PRACTICE 6   EDITING ADJECTIVES

LEARNING JOURNAL
Which topic in this chapter is most difficult for you? How could you explain that problem to someone else? How can you try to avoid it in your own writing?

For each item, write a sentence using the noun listed and the adjectives in parentheses. Be sure to put the adjectives in the correct order: judgment or overall opinion, size, shape, age, color, nationality or location, and material.

EXAMPLE: program (television, silly, black-and-white, old)

We watched a silly old black-and-white television program last night.

1. handkerchief (faded, lace)

_____

2. creature (green, frightening, Martian)

_____

3. stairway (marble, massive, new)

_____

_____

4. classroom (cold, downstairs, little)

_____

5. tomatoes (red, New Jersey, delicious)

_____

PART SIX

Word Use

34

Word Choice

Avoiding Language Pitfalls

Understand the Importance of Choosing Words Carefully

In conversation, much of your meaning is conveyed by your facial expression, your tone of voice, and your gestures. In writing, you have only the words on the page to make your point, so you must choose them carefully. If you use vague or inappropriate words, your readers may not understand what you have to say. Carefully chosen, precise words tell your readers exactly what you mean.

Two resources will help you find the best words for your meaning: a dictionary and a thesaurus.

LEARNING JOURNAL
Use your learning journal as a place to record sentences with the types of problems covered in this chapter. Also write down edited versions of these sentences, with the problems corrected.

DICTIONARY

You need a dictionary. For a very small investment, you can have a complete word resource for all kinds of useful information about words: spelling, division of words into syllables, pronunciation, parts of speech, other forms of words, definitions, and examples of use. Following is a sample dictionary entry.

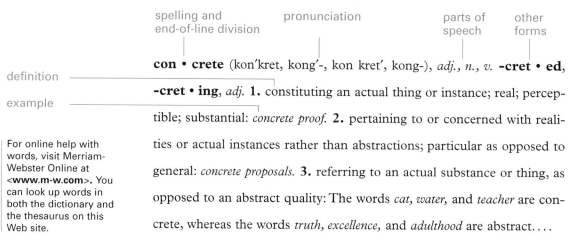

spelling and end-of-line division | pronunciation | parts of speech | other forms

definition ——————

example ——————

con • crete (kon′krēt, kong′-, kon krēt′, kong-), *adj., n., v.* **-cret • ed**, **-cret • ing**, *adj.* **1.** constituting an actual thing or instance; real; perceptible; substantial: *concrete proof.* **2.** pertaining to or concerned with realities or actual instances rather than abstractions; particular as opposed to general: *concrete proposals.* **3.** referring to an actual substance or thing, as opposed to an abstract quality: The words *cat, water,* and *teacher* are concrete, whereas the words *truth, excellence,* and *adulthood* are abstract....

—*Random House Webster's College Dictionary*

For online help with words, visit Merriam-Webster Online at <**www.m-w.com**>. You can look up words in both the dictionary and the thesaurus on this Web site.

THESAURUS

For a map of synonyms for any word, visit the Plumb Design Visual Thesaurus at <**www.plumbdesign .com/thesaurus**>.

A thesaurus gives *synonyms* (words that have the same meaning) for the word you look up. Like a dictionary, it comes in inexpensive and even electronic editions. Use a thesaurus when you can't find the right word for what you mean. Be careful, however, to choose a word that has the precise meaning you intend. If you are not sure how a word should be used, look it up in the dictionary.

Concrete, *adj.* **1.** Particular, specific, single, certain, special, unique, sole, peculiar, individual, separate, isolated, distinct, exact, precise, direct, strict, minute; definite, plain, evident, obvious; pointed, emphasized; restrictive, limiting, limited, well-defined, clear-cut, fixed, finite; determining, conclusive, decided.

—J. I. Rodale, *The Synonym Finder*

Practice Avoiding Four Common Word-Choice Problems

Four common problems with word choice may make it hard for you to get your point across. You can eliminate them by using specific words that fit your meaning and make your writing clearer.

VAGUE AND ABSTRACT WORDS

Your words need to create a clear picture for your readers. Vague and abstract words are too general. They don't give your readers a clear idea of what you mean. Here are some common vague and abstract words.

Vague and Abstract Words

a lot	dumb	nice	school
awful	good	OK (okay)	small
bad	great	old	thing
beautiful	happy	person	very
big	house	pretty	whatever
car	job	sad	young

When you see one of these words or another general word in your writing, try to replace it with a concrete or more specific word. A **concrete word** names something that can be seen, heard, felt, tasted, or smelled. A **specific word** names a particular individual or quality. Compare these two sentences:

VAGUE AND ABSTRACT	It was a beautiful day.
CONCRETE AND SPECIFIC	The sky was a bright, cloudless blue; the sun was shimmering; and the temperature was a perfect 78 degrees.

The first version is too general to be interesting. The second version creates a clear, strong image. Some words are so vague that it is best to avoid them altogether.

VAGUE AND ABSTRACT   It's like *whatever.*

[This sentence is neither concrete nor specific.]

PRACTICE 1   AVOIDING VAGUE AND ABSTRACT WORDS

In the following sentences, underline any words that are vague or abstract. Then edit each sentence by replacing any vague or abstract words with concrete, specific ones. You may invent any details you like.

cousin Jonathan collects teeth, and my Aunt Farielle has the world's
EXAMPLE: My <u>relatives</u> are weird.   *loudest laugh.*

Well Behaved

1. My little sister is a good girl.

every night

2. Both of my parents work a lot, so I babysit pretty often.

enjoy each others company

3. My sister and I have fun together.

every month

4. Our relatives visit very frequently.

5. My grandmother is the nicest person I know.

6. She likes to cook things that remind her of home.

7. One of my uncles is a little crazy.

throws papers

8. He does dumb things to get my attention.

9. He treats me as if I were very young.

10. I guess he is just happy to see me.

SLANG

DEFINITION: Slang is informal and casual language, shared by the group that uses it. Slang should be used only in informal and casual situations. Avoid it when you write, especially for college classes or at work. Use language that is appropriate for your audience and purpose.

SLANG	EDITED
The kid in the store was *freakin'*.	The child was screaming and crying.
I'll give you the *411* tonight.	I'll give you the information tonight.
Getting fired really *bites*.	Getting fired is upsetting.

PRACTICE 2   AVOIDING SLANG

In the following sentences, underline any slang words. Then edit the sentences by replacing the slang with language appropriate for a formal audience and purpose. Imagine that you are writing to a supervisor at work.

EXAMPLE: The company's offer of paid paternity leave to full-time

generous

employees is ~~way cool~~.

1. I wanted to express my appreciation for the fab new benefits package.

2. If I didn't have insurance through the company, the premiums would really put the hurt on my paycheck.

3. Now that my wife and I are starting a family, insurance is a biggie.

4. I am planning to take two weeks of paternity leave in October when our rug rat arrives.

5. Without the company paying for this leave, I would no way be able to afford the time off.

6. Doing the quality-time thing with my wife and baby is very important to me.

7. I know that adjusting to fatherhood will not be cake.

8. We are both mad grateful that the company is rewarding its employees in this way.

9. If I can do anything to make my absence easier on my coworkers, please give me a shout.

10. This new company policy really is all that, and my family and I thank you.

WORDY LANGUAGE

People sometimes use too many words to express their ideas. They may think that using more words will make them sound smart and important. But too many words can get in the way of a writer's point and weaken it.

Wordy language includes phrases that contain too many words, unnecessarily qualify (comment on) a statement, or use slightly different words without adding any new ideas.

WORDY	We have no openings *at this point in time*.
EDITED	We have no openings now.

[The phrase *at this point in time* uses five words to express what could be said in one word: *now*.]

WORDY	*In the opinion of this writer,* tuition fees are too high.
EDITED	Tuition fees are too high.

[The qualifying phrase *in the opinion of this writer* is not necessary and weakens the statement.]

WORDY	The suspect was *evasive* and *avoided answering the questions.*
EDITED	The suspect was evasive.

[The words *evasive* and *avoided answering the questions* repeat the same idea without adding anything new.]

Common Wordy Expressions

WORDY	EDITED
As a result of	Because
Due to the fact that	Because
In spite of the fact that	Although
It is my opinion that	I think
In the event that	If
The fact of the matter is that	(Just state the point.)
A great number of	Many
At that time	Then
In this day and age	Now
At this point in time	Now
In this paper I will show that . . .	(Just make the point; don't announce it.)

PRACTICE 3   AVOIDING WORDY LANGUAGE

In the following sentences, underline the wordy language. Then edit each sentence to make it more concise.

EXAMPLE: Television shows <u>are things that</u> contribute to our view of the world.

1. <u>The fact of the matter</u> is that many young people get their first ideas

   about interesting jobs from watching television.

2. Some American scientists became interested in science as a result of the fact that they watched *Star Trek* as children.

watching

3. Shows like *L.A. Law* made the legal profession attractive to a great number of future lawyers.

4. For a long period of time, political careers were not portrayed positively on television.

5. There are some people who believe that declining respect for politicians began with television shows.

6. It is very true that popular shows like *The Simpsons* and *Spin City* have portrayed politicians as stupid, corrupt, or both.

7. In this day and age, however, more young people are becoming interested in careers in government.

8. Now there are sympathetic people with political careers who appear on *West Wing* each week.

9. Will the United States have a crop of idealistic young politicians in the next decade due to the fact that they watched *West Wing* as impression-able teens?

Because

10. Motivated political workers are an essential part of any democracy, so in actual fact *West Wing* may even be good for our country.

CLICHÉS

DEFINITION: **Clichés** are phrases used so often that people no longer pay attention to them. To get your point across and to get your readers' attention, replace clichés with fresh language that precisely expresses your meaning.

CLICHÉS	EDITED
Passing the state police exam is no *walk in the park*.	Passing the state police exam requires careful preparation.
I was *sweating bullets* until the grades were posted.	I was anxious until the grades were posted.

COMMON CLICHÉS

as big as a house	light as a feather
the best/worst of times	no way on earth
better late than never	110 percent
break the ice	playing with fire
the corporate ladder	spoiled brat
crystal clear	spoiled rotten
a drop in the bucket	starting from scratch
easier said than done	sweating blood/bullets
hard as a rock	work like a dog
hell on earth	worked his/her way up
last but not least	

PRACTICE 4   AVOIDING CLICHÉS

In the following sentences, underline the clichés. Then edit each sentence by replacing the clichés with fresh language that precisely expresses your meaning.

EXAMPLE: Keeping children safe is ~~easier said than done~~. *a challenging task.*

1. People with young children need eyes in the back of their heads.

2. Children can put themselves in danger faster than lightning.

3. Parents of a toddler should have their heads examined if they do not lock cabinets containing household chemicals.

4. Toddlers grow by leaps and bounds, and new levels of childproofing must be done as children learn to climb gates and open doors.

5. Parents sometimes recognize dangers in the nick of time and stop their children from injuring themselves.

6. When their children play at another child's house, some parents may worry that the other parents will not keep an eagle eye on their youngsters.

7. Parents have mortal fears of their young children running into traffic to chase a ball.

8. Swimming pools can be deathtraps unless they are surrounded by a high fence with a locked gate.

9. Children must be taught to keep their hands to themselves and leave the area immediately if they find a gun in someone's home.

10. Someday young children will be old enough to be independent, but their independence can also drive parents out of their minds with worry.

Edit Paragraphs and Your Own Writing

PRACTICE 5   EDITING PARAGRAPHS FOR WORD CHOICE

Find and edit any examples of vague and abstract language, slang, wordy language, or clichés in the following paragraphs. You may want to refer to the Quick Review Chart on page 540.

(1) Being the big kahuna at a major American corporation almost always pays extremely well. (2) CEOs earn millions of dollars each and every year, and most also get stock options. (3) Even if the company goes off the rails and the CEO gets fired, he (and it is almost always a guy thing)

often gets a severance package that is worth additional millions. (4) A CEO's salary in the United States is usually several hundred times larger than the average that is paid for a company worker's wages. (5) This ratio is pretty big compared with the ratios in other industrialized countries. (6) In Japan, for example, a CEO's salary maxes out at about ten times that of a worker. (7) Are American CEOs really that great? (8) Are they, in actual fact, worth what they are paid?

(9) The fact of the matter is that highly paid CEOs can rarely do what corporate directors hope. (10) They may have earned sky-high profits at a previous corporation, but every business is different. (11) There is no guarantee that these men will be able to keep up the good work. (12) If a company promoted a worker from within, he or she probably would not only know the biz inside and out but also work for fewer bucks than a hired gun from outside. (13) Then the corporation would be ahead of the game to the tune of a few million dollars. (14) Why, then, are corporations willing to pay a lot of money to recruit expensive outsiders as CEOs?

(15) The problem with promoting a CEO from within the company is the fact that few companies want to take risks. (16) For a decade or more, hiring a CEO has meant finding the CEO of another company and paying him enough to get him to jump ship. (17) Company directors think that their stockholders have the expectation that the company will bring in a highly paid outsider. (18) The directors are freaked out by the idea that an insider might fail and disappoint stockholders. (19) Of course, most CEOs brought in from elsewhere also end up in the dumpster, but

the corporate boards can at least reassure themselves that their choice has a track record when he arrives. (20) Corporations claim to want leaders who can think outside the box. (21) However, there are few corporate boards of directors who are willing to look anywhere other than conventional places for their next leaders. (22) This conventional thinking will eventually be lousy for business; perhaps only then will the trend toward hiring expensive CEOs change.

 PRACTICE 6   EDITING YOUR OWN WRITING FOR WORD CHOICE

As a final practice, edit a piece of your own writing for word choice. It can be a paper you are working on for this course, a paper you've already finished, a paper for another course, or a recent piece of writing from your work or everyday life. Record in your learning journal any problem sentences you find, along with their corrections. You may want to use the following Quick Review Chart.

Quick Review Chart

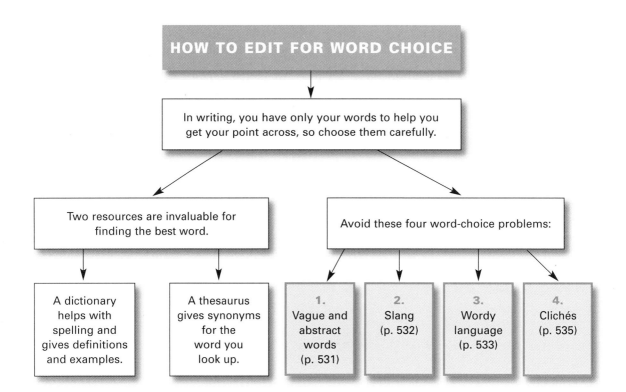

HOW TO EDIT FOR WORD CHOICE

In writing, you have only your words to help you get your point across, so choose them carefully.

Two resources are invaluable for finding the best word.

Avoid these four word-choice problems:

A dictionary helps with spelling and gives definitions and examples.

A thesaurus gives synonyms for the word you look up.

1.
Vague and abstract words
(p. 531)

2.
Slang
(p. 532)

3.
Wordy language
(p. 533)

4.
Clichés
(p. 535)

35

Commonly Confused Words

Avoiding Mistakes with Sound-alikes

Understand Why Certain Words Are Commonly Confused

People often confuse certain words in English because they sound alike and may have similar meanings. In writing, words that sound alike may be spelled differently, and readers rely on the spelling to understand what you mean. When you mean one word but write another that sounds the same, the different spelling and different meaning may confuse your readers. Edit your writing carefully to make sure that you have used the correct words.

To understand this chapter, you need to know what nouns, verbs, adjectives, and adverbs are. For a review, see Chapters 22, 26, and 28.

STRATEGIES FOR EDITING SOUND-ALIKES

1. Proofread carefully, using the techniques discussed on page 557.

2. Use a dictionary to look up any words you are unsure of.

3. Focus on finding and correcting mistakes you make with the twenty-seven sets of commonly confused words covered in this chapter.

4. Develop a personal list of words you confuse often. In your learning journal or on an index card, record the words that you confuse in your writing, and jot down their meanings. Before you turn in any piece of writing, consult your personal list to make sure you have used the correct words.

Practice Using Commonly Confused Words Correctly

LEARNING JOURNAL
Use your learning journal as a place to start a personal list of words you commonly confuse. When you edit your papers, be sure to check for those words.

Study the different meanings and spellings of these twenty-seven sets of commonly confused words. Complete the sentence after each set of words, filling in each blank with the correct word.

A/An/And

Some commonly confused words—such as *conscience* and *conscious, loose* and *lose,* and *of* and *have*—sound similar but not exactly alike. To avoid confusing these words, practice pronouncing them correctly.

a: used before a word that begins with a consonant sound
  A bat was living behind the shutter.

an: used before a word that begins with a vowel sound
  An elderly lady sat beside me.

and: used to join two words
  My sister *and* I went to the amusement park.

A friend *and* I got lost in an old maze.

Most classrooms have _____ worn-out chair _____ _____ old desk

for the teacher.

A **noun** is a word that names a person, place, or thing.

Accept/Except

A **verb** tells what action the subject performs or links the subject to a word that describes it.

accept: to agree to receive or admit (verb)
  I plan to *accept* the offer.

except: but, other than (conjunction)
  The whole family was there *except* my brother.

I *accept* all your requests *except* the one to borrow my car.

An **adjective** describes or adds information about a noun or a pronoun.

Do not _____ anything from people at airports _____

from family members.

An **adverb** describes or adds information about a verb, an adjective, or another adverb.

Advice/Advise

advice: opinion (noun)
  I would like your *advice* on this decision.

advise: to give an opinion (verb)
  My boyfriend *advises* me about car repairs.

Please *advise* me what to do; your *advice* is always helpful.

_____ me of your plans, particularly if you don't follow my

_____ .

Affect/Effect

affect: to have an impact on, to change something (verb)
  The whole region was *affected* by the drought.

effect: a result (noun)
  The lack of water will have a tremendous *effect* on many businesses.

The sunny weather has had a positive *effect* on people's moods, but it will negatively *affect* the economy.

Since this year's drought will _____ the cost of food, we'll be

feeling its _____ personally.

Are/Our

are: a form of the verb *be*
  The flowers *are* ready to bloom.

our: a pronoun showing ownership
  I am proud of *our* garden.

Gardens *are* rare in *our* neighborhood.

_____ bulbs _____ arriving this week.

By/Buy

by: next to or before
  I'll be standing *by* the door.
  We have to be at the restaurant *by* 8:00.

buy: purchase (verb)
  I would like to *buy* a new car.

By the time I'm ready to leave the dollar store, I have found too much I want to *buy*.

I have decided to _____ the model _____ the showroom entrance.

Conscience/Conscious

conscience: a personal sense of right and wrong (noun)
  My *conscience* keeps me from doing bad things.

conscious: awake, aware (adjective)
  The patient is now *conscious*.
  Shelly was *conscious* of Sam's feelings.

Danny made a *conscious* decision to listen to his *conscience*.

Remember that one of the words is con-science; the other is not.

The burglar was ＿＿＿＿＿＿＿ that someone else was in the house and

for a moment felt a twinge of ＿＿＿＿＿＿＿.

Fine/Find

fine: of high quality; feeling well; a penalty for breaking a law
> She works in the *fine* jewelry department.
> After taking some aspirin, Shana felt *fine*.
> The *fine* for exceeding the speed limit is $100.

find: locate, discover (verb)
> Can you help me *find* the key?

You will *find* a *fine* leather jacket in the coat department.

A ＿＿＿＿ partner is hard to ＿＿＿＿.

Its/It's

It's is a contraction, short for *it is*. If you are not sure whether to use *its* or *it's* in a sentence, try substituting *it is*. If the sentence doesn't make sense with *it is*, use *its*.

its: a pronoun showing ownership
> The bird went back to *its* nest.

it's: a contraction of the words *it is*
> *It's* important for you to be on time.

It's amazing to see a butterfly come out of *its* cocoon.

＿＿＿＿ good news for us that the bus changed ＿＿＿＿ route.

Knew/New/Know/No

knew: understood; recognized (past tense of the verb *know*)
> I *knew* we took the wrong turn.

new: unused, recent (adjective)
> Jane has a *new* boyfriend.

know: to understand, to have knowledge of (verb)
> I *know* him from work.

no: used to form a negative
> There are *no* other classes at that time.

I *knew* that Jason would need *new* shoes.

The ＿＿＿＿ employee already ＿＿＿＿ some of the other employees.

There is *no* way to *know* what will happen.

Do you _____ what _____ means?

Loose/Lose

loose: baggy, not fixed in place (adjective)
    That button is *loose*.

lose: to misplace, to forfeit possession of (verb)
    I don't want to *lose* my job.

If the muffler is *loose*, you might *lose* it.

You will _____ that bracelet if it's too _____.

Mind/Mine

mind: object to; the thinking or feeling part of one's brain
    I don't *mind* loud music.
    Sometimes I think I am losing my *mind*.

mine: belonging to me; a source of ore and minerals
    That parking space is *mine*.
    That store is a gold *mine*.

Keep in *mind* that the sweater is *mine*.

Your _____ is a lot sharper than _____.

Of/Have

of: coming from; caused by; part of a group; made from (preposition)
    The president *of* the company pleaded guilty to embezzlement.

have: to possess (verb). Also used as a helping verb.
    Do you *have* a schedule?
    Jeannie should *have* been here by now.

I would *have* helped if you had told me you were out *of* change.

Joe might _____ been part _____ the band.

Do not use *of* after *would, should, could,* and *might.* Use *have* after those words.

Passed/Past

passed: went by or went ahead (past tense of the verb *pass*)
Tim *passed* us a minute ago.

past: time that has gone by (noun); gone by, over, just beyond
The school is just *past* the traffic light.

This past school year, I *passed* all of my exams.

If you go _____ the church, you have _____ the

right turn.

Peace/Piece

peace: no disagreement; calm
The sleeping infant is at *peace*.

piece: a part of something larger
May I have a *piece* of paper?

We will have no *peace* until we give the dog a *piece* of that bread.

For the sake of _____, please share that _____ of pie.

Principal/Principle

principal: main (adjective); chief; head of a school (noun)
Making sales calls is your *principal* responsibility.
Darla is a *principal* of the company.
Mr. Tucker is the *principal* of the Sawyer School.

principle: a standard of beliefs or behaviors (noun)
The issue is really a matter of *principle*.

The *principle* at stake is the *principal* issue of the court case.

The _____ problem with many criminals is that they do not

have good _____.

Quiet/Quite/Quit

quiet: soft in sound; not noisy (adjective)
The library was very *quiet*.

quite: completely, very (adverb)
I have had *quite* enough to eat after that half-pounder and fries.

quit: to stop (verb)
Will you please *quit* bothering me?

It is not *quite* time to *quit* yet.

The machine _____ running, and the office was _____.

Right/Write

right: correct; in a direction opposite from left (adjective)
Are you sure this is the *right* way?
Take a *right* after the bridge.

write: to put words on paper (verb)
I will *write* soon.

Please be sure to *write* the *right* address.

_____ your name in the _____ column.

Set/Sit

set: a collection of something (noun); to place an object somewhere (verb)
Junior has a great train *set*.
Please *set* the package on the table.

sit: to rest with one's rear end supported by a chair or other surface
You can *sit* right over there.

Set your coat down before you *sit*.

Let's _____ and look over my _____ of travel photos.

Suppose/Supposed

suppose: imagine or assume to be true
Suppose you could go anywhere in the world.
I *suppose* you want some dinner.

supposed: past tense of *suppose*; intended
The clerk *supposed* the man was over twenty-one.

You are *supposed* to call when you are going to be late, but I *suppose* that's too much to expect.

I was _____ to take the ten o'clock train, but I _____

the eleven o'clock is okay.

Than/Then

than: a word used to compare two or more things or persons
Joanne makes more money *than* I do.

then: at a certain time
I will look forward to seeing you *then*.

I weigh a lot more *than* I used to back *then*.

If you want to lose weight, _____ you will have to eat less

_____ you do.

Their/There/They're

If you aren't sure whether to use *their* or *they're,* substitute *they are* for *they're.* If the sentence doesn't make sense, use *their.*

their: a pronoun showing ownership
Their new apartment has two bedrooms.

there: a word indicating placement or existence
Your desk is over *there*.
There is more work than I can handle.

they're: a contraction of the words *they are*
They're going to Hawaii.

Their windows are open, and *there* is a breeze, so *they're* not hot.

_____ going to be away, so my friend will be staying

_____ and taking care of _____ cat.

Though/Through/Threw

though: however; nevertheless; in spite of
I'll be there, *though* I might be a little late.

through: finished with (adjective); from one side to the other (preposition)
Jenna is *through* with school in May.
Go *through* the first set of doors.

threw: hurled, tossed (past tense of the verb *throw*)
    She *threw* away the garbage.

Jimmy *threw* the ball, and it went *through* the window, *though* he had not aimed it there.

_____ she loved him, she _____ him out because she

couldn't go _____ the pain he caused.

To/Too/Two

to: a word indicating a direction or movement (preposition); part of the infinitive form of a verb
    I am going *to* the food store.
    Do you want *to* see a movie?
too: also; more than enough; very (adverb)
    Toni was sick, *too*.
    The car was going *too* fast.
two: the number between one and three
    There are *two* tables.

They went *to* a restaurant and ordered *too* much food for *two* people.

The _____ friends started _____ dance, but it was _____ crowded

to move.

Use/Used

use: to employ or put into service (verb)
    I *use* this grill all the time.
used: past tense of the verb *use*. *Used to* can indicate a past fact or state, or it can mean "familiar with."
    I *used* the grill last night to cook chicken.
    I *used to* do yoga.
    I am *used* to juggling school and work.

Paolo *used* to be a farmer, so he knows how to *use* all the equipment.

When you last _____ the oven, what did you _____ it for?

Who's/Whose

who's: a contraction of the words *who is* or *who has*
   Who's hungry?
   Who's been here the longest?

whose: a pronoun showing ownership
   Whose bag is this?

The person *whose* name is first on the list is the one *who's* going next.

_____ the man _____ shoes are on the table?

If you aren't sure of whether to use *your* or *you're,* substitute *you are.* If the sentence doesn't make sense, use *your.*

Your/You're

your: a pronoun showing ownership
   I like *your* shirt.

you're: a contraction of the words *you are*
   You're going to run out of gas.

You're about to get paint all over *your* hands.

_____ teacher says _____ always late to class.

PRACTICE 1   USING THE RIGHT WORD

In each of the following items, circle the correct word in parentheses.

   EXAMPLE: (You're/Your) résumé is a critical computer file.

1. I tell all my friends to back up important data on (their / there) computers.

2. Unfortunately, I sometimes forget to take my own (advice / advise).

3. My computer had a serious crash, and now I cannot (find / fine) the most recent copy of my résumé.

4. I should (have / of) made a hard copy and a backup on a floppy disk, but I didn't.

5. Today I have (a / an / and) interview for a job I really want, and I can't locate any résumés (accept / except) one from 1998.

6. (Loosing / Losing) a résumé is not the end of the world, but it will be (quiet / quite) a job reconstructing it.

7. It took me hours to (right / write) and proofread my most recent résumé.

8. This morning I quickly (set / sit) down some information to give to the interviewer, but this version is sloppier (than / then) the résumé I (use / used) to have.

9. (Though / Through) I feel that I am well qualified for this job, I'm afraid that this résumé may have a bad (affect / effect) on my chances of being hired.

10. An interviewer (who's / whose) task is to hire the best person must pay attention (to / too / two) small details.

Edit Paragraphs and Your Own Writing

▨ **PRACTICE 2** **EDITING PARAGRAPHS FOR COMMONLY CONFUSED WORDS**

Edit the following paragraphs to correct errors in the use of commonly confused words.

1. (1) Most people no that Americans love to drive there cars. (2) However, many people may not be conscience of how much the government does to support our car culture. (3) For instance, the United States would never of had so many good highways without federal and state assistance

for road construction and maintenance. (4) New highways are usually paid for mainly buy tax money. (5) It is rare for a new road too be paid for with tolls, which would come exclusively from the people driving on it. (6) Americans also expect they're roads to be well maintained, and they may right to their representatives to complain about potholes and aging road surfaces. (7) The government is even responsible for keeping gas prices lower here then in most other industrialized nations.

(8) Few people mine that the government assists drivers in these ways. (9) Some would argue that its a government's job to help pay for transportation. (10) However, other forms of transportation in this country are often past over when Congress hands out funds. (11) Amtrak, the U.S. railroad, will soon loose all government funds, even though many government officials are skeptical of it's ability to keep operating without government assistance. (12) Accept for a few places like New York and San Francisco, most U.S. cities do not have good mass transit systems. (13) Americans who's travels have taken them to certain parts of the world praise the national train systems and city transit systems they find there. (14) As traffic gets worse in our nation's urban and suburban areas, some people fine it odd that the United States does not invest more in transportation that would allow people to leave there cars at home.

2. (1) Hoping to keep are nation's blood supply safe, the U.S. government has placed restrictions on donating blood. (2) Anyone whose spent more than five years in Europe or more than three months in England since 1980 is not allowed to give blood. (3) Officials hope that asking about time in Europe will help them fine people who might of been exposed to mad cow disease. (4) Men are also asked whether they have

had sexual relations with other men in the passed ten years. (5) If they have, their asked not to give blood. (6) This is suppose to protect the blood supply from the AIDS virus. (7) Of course, they're are some problems with these restrictions. (8) First, know one knows how much exposure to infected meat can give a person mad cow disease, and know one is sure how long the disease can hide in a human body. (9) Second, many gay men our not infected with HIV, and many women, who are not asked about sexual activity, are infected. (10) Restricting certain groups of people from giving blood may not do anything to protect the blood supply, but it will certainly effect the amount of blood available. (11) Is it better to allow the blood supply to become dangerously low then to allow people who's blood might carry a disease to donate blood?

PRACTICE 3   EDITING YOUR OWN WRITING FOR COMMONLY CONFUSED WORDS

As a final practice, edit a piece of your own writing for commonly confused words. It can be a paper you are working on for this course, a paper you've already finished, a paper for another course, or a recent piece of writing from your work or everyday life. Add any misused words you find to your personal list of confusing words.

LEARNING JOURNAL
Which of the sets of commonly confused words do you mix up most often? How could you explain the different words to someone else? How could you try to avoid them in your own writing?

36

Spelling

Using the Right Letters

Understand the Importance of Spelling Correctly 554

Practice Spelling Correctly 556

Edit Paragraphs and Your Own Writing 562

DEFINITION: As part of their editing, successful writers **proofread** their writing to find and correct their spelling, punctuation, and capitalization errors before they submit their writing.

Understand the Importance of Spelling Correctly

Some very smart people are very poor spellers. Unfortunately, spelling errors are easy for readers to spot, and they make a bad impression. In fact, spelling errors can be considered the fifth most serious error that writers make.

Read the following paragraph, the body of a follow-up letter one student wrote to a prospective employer after an interview:

Thank you for the oportunity to meet about the summer internship at Margate Associates. I hope you will find that my coursework in graphic design and my excellant communication skills make me a promiseing candidate for the position. I look forward to hearing from you soon. I am happy to provide you with referances if you need them.

554

Can you find the four spelling mistakes? If you make such mistakes in your writing, your reader may become confused or frustrated—and your message may get lost. In the case of the summer internship at the design firm, another student got the job.

TWO IMPORTANT TOOLS: DICTIONARY AND SPELLING LIST

If you are serious about improving your spelling, you need to have a dictionary and a spelling list—and to use them.

Dictionary

A dictionary contains the correct spellings of words, along with information on how they are pronounced, what they mean, and where they came from. Buy a dictionary; everyone needs one. When proofreading your papers, use a dictionary whenever you are unsure about the spelling of a word. *Checking a dictionary is the single most important thing you can do to improve your spelling.*

For a sample dictionary entry, see page 530.

Buy a current dictionary rather than an old one because current editions have up-to-date definitions and words that are new to the language, such as *Internet, online, downsizing,* and *Web page.* If you have trouble finding words in a regular dictionary, get a spelling dictionary, which is designed to help you find a word even if you have no idea how to spell it.

Spelling List

Most people misspell the same words over and over. Keeping a spelling list will help you identify your problem words and learn to spell them correctly.

Set aside a section of your course notebook or journal for your spelling list. Every time you edit a paper, write down the words that you have misspelled. Write the correct spelling first, and then in parentheses note the way you actually wrote the word. After you have recorded the spelling errors for three pieces of writing, spend ten minutes analyzing your spelling list. Ask yourself:

- What words have I misspelled more than once?
- What do I get wrong about them? Do I always misspell them the same way?
- What are my personal spelling demons? ("Demons" are the five to ten words that you tend to spell wrong over and over.)

Online dictionaries can also help you with spelling. Here are the names and Web addresses of some popular ones.

• Merriam-Webster Online at <**www .m-w.com**>. This dictionary has a feature called the wild card search. If you are fairly sure how the beginning of a word is spelled, you can enter those letters and then an asterisk (*) and get a list of the words that begin with them. From the list, you can choose the word you want.

• Your Dictionary at <**www .yourdictionary .com**>. This site even features specialty dictionaries for business, computers, law, medicine, and other work-related areas.

• What other mistakes do I repeat (leaving the final -*s* off words, for example)?

Write your personal demons (five to ten words), spelled correctly, on an index card, and keep it somewhere handy so that you can consult the card whenever you write.

Every few weeks, go back to your spelling list to see whether your problem words have changed. Are you misspelling fewer words in each paper? What are your current spelling demons? Using a spelling list will definitely improve your spelling.

Practice Spelling Correctly

You can improve your spelling in several ways. First, learn to find and correct spelling mistakes in your writing. At the same time, work on becoming a better speller so that you make fewer mistakes to begin with.

THREE STEPS FOR FINDING AND CORRECTING MISTAKES

Every time you write a paper, proofread it for spelling errors by focusing only on spelling. Don't try to correct your grammar, improve your message, and check your spelling at the same time. Remember to check the dictionary whenever you are unsure about the spelling of a word and to add all the spelling mistakes you find to your personal spelling list.

Step 1. *Use a Spell Checker*

Most word-processing programs have spell checkers. A spell checker finds and highlights a word that may be misspelled, suggests other spellings, and gives you the opportunity to change the spelling of the word. Use this feature after you have completed a piece of writing but before you print it out.

However, since no spell checker can catch every mistake in a piece of writing, never rely on a spell checker to do your editing for you. A spell checker ignores anything it recognizes as a word, so it will not help you find words that are misused or misspellings that are also words. For example, a spell checker would not highlight any of the problems in these phrases:

Just to it.	(Correct: Just do it.)
pain in the nick	(Correct: pain in the neck)
my writing coarse	(Correct: my writing course)

Step 2. Use Proofreading Techniques

Use some of the following proofreading techniques to focus on the spelling of one word at a time. Different techniques work for different people, so try them all and then decide which ones work for you.

> Some word-processing programs will automatically highlight words that may be misspelled as you write and suggest alternatives if you click the mouse.

PROOFREADING TECHNIQUES

- Put a piece of paper under the line that you are reading.
- Cut a "window" in an index card that is about the size of a long word (such as *misunderstanding*), and place it over your writing to focus on one word at a time.
- Proofread your paper backward, one word at a time.
- If you are using a computer, print out a version of your paper that looks noticeably different: Make the words larger, make the margins larger, triple-space the lines, or do all of these. Read this version carefully.
- Read your paper aloud. This strategy will help you if you tend to leave words out.
- Exchange papers with a partner for proofreading. Your only task as you proofread your partner's paper should be to identify possible misspellings. The writer of the paper should be responsible for checking the spelling and correcting any spelling errors.

Step 3. Check Your Personal Spelling List

After you proofread each word in your paper, look at your personal spelling list and your list of demon words one more time. Have you used any of these words in your paper? If so, go back and check their spelling again. You may be surprised to find that you missed seeing the same old spelling mistakes.

> Most word-processing programs allow you to search for specific words using Find or Search commands from the Edit menu.

PRACTICE 1   USING THE THREE STEPS FOR FINDING AND CORRECTING MISTAKES

Take the last paper you wrote — or one that you are working on now — and use the three steps for finding and correcting spelling mistakes. How many spelling mistakes did you find? Were you surprised? How was the experience different from what you normally do to edit for spelling? How confident are you that your paper now contains no spelling mistakes?

THREE STRATEGIES FOR BECOMING A BETTER SPELLER

Learning to find and correct spelling mistakes that you have already made is only half the battle. You also need to become a better speller so that you do not make so many mistakes in the first place. Here are three strategies.

Strategy 1. Master Your Personal Spelling Demons

Once you know what your spelling demons are, you can start to conquer them. If your list of spelling demons is long, you may want to start by focusing on the top five or the top three. When you have mastered these, you can go on to the next few. Different techniques work for different people. Try them all, and then stick with the ones that work for you.

TECHNIQUES FOR MASTERING YOUR SPELLING DEMONS

- Create a memory aid, an explanation or saying that will remind you of the correct spelling. For example, "*surprise* is no *prize*" may remind you to spell *surprise* with an *s*, not a *z*.
- Break the word into parts, and try to master each part. You can break it into syllables (*Feb ru ar y*) or separate the prefixes and endings (*dis ap point ment*).
- Write the word correctly ten times.
- Say the letters of the word out loud. See if there's a rhythm or a rhyme you can memorize.
- Write a paragraph in which you use the word at least three times.
- Say the word out loud, emphasizing each letter and syllable even if that's not the way you normally say it. For example, say *prob a bly* instead of *prob ly*. Try to pronounce the word this way in your head each time you spell it.
- Ask a partner to give you a spelling test.

Strategy 2. Master Commonly Confused Words

Chapter 35 covers twenty-seven sets of words that are commonly confused because they sound alike, such as *write/right* and *its/it's*. If you can master these commonly confused words, you will avoid many spelling mistakes.

Strategy 3. Learn Six Spelling Rules

This section of the chapter covers spelling situations in which people often think, "What do I do here?" If you can remember the rules, you can avoid or correct many of the spelling errors in your writing.

Before the six rules, here is a quick review of vowels and consonants.

ⓐ b c d ⓔ f g h ⓘ j k l m n ⓞ p q r s t ⓤ v w x y z

Vowels

Consonants are all the letters that are not vowels.

The letter *y* can be either a vowel or a consonant. It is a vowel when it sounds like the *y* in *fly* or *hungry*. It is a consonant when it sounds like the *y* in *yellow*.

Should I Use *ie* or *ei*?

RULE 1:   *I* before *e*
          Except after *c*.
          Or when sounded like *a*
          As in *neighbor* or *weigh*.

Many people repeat this rhyme to themselves as they decide whether a word is spelled with an *ie* or an *ei*.

piece (*i* before *e*)

receive (except after *c*)

eight (sounds like *a*)

EXCEPTIONS: either, neither, foreign, height, seize, society, their, weird

Should I Drop the Final *e* or Keep It When Adding an Ending to a Word?

RULE 2:   Drop the final *e* when adding an ending that begins with a vowel.

hope + ing = hoping

imagine + ation = imagination

Keep the final *e* when adding an ending that begins with a consonant.

achieve + ment = achievement

definite + ly = definitely

EXCEPTIONS: argument, awful, simply, truly (and others)

Should I Change the *y* to *i* when Adding an Ending?

RULE 3:   When adding an ending to a word that ends in *y*, change the *y* to *i* when a consonant comes before the *y*.

lonely + est = loneliest

happy + er = happier

apology + ize = apologize

likely + hood = likelihood

Do not change the *y* when a vowel comes before the *y*.

boy + ish = boyish

pay + ment = payment

survey + or = surveyor

buy + er = buyer

EXCEPTIONS: 1. When adding *-ing* to a word ending in *y*, always keep the *y*, even if a consonant comes before it: study + ing = studying.
2. Other exceptions include *daily, dryer, said,* and *paid.*

Should I Double the Final Consonant When Adding an Ending?

RULE 4:   When adding an ending that starts with a vowel to a one-syllable word, follow these rules.

Double the final consonant only if the word ends with a consonant-vowel-consonant.

strap + ed = strapped

occur + ence = occurrence

prefer + ed = preferred

commit + ed = committed

Do not double the final consonant if the word ends with some other combination.

VOWEL-VOWEL-CONSONANT	VOWEL-CONSONANT-CONSONANT
clean + est = cleanest	slick + er = slicker
poor + er = poorer	teach + er = teacher
clear + ed = cleared	last + ed = lasted

RULE 5:   When adding an ending that starts with a vowel to a word with two or more syllables, follow these rules.

Double the final consonant only if the word ends with a consonant-vowel-consonant and the stress is on the last syllable.

admit + ing = admitting

control + er = controller

admit + ed = admitted

Do not double the final consonant in other cases.

problem + atic = problematic

understand + ing = understanding

offer + ed = offered

Should I Add -*s* or -*es*?

The endings -*s* and -*es* are used to make the plural form of most nouns (*two books*) and the he/she/it form of most verbs (*he runs*).

RULE 6:   Add -*s* to most words, including words that end in *o* preceded by a vowel.

MOST WORDS	WORDS THAT END IN VOWEL PLUS *O*
book + s = books	video + s = videos
college + s = colleges	stereo + s = stereos
jump + s = jumps	radio + s = radios

Add -*es* to words that end in words that end in *s*, *sh*, *ch*, or *x* and *o* preceded by a consonant.

WORDS THAT END IN *S, SH, CH,* OR *X*	WORDS THAT END IN CONSONANT PLUS *O*
class + es = classes	potato + es = potatoes
push + es = pushes	hero + es = heroes
bench + es = benches	go + es = goes
fax + es = faxes	

EXCEPTIONS: pianos, solos (and others)

One Hundred Commonly Misspelled Words

Use this list as an easy reference to check your spelling.

absence	already	athlete	believe
achieve	analyze	awful	business
across	answer	basically	calendar
aisle	appetite	beautiful	career
a lot	argument	beginning	category

(continued)

chief	exercise	lightning	roommate
column	fascinate	loneliness	schedule
coming	February	marriage	scissors
commitment	finally	meant	secretary
conscious	foreign	muscle	separate
convenient	friend	necessary	sincerely
cruelty	government	ninety	sophomore
daughter	grief	noticeable	succeed
definite	guidance	occasion	successful
describe	harass	occurrence	surprise
dictionary	height	perform	truly
different	humorous	physically	until
disappoint	illegal	prejudice	usually
dollar	immediately	probably	vacuum
eighth	independent	psychology	valuable
embarrass	interest	receive	vegetable
environment	jewelry	recognize	weight
especially	judgment	recommend	weird
exaggerate	knowledge	restaurant	writing
excellent	license	rhythm	written

Edit Paragraphs and Your Own Writing

■ **PRACTICE 2 EDITING PARAGRAPHS FOR SPELLING**

Find and correct any spelling mistakes in the following paragraphs.

1. (1) Anyone interested in wierd events should visit New York City on

October 31, when the bigest Halloween parade in the country takes place.

(2) Everyone in the city, it seems, marchs in the parade, yet they're are

still an estimated two million people watching from the sidewalks. (3) The parade had its beginings in Greenwich Village, and original parade-goers walked though the small, winding streets of that old New York nieghborhood. (4) Buy now the parade has goten so large that it has to go down one of the city's broad avenues. (5) The Halloween parade suprises alot of people who see it for the first time. (6) The merryment begins early in the evening, as costumed paraders line up. (7) Your likely to see a huge group of freinds dressed as one hunderd and one dalmatians or perhaps some comicaly exagerated versions of goverment officials. (8) Every kind of costume is permited in the parade, and some people attend skimpyly dressed, aparently without embarassment, in spite of the October chill. (9) For a fascinateing look at how strangly people can behave on Halloween, the New York City Halloween parade is the place to bee.

2. (1) During the summer months, people love to head to the beachs. (2) Accept for those who have recently seen *Jaws,* most people don't consider going to the ocean a dangerous activity. (3) Usualy, people can swim safly at the beach, but its always wise to be cautious. (4) Shark attacks are very rare — their were only seventy-nine in the world in 2000 — but a majority of them happen in the waters around the United States. (5) Shiney jewelery can attract sharks because it resembles fish scales, and swimers in the early morning or late evening are more likely to encounter sharks who are hopeing to grab a byte to eat. (6) Of course, people are much more apt to meet up with jellyfish than with sharks, but even a jellyfish sting can leave a beachgoer acheing for hours. (7) Finaly, everyone ought to be aware that waist sometimes gets into seawater, specially near urban areas. (8) Testing is suppose to be done periodicaly, and any beach with unsafe water should be closed; anyone who doesn't

trust government testing can by a kit and do the job at home. (9) People who think to much about the dangers of going in the ocean may feel safer lying peacfully in the sand. (10) That's probaly fine—as long as they wear plenty of sonscreen.

■ PRACTICE 3   EDITING YOUR OWN WRITING FOR SPELLING

LEARNING JOURNAL
Which spelling strategy is most helpful for you? What spelling advice would you give to someone else?

As a final practice, edit a piece of your own writing for spelling, using the techniques described in this chapter. It can be a paper you are working on for this course, a paper you've already finished, a paper for another course, or a recent piece of writing from work or everyday life. Record in your learning journal any mistakes you find, along with their corrections.

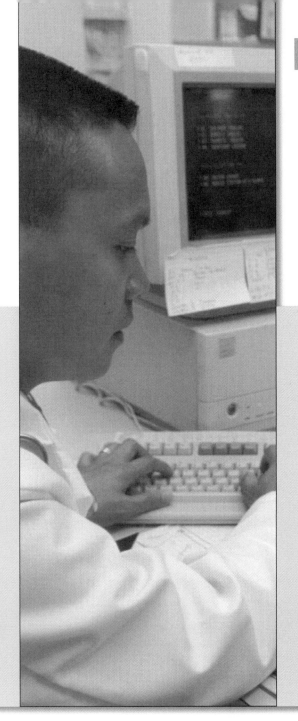

PART SEVEN

Punctuation and Capitalization

37

Commas

,

Understand What Commas Do

To understand this chapter, you need to know what nouns, sentences, phrases, and clauses are. If you need to review, see Chapter 22.

DEFINITION: **Commas (,)** are punctuation marks that separate words and word groups to help readers understand a sentence. Read aloud the following three sentences. How does the use of commas change the meaning?

NO COMMA	After you call Jim I'll leave for the restaurant.
ONE COMMA	After you call Jim, I'll leave for the restaurant.
TWO COMMAS	After you call, Jim, I'll leave for the restaurant.

Using commas correctly helps your readers understand what you mean. Commas signal particular meanings to your readers, so it is important that you understand when and how to use them.

567

Practice Using Commas Correctly

COMMAS BETWEEN ITEMS IN A SERIES

Use commas to separate the items in a series (three or more items). This includes the last item in the series, which usually has *and* before it.

When you go to the store, please pick up *milk, bread, orange juice,* and *bananas.*

Last semester I took *math, reading,* and *composition.*

Students may take the course as a *regular classroom course,* as an *online course,* or as a *distance learning course.*

NOTE: In magazines and newspapers, as well as in some business writing, the comma before the final item is sometimes left out. In college writing it is always best to include it, however, so that your meaning will be clear.

LEARNING JOURNAL
Use your learning journal as a place to record sentences with comma problems. Also write down edited versions of these sentences, with the problems corrected.

How does a comma change the way you read a sentence aloud? Most readers pause when they come to a comma.

For more practice, visit Exercise Central at <**www .bedfordstmartins .com/realessays**>.

PRACTICE 1   USING COMMAS IN SERIES

Edit the following sentences by underlining the items in the series and adding commas where they are needed. If a sentence is already correct, put a "C" next to it.

> **EXAMPLE**: The money we touch͵ carry in our wallets͵and give to other people may be covered with germs.

1. Money has been called "the root of all evil" and "filthy lucre."

2. Apparently, money actually is dirty tainted and germ-covered.

3. A recent study of sixty-eight dollar bills found five carrying germs that could infect healthy people fifty-nine harboring bacteria that could sicken people with depressed immune systems, and only four that were free of dangerous infectious agents.

4. The bills were selected randomly taken to a laboratory and tested for germs.

5. Of course, this study involved a very small localized and not necessarily representative sample of bills.

6. My mother, a highly trained, experienced, and conscientious nurse, always told me to wash my hands after handling money.

7. Once, when I was attempting to open my purse accept a receipt from a cashier and hold my change at the same time, I stuck some dollar bills in my mouth for a moment.

8. My mother was astonished concerned and a little angry as she snapped at me to get the money out of my mouth.

9. Although the study of the sixty-eight dollar bills does not reveal whether germs can transfer from bills to people survive for long periods on money, or otherwise contribute to human illness, reading about it made me realize that my mother had been right to be worried.

10. I wonder what would happen if researchers tested random bathroom doors bus seats or any other public and frequently touched objects.

COMMAS IN COMPOUND SENTENCES

DEFINITION: A **compound sentence** contains two independent clauses (sentences) joined by one of these words: *and, but, for, nor, or, so, yet*. Use a comma before the joining word to separate the two clauses.

> The words *and, but, for, nor, or, so,* and *yet* are called coordinating conjunctions.

| Sentence | , | *and, but, for, nor, or, so, yet* | Sentence. |

Tom missed class yesterday, *and* he called to ask me what he missed.

I would have been happy to help him, *but* I was absent, too.

I told him I wasn't there, *so* he said he would email the professor.

NOTE: A comma is not needed if the word *and, but, for, nor, or, so,* or *yet* joins two sentence elements that are not independent clauses.

■   **PRACTICE 2   USING COMMAS IN COMPOUND SENTENCES**

Edit the following compound sentences by adding commas where they are needed. If a sentence is already correct, put a "C" next to it.

> EXAMPLE: The population of the United States is getting older, but the number of people trained to care for the elderly is declining.

1. Working in a nursing home is a difficult job for elderly patients can seldom do much for themselves.

2. The labor is sometimes physically difficult but it can also be mentally draining.

3. Few trained nurses and nurse's aides want nursing-home jobs for the pay is also usually lower than that offered by hospitals.

4. Nursing-home workers have high turnover rates and the facilities are constantly in need of new personnel.

5. More workers will be needed as the baby boomers become elderly yet there is already a shortage of people willing to do the tough and often unpleasant work.

6. A director sometimes must hire undertrained workers or the nursing home will face a severe staff shortage.

7. Workers without education and training may have difficulty understanding a doctor's orders, so the patients' care may suffer.

8. Home health aides and hospice workers are also in short supply and the need for such workers is growing every day.

9. Solving these problems will be difficult for long-term care for the elderly is already very expensive.

10. People caring for elderly patients must get better pay or no one will be available to do the work in a few years.

COMMAS AFTER INTRODUCTORY WORD GROUPS

Use a comma after an introductory word or word group. An introductory word group can be a word, phrase, or clause. The comma lets your readers know when the main part of the sentence is starting.

| Introductory word or word group | , | Main part of sentence. |

INTRODUCTORY WORD: *Happily,* I turned in my final paper.

INTRODUCTORY PHRASE: *According to the paper,* the crime rate went down.

INTRODUCTORY CLAUSE: *As you know,* the store is going out of business.

PRACTICE 3   USING COMMAS AFTER INTRODUCTORY WORD GROUPS

In each item, underline any introductory word or word group. Then add commas after introductory word groups where they are needed.

EXAMPLE: Every year, more than two hundred motorists die in collisions with animals.

1. Along roadsides all across this country, drivers see the bodies of animals hit by cars.

2. Usually the victims are common species of wildlife, such as deer and raccoons.

3. Of course hitting a deer is not only disturbing but also potentially harmful or fatal to the occupants of a car.

4. However the deer population has not suffered much of a decline from traffic accidents.

5. On the other hand drivers in wilderness areas may accidentally kill endangered species.

6. For instance wildlife experts believe that 65% of the population of endangered Florida panthers has been killed on highways in the past twenty years.

7. Maintaining the world's largest network of roads the U.S. Forest Service tries to balance the needs of humans and wildlife.

8. To get access to wilderness areas humans, many of whom strongly favor protecting the environment, need roads.

9. Unfortunately wilderness roads may isolate populations of animals that will not cross them and kill animals that make the attempt.

10. Although expensive underpasses and overpasses have been successful in some areas at reducing human collisions with animals.

COMMAS AROUND APPOSITIVES AND INTERRUPTERS

DEFINITION: An **appositive** comes directly before or after a noun or pronoun and renames it.

For more on appositives, see pages 504–506.

Dick, *my neighbor,* is being sued by a builder.

Apartment prices are high at Riverview, *the new complex.*

An interrupter that appears at the beginning of a sentence can be treated the same as an introductory word group.

DEFINITION: An **interrupter** is an aside or transition that interrupts the flow of a sentence and does not affect its meaning.

Campus parking fees, *you should know,* are going up by 30 percent.

A six-month sticker will now be $45, *for example.*

Putting commas around appositives and interrupters tells readers that these elements give extra information but are not essential to the meaning of a sentence. If an appositive or interrupter is in the middle of a sentence, set it off with a pair of commas, one before and one after. If an appositive or interrupter comes at the beginning or end of a sentence, separate it from the rest of the sentence with one comma.

Incidentally, your raise has been approved.

Your raise, *incidentally,* has been approved.

Your raise has been approved, *incidentally.*

NOTE: Sometimes an appositive is essential to the meaning of a sentence. When a sentence would not have the same meaning without the appositive, the appositive should not be set off with commas.

The actor *John Travolta* has never won an Academy Award.

[The sentence *The actor has never won an Academy Award* does not have the same meaning.]

The lawyer *Clarence Darrow* was one of history's greatest speakers.

[The sentence *The lawyer was one of history's greatest speakers* does not have the same meaning.]

PRACTICE 4   USING COMMAS TO SET OFF APPOSITIVES AND INTERRUPTERS

Underline any appositives or interrupters in the following sentences. Then use commas to set them off.

> **EXAMPLE**: The reason for the delay, a mechanical problem with the airplane, was not mentioned.

1. Road rage as most people have heard occurs when an angry driver overreacts.

2. Another phenomenon air rage involves out-of-control and often intoxicated passengers on an airplane.

3. One famous air rage incident a confrontation between a drunken businessman and a flight attendant ended with the passenger tied to his seat for the rest of the flight.

4. Ground rage like air rage is a term used for incidents between airline passengers and airline employees.

5. Ground rage however occurs in the terminal, not in the air.

6. Gate agents the people who check tickets and allow passengers to board the plane are frequent victims of ground rage.

7. Oversold seats a common occurrence in air travel can mean that some passengers are forced to miss a flight.

8. Passengers many of whom are on a tight schedule or have a connecting flight to catch find delayed flights infuriating as well.

9. Some delayed or bumped passengers take out their anger on the gate agent a convenient target.

10. Although some airline employees may not be helpful or friendly, their attitudes do not excuse passengers who commit assault a serious crime.

COMMAS AROUND ADJECTIVE CLAUSES

DEFINITION: An **adjective clause** is a group of words that begins with *who,* *which,* or *that,* has a subject and verb, and describes the noun right before it in a sentence. Whether or not an adjective clause should be set off from the rest of the sentence by commas depends on its meaning in the sentence.

If an adjective clause can be taken out of a sentence without completely changing the meaning of the sentence, put commas around the clause.

> Use *who* to refer to a person, *which* to refer to places or things (but not to people), and *that* for people, places, or things. When referring to a person, *who* is preferable to *that*.

The mayor, *who was recently elected,* has no political experience.

SuperShop, *which is the largest supermarket in town,* was recently bought by Big Boy Markets.

I have an appointment with Dr. Kling, *who is the specialist.*

If an adjective clause is essential to the meaning of a sentence, do not put commas around it. You can tell whether a clause is essential by taking it out and seeing if the meaning of the sentence changes significantly, as it would if you took the clauses out of the following examples:

The hair salon *that I liked* recently closed.

Salesclerks *who sell liquor to minors* are breaking the law.

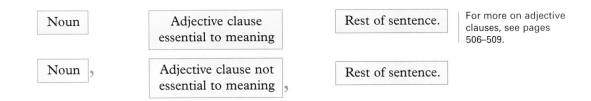

For more on adjective clauses, see pages 506–509.

PRACTICE 5   USING COMMAS TO SET OFF ADJECTIVE CLAUSES

Edit the following sentences by putting any needed commas around adjective clauses. Remember that if an adjective clause is essential to the meaning of the sentence, you should not use commas. If a sentence is already correct, put a "C" next to it.

EXAMPLE: Stephen King, who understands how to frighten his readers, has depicted evil clowns in his work.

1. The only thing that terrifies Maria is a person dressed as a clown.

2. The fear of clowns which is called coulrophobia is fairly common among children.

3. Some young children who develop this fear are not prepared adequately before seeing a clown for the first time.

4. Clowns who usually wear heavy makeup and brightly colored wigs do not look like ordinary people.

5. Clowns also make sudden and surprising movements that frighten many youngsters.

6. Most children who fear clowns will get over their phobia as they grow up.

7. Such people who may never love clowns will still be able to tolerate having them around.

8. Many adults have read books and seen movies that show clowns as evil killers.

9. Few adults admit to having coulrophobia which is most effectively treated when the sufferer confronts the fear.

10. Unlike some other phobias which can trap people in their homes or make them unable to work, coulrophobia has little effect on most sufferers who are not likely to meet clowns frequently in everyday life.

OTHER USES FOR COMMAS

Commas with Quotation Marks

For more on quotation marks, see Chapter 39.

DEFINITION: **Quotation marks** are used to show that you are using a **direct quotation**, repeating exactly what someone said or wrote. Generally use commas to set off the words inside quotation marks from the rest of the sentence.

"Excuse me," said the old woman in back of me.

"Did you know," she asked, "that you just cut in front of me?"

I exclaimed, "Oh, no. I'm so sorry!"

Notice that a comma never comes directly after a quotation mark.

Commas in Addresses

Use commas to separate the elements of an address included in a sentence. However, do not use a comma before a zip code.

My address is 4498 Main Street, Bolton, Massachusetts 01740.

If a sentence continues after the address, put a comma after the address. Also use a comma after individual elements used to name a geographical location such as a city and state.

The house was moved from Cripple Creek, Colorado, to the lot on Forest Street.

Commas in Dates

Separate the day from the year with a comma. If you give the month and year, do not separate them with a comma.

She wrote the letter on April 1, 2003.

The next session is in January 2010.

If a sentence continues after the date, put a comma after the date.

He waited until April 15, 2002, to file his 2001 tax return.

Commas with Names

Put commas around the name of someone you are addressing by name.

Don, I want you to come look at this.

Unfortunately, Marie, you need to finish the report by next week.

Commas with Yes or No

Put a comma after the word *yes* or *no* in response to a question.

No, that isn't what I meant.

PRACTICE 6   **USING COMMAS IN OTHER WAYS**

Edit the following sentences by adding commas where they are needed. If a sentence is already correct, put a "C" next to it.

EXAMPLE: The new regulations went into effect on April 1, 2001.

1. My sister asked "James do you get a lot of telemarketing calls?"

2. "Yes I do" I replied "and they always come at dinnertime."

3. She told me that in April 2001 new laws that could help me protect my privacy had taken effect.

4. I wrote to the governor's office in Albany New York for information about the telemarketing registry.

5. My address, which is 21 Highland Road Binghamton New York, has now been added to the state registry.

6. For a while I still got occasional calls that began with an unfamiliar voice saying "James I have an exciting offer for you."

7. I simply replied "No I have news for you."

8. I pointed out that on August 11 2001 I had added my name and address to a list of people who do not want to receive calls about exciting offers.

9. "As you probably know" I told my unwanted callers "it is illegal for you to contact me in this way."

10. The marketing calls had stopped completely by November 1.

Edit Paragraphs and Your Own Writing

PRACTICE 7   EDITING PARAGRAPHS FOR COMMAS

Edit the following paragraphs by adding commas where they are needed. If a sentence is already correct, put a "C" next to it.

1. (1) Everyone who uses cleaning products at home has probably seen warning labels on those products for most household cleaners contain harsh chemicals. (2) The warnings which are required by law are so common that many users probably ignore them. (3) However all cleaning products should be used with care and some of them can seriously injure children or anyone else who misuses them. (4) Drain cleaners toilet bowl cleaners and chlorine bleach can all cause serious damage to skin eyes and other sensitive tissue. (5) Glass cleaners can react with bleach to produce toxic fumes. (6) Alternative cleansers nontoxic products that can be made from items in an average kitchen are cheaper than brand-name cleaning products and usually work just as well. (7) For most cleaning jobs a solution of vinegar and water or baking soda and water is effective. (8) A plunger can often fix a clogged drain as well as a drain cleaner can and club soda cleans windows nicely. (9) As for air fresheners one expert

advises "Open your windows." (10) Economy efficiency and safety are three excellent reasons for choosing homemade cleansers.

2. (1) A few days ago I received an email that told a terrifying story. (2) At a large discount store in Austin Texas a four-year-old girl had disappeared and her mother had asked for the store employees' help in finding the child. (3) Thinking quickly the employees locked all of the doors posted an employee at every exit and systematically searched the store. (4) The child who was found in a bathroom was safe but half of her head had been shaved. (5) In addition someone had changed her clothes so it seemed obvious that an abductor had been trying to slip her out of the store unnoticed. (6) The email message which came from a distant acquaintance ended by advising me "Don't let your children out of your sight!"

(7) Later that day I was talking to my neighbor and I happened to mention the message. (8) She too had seen it and the story had shocked her. (9) Something about the story made me suspicious however so I decided to do some Internet research. (10) I found a site that discussed urban legends Internet hoaxes and chain letters. (11) On the site I discovered an exact copy of the email I had received. (12) I also learned that my neighbor and I were not the first people to fall for this hoax for Ann Landers had even printed a version of it several years earlier. (13) When she learned that she had been fooled she printed a retraction a column explaining that the story was fictional. (14) A reader wrote to her and said "Reminding people to be cautious is one thing. Scaring the pants off of them is another."

(15) After doing the research I felt better about the scary email story but I felt sad that we are so distrustful of one another. (16) Such stories can make us fear that potential abductors are everywhere. (17) Thirty years ago most parents were not usually afraid to let children walk to school alone or play outside but today's parents rarely let children out of their sight until the kids are in their teens. (18) The difference is not in the number of abductions of children a very small number that has remained nearly constant over the decades. (19) No the difference is that people

now hear about these unusual and terrifying instances over and over. (20) Eventually they reach the conclusion that these stories must be true and they are convinced that such dreadful things must happen frequently. (21) The email I had received was contributing I decided to this climate of irrational fear. (22) "Ann Landers's reader was right" I said to myself. (23) "We should teach our children caution but we can harm them and ourselves by making them believe that evil strangers are lurking around every corner."

PRACTICE 8   EDITING YOUR OWN WRITING FOR COMMAS

LEARNING JOURNAL
What mistake with commas do you make most often? Why do you think you make this mistake?

As a final practice, edit a piece of your own writing for commas. It can be a paper you are working on for this course, a paper you've already finished, a paper for another course, or a recent piece of writing from your work or everyday life. In your learning journal, record any examples of sentences with comma problems that you find, along with the edited versions.

38

Apostrophes

'

Understand What Apostrophes Do

To understand this chapter, you need to know what nouns and pronouns are. For a review, see Chapters 27 and 33.

DEFINITION: An **apostrophe** (') is a punctuation mark that either shows ownership (*Susan's*) or indicates that a letter has been intentionally left out to form a contraction (*I'm, that's, they're*). Although an apostrophe looks like a comma (,), it is not used for the same purpose, and it is written higher on the line than commas are.

apostrophe'   comma,

Practice Using Apostrophes Correctly

APOSTROPHES TO SHOW OWNERSHIP

Singular means one; plural means more than one.

• Add -*'s* to a singular noun to show ownership even if the noun already ends in -*s*.

581

Darcy's car is being repaired.

Joan got all the information she needed from the hotel's Web site.

Chris's house is only a mile away.

- If a noun is plural and ends in -s, just add an apostrophe to show ownership. If it is plural but does not end in -s, add -'s.

  The actors' outfits were dazzling. [More than one actor]

  Seven boys' coats were left at the school.

  The children's toys were all broken.

- The placement of an apostrophe makes a difference in meaning.

  My neighbor's twelve cats are howling. [One neighbor who has twelve cats]

  My neighbors' twelve cats are howling. [Two or more neighbors who together have twelve cats]

- Do not use an apostrophe to form the plural of a noun.

  Use the stair's or the elevator.

  All of the plant's in the garden are blooming.

- Do not use an apostrophe with a possessive pronoun. These pronouns already show ownership (possession).

  Do you want to take my car or your's?

  That basket is our's.

Possessive Pronouns

my	his	its	their
mine	her	our	theirs
your	hers	ours	whose
yours			

Its or It's

The single most common error with apostrophes and pronouns is confusing *its* (a possessive pronoun) with *it's* (a contraction meaning "it is"). Whenever you write *it's*, test to see if it's correct by reading it aloud as *it is* to hear if it makes sense.

■ **PRACTICE 1   USING APOSTROPHES TO SHOW OWNERSHIP**

Edit the following sentences by adding -*'s* or an apostrophe alone to show ownership and by crossing out any incorrect use of an apostrophe or -*'s*.

For more practice, visit Exercise Central at <**www. bedfordstmartins.com/ realessays**>.

> *Fevers*   *body's*
> EXAMPLE: **Fever's are an important part of the human bodys system**
>   of defense against infection.

1. A thermometers indicator mark at 98.6 degrees is supposed to show a persons normal body temperature.

2. However, normal body temperature can range from 97 degrees to 100.4 degrees, so most doctors view of a temperature lower than 100.5 is that its not a fever at all.

3. Fever's help the body combat virus's and stimulate the immune system.

4. Unless a persons temperature is raised by an outside source, the bodys regulatory system will not usually let a fever go higher than 106 degrees.

5. A fevers appearance is not necessarily a reason to take fever-reducing medication's, which can lower a bodys temperature without doing anything to fight the infection.

6. Taking fever-reducing drug's can actually make an illness take longer to run it's course.

7. Many doctors' do not recommend using any drugs to treat a fever if its lower than 102 degrees.

8. Parents should be aware that childrens fevers can go even higher than their's.

9. Some parents fears of fever are so intense that they suffer from "fever phobia" and overreact to their childrens' symptoms.

10. Fever phobia can cause parent's to give their child extra medicine, but overdoses of ibuprofen and other fever reducers can impair the livers' ability to work properly and can therefore complicate the childs sickness.

APOSTROPHES IN CONTRACTIONS

DEFINITION: A **contraction** is formed by joining two words and leaving out one or more of the letters. When writing a contraction, put an apostrophe where the letter or letters have been left out, not between the two words.

Carol's studying to be a nurse. = *Carol is* studying to be a nurse.

I'll go when you come back. = *I will* go when you come back.

Be sure to put the apostrophe in the right place.

Don does'n't work here anymore.

> Do not use contractions in formal papers or reports for college or work.

Common Contractions

aren't = are not	she'll = she will
can't = cannot	she's = she is, she has
couldn't = could not	there's = there is
didn't = did not	they'd = they would, they had
don't = do not	they'll = they will
he'd = he would, he had	they're = they are
he'll = he will	they've = they have
he's = he is, he has	who'd = who would, who had
I'd = I would, I had	who'll = who will
I'll = I will	who's = who is, who has

I'm = I am

I've = I have

isn't = is not

it's = it is, it has

let's = let us

she'd = she would, she had

won't = will not

wouldn't = would not

you'd = you would, you had

you'll = you will

you're = you are

you've = you have

PRACTICE 2   **USING APOSTROPHES IN CONTRACTIONS**

Read each sentence carefully, looking for any words that have missing letters. Edit these words by adding apostrophes where needed. Or, if apostrophes are misplaced, cross out and correct the error.

         I've

EXAMPLE: Ive never read a book that I enjoyed more than this one.

1. If youv'e ever read a book that was so wonderful you wanted all of your friends to read it, you may have considered the question "What makes a book great?"

2. Thats the question many students and teachers of literature have been asking for several years now, and they still are'nt close to coming up with a definite answer.

3. Theres a problem with trying to establish which books are worth reading: Whos going to decide?

4. Some people argue that a book shouldve passed the test of time before college students should be required to study it.

5. This requirement may mean, however, that a book written a hundred years ago is frequently taught and a newer book thats just as good is'nt.

6. Its also true that books whose authors are women or members of minority groups dont appear as frequently on lists of great books of the past as books by white men.

7. In many cases, female and minority writers of the past didnt have the money or connections to get a book published or could'nt find an audience for a book that was ahead of its time.

8. Some scholars argue that it should'nt matter what the background of the author is because great literature is universal.

9. Others think that its important to introduce college students to books by female and minority writers because books by dead white men arent going to interest a large percentage of today's students.

10. Youre probably aware that when instructors decide which books to teach, theyr'e making political as well as literary choices thatll affect their students.

APOSTROPHES WITH LETTERS, NUMBERS, AND TIME

• Use -'s to make letters and numbers plural. The apostrophe prevents confusion or misreading.

> *Mississippi* has four i's.

> In women's shoes, size 8's are more common than size 10's.

• Use an apostrophe or -'s in certain expressions in which time nouns are treated as if they possess something.

> I get two weeks' vacation next year.

> Last year's prices were very good.

PRACTICE 3   USING APOSTROPHES WITH LETTERS, NUMBERS, AND TIME

Edit the following sentences by adding apostrophes where needed and fixing incorrectly used apostrophes.

EXAMPLE: Changing the marquee was supposed to be just a few
                                                                   minutes'
minute's work.
                  ^

1. Last year, I turned down a summers worth of beachgoing to stay in town and work at the local movie theater.

2. When I had two week's experience, the manager handed me a ladder and a box of letters to change the marquee outside.

3. I was trying to write *O Brother, Where Art Thou?* and *George Clooney,* but I ran out of Es.

4. The manager gave me a box of numbers and told me to use backward 3s.

5. When I discovered that I didn't have two more os for *Clooney* and turned an 8 on its side instead, the manager told me I would go far in the movie business.

Edit Paragraphs and Your Own Writing

PRACTICE 4   EDITING PARAGRAPHS FOR APOSTROPHES

Edit the following paragraphs by adding apostrophes where needed and crossing out incorrectly used apostrophes. If a sentence is already correct, put a "C" after it.

1. (1) Some of the first discussion's of global warming focused attention on one of the gas's that contributes to the greenhouse effect: methane. (2) Like other greenhouse gases, methane helps to keep the earths' heat trapped in our atmosphere, and the temperature of the earth goes up as a result. (3) Humans are'nt the only producers of methane; its also a by-product of cow's digestion of their food. (4) For a while, many Americans knowledge of global warming didnt go much further than cow jokes. (5) As scientists' have become more convinced that global warming is real and a potential threat to human's, our knowledge of the causes of the greenhouse effect has expanded. (6) Cows arent completely

off the hook, but theyre far less guilty of contributing to global warming than humans and cars are. (7) The amount of methane produced by cows' adds up to about 3 percent of the total amount of greenhouse gases produced by people. (8) Getting a cow to change it's diet wo'nt solve the worlds warming problem.

2. (1) Some people are terribly annoyed by misplaced apostrophes, and some people are'nt. (2) In England, John Richards, a man whos annoyed by incorrect apostrophe placement, has founded an organization called the Apostrophe Protection Society to campaign for the correct use of apostrophe's. (3) He has attracted dozen's of supporters who are infuriated by signs, menu's, and other notices in public places that contain apostrophe errors. (4) One woman who joined the society carries small apostrophes on sticky piece's of paper so that she can correct signs with missing punctuation. (5) She admits that her husbands view of punctuation is not as strict as her's, and she says that this sometimes causes arguments between them. (6) An article about the Englishman appeared in a major U.S. newspaper, and afterward the papers editors were flooded with letters related to the subject of apostrophes. (7) Although a few people thought Richards crusade shouldnt be taken seriously, the majority of letter writers supported his view, and one or two couldn't wait to start a chapter of the society in the United States. (8) It seems that no matter how relaxed some people get about punctuation, there will always be some other's who want to make sure that all the *i*s are dotted, all the *t*s are crossed, and all the apostrophe's are in their proper places.

3. (1) In March of 2001, the keyless entry systems of cars in Bremerton, Washington, suddenly stopped working, and no one knows why.

(2) The cars locks were supposed to respond when their owner's pushed a button, and all at once they wouldnt. (3) After a few days wait, the entry systems began functioning again. (4) Many resident's of Bremerton, the home of a Navy shipyard, were convinced that the militarys' technological activity had affected the cars, but Navy official's denied it. (5) Other people wondered if radio transmissions might have jammed the frequency and prevented the keyless systems' from functioning. (6) Fortunately, people whose cars have keyless entry systems were'nt locked out for those days. (7) These owners simply had to resort to a backup system to open and lock their car's — its called a "key."

PRACTICE 5   EDITING YOUR OWN WRITING FOR APOSTROPHES

As a final practice, edit a piece of your own writing for apostrophes. It can be a paper you are working on for this course, a paper you've already finished, a paper for another course, or a recent piece of writing from your work or everyday life. In your learning journal, record any examples of sentences with apostrophe problems that you find, along with the edited versions.

LEARNING JOURNAL
What type of mistake with apostrophes do you make most often? How can you avoid this mistake or be sure to edit for it?

39

Quotation Marks

" "

Understand What Quotation Marks Do 590

Practice Using Quotation Marks Correctly 591

Edit Paragraphs and Your Own Writing 597

Understand What Quotation Marks Do

To understand this chapter, you need to know what a sentence is. For a review, see Chapter 22.

DEFINITION: **Quotation marks (" ")** are punctuation marks with two common uses in college writing: They are used with some quotations, and they are used to set off titles. They always appear in pairs.

DEFINITIONS: A **quotation** is the report of another person's words. There are two types of quotations: **direct quotations** (the exact repetition, word for word, of what someone said or wrote) and **indirect quotations** (a restatement of what someone said or wrote, not word for word). Quotation marks are used only for direct quotations.

DIRECT QUOTATION   George said, "I'm getting a haircut."

INDIRECT QUOTATION   George said that he was getting a haircut.

Practice Using Quotation Marks Correctly

QUOTATION MARKS FOR DIRECT QUOTATIONS

When you write a direct quotation, you need to use quotation marks around the quoted words. These marks tell readers that the words used are exactly what was said or written.

1. "My license expires tomorrow," Gerri told me.

2. I asked, "Are you going to get it renewed?"

3. "Well, I should," Gerri admitted, "but I don't think I have time to get to the Registry of Motor Vehicles. What will happen if I'm late?"

4. "Probably nothing," I replied. "I wouldn't risk it, though."

5. After thinking for a moment, Gerri said, "I think I'll take my chances."

When you are writing a paper in which you use outside sources, use quotation marks to indicate the exact words that you quote from a source. You'll then have to cite, or give credit to, the source.

> The government needs to ensure that when a company fails, employees' pensions are protected. A recent article in the *Boston Globe* reported, "When Polaroid collapsed, pension funds and employee stock programs were suddenly worthless. At the same time, however, the chief financial officer walked away with a package worth more than $2 million." (Richardson B3)

Quoted words are usually combined with words that identify who is speaking, such as *Gerri told me* in the first example. The identifying words can come after the quoted words (example 1), before them (example 2), or in the middle (example 3). Here are some guidelines for capitalization and punctuation:

- Capitalize the first letter in a complete sentence that's being quoted, even if it comes after some identifying words (example 2).

- Do not capitalize the first letter in a quotation if it's not the first word in a complete sentence (*but* in example 3).

- If it is a complete sentence and its source is clear, you can let a quotation stand on its own, without any identifying words (example 4).

LEARNING JOURNAL
Use your learning journal as a place to record sentences with mistakes in the use of quotation marks. Also write down edited versions of these sentences, with the problems corrected.

For information about how to use quotations in research papers, see Chapter 20.

For more on commas with quotation marks, see page 576.

For more on citing sources, see pages 318–321.

- Attach identifying words to a quotation; these identifying words cannot be a sentence on their own.

- Use commas to separate any identifying words from quoted words in the same sentence.

- Always put quotation marks after commas and periods. Put quotation marks after question marks and exclamation points if they are part of the quoted sentence.

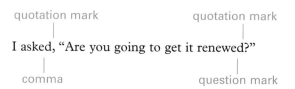

- If a question mark or exclamation point is part of your own sentence, put it after the quotation mark.

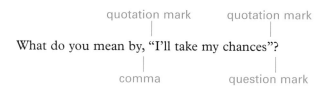

Setting Off a Quotation within Another Quotation

Sometimes you may directly quote someone who quotes what someone else said or wrote. Put single quotation marks (' ') around the quotation within a quotation so that readers understand who said what.

> The student handbook said, "Students must be given the opportunity to make up work missed for legitimate reasons."
>
> Terry told his instructor, "I'm sorry I missed the exam, but I would like to take a makeup exam. Our student handbook says, 'Students must be given the opportunity to make up work missed for legitimate reasons,' and I have a good reason."

Terry's entire quotation.

Here, Terry is including a quotation from the student handbook.

■ **PRACTICE 1**   **PUNCTUATING DIRECT QUOTATIONS**

For more practice, visit Exercise Central at <**www .bedfordstmartins.com/ realessays**>.

Edit the following sentences by adding quotation marks and commas where needed.

EXAMPLE: She asked ,"Did the Supreme Court make the right decision
in ending the Florida recount and settling the 2000
presidential election?"

1. Writing about the United States in the nineteenth century, Alexis de
   Tocqueville noted If ever the Supreme Court came to be composed of
   rash or corrupt men, the confederation would be threatened by anarchy
   or by civil war.

2. After reading us this quote, Professor Patel asked What do you suppose
   Tocqueville would have thought of the Supreme Court's decision in
   Bush v. Gore?

3. Were the justices 'rash' or 'corrupt' she continued or did they do the
   right thing when they ended the long election?

4. Natalie announced I think that more people in Florida intended to vote
   for Gore than for Bush.

5. But Roberto interrupted we can't ever know people's intentions for
   certain, so the only important question is how the Florida citizens
   actually voted.

6. How are we supposed to know that when the Supreme Court stopped
   the recount? Natalie retorted.

7. Professor Patel reminded us No one has answered my question yet.

8. Roberto said The country was suffering because no one knew who
   would be the next president, so the Supreme Court did the right thing.

9. The justices who stopped the recount were motivated by conservative
   political views Natalie fumed. The decision was obviously corrupt!

10. Why was Professor Patel smiling when she said This will be the topic of

your first research paper ?

NO QUOTATION MARKS FOR INDIRECT QUOTATIONS

When you report what someone said or wrote but do not use the person's exact words, you are writing an indirect quotation. Do not use quotation marks for indirect quotations. Indirect quotations often begin with the word *that*.

INDIRECT QUOTATION	DIRECT QUOTATION
Sophie said that the exam was postponed.	Sophie said, "The exam was postponed."
The boy asked me what time it was.	"What time is it?" asked the boy.
Carolyn told me that she had an accident.	Carolyn told me, "I had an accident."

PRACTICE 2   PUNCTUATING DIRECT AND INDIRECT QUOTATIONS

Edit the following sentences by adding quotation marks where needed and crossing out quotation marks that are incorrectly used. If a sentence is already correct, put a "C" next to it.

EXAMPLE: After being laid off, Sarita told me that "she would never work for another dot-com."

1. I loved the informal office at first, she said.

2. Sarita remembered "how much she had enjoyed setting her own hours."

3. She admitted, I have never been a business-suit kind of person, so I

liked the fact that every day was casual.

4. "But after a while, I wondered how on earth the company was supposed

to earn a profit," she told me.

5. Sarita had asked the company's founder what his plans for the future

were.

6. She began to worry when he told her that "he hadn't thought that far ahead yet."

7. "He apparently thought that people would keep giving us money just because the company was cool," she said exasperatedly.

8. Sarita told a colleague that "she was looking for a new job because she didn't think the dot-com would last."

9. I was just starting to send out résumés when I got laid off, she recalled, and fortunately I found something before my severance pay ended.

10. She told me that other people at the company had not been as fortunate as she was, and when the dot-com went bankrupt, the remaining employees were suddenly left without paychecks.

QUOTATION MARKS FOR CERTAIN TITLES

When you refer to a short work such as a magazine or newspaper article, a chapter in a book, a short story, an essay, a song, or a poem, put quotation marks around the title of the work.

NEWSPAPER ARTICLE	"Mayor Warns of Budget Cuts"
SHORT STORY	"Everyday Use"
ESSAY	"Spice of Life"

Usually titles of longer works, such as novels, books, magazines, newspapers, movies, television programs, and CDs, are underlined or italicized. The titles of sacred books such as the Bible or the Koran are neither underlined, italicized, nor surrounded by quotation marks.

BOOK	<u>The Chocolate War</u> or *The Chocolate War*
NEWSPAPER	<u>Washington Post</u> or *Washington Post*

[Do not underline, italicize, or capitalize the word *the* before the name of a newspaper or magazine, even if it is part of the title: I saw that in the *New York Times*. But do capitalize *The* when it is the first word in titles of books, movies, and other sources.]

If you are writing a paper with many outside sources, your instructor will probably refer you to a particular system of citing sources. Follow that system's guidelines when you use titles in your paper.

NOTE: Do not enclose the title of a paragraph or an essay that you have written in quotation marks when it appears at the beginning of your paper. Do not underline it either.

 PRACTICE 3 USING QUOTATION MARKS FOR TITLES

Edit the following sentences by adding quotation marks around titles as needed. Underline any book, magazine, or newspaper titles.

EXAMPLE: As we rode the elevator to our meeting on the fortieth

floor, we had to listen to a piped-in instrumental version

of "Oops, I Did It Again."

1. At the meeting, an outside consultant tried to motivate us by quoting from an article in USA Today called How to Get the Job Done.

2. Then he gave each of us a copy of a well-known CEO's autobiography and asked us to read Chapter 4, The Road to the Top.

3. Marta looked as if she were taking careful notes, but I knew that she was working on the final draft of an essay she was hoping to publish in Business Review, her favorite magazine.

4. When she had told me earlier that the essay would be called Why Meetings Are Usually Useless, I had volunteered to provide many personal examples to prove her point.

5. When the grueling meeting was over, Marta reminded me that Wallace Stevens, the poet who wrote Sunday Morning, had found a way to be creative while he spent his days working at an insurance company.

Edit Paragraphs and Your Own Writing

PRACTICE 4   **EDITING PARAGRAPHS FOR QUOTATION MARKS**

Edit the following paragraphs by adding quotation marks where needed and crossing out any incorrectly used quotation marks. Correct any errors in punctuation.

1. (1) After Michael saw an advertisement in his local newspaper for a concert featuring The Pink Panther Theme, Charade, and other songs by Henry Mancini, he immediately bought a ticket. (2) He had just finished reading a book about the film composer, and he told me that "he couldn't wait to hear the music played live." (3) He said that "I should go, too," but I stayed home and watched television. (4) After he went to the show, he told me I thought that they saved the best for last. (5) He described the final number, when a young woman stepped onto the stage and sang, Moon river, wider than a mile, I'm crossing you in style someday. (6) He knew Moon River from the movie Breakfast at Tiffany's and as a hit song for Andy Williams in the 1960s, but he had never found the song as beautiful as it seemed that night at the concert. (7) "It was an amazing evening ", he told me. (8) His description of the concert was so vivid that I went out and bought a CD called "Henry Mancini's Greatest Hits." (9) Now I regret my decision: Why didn't I go to the concert when Michael said, "Come with me; you'll love the music? " (10) As I listen to the CD, I realize that he was right, and next time he tells me about a show that "he thinks I'll love," I'm going to go along.

2. (1) "Did you know that people our age could experience a life crisis"? my twenty-five-year-old friend Beth asked as we browsed at the newsstand. (2) She showed me an article called The Trouble with Being 25 in a magazine she was looking at.

(3) I told her that "she was crazy." (4) You wait until midlife for your crisis, silly, I said. (5) I was imagining a middle-aged businessman suddenly buying an expensive sports car and driving around listening to Prince singing Little Red Corvette.

(6) Beth pointed out that she had plenty of anxiety about being twenty-five. (7) It's as if people look at me and think I'm still basically a teenager, yet I have a grown-up job and grown-up responsibilities to go with it, she said.

(8) I asked her "what kinds of responsibilities she was talking about." (9) I have rent and bills to pay, she said, and I'm trying to decide if I should take a couple of classes at night to get a better job. (10) She thought for a moment and then added, "And sooner or later I'll need to figure out whether I want to get married and have children". (11) She picked up a newspaper and idly turned the pages until she found a headline that said Confusion Reigns among Young Singles.

(12) "Wow! You're right"! I blurted out. (13) It's a good thing you read those stupid magazines, I said to Beth. (14) I was only partly kidding when I added that "she and I would never have realized that we were supposed to be having a crisis if we hadn't read about it."

(15) Let's do something to celebrate, said Beth. (16) That's why we spent the rest of the afternoon sitting around my kitchen table drinking coffee, listening to Beck singing Loser, and reading out loud to each other from How to Tell If You're Ready to Settle Down in the new issue of Cosmopolitan.

PRACTICE 5   EDITING YOUR OWN WRITING FOR QUOTATION MARKS

As a final practice, edit a piece of your own writing for quotation marks. It can be a paper you are working on for this course, a paper you've already finished, a paper for another course, or a recent piece of writing from your work or everyday life. In your learning journal, record any examples you find of sentences with mistakes in the use of quotation marks. Also write down the edited versions.

LEARNING JOURNAL
In your own words, explain the difference between direct quotations and indirect quotations. Write one example of each.

40

Other Punctuation

; : ( ) — -

Understand What Punctuation Does

To understand this chapter, you need to know what sentences and independent clauses are. For a review, see Chapter 22.

Punctuation helps readers understand your writing. If you use punctuation incorrectly, you send readers a confusing message—or, even worse, a wrong one. This chapter covers five marks of punctuation that people sometimes use incorrectly. Knowing what functions these marks of punctuation serve can help you avoid such mistakes.

SEMICOLON ;	Joins two independent clauses into one sentence
	Separates complete items in a list that already has commas within individual items
COLON :	Introduces a list
	Announces an explanation
PARENTHESES ( )	Set off extra information that is not essential to the sentence
DASH —	Sets off words for emphasis
	Indicates a pause
HYPHEN -	Joins two or more words that together form a single description
	Shows a word break at the end of a line

600

Practice Using Punctuation Correctly

SEMICOLON ;

Semicolons to Join Independent Clauses

Use a semicolon to join two very closely related sentences and make them into one sentence.

For more on using semicolons to join sentences, see Chapter 30.

> In an interview, hold your head up, and don't slouch; it is important to look alert.

> Make good eye contact; looking down is not appropriate in an interview.

Semicolons in Lists Containing Commas

When one or more items in a list contain commas, use semicolons to separate the items. Otherwise, it is difficult for readers to tell where one item ends and another begins.

LEARNING JOURNAL
Use your learning journal as a place to record sentences in your writing that should have semicolons, colons, parentheses, dashes, and hyphens. Try to find one sample sentence for each of these punctuation marks. Write the sentence both before and after you edit it.

> Jim's younger sister, Toni, lives in San Francisco; his older sisters, Patti and Lori, live in Denver; and his brother, Marty, lives in Boca Raton.

COLON :

Colons before Lists

Use a colon after an independent clause to introduce a list.

See Chapter 37, Chapter 38, and Chapter 39 for coverage of commas, apostrophes, and quotation marks, respectively.

> In the United States, three ice cream flavors are the most popular: vanilla, chocolate, and strawberry.

> I have three stops to make on the way home: the grocery store, the post office, and the police station.

Colons before Explanations or Examples

Use a colon after an independent clause to let readers know that you are about to provide an explanation or example of what you just wrote. If the explanation or example is also an independent clause, capitalize the first letter after the colon.

An independent clause contains a subject and a verb, and it expresses a complete thought. It can stand on its own as a sentence.

> Sometimes the choice of cereals is overwhelming: My supermarket carries at least five different types of raisin bran.

I use one criterion to choose a cereal: price.

NOTE: A colon in a sentence must follow an independent clause. A common misuse is to place a colon after a phrase instead of an independent clause. Watch out especially for colons following the phrase *such as* or *for example*.

INCORRECT	The resort offers many activities such as: snorkeling, golf, and windsurfing.
CORRECT	The resort offers many activities: snorkeling, golf, and windsurfing.
CORRECT	The resort offers many activities such as snorkeling, golf, and windsurfing.
INCORRECT	Suzy has many talents. For example: writing, drawing, and painting.
CORRECT	Suzy has many talents: writing, drawing, and painting.

Colons in Business Correspondence

Use a colon after a greeting (called a salutation) in a business letter and after the standard heading lines at the beginning of a memorandum.

Dear Mr. Latimer:

To: Jeffery Siddall

From: Susan Anker

PARENTHESES ( )

Use parentheses to set off information that is not essential to the meaning of a sentence. Parentheses are always used in pairs and should be used sparingly.

My grandfather's most successful invention (his first) was the electric blanket.

My worst habit (and also the hardest to break) is interrupting.

When people speak too slowly, I often finish their sentences (at least in my mind).

DASH —

Dashes can be used like parentheses to set off additional information, particularly information that you want to emphasize.

> The essay question—worth 50 percent of the whole exam—will be open book.

> Your answers should be well developed, and points—2 per error—will be deducted for major grammar mistakes.

A dash can also indicate a pause, much as a comma does.

> My son wants to buy a car—more power to him.

Make a dash by typing two hyphens together. Do not leave any extra spaces around a dash.

HYPHEN -

Hyphens to Join Words That Form a Single Description

Writers often join two or more words that together form a single description of a person, place, or thing. To join the words, use a hyphen.

> The eighty-year-old smoker was considered a high-risk patient.

> I followed the company's decision-making procedure.

> I can't wait to see my end-of-the-year grade.

Hyphens to Divide a Word at the End of a Line

Use a hyphen to divide a word when part of the word must continue on the next line.

> If you give me the receipt for your purchase, I will imme-
> diately issue a refund.

If you are not sure where to break a word, look it up in a dictionary. The word's main entry will show you where you can break the word: dic • tio • nary. If you still aren't confident that you are putting the hyphen in the right place, don't break the word; write it all on the next line.

Edit Paragraphs and Your Own Writing

■ **PRACTICE 1 EDITING PARAGRAPHS FOR OTHER PUNCTUATION MARKS**

For more practice, visit Exercise Central at <www .bedfordstmartins.com /realessays>.

Edit the following paragraphs by adding semicolons, colons, parentheses, dashes, and hyphens where needed. Keep in mind that in some places, more than one type of punctuation may be acceptable.

1. (1) The International Olympic Committee met in 2001 to choose the site of the 2008 Olympic Games the winner was Beijing, China's capital. (2) Beijing the loser to Sydney, Australia, for the 2000 Olympics by just two votes had campaigned heavily for the honor of hosting the Olympics. (3) The 2001 vote which had some vocal opponents granted the Olympic Games to China for the first time in history. (4) Those who objected to the Olympic Committee's choice had several strong reasons China has a history of environmental problems, including severe smog in Beijing as a result of coal burning factories, polluting buses, and heavy automobile traffic and, even more important, the country has been scrutinized for human rights abuses. (5) Chinese officials had announced a twelve billion dollar project to cut air pollution in the city before the Olympic Committee made its decision. (6) Human rights abuses are not as easily answered several members of Congress were among those complaining about China's treatment of political and religious dissidents.

(7) Supporters of Beijing's bid to host the Olympics believe that the Games will make China a more open society reporters, athletes, and spectators will flood Beijing in 2008. (8) Some members of the Olympic Committee including the outgoing president, said to be a strong supporter of Beijing's bid hope the vote will lead to improved human rights

situations in China. (9) There are many skeptics some argue that Beijing will see the Olympics as a reward, not as an opportunity for change. (10) Some even compare the Beijing Olympics to the 1936 Olympics in Hitler's Berlin one difference, however, is that billions of people will be watching the Games on television in 2008. (11) Whatever happens in China as a result of holding the Games in Beijing, the Chinese people strong supporters of the Beijing Olympics are overjoyed at the chance to show off their capital city. (12) Sports fans and freedom loving people all over the world will be watching China as 2008 approaches.

2. (1) In every state, there are minimum ages for driving these can range from fourteen to eighteen. (2) Eighteen year olds may have to pass a driving test, but sometimes they can renew their licenses by mail. (3) In some states, people can go on renewing drivers' licenses indefinitely or at least until they die or have their licenses revoked. (4) However, as people age, they can become less able to handle an automobile well reflexes get slower, eyesight often becomes less acute, and forgetfulness may increase. (5) Not every driver over seventy is unfit however, some older drivers can pose a danger on the road. (6) Some people argue that drivers no matter what their age should have to prove their physical and mental fitness for keeping a license. (7) Children and friends of the elderly worry about accidents involving older drivers, but they are also concerned about the effects that losing a driver's license may have on an independent minded senior. (8) As the population of the United States ages, the need to balance fairness to older drivers with traffic safety concerns is likely to grow more urgent most of us like it or not will have to face this question whether we are worried about our parents or ourselves.

**PRACTICE 2   EDITING YOUR OWN WRITING FOR OTHER
PUNCTUATION MARKS**

As a final practice, edit a piece of your own writing for semicolons, colons,
parentheses, dashes, and hyphens. It can be a paper you are working on for
this course, a paper you've already finished, a paper for another course, or
a piece of writing from your work or everyday life. You may want to try
more than one way to use these marks of punctuation in your writing. In
your learning journal, record any examples of sentences you edited, showing the sentences both before and after you edited them.

41

Capitalization

Using Capital Letters

Understand Three Rules of Capitalization

There are three basic rules of capitalization.

THE THREE RULES OF CAPITALIZATION
Capitalize the first letter

1. Of every new sentence
2. Of names of specific people, places, dates, and things
3. Of important words in titles

To understand this chapter, you need to know what a sentence is. For a review, see Chapter 22.

If you can remember these three rules, you will avoid the most common errors in capitalization.

Practice Capitalization

CAPITALIZATION OF SENTENCES

Capitalize the first letter in each new sentence, including the first word in a direct quotation.

LEARNING JOURNAL
Use your learning journal as a place to record any capitalization problems that you find in your writing. Also write down edited versions of the sentences, with the problems corrected.

Mary was surprised when she saw all the people.

She asked, "What's going on here?"

For more practice, visit Exercise Central at <www.bedfordstmartins.com/realessays>.

███   **PRACTICE 1   CAPITALIZING THE FIRST WORD IN A SENTENCE**

Edit the following paragraph, changing lowercase letters to capital letters as needed. If a sentence is already correct, put a "C" next to it.

(1) Many fans of classic films point to 1939 as the greatest year in cinema history. (2) Moviegoers that year were mesmerized by Rhett Butler telling Scarlett O'Hara, "frankly, my dear, I don't give a damn." (3) the same year, audiences thrilled to the story of little Dorothy, who clicked her heels together and chanted, "there's no place like home." (4) the films of 1939 still make movie buffs shake their heads and mutter, "they don't make movies like that anymore!"

CAPITALIZATION OF NAMES OF SPECIFIC PEOPLE, PLACES, DATES, AND THINGS

The general rule is to capitalize the first letter in names of specific people, places, dates, and things. Do not capitalize general words such as *college* as opposed to the specific name: *Lincoln College*. Look at the examples for each group.

The word president *is not capitalized unless it comes directly before a name as part of that person's title: President George W. Bush.*

People

Capitalize the first letter in names of specific people and in titles used with names of specific people.

SPECIFIC	NOT SPECIFIC
Joan Feinberg	my friend
Dr. James	the physician
Professor Clark	your professor
Aunt Jane, Mother	my aunt, my mother

The name of a family member is capitalized when the family member is being addressed directly or when the family title is standing in for a first name.

> Do not capitalize directions in a sentence: *Drive south for five blocks.*

Happy Birthday, Sister.

I see Mother is now taking classes.

In other instances, do not capitalize.

It is my sister's birthday.

My mother is taking classes.

Places

Capitalize the first letter in names of specific buildings, streets, cities, states, regions, and countries.

SPECIFIC	NOT SPECIFIC
Bolton Police Department	the police department
Washington Street	our street
Boston, MA	my hometown
Texas	this state
the West	the western part of the country
Italy	that country

Dates

Capitalize the first letter in the names of days, months, and holidays. Do not capitalize the names of the seasons (winter, spring, summer, fall).

SPECIFIC	NOT SPECIFIC
Monday	today
January 4	winter
Presidents' Day	my birthday

Organizations, Companies, and Groups

SPECIFIC	NOT SPECIFIC
Bradford College	my college
Toys "R" Us	the toy store
Merrimack Players	the theater group

Languages, Nationalities, and Religions

The names of languages should be capitalized even if you aren't referring to a specific course: I am taking nutrition and Spanish.

SPECIFIC	NOT SPECIFIC
English, Greek, Spanish	my first language
Christianity, Buddhism	your religion

Courses

SPECIFIC	NOT SPECIFIC
English 100	a writing course
Nutrition 100	the basic nutrition course

Commercial Products

SPECIFIC	NOT SPECIFIC
Diet Coke	a diet cola
Hershey bar	a chocolate bar

PRACTICE 2   CAPITALIZING NOUNS

Edit the following sentences by adding capitalization as needed or removing capitalization where it is inappropriate.

EXAMPLE: My High School had a painting by Birger Sandzen on display in an Art classroom.

1. Lindsborg is a small town in McPherson county, Kansas, that calls itself "little sweden, U.S.A."

2. Lindsborg's Restaurant, the Swedish crown, serves Swedish Meatballs at its sunday smorgasbord.

3. The Town's most famous resident was probably a swedish immigrant Artist named Birger Sandzen.

4. He read a book by the founder of Bethany college in lindsborg and came to kansas to teach at the College in 1894.

5. Sandzen intended to stay in kansas for two or three years, but he loved the great plains and ended up remaining in lindsborg for the rest of his life.

6. Sandzen taught Art, but he also taught Languages, and he sang as a Tenor with the Bethany oratorio society.

7. Although Sandzen worked mainly in the midwest, the Rocky mountains, and other relatively unpopulated parts of The United States, he exhibited widely.

8. His show at the Babcock galleries in new york received an enthusiastic Critical response.

9. Sandzen's use of vivid color showed the beauty of the natural landscapes of the west.

10. Sandzen's name may not be familiar to every Art Lover, but his paintings and engravings—which are found in private collections, at Schools in Kansas, and at the Sandzen memorial gallery in Lindsborg— are quite valuable today.

CAPITALIZATION OF TITLES

When you write the title of a book, movie, television program, magazine, newspaper, article, story, song, paper, poem, and so on, capitalize the first word, the last word, and all important words in between. Words that do not need to be capitalized (unless they are the first word) include articles (*the, a, an*); coordinating conjunctions (*and, but, for, nor, or, so, yet*); and prepositions.

For more on punctuating titles, see Chapter 39. For a list of common prepositions, see Chapter 22.

West Wing is a very popular television program.

Newsweek and *Time* often have similar cover stories.

"Once More to the Lake" is one of Chuck's favorite essays.

■ **PRACTICE 3   CAPITALIZING TITLES**

Edit the following sentences by capitalizing titles as needed.

> EXAMPLE: Kermit the Frog sang "it's not easy being green" in *the muppet movie.*

1. The television show *sesame street,* which began in 1969, was an innovator in programming for children.

2. My favorite among the show's friendly puppets, known as the Muppets, was Ernie, who liked to sing "rubber ducky."

3. The popular Muppets Kermit the Frog and Miss Piggy starred in several films, including one based on Charles Dickens's classic *a christmas carol* and one based on Robert Louis Stevenson's *treasure island.*

4. The show contained no advertising, but magazines such as *sesame street parents* and toys based on the characters brought in huge amounts of money.

5. "Elmo's world," a segment added to the show in the 1990s, introduced the small red monster who would become one of the most popular toys in history.

Edit Paragraphs and Your Own Writing

■ **PRACTICE 4   EDITING PARAGRAPHS FOR CAPITALIZATION**

Edit the following paragraphs by capitalizing as needed and removing any unnecessary capitalization.

(1) Are Pennies necessary? (2) In 2001, representative Jim Knowles of arizona introduced legislation, the legal tender modernization act, to

require that prices be rounded up or down to the nearest nickel, eliminating the need for pennies. (3) according to the group Americans For Common cents, however, "pennies are a part of our culture and our economy." (4) Should the united states keep its least valuable coin?

(5) Opponents of the Copper coin—which has been made of Zinc with a Copper coating since 1982—say that people don't like to use Pennies. (6) Although many of us are familiar with the saying, "find a penny, pick it up; All day long you'll have good luck," a majority of americans do not think that picking up a dropped penny is worth their time and effort. (7) many stores place Penny trays on the counter so that Customers can either leave unwanted pennies or pick a few up for the Cashier to avoid getting any pennies in change. (8) The U.S. mint says that there are over 130 Billion pennies in circulation, but in 2000 it had to produce fourteen Billion more—70 Percent of the total number of coins minted—because people tend to throw loose change in a jar and leave it there.

(9) Yet the penny is undeniably a part of American History. (10) Pennies were the first coins minted in the united states, in 1793. (11) Only four of these original coins survive, and they are valued at more than a quarter of a Million dollars each. (12) Pennies were the first U.S. Coins to carry the image of a historical figure: They have featured the likeness of president abraham lincoln since 1909, the one hundredth anniversary of his birth. (13) fifty years later, the lincoln memorial was added to the reverse side, replacing the stalks of wheat on earlier Pennies.

(14) Pennies are part of the culture, too. (15) Everyone has heard, "a penny saved is a penny earned," and that saying is not likely to change even though a penny doesn't buy much today. (16) Music lovers may know the popular song "pennies from Heaven," which was a hit for frank sinatra, and film buffs might have seen either the bing crosby or the steve

martin movie with the same name. (17) finally, unlike the john f. kennedy half-dollar coin, which is no longer minted, people simply expect pennies to be there.

(18) Of course, other american coins have disappeared over the years, and perhaps the Penny has outlived its usefulness. (19) But many U.S. Citizens care about the fate of the penny and don't want it to disappear.

PRACTICE 5   EDITING YOUR OWN WRITING FOR CAPITALIZATION

LEARNING JOURNAL
What problem with capitalization do you have most often? How can you edit more effectively for this problem in the future?

As a final practice, edit a piece of your own writing for capitalization. It can be a paper you are working on for this course, a paper you've already finished, a paper for another course, or a recent piece of writing from your work or everyday life. In your learning journal, record any examples of sentences with capitalization problems that you find, along with the edited versions.

Appendix A

How to Write Email and Memos

Understand and Write Email

DEFINITION: **Email,** the term used for electronic mail, is a form of written communication sent over a computer network. It is fast, and it is not time-dependent: You can send an email anytime, and the recipient can read it anytime. Like any other form of written communication, however, email requires following certain conventions. You might use email to communicate in all sorts of ways, as shown in the following examples.

COLLEGE

- You are assigned a group project, and you and other members of the group communicate by email rather than always having to get together at the same time in the same place.

WORK

- You send a group message to your coworkers by email rather than printing it out, copying it, and distributing it.

EVERYDAY LIFE

- You have a friend or family member who lives far away, and you keep in touch by email.

AUDIENCE: When you are writing an email message, consider your audience and your purpose just as you do when you are writing a paragraph or an essay. People often think of email as very informal, and if you are communicating with a friend or family member for personal reasons, an informal, chatty tone is certainly appropriate. But when you are writing an email that will go out to your instructor, other students, or anyone at work, it should be more formal.

PURPOSE: If you are writing an email to family or friends, your purpose is probably to stay in touch, and you don't need to think too much about it. Be careful, though, about what you say and how you say it. Unlike speech, email is a written document. The recipient can't see your facial expressions or hear your tone of voice. Before sending even an informal email, read it over to make sure that it serves your purpose and doesn't include anything that could be misinterpreted.

If you are writing a formal email, decide what your purpose is before you write. State your purpose clearly at the beginning of the message so that your readers know why you are writing and what they should be looking for. A formal email should have a clear topic and related points just as any other piece of formal writing does.

Differences between Informal and Formal Email

INFORMAL EMAIL	FORMAL EMAIL
Audience	
Family, friends	Instructor, other students, coworkers, or customers
Purpose	
To keep in touch	To discuss your coursework or your company's business
Tone	
Informal, chatty, familiar	More formal, concise, and to the point
Format	
• Does not need to state the purpose	• Under "Subject," states the subject of the email
• Does not need to follow paragraph or essay format	• States the purpose at the start of the email
	• Is organized so that points are made clearly and briefly (may used bulleted lists—as in the example of formal email that follows—or numbered lists)
• Needs to be reread before sending	• Needs to be carefully reread and revised for clarity and accuracy before sending
• Is not always perfectly correct in grammar, spelling, and punctuation	• Should be correct in grammar, spelling, and punctuation

EXAMPLE: INFORMAL EMAIL TO A FRIEND

From: Isabel DeSimone
Sent: Thu 10/2/03 9:48 AM
To: Lynn Vargas
Subject: Need a vacation

Hi,

This week is like never-ending! I just finished a huge data entry project, and my manager handed me this new top-priority research thing two minutes ago. Does she expect me to finish this before I leave for my vacation? Maybe she's forgotten. I sure haven't, though. I can't wait to get on that plane and leave phones, email, filing, and faxing behind for one blessed week! What's going on with you?

EXAMPLE: FORMAL EMAIL TO A MANAGER

From: Robert Sullivan
Sent: Thu 10/2/03 1:52 PM
To: Will Stepney
Subject: Visit to competing test lab   ——————— States topic

Mr. Stepney: ————————————————— Formal, businesslike

My more formal report will follow, but here are my quick impressions based on a visit to Front Range Testing Services, ——— States purpose of email
Inc., a new key player in product safety testing:

- Ample product testing support for manufacturers and distributors of goods to Europe, Canada, and Mexico; no support for South America.
- The Boulder facility has two 3-meter indoor open area test sites; one 10-meter indoor open area test site; and three RF Shielded Rooms. All seem to be in good condition.

Uses a bulleted list to present points briefly

- The Estes Park facility has an acoustical sound room and two brand-new environmental chambers.
- Rates are high—especially for testing performed at the Estes Park facility.

My complete report, which I will submit to you next week, will make recommendations for competing against Front Range and other labs.

Has a conclusion

Thank you.

Robert Sullivan

PRACTICE 1   WRITING EMAILS FOR DIFFERENT AUDIENCES

For each of the following topics, write two different emails to the two audiences indicated. Put each email on a separate piece of paper or in a separate computer file. Keep all of the emails brief. Use the list on page 616 to help you.

1. **TOPIC:** A difficult customer

   INFORMAL AUDIENCE: A friend

   FORMAL AUDIENCE: A boss

2. **TOPIC:** Two days without heat in your apartment

   INFORMAL AUDIENCE: A friend

   FORMAL AUDIENCE: Your landlord

SOME CAUTIONS ABOUT EMAIL

- Avoid emailing friends from work. Most companies regard personal use of email in the same way that they regard personal phone calls.

- Do not put anything in an email that you would not want to be seen by anyone else. Deleting an email does not make it disappear altogether, and others may have access to it.

- If you communicate an important message via email, send a hard copy to your reader as well. Also make a file copy. Too often people forget to print out copies of email communications and don't have the information available in their files.

- Do not use email to replace face-to-face or phone communications. Although email is efficient and valuable, it can isolate people from personal contact with customers, coworkers, and even friends and family.

Understand and Write Memos

DEFINITION: Memos are a very common form of internal written communication in the workplace, and you will almost certainly need to know how to write them. Because people at work are busy, effective memos provide accurate information that they can quickly read and understand.

Memos are similar to formal emails. When you have a message to communicate, your choice of either a memo or a formal email will depend on your individual situation. When you write and send a memo, make a file copy of it.

SEVEN BASICS OF A GOOD MEMO

1. It has a businesslike tone: courteous but to the point.
2. It uses the fewest words possible to convey the necessary information to the particular reader(s).
3. It states the purpose clearly.
4. It allows readers to find points of information easily.
5. It presents points in a logical order.
6. It follows standard memo format.
7. It is correct in grammar, spelling, and punctuation.

AUDIENCE: Because memos are used most commonly in the workplace, keeping your audience in mind is essential. Give the information that the reader or group of readers needs, and express it in terms that they will understand. Otherwise, you may be misunderstood, and your memo could result in errors that affect you and your fellow workers.

PURPOSE: Know exactly what your purpose is when you write a memo, and make that purpose clear to your readers from the start. You should also know what information you need to include to fulfill that purpose.

FORMAT: All memos should include the following information, usually in this order. Many companies have preprinted memo forms, and many word-processing programs have a memo-format feature.

Date:
To:
From:
Subject:
cc: (people to whom you are sending copies of the memo)

Depending on their purpose, some memos may be very brief, as in the following example.

Date: June 15, 2003
To: Tamara Shue
From: Susan Anker
Subject: Vacation time
cc: M. Weiser, Human Resources

I would like to take five days of vacation from 7/31/03–8/4/03.
Thank you for your consideration.

Memos can also be longer, but they should be no longer than it takes you to convey necessary information. As with emails, memos often make use of bulleted lists to highlight main points.

MEMORANDUM
Date: October 30, 2003
To: All sales associates
From: Karen Eisenhauer
Subject: Change in employee benefits

Effective January 1, 2004, all full-time sales associates will be eligible for tuition reimbursement benefits. The company recognizes that when comparable training is not available at the corporate training center, employees miss out on advancement opportunities. The company has established a policy with the aim of retaining valuable long-term employees. Brief details of the plan are as follows:

- "Full-time" is considered twenty-eight or more hours in a week.
- Employees are eligible to be reimbursed up to $75 per credit hour.
- Employees are eligible to be reimbursed only for those courses in which they earned a "Pass" grade (Pass/Fail) or "C" or better in a graded course.

I will describe the benefits in greater detail at our regularly scheduled staff meeting next Tuesday, November 4.

PRACTICE 2   WRITING MEMOS

On separate pieces of paper, or in separate computer files, write memos on the following topics. Use the list on page 619 to help you.

1. **TOPIC**: Announcement of a company holiday

   AUDIENCE: Employees

2. **TOPIC**: Process for evacuating the building when the fire alarm sounds

   AUDIENCE: People in this classroom

Appendix B

How to Write a Résumé and a Letter of Application

DEFINITION: A **résumé** presents your experience and skills in brief written form. When you apply for a job, you should have an up-to-date résumé that you can send to a prospective employer or carry with you to an interview. Because the quality of your résumé will often determine whether you are called for an interview, it is worth your time to put together a good one.

DEFINITION: A **letter of application** is the letter you write to a prospective employer when you are interested in applying for a position. Usually, you will send a letter of application with your résumé.

How to Write a Good Résumé

The following descriptive guide was written by Jill Lee, formerly coordinator of career services at the University of Toledo Community and Technical College.

The appearance of your résumé is very important. Use a good-quality paper, and print copies of your résumé on a laser printer. Spelling and grammar are also important. A spelling error or an obvious grammar error may eliminate you as a job candidate, so proofread your résumé carefully. Emphasize your positive qualities in your résumé, highlighting your skills and accomplishments. Within each section, list the most recent information first and then work back in time. For example, under "Experience" or "Employment" you should list your current or most recent position first, then the one before that, and so on.

A competitive résumé must be concise and well organized. Prospective employers spend an average of six to eight seconds deciding whether to give a résumé serious consideration, so you should be brief and highlight your skills and experience. Try to keep your résumé to one page.

A résumé should include the following categories of information. (See the sample résumé on p. 626.)

IDENTIFYING INFORMATION

At the top of the page, put your identifying information: your full name, address, telephone number (including area code), and email address if you have one. Include your work number if it's all right for someone to contact you there. It's important to include a number where a caller can leave a message. Each piece of information should be on its own line and centered.

CAREER OBJECTIVE

If you have a specific career objective, you can list it under this category. It should be a clearly defined, short-term goal.

> OBJECTIVE: To obtain a position as an engineering technician

> OBJECTIVE: To obtain an accounting position

Make sure that your objective matches the career opportunities available at the company you are sending your résumé to.

EDUCATION

Under "Education," be sure to correctly identify your degree(s). Include the date you received each degree, or your "anticipated" or "expected" graduation date. Under most circumstances, you should not include your high school. Note: Associate degrees do not have an -s at the end of the word *associate*.

> Associate of Applied Business/Science degree in Medical Technology, May 2000

> B.A. in Communication, May 2002 (anticipated)

Under the appropriate degree(s), include the complete name of each school you attended, along with the city and state where it is located.

> The University of Toledo Community and Technical College, Toledo, Ohio

List any relevant additional information, such as grade point average (GPA) if it was 3.0 or higher, dean's list, honorary society, or other academic honors or awards.

EXPERIENCE

List both paid employment and volunteer work or internships, focusing on the experience that is most relevant to your career objective. If you like, you can create both an "Employment" category listing paid positions and a separate "Related Experience" section listing unpaid positions such as computer-lab tutor, campus guide, or senior mentor.

Each entry in the experience section should include the following information:

Title of position

Company name and location (city, state)

Dates of employment/experience

Summarize the positions you've held, and highlight your accomplishments. Include all of the concrete skills and abilities you have developed, particularly those skills relevant to your current career goals. Remember that a résumé is not the place for undue modesty about your achievements. You need to emphasize your skills to prospective employers. Tell an employer what you can do for the company or organization. Imagine a reader who is asking the question, "Why should I hire you?" and provide reasons. Use action verbs to describe your achievements.

Developed a proposal for marketing career services.

Assisted with legal research.

Analyzed reports and data and *compiled* results.

SKILLS

List any special abilities and skills in this category, such as computer, budgeting, or math skills; language skills; telephone abilities; and equipment skills. Don't skimp on this section. Brainstorm to make a list of everything you can do. Then pare down your list to the skills that may be relevant to an employer.

REFERENCES

References are people who will vouch for you. They should be people who have worked closely with you, such as former employers or instructors, who you think will say positive things about you. Be sure to check with the people you plan to list to make sure it's okay to use them as references.

On your résumé, you may list the names, positions, companies, and telephone numbers of your references, or you may simply write "References available upon request." If you state that references are available, make sure you have people and contact numbers lined up.

OTHER POSSIBLE HEADINGS

You may have qualifications or abilities that you want to include on your résumé but that don't fit neatly into any of the categories. Don't omit them; consider adding categories to fit your qualifications, such as "Special Training" or "Certifications." You want your résumé to include any information that will strengthen your appeal as a potential employee.

■ **ASSIGNMENT** **WRITING A RÉSUMÉ**

Using the model résumé and the Checklist: How to Write a Résumé, which follows, write your own résumé.

SAMPLE RÉSUMÉ

Megan Ormsby
2005 Garden Park Drive
Toledo, OH 43612
(419) 555-0622
mormsby@hotmail.net

CAREER OBJECTIVE	To obtain a position as a legal secretary
EDUCATION	Associate degree in Legal Secretarial Technology, June 2002
	The University of Toledo Community and Technical College, Toledo, Ohio
	GPA: 3.5 (A = 4.0)
	• Dean's list
	• Golden Key National Honor Society
EXPERIENCE	**March 2000–present:**
	Legal secretary
	Johnson's Legal Services,
	Perrysburg, Ohio
	• Combined and entered expert testimony into database
	• Drafted distribution and settlement letters
	• Entered and updated claims in Lawtrac
	• Filled out and filed probate forms
	• Attended administrative hearings
	• Helped organize information for spreadsheets
	January 1996–March 2000:
	Secretary
	The University of Toledo, Toledo, Ohio
	• Developed an office procedures manual
	• Typed documents
	• Organized the office
	• Provided courteous, personal service
SKILLS	• Proficient in WordPerfect, Excel, Windows, Lotus Notes, Microsoft Word, PageMaker, QuarkXPress
	• Excellent written and oral communication skills
	• Excellent editing and proofreading skills
	• Certified legal secretary
REFERENCES	Available upon request

▨ CHECKLIST   **HOW TO WRITE A RÉSUMÉ**

Check off the items as you write your résumé.

1. **Put your name, address, telephone number, and email address centered at the top of the page.**

2. **State your career objective; keep it brief and as specific as possible.**

3. **Complete the "Education" category.**

_____   List degrees received, the date you received each degree, and the institution for each.

4. **Complete the "Experience" category.**

_____   Start with your most recent position.

_____   List the title of each position, the company name and location, and the dates of employment.

_____   For each position, particularly the most recent one, list your achievements and/or responsibilities. Start with an action verb (*Designed* a brochure using QuarkXPress).

5. **Complete the "Skills" category.**

_____   List any skills you have that are relevant to the position you are seeking (computer, language, office machines, and so on).

6. **Provide a list of references, or state "References available upon request."**

_____   Check with the people you are listing to make sure that they are willing to give you a reference and that you have their most current contact information.

7. **Revise your draft résumé.**

_____   Add any experiences or skills that you overlooked.

_____   Make sure that all information is complete and accurate.

8. **Edit your résumé.**

_____   Carefully read your résumé, checking for and correcting errors in grammar, spelling, or punctuation.

(*continued*)

_____ Leave enough space between items so that the résumé looks easy to read and attractive.

9. Print your résumé.

_____ Use a high-quality printer, or go to a copy shop to print your résumé. It is important that it look clean, crisp, and professional.

How to Write a Letter of Application

Although your résumé provides detailed information about your experience and skills, your letter of application is the first item a prospective employer sees, so it is a very important piece of writing.

SIX BASICS OF A GOOD LETTER OF APPLICATION

1. It considers your audience (the prospective employer), what information that person would value, and the appropriate tone with which to address that person.
2. It keeps your purpose (to become a candidate for employment) in mind.
3. It follows a standard business-letter format.
4. It briefly but specifically summarizes what position(s) you are interested in, what your qualifications are, and why you should be considered for a position.
5. It provides contact information.
6. It is free of grammar, punctuation, and spelling errors.

The letter of application on page 629 uses a correct business format, and its parts are labeled to show you how the letter should be set up and what it should include. Note that the writer tells the prospective employer exactly how to reach her.

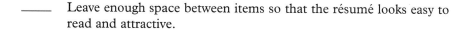 **ASSIGNMENT   WRITING A LETTER OF APPLICATION**

Write a letter of application to a company that you would like to work for. If possible, look up the address and the name of the director of human resources for that company. Use the sample letter of application and the Checklist: How to Write a Letter of Application, which follows, to help you.

Megan Ormsby
2005 Garden Park Drive
Toledo, OH 43612
(419) 555-0622
mormsby@hotmail.net

Letterhead should match heading of résumé.

January 4, 2003

Date of letter

Donna Contini, Manager
Human Resources
Carter, Jonas, and Abrams
1027 Center Drive
Canton, OH 44011

Name and title of person you are writing to

Department

Name of company and address

Dear Ms. Contini:

Uses formal *Mr., Ms.,* or *Mrs.* followed by a colon

I am interested in the position of legal secretary at your firm, which you recently advertised in the *Canton News*. Carter, Jonas, and Abrams is a well-respected, large, and busy law firm, and I would like to be part of just such an organization. I believe that my education, my experience, and my skills fit the requirements for this position.

States position writer is interested in

Makes positive statement about company and writer's fit for position

In June 2002, I received a degree in Legal Secretarial Technology from the University of Toledo Community and Technical College, where I maintained a consistently high grade point average. While pursuing my degree, I worked full-time as a legal secretary at a small firm where I am still employed. During my years there I have had the opportunity to sharpen my computer and communication skills and have learned to organize and keep track of a large number of tasks.

Summarizes experience, education, and skills

I am ready to move to a more challenging atmosphere and am eager to apply myself to a new and demanding position at a dynamic firm such as Carter, Jonas, and Abrams. Because of my experience, I can be productive from my first day on the job, though I know I will have much to learn. I am enthusiastic about that prospect.

Shows benefit of hiring writer and enthusiasm

I have enclosed a résumé that details my education, experience, and skills. I hope you will agree that they are a good match for the position at Carter, Jonas, and Abrams, and I will look forward to hearing from you. Because I am at work during the day, the best way to reach me is to call the number listed above and leave a message letting me know when it would be convenient for me to return your call. Thank you for your consideration.

Lets reader know how to reach writer

Ends with enthusiasm, confidence, and polite thanks

Sincerely,

Megan Ormsby

Megan Ormsby

CHECKLIST   **HOW TO WRITE A LETTER OF APPLICATION**

Check off the items as you write your letter.

1. **Put your name, address, telephone number, and email address in a letterhead that is centered at the top of the page.**

2. **Write the date and address of your letter.**

_____ Write the date and skip two or three spaces.

_____ Write the name, title, and address of the person you are writing to. Skip two more spaces.

3. **Write your salutation.**

_____ Write *Dear Mr./Ms./Mrs./Dr.* and the person's last name. Put a colon (:) after the name.

_____ Skip two spaces.

4. **Write the body of your letter.**

_____ In the first paragraph, state the position you are interested in.

_____ In the second paragraph, briefly but specifically state your qualifications, skills, and strengths.

_____ In the third paragraph, restate your interest in the position, your enthusiasm, and your confidence in your ability to succeed in the position; indicate how the prospective employer can contact you; and thank him or her for considering you.

_____ Skip two spaces.

5. **Write your closing.**

_____ Write *Sincerely* followed by a comma (,).

_____ Skip four spaces and type your name.

6. **Revise your letter.**

_____ Reread what you have written, and add anything that would strengthen your appeal to the prospective employer.

7.   **Edit your letter.**

_____   Carefully edit your letter, making sure that it has no errors in spelling, grammar, or punctuation.

_____   Make sure that it follows the standard format for a letter of application and includes all of the elements.

8.   **Print and sign your letter.**

_____   Use a high-quality printer, or go to a copy shop to print your letter. It is important that it look clean, crisp, and professional.

_____   Sign your name, neatly, above the typed signature.

_____   Make a copy of your letter for your files.

Appendix C
How to Make an Oral Presentation

Five Surefire Strategies

In college, at work—sometimes even in your everyday life—you will need to make oral presentations. Most people rate public speaking as one of life's most stressful experiences. A number of practical strategies, however, can help you cope with the anxiety that may be caused by this task. Knowing how to prepare for an oral presentation will help you feel confident and in control of the situation.

You have probably witnessed an embarrassing oral presentation, a situation in which the speaker fell apart and the audience felt as uncomfortable as the speaker. The following is an example of such an occurrence.

SITUATION: Jean is in the middle of reviewing her presentation notes when she hears herself being introduced. Startled, she gathers her materials into a messy stack of notes and papers, apologizes for not being ready, and walks quickly to the front of the room.

Obviously flustered, she tries to reorganize her notes, shuffling papers, frowning, and sighing loudly. She begins reading her presentation with her head down, speaking quickly and softly. Several people call out, "I can't hear you" or "Speak up."

Jean clears her throat and starts from the beginning. She's so rattled that her voice quivers and then breaks. She looks up, red in the face, and says, "Sorry. I'm really nervous."

She continues but moves too quickly from one point to the next because she doesn't want to bore people. She forgets to introduce or summarize any of her points, so the audience finds it difficult to follow her speech. People start to tune out.

Aware that she's not doing very well, Jean nervously fiddles with her hair while speaking. She reads quickly and with no emphasis, thinking that the sooner she gets through this, the sooner she can sit down. The words that looked so good when she wrote them sound stupid and awkward when she says them aloud.

As Jean turns to the second page, she realizes that her papers are out of order. There is an awkward silence as she searches desperately for the right page. She finally finds it and begins again. Soon she comes to a word that she can't read, and she has to stop again to figure it out. Still fiddling with her hair, she now looks as if she's about to pull it out.

Jean skips the word and continues. Her only goal now is to finish. But she's run out of time because of her fumbling and because her presentation was too long to begin with. The warning signal goes off, indicating that one minute remains.

This is the last straw for Jean. She looks up, bright red and nearly in tears, and says, "I guess I've run out of time. I only got through one of my points. I don't have time for what I really wanted to say." She grabs her papers and returns to her seat.

Jean sits in total misery, sure that everyone is looking at her. She can't listen to anyone else's presentation. All she can do is stare at the floor and wait impatiently for the moment she can escape from the room.

ANALYSIS: Jean's presentation was not successful because of some common pitfalls she could easily have avoided. She wasn't adequately prepared, she was obviously very nervous, she hadn't structured her presentation to make her points clear to her audience, she hadn't practiced reading her presentation aloud, and she fled at the end. If she had practiced five simple strategies for making an oral presentation, her experience would have been much less painful, and her presentation would have been much better.

Strategy 1. Be Prepared

Jean's first mistake was not being well prepared. She wasn't psychologically ready to speak, and she hadn't organized the materials for her presentation properly. Because she was busy reviewing her notes at the last minute, she was caught off guard. Her papers got messed up, she was startled, and she was off to a bad start.

ORGANIZE YOUR NOTES

Before you go into the room where you are giving your presentation, make sure all of your notes are in order. Number all pages or notecards so you can quickly reorganize them if they get mixed up, and carry all of your materials in a folder.

KEEP YOUR NOTES IN ORDER

If you want to review your key points while waiting to make your presentation, try to run through them in your head. Leave the folder closed. If you need to refresh your memory on a particular point, open the folder and carefully go through your notes until you find the answer.

USE YOUR ENERGY

Be aware of when your turn is coming, and focus on being calm. Tell yourself that you're prepared and you know what you're doing. Breathe deeply. Don't worry if your heart is beating hard and fast; that's normal. Nervous energy before a performance of any sort is natural and can make you a more engaging speaker. You just need to learn to channel that energy and make it work *for* you. Use that adrenaline to fuel your enthusiasm for your topic.

BUILD YOURSELF UP

Keep breathing normally. However silly it may seem, remind yourself of your strengths and repeat them in your head as your turn to speak approaches: "I know what I'm talking about." "I look good today." "I have a good voice." Remember that your audience isn't waiting for you to fail. Most people understand the stress of oral presentations and are sympathetic. Your audience wants you to do well.

CARRY YOURSELF LIKE ROYALTY

When it's your turn, take a deep breath, calmly pick up your folder, and walk to the front of the room. Walk slowly, stand straight, and focus on projecting a confident image. Remember that you're in control.

Strategy 2. Act with Confidence

Jean's second mistake was not acting with confidence and authority. She was visibly upset as she tried to get her notes in order, and when she did start, she spoke too softly to be heard. When her voice broke, she apologized to the audience and announced her nervousness. Practicing several techniques would have made her appear confident and in control.

TAKE YOUR TIME

After you've walked to the front of the room, take a few moments to calmly arrange your notes and papers before you begin. Relax. The timing of your presentation won't start until you begin speaking, so make sure your materials are where you need them before beginning. Remember that even professional speakers need a few moments to lay out their notes and compose themselves.

TAKE COMMAND AND GREET YOUR AUDIENCE

When you're ready to begin, stand up straight and look up and out at the audience. Remember that you are in command of the room. Pause for a few seconds to let people know you're about to begin, and wait for them to give you their attention. When you have their attention, take a deep breath and begin.

Smile and greet the audience, surveying the room as you do so. Your greeting should be simple, like "Good morning and thank you all for coming." If some people in the audience don't know you, be sure to introduce yourself. Don't forget to smile: It will relax you as well as your audience.

SLOW DOWN AND SPEAK UP

Make sure that you speak slowly, clearly, and loudly. If you're nervous, you will tend to speak too quickly, so try to slow down your speech a bit. Try to project your voice so that the people in the last row can hear you. It may feel as if you're shouting, but you won't be. Don't be embarrassed to ask if everyone can hear you. Experienced speakers often break the ice by encouraging an audience to tell them if they need to speak up.

Strategy 3. Structure Your Presentation

Jean's third mistake was not giving her presentation a clear structure, which would have made it easy for her audience to follow her key points. Your presentation should include lots of verbal cues that let people know when you're making a point, what it is, and when you're moving to another point. The structure of an oral presentation must be much more obvious than the structure of a written paper so that people can understand as they are listening.

LIMIT YOUR TOPIC

Choose a manageable topic for the time allotted, and limit the number of points you plan to make. Listening is hard work, and most people can absorb only a few key points from a speech. In any presentation, try to limit yourself to three key points, and be sure to support each of them with concrete examples. When you give more complex presentations, you may need to use visual aids—such as transparencies or slides—that will allow you to illustrate and reinforce your points.

STATE YOUR THESIS AND PREVIEW YOUR KEY POINTS

Let your audience know what your topic is and the main point you are going to make about it. State your thesis (your main point) slowly so that people understand the purpose of your presentation. Tell them: "My topic today is _____," and "I will be arguing [or showing, or explaining] _____."

Tell your audience about the structure of your presentation by giving them a preview of your key points. You might say: "There are three major points I'd like to make about _____. First I'll present _____. Second I'll discuss _____. And my third point will be _____. This presentation should take approximately three minutes, and there will be time for questions at the end."

USE TRANSITIONS TO MOVE FROM POINT TO POINT

Use transitions to let your audience know when you're finished with one point and are about to make another. In your preview, you told the audience what your key points would be. As you speak, you should give clear verbal cues when introducing and summarizing each point. Here is one way to do so.

- My first point is _____.
- Give examples/explanation.
- Repeat or summarize the first point (to remind the audience of what it is and to let them know you're about to move to another point).
- My second point is _____.
- Give examples/explanation.
- Repeat or summarize second point.
- My third and final point is _____.
- Give examples/explanation.
- Repeat or summarize third point.

CONCLUDE BY REVIEWING YOUR KEY POINTS

Let people know when you're coming to the end of your presentation by using a verbal cue such as *in conclusion, to summarize,* or *to review.* Then review your key points. Conclude with a simple, strong sentence that restates the overall purpose of your presentation—the main point you want to make.

Strategy 4. Practice Your Presentation

Like many people, Jean made the mistake of not adequately practicing her presentation. The right kind of practice would have helped her avoid the following problems: fidgeting with her hair, writing a presentation that sounded awkward when presented orally, losing her place in the middle of her talk, being unable to read her handwriting, and running out of time.

Even professional speakers practice their speeches. You should allow plenty of time to practice giving your oral presentation.

PRACTICE ALOUD

Phrases and sentences that sound good in writing often sound awkward when spoken. Read your presentation aloud—several times—to make sure that it sounds right. You'll feel silly, but do it anyway. Stop and make changes when a sentence sounds awkward. Be aware of any distracting habits you may have, such as interrupting your speech with expressions like "uh," or "you know."

Practicing aloud will also help you remember your key points. Practice your speech again and again until you feel comfortable with it. Be sure to practice aloud a final time on the day of your presentation.

PRACTICE IN FRONT OF A MIRROR

You need to see what you look like as you give your presentation, so try practicing in front of a mirror. This may make you feel even sillier than just saying the speech aloud, but it will also make you feel much more confident when you actually give the presentation.

- Stand straight and look up at the mirror frequently. Pretend you are looking out at an audience.

- Be aware of any distracting habits you have while speaking, such as fidgeting with your hair, as Jean did. Some people shift their weight from one leg to another, or sway back and forth, or stand with their legs far apart in a military stance.

- Practice keeping your hands still, except when you want to gesture or point to something for emphasis. You can hold your notes at your side or in front of you, or you can place them on a table or podium.

- Practice keeping your feet slightly apart and your weight evenly distributed. Don't shift back and forth or rock.

- If you know you will be seated when giving your presentation, you should sit in a chair while practicing. Don't jiggle your feet or swing your legs. Keep your feet flat on the floor.

PRACTICE WORKING WITH YOUR MATERIAL

Figure out in advance how you will handle your notes and papers. After you've said your presentation aloud a couple of times to get the wording right, decide whether you will work with the whole presentation written out, an outline, or notecards.

THE WHOLE PRESENTATION: If you think you need the whole presentation—written out word for word—to read from, that's fine, but you still have to practice. You have to be comfortable enough with the written version to be able to deliver it naturally, not as if you're reading, and to look up at your audience without fear of losing your place. If your eyes are glued to the page, you'll lose your audience's attention.

In addition to practicing, you should format your presentation so that it will be easy for you to find your place.

- Highlight your key points in color or by obvious underlining so that you'll be able to find your place quickly if you get lost.

- Double-space between the lines of your presentation so that you won't have trouble reading it.

- Use a large type size. If you must handwrite your presentation, make sure that you can read your handwriting.

- Write the numbers of your key points in the margin (next to the paragraphs where you introduce those points), write "conc." next to your conclusion, and so on.

- Make sure your pages are clearly numbered so that they can easily be put in order if you mix them up.

OUTLINE: Instead of writing out your entire presentation, word for word, you may want to write your key points in outline form. An outline should include all of the major points you want to make, with examples or explanations. It should also include the points to be made in the introduction and conclusion.

NOTECARDS: Some people prefer to work from 3″ × 5″ notecards rather than pieces of paper. They prepare a separate notecard for each major point, listing the point and an example. If you use notecards, be sure to number them in the top right corner so that you can easily reassemble them if they get out of order.

TIME YOURSELF

As you practice aloud, time yourself. You need to be sure that you can finish your presentation within the time limit you've been given.

If you find that you don't have enough time to make your major points, don't just speak more quickly. Go back and revise your presentation. Keep the points simple and the examples clear. If necessary, cut back on the number of points you are making, keeping only the strongest ones.

Be sure to time yourself at least twice after you have your presentation in final form.

Strategy 5. Create a Good Final Impression

Jean's last mistake was that when she ran short on time, she panicked and ended on a bad note. Practicing aloud and timing yourself will help you avoid this problem, but if you do run short on time, don't panic.

Usually speakers are given a warning signal of some sort to let them know that they need to finish. If you get a warning signal before you've said all you wanted to, remember that it's a warning. You have a little time left to conclude your presentation.

You may have enough time to finish your speech as planned, but if you know you can't cover all of it in the time remaining, you will need to condense it. Reduce the details about your points, and move to a very brief conclusion. You may need to move to your final point and give it without an example. Then say, "Again, here are the major points," repeat them briefly, and conclude.

When the time is over, look up, smile at your audience, thank them for their attention, and ask if they have any questions. Give the audience time to respond. It may take them a while to start asking questions. Wait calmly, and look around the room. If there are no questions, thank the audience again and return to your seat.

Answers to Odd-Numbered Exercises

CHAPTER 22: THE BASIC SENTENCE

Practice 22-1, page 347

Answers: **1.** Subject: thousands; prepositional phrases: of young people; from all over the country; to New York City **3.** Subject: artists; prepositional phrases: with big talent and very little money; of finding an apartment; in New York. **5.** Subject: advice; prepositional phrase: of a real estate broker **7.** Subject: apartment; prepositional phrases: with no closets and no view; on the island of Manhattan **9.** Subject: people; prepositional phrases: without money; with roommates

Practice 22-2, page 350

Answers: **1.** Subject: family; action verb: moved **3.** Subject: Miguel; helping verb + main verb: was learning **5.** Subject: he; linking verb: was **7.** Subject: plan; helping verb + main verb: had been **9.** Subject: family; linking verb: is

Practice 22-3, page 352

Answers and possible edits: **1.** I (incomplete thought); He walked down the red carpet, smiling broadly as the cameras flashed all around him. **3.** I (incomplete thought); The man who lives in the big brick house on Valley Street is my new boss. **5.** C (complete thought) **7.** I (incomplete thought); Sandra had her appendix removed, which explains why she missed class last week. **9.** C (complete thought)

CHAPTER 23: FRAGMENTS

Practice 23-1, page 356

Possible edits: **1.** Fingerprinting must have seemed like magic to the public a hundred years ago. **3.** With the development of techniques for finding and preserving fingerprints, detectives gained an advantage over criminals who did not wear gloves. **5.** Until recently, few people realized that identifying fingerprints was not an exact science. **7.** When two prints were very similar, there have even been a few cases of mistaken fingerprint identification. **9.** DNA evidence has become the new industry standard in the past decade.

Practice 23-2, page 359

Answers and possible edits: **1.** Dependent word: if. If a company mainly sells information, its workers are more likely than employees of other businesses to be allowed to do their jobs at home. **3.** Dependent word: unless. Some companies are reluctant to approve telecommuting, unless their workers already have the necessary computer equipment at home. **5.** Dependent word: while. While going to work in a bathrobe may be appealing, telecommuters sometimes discover that working at home also has drawbacks. **7.** Dependent word: so. A telecommuter needs motivation and discipline so that he or she can concentrate on the job while surrounded by all the distractions of home. **9.** Dependent word: which. Finally, telecommuters may find the pace of their work slowed down by their home Internet connection, which may not be as fast as an office's high-speed line.

Practice 23-3, page 362

Answers and possible edits: **1.** *–ing* verb: living. My grandmother spent her entire life living on a farm in eastern Wyoming. **3.** *–ing* verb: creating. She was a natural seamstress. My grandmother created shirts and dresses more beautiful than anything available in a store. **5.** *–ing* verb: using. The quilting circle made quilts for special occasions using scraps of cloth left over from other sewing projects. **7.** *–ing* verb: celebrating. Celebrating the birth of her first child, my father, the quilting circle gave my grandmother a baby quilt that is now a treasured heirloom. **9.** *–ing* verb: looking. Looking at each bit of cloth in that quilt, my grandmother could still describe, years later, the garment she had made from it.

Practice 23-4, page 364

Answers and possible edits: **1.** *To* + verb: to refuse. In 1976, several oil-producing countries in the Middle East made an agreement to refuse to sell oil to the United States. **3.** *To* + verb: to meet. American automakers increased the fuel efficiency of their cars to meet consumers' demands for vehicles with better gas mileage. **5.** *To* + verb: to stop. Oil and gasoline soon became widely available again, so many Americans made a decision to stop worrying about conserving energy. **7.** *To* + verb: to deal. The nation had to deal with energy shortages in California and rising gas prices across the country in 2001. Some people suggested that Americans needed to consume less energy. **9.** *To* + verb: to consider. Perhaps the booming economy of the 1990s convinced too many Americans that there would never be a need for them to consider a less wasteful lifestyle.

Practice 23-5, page 367

Possible edits: **1.** Many parents believe that they would know if their daughters were being abused, either physically or emotionally. **3.** A young man can be abusive without laying a finger on his girlfriend. He might monitor her actions and keep her from spending time with other friends. **5.** Around her parents, a teenager's boyfriend may act like a perfect gentleman. He may be polite, attentive, and kind to the young woman. **7.** A young woman with an abusive boyfriend may develop psychological problems that will be difficult to treat, such as low self-esteem. **9.** Friends who think that a young woman is involved in an abusive relationship should try to be supportive of her, not turn away even if she will not leave her boyfriend.

Practice 23-6, page 369

Answers and possible edits: **1.** (1/2) Genetically modified foods are being marketed as the foods of the future. (3) Correct (4) Correct (5/6) A gene from a fish may be found to make tomatoes more resistant to disease. (7/8/9) Of course, this genetic modification may have unintended effects, as in the case of genetically modified corn, which may harm monarch butterfly caterpillars. (10/11) Arguing that the long-term effects of genetic modification may not be known for years to come, some scientists urge caution before marketing genetically modified foods. **3.** (1/2) The term *organic* means different things to different people. (3/4) Organic foods are supposed to be grown without pesticides, a method that reduces a farm's impact on the environment. (5) Correct (6) Correct (7/8) They pay premium prices for organic products because they think the food is good for their own well-being, not just that of the environment. (9) Correct (10/11) The label merely means that the ingredients meet a certain government standard, while guaranteeing nothing about the nutritional content or health benefits of the food. **5.** (1) Correct (2/3) Doctors have begun to explain to their patients that antibiotics are useful only for certain kinds of infections and that patients must finish every course of antibiotics they start. (4/5) Antibiotic use in agriculture, however, has continued to increase. (6/7) The government does not even keep records of antibiotic use in farm animals. (8/9) Many cattle, pigs, and chickens get antibiotics for economic reasons, such as to keep them

healthy and to make them grow faster. (10) Correct (11) Correct

CHAPTER 24: RUN-ONS

Practice 24-1, page 376

Answers and possible edits: **1.** FS (fused sentence). The invention of cell phones made telephoning from a car possible. People could telephone for help if they were stranded on the highway. **3.** CS (comma splice). Some communities in the United States have banned drivers from talking on handheld cell phones; a driver must stop the car to place a call legally in those areas. **5.** FS (fused sentence). No one debates that drivers can be distracted by cell phones. Some people wonder, however, whether the problem is really the fact that a driver is holding the phone. **7.** FS (fused sentence). Some people worry that drivers are distracted not by holding the telephone, but by holding a conversation. A tense discussion with the boss or good news from a relative can take the driver's attention from traffic. **9.** CS (comma splice) There are differences, however, between talking on a cell phone and listening to music in the car. The telephone requires interaction from the driver, but the radio calls for passive listening.

Practice 24-2, page 379

Answers and possible edits: **1.** Subjects: penguins; birds. Verbs: live; have been. Fairy penguins, a small breed of penguin, live in Tasmania, and these birds have often been the victims of oil spills. **3.** Subjects: attempts; oil. Verbs: can be; is. Unfortunately, the penguins' attempts to clean off their feathers can be fatal, for crude oil is poisonous to penguins. **5.** Subjects: one; volunteers; Verbs: created; knitted. One of the conservationists created a pattern for a sweater for the penguins, and volunteers from around the world knitted these unusual sweaters. **7.** Subjects: most; some. Verbs: were made; were sent. Most of the sweaters were made by elderly nursing-home residents in Tasmania, but some were sent from as far away as Japan. **9.** Subjects: some; few. Verbs: made; have. Some creative knitters made tuxedo-patterned sweaters, and a few of these penguin suits even have bow ties.

Practice 24-3, page 381

Answers and possible edits: **1.** Subjects: neighbor; children. Verbs: began; were. My neighbor, Mr. Johnson, began his hobby because his children were worried about his ability to keep busy after retirement. **3.** Subjects: he; he. Verbs: made; was. He made the models out of sheet metal because he was used to working with that material. **5.** Subjects: he; Mr. Johnson. Verbs: finished; painted. After he finished the metal work, Mr. Johnson painted the house white with a green roof, just like the original. **7.** Subjects: he; he. Verbs: was working; found. While he was working on the model courthouse, he found photographs of his childhood home.   **9.** Subjects: he; family. Verbs: finished; began. When he finished his model of the old house, his family began to show the models to other people.

Practice 24-4, page 383

Answers and possible edits: **1.** (1) Correct (2) It's often easy to forget things when you want desperately to remember them. (3) You have probably had the experience of forgetting an acquaintance's name, which comes to your mind only when it's too late. (4) You have also probably been unable to find your keys once in a while because you put them down somewhere without thinking. (5) At other times, however, you may find it difficult to forget some things even though you wish you could never think of them again. (6) Correct (7) Sometimes you may find yourself forced to relive your most embarrassing moment over and over again in your mind; your memory won't let you leave that part of your past behind. (8) Some scholars believe that these annoying habits of memory evolved for a reason. It's hard to imagine, though, any good reason for developing the ability to forget where you left your keys.

CHAPTER 25: PROBLEMS WITH SUBJECT-VERB AGREEMENT

Practice 25-1, page 391

Answers: **1.** Subject: I; verb: was   **3.** Subject: I; verb: have   **5.** Subject: games; verb: are   **7.** Subject: incidents; verb: do   **9.** Subject: children; verb: do

Practice 25-2, page 391

Answers: **1.** Subject: students; verb: are   **3.** Subject: computer; verb: does   **5.** Subject: program; verb: has   **7.** Subject: teachers; verb: are   **9.** Subject: computer; verb: does

Practice 25-3, page 393

Answers: **1.** Prepositional phrase: with hearing loss; verb: have   **3.** Prepositional phrase: with words; verb: comes   **5.** Prepositional phrase: in this country; verb: feel   **7.** Prepositional phrase: in a deaf household; verb: resembles   **9.** Prepositional phrase: to the hearing world and the deaf world; verb: pull

Practice 25-4, page 395

Answers: **1.** Dependent clause: which is a job applicant's first contact with many prospective employers; verb: contains   **3.** Dependent clause: who held a previous job for two months; verb: claims   **5.** Dependent clause: who never completed a college degree; verb is OK   **7.** Dependent clause: who like a résumé; verb: check   **9.** Dependent clause: who invent material on a résumé; verb: forget

Practice 25-5, page 396

Answers: **1.** Subject joined by: and; verb: do   **3.** Subject joined by: or; verb: is   **5.** Subject joined by: and; verb: contain   **7.** Subject joined by: and; verb: contribute   **9.** Subject joined by: nor; verb: are

Practice 25-6, page 398

Answers: **1.** Subject: anyone; verb: needs; dependent clause: who wants to take college courses   **3.** Subject: several; verb: offer; prepositional phrase: of the hundreds of accredited colleges in the United States   **5.** Subject: everyone; verb: has; dependent clause: who takes online courses   **7.** Subject: someone; verb: is; dependent clause: who learns best by listening   **9.** Subject: anybody; verb: needs; dependent clause: who is considering an online class

Practice 25-7, page 400

Answers: **1.** Where are the corporation's main offices located?   **3.** How well does the average employee abroad speak English?   **5.** How many languages is the manual written in?   **7.** There are some machines that can do translation.   **9.** OK

Practice 25-8, page 401

Answers: **1.** (1) School systems around the country are embracing educational standards. (2) The idea of standards sounds reasonable. (3) Correct (4) A national standard for all American students has many supporters, too. (5) If the requirements for graduation in Oregon and Tennessee are the same, everyone with a high school diploma gets a similar education. (6) Correct (7) Correct (8) Mathematics and writing are important, but so are music and physical education. (9) How are parents, teachers, and administrators ever going to find standards that everyone accepts?   **3.** (1) Correct (2) Most school districts that have a testing program use tests that can be scored by a computer. (3) Computers cannot read, so the tests that they grade usually offer multiple-choice questions. (4) A multiple-choice test in science or mathematics does not allow students to demonstrate critical thinking. (5) How do students show their writing ability on such a test? (6) There are tricks to answering multiple-choice questions that many students learn. (7) Correct (8) Nevertheless, the quick results and low cost of a multiple-choice computer-graded test mean that this imperfect testing system is used in many school systems.   **5.** (1) Many parents who send their children to public school fear that the schools are not teaching the students adequately. (2) As these fears increase, the number of states that require tests rises as well. (3) But there have been some teachers and parents willing to resist standardized testing. (4) A few parents have kept their children home on test days. (5) In rare cases, teachers who oppose testing have refused to administer standardized tests to their students. (6) In the places that require students to pass tests in order to graduate, rebellion against tests has serious consequences for the student. (7) Correct (8) People who believe that standardized testing is not the answer are still trying to change this growing national trend.

CHAPTER 26: VERB PROBLEMS
Practice 26-1, page 407
Answers: **1.** Subject: I; verb: enjoy **3.** Subject: I; verb: work **5.** Subject: he; verb: loves **7.** Subject: they; verb: use **9.** Subject: hospital; verb: allows

Practice 26-2, page 408
Answers: **1.** faced **3.** covered; wanted; realized; involved **5.** called **7.** needed **9.** offered; failed **11.** freed; carried

Practice 26-3, page 409
Answers: **1.** Helping verb: has; verb: forced **3.** Helping verb: had; verb: attended **5.** Helping verb: have; verb: objected **7.** Helping verb: have; verb: traveled **9.** Helping verb: had; verb: hoped

Practice 26-4, page 413
Answers: **1.** am **3.** has **5.** are **7.** has **9.** are

Practice 26-5, page 414
Answers: **1.** were; were **3.** was; were **5.** was; was **7.** was **9.** were; were

Practice 26-6, page 415
Answers: **1.** built **3.** hung **5.** struck **7.** began **9.** left; stood

Practice 26-7, page 416
Answers: **1.** Two years ago, my high school set up a student court to give students a voice in disciplining rule breakers. **3.** Some of us served as members of juries, and others became advocates or even judges. **5.** Then, last spring, my friend Dewayne appeared before the student court after he lost his temper and struck a fellow student. **7.** I told the jury that he knew his violent reaction was a mistake. **9.** After hearing the verdict, Dewayne shook hands with all the jurors and thanked them for their fairness.

Practice 26-8, page 417
Answers: **1.** Helping verb: had; verb: taken **3.** Helping verb: had; verb: begun **5.** Helping verb: had; verb: been **7.** Helping verb: had; verb: bought **9.** Helping verb: had; verb: sold

Practice 26-9, page 419
Answers: **1.** have been **3.** have found **5.** have begun **7.** discovered **9.** have faced; have been

Practice 26-10, page 420
Answers: **1.** got **3.** had heard **5.** had just learned **7.** raised **9.** had warned

Practice 26-11, page 422
Possible edits: **1.** The Senate denied Robert Bork's nomination to the Supreme Court. **3.** Genzyme, Inc., is laying off eighty employees. **5.** I mailed the check last Tuesday.

Practice 26-12, page 423
Answers: **1.** Verbs: love, wanted; corrected verb: want **3.** Verbs: is, counted; corrected verb: counts **5.** Verbs: appear, had; corrected verb: have **7.** Verbs: had, go; corrected verb: went **9.** Verbs: had, can offer; corrected verb: have

Practice 26-13, page 424
Answers: **1.** (1) Since 1835, trapeze artists have considered the triple somersault the most dangerous maneuver. (2) That year, a performer tried to do a triple somersault on a trapeze for the first time and died in the attempt. (3) Only one person managed to do the trick successfully for the next sixty-three years. (4) That man, a trapeze artist named Armor, did a triple somersault in 1860 and was afraid to try it again. (5) According to circus legend, the second person to survive the triple, Ernie Clarke, once did a quadruple somersault in private. (6) Correct (7) Circus historians now believe that Alfredo Codona, a performer in the 1920s and 1930s, was the greatest master of the triple somersault. (8) He has gone down in history as the King of Trapeze. **3.** (1) The Olympic Games first let women compete in swimming events in 1912, and with that, the swimsuit revolution began. (2) Correct (3) Before that year, women had only been able to wade at the beach in bathing costumes with long, baggy legs. (4) The 1913 suits, designed by Carl Jantzen, were ribbed one-piece outfits that allowed actual swimming. (5) An engineer, Louis Réard, came up with the next major development in swimwear in 1946 while working in the lingerie business (6) He called it the "bikini," after a Pacific island used for testing the atomic bomb. (7) In the 1950s, few Americans dared to wear bikinis, which were considered scandalous. (8) Two-piece swimsuits caught on in the 1960s and 1970s. (9) The bikini lost some popularity in the last decades of the twentieth century, but it has made a triumphant return in the new millennium.

CHAPTER 27: PRONOUNS
Practice 27-1, page 431
Answers: **1.** Pronoun: they; noun: people **3.** Pronoun: it; noun: microlending **5.** Pronoun: them; noun: owners **7.** Pronoun: her; noun: woman **9.** Pronoun: his or her; noun: entrepreneur

Practice 27-2, page 434

Answers: **1.** his or her **3.** their **5.** himself or herself **7.** they need **9.** their

Practice 27-3, page 436

Answers: **1.** its **3.** its **5.** its **7.** its **9.** its

Practice 27-4, page 438

Possible edits: **1.** In a psychology study, volunteers who watched a video of two basketball teams had to count the number of passes. **3.** Later, when meeting with the researchers, many of the volunteers asked, "What gorilla?" **5.** The way the human brain processes visual information may keep people from using that information wisely. **7.** A stop sign appearing at an intersection cannot prevent an accident if drivers do not see the sign. **9.** However, the study indicates that drivers make mistakes because they may not see problems ahead.

Practice 27-5, page 439

Answers: **1.** Robots have been part of many science-fiction classics, from *The Jetsons* to *Star Wars.* **3.** In some industries, robots are already part of the workforce. **5.** A factory might use robots to handle substances that are dangerous for humans to touch. **7.** Some children who wanted a robot friend have already gotten their wish. **9.** The robot dog was first on many holiday and birthday gift lists for children in the past few years.

Practice 27-6, page 442

Answers: **1.** I met Jun when we were students in an engineering program, and he and I both decided that we were interested in business careers. **3.** C **5.** He and I were convinced that smart people with master's degrees in engineering would be useful in the business world, with or without an MBA. **7.** C **9.** Nancy said that she and Andrew had learned that people without MBAs perform just as well in corporate America as people who have business degrees.

Practice 27-7, page 443

Answers: **1.** My mother and father had a garden in their backyard, but she spent much more time there than he. **3.** The garden was filled with tomatoes because my mother loved no other vegetable as much as them. **5.** C **7.** He made sure that the leaf of each plant was free of slugs, for few other garden pests are as destructive as they. **9.** I spend just as much time as he working in the garden, however.

Practice 27-8, page 444

Answers: **1.** whom **3.** whom **5.** who

Practice 27-9, page 446

Possible edits: **1.** Experts agree that the percentage of people with allergies to foods is rising, but they don't know why. **3.** If a person has a severe allergy to a food and unknowingly eats even a small amount of that food, he or she could die. **5.** When young children have severe allergies, their parents can be extremely cautious. **7.** He carries an adrenaline pen that can save his life if he goes into shock from a food allergy. **9.** My mother will not take my brother to any public place where she can even smell peanuts.

Practice 27-10, page 447

Possible edits: **1.** The picture phone never caught on with consumers, but videoconferencing uses the same idea. (2) Anyone who has a video camera hooked up to a home computer can connect to someone else with a similar setup. (3) A person simply sits in front of the camera and talks; a person or group of people on the other end is able to see and hear him or her. (4) Videoconferencing has been wonderful for both businesses and families. (5) In the new global economy, a company often has its offices all over the world. (6) Once, a businessperson might have had to travel a great deal to keep in touch with his or her clients, suppliers, and fellow employees around the globe. (7) Today, much business can be done with videoconferencing. (8) People can attend a meeting and see their clients face to face while remaining on a different continent. (9) The technology has improved so that anyone can transmit high-quality images and sound, and the cost of videoconferencing continues to drop. (10) And of course, a videoconferencing businessperson with competitors who travel the world will save much more money than they on airfare and accommodations. (11) Correct (12) A family today may find that they often must spend time apart. (13) A parent traveling for business may not see his or her spouse or children for days at a time. (14) People move across the country from where they grew up, leaving parents and siblings behind. (15) Parents sometimes divorce, and sometimes one starts a new job far away from the children. (16) Today, however, people who cannot be present to kiss their children goodnight or wish their sister a happy birthday can see family members across the miles through videoconferencing. (17) Divorced parents whom judges have allowed to move to another state have actually been required by law to buy videoconferencing technology to keep in touch with their children. (18) Most people do not feel that videoconferencing can replace being physically present with family members and clients, but videoconferences cost less than regular visits while offering more intimacy than a telephone call. (19) If the eyes are the windows of the soul, videoconferencing helps people look into those windows and stay connected.

CHAPTER 28: ADJECTIVES AND ADVERBS

Practice 28-1, page 452

Answers: **1.** *Easy* modifies *jobs.* **3.** *Frequent* modifies *employer.* **5.** *Interesting* modifies *work.* **7.** *Responsibly* modifies *behaving.* **9.** *Financially* modifies *independent.*

Practice 28-2, page 454

Answers: **1.** most commonly   **3.** longer   **5.** smaller   **7.** highest   **9.** more difficult

Practice 28-3, page 456

Answers: **1.** *Well* modifies *known.*   **3.** *Well* modifies *contrasts.*   **5.** *Good* modifies *tale.*   **7.** *Well* modifies *lives.*   **9.** *Well* modifies *jump.*

Practice 28-4, page 457

Answers: **1.** better   **3.** worst   **5.** worst   **7.** best   **9.** worse

Practice 28-5, page 458

Answers: **1.** (1) For an average European in the Middle Ages, wearing stripes was not simply a fashion mistake. (2) According to Michel Pastoureau, a scholar of the medieval period, wearing stripes was one of the worst things a European Christian could do in the thirteenth and fourteenth centuries. (3) Stripes might be taken as a sign that the wearer was sillier than other people; jesters, for example, often wore them. (4) Prostitutes also wore striped clothes, so stripes might be seen as an indication that the person was more sinful than others. (5) Wearing stripes was most dangerous for clergymen. (6) At least one clergyman in fourteenth-century France was executed because he had been foolish enough to wear striped clothes. (7) Carmelite monks who wore striped cloaks were frequently attacked, and several popes insisted that the monks change to a simpler costume. (8) People in medieval Europe certainly took their clothing seriously.   (9) Correct

CHAPTER 29: MISPLACED AND DANGLING MODIFIERS

Practice 29-1, page 464

Possible edits: **1.** Are there energy fields in a human body that can be touched by trained professionals?   **3.** According to believers in therapeutic touch, an energy field that is out of alignment can cause pain and illness.   **5.** After a session of therapeutic touch, many patients report that they just felt better without knowing why.   **7.** In her experiment, practitioners who could not see Emily were supposed to use the invisible energy field to determine when her hands were near theirs.   **9.** Anyone who can demonstrate the ability to detect a human energy field in a similar experiment can claim a million-dollar prize.

Practice 29-2, page 466

Possible edits: **1.** Trading in a used car, a seller will get a better price if the car is clean.   **3.** With the used car looking like new, the owner can get the best price for a trade-in or a resale.   **5.** Approved as safe and drivable by a reputable mechanic, a used car may still have minor mechanical problems that do not have to be fixed.   **7.** By deducting the cost

of repairing minor problems from the asking price, the owner can be fair with a buyer.   **9.** With higher than usual mileage, a used car might need a reduced asking price.

Practice 29-3, page 467

Possible edits: **1.** (1) Shipping and handling costs can make or break a business that sells online. (2) By charging too much, a site may force customers to abandon their order. (3) A customer who feels that shipping and handling charges are too high may never return to the site. (4) Most people have shipped packages at least occasionally, so they know how much shipping costs. (5) Going too far in the other direction, some online sites offer their customers free shipping and handling. (6) The sites that offer free shipping lose money, and may have to either close down for good or start charging shipping fees. (7) Correct (8) Using these shippers, the online sites must either charge a flat fee, which may be too much or too little, or make the customer wait until the order is complete to find out the shipping fee. (9) Neither option is perfect, so a business that wants to keep expanding its customer base must choose the least unattractive solution.

CHAPTER 30: COORDINATION AND SUBORDINATION

Practice 30-1, page 473

Possible edits: **1.** or   **3.** and   **5.** so   **7.** for   **9.** and

Practice 30-2, page 474

Possible edits: **1.** Gasoline prices are lower in the United States than in many other industrialized countries, but most Americans do not find this news comforting.   **3.** In 2000, Hong Kong drivers paid over three times as much as Americans paid for gasoline, and Italians and Japanese were buying gas at more than four dollars a gallon.   **5.** Few people would argue that gasoline prices in the United States are too low, but the reason for these relatively cheap prices is that gasoline is not heavily taxed.   **7.** Gasoline taxes can help to pay for roads, or they can raise money for research into fuel efficiency.   **9.** Many Americans do not want to pay gas taxes of even two or three cents per gallon, nor do most want to spend tax money on mass transit systems.

Practice 30-3, page 477

Answers: **1.** Legal differences can cause problems in the global marketplace; businesses from two different countries working together will probably not use the laws of either country when they draw up a contract.   **3.** The American legal system is set up to deal with corporations and business interests; it is not surprising that many international businesses choose to follow U.S. laws.   **5.** International students can often find good jobs after finishing law school;

they usually know more than one language and understand more than one culture.

Practice 30-4, page 477

Possible edits: **1.** Some high school graduates want to grow up as quickly as possible; however, others want to enjoy a period with limited responsibilities. **3.** Some students are not ready to think about college yet; therefore, they should choose another option. **5.** Many high school graduates have minimal living expenses; as a result, they can experiment with careers and find out what they enjoy doing. **7.** Volunteer work allows many high school graduates to help causes they believe in; in addition, they may get to visit other parts of the world. **9.** Some high school graduates work, volunteer, or join the military as an intermediate step; in fact, they may plan to go to college after spending some time away from school.

Practice 30-5, page 479

Possible edits: **1.** because **3.** after **5.** so that **7.** where **9.** if

Practice 30-6, page 481

Possible edits: **1.** Although toddlers do not get to make many decisions, they want to have some power over their own lives. **3.** If parents want to avoid power struggles with their toddlers, the parents should learn to pick their battles. **5.** Parents should not let a child do anything dangerous even though the child may want to. **7.** Although adolescents need to establish their independence from their parents, they also want their parents to set some limits. **9.** Food, sleep, clothes, and grooming are often battlefields for children and parents unless parents remember their own rebellious phases and try to understand what their children are feeling.

Practice 30-7, page 482

Possible edits: **1.** (1/2) Lyme disease, which is carried by deer ticks, appears most frequently in the northeastern United States. (3) No change (4/5) After people venture into tall grass or brush against other foliage, they should inspect any exposed skin carefully for the minuscule ticks. (6) No change (7/8) Limiting exposed skin by wearing socks, long pants, and long sleeves gives ticks fewer chances to attach themselves; so does washing exposed skin within about ninety minutes of being outdoors. (9) No change

CHAPTER 31: PARALLELISM

Practice 31-1, page 486

Answers and possible edits: **1.** Parts that should be parallel: to remain safe/so that assistance will come quickly. When your car breaks down on the road, you should follow simple rules to remain safe and get assistance quickly. **3.** Parts that should be parallel: open the hood/put on emergency flashers/

you could tie a handkerchief to the antenna. All of the cars in a parking lot look similar, so a mechanic may have trouble finding your car unless you open the hood, put on emergency flashers, or tie a handkerchief to the antenna. **5.** Parts that should be parallel: sees no obviously broken-down car/he or she has other calls to deal with. A mechanic who sees no obviously broken-down car and has other calls to deal with may simply go on to the next customer. **7.** Parts that should be parallel: about problems/if there are delays. Most pay phones nowadays do not receive incoming calls, so the garage may not be able to call you back on a pay phone to let you know about problems or delays. **9.** Parts that should be parallel: sitting in a car/if you stand behind it. Sitting in a car or standing behind it can be very dangerous when a breakdown occurs on the side of the highway.

Practice 31-2, page 488

Answers and possible edits: **1.** Parts that should be parallel: getting the household electric bill/to pay the rent each month. For many people, getting the household electric bill is more worrisome than paying the rent each month. **3.** Parts that should be parallel: saving money/to use less electricity. Saving money appeals to many consumers more than using less electricity. **5.** Parts that should be parallel: running the refrigerator/the use of all other appliances. In most households, running the refrigerator uses more energy than using all other appliances. **7.** Parts that should be parallel: an energy-efficient new refrigerator/running an inefficient older model. However, running an energy-efficient new refrigerator uses much less electricity than running an inefficient older model. **9.** Parts that should be parallel: to buy an efficient new refrigerator/it would take to run the old one for another five years. Householders might spend less money to buy an efficient new refrigerator than to run the old one for another five years.

Practice 31-3, page 489

Answers and possible edits: **1.** Paired words: both/and. Parts that should be parallel: pressed for time/have gotten used to convenient but fattening foods. People in the United States are both pressed for time and used to convenient but fattening foods. **3.** Paired words: rather/than. Parts that should be parallel: look thinner/to stay the same size and get in better shape. Being overweight can be unhealthy, but many Americans would rather look thinner than stay the same size and get in better shape. **5.** Paired words: both/and. Parts that should be parallel: overweight people/it even influences people of normal weight. The idea that thinner is better affects both overweight people and people of normal weight. **7.** Paired words: either/or. Parts that should be parallel: surgical procedures to remove fat/they have died from dangerous diet drugs. Dozens of healthy, average-sized Americans in the past ten years have died from either surgical procedures to remove fat or dangerous diet drugs. **9.** Paired words: not only/but also. Parts that should be parallel: in good health/can be physically fit. Some people who are larger than average are not only in good health but also physically fit.

Practice 31-4, page 491
Possible edits: **1.** but also leadership experience. **3.** nor allows flexibility. **5.** and from other students.

Practice 31-5, page 491
Possible edits: **1.** (1) Some employees who want to advance their careers would rather transfer within their company than look for a new job elsewhere. (2) In-house job changes are possible, but employees should be sure that they both meet the criteria of the job and avoid making their present boss angry. (3) Because businesses invest money in each person they hire, many companies would rather hire from within than bring an outsider into a position. (4) By hiring an employee from another department, a company neither needs to make an investment in a new employee nor loses a current employee. (5) Transfers usually go more smoothly now than in the past; however, an in-house job move can still require diplomacy and honesty. (6) Experts caution employees who are considering an in-house transfer to tell their current manager the truth and to discuss their wish to transfer with the potential new manager. (7) Employees should neither threaten to quit if they do not get the new job nor spread the word around the department that they are anxious to leave their present job. (8) Employees' goals for in-house transfers should be advancing their careers and making sure that they create no bad feelings with the move.

CHAPTER 32: SENTENCE VARIETY
Practice 32-1, page 497
Answers: **1.** Annually, harsh weather takes a toll on sandy beaches. **3.** Eventually, the ocean washed the ground out from under it. **5.** Now it is going to be demolished.

Practice 32-2, page 497
Possible edits: **1.** Once **3.** Overnight, **5.** Later,

Practice 32-4, page 499
Possible edits: **1.** Paying attention to role models, some children learn aggression from people at home, at school, or on television. **3.** Acting violently under stress, his favorite television characters do not model good behavior, either. **5.** Punishing my son for his angry outbursts, I used to take away his toys and privileges. **7.** Giving him something to focus on before lashing out, I taught my son concrete ways to react to his anger. **9.** Counting to ten when he gets angry, Sean now gives himself time to cool off.

Practice 32-5, page 500
Possible edits: **1.** Staring **3.** Pounding **5.** Returning

Practice 32-7, page 502
Possible edits: **1.** Many New Yorkers refused to believe in the existence of the alligator spotted in a pond in Central Park in New York City in June of 2001. **3.** Believed by some gullible people, the rumors about giant sewer alligators were untrue. **5.** Reported by several New Yorkers, the Central Park alligator sightings were confirmed when a television news crew filmed a reptile in the pond. **7.** Surrounded by news cameras and curious onlookers, the pond in Central Park was brightly lit just before 11:00 P.M. on June 22. **9.** Surprised to find that the caiman was only two feet long, some New Yorkers may have felt a bit foolish for expecting to see a giant alligator in the park.

Practice 32-8, page 503
Possible edits: **1.** Trained **3.** Treated **5.** Asked

Practice 32-10, page 505
Possible edits: **1.** In the late 1980s, political activists, a rare breed, were almost unknown on many college campuses. **3.** Protests made the news again in 1999, the year activists targeted the Seattle meeting of the World Trade Organization. **5.** But the Seattle protests publicized the idea of social activism, a concept that was out of fashion at the time. **7.** Most social activists share a common goal, to have a positive effect on others' lives. **9.** College courses can provide young activists with a knowledge of history, an essential subject for anyone who hopes to improve society.

Practice 32-11, page 506
Possible edits: **1.** *Love and Desire* **3.** an aging but reliable machine **5.** a pile over two feet high

Practice 32-12, page 507
Possible edits: **1.** Cats produce a protein that keeps their skin soft. **3.** Some cat lovers who are allergic to cats can control their allergies with medication. **5.** Scientists have successfully cloned mice that have been genetically engineered for scientific study. **7.** According to cat experts, more than 10 percent of those people who have allergic reactions to cats are allergic to something other than the skin-softening protein. **9.** However, owning a genetically engineered cat would allow an allergic person to avoid taking allergy medications, which can sometimes cause dangerous side effects.

Practice 32-13, page 509
Possible edits: **1.** that receive hundreds or thousands of hits each day **3.** , which is becoming rarer every day, **5.** , which companies use to target potential customers,

Practice 32-14, page 509

Possible edits: (1) Lotteries, which were illegal until recently in most U.S. states, have now been legalized in most parts of this country. (3) Run by state governments in many places, lotteries allow the governments to raise money without raising taxes. (5) The money can help fund education and other projects that are necessary and expensive. (7) Many citizens who consider lotteries an ideal way to raise funds reason that no one is forced to buy a lottery ticket. (9) No change (10/11) Many experts on gambling worry about the increasing numbers of state lotteries, which are difficult for many people to resist. (12/13) Offering prizes of millions of dollars, lotteries make people fantasize about easy wealth. (14/15) Costing very little, lottery tickets are sold in grocery stores and shops in every neighborhood. (16/17) Unfortunately, the people least able to afford lottery tickets spend the most money on them, convinced that they will strike it rich someday. (18/19) In many impoverished areas, large numbers of people regularly buy several lottery tickets each week, hoping to escape boring, low-paying jobs. (20) No change (21) Many people addicted to gambling do not consider the nearly impossible odds of winning a lottery jackpot. (23/24) Hooked by occasional small payoffs of two or three dollars, addicted gamblers will keep buying tickets until they have no money left. (25/26) Promising a big payoff for a little investment, lotteries bring vast amounts of money into state treasuries. (27/28) But lottery supporters, believing that lotteries save everyone money, seldom think about the victims of lotteries. (29) No change (31) No change

CHAPTER 33: ESL CONCERNS
Practice 33-1, page 516

Answers: **1.** I am a waitress at a restaurant four days a week. **3.** There is a university close by, so many college students eat at my restaurant because it serves cheap food. **5.** They seem to think that it is okay to be rude to the person serving them. **7.** I do not make a high salary, so I need the tips from my customers to make a good living. **9.** However, I think that people who cannot afford to leave a tip should not eat in a restaurant.

Practice 33-2, page 518

Answers: **1.** Marlene and Agnetha wanted to see a certain movie after they saw the advertisement for it in the newspaper. **3.** The two women did not want to miss seeing the film at their neighborhood theater, so they arranged their schedules carefully. **5.** After they saw the movie, they were very angry that they had wasted their time and money. **7.** Then Marlene read in a different newspaper that the movie studio had admitted to inventing David Manning. **9.** Therefore, the studio executives had decided to publish advertisements that contained a made-up quotation saying that the film was wonderful.

Practice 33-3, page 521

Answers: **1.** During World War II, more than 120,000 Japanese Americans were shut up in internment camps. **3.** These soldiers often had to fight against prejudice as well as the enemy. **5.** After the war, many Japanese Americans who had been interned were ashamed of their experience. **7.** They wanted to make other Americans aware of the sacrifices of Japanese Americans during World War II. **9.** For the center of the memorial park, the designers picked out a sculpture by a Japanese American artist, Nina Akamu, featuring two cranes tangled in barbed wire.

Practice 33-4, page 522

Answers: **1.** Students who are anxious about mathematics take fewer math classes and perform worse in them than students who do not have math anxiety. **3.** It turns out that worry prevents students from understanding mathematics as well as they could. **5.** Starting at about the age of twelve, students with math anxiety become less able to compensate for the loss of working memory. **7.** Students who once thought they would never be able to understand math may someday find out that they can conquer their anxiety and cope with numbers.

Practice 33-5, page 524

Answers: **1.** Negative: We will not have to cancel the picnic. Question: Will we have to cancel the picnic? **3.** Negative: The garden does not need water this year. Question: Does the garden need water this year? **5.** Negative: Carrying an umbrella was not a good idea. Question: Was carrying an umbrella a good idea?

Practice 33-6, page 526

Possible edits: **1.** We found a faded lace handkerchief lying in the drawer. **3.** During the restoration, builders added a massive new marble stairway to the entrance. **5.** I put several delicious red New Jersey tomatoes in the salad.

CHAPTER 34: WORD CHOICE
Practice 34-1, page 531

Answers and possible edits: **1.** Vague or abstract words: little; good. My four-year-old sister cleans up her room, puts away her toys and books, and helps my parents and me with simple chores. **3.** Vague or abstract words: fun. My sister and I enjoy playing board games and reading books together. **5.** Vague or abstract words: nicest. My grandmother hugs me enthusiastically and has been encouraging me to try to get a dance scholarship. **7.** Vague or abstract words: one of my uncles; a little crazy. My uncle Mahmoud wears loud purple suits and spikes his hair straight up. **9.** Vague or abstract words: treats me; very young. He pinches my cheeks as if I were a kindergartner instead of a college student.

Practice 34-2, page 532

Answers and possible edits: **1.** Slang: fab. I wanted to express my appreciation for the wonderful new benefits package. **3.** Slang: biggie. Now that my wife and I are starting a family, insurance is a major factor.   **5.** Slang: no way. Without the company paying for this leave, I would not be able to afford the time off.   **7.** Slang: cake. I know that adjusting to fatherhood will not be easy.   **9.** Slang: give me a shout. If I can do anything to make my absence easier on my coworkers, please let me know.

Practice 34-3, page 534

Answers and possible edits: **1.** Wordy language: the fact of the matter is that. Many young people get their first ideas about interesting jobs from watching television.   **3.** Wordy language: a great number of. Shows like *L.A. Law* made the legal profession attractive to many future lawyers.   **5.** Wordy language: there are some people who. Some believe that declining respect for politicians began with television shows. **7.** Wordy language: in this day and age. Now, however, more young people are becoming interested in careers in government.   **9.** Wordy language: due to the fact that. Will the United States have a crop of idealistic young politicians in the next decade because they watched *West Wing* as impressionable teens?

Practice 34-4, page 536

Answers and possible edits: **1.** Cliché: eyes in the back of their heads. People with young children need to be constantly alert.   **3.** Cliché: have their heads examined. Parents of a toddler should rethink their safety policies if they do not lock cabinets containing household chemicals.   **5.** Cliché: in the nick of time. Parents sometimes recognize dangers moments before a mishap and stop their children from injuring themselves.   **7.** Cliché: mortal fears. Parents worry about their young children running into traffic to chase a ball.   **9.** Cliché: to keep their hands to themselves. Children must learn not to touch the weapon and to leave the area immediately if they find a gun in someone's home.

Practice 34-5, page 537

Possible edits: (1) Being the chief executive officer at a major American corporation almost always pays extremely well. (3) Even if the company performs poorly and the CEO gets fired, he (and it is almost always a man) often gets a severance package that is worth additional millions. (5) This ratio is enormous compared with the ratios in other industrialized countries. (7) Are American CEOs really exceptional? (9) In fact, highly paid CEOs can rarely do what corporate directors hope. (11) There is no guarantee that these men will be able to make another business succeed. (13) Then the corporation would be able to spend a few million dollars less on its chief officer. (15) The problem with promoting a

CEO from within the company is that few companies want to take risks. (17) Company directors think that their stockholders expect the companies to bring in a highly paid outsider. (19) Of course, most CEOs brought in from elsewhere also fail to satisfy the shareholders, but the corporate boards can at least reassure themselves that their choice has a track record when he arrives. (21) However, few corporate boards of directors are willing to look anywhere other than conventional places for their next leaders.

CHAPTER 35: COMMONLY CONFUSED WORDS

Practice 35-1, page 550

Answers: **1.** their **3.** find **5.** an; except **7.** write **9.** though; effect

Practice 35-2, page 551

Answers: **1.** (1) Most people know that Americans love to drive their cars. (2) However, many people may not be conscious of how much the government does to support our car culture. (3) For instance, the United States would never have had so many good highways without federal and state assistance for road construction and maintenance. (4) New highways are usually paid for mainly by tax money. (5) It is rare for a new road to be paid for with tolls, which would come exclusively from the people driving on it. (6) Americans also expect their roads to be well maintained, and they may write to their representatives to complain about potholes and aging road surfaces. (7) The government is even responsible for keeping gas prices lower here than in most other industrialized nations. (8) Few people mind that the government assists drivers in these ways. (9) Some would argue that it's a government's job to help pay for transportation. (10) However, other forms of transportation in this country are often passed over when Congress hands out funds. (11) Amtrak, the U.S. railroad, will soon lose all government funds, even though many government officials are skeptical of its ability to keep operating without government assistance. (12) Except for a few places like New York and San Francisco, most U.S. cities do not have good mass transit systems. (13) Americans whose travels have taken them to certain parts of the world praise the national train systems and city transit systems they find there. (14) As traffic gets worse in our nation's urban and suburban areas, some people find it odd that the United States does not invest more in transportation that would allow people to leave their cars at home.

CHAPTER 36: SPELLING

Practice 36-2, page 562

Answers: **1.** (1) Anyone interested in weird events should visit New York City on October 31, when the biggest Halloween parade in the country takes place. (2) Everyone in the city, it seems, marches in the parade, yet there are still an estimated two million people watching from the side-walks. (3) The parade had its beginnings in Greenwich Village, and original parade-goers walked though the small, winding streets of that old New York neighborhood. (4) By now the parade has gotten so large that it has to go down one of the city's broad avenues. (5) The Halloween parade surprises a lot of people who see it for the first time. (6) The merriment begins early in the evening, as costumed paraders line up. (7) You're likely to see a huge group of friends dressed as one hundred and one dalmatians or perhaps some comically exaggerated versions of government officials. (8) Every kind of costume is permitted in the parade, and some people attend skimpily dressed, apparently without embarrassment, in spite of the October chill. (9) For a fascinating look at how strangely people can behave on Halloween, the New York City Halloween parade is the place to be.

CHAPTER 37: COMMAS
Practice 37-1, page 568
Answers: **1.** C **3.** A recent study of sixty-eight dollar bills found five carrying germs that could infect healthy people, fifty-nine harboring bacteria that could sicken people with depressed immune systems, and only four that were free of dangerous infectious agents. **5.** Of course, this study involved a very small, localized, and not necessarily representative sample of bills. **7.** Once, when I was attempting to open my purse, accept a receipt from a cashier, and hold my change at the same time, I stuck some dollar bills in my mouth for a moment. **9.** Although the study of the sixty-eight dollar bills does not reveal whether germs can transfer from bills to people, survive for long periods on money, or otherwise contribute to human illness, reading about it made me realize that my mother had been right to be worried.

Practice 37-2, page 570
Answers: **1.** Working in a nursing home is a difficult job, for elderly patients can seldom do much for themselves. **3.** Few trained nurses and nurse's aides want nursing-home jobs, for the pay is also usually lower than that offered by hospitals. **5.** More workers will be needed as the baby boomers become elderly, yet there is already a shortage of people willing to do the tough and often unpleasant work. **7.** C **9.** Solving these problems will be difficult, for long-term care for the elderly is already very expensive.

Practice 37-3, page 571
Answers: **1.** Along roadsides all across this country, drivers see the bodies of animals hit by cars. **3.** Of course, hitting a deer is not only disturbing but also potentially harmful or fatal to the occupants of a car. **5.** On the other hand, drivers in wilderness areas may accidentally kill endangered species. **7.** Maintaining the world's largest network of roads, the U.S. Forest Service tries to balance the needs of humans and wildlife. **9.** Unfortunately, wilderness roads may isolate populations of animals that will not cross them and kill animals that make the attempt.

Practice 37-4, page 573
Answers: **1.** Road rage, as most people have heard, occurs when an angry driver overreacts. **3.** One famous air rage incident, a confrontation between a drunken businessman and a flight attendant, ended with the passenger tied to his seat for the rest of the flight. **5.** Ground rage, however, occurs in the terminal, not in the air. **7.** Oversold seats, a common occurrence in air travel, can mean that some passengers are forced to miss a flight. **9.** Some delayed or bumped passengers take out their anger on the gate agent, a convenient target.

Practice 37-5, page 575
Answers: **1.** C **3.** C **5.** C **7.** Such people, who may never love clowns, will still be able to tolerate having them around. **9.** Few adults admit to having coulrophobia, which is most effectively treated when the sufferer confronts the fear.

Practice 37-6, page 577
Answers: **1.** My sister asked, "James, do you get a lot of telemarketing calls?" **3.** She told me that in April 2001, new laws that could help me protect my privacy had taken effect. **5.** My address, which is 21 Highland Road, Binghamton, New York, has now been added to the state registry. **7.** I simply replied, "No, I have news for you." **9.** "As you probably know," I told my unwanted callers, "it is illegal for you to contact me in this way."

Practice 37-7, page 578
Answers: **1.** (1) Everyone who uses cleaning products at home has probably seen warning labels on those products, for most household cleaners contain harsh chemicals. (2) The warnings, which are required by law, are so common that many users probably ignore them. (3) However, all cleaning products should be used with care, and some of them can seriously injure children or anyone else who misuses them. (4) Drain cleaners, toilet bowl cleaners, and chlorine bleach can all cause serious damage to skin, eyes, and other sensitive tissue. (5) Glass cleaners can react with bleach to produce toxic fumes. (6) Alternative cleansers, nontoxic products that can be made from items in an average kitchen, are cheaper than brand-name cleaning products and usually work just as well. (7) For most cleaning jobs, a solution of vinegar and water or baking soda

and water is effective. (8) A plunger can often fix a clogged drain as well as a drain cleaner can, and club soda cleans windows nicely. (9) As for air fresheners, one expert advises, "Open your windows." (10) Economy, efficiency, and safety are three excellent reasons for choosing home-made cleansers.

CHAPTER 38: APOSTROPHES

Practice 38-1, page 583

Answers: **1.** A thermometer's indicator mark at 98.6 degrees is supposed to show a person's normal body temperature. **3.** Fevers help the body combat viruses and stimulate the immune system. **5.** A fever's appearance is not necessarily a reason to take fever-reducing medications, which can lower a body's temperature without doing anything to fight the infection. **7.** Many doctors do not recommend using any drugs to treat a fever if it's lower than 102 degrees. **9.** Some parents' fears of fever are so intense that they suffer from "fever phobia" and overreact to their children's symptoms.

Practice 38-2, page 585

Answers: **1.** If you've ever read a book that was so wonderful you wanted all of your friends to read it, you may have considered the question "What makes a book great?" **3.** There's a problem with trying to establish which books are worth reading: Who's going to decide? **5.** This requirement may mean, however, that a book written a hundred years ago is frequently taught and a newer book that's just as good isn't. **7.** In many cases, female and minority writers of the past didn't have the money or connections to get a book published or couldn't find an audience for a book that was ahead of its time. **9.** Others think that it's important to introduce college students to books by female and minority writers because books by dead white men aren't going to interest a large percentage of today's students.

Practice 38-3, page 586

Answers: **1.** Last year, I turned down a summer's worth of beachgoing to stay in town and work at the local movie theater. **3.** I was trying to write *O Brother, Where Art Thou?* and *George Clooney,* but I ran out of *E*'s. **5.** When I discovered that I didn't have two more *o*'s for *Clooney* and turned an *8* on its side instead, the manager told me I would go far in the movie business.

Practice 38-4, page 587

Answers: **1.** (1) Some of the first discussions of global warming focused attention on one of the gases that contributes to the greenhouse effect: methane. (2) Like other greenhouse gases, methane helps to keep the earth's heat trapped in our atmosphere, and the temperature of the earth goes up as a result. (3) Humans aren't the only producers of methane; it's also a by-product of cows' digestion of their food. (4) For a while, many Americans' knowledge of global warming didn't go much further than cow jokes. (5) As scientists have become more convinced that global warming is real and a potential threat to humans, our knowledge of the causes of the greenhouse effect has expanded. (6) Cows aren't completely off the hook, but they're far less guilty of contributing to global warming than humans and cars are. (7) The amount of methane produced by cows adds up to about 3 percent of the total amount of greenhouse gases produced by people. (8) Getting a cow to change its diet won't solve the world's warming problem. **3.** (1) In March of 2001, the keyless entry systems of cars in Bremerton, Washington, suddenly stopped working, and no one knows why. (2) The cars' locks were supposed to respond when their owners pushed a button, and all at once they wouldn't. (3) After a few days' wait, the entry systems began functioning again. (4) Many residents of Bremerton, the home of a Navy shipyard, were convinced that the military's technological activity had affected the cars, but Navy officials denied it. (5) Other people wondered if radio transmissions might have jammed the frequency and prevented the keyless systems from functioning. (6) Fortunately, people whose cars have keyless entry systems weren't locked out for those days. (7) These owners simply had to resort to a backup system to open and lock their cars — it's called a "key."

CHAPTER 39: QUOTATION MARKS

Practice 39-1, page 592

Answers: **1.** Writing about the United States in the nineteenth century, Alexis de Tocqueville noted, "If ever the Supreme Court came to be composed of rash or corrupt men, the confederation would be threatened by anarchy or by civil war." **3.** "Were the justices 'rash or corrupt,'" she continued, "or did they do the right thing when they ended the long election?" **5.** "But," Roberto interrupted, "we can't ever know people's intentions for certain, so the only important question is how the Florida citizens actually voted." **7.** Professor Patel reminded us, "No one has answered my question yet." **9.** "The justices who stopped the recount were motivated by conservative political views," Natalie fumed. "The decision was obviously corrupt!"

Practice 39-2, page 594

Answers: **1.** "I loved the informal office at first," she said. **3.** She admitted, "I have never been a business-suit kind of person, so I liked the fact that every day was casual." **5.** C **7.** C **9.** "I was just starting to send out résumés when I got laid off," she recalled, "and fortunately I found something before my severance pay ended."

Practice 39-3, page 596

Answers: **1.** At the meeting, an outside consultant tried to motivate us by quoting from an article in USA Today called, "How to Get the Job Done." **3.** Marta looked as if she were taking careful notes, but I knew that she was working on the final draft of an essay she was hoping to publish in Business Review, her favorite magazine. **5.** When the grueling meeting was over, Marta reminded me that Wallace Stevens, the poet who wrote "Sunday Morning," had found a way to be creative while he spent his days working at an insurance company.

Practice 39-4, page 597

Answers: **1.** (1) After Michael saw an advertisement in his local newspaper for a concert featuring "The Pink Panther Theme," "Charade," and other songs by Henry Mancini, he immediately bought a ticket. (2) He had just finished reading a book about the film composer, and he told me that he couldn't wait to hear the music played live. (3) He said that I should go, too, but I stayed home and watched television. (4) After he went to the show, he told me, "I thought that they saved the best for last." (5) He described the final number, when a young woman stepped onto the stage and sang, "Moon river, wider than a mile, I'm crossing you in style someday." (6) He knew "Moon River" from the movie Breakfast at Tiffany's and as a hit song for Andy Williams in the 1960s, but he had never found the song as beautiful as it seemed that night at the concert. (7) "It was an amazing evening," he told me. (8) His description of the concert was so vivid that I went out and bought a CD called Henry Mancini's Greatest Hits. (9) Now I regret my decision: Why didn't I go to the concert when Michael said, "Come with me; you'll love the music"? (10) As I listen to the CD, I realize that he was right, and next time he tells me about a show that he thinks I'll love, I'm going to go along.

CHAPTER 40: OTHER PUNCTUATION

Practice 40-1, page 604

Possible edits: **1.** (1) The International Olympic Committee met in 2001 to choose the site of the 2008 Olympic Games; the winner was Beijing, China's capital. (2) Beijing (the loser to Sydney, Australia for the 2000 Olympics by just two votes) had campaigned heavily for the honor of hosting the Olympics. (3) The 2001 vote—which had some vocal opponents—granted the Olympic Games to China for the first time in history. (4) Those who objected to the Olympic Committee's choice had several strong reasons: China has a history of environmental problems, including severe smog in Beijing as a result of coal-burning factories, polluting buses, and heavy automobile traffic; and, even more important, the country has been scrutinized for human rights abuses. (5) Chinese officials had announced a twelve-

billion-dollar project to cut air pollution in the city before the Olympic Committee made its decision. (6) Human rights abuses are not as easily answered; several members of Congress were among those complaining about China's treatment of political and religious dissidents. (7) Supporters of Beijing's bid to host the Olympics believe that the Games will make China a more open society: Reporters, athletes, and spectators will flood Beijing in 2008. (8) Some members of the Olympic Committee (including the outgoing president, said to be a strong supporter of Beijing's bid) hope the vote will lead to improved human rights situations in China. (9) There are many skeptics; some argue that Beijing will see the Olympics as a reward, not as an opportunity for change. (10) Some even compare the Beijing Olympics to the 1936 Olympics in Hitler's Berlin; one difference, however, is that billions of people will be watching the Games on television in 2008. (11) Whatever happens in China as a result of holding the Games in Beijing, the Chinese people—strong supporters of the Beijing Olympics—are overjoyed at the chance to show off their capital city. (12) Sports fans and freedom-loving people all over the world will be watching China as 2008 approaches.

CHAPTER 41: CAPITALIZATION

Practice 41-1, page 608

Answers: (1) C (3) The same year, audiences thrilled to the story of little Dorothy, who clicked her heels together and chanted, "There's no place like home."

Practice 41-2, page 610

Answers: **1.** Lindsborg is a small town in McPherson County, Kansas, that calls itself "Little Sweden, U.S.A." **3.** The town's most famous resident was probably a Swedish immigrant artist named Birger Sandzen. **5.** Sandzen intended to stay in Kansas for two or three years, but he loved the Great Plains and ended up remaining in Lindsborg for the rest of his life. **7.** Although Sandzen worked mainly in the Midwest, the Rocky Mountains, and other relatively unpopulated parts of the United States, he exhibited widely. **9.** Sandzen's use of vivid color showed the beauty of the natural landscapes of the West.

Practice 41-3, page 612

Answers: **1.** The television show *Sesame Street*, which began in 1969, was an innovator in programming for children. **3.** The popular Muppets Kermit the Frog and Miss Piggy starred in several films, including one based on Charles Dickens's classic *A Christmas Carol* and one based on Robert Louis Stevenson's *Treasure Island*. **5.** "Elmo's World," a segment added to the show in the 1990s, introduced the small red monster who would become one of the most popular toys in history.

Practice 41-4, page 612

Answers: (1) Are pennies necessary? (3) According to the group Americans for Common Cents, however, "Pennies are a part of our culture and our economy." (5) Opponents of the copper coin—which has been made of zinc with a copper coating since 1982—say that people don't like to use pennies. (7) Many stores place penny trays on the counter so that customers can either leave unwanted pennies or pick a few up for the cashier to avoid getting any pennies in change. (9) Yet the penny is undeniably a part of American history. (11) Only four of these original coins survive, and they are valued at more than a quarter of a million dollars each. (13) Fifty years later, the Lincoln Memorial was added to the reverse side, replacing the stalks of wheat on earlier pennies. (15) Everyone has heard, "A penny saved is a penny earned," and that saying is not likely to change even though a penny doesn't buy much today. (17) Finally, unlike the John F. Kennedy half-dollar coin, which is no longer minted, people simply expect pennies to be there. (19) But many U.S. citizens care about the fate of the penny and don't want it to disappear.

Index

Correction Symbols

This chart lists typical symbols that instructors use to point out writing problems. The explanation of each symbol includes a step you can take to revise or edit your writing. Included also are suggested chapters to check for more help and information. If your instructor uses different symbols for some errors, write them in the left-hand column for future reference.

YOUR INSTRUCTOR'S SYMBOL	STANDARD SYMBOL	HOW TO REVISE OR EDIT (NUMBERS IN BOLDFACE ARE CHAPTERS WHERE YOU CAN FIND HELP)
	adj	Use correct adjective form **28**
	adv	Use correct adverb form **28**
	agr	Correct subject-verb agreement or pronoun agreement **25; 27**
	awk	Awkward expression: edit for clarity **7**
	cap	Use capital letter correctly **41**
	case	Use correct pronoun case **27**
	cliché	Replace overused phrase with fresh words **34**
	coh	Revise paragraph or essay for coherence **7**
	combine	Combine sentences **32**
	con t	Correct the inconsistent verb tense **26**
	coord	Use coordination correctly **30**
	cs	Comma splice: join the two sentences correctly **24**
	d or dic	Diction: edit word choice **34**
	dev	Develop your paragraph or essay more completely **4; 6**
	dm	Revise to avoid a dangling modifier **29**
	frag	Attach the fragment to a sentence or make it a sentence **23**
	fs	Fused sentence: join the two sentences correctly **24**
	intro	Add or strengthen your introduction **6**
	ital	Use italics **39**
	lc	Use lowercase **41**
	mm	Revise to avoid a misplaced modifier **29**
	pl	Use the correct plural form of the verb **26**
	ref	Make pronoun reference clear **27**
	ro	Run-on sentence: join the two sentences correctly **24**
	sp	Correct the spelling error **35; 36**
	sub	Use subordination correctly **30**
	sup	Support your point with details, examples, or facts **4**
	tense	Correct the problem with verb tense **26**
	trans	Add a transition **7**
	ts	Add or strengthen your topic sentence or thesis statement **3**
	u	Revise paragraph or essay for unity **7**
	w	Delete unnecessary words **34**
	?	Make your meaning clearer **7**
	,	Usc comma correctly **37**
	; : ( ) - —	Use semicolon/colon/parentheses/hyphen/dash correctly **40**
	" "	Use quotation marks correctly **39**

Useful Lists, Checklists, and Charts